SELECTED REPRINTS ON
Dataflow and Reduction Architectures

Edited by S. S. Thakkar

COMPUTER SOCIETY ORDER NUMBER 759
LIBRARY OF CONGRESS NUMBER 87-70817
IEEE CATALOG NUMBER EH0260-0
ISBN 0-8186-0759-9
SAN 264-620X

 **THE COMPUTER SOCIETY** OF THE IEEE

 IEEE   THE INSTITUTE OF ELECTRICAL AND ELECTRONICS ENGINEERS, INC.

IEEE **COMPUTER SOCIETY PRESS**

SELECTED REPRINTS ON
Dataflow and Reduction Architectures

Edited by S. S. Thakkar

COMPUTER SOCIETY ORDER NUMBER 759
LIBRARY OF CONGRESS NUMBER 87-70817
IEEE CATALOG NUMBER EH0260-0
ISBN 0-8186-0759-9
SAN 264-620X

 **THE COMPUTER SOCIETY**
®OF THE IEEE

IEEE THE INSTITUTE OF ELECTRICAL AND ELECTRONICS ENGINEERS, INC.

IEEE
**COMPUTER
SOCIETY
PRESS**®

Published by Computer Society Press of the IEEE
1730 Massachusetts Avenue, N.W.
Washington, D.C. 20036-1903

Cover designed by Jack I. Ballestero

Computer Society Order Number 759
Library of Congress Number 87-70817
IEEE Catalog Number EH0260-0
ISBN 0-8186-0759-9 (Paper)
ISBN 0-8186-4759-0 (Microfiche)
SAN 264-620X

Order from: Computer Society of the IEEE   IEEE Service Center   Computer Society of the IEEE
            Post Office Box 80452   445 Hoes Lane   13, Avenue de l'Aquilon
            Worldway Postal Center   P.O. Box 1331   B-1200 Brussels
            Los Angeles, CA 90080   Piscataway, NJ 08855-1331   BELGIUM

THE INSTITUTE OF ELECTRICAL AND ELECTRONICS ENGINEERS, INC.

Acknowledgments

I would like to thank all the authors who have contributed to this reprint collection and apologize to the authors whose papers were not selected due to space limitations. I also extend thanks to my wife Kit and son Nalin for their support and help. Special thanks go to my wife for making time available for me to complete this work.

Finally I would like to thank Diane Bailey for her secretarial help and Sequent Computer Systems for the use of their facilities.

Preface

Computer architecture is going through a radical change as advances in technology and programming languages continue to open new possibilities. As the physical limits for speed are approaching, researchers are looking at alternatives to von Neumann architecture. The alternatives are parallel architectures that can be constructed out of identical processing elements. This reprint collection looks at alternatives to von Neumann architecture: dataflow and reduction architectures.

This collection is intended for computer science and engineering professionals who need to understand these new exciting architectures. It can be used as a textbook for a course on Dataflow and Reduction Architectures, as a supplementary reading for a course on Multiprocessor Architectures, or as a reference for students pursuing computer architecture research.

The reprint collection is organized into eight chapters that cover: different dataflow systems, dataflow solution to multiprocessing, dataflow languages and dataflow graphs, functional programming languages and their implementation, uniprocessor architectures that provide support for reduction, parallel graph reduction machines, and hybrid multiprocessor architectures.

Table of Contents

Chapter 1: Introduction

Background

New architectures based on data-driven and demand-driven principles depart from the inherently sequential von Neumann architectures and show a potential to take advantage of rapidly changing hardware technology, namely, very large scale integration (VLSI). These architectures can be realized from a number of identical units that can achieve highly parallel operations, which makes them well suited to VLSI technology. They are based on single assignment and functional programming languages, allowing them to implicitly exploit parallelism in an application. Thus, these architectures show promise of making better use of VLSI and parallelism.

The data-driven architectures are based on the dataflow model of computation. In this model, data are active and flow asynchronously through the program, activating each instruction when all the required input data have arrived. This contrasts to the von Neumann model in which data passively reside in memory while instructions are executed in a sequence controlled by a program counter. In a dataflow machine, the program is represented as a graph. The nodes of the graph represent the functions to be performed (i.e., instructions) and data appear as input to the nodes. Tokens (data carriers) containing one data value flow on arcs of the graph. When a pair of matching tokens arrive at a node, the instruction is executed and the token removed from its inputs. The resulting data are then dispatched with a token. This kind of architecture is called *dataflow* because the data appear to flow through the graph.

For example, consider the evaluation of the following expression:

$$X = (B + 1) * (A-C)$$

where $A = 10$, $B = 5$, and $C = 3$. The expression can be represented as the dataflow graph as shown in Figure 1.1. There are three instructions I1, I2, and I3. Each instruction consists of an operator; two inputs, which are either literals or unknown operands defined by the empty parenthesis; and a reference of the destination instruction and argument position for the result data token. The black dots indicate the availability of the data token. The instruction is enabled when all its operands are *known*. The operator then consumes the data tokens, performs the required operation, and by using the embedded reference, stores the copy of the

result data token into the destination instruction(s). In the example, the arrival of data token 5 triggers the execution of I1, and similarly, the arrival of 10 and 3 triggers the execution of I2. Subsequently, the tokens 6 and 7 are passed to I3, and finally, the result 42 is passed as an argument to some other expression.

Figure 1.1 illustrates the natural parallelism in dataflow computation; the programmer does not have to specify evaluation explicitly. Instructions I1 and I2 can be evaluated in parallel if the processing resources are available.

The main features of the dataflow [1], resulting from its choice of mechanisms, include (1) data are passed directly between instructions; (2) literals are again stored in instructions; (3) execution consumes data tokens, so the values are no longer available to be reused; (4) there is no concept of shared data as embodied in the traditional notion of a variable; and, (5) flows of control and data are identical.

Thus the sharing is only supported by copying the values. This makes the dataflow computation very efficient for evaluating simple expressions but less efficient for handling data structures. The dataflow computation can be wasteful for evaluation of conditional expression since both alternatives will be evaluated. Chapter 2 describes how the dataflow machines handle the data structures.

The demand-driven architectures have their foundation in functional or declarative programming languages. These languages are based on lambda calculus, and programming by using them is closer to writing mathematical equations

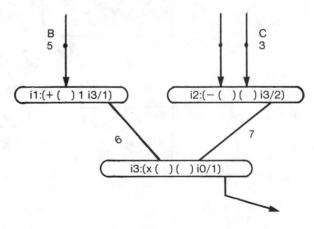

Figure 1.1

than to conventional programming. The expressions are represented as graphs that are reduced by evaluation of their branches or sub-graphs. The reduction is done only when the result of the sub-graph is required; that is, on demand *(lazily)*. Different parts of the graphs can be reduced or evaluated in parallel.

There are two reduction models [1]: string reduction and graph reduction. String reduction has a *by value* data mechanism and graph reduction has a *by reference* data mechanism. Both forms of recursion have a *recursive* control mechanism. Demanding the result of the expression (definition) X, where X = (B + 1)*(B-C) means we require that the embedded reference X, causing the execution, is rewritten in a simple form. Because of these attributes only one definition of X may occur in a program and all references give the same value, a property known as *referential transparency*.

In string reduction, the instruction accessing a particular definition will take and manipulate a separate copy of the definition. Each instruction consists of an operator followed by literals or embedded references used to demand the corresponding input operands. The example (Figure 1.2) shows the evaluation of the definition X by using string reduction. The reference X is overwritten by the definition. Next, the operation of a multiply operator is suspended while its arguments I1 and I2 are evaluated. Finally, the expression is said to be reduced when all the arguments of the expressions are replaced by literal values and the expression is evaluated.

In graph reduction, the instruction accessing a particular definition will manipulate references to that definition. The arguments are shared, using pointers unlike string reduc-

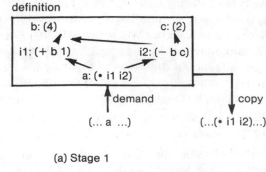

(a) Stage 1

$(...(\bullet (+ 4 1) (- 4 2))...) (...(\bullet 5 2)...) (...10...)$

(b) Stage 3 to 5

Figure 1.2: String Reduction Program for a=(b+1)*(b-c).

tion. In the example (Figure 1.3), some instruction demands the value associated with X, but, instead of taking a copy of the definition, the reference is traversed until it is reduced and value is returned. One way to identify the original source of the definition is to embed a reference in the definition. This traversal of the reference is continued until the expression is reduced and the value is returned.

The main features of reduction are [1]: (1) program structures, instructions, and arguments are all expression; (2) there is no concept of data storage such as a variable; (3) there are no additional sequencing constraints over and above those implied by demands for operands; and (4) demands may return simple or complex arguments such as a function (as input to a higher-order function).

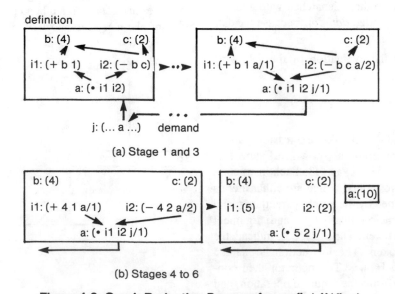

(a) Stage 1 and 3

(b) Stages 4 to 6

Figure 1.3: Graph Reduction Program for a=(b+1)*(b-c).

The type of sharing embodied by string reduction is that of separate copies, whereas that of graph reduction is update in place. These features make string reduction (innermost evaluation) more suitable for simple expression evaluation and graph reduction (outermost evaluation) more suitable when larger structures are involved. Both forms of reduction are constrained by the absence of explicit output arguments.

This reprint collection is organized to give an understanding of the data-driven and demand-driven architectures and their programming. The chapters contain descriptions of several practical data-driven and demand-driven architectures. Additional references are provided for readers who would like to pursue a further study of the subject.

This chapter contains two tutorial papers on existing demand-driven and data-driven architectures. The papers present a brief description of the principles and each of the existing systems. Each paper also contains an extensive bibliography on the subject matter.

Article Summary

Treleaven et al., in "Data-Driven and Demand-Driven Computer Architecture," examine the data-driven and demand-driven computer systems with respect to their computation organization, (stored) program organization, and machine organization. The three models for comparison are classified as control flow, dataflow, and reduction. The computation organizations are classified by how they select instructions to be executed, how the instruction is examined to determine if it is executable, and how the instruction is executed. The program organization refers to the way machine code programs are represented and executed in a computer architecture. The data and the control mechanisms govern the program representation and execution for three models. The machine organization refers to the way machine resources are configured and allocated to support the program organization. A survey of early data- and demand-driven architectures using these classifications follows.

Vegdahl, in "A Survey of Proposed Architectures for Execution of Functional Languages," examines functional programming languages with regard to programming style and efficiency and then compares them with imperative languages. However, a major drawback to using functional programming languages is that they have been perceived to run slowly on von Neumann architectures. Hence, architectures are examined that have been proposed or built to give hardware support to functional programming languages. Vegdahl also examines the suitability of functional programming languages for parallel execution.

References

[1] Treleaven, P.C., "Decentralised Computer Architectures," *New Computer Architectures*, Academic Press, London, England, 1984, pp. 1-55.

Data-Driven and Demand-Driven Computer Architecture

PHILIP C. TRELEAVEN, DAVID R. BROWNBRIDGE, AND RICHARD P. HOPKINS

Computing Laboratory, University of Newcastle upon Tyne, Newcastle upon Tyne, NE1 7RU, England

Novel data-driven and demand-driven computer architectures are under development in a
large number of laboratories in the United States, Japan, and Europe. These computers
are not based on the traditional von Neumann organization; instead, they are attempts to
identify the next generation of computer. Basically, in data-driven (e.g., data-flow)
computers the availability of operands triggers the execution of the operation to be
performed on them, whereas in demand-driven (e.g., reduction) computers the
requirement for a result triggers the operation that will generate it.

Although there are these two distinct areas of research, each laboratory has developed
its own individual model of computation, stored program representation, and machine
organization. Across this spectrum of designs there is, however, a significant sharing of
concepts. The aim of this paper is to identify the concepts and relationships that exist
both within and between the two areas of research. It does this by examining data-driven
and demand-driven architecture at three levels: computation organization, (stored)
program organization, and machine organization. Finally, a survey of various novel
computer architectures under development is given.

Categories and Subject Descriptors: C.0 [**Computer Systems Organization**]:
General— *hardware/software interfaces; system architectures;* C.1.2 [**Processor
Architecture**]: Multiple Data Stream Architectures (Multiprocessors); C.1.3 [**Processor
Architecture**]: Other Architecture Styles—*data-flow architectures; high-level language
architectures*; D.3.2 [**Programming Languages**]: Language Classifications—*data-flow
languages; macro and assembly languages; very high-level languages*

General Terms: Design

Additional Key Words and Phrases: Demand = driven architecture, data = driven
architecture

INTRODUCTION

For more than thirty years the principles of
computer architecture design have largely
remained static [ORGA79], based on the von
Neumann organization. These von Neumann principles include

(1) a single computing element incorporating processor, communications, and
memory;
(2) linear organization of fixed-size memory cells;
(3) one-level address space of cells;
(4) low-level machine language (instructions perform simple operations on elementary operands);
(5) sequential, centralized control of computation.

Over the last few years, however, a number of novel computer architectures based
on new "naturally" parallel organizations
for computation have been proposed and
some computers have even been built. The
principal stimuli for these novel architectures have come from the pioneering work
on data flow by Jack Dennis [DENN74a,
DENN74b], and on reduction languages and
machines by John Backus [BACK72,
BACK73] and Klaus Berkling [BERK71,
BERK75]. The resulting computer architecture research can be broadly classified as
either data driven or demand driven. In
data-driven (e.g., data-flow) computers the
availability of operands triggers the execution of the operation to be performed on
them, whereas in demand-driven (e.g., re-

CONTENTS

duction) computers the requirement for a result triggers the operation that will generate it.

Although the motivations and emphasis of individual research groups vary, there are basically three interacting driving forces. First, there is the desire to utilize concurrency to increase computer performance. This is based on the continuing demand from areas such as weather forecasting and wind tunnel simulation for computers with a higher performance. The natural physical laws place fundamental limitations on the performance increases obtainable from advances in technology alone. And conventional high-speed computers like CRAY 1 and ILLIAC IV seem unable to meet these demands [TREL79]. Second, there is the desire to exploit very large scale integration (VLSI) in the design of computers [SEIT79, MEAD80, TREL80b]. One effective means of employing VLSI would be parallel architectures composed of identical computing elements, each containing integral capabilities for processing, communication, and memory. Unfortunately "general-purpose" organizations for interconnecting and programming such architectures based on the von Neumann principles have not been forthcoming. Third, there is the growing interest in new classes of very high level programming languages. The most well-developed such class of languages comprises the functional languages such as LISP [McCA62], FP [BACK78], LUCID [ASHC77], SASL [TURN79a], Id [ARVI78], and VAL [ACKE79b]. Because of the mismatch between the various principles on which these languages are based, and those of the von Neumann computer, conventional implementations tend to be inefficient.

There is growing agreement, particularly in Japan and the United Kingdom, that the next generation of computers will be based on non-von Neumann architecture. (A report [JIPD81a] by Japan's Ministry of International Trade and Industry contains a good summary of the criteria for these fifth-generation computers.) Both data-driven and demand-driven computer architecture are possible fifth-generation architectures. The question then becomes, which architectural principles and features from the various research projects will contribute to this new generation of computers?

Work on data-driven and demand-driven architecture falls into two principal research areas, namely, data flow [DENN79b, GOST79a] and reduction [BERK75]. These areas are distinguished by the way computation, stored programs, and machine resources are organized. Although research groups in each area share a basic set of concepts, each group has augmented the concepts often by introducing ideas from other areas (including traditional control-flow architectures) to overcome difficulties. The aim of this paper is to identify the concepts and relationships that exist both within and between these areas of research. We start by presenting simple operational models for control flow, data flow, and reduction. Next we classify and analyze the way computation, stored programs, and machine resources are organized across the three groups. Finally, a survey of various novel computer architectures under development is given in terms of these classifications.

1. BASIC CONCEPTS

Here we present simple operational models of control flow, data flow, and reduction. In order to compare these three models we discuss each in terms of a simple machine code representation. These representations are viewed as instructions consisting of sequences of arguments—operators, literal operands, references—delimited by parentheses:

$$(\text{arg0 arg1 arg2 arg3} \cdots \text{arg}n-1 \text{ arg}n).$$

However, the terms "instruction" and "reference" are given a considerably more general meaning than their counterparts in conventional computers. To facilitate comparisons of control flow, data flow, and reduction, simple program representations for the statement a = (b + 1) * (b − c) are used. Although this statement consists of simple operators and operands, the concepts illustrated are equally applicable to more complex operations and data structures.

1.1 Control Flow

We start by examining control flow, the most familiar model. In the control-flow program representations shown in Figure 1, the statement a = (b + 1) * (b − c) is specified by a series of instructions each consisting of an operator followed by one or more operands, which are literals or references. For instance, a dyadic operation such

as + is followed by three operands; the first two, b and 1, provide the input data and the last, t1, is the reference to the shared memory cell for the result. Shared memory cells are the means by which data are passed between instructions. Each reference in Figure 1 is also shown as a unidirectional arc. Solid arcs show the access to stored data, while dotted arcs define the flow of control.

In traditional sequential (von Neumann) control flow there is a single thread of control, as in Figure 1a, which is passed from instruction to instruction. When control reaches an instruction, the operator is initially examined to determine the number and usage of the following operands. Next the input addresses are dereferenced, the operator is executed, the result is stored in a memory cell, and control is passed implicitly to the next instruction in sequence. Explicit control transfers are caused by operators such as GOTO.

There are also parallel forms of control flow [FARR79, HOPK79]. In the parallel form of control flow, shown in Figure 1b, the implicit sequential control-flow model is augmented by parallel control operators. These parallel operators allow more than one thread of control to be active at an instance and also provide means for synchronizing these threads. For example, in Figure 1b the FORK operator activates the subtraction instruction at address i2 and passes an implicit flow of control on to the addition instruction. The addition and subtraction may then be executed in parallel. When the addition finishes execution, control is passed via the GOTO i3 instruction to the JOIN instruction. The task of the JOIN is to synchronize the two threads of control that are released by the addition and subtraction instruction, and release a single thread to activate the multiply instruction.

In the second parallel form of control flow, shown in Figure 1c, each instruction explicitly specifies its successor instructions. Such a reference, i1/0, defines the specific instruction and argument position for the control signal, or *control token*. Argument positions, one for each control signal required, are represented by empty bracket symbols ( ), and an instruction is

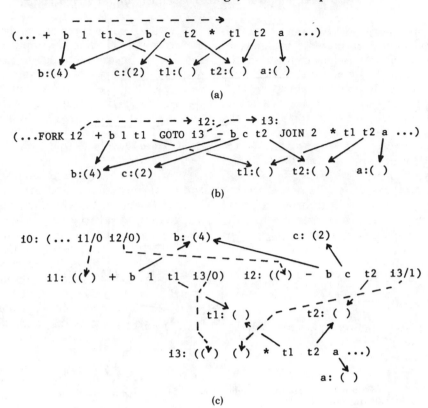

Figure 1. Control-flow programs for a = (b + 1) * (b − c): (a) sequential; (b) parallel "FORK–JOIN"; (c) parallel "control tokens."

executed when it has received the required control tokens. The two parallel forms of control flow, illustrated by Figures 1b and 1c, are semantically equivalent; FORKS are equivalent to multiple successor instruction addresses and JOINs are equivalent to multiple empty bracket arguments.

The sequential and parallel control-flow models have a number of common features: (1) data are passed indirectly between instructions via references to shared memory cells; (2) literals may be stored in instructions, which can be viewed as an optimization of using a reference to access the literal; (3) flow of control is implicitly sequential, but explicit control operators can be used for parallelism, etc.; and (4) because the flows of data and control are separate, they can be made identical or distinct.

1.2 Data Flow

Data flow is very similar to the second form of parallel control flow with instructions activated by tokens and the requirement for tokens being the indicated ( ) symbols. Data-flows programs are usually described in terms of directed graphs, used to illustrate the flow of data between instructions. In the data-flow program representation shown in Figure 2, each instruction consists of an operator, two inputs which are either literal operands or "unknown" operands defined by empty bracket ( ) symbols, and a reference, i3/1, defining the specific instruction and argument position for the result. A reference, also shown as a unidirectional arc, is used by the producer instruction to store a *data token* (i.e., result) into the consumer. Thus data are passed directly between instructions.

An instruction is enabled for execution when all arguments are known, that is, when all unknowns have been replaced by partial results made available by other instructions. The operator then executes, removing the inputs from storage, processing them according to the specified operation,

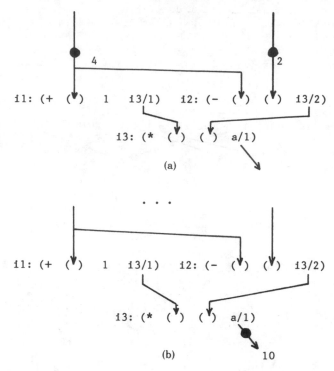

Figure 2. Data-flow program for a = (b + 1) * (b − c): (a) Stage 1; (b) Stage 4.

and using the embedded reference to store the result at an unknown operand in a successor instruction. In terms of directed graphs, an instruction is enabled when a data token is present on each of its input arcs. During execution the operator removes one data token from each input arc and releases a set of result tokens onto the output arcs.

Figure 2 illustrates the sequence of execution for the program fragment a = (b + 1) * (b − c), using a black dot on an arc to indicate the presence of a data token. The two black dots at Stage 1 in Figure 2 indicate that the data tokens corresponding to the values of b and c have been generated by predecessor instructions. Since b is required as input for two subsequent instructions, two copies of the token are generated and stored into the respective locations in each instruction. The availability of these inputs completes both the addition and the subtraction instruction, and enables their operators for execution. Executing completely independently, each operator consumes its input tokens and stores its result

into the multiplication instruction "i3." This enables the multiplication, which executes and stores its result corresponding to the identifier "a," shown at Stage 4.

In the data-flow model there are a number of interesting features: (1) partial results are passed directly as data tokens between instructions; (2) literals may be embedded in an instruction that can be viewed as an optimization of the data token mechanism; (3) execution uses up data tokens—the values are no longer available as inputs to this or any other instruction; (4) there is no concept of shared data storage as embodied in the traditional notion of a variable; and (5) sequencing constraints— flows of control—are tied to the flow of data.

1.3 Reduction

Control-flow and data-flow programs are built from fixed-size instructions whose arguments are primitive operators and operands. Higher level program structures are built from linear sequences of these primitive instructions.

Computing Surveys, Vol. 14, No. 1, March 1982

In contrast, reduction programs are built from nested expressions. The nearest analogy to an "instruction" in reduction is a function application, consisting of ⟨function⟩ ⟨argument⟩, which returns its result in place. Here a ⟨function⟩ or ⟨argument⟩ is recursively defined to be either an atom, such as + or 1, or an expression. Likewise, a reference may access, and function application may return, either an atom or an expression. Higher level program structures are reflected in this machine representation, being themselves function applications built from more primitive functions. In reduction, a program is mathematically equivalent to its result in the same way that the expression 3 + 3 is equivalent to the number 6. Demanding the result of the *definition* "a," where a = (b + 1) * (b − c), means that the embedded reference to "a" is to be rewritten in a simpler form. (It may be helpful for the reader to view this evaluation of a reference as calling the corresponding definition, giving reduction a CALL–RETURN pattern of control.) Because of these attributes, only one definition of "a" may occur in a program, and all references to it give the same value, a property known as *referential transparency*. There are two forms of reduction, differentiated in the way that arguments in a program are manipulated, called string reduction and graph reduction.

The basis of string reduction is that each instruction that accesses a particular definition will take and manipulate a separate copy of the definition. Figure 3 illustrates string manipulation for a reduction execution sequence involving the definition a = (b + 1) * (b − c). Each instruction consists of an operator followed by literals or embedded references, which are used to demand its input operands. At Stage 1 in Figure 3 some instruction, containing the reference "a," demands the value corresponding to the definition "a." This causes a copy of the definition to be loaded into the instruction overwriting the reference "a," as also shown in Figure 3. Next the multiplication operator demands the values corresponding to i1 and i2, causing them to be overwritten by copies of their definitions. The multiplication then suspends and the addition and subtraction operators demand the values of b and c. The substitution of the values 4 and 2 is shown at Stage 3 in Figure 3. The reducible subexpressions (+ 4 1) and (− 4 2) are then rewritten, causing the multiplication to be reenabled. Finally at Stage 5 the multiplication is replaced by the constant 10, which is the value of "a."

The basis of graph reduction is that each instruction that accesses a particular definition will manipulate references to the definition. That is, graph manipulation is based on the sharing of arguments using pointers. Figure 4 illustrates graph reduction using the same program definition a = (b + 1) * (b − c) as above. At Stage 1 in Figure 4 an instruction demands the value corresponding to "a," but instead of a copy of the definition being taken, the reference is traversed in order to reduce the definition and return with the actual value. One of the ways of identifying the original source of the demand for "a," and thus supporting the return, is to reverse the arcs (as shown in Figure 4) by inserting a source reference in the definition.

This traversal of the definition and the reversal of the references is continued until constant arguments, such as b and c in Figure 4, are encountered. In Figure 4, reduction of the subexpressions in the definition starts with the rewriting of the addition and the subtraction as shown at Stage 4. This proceeds until the value of "a" is calculated and a copy is returned to the instruction originally demanding "a." (If there are no further references to b, c, i1, and i2, then they can be "garbage collected.") Any subsequent requests for the value of "a" will immediately receive the constant 10—one of the major benefits of graph reduction over string reduction.

In reduction the main points to note are that: (1) program structures, instructions, and arguments are all expressions; (2) there is no concept of updatable storage such as a variable; (3) there are no additional sequencing constraints over and above those implied by demands for operands; and (4) demands may return both simple or complex arguments such as a function (as input to a higher order function).

Control flow, data flow, and reduction clearly have fundamental differences,

definition

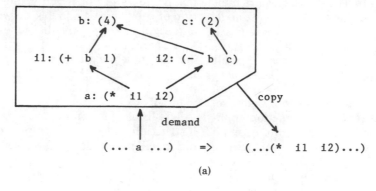

(...a...)   =>   (...(* i1 i2)...)

(a)

. . .

(...(* (+ 4 1) (- 4 2))...)   =>   (...(* 5 2)...)   =>   (...10...)

(b)

Figure 3. String reduction program for a = (b + 1) * (b − c): (a) Stages 1 and 3; (b) Stages 3–5.

definition

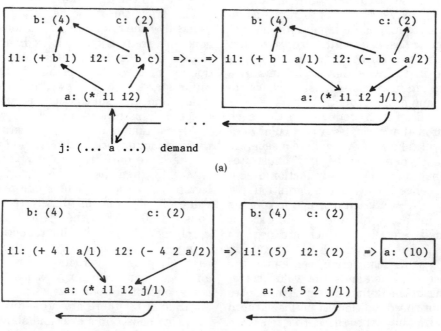

(a)

(b)

Figure 4. Graph reduction program for a = (b + 1) * (b − c): (a) Stages 1 and 3; (b) Stages 4–6.

which relate to their advantages and disadvantages for representing programs. However, they also have interesting underlying similarities. In the next two sections on computation organization and program organization we attempt to identify and classify these underlying concepts.

2. COMPUTATION ORGANIZATION

In this section we examine, at an abstract level, the way computation progresses. This progress takes the form of successive changes in the state of the computation brought about by executing instructions. Computation organization describes how these state changes come to take place by describing the sequencing and the effect of instructions. We describe the rules determining which instructions are selected for execution and how far reaching the effects of their execution may be.

This abstract level of classification enables a clear distinction to be drawn between the terms: control driven, data driven, and demand driven. These three classes are often identified with, respectively, the operational models control flow, data flow, and reduction. Here we define the notions of control-driven, data-driven, and demand-driven computation organizations and identify their relationships to the three operational models.

2.1 Classification

Computation organizations may be classified by considering computation to be a continuous repetition of three phases: select, examine, and execute. It needs to be emphasized that this description does not necessarily reflect the way in which particular computer implementations operate but rather that it is a logical description of the affects achieved.

(1) *Select*. At the select phase a set of instructions is chosen for possible execution. The rule for making this choice is called a *computation rule*. The computation rule selects a subset of instructions in the program. Only instructions chosen by the select phase may be executed, but selection does not guarantee execution. Three of the computational rules used in this clas-

sification are imperative, innermost, and outermost. The imperative computation rule selects the instructions indicated by, for example, a special ("program counter") register or the presence of control tokens. This selection is made regardless of the position of the instruction in the program structure. Innermost and outermost computation rules select, respectively, the instructions most deeply nested and least deeply nested in the program structure. An innermost instruction has no instructions as arguments to it (only values). An outermost instruction is not nested as an argument of any other instruction. The instructions selected by the three rules are illustrated in Figure 5.

(2) *Examine*. At the examine phase, each of the instructions previously chosen in the select phase is examined to see if it is executable. The decision is based on examination of each instruction's actual arguments. The rule for making this decision is called a *firing rule*. For instance, the firing rule may require all operands to be data values, or it may require only one operand to be a value as, for example, in a conditional. If an instruction is executable, it is passed on to the next phase for execution; otherwise, the examine phase may take some action, such as delaying the instruction or attempting to coerce arguments so as to allow execution.

(3) *Execute*. At the execute or "target" phase, which is broadly similar in all computation organizations, instructions are actually executed. The result of execution is to change the state of the computer. Results are made available and are passed to other parts of the program. Execution may produce globally perceived changes, perhaps by changing the state of a globally shared memory, or it may produce localized changes as when an expression is replaced by its value.

2.2 Control Flow

The select phase of control-flow computation corresponds to the fetch part of the fetch–execute control cycle. Each control-flow computing element has a program counter naming the next instruction to execute. In the select phase, the program

The expression denotes the product of two complex numbers:
`(a,b) * (c,d)`

Imperative
```
    ( (a*c) - (b*d) , (a*d) + (b*c) )
       ↑

       PC
```

Instructions selected depending on the value of PC

Innermost
```
    ( (a*c) - (b*d) , (a*d) + (b*c) )
       ↑       ↑        ↑       ↑
```

Instructions selected are the most deeply nested

Outermost
```
    ( (a*c) - (b*d) , (a*d) + (b*c) )
            ↑                ↑
```

Instructions selected are those un—nested

Figure 5.   Three computation rules applied to an expression.

counter is used to choose the instructions to be used. Once chosen by select, instructions are not checked by an examine phase, but are automatically passed on to execution. The execute phase of control-flow instructions is allowed to change any part of the state. Control flow uses a shared memory to communicate results. The state of computation is represented by the contents of this shared memory and of the program counter register(s). A program counter is updated at the end of each cycle either implicitly or, in the case of GOTOs, explicitly.

We define the term *control driven* to denote computation organizations in which instructions are executed as soon as they are selected. The select phase alone determines which instructions are to be executed. For all computation organizations in this class the examine phase is redundant, and instruction sequencing is independent of program structure.

2.3 Data Flow

There are many varieties of data-flow computers; here we restrict ourselves to "pure" data-flow computation as described in Section 1.2. In pure data flow, instructions are executed as soon as *all* their arguments are available. Logically at least, each instruction has a computing element allocated to it continuously, just waiting for arguments to arrive. So the select phase of data-flow computation may be viewed as logically allocating a computing element to every instruction. The examine phase implements the data-flow firing rule, which requires all arguments to be available before execution can take place. Arguments must be data items, not unevaluated expressions. If values are not yet available, the computing element will not try to execute the instruction but will remain dormant during the execute phase. The execute phase in data flow changes a local state consisting of the executing instruction and its set of successor instructions. The instruction consumes its arguments and places a result in each successor instruction.

We define the term *data driven* to denote computation organizations where instructions passively wait for some combination of their arguments to become available. This implies a select phase, which (logically) allocates computing elements to all instructions, and an examine phase, which suspends nonexecutable instructions. In data-driven computation organizations, the key factor governing execution is the availability of data. For this reason "data driven" is the same as "availability driven."

2.4 Reduction

Reduction computers each have different rules embodied in their select phase. The choice of computation rule is a design choice for a particular reduction computer. The commonest rules used are *innermost* and *outermost* (see Figure 5), and in fact the discussion of reduction in Section 1 was restricted to outermost reduction. The computation rule in a reduction computer determines the allocation of computing elements at the beginning of each computation cycle. In the examine phase the arguments are examined to see whether execution is possible. If it is, the instruction is executed. Otherwise, the computing element tries to coerce the arguments into the required pattern. This coercion demands the evaluation of argument(s) until sufficient are available for execution. Logically, this demand consists of spawning one or more subcomputations to evaluate operands and waiting for them to return with a value. The instruction set of a reduction computer may contain many different firing rules, each instruction having the rule most suited to it. For example, all arithmetic operations will have a firing rule that forces their arguments to be values. The execute phase in a reduction machine involves rewriting an instruction in situ. The instruction is replaced by its result where it stands. Only the local state consisting of the instruction itself and those instructions that use its results are changed. Execution may thus also enable another instruction.

We define the term *demand driven* to denote a computation organization where instructions are only selected when the value they produce is needed by another, already selected instruction. All outermost reduction architectures fall into this category but innermost reduction architectures do not. The essence of a demand-driven computation organization is that an instruction is executed only when its result is demanded by some other instruction and the arguments may be recursively evaluated where necessary. In reduction computers with an innermost computation rule, instructions are never chosen by select until their arguments are available. This restriction means that all arguments reaching the examine stage are preevaluated and hence no coercions need ever take place. It also means that all instructions have all their arguments evaluated whether or not this is necessary, exactly as occurs in data flow. Thus we believe innermost computation organizations are data driven.

2.5 Implications

The implications of the computation organization classification can now be summarized. Control-flow computers have a control-driven computation organization; instructions are arbitrarily selected, and once selected they are immediately executed. Data-flow computers have a data-driven computation organization; all instructions are in principle active, but only execute when their arguments become available. Some reduction computers are demand driven and some are data driven.

Control-flow computers all have a control-driven computation organization. The control-driven organization is characterized by the lack of an examine stage, and by a computation rule that selects instructions independently of their place in the program's structure. This implies that the program has complete control over instruction sequencing. Once selected, instructions will always be executed regardless of the state of their operands. There is no wait for arguments, or demand for arguments, apart from the dereferencing of an address. It is up to the programmer to ensure that arguments are set up before control reaches an instruction. The advantage of control-driven computation is full control over sequencing. The corresponding disadvantage is the programming discipline needed to avoid run-time errors. These errors are harder to prevent and detect than exceptions (overflow, etc.), which occur at the execute phase in all computation organizations. A typical example of the twin generalities and dangers of control-driven computation organization is the ability to execute data as a program.

Data-flow computers have a data-driven computation organization that is characterized by a passive examine stage. Instructions are examined, and if they do not pass the firing rule, no action is taken to force them to become executable. The data-flow firing rule requires all arguments to arrive before an instruction will execute. However, some data-flow implementations have found this too restrictive and have added non-data-driven instructions to provide some degree of explicit control. The advantage of data-driven computation is that instructions are executed as soon as their arguments are available, giving a high degree of implicit parallelism. The disadvantages are that instructions may waste time waiting for unneeded arguments. This becomes increasingly apparent when the implementation of data-flow procedures is considered. In addition, operators such as an if–then–else operator, which will use only two of its three arguments, discarding the other, will always be forced to wait for all three. In the worst case this can lead to nontermination through waiting for an unneeded argument, which is, for example, an infinite iteration.

A reduction computer having a demand-driven organization is characterized by an outermost computation rule coupled with the ability to coerce arguments at the examine stage. Instruction sequencing is driven by the need to produce a result at the outermost level, rather than to insist on following a set pattern. Each instruction chosen by the outermost select can decide to demand further instructions. Instructions actively coerce their arguments to the required form if they are not already in it. Reduction computers not possessing (1) an outermost select and (2) a coercing examine phase cannot be classified as demand driven. The advantage of the demand-driven computation organization is that only instructions whose result is needed are executed. A procedure-calling mechanism is built in, by allowing the operator of an instruction to be defined as a block of instructions. The disadvantage of demand-driven computation is in processing, say, arithmetic expressions, where every instruction (+, *, etc.) always contributes to the final result. Propagating demand from outermost to innermost is wasted effort; only operator precedence will determine sequencing, and every instruction must be activated. In these cases, data-driven computation organization is better since the

sequencing is determined solely by operator priorities. Demand driven is superior only for "nonstrict" operators such as "if–then–else," which do not require all their arguments.

Last, the execute phase of any computation organization has important consequences for the underlying implementation. Global changes may have far-reaching effects, visible throughout the computer. Local changes can only alter the state of a small part of the computation. To support a computation organization allowing global state changes, some form of global communications between instructions is required. On the other hand, if only local changes are to be supported, this locality can be exploited in a distributed architecture. In general, data-flow and reduction programs are free from side effects, another feature making them suitable for distributed implementation.

3. PROGRAM ORGANIZATION

We use the term program organization to cover the way machine code programs are represented and executed in a computer architecture. This section starts by classifying the underlying mechanisms of program organization for control-flow, data-flow, and reduction models.

3.1 Classification

Two computational mechanisms, which we refer to as the data mechanism and the control mechanism, seem fundamental to these three groups of models. The *data mechanism* defines the way a particular argument is used by a number of instructions. There are three subclasses:

(1) *by literal*—where an argument is known at compile time and a separate copy is placed in each accessing instruction (found in all the operational models);

(2) *by value*—where an argument, generated at run time, is shared by replicating it and giving a separate copy to each accessing instruction, this copy being stored as a value in the instruction (as seen in data flow and string reduction);

Data Mechanisms

	by value (& literal)	by reference (& literal)
sequential		von Neumann control flow
parallel	data flow	parallel control flow
recursive	string reduction	graph reduction

Control Mechanisms

Figure 6. Computational models: control and data mechanisms.

(3) *by reference*—where an argument is shared by having a reference to it stored in each accessing instruction (as seen in control flow and graph reduction).

The *control mechanism* defines how one instruction causes the execution of another instruction, and thus the pattern of control within the total program. There are again three subclasses:

(1) *sequential*—where a single thread of control signals an instruction to execute and passes from one instruction to another (as seen in traditional sequential control flow);

(2) *parallel*—where control signals the availability of arguments and an instruction is executed when all its arguments (e.g., input data) are available (as seen in data flow and parallel control flow);

(3) *recursive*—where control signals the need for arguments and an instruction is executed when one of the output arguments it generates is required by the invoking instruction. Having executed, it returns control to the invoking instruction (as seen in string reduction and graph reduction).

The relationship of these data and control mechanisms to the three groups of operational model is summarized in Figure 6. Using this classification as a basis, we now examine the advantages and disadvantages for program representation and execution of control flow, data flow, and reduction.

3.2 Control Flow

Control flow is based on a "sequential" or "parallel" control mechanism. Flow of control is implicitly sequential with explicit sequential and parallel patterns of control being obtained from, respectively, GOTO and FORK–JOIN style control operators. The basic data mechanism of control flow is a by-reference mechanism, with references embedded in instructions being used to access shared memory cells. This form of data sharing is *shared update*, in which the effects of changing the contents of a memory cell are immediately available to other users.

In computers based on parallel program organizations such as parallel control flow, special precautions must be taken in a program's representation (style of machine code generated) to ensure that the natural asynchronous execution does not lead to unwanted indeterminacy. This is basically a problem of synchronizing the usage of shared resources, such as a memory cell containing an instruction or data. It is appropriate to examine the support in parallel control-flow computers of two important programming mechanisms—iteration and procedures—because they illustrate how these synchronization problems are controlled and also the style of program representation used.

Iteration becomes a potential problem for parallel control flow because program fragments with loops may lead to logically cyclic graphs in which each successive it-

15

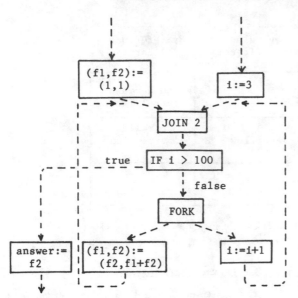

Figure 7. Control-flow iteration using feedback.

eration of a loop could execute concurrently, giving the possibility, for instance, of multiple-data items being stored in the same memory cell. Two possible schemes may, in general, be used to control potentially concurrent iteration. The first uses the feedback of control to synchronize reference usage and the second represents iteration by the equivalent recursion, thereby creating unique contexts for references.

To illustrate these two schemes for representing iteration, we use as an example a program fragment that calculates the one-hundredth number in the Fibonacci series:

(f 1, f 2) := (1, 1);
FOR i = 3 TO 100 DO
    (f 1, f 2) := (f 2, f 1 + f 2) OD;
answer := f 2;

This fragment, using concurrent assignment, consists of two calculations, one producing the Fibonacci series as successive values of f2, and the other incrementing the iteration count i. Since i is not used within the DO ... OD, these two calculations may execute in parallel.

The first scheme for supporting iteration based on the feedback of control to synchronize resource usage is shown in Figure 7. This ensures that only a single copy of an instruction can be active or that a single data item may occupy a memory cell, at an instant. This synchronization is achieved

by the JOIN instruction. Next the IF instruction, if false, performs a new iteration or, if true, transfers the value of f2 to memory cell "answer." Since memory cells are continually updated in this iteration scheme, it may be necessary in specific implementations to execute the concurrent assignment (f1, f2) := (f2, f1 + f2) sequentially to exclude indeterminacy. The second iteration scheme makes use of the procedure mechanism to provide separate contexts for each iteration, by transforming the iterative program into the equivalent recursion:

fib(f1, f2, i) := IF i > 100
                  THEN f2
                  ELSE fib(f2, f1 + f2, i + 1) FI;
answer := fib(1, 1, 3);

Each time a new call of the function fib is made, a new process, with a separate context, is created.

At a logical level there are two instructions involved in procedure invocation. (Figure 8 illustrates this procedure mechanism.) In a calling process P1, there is a CALL instruction that first obtains a new (globally unique) process identifier P2 and then changes the context of the input parameters from P1 to the new context P2. At the end of the called procedure, there must be a RETURN instruction that changes the context of the computed results back to

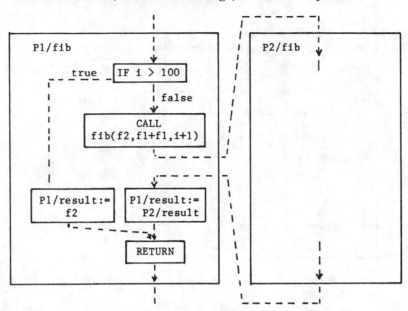

Figure 8.   Control-flow iteration using recursion.

the calling context P1. To achieve this, the CALL instruction must pass the caller's process identifier P1 to the RETURN. When all the results have been returned to the calling process, the called process P2 is deleted by the RETURN instruction.

3.3 Data Flow

Data flow is based on a by-value data mechanism and a parallel control mechanism, supported by data tokens. Thus flows of data and control are identical in data flow. A data token is used to pass a copy of a partial result directly from the producer to the consumer instruction. This form of data sharing is that of *independent copies*, in which the effect of a consumer instruction accessing the contents of a received data token is hidden from other instructions.

When an instruction is executed, the role of an embedded reference is to specify the consumer instruction and argument position for a data token. In terms of directed graphs, the role of the reference is to provide a "name" that identifies uniquely a particular data token generated by a program at an instant, by specifying the arc on which it is traveling and the node to which it is destined. Unfortunately the two-field (instruction/argument position) name for-

mat does not provide such uniqueness. For instance, more than one copy of a particular instruction may be executing in parallel. Thus tokens are no longer uniquely named, leading to the possibility of tokens being inserted in the wrong instruction. To distinguish the separate contexts of instances of a procedure, an additional "process" field is logically appended to a reference. In summary, the basic format of a reference is [ARVI77a, TREL78]

$$\langle P \ / \ N \ / \ A \rangle$$

process ───────┘ │ │
instruction (node) ──────┘ │
argument (arc) ───────────────┘

and the fields are used for the following:

(1) The process (P) field distinguishes separate instances of an instruction N that may be executing in parallel, either within a single program or within distinct programs.
(2) The instruction (N) field identifies the consuming instruction to which the data token is being passed.
(3) The argument (A) field identifies in which argument position in the instruction N the token is to be stored.

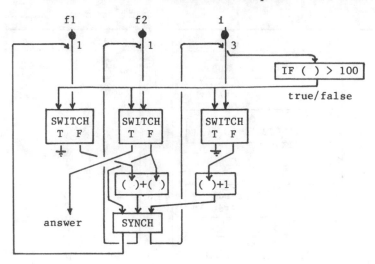

Figure 9. Data-flow iteration using feedback of tokens.

In the machine code of a data-flow computer, the values of the N and the A fields are usually statically embedded in the code at compile time, whereas the value of the P is dynamically generated at run time by the system.

Recall in our discussion of parallel control flow that special precautions need to be taken in the style of machine code generated for a program to exclude unwanted indeterminacy. Similar precautions must be taken for data flow. Here we examine data-flow program representations for iteration and procedures, using the two schemes for iteration previously discussed for control flow. Again, the program fragment that calculates the one-hundredth number in the Fibonacci series is used for examples. It is interesting to compare these examples with those previously given for control flow.

The first scheme for supporting iteration is illustrated by Figure 9. Here the feedback of data tokens synchronizes the usage of references, thereby ensuring that only a single data token can ever be on a logical arc at an instant. At the start of each iteration the IF instruction releases a true/false data token, a copy of which is passed to each SWITCH. A SWITCH takes two types of inputs: one being a true/false token, which selects either the true or the false outputs, and the other the data token to be switched. If the token is false, the other tokens are fed into the iteration,

whereas a true token causes the data token corresponding to f2 to be routed to answer and the other tokens to be discarded, as shown by the "earth" symbols. To ensure that all calculations within the loop have terminated before feeding back the tokens into the next iteration, a SYNCHronizer instruction is used. The SYNCH fires when all inputs are present and releases them onto the corresponding output arcs.

The second scheme for supporting iteration is based on a data-flow procedure mechanism [ARVI78, MIRA77, HOPK79], which allows concurrent invocations of a single procedure through the use of the process (P) field. This mechanism is essential to provide distinct naming contexts for each procedure invocation, thus isolating the data tokens from those belonging to any other invocation. The second iteration scheme that represents iteration by the equivalent recursion is shown in Figure 10. In this example parallelism is only obtained when a new invocation of the procedure fib is to be used, by calculating the value parameters (f2, f1 + f2, i + 1) concurrently. As in the control-flow procedure mechanism, discussed above, the CALL instruction creates a new process and inserts the parameters, and the RETURN changes back the context of the results and deletes the invoked process.

There is, in fact, a third scheme for supporting iteration in use in data-flow com-

Computing Surveys, Vol. 14, No. 1, March 1982

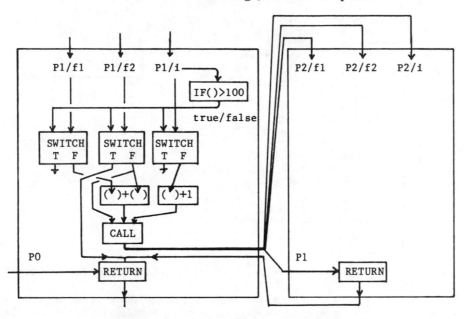

Figure 10. Data-flow iteration using recursion.

puters, based on an additional *iteration number* field [ARVI77a, TREL78] in each reference, for example, P/N/A/I. This iteration number field distinguishes individual data tokens, logically flowing on a particular arc, by giving each token a unique I value, for example, 1, 2, 3, ... Using this third scheme for the Fibonacci example, basically three sequences of data tokens would be generated: f2/1, f2/2, ... ; f1/1, f1/2, ...; and i/1, i/2, ... Some of the data-flow computer designs [ARVI77a, WATS79] support this concept of an iteration number field, but the field is only directly applicable for a single level of iteration. Using only iteration numbers for nested iterations such as

FOR x = 1 TO 3 DO
  FOR y = 1 TO 3 DO
    FOR z = 1 TO 3 DO
      ... N ...
    OD
  OD
OD

it would be necessary to provide three iteration number fields in a reference to give unique names for the 27 tokens for, say, argument A of N, that is, P/N/A/1/1/1 ... P/N/A/1/2/3 ... P/N/A/3/3/3. (In fact, this case can be avoided by treating each FOR ... OD as a procedure with a unique process number and using a single iteration number for its one level of internal iteration.)

3.4 Reduction

Reduction is based on a recursive control mechanism and either a by-value or a by-reference data mechanism. String reduction has a by-value data mechanism, and graph reduction has a by-reference data mechanism. Reduction programs are essentially expressions that are rewritten in the course of execution. They are built (as described in Section 1.3) from functions applied to arguments. Recall that both functions and arguments can be simple values or subexpressions. In string reduction, copies of expressions are reduced. In graph reduction, subexpressions are shared using references. Referential transparency (see Section 1.3) means that a reduction program will give the same result whether data are copied or shared. Below, string reduction and graph reduction are described in more detail. Note that because reduction is inherently recursive, we only show a recursive version of the Fibonacci program. In reduction programs iteration is represented as tail recursion.

```
Initial Expression:

  ( answer ) WHERE
                   answer = fib (1, 1, 3);
            fib (f1, f2, i) = IF i > 100 THEN f2
                                        ELSE fib (f2, f1+f2, i+1) FI;

First Reduction:

  ( IF 3 > 100 THEN 1
             ELSE fib (1, 1+1, 3+1) FI )

Next Reductions:

  ( IF FALSE THEN 1
             ELSE fib (1, 1+1, 3+1) FI )

  ( fib (1, 1+1, 3+1) )

  ( fib (1, 2, 4) )

  ( fib (2, 3, 5) ) ... ( fib (3, 5, 6) ) ... ( fib (5, 8, 7) )
```

Figure 11.   String reduction of Fibonacci program.

String reduction programs are expressions containing literals and values. They are conveniently represented as a bracketed expression, with parentheses indicating nesting, as shown in Figure 11. In Figure 11 the initial expression (answer) is first reduced using the definition fib(f1, f2, i), with f1, f2, and i replaced by 1, 1, and 3. The next reduction evaluates $3 > 100$, giving (IF FALSE ...) followed by (fib(1, 1 + 1, 3 + 1)) and so on. Execution terminates with the original expression, answer, being replaced by the one-hundredth Fibonacci number. Because the form of this function is tail recursive, its execution behaves like iteration; the final result is passed out directly to the original computation, and no intermediate values are preserved.

In Figure 11, an innermost computation rule (Section 2.1) was used, forcing all arguments to be evaluated before being substituted into definitions. If another rule were chosen, a different sequence of reductions would occur before the same answer was found. In string reduction, because a by-value data mechanism is used, separate copies of actual arguments are generated for each formal parameter occurrence. This may increase parallelism, in the sense that many processors can work simultaneously on their own copies of subexpressions. But most of this work may be needlessly dupli-

cated effort as in the example above. For this reason, we conclude that string manipulation is best suited to innermost computation rules where functions are only applied to already evaluated arguments. In this case work will not be duplicated.

Graph reduction programs are expressions containing literals, values, and references. In graph reduction, parameters are substituted by reference into the body of a defined function. For simplicity we assume that the substitution occurs automatically when a definition is dereferenced. In practice, a special mechanism such as lambda substitution or combinators [TURN79a] is used to achieve this formal-to-actual parameter binding. Because of the by-reference mechanism, in Figure 12, it is more suitable to use a graphic notation to represent the Fibonacci program. Nodes of the graph represent a function and its arguments, while arcs represent references and structuring.

Figure 12 shows a graph reduction program for Fibonacci. This example uses a parallel outermost computation rule. The loss of efficiency that can occur with outermost string reduction does not occur here because graph reduction permits sharing of expressions. If an innermost computation rule had been used, no real use would have been made of the graph reduction's by-ref-

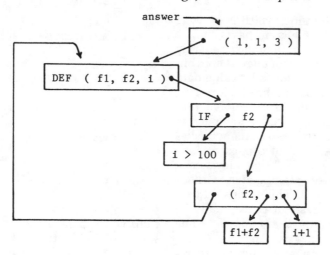

Figure 12. Graph reduction of Fibonacci program.

erence data mechanism. This is because all subexpressions would be reduced before the functions referring to them. Thus the only references in functions would be to values, and there would be no sharing of subexpressions. For this reason, graph reduction is suited to outermost computation rules.

3.5 Implications

Control-flow program organizations, owing to the separation of flows of control from flows of data and the way operands are accessed, tend to be less efficient than, say, data flow when evaluating simple expressions. For example, to pass the partial result of a subexpression to the enclosing expression requires three operations—store result, send control flow, load result—in control flow, but only one operation—send data token—in data flow. However, control flow has advantages when manipulating data structures that are to be manipulated in place, or where a specific pattern of control is required, as, for instance, with conditional evaluation of alternatives. In addition, since instructions have both input and output references, the pattern of data accesses is unconstrained, with execution manipulating a global state composed of all the memory cells of a program. As a general-purpose program organization control flow is surprisingly flexible, particularly with respect to memory changes, interaction, and complex control structures. The

criticisms of control-flow organizations have been well documented by Backus [BACK78]. Basically, they lack useful mathematical properties for reasoning about programs, parallelism is in some respect bolted on, they are built on low-level concepts, and there is a major separation between the representation and execution of simple instructions and of procedures and functions.

The major advantage of data flow is the simplicity and the highly parallel nature of its program organization. This results from the data token scheme combining both the by-value data mechanism and the parallel control mechanism. The data-flow program organization is very efficient for the evaluation of simple expressions and the support of procedures and functions with call-by-value parameters. However, where shared data structures are to be manipulated in place or where specific patterns of control are required, such as sequential or conditional, data flow seems at a disadvantage. Implementation of data-flow program organizations often separate the storage for data tokens and instructions, which makes compilation at least conceptually difficult. Thus as a general-purpose program organization pure data flow is questionable, but for more specialist applications like process control or even robotics it may be highly suitable [JIPD81c].

String and graph reduction are both notable for providing efficient support for functional programming, which is growing in interest. Graph reduction has a by-reference data mechanism that allows sharing and allows manipulation of unevaluated objects. String reduction has a by-value data mechanism and so has minimal addressing overheads. The nature of functional programs makes them suitable for parallel evaluation; referential transparency makes reductions independent of context and sequencing. Graph manipulation allows arbitrary objects to be manipulated without their being evaluated. This means that infinite data structures can conceptually be used as long as only the values of some finite part of them are demanded.

In graph reduction, structures are represented by a reference until their contents are needed; because references are generally smaller than structures, they are more efficient to manipulate. In string reduction, structures are represented by value, and so their contents are duplicated at many points in the program; thus their contents are available locally, without a referenced value being fetched from elsewhere. Last, for reduction program organizations to become candidates for general-purpose computing, it is necessary for functional programming language to become the most widely used style of programming.

4. MACHINE ORGANIZATION

We use the term machine organization to cover the way a machine's resources are configured and allocated to support a program organization. This section starts by classifying the machine organizations being used in data-driven and demand-driven computers.

4.1 Classification

An examination of the data- and demand-driven computer architectures under development reveals three basic classes of machine organization, which we call centralized, packet communication, and expression manipulation.

(1) *Centralized.* Centralized machine organization consists of a single processor, communication, and memory resource, as shown in Figure 13. It views an executing program as having a single active instruction, which passes execution to a specific successor instruction. The state of execution is often held in registers or stacks.

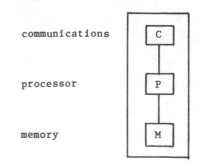

Figure 13. Centralized machine organization.

tion, which passes execution to a specific successor instruction. The state of execution is often held in registers or stacks.

(2) *Packet communication.* Packet communication machine organization consists of a circular instruction execution pipeline of resources in which processors, communications, and memories are interspersed with "pools of work." This is illustrated by Figure 14. The organization views an executing program as a number of independent information packets, all of which are active, and may split and merge. For a parallel computer, packet communication is a very simple strategy for allocating packets of work to resources. Each packet to be processed is placed with similar packets in one of the pools of work. When a resource becomes idle, it takes a packet from its input pool, processes it, places a modified packet in an output pool, and then returns to the idle state. Parallelism is obtained either by having a number of identical resources between pools, or by replicating the circular pipelines and connecting them by the communications.

(3) *Expression manipulation.* Expression manipulation machine organization consists of identical resources usually organized into a regular structure such as a vector or tree, as shown in Figure 15. Each resource contains a processor, communication, and memory capability. The organization views an executing program as consisting of one large nested program structure, parts of which are active while other parts are temporarily suspended. In an expression manipulation organization the adjacency of items in the program structure is significant, and the memories in this ma-

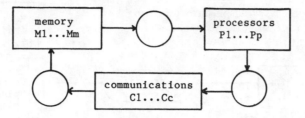

Figure 14. Packet communication machine organization.

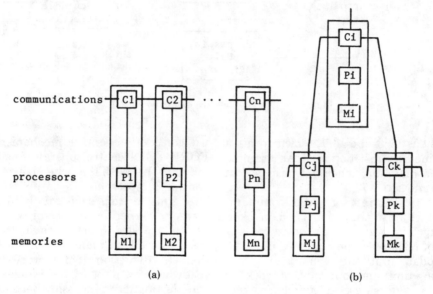

Figure 15. Expression manipulation machine organization: (a) vector; (b) tree.

chine structure maintain the adjacency of items in the program structure. Each resource examines its part of the overall program structure looking for work to perform.

Since these machine organizations relate closely to the way programs are represented and executed, the three are often equated and confused with, respectively, control-flow, data-flow, and reduction program organizations. However, as we discuss below, other less obvious pairings of machine and program organizations are possible.

4.2 Control Flow

The most obvious means of supporting control flow is to use a centralized machine organization for sequential forms and either a packet communication or an expression manipulation machine organization for parallel control flow. Sequential control flow supported by a centralized machine orga-

nization, where the active instruction is specified by the program counter register, is clearly the basis of all traditional computers. Their familiarity does not warrant further discussion, and we shall concentrate on the support of parallel control flow.

For parallel control flow two basic methods were discussed in Section 1.1 for synchronizing the execution of instructions, namely, FORK–JOIN control operators and the use of control tokens. We start by examining a packet communication machine organization supporting control tokens. In such a machine organization, one of the ways of synchronizing a set of control tokens activating an instruction is to use a *matching* mechanism. This matching mechanism intercepts tokens and groups them into sets with regard to their common consumer instruction. When a set is complete, control is released to activate the instruction, as, for instance, in Figure 1c

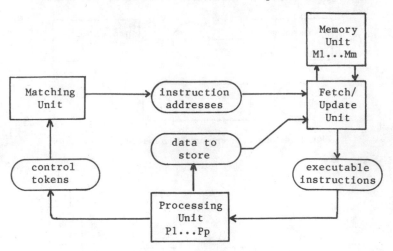

Figure 16. Control-flow packet communications.

with tokens i3/0 and i3/1, which forms a set destined for instruction i3. An example of such a matching scheme is proposed in FARR79 and HOPK79.

Figure 16 illustrates a packet communication machine organization based on token matching. The organization consists of four groups of resources: the matching unit, the fetch/update unit, the memory unit, and processing unit; and four pools of work for instruction addresses, executable instructions, data to store, and control tokens. The task of the matching unit is to group tokens by taking individual tokens from the control tokens pool and storing them in their respective sets in its local memory. When a set of tokens is complete, their common instruction address is placed in the output pool and the set is deleted. The fetch/update unit has two input pools, one containing addresses of instructions to be activated and the other data to be stored. This unit interacts with the memory unit, which stores instructions and data. For each address consumed, the fetch/update unit takes a copy of the corresponding instruction, dereferences its input arguments and replaces them by their corresponding values, and outputs this executable instruction. Last, the processing unit takes executable instructions, processes them, and outputs data to store and control tokens to the respective pools.

For parallel control flow supported by an expression manipulation organization,

we consider a control mechanism using FORK–JOIN control operators, as shown in Figure 1b. With this scheme each flow of control is represented by a processor executing instructions sequentially in its local memory. When a processor executes a FORK operator, it activates another processor whose local memory contains the addressed instruction. If this processor is already busy, then the FORK is delayed until the destination processor becomes idle. On completion, the processor issuing the FORK resumes sequential execution. JOIN operators synchronize execution by logically consuming flows of control. The processor executing the JOIN n must be reactivated n times before it resumes sequential execution. The memories of an expression manipulation organization, as shown in Figure 15, maintain the adjacency of instructions in the program structure. Thus a processor sequentially executing instructions may run off the end of its memory. In this case control is passed, in the same way as a FORK operator, to the adjacent processor.

4.3 Data Flow

Since a data-flow computer needs to record the large set of potentially executable instructions, it is difficult to conceive of supporting data flow with a centralized machine organization. We therefore proceed to examine packet communication, the

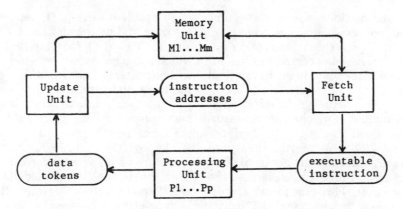

Figure 17. Data-flow packet communication with token storage.

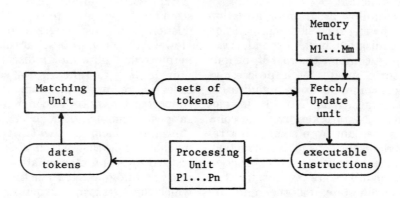

Figure 18. Data-flow packet communication with token matching.

most obvious machine organization for supporting data flow.

Instruction execution in data-flow computers is, in general, controlled by either of two synchronization schemes [DENN79b], which we refer to as *token storage* and *token matching*. In the first scheme data tokens are actually stored into an instruction or a copy of the instruction, and an instruction executes when it has received all its inputs. Examples of this scheme include the Massachusetts Institute of Technology [DENN79a] and Texas Instruments [CORN79] data-flow computers. In the second scheme a token-matching mechanism, as described above, is employed. When a set of data tokens is complete, the set is released to activate the consumer instruction—as, for instance, in Figure 2, with i2/1 := 4 and i2/2 := 2, which form a set of tokens (4, 2) for instruction i2. Examples of this scheme include Irvine Data Flow

[ARVI80a], the Manchester Data Flow System [WATS79], and the Newcastle Data-Control Flow Computer [HOPK79].

Packet communication organizations based on these two schemes for synchronizing instruction execution are illustrated by Figures 17 and 18. A point of commonality in the two organizations is the processing unit consisting of a number of independent processing elements that asynchronously evaluate the executable instruction packets. Such a packet contains all the information required to process the instruction and distribute the results: the operation code, the input values, and the references for the result tokens.

In Figure 17 the data token packets are in the input pool of the update unit. This unit takes in single data tokens and stores them in the memory unit. Certain of these data tokens may complete the inputs for an instruction, thus enabling it for execution.

For these instructions the update unit places their addresses in its output pool. The fetch unit uses these instruction addresses to retrieve the corresponding instructions and place them in its output pool for execution.

In Figure 18, where synchronization is based on a matching mechanism, data token packets form the input pool of the matching unit. This unit forms them into sets, temporarily storing the set until complete, whereupon the set is released to the fetch/update unit. This unit forms executable instructions by merging the values from a set of tokens with a copy of their consumer instruction.

When a data-flow program organization is supported by an expression manipulation machine organization, each of the identical resources must combine the role of the four units (memory, update, fetch, processing) of the packet communication organization with token storage. When a processing element receives a data token over the communications medium from some other resource, it updates the consumer instruction. The element then inspects the instruction to see if all the inputs are present; if not, it returns to the idle state. If all the inputs are present, the processing element performs the operation and deletes the inputs from its memory. Next it passes the data tokens containing the results to their consumer instructions and returns to the idle state. We place the Utah Data-Driven Machine [DAVI78] in this category.

4.4 Reduction

In reduction computers instruction execution is based on the recognition of reducible expressions and the transformation of these expressions. Execution is by a substitution process, which traverses the program structure and successively replaces reducible expressions by others that have the same meaning, until a constant expression representing the result of the program is reached. There are two basic problems in supporting this reduction on a machine organization: first, managing dynamically the memory of the program structure being transformed and, second, keeping control information about the state of the transformation. Solutions to the memory manage-

ment problem include (1) representing the program and instructions as strings, for example, "((*) ((+) (b) (1)) ((−) (b) (c)))," which can be expanded and contracted without altering the meaning of the surrounding structure, and (2) representing the program as a graph structure with pointers, and using garbage collection. Solutions to the control problem are (1) to use control stacks, which record, for example, the ancestors of an instruction, that is, those instructions that demanded its execution; and (2) pointer reversal, where the ancestor is defined by a *reversed* pointer stored in the instruction.

Expression manipulation organizations seem most applicable to supporting the reduction form of program organization. However, the computational rules (e.g., innermost and outermost) discussed above provide us with schemes for sequentially executing reduction programs that may be supported by centralized machine organizations. Examples of such centralized organizations includes the GMD reduction machine [KLUG79], which uses seven specialized stacks for manipulating strings, and the Cambridge SKIM machine [CLAR80], which supports graph structures.

Packet communication organizations are also being used to support reduction. An example of such an organization is the Utah Applicative Multiprocessing System [KELL79]. In these organizations, which support demand-driven graph reduction, instruction execution is controlled by two types of token. A consumer instruction dispatches a demand token (containing a return reference) to a producer instruction signaling it to execute and return its results. This producer instruction returns the result in a *result* token, which is basically a data token as in data flow. Two synchronization schemes are required for reduction to be supported by packet communication. The first ensures that only a single demand token for a particular instruction can actually activate the instruction, while the second provides synchronization for result tokens, as was provided for data tokens in data flow.

The final machine organization discussed here is the support of reduction by expression manipulation. Examples of such orga-

Memories

Stage	M1	M2	M3	M4	M5	M6
1	(* i1 i2)	–	–	i1:(+b1)	i2:(-bc)	b:(4) c:(2)
2	(* (+ b 1) i2)	–		"	"	" "
3	(* (+ b 1)	(-bc))		"	"	" "
4	(*	(+ 4 1)	(- 4 2))	"	"	" "
5	(* 5 2)	–	–	"	"	" "

Figure 19.   Reduction expression manipulation.

nizations are the Newcastle Reduction Machine [TREL80a] and the North Carolina Cellular Tree Machine [MAGO79a]. The example expression manipulation organization we shall examine [WILN80] is one in which the program structure is represented as nested delimited strings and each memory in the machine is connected to its two adjacent memories to form what may be viewed as a large bidirectional shift register. Substitution of an expression into a memory causes the adjacent information to shift apart, which may cause its migration into adjacent memory elements. Figure 19 illustrates this migration of instructions.

To find work each processing element P_i traverses the subexpression in its memory M_i, looking for a reducible expression. Since the "window" of a processing element into the overall expression under evaluation is limited to the contents of its own memory element, it is not possible for two processing elements to attempt simultaneously to reduce the same subexpression—one of the key implementation problems of expression manipulation machines. When a processing element locates a reference to be replaced by its corresponding definition, it sends a request to the communications unit via its communications element C_i. The communications units in such a computer are frequently organized as a tree-structured network on the assumption that the majority of communications will exhibit properties of locality of reference. Concurrency in such reduction computers is related to the number of reducible subexpressions at any instant and also to the number of processing elements to traverse these expressions. Additional concurrency is obtained by increas-

ing the number of M_i-P_i-C_i elements, and also by reducing the size of each memory element, thus increasing the physical distribution of the expressions.

4.5 Implications

From the above discussions of control flow, data flow, and reduction, it is clear that they gravitate toward, respectively, centralized, packet communications and expression manipulation organizations. However, we have also shown, and the fact is being demonstrated by various research groups, that other pairings of program organizations and machine organizations are viable.

Control flow can be efficiently supported by either of the three machine organizations. A centralized organization is most suited to sequential control flow. The advantage of this organization is its simplicity, both for resource allocation and implementation; its disadvantage is the lack of parallelism. A packet communication organization favors a parallel "control token" form of control flow. Although relatively simple, it lacks the concept of an implicit next instruction, thereby incurring additional explicit references in instructions and extra resource allocation. Last, an expression manipulation machine organization is most suited to a parallel FORK–JOIN style of control flow. This organization combines the advantages of the above two by being parallel but also supports the concept of an implicit next instruction. It does, however, incur additional FORK and JOIN style control operators.

For data flow it is difficult to envisage a centralized machine organization because of the need to record a large number of potentially executable instructions. However, packet communication provides two alternative organizations for the efficient support of data flow. The first packet communication scheme is based on storing data tokens into an instruction and executing the instruction when it is complete. This form of machine organization may be viewed as supporting self-modifying programs and has the advantage of conceptually allowing one data-flow program to generate another for execution. The second packet communication scheme is based on matching data tokens. This form of organization has the advantage of supporting reentrant code, but the disadvantage of being conceptually difficult to generate code for. Data flow may also be supported by expression manipulation, but it is difficult to assess the advantages and disadvantages of this approach.

Finally, we consider machine organization for reduction. Because of the various computational rules for reduction, it can be efficiently supported by any of the three machine organizations. For all these organizations, the two basic problems are, first, managing dynamically the memory and, second, managing the control information. A centralized organization is best suited to a sequential form of reduction. It can implement with reasonable efficiency either string or graph manipulation. A packet communication and expression manipulation organization favor a parallel computational rule.

5. DATA-FLOW COMPUTERS

The number of extremely interesting data-driven and demand-driven computer architectures under investigation has made our task of choosing the set to survey particularly difficult. Since this paper is concerned with identifying related concepts rather than describing implementations, we have chosen to give brief overviews of a number of architecture schemes, described in the open literature, whose concepts seem particularly interesting. Our examination of data-driven computers clearly must start with the Massachusetts Institute of Technology architecture.

5.1 M.I.T. Data-Flow Computer

The contribution of the M.I.T. project to data-flow research has been significant, forming the basis for most other data-flow projects. There are extensive references to this M.I.T. work, which covers data-flow graphs [RODR69, DENN71, DENN72, DENN74a], computer architecture [DENN74b, DENN75b, RUMB77, DENN79a], and the design of high-level programming languages [WENG75, ACKE79a], including the single-assignment language VAL [ACKE79b], based on the abstract-data-type language CLU. (Data-flow languages are in general based on the single-assignment principle [TESL68, CHAM71].) This description of the M.I.T. work concentrates on the computer architecture and is based on a description given in DENN79a.

The program organization used in the M.I.T. computer is clearly data flow; however, only one token may occupy an arc at an instance. This leads to a firing rule which states that an instruction is enabled if a data token is present on each of its input arcs and no token is present on any of its output arcs. Thus the M.I.T. program organization contains control tokens, as well as data tokens, that contribute to the enabling of an instruction but do not contribute any input data. These control tokens act as acknowledge signals when data tokens are removed from output arcs. In the program, organization values from data tokens are stored into locations in an instruction and control tokens signal to a producer instruction when particular locations become unoccupied.

The M.I.T. organization is what we term a packet communication organization with token storage. This organization is shown in Figure 20. It consists of five major units connected by channels through which information packets are sent using an asynchronous transmission protocol. The five units are (1) the Memory Section, consisting of Instruction Cells that hold the instructions and their operands; (2) the Processing Section, consisting of specialist processing elements that perform operations on data values; (3) the Arbitration Network, delivering executable instruction packets from the Memory Section to the Processing Section; (4) the Control Network, deliver-

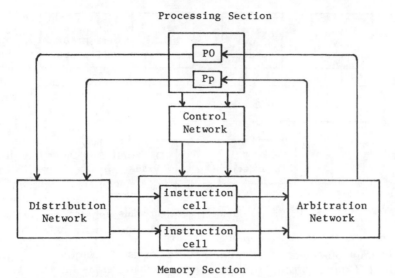

Processing Section

Memory Section

Figure 20. M.I.T. data-flow computer.

ing control packets from the Processing Section to the Memory Section; and (5) the Distribution Network, delivering data packets from the Processing Section to the Memory Section.

Instructions held in the Memory Section are enabled for execution by the arrival of their operands in data packets from the Distribution Network and in control packets from the Control Network. Each Instruction Cell in the Memory Section holds one instruction of the data-flow program and is identified by a unique address. When occupied, an Instruction Cell holds an instruction consisting of an operation code and several references (i.e., destination addresses) for results and contains, in addition, three registers, which await the arrival of values for use as operands by the instruction. Once an Instruction Cell has received the necessary operand values and acknowledge signals, the cell becomes enabled.

Enabled instructions together with their operands are sent as operation packets to the Processing Section through the Arbitration Network. This network provides a path from each Instruction Cell to each specialist element in the Processing Unit and sorts the operation packets among its output ports according to the operation codes of the instructions they contain. The results of instruction execution are sent through the Distribution and Control Networks to

the Memory Section, where they become operands of other instructions.

Each result packet consists of a result value and a reference derived from the instruction by the processing element. There are two kinds of result packet: (1) control packets containing Boolean values (Boolean data tokens) and acknowledge signals (control tokens), which are sent through the Control Network; and (2) data packets (data tokens) containing integer or complex values, which are sent through the Distribution Network. The two networks deliver result packets to the Instruction Cells specified by their destination field and a cell becomes enabled when all result packets have been received.

The current status of the M.I.T. dataflow project is that hardware for the above computer architecture is under development and a compiler is being written for the VAL programming language. A number of supportive projects on fault tolerance, hardware description languages, etc. are also in progress.

5.2 Texas Instruments Distributed Data Processor

The Distributed Data Processor (DDP) is a system designed by Texas Instruments to investigate the potential of data flow as the basis of a high-performance computer, con-

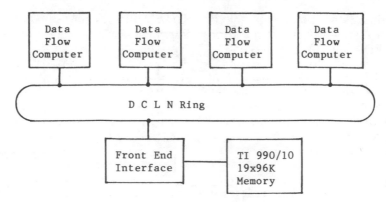

Figure 21.   Texas Instruments distributed data processor.

structed using only off-the-shelf technology. This project [CORN79, JOHN79] began in mid-1976, and DDP plus its supporting software has been operational since September 1978. A most interesting aspect of the DDP project is that the computer is largely programmed in FORTRAN 66. A cross compiler, based on the Texas Instruments Advanced Scientific Computer's optimizing FORTRAN compiler, translates FORTRAN subprograms separately into directed graph representations and a linkage editor combines them into a single program [JOHN79]. The following description of DDP is largely taken from the paper by Cornish [CORN79].

Conceptually, DDP and the M.I.T. computer discussed above are based on a similar data-flow program organization. An instruction is enabled if a data token is present on each of its input arcs and no token is present on any of its output arcs. Only one token may occupy an arc at an instance. In addition, control tokens are used as acknowledge signals, for instance, to handle FORTRAN language constructs that are resistant to representation by "pure" data-flow code.

A DDP instruction consists of the following fields: (1) an operation code, (2) a so-called predecessor count of the input tokens yet to arrive, (3) a field reserved for a hardware-maintained linked list of instructions ready for execution, (4) an original count of tokens used to restore the predecessor count after the instruction executes, (5) an operand list with space reserved for incoming token operands, and finally (6) a

successor list containing the destination instruction addresses for the result tokens. The size of instructions and whether they are of fixed or variable length are unclear from the references.

The DDP machine organization is what we term a packet communication organization with token storage, because operands are stored into unoccupied locations in an instruction. Although this is the same class of machine organization as the M.I.T. computer, the computer architecture of DDP is significantly different. A block diagram of the DDP system is shown in Figure 21. It consists of five independent computing elements: four identical data-flow computers that cooperate in the execution of a computation and a Texas Instruments 990/10 minicomputer, acting as a front-end processor for input/output, providing operating system support, and handling the collection of performance data. (A data-flow program to be executed is statistically partitioned and allocated among the four data-flow computers.) These five computing elements in the DDP are connected together by a variable-length, word-wide, circular shift register known formally as a DCLN ring. This shift register is daisy chained through each element and may therefore carry up to five variable-length packets in parallel.

Each data-flow computer consists of four principle units. These units are (1) the Arithmetic Unit, which processes executable instructions and outputs tokens; (2) the Program Memory, built out of standard random-access-memory (RAM) chips and holding the data-flow instructions; (3) the Update Controller, which updates instructions with tokens; and (4) the Pending Instruction Queue, which holds executable instructions that have been enabled. Executable instructions are removed from this queue by the Arithmetic Unit and processed. When an instruction completes execution, a series of token packets are released to the Update Controller. Using the address in a packet the Update Controller stores the token operand in the instruction and decrements by one its predecessor count. If this count is zero, the instruction is ready to execute; a copy is placed on the Pending Instruction Queue and the stored version of the instruction is reinitialized. It is unclear whether the Pending Instruction Queue may contain more than one executable instruction. However, when the capacity of the queue is exceeded, the enabled instructions are linked, in memory, to the Pending Instruction Queue via their link field already reserved for this purpose. This method has the advantage that no amount of program parallelism overflows the capacity of the hardware resource.

DDP is implemented in transistor–transistor logic (TTL) on wire-wrap boards and chassis from Texas Instruments 990 minicomputer components. Each data-flow computer contains 32K words of metal-oxide-semiconductor (MOS) memory with each word divided as a 32-bit data field and a 4-bit tag field holding the predecessor count. Each of these computers contains about the same number of components as a minicomputer and provides approximately the same raw processing power. Thus, as remarked by Cornish [CORN79, pp. 19–25], "data flow designs place no particular burden on the implementation other than using more memory for program storage."

5.3 Utah Data-Driven Machine

Data-Driven Machine #1 (DDM1) is a computing element of a recursively structured data-flow architecture designed by Al Davis and his colleagues while working at Burroughs Interactive Research Center in La Jolla, California. DDM1 [DAVI78, DAVI79a, DAVI79b] was completed in July 1976 and now resides at the University of Utah, where the project is continuing under support from Burroughs Corporation. Here we examine the structure of this recursive architecture and the operation of DDM1, descriptions primarily taken from Davis [DAVI78].

The program and machine organization, both based on the concept of recursion, contrasts markedly with the previous data-flow systems we have examined. The computer is composed of a hierarchy of computing elements (processor–memory pairs), where each element is logically recursive and consists of further inferior elements. Physically the computer architecture is tree structured, with each computing element being connected to a superior element (above) and up to eight inferior elements (below), which it supervises. Only recently have other groups come to recognize the fundamental importance of hierarchy for decentralized systems, particularly those exploiting VLSI [SEIT79, MEAD80, TREL80b], since it is able to utilize locality of reference to reduce the critical problems of system-wide communication and control.

In the Utah data-flow program organization, referred to as Data-Driven Nets [DAVI79a], data tokens provide all communication between instructions—there are no control tokens. In addition, the arcs of the directed graph are viewed as first-in/first-out (FIFO) queues, a model that is supported by the architecture. The actual program representation corresponding to these Data-Driven Nets consists of hierarchically nested structure of variable-length character strings. A data-flow program, its subprograms, and their individual instructions are each viewed as a parenthesized string, for example,

$$\text{``(( ) (( ) } \ldots \text{) } \ldots \text{).''}$$

The notion of an arc being a FIFO queue is supported by storing the data tokens that have arrived but have not been consumed with the instruction in the program structure. Each instruction therefore consists of an operation code and a list of destination addresses for the results, together with a variable number of sets of data tokens waiting either for a set to be complete or for consumption by the instruction. An advan-

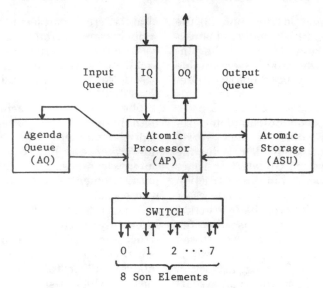

Figure 22. Utah data-driven machine (DDM1).

tage of the parenthesized string form of representation is that it supports dynamic, and localized, variation of the program structure. Because of the nature of this program representation and the method of allocating work to resources, discussed below, we classify the Utah architecture as an expression manipulation machine organization.

A block diagram of the computing element DDM1 is shown in Figure 22. DDM1 consists of six major units: (1) the Atomic Storage Unit (ASU) provides the program memory; (2) the Atomic Processor (AP) executes the instructions; (3) the Agenda Queue (AQ) stores messages for the local Atomic Storage Unit; (4) the Input Queue (IQ) buffers messages from the superior computing element; (5) the Output Queue (OQ) buffers messages to the superior element; and finally (6) the SWITCH connects the computing element with up to eight inferior elements. All paths between these units, except for that between the Atomic Storage Unit and Atomic Processor are six wire paths (a two-wire request–acknowledge control link and the four-wire, character-width data bus). The units communicate asynchronously using a four-phase request–acknowledge protocol.

Work in the form of a program fragment is allocated to a computing element by its superior, being placed as a message in the Input Queue. The action taken by the computing element depends on the structure of the fragment and whether there are further inferior elements. If there exists some set of concurrent subprograms and the computing element has substructure, then it will decompose and allocate the subprograms to its inferior elements. Otherwise, the program fragment is placed in the element's own Atomic Storage Unit. The Atomic Storage Unit of DDM1 contains a 4K × 4-bit character store, using RAM devices, and also performs storage management functions on the variable-length parenthesized strings, such as initialize, read, write, insert, and delete. All target locations in the store are found by an access vector into the tree-organized storage structure. Free space is managed automatically.

When a data token arrives as a message, for example, in the Input Queue, it is either passed on via the appropriate queue to a computing element at some other level, or if the program fragment is in the local Atomic Storage Unit, it is inserted into the instruction. When such an instruction becomes enabled, it is executed immediately by the Atomic Processor and the result tokens distributed. These are placed in the Output Queue or SWITCH, or if the receiving instruction is in the local Atomic Storage Unit, they are placed in the Agenda Queue. After the processor has generated all the result tokens, it will service messages from the SWITCH, the Agenda Queue, and the Input Queue, in descending order of priority.

Current status of the project is that DDM1 is operational and communicates with a DEC-20/40, which is used for software support of compilers, simulators, and performance measurement programs. The current programming language is a statement description of the directed graph; however, an interactive graphical programming language is also under development.

5.4 Irvine Data Flow Machine

The Irvine data-flow (Id) machine is motivated by the desire to exploit the potential of VLSI and to provide a high-level, highly concurrent program organization. This project originated at the University of California at Irvine [ARVI75, ARVI77a, ARVI77b, GOST79a, GOST79b] and now continues at the Massachusetts Institute of Technology [ARVI80a, ARVI80b]. It has made significant contributions to data-flow research, in particular the Id language [ARVI78]. The description given here is principally based on ARVI80a.

The program organization used in the Id machine is pure data flow, with an instruction being enabled when all its input tokens are available. Each instruction may have one or two inputs and any number of outputs. There are a number of interesting features in the Id program organization. The first feature is the sophisticated token identification scheme, similar to the P/N/A/I format discussed in Section 3.3. A token identifier consists of (1) a code block name identifying a particular procedure or loop; (2) a statement number within the code block; (3) an initiation number for the loop; and (4) a context name identifying the activity invoking this procedure or loop. The second interesting feature is its support for data structures, such as arrays, by the inclusion of *I structures* [ARVI80b]. An I structure is a set of components, with each component having a unique selector (for an array the selectors are the indexing integers) and being either a value or an un-

known if the value is not yet available. This feature uses the by-reference mechanism of control flow. Two further features are that Id supports the nondeterminism required for implementing resource managers and, by treating procedure definitions as manipulable values, supports higher order functions, abstract data types, and operator extensibility. These features are discussed in detail in ARVI78.

The Id machine has a packet communication organization with token matching. It consists of N processing elements and an $N \times N$ communications network for routing a token from the processing element generating it to the one consuming the token. This machine organization attempts to minimize communications overhead in two ways. First, the matching unit for tokens destined for a particular instruction is in the same processing element as is the storage holding that instruction. Second, there is a short-circuit path from a processing element to itself so that there is no need to use the full $N \times N$ network if a token is destined for the same processing element as generated it. The mapping algorithm, determining in which processing element an instruction is stored, is intended to obtain maximum usage of this short circuit, while still giving good processor utilization.

Figure 23 illustrates a processing element of the proposed Irvine data-flow machine. Each processing element is essentially a complete computer with an instruction set, up to 16K words each of program storage and data structure storage, and certain special elements. These specialist elements include: (1) the input section, which accepts inputs from other processing elements; (2) the waiting–matching section, which forms data tokens into sets for a consumer instruction; (3) the instruction fetch section, which fetches executable instructions from the local program memory; (4) the service section, that is, a floating-point arithmetic-logic unit (ALU) (e.g., Intel 8087); and (5) the output section, which routes data tokens containing results to the destination-processing element.

The current status of the project is that a computer with 64 processing elements is currently being designed at the Massachusetts Institute of Technology and is ex-

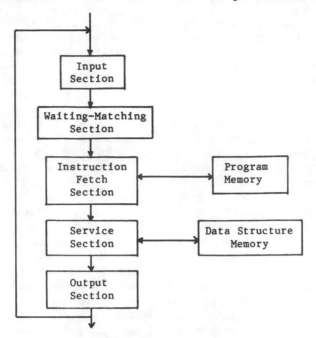

Figure 23. Irvine data-flow processing element.

pected to be ready for MOS fabrication by the end of 1982.

5.5 Manchester Data-Flow Computer

The data-flow project at Manchester University, like a number of other projects, is investigating the use of data flow as the basis for a high-performance computer. This project, starting in 1975, has included the design of a high-level, single-assignment programming language LAPSE, the implementation of translators for LAPSE and a subset of PASCAL, and the production of a detailed stimulator for the Manchester computer architecture. Currently the group is implementing a 20-processor data-flow computer prototype. Early ideas on this design are given in TREL78; this description of the computer is based on WATS79.

The program organization used by the Manchester computer is pure data flow, with an instruction being enabled when all its input arcs contain tokens (its output arcs may also contain unconsumed data tokens), and an arc is viewed as a FIFO queue providing storage for tokens. The program representation is based on a two-address format, with an instruction consisting of an operation code, a destination in-

struction address for a data token, and either a second destination address or an embedded literal. Each instruction consumes either one or two data tokens, and emits either one or two tokens. A token consists of three fields: the value field holding the operand, an instruction address field defining the destination instruction, and last a label field. This label is used for matching tokens into sets and provides three types of information, identifying the process to which the token belongs, the arc on which it is traveling, and also an iteration number specifying which particular token on an arc this is. Thus tokens have a four-field name, as discussed in Section 3.3, serving a number of roles in the architecture, including supporting the notion of arcs being FIFO queues, allowing tokens to be matched into sets, and allowing a program's instructions to be used reentrantly.

The machine organization of the computer is a packet communication organization with token matching. Figure 24 shows a block diagram of the Manchester data-flow computer. It consists of five principal units: (1) the Switch provides input–output for the system; (2) the Token Queue is a FIFO buffer providing temporary storage

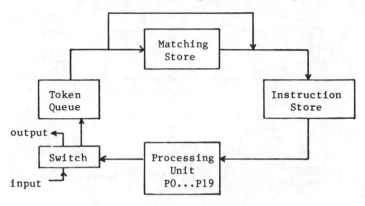

Figure 24. Manchester data-flow computer.

for tokens; (3) the Matching Store matches pairs of tokens; (4) the Instruction Store is the memory holding the data-flow programs; and (5) the Processing Unit, consisting of a number of identical processing elements, executes the instructions. The Switch is used for passing data tokens into or out of the computer, either communicating with peripherals or other, possibly data-flow, computers. To start execution of a program fragment, initialization tokens are inserted at the Switch and directed by their labels to the starting instructions of the computation. A special destination address in the final instructions of the program fragment allows tokens to be output.

A token on reaching the front of the Token Queue can access (if one of a pair) or bypass (if a single input) the Matching Store, depending on information in the token label. An access to the Matching Store will cause a search of the store. The Matching Store is associative in nature, although it is implemented using RAM with hardware hashing techniques, and is based on the work of Goto and Ida [GOTO77]. If a token is found with the same label and instruction address, it is removed to form a token pair. If no match is found, the incoming token is written to the store. Token pairs from the Matching Store, or single tokens that have bypassed it, are routed to the Instruction Store. At this store, which is a RAM addressed by the contents of the instruction address field, the tokens are combined with a copy of the destination instruction to form an executable instruc-

tion that is released to the Processing Unit. This unit consists of a distribution and arbitration system, and a group of microprogrammed microprocessors. The distribution system, on receipt of an executable instruction, will select any processor that is free and allocate the instruction. After execution, the arbitration system controls the output of result tokens from the processing elements.

The current status of the project is that a 20-processing-element computer is under construction. Each processing element is built from Schottky bit–slice microprocessors and is estimated to give an average instruction execution time of 3 microseconds for the data-flow arithmetic operations. If all 20 processing elements can be utilized fully, this will give an approximately 6-million-instruction-per-second rate for the computer as a whole. To support this rate, the following operation times [WATS79] are required: (1) Token Queue read 202 nanoseconds; (2) Matching Store access 303 nanoseconds; (3) Instruction Store read 303 nanoseconds; (4) SWITCH operation 202 nanoseconds; and (5) Token Queue write 202 nanoseconds. These speeds require a storage access time of the order of 200 nanoseconds, which is achievable with low-cost MOS storage devices.

5.6 Toulouse LAU System

"*Language à assignation unique*" is the French translation for the phrase "single-assignment language." The LAU system [COMT76, GELL76, PLAS76, SYRE77,

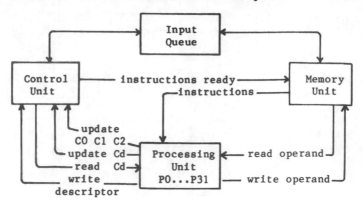

Figure 25. LAU system.

COMT79b] is a data-driven computer designed to execute such languages. The LAU project is based at the CERT Laboratory in Toulouse. Notably this extensive project, starting in 1976, initially designed the LAU high-level language, which was used to program a large number of problems. Subsequently, the group implemented a compiler for the language and a detailed simulator, which yielded a large number of simulation data [PLAS76]. This led to the design and current construction of a powerful 32-processor data-driven computer. The description of the LAU computer given here is based on the paper by Comte and Hifdi [COMT79b].

The LAU programming language has a data-flow model, but the computer's program organization is in fact based on control-flow concepts. In the computer data are passed via sharable memory cells that are accessed through addresses embedded in instructions, and separate control signals are used to enable instructions. However, it should be stressed that, as in data flow, the flow of control is tied to the flow of data (i.e., the control graph and the data graph are identical).

Program representation is based on three logical types of memory, for instructions, for data, and for control information. An instruction (66 bits in length) has a three-address format and consists of an operation code, two data memory addresses for input operands, and a data memory address for the result operand. Following conventional practice, if an input operand is a literal, it replaces the address in the instruction. Each cell in the data memory consists of a value field providing storage for the operand and of two link fields that contain instruction memory addresses of instructions using the operand as an input.

Corresponding to each instruction and data operand are sets of control bits which synchronize execution. Three control bits referred to as $C0, C1$, and $C2$ denote the state of an instruction. $C1$ and $C2$ define whether the two corresponding input operands are available, while $C0$ provides environment control, as, for instance, for instructions within loops. An instruction is enabled when $C0 C1 C2$ match the value 111. A final control bit, referred to as Cd, is associated with each data operand and specifies if the operand is available. Execution of an enabled instruction consists of fetching the two input operands from the data memory using the embedded operand addresses, and performing the specified operation. Next, the result operand is written to the data memory using the result address, which causes the corresponding link addresses to be returned to the processor, and is used to update the corresponding $C1$ and $C2$ of instructions using the result as inputs.

The LAU machine organization is a packet communication organization with token storage, owing to the form of program organization, notably the association of $C0 C1 C2$ control bits with each instruction. Figure 25 illustrates the system organization of the LAU computer. It comprises the memory unit providing storage for instructions and data, the control unit maintaining the control memory, and the processing unit consisting of 32 identical processing elements. Each element is a 16-bit microprogrammed processor built around the AMD 2900 bit–slice microprocessor. Perhaps the most interesting part is the control unit, where the von Neumann program counter is replaced by two memories: the Instruction Control Memory (ICM) and the Data Control Memory (DCM). ICM handles the three control bits C0 C1 C2 associated with each instruction and DCM manages the Cd bit associated with each data operand.

As an illustration of the operation of the LAU computer let us consider the processing of an enabled instruction. Processing starts in the control unit at the Instruction Control Memory. ICM is composed of 32K three-bit-wide words, with the control bits in word i corresponding to the instruction in word i in the memory unit. Two processors scan this memory: the Update Processor sets particular bits of C0 C1 C2, and the Instruction Fetch Processor associatively accesses the memory for 111 patterns. When an enabled instruction is found, its address is sent to the memory unit and the control bits are reset to 011.

The address of the enabled instruction is queued, if necessary, in a 16-bit × 64-word FIFO queue, which is a pool of work for the memory unit. This unit consumes the address and places the corresponding instruction on the instruction bus, which is also a 64-bit × 128-word FIFO queue, where it is eventually accessed by an idle processing element. Once in a processing element, the instruction is decoded and the input addresses are dispatched to the memory unit to access the data operands. When the inputs return, the operation is performed and the result generated. Next the processing element issues a write–read request to the memory unit giving the result and its address. The result will be stored in the value field and the contents of the two link fields will be returned to the element. Once the link fields have been returned, the processing element sends the links to the Update Processor, which uses them to set the corresponding C1 or C2 bits in the instruction

control memory. In parallel to the storing of the result, the processing element sends the result address to the data control memory where the Cd bit is set. This memory is *n* 1-bit words. Like the ICM, the DCM is served by two processors, one that updates the Cd bits and the other that checks that accesses to operands in the memory unit are in fact available (i.e., the Cd bit is set).

Regarding the status of the LAU project, the first of the 32 processors became operational in September 1979, and the remainder have been constructed since then. Predicted performance figures for this hardware are given in COMT79b.

5.7 Newcastle Data-Control Flow Computer

Most of the data-driven projects discussed above are based on a single program organization and are concerned, specifically, with studying its embodiment in a suitable machine organization. In contrast, the group at the University of Newcastle upon Tyne are interested in the actual program organizations, their suitability for a general-purpose decentralized computer, and the possibilities for combining them. In this respect the group has investigated, using software and hardware simulators, data flow [TREL78], "multithread" control flow [FARR79], and reduction [TREL80a] organizations, and also combinations of more than one organization in a single computer. Here we describe the JUMBO computer architecture [HOPK79, TREL82] built to study the integration of data-flow and control-flow computation.

The program organization has both data tokens and control tokens, and some specific combination of tokens causes the enabling of a particular instruction. In the organization there are two ways in which an instruction may obtain its input operands, namely, (1) by receiving data tokens, which may carry a value or an address of the stored value; or (2) by means of embedded inputs stored in the instruction, which, like the contents of data tokens, may be literal values or addresses. When an instruction is enabled, the token inputs and embedded inputs are merged to produce a set of values and addresses. The addresses of inputs are then dereferenced and re-

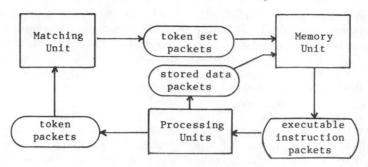

Figure 26. Newcastle data-control flow computer.

placed by their corresponding values from memory. The resulting executable instruction then has a complete set of value arguments on which to compute.

An instruction consists of an operation code and up to eight arguments, certain arguments being embedded in the stored instruction and others being supplied by data tokens at run time. Each operation code uses arguments in specific positions for inputs and places its results in other positions. A stored instruction therefore consists of (1) an operation code, (2) up to eight embedded arguments, (3) a position field defining those arguments that are present, (4) an input mode field defining which of the merged token and embedded arguments are to be dereferenced, and (5) an output mode field specifying which arguments and results are to be combined to produce the outputs of the instruction after execution. Three types of output may be produced by an instruction, namely, data to store in memory, data tokens, and control tokens. Each consists of a reference and a value. For data to store, the name gives the address of the memory cell; for tokens it gives the address of the destination instruction and information to control the token's matching with other tokens in the set, such as the count of tokens. In the computer up to four tokens may be grouped together in a set.

The machine organization of the JUMBO computer is a packet communication organization with token matching. A block diagram of the computer, as shown in Figure 26, consists of three principal units interconnected by FIFO buffers. The Matching Unit controls the enabling of in-

structions by matching sets of tokens, which are released to the Memory Unit when complete. The Memory Unit provides storage for data and instructions. It places the contents of stored data packets in the appropriate memory cell, and for token set packets it constructs executable instructions, which are released to the Processing Unit. Finally, the Processing Unit supports instruction execution and the distribution of results.

When a token set packet is released by the Matching Unit, it contains between zero and four input arguments supplied by data tokens. Using the destination instruction address in the packet, the Memory Unit takes a copy of the target instruction and merges the token arguments with those already embedded in the instruction. The copy of the instruction now has a complete set of arguments. Next, the input mode field, which is an 8×1-bit vector, is extracted, and for each bit set the corresponding argument is assumed to be a memory address and is dereferenced and replaced by its corresponding value to give an executable instruction.

Each of the three units of the JUMBO computer is built from a Motorola M6800 microcomputer system. Storage in the JUMBO computer is divided into 1-kbyte pages. Each process executing in the computer has three pages, one for its tokens in the Matching Unit, and one each for its code and data in the Memory Unit. Processes can be dynamically created and killed, and the token page can be reallocated, implicitly deleting residual tokens so that graphs do not have to be self-cleaning as on other data-driven computers.

5.8 Other Projects

Research into data flow is a rapidly expanding area in the United States, Japan, and Europe. Besides the projects briefly described above, there are a number of other interesting data-flow projects worthy of description in this survey. These include: the MAUD single-assignment system at the University of Lille, France [LECO79]; work at the Mathematical Center, Amsterdam on compiling conventional languages for data-flow machines [VEEN80]; the PLEXUS project at the University of Tampere, Finland [ERKI80]; the FLO project at the University of Manchester, England [EGAN79]; work on a hierarchical data-flow system at the Clarkson College of Technology, New York [SHRO77]; and a number of machines that have been built or are under development in Japan [JIPD81b] such as a high-speed, data-flow machine being developed at Nippon Telegraph and Telephone [AMAM80, JIPD81b].

6. REDUCTION COMPUTERS

Apart from the pioneering work of Klaus Berkling, the stage of development of reduction computers somewhat lags behind that of data-flow computers. This is probably due to reduction semantics being an unfamiliar form of program execution for most computer architects.

6.1 GMD Reduction Machine

The reduction machine project based on the GMD (Gesellschaft für Mathematik und Datenverarbeitung) Laboratory in Bonn, West Germany, aimed to demonstrate that reduction machines are a practical alternative to conventional architectures. In particular, the aim was to build a computer easy to program directly in a high-level, functional language based on the lambda calculus. Early ideas on this theme are given in BERK71 and consolidated in BERK75. This description of the GMD reduction machine is based on the account in KLUG79, supplemented by information from HOMM79 and KLUG80.

The GMD machine's program organization is string reduction. A design objective was the elimination of addresses entirely, and this is achieved by always using substi-

tution copies of code and data instead of sharing by using addresses. In the machine a program is represented as a prefix expression, the binary tree structuring being uniquely exhibited by a string of symbols. These expressions may be atoms—single symbols or values—or may themselves be strings. Each subtree consists of three parts, namely, a *constructor*, a *function*, and its *argument*.

One task of the constructor is to indicate which of its offspring in the tree is the function and which the argument. Since the reduction machine is designed to traverse expression trees in preorder (i.e., left subtree before the right), it is necessary to know whether the function or the argument should be reduced first, and the order in which they occur in the expression. This is provided by two types of constructor represented by the symbols ":" and "←." The constructor ":", used in the format ": argument function", evaluates the argument expression, by reduction to a constant expression, before the function is applied to it. The constructor "←", used in the form "← function argument", applies (reduces) the function expression before the argument is evaluated.

Expressions may in general be built from either constructor and identical constant expressions obtained. For instance, the arithmetic expression 4 + 2 can be represented either as : 2 : 4 + or as ← ← + 4 2. Differences arise when constructors are applied to function bodies as they give rise to by-value and by-name parameter substitution. Special symbols for function–argument binding are also provided in the form of a pair of constructors lambda and alpha. The former implements standard lambda substitution, while the latter is used to implement recursion. Lambda simply causes the actual parameter to be substituted for a formal parameter in an expression (the operation being known in lambda calculus as a beta reduction). Alpha is used to bind function bodies to occurrences of the function name in recursive expressions, with occurrences of the name being replaced by a new application of alpha, for example,

ALPHA.f(. . . f . . .)
   reduces to f(. . . ALPHA.f . . .)

Obviously the bracketed body of f must

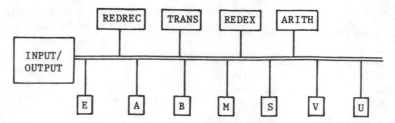

Figure 27. GMD reduction machine.

contain a terminating condition to prevent the recursion's being infinite.

The GMD machine organization is classified as a centralized organization, particularly by the way it represents and executes programs. A block diagram of the machine architecture is shown in Figure 27. It consists of the reduction unit (comprising four subunits named TRANS, REDREC, REDEX, and ARITH), a set of seven 4-kbyte push-down stacks (of which E, A, B, U, V, and M are used to process expressions, and S serves as the system control stack), and a 1-byte-wide bus system for communication between the various units. In the reduction unit the four subunits perform the following tasks. TRANSport performs all traversal algorithms; REDuction–RECognition looks for an instance of a reducible expression during traversal and, upon finding one, halts the TRANS unit and passes control to the REDEX unit. REDuction–EXecution essentially provides a fast control memory containing all the control programs to perform the reductions. In this task it is assisted by the ARITHmetic unit, which performs all the arithmetic and logical operations.

In the traversal of an expression by the machine, three principal stacks are used. These are E, M, and A, referred to as *source, intermediate,* and *sink.* The source stack holds the tree expression to be reduced with the root constructor on top of the stack. As the expression is traversed, a succession of pop operations moves the symbols off the source stack onto the sink stack. For reasons of consistency, the expression ending up on the sink stack must appear with the constructors on top of their respective subtrees. To accomplish this, the third intermediate stack is used as temporary storage for constructors that emerge from the source stack ahead of their subexpressions, but must enter the sink stack after them.

The GMD reduction machine has been built and is connected to a microcomputer system supporting a library and programming tools. The whole system has been operational since 1978. An attempt has also been made to implement Backus' FP language [BACK78], but in general this is less successful than the original lambda calculus language for which the machine was designed. The main contribution of the GMD project is to demonstrate that there is sufficient understanding of reduction to implement a workable machine. The project has also shown that string manipulation is a useful technique but may be inefficient when adhered to rigorously.

6.2 Newcastle Reduction Machine

The Newcastle reduction machine project aimed to investigate the use of parallelism in such machines and also explore the feasibility of basing these designs on a few replicated large-scale integrated (LSI) parts. This project resulted in the design and simulation of a parallel string reduction machine, the major feature of the design being the use of state-table-driven processors that allowed the computer to be used as a vehicle for testing different reduction (language) schemes. The presentation given here is based on TREL80a and uses an example reduction language described there.

The program organization uses string manipulation; references may occur in a string, and these are substituted by the corresponding definition at run time. A parallel innermost computation rule is used. An expression in the program representa-

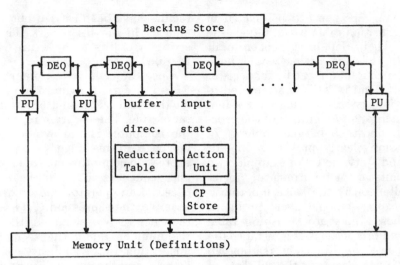

Figure 28.   Newcastle reduction machine.

tion is delimited by left bracket "(" and right bracket ")" symbols, and consists of a function followed by a list of arguments "(function arg 1 arg 2 ···)." Here function is a simple operator, but an argument may be a literal value, a reference to a definition, or a bracketed expression to be reduced.

Besides the normal arithmetic, logical, and conditional operators, there are LOAD, STORE, and APPLY operators used to access definitions explicitly. LOAD is used for dereferencing and replaces the reducible expression (LOAD ref) by the definition corresponding to ref. STORE is used (STORE ref def) to create or update stored definitions and can, if not used carefully, violate the referential transparency property of reduction machines. APPLY is used to bind arguments to a parameterized function.

The machine organization, an expression manipulation type, of the Newcastle reduction machine is shown in Figure 28. It consists of three major parts: (1) a common memory unit containing the definitions; (2) a set of identical, asynchronous processing units (PU); and (3) a segmented shift register containing the expression being evaluated. This shift register comprises a number of double-ended queues (DEQ) containing the parts of the expression being traversed, and a backing store to hold the inactive parts of the expression. Each processing unit has direct access to the whole

memory unit and two double-ended queues. Figure 28 also shows the architecture of an individual processing unit. It consists of four registers containing information on the subexpression being traversed, the reduction table that contains the user-defined state transition table controlling the evaluation, an action unit performing the actions specified by the reduction table, and the operation store holding user-defined code for the action unit.

The basic aim of each processing unit is to build up a reducible expression "(operator constant . . .)" in its buffer register and then rewrite it. Each processing unit can read or write to either of its double-ended queues, the current direction being maintained by the direction register. When an item is read and removed from a DEQ, it is transferred into the input register. Associated with each item is a type field (e.g., operator, operand, left bracket, right bracket, empty), which is used in conjunction with the current state, held in the state register, to index into the reduction table. The selected reduction table entry defines an action to be performed, such as move item to buffer register and new values for the state and direction registers. For instance, the registers of a processing unit might contain the following—buffer: "(+ 4 2"; input ")"; direction: "right"; state: "3"— when reading from the right and a right bracket is encountered. For the example reduction language the action selected in the state transition table would reduce the expression. Had a left bracket been input instead, the selected action would have emptied the contents of the buffer register into the left-hand DEQ, and attempted to find a new innermost reducible expression.

The asynchronous operation of the processing units and their parallel traversal of the expression clearly provide scope for deadlock and starvation. For example, two adjacent units might be attempting to reduce simultaneously the same innermost, reducible expression. To avoid problems such as these, the state transition table obeys certain protocols; in this instance the processing unit on the right reading an empty DEQ would output the contents of its buffer register and reverse direction. To enforce the use of these protocols, a software package called the reduction table generator is used to automatically generate a consistent reduction table for a user's language, input as a Backus–Naur Form (BNF) syntax. This package employs ideas similar to compiler–compilers that are used to generate table-driven LR parsers.

For this proposed reduction machine design, the novel features stated are the use made of state tables to support a class of user-defined reduction schemes and the use made of parser generator concepts for generating these tables. The main disadvantages of the proposal seem to be the normal ones of innermost reduction, such as correctly handling conditionals, and the global memory unit, which is a bottleneck.

6.3 North Carolina Cellular Tree Machine

The cellular computer architecture project [MAGO79a, MAGO79b, MAGO80] at the University of North Carolina, Chapel Hill, is strongly influenced both by VLSI and functional programming. Specifically, the computer has the following four properties: (1) it has a cellular construction, that is, the machine is obtained by interconnecting large numbers of a few kinds of chip in a regular pattern; (2) it executes Backus' FP class of languages [BACK78]; (3) it automatically exploits the parallelism present in FP programs; and (4) its machine language is, in fact, the FP language. Extensive simulation studies of the computer archi-

tecture have been carried out and are referenced in Mago's papers. This brief description of the architecture is based on MAGO80.

Since the cellular computer is based on FP, its program organization is string reduction with a parallel innermost computation rule. The program representation in the computer is the symbols of the FP language. In this language, a program is an expression consisting of nested applications and sequences. Each application is composed of an operator and an operand. For example, the expression $\langle 7, (+ : \langle 2, 5 \rangle) \rangle$ is a sequence of two elements, the first being the number 7 and the second being an application. In the application the operator is the + and the operand is the sequence of two numbers $\langle 2, 5 \rangle$.

An FP machine program is a linear string of symbols that are mapped into a vector of memory cells in the computer one symbol per cell, possibly with empty cells interspersed. This is illustrated by Figure 29. Some of the symbols used to separate expressions in the written form of FP programs are omitted in the machine representation, since their function is served by cell boundaries. In addition, to simplify the operation of the computer, closing application and sequencing brackets are omitted and instead an integer is stored with every remaining FP symbol, indicating the nesting level of that symbol. This is also shown in Figure 29.

The cellular computer's machine organization—an expression manipulation type—is a binary tree structure with two different kinds of cell. Leaf cells (called L cells) serve as memory units, and nonleaf ones (called T cells) provide a dual processing/communication capability. An FP expression is mapped onto this tree structure, each FP symbol being stored in an L cell and a subtree of symbols (i.e., a subexpression) being linked by some dedicated T cells, as shown in Figure 29. A particular set of L and T cells will be dedicated to a subtree for at least the duration of one machine cycle.

Having partitioned the expression to be executed into a collection of cells, itself a cellular computer, the interaction of these cells in the reduction of an innermost ap-

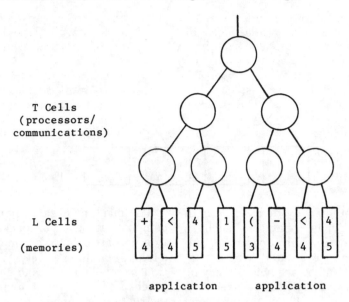

T Cells
(processors/
communications)

L Cells

(memories)

application   application

Figure 29.   Cellular tree machine.

plication is handled by microprograms. Microprograms normally reside outside the network of cells and are brought in on demand. Once a microprogram is demanded, it is placed in registers in the L cells, each cell receiving a fraction of the microprogram, that part necessary to make its contribution to the total reduction. For example, if one of the L cells wants to broadcast some information to all other L cells involved in reducing a subexpression, it executes a SEND microinstruction [MAGO79a], explicitly identifying the information item to be broadcast. As a result, this information is passed to the root of the subexpression and broadcast to all appropriate L cells.

It often happens that the result expression is too large to be accommodated in the L cells that held the initial expression. In such a case, if the required number of L cells are available elsewhere, then cell contents are repositioned. This storage management is the only kind of resource management needed in the processor because whenever an expression has all the L cells needed, it is guaranteed to have the necessary T cells.

The operation of the cells in the network is coordinated, not by a central clock, but by endowing each cell with a finite-state control, and letting the state changes sweep

up and down the tree. This allows global synchronization, even though the individual cells work asynchronously and only communicate with their immediate neighbors.

For a detailed description of the cellular computer's structure and operation the reader should consult Parts 1 and 2 of MAGO79a. Last, a particularly interesting claim made by Magó [MAGO80] is that parallelism in the computer overcomes the overheads associated with copying in a string reduction machine.

6.4 Utah Applicative Multiprocessing System

The Applicative Multiprocessing System (AMPS) is a loosely coupled, tree-structured computer architecture designed to incorporate a large number (say 1000) of processors. The project [KELL78, KELL79] under investigation at the University of Utah aims to increase the programmability of this parallel computer by basing its machine language on a dialect of LISP employing lenient CONS [FRIE76, HEND76]. AMPS uses dynamic strategies for allocating work to processors and also attempts to exploit locality of reference in its programs. This description of AMPS is taken from KELL79.

AMPS is based on a parallel graph reduction program organization, with paral-

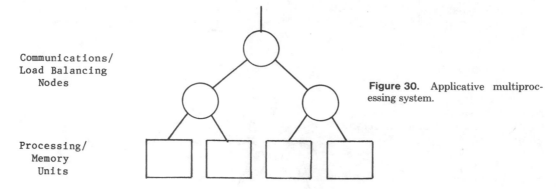

Communications/
Load Balancing
    Nodes

Processing/
 Memory
  Units

Figure 30. Applicative multiprocessing system.

lelism being obtained by demanding both arguments of dyadic operators, such as PLUS, concurrently. The program organization also updates evaluated structures in place but copies subgraphs before applying them. This is necessary because execution overwrites an expression, and unless a copy is taken, a definition would be lost the first time it was used.

Program representation in AMPS is a compiled dialect of LISP called FGL (Flow Graph LISP). A program in FGL consists of a main function graph, together with what are called productions for programmer-defined functions. These productions specify how a node containing a function reference (the antecedent of the production) is to be replaced by a function graph (the consequent of the production). FGL provides a repertoire of basic operators (e.g., the primitive functions of LISP) that may be used in constructing graphs.

Programs are divided into "blocks," a block being either a code block or a data block. The contents of a code block form a linear representation of an FGL graph, which is copied as the source of initial code to be stored in a newly allocated data block. This copying may be viewed as the application of an FGL production, that is, replacing the antecedent node with its consequent graph. Each entry in a data block is either a literal value or an instruction, defining an operator and its arguments. In detail an instruction may contain four types of argument, namely, (1) an operator, (2) references to input operands, (3) so-called *notifiers*, which are references to instructions that have demanded this instruction's value, and (4) a single global reference providing linkage across blocks.

The machine organization of the AMPS computer is based on packet communication, in particular, what may be viewed as a token-matching variety. When an instruction is invoked, demand packets are dispatched for the input operands, and the instruction suspends execution. The instruction is reenabled by the arrival of result packets on which it executes. The physical arrangement of components in AMPS, shown in Figure 30, is a binary tree structure with two types of node. Combined processing/memory units are attached as leaf nodes, while the internal nodes of the tree structure are dual communication and load-balancing units.

The packet-switched communication network in AMPS is designed to take advantage of locality of information flow, to reduce communication costs. Information first travels up the tree toward the root node until it encounters a node that spans the destination leaf, at which point it proceeds down the tree. Thus relatively local communication is separated from more global flows and takes less time. In its load-balancing role, a node periodically obtains load-monitoring signals from its subordinates, which it uses to reallocate work to underutilized nodes, while attempting to maintain physical locality of references.

A processing unit, roughly the size of a conventional microcomputer, is able to execute program tasks sequentially and also to allocate storage in response to the execution of *invoke* instructions. An invoke instruction creates a task, which is then executed in the local processing unit or in another unit, as dictated by system loading. Execution of an invoke causes the allocation of storage for a data block, the copying of a code block into the storage, and the initialization of various linkage instructions. These provide linkage between the nodes of the graph containing the antecedent of the production and those of the consequent.

Tasks to be executed (i.e., operators with their associated arguments) are placed in pools of work. There are two classes of pools:

(1) demand—containing references to operators for which evaluation is to be attempted;

(2) result—containing references to operators, along with their corresponding values after evaluation.

Each processing unit has its own demand pool, called the invoke list, but it is unclear from KELL79 whether the result pool is also distributed.

At the start of executing a program, a reference to the instruction producing the result is placed on an invoke list and the instruction is then fetched. If the arguments of the instruction are ready, then the instruction is executed; otherwise, a reference to each argument, together with a notifier so it may return the result, is placed on the invoke list. These notifiers support graph reduction by the reversal of pointers, as discussed in Section 1.4. Several notifiers may be contained in an entry in an invoke list, defining all the instructions that have demanded the result. Once evaluated, a result value replaces the instruction that calculates it. Via the result list, any instructions that were specified by notifiers as awaiting this result as an argument are then notified by being placed on an invoked list to be retried.

Current status of the project is that a simulator for the program organization has been written in PASCAL and another one, in SIMULA-67, is being written to evaluate the tree architecture. Apparently [KELL79] there are no immediate plans for construction of a physical realization of the machine.

6.5 S–K Reduction Machine

Turner's S–K reduction machine [TURN79a, TURN79b], unlike the other projects we have examined, is not strictly a proposal for a new computer architecture;

instead, it is a novel implementation technique for functional languages. This work has attracted considerable attention and is sufficiently relevant to warrant discussion here. Using a result of Schonfinkel [SCHO24] from combinatory logic, Turner has devised a variable free representation for programs which contain bound variables. He has also designed a graph reduction machine that efficiently executes that representation as machine code. Our discussion of the S–K reduction machine and its use of combinators is taken from TURN79a.

The program organization of the S–K reduction machine is lazy evaluation [HEND76], based on graph manipulation with a leftmost outermost computation rule. However, the central feature of the machine design is its use of combinators, special operators that serve the role of bound variables in a program and hence allow them to be removed from the code. Let us consider the role of bound variables. A bound variable in a programming language and a corresponding reference in the machine code provide access to an object. The logical role of this reference is to associate or bring together some operand and operator at run time, since it is not physically possible to place each operand next to its operator.

Compilation into combinators removes bound variables from the program. Execution of the resulting machine code routes actual values back into the places in the program where bound variables formerly occurred. Compilation and execution are thus symmetric. The following illustrates the combinators and their transformations in the S–K machine:

Combinators	Transformations
S f g x	f x (g x)
K x y	x
C f g x	(f x) g
B f g x	f (g x)
I x	x
COND TRUE x y	x
COND FALSE x y	y

For example, the definition "DEF fac" will be represented as

DEF fac = S(C(B COND(EQ 0))1)
(S TIMES(B fac(C MINUS 1))).

The compiler transforms each incoming expression into a variable free machine code. Code is stored as a binary tree whose internal nodes represent function applications and whose leaves will be constants such as 1, PLUS, or S. The trees are built using references, and these references may be manipulated at run time without the contents of the corresponding subtree being known. Recursive definitions are handled using an additional Y combinator. Execution of Y produces a cyclic reference at run time.

The run-time system consists of a reduction machine (currently implemented in software), which progressively transforms the combinator code as discussed above. To schedule the sequence of leftmost reductions, a *left ancestor stack*, which initially contains only (a pointer to) the expression to be evaluated, is used. This is illustrated by Figure 31. As long as the expression at the front of the stack is an application, the machine continues to take its left subtree (the function of the function–argument pair), pushing it onto the stack. Eventually an atom is at the front of the stack. If it is a combinator, then the appropriate transformation rule is applied, using the pointers on the stack to gain access to the arguments where necessary. Figure 31 shows the state of the stack before and after applying the C transformation. All structures manipulated by the run-time system are built out of two-field cells, and a LISP-style storage allocation scheme is used with mark bits and a garbage collector.

Turner has compared his S–K reduction machine with the more conventional SECD machine of Landin [LAND64] used for implementing functional languages and has noted the following [TURN79a]. First, the object code of the S–K machine seems to be consistently twice as compact as the SECD code. Second, the execution speed of the S–K machine is slightly slower than a nonlazy SECD machine, but much superior when a lazy (evaluation) SECD machine is used. Further details of these comparisons are given in TURN79a.

6.6 Cambridge SKIM Machine

The SKIM reduction machine [CLAR80] at Cambridge University is, to our knowledge,

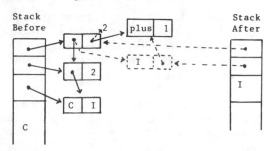

Figure 31. The S–K reduction machine's stack behavior.

the first hardware graph reduction machine to be built. A conventional microprocessor is microcoded to emulate combinators as used above in the S–K reduction machine. The technique of using combinators to support applicative programming was first developed by Turner in his software reduction machine, which is described above. The SKIM machine is fully operational, and some interesting performance measurements have been obtained. This present account of the machine is based in information from Clark et al. [CLAR80].

SKIM employs lazy evaluation. Programs are evaluated outermost first and, wherever possible, common subexpressions are shared. The instruction set is similar to that of the S–K reduction machine, containing combinators (S, K, I, . . .), list operators (HD, TL, . . .), and standard operators (+, −, . . .). Programs in SKIM are represented by a graph built of two element cells. In SKIM, these are implemented by dividing the memory into two banks, HEAD and TAIL, and using a microcoded garbage collector to handle memory management. SKIM has no stacks; instead, programs are traversed by pointer reversal.

SKIM is driven by a combinator reducer that scans down the leftmost branch of the program tree to find an operator (combinator) at the leaf. When a pointer has been used to go down one level in the tree, it is reversed to indicate the return route back up the tree. Eventually a sequence of pointers from root to leaf is transformed into a sequence of pointers from leaf to root (see Figure 32). The leaf operator is now executed, using the back pointers to access its arguments in a way analogous to accessing the top few elements of a stack.

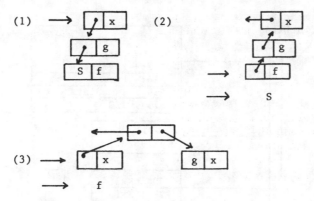

Figure 32. Pointer-reversing traversal and execution.

Some operators (mainly the arithmetic and Boolean ones) are strict. That is, their arguments must be reduced to values before being used. For instance, if we wish to add together two arithmetic expressions E1 + E2, both E1 and E2 must be reduced to their values n1, n2 before the operator + can be executed. This case arises as a consequence of the outermost computation rule of lazy evaluation, which means an operator is always reached before its arguments. SKIM handles this recursive evaluation of arguments by simulating a stack by a linked list in the main HEAD–TAIL memory. This mechanism, coupled with the pointer-reversing traversal, means that no special fixed storage area is set aside for evaluation stacks.

The SKIM machine organization (see Figure 33) consists of 16 internal registers and 32K words of 16-bit memory. Only three microinstruction types are provided: memory read, memory write, and ALU operations. The microinstruction cycle time is given as 600 nanoseconds. As mentioned above, memory is divided into two banks, HEAD and TAIL. These are accessed by 15-bit addresses, one bit being used to select the appropriate bank.

The SKIM experiment has demonstrated that combinators form a simple elegant machine code to support functional programming. The main difference between SKIM and a conventional microcomputer is that it is a reduction machine. Execution progresses by rewriting the program. The performance measures obtained indicate that SKIM compares favorably with conventional architectures. For example, in comparison with BASIC on a microprocessor, SKIM was about twice as fast as interpreted BASIC and a little slower than compiled BASIC. In comparison with LISP running on a large IBM/370 mainframe, SKIM was found to be about half as fast as interpreted LISP and eight times slower than compiled LISP. The performance figures seem to justify their claim that minicomputer performance was obtained at microcomputer cost simply by using an instruction set suited to the application.

6.7 Other Projects

Research into reduction machines, although not as firmly established as dataflow computers, is starting to expand rapidly. Besides the projects described above, there are a number of others worthy of description, including those of Darlington [Darl81] at Imperial College, London, and Sleep [Slee80, Slee81] at the University of East Anglia, who are both investigating interesting packet communication machine organizations that support parallel graph reduction.

7. FUTURE DIRECTIONS

The research described above into data-driven and demand-driven computer architecture is motivated by the growing belief [JIPD81c] that the next, the fifth, generation of computers will not be based on the traditional von Neumann organization. The question we have been addressing is: Which architectural principles and features from

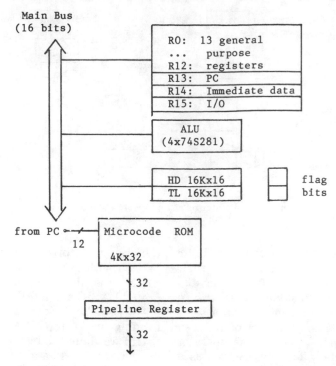

Figure 33. SKIM machine block diagram.

the various research projects will contribute to this future general-purpose computer?

One means of evaluating the potential of the various control-flow, data-flow, and reduction approaches is to compare them to the motivations for data-driven and demand-driven computing discussed in the introduction. These are

(1) utilization of concurrency;
(2) exploitation of VLSI;
(3) new forms of programming.

For the computation organization it is clear that the sequential control-driven model, which has long been predominant, has not encouraged the use of highly concurrent programs. (However, parallel control-driven computation organizations are possible.) It is also clear that the new forms of programming, such as functional languages, are naturally matched with data-driven and demand-driven computation organizations, and that these models allow utilization of concurrency. The differences between data-driven and demand-driven

computation organizations are still being explored.

For the program organization it is significant that control flow, data flow, and reduction regard the by-value and by-reference data mechanisms and the sequential, parallel, and recursive control mechanisms as sets of alternatives. This results in each program organization having specific advantages and disadvantages for program representation and execution. For example, in comparing by-value and by-reference data mechanisms, the former is more effective when manipulating integers and the latter is more effective when manipulating arrays. Each program organization is suited to a particular form of programming language. Thus each program organization is, although "universal" in the sense of a Turing machine, somewhat restricted in the classes of computation it can efficiently support. We may speculate that it should be possible and indeed desirable for general-purpose computing to design computer architectures whose program organization is a synthesis of both sets of data and control mechanisms [TREL81b].

For the machine organization it is clear that centralized, packet communication, and expression manipulation gravitate toward, respectively, control flow, data flow, and reduction. However, we have shown that other pairings of the machine organizations and the program organizations are viable. When evaluating the three machine organizations against the motivations for data-driven and demand-driven computers listed above, the utilization of concurrency would seem to preclude centralized organizations in favor of the other two organizations. In addition, VLSI requires an organization in which a replication of identical computing elements can be plugged together to form a larger parallel computer. But it is also necessary for a computing element to have a centralized organization so that it can function independently. Thus the three machine organizations, instead of being competitive, seem in fact to be complementary organizations. Each organization is based on a sequential building block: a computing element containing a processor, communications, and memory. The centralized organization defines how a single computing element must be able to function as a self-contained computer. The packet communication organization shows how concurrency within a computing element may be increased by replicating resources. Last, the expression manipulation organization specifies how a group of computing elements may be interconnected, at a system level, to satisfy the VLSI attributes of replication.

In conclusion, having examined the computation organizations, program organizations, and machine organizations for control flow, data flow, and reduction, and also the approaches taken by the individual research groups, it is regrettably impossible at this time to identify the future "von Neumann." We were, however, able to analyze the advantages and disadvantages of the various approaches. Using such knowledge it is even possible to "engineer" new program organizations and machine organizations [WILN80, TREL81a].

ACKNOWLEDGMENTS

In acknowledging all the people who have contributed to the writing of this paper it is difficult not to list a significant proportion of the computing science community. First, let us thank those people investigating data-driven and demand-driven computing, whose work was discussed above, for taking time to read this document and comment on our description of their work. Second, we express our gratitude to Klaus Berkling, Jean-Pierre Banatra, Al Davis, Ronan Sleep, and Graham Wood for their detailed comments on an early version of this paper. Third, we would like to thank our colleagues at the University of Newcastle upon Tyne, in particular, current and past members of the Computer Architecture Group. Fourth, we thank the referees for their helpful comments. Finally, we wish to thank the Distributed Computing Systems Panel (its current and past members) of the United Kingdom Science and Engineering Research Council, which not only funds our research but has also been largely responsible for establishing and encouraging data-driven and demand-driven computing research in the United Kingdom.

REFERENCES

ACKE79a   ACKERMAN, W. B. "Data flow languages," in *Proc. 1979 Nat. Computer Conf.* (New York, N.Y., June 4–7), vol. 48, AFIPS Press, Arlington, Va, 1979, pp. 1087–1095.

ACKE79b   ACKERMAN, W. B., AND DENNIS, J. B. "VAL—A value oriented algorithmic language, preliminary reference manual," Tech. Rep. TR-218, Lab. for Computer Science, Massachusetts Institute of Technology, June 1979.

AMAM80   AMAMIYA, M., HASEGAWA, R., AND MIKAMI, H. "List processing and data flow machine," Lecture Note Series, No. 436, Research Institute for Mathematical Sciences, Kyoto Univ., Sept. 1980.

ARVI75   ARVIND AND GOSTELOW, K. P. "A new interpreter for dataflow and its implications for computer architecture," Tech. Rep. 72, Dep. Information and Computer Science, Univ. of California, Irvine, Oct. 1975.

ARVI77a   ARVIND AND GOSTELOW, K. P. "A computer capable of exchanging processors for time," in *Proc. IFIP Congress* (1977), 849–854.

ARVI77b   ARVIND AND GOSTELOW, K. P. "Some relationships between asynchronous interpreters of a dataflow language," in *Proc. IFIP Working Conf. Formal Description of Programming Languages*

(Aug. 1977), E. J. Neuhold, Ed., Elsevier North-Holland, New York, 1977.

ARVI78   ARVIND, GOSTELOW, K. P., AND PLOUFFE, W. "An asynchronous programming language and computing machine," Tech. Rep. 114a, Dep. Information and Computer Science, Univ. of California, Irvine, Dec. 1978.

ARVI80a   ARVIND, KATHAIL, V., AND PINGALI, K. "A processing element for a large multiprocessor dataflow machine," in *Proc. Int. Conf. Circuits and Computers* (New York, Oct. 1980), IEEE, New York, 1980.

ARVI80b   ARVIND AND THOMAS, R. E. "I-structures: An efficient data type for functional languages," Rep. LCS/TM-178, Lab. for Computer Science, Massachusetts Institute of Technology, June 1980.

ASHC77   ASHCROFT, E. A., AND WADGE, W. W. "LUCID, a nonprocedural language with iteration," *Commun. ACM* **20**, 7 (July 1977), 519–526.

BACK72   BACKUS, J. "Reduction languages and variable free programming," Rep. RJ 1010, IBM Thomas J. Watson Research Center, Yorktown Heights, N.Y., Apr. 1972.

BACK73   BACKUS, J. "Programming languages and closed applicative languages," in *Proc. ACM Symp. Principles of Programming Languages*, ACM, New York, 1973, pp. 71–86.

BACK78   BACKUS, J. "Can programming be liberated from the von Neumann style? A functional style and its algebra of programs," *Commun. ACM* **21**, 8 (Aug. 1978), 613–641.

BERK71   BERKLING, K. J. "A computing machine based on tree structures," *IEEE Trans. Comput.* **C-20**, 4 (Jan. 1971), 404–418.

BERK75   BERKLING, K. "Reduction languages for reduction machines," in *Proc. 2nd Int. Symp. Computer Architecture* (Houston, Tex., Jan. 1975), IEEE, New York, 1975, pp. 133–140.

CHAM71   CHAMBERLIN, D. D. "The single assignment approach to parallel processing," in *Proc. Nat. Computer Conf.* (Las Vegas, Nev., Nov. 16–18), vol. 39, AFIPS Press, Arlington, Va., 1971, pp. 263–269.

CLAR80   CLARKE, T. J. W., GLADSTONE, P. J. S., MACLEAN, C. D., AND NORMAN, A. C. "SKIM—The S, K, I reduction machine," in *Proc. LISP-80 Conf.* (Stanford, Calif., Aug. 1980), pp. 128–135.

COMT76   COMTE, D., DURRIEU, A., GELLY, O., PLAS, A., AND SYRE, J. C. "TEAU 9/7: SYSTEME LAU—Summary in English," CERT Tech. Rep. #1/3059, Centre d'Études et de Recherches de Toulouse, Oct. 1976.

COMT79b   COMTE, D., AND HIFDI, N. "LAU Multiprocessor: Microfunctional description and technological choices," in *Proc. 1st European Conf. Parallel and Distributed Processing* (Toulouse, France, Feb. 1979), pp. 8–15.

CORN79   CORNISH, M. "The TI data flow architectures: The power of concurrency for avionics," in *Proc. 3rd Conf. Digital Avionics Systems* (Fort Worth, Tex., Nov. 1979), IEEE, New York, 1979, pp. 19–25.

DARL81   DARLINGTON, J., AND REEVE, M. "ALICE: A multiprocessor reduction machine for the parallel evaluation of applicative languages," in *Proc. Int. Symp. Functional Programming Languages and Computer Architecture* (Göteborg, Sweden, June 1981), pp. 32–62.

DAVI78   DAVIS, A. L. "The architecture and system method of DDM1: A recursively structured data driven machine," in *Proc. 5th Annu. Symp. Computer Architecture* (Palo Alto, Calif., Apr. 3–5), ACM, New York, 1978, pp. 210–215.

DAVI79a   DAVIS, A. L. "DDN's—A low level program schema for fully distributed systems," in *Proc. 1st European Conf. Parallel and Distributed Processing* (Toulouse, France, Feb. 1979), pp. 1–7.

DAVI79b   DAVIS, A. L. "A data flow evaluation system based on the concept of recursive locality," in *Proc. 1979 Nat. Computer Conf.* (New York, N.Y., June 4–7), vol. 48, AFIPS Press, Arlington, Va., 1979, pp. 1079–1086.

DENN71   DENNIS, J. B. "On the design and specification of a common base language," in *Proc. Symp. Computers and Automata*, Polytechnic Institute of Brooklyn, Brooklyn, N.Y., 1971.

DENN72   DENNIS, J. B., FOSSEEN, J. B., AND LINDERMAN, J. P. "Data flow schemas," in *Int. Symp. on Theoretical Programming*, A. Ershov and V. A. Nepomniascuy, Eds., *Lecture notes in computer science*, vol. 5, 1972, Springer-Verlag, New York, pp. 187–216.

DENN74a   DENNIS, J. B. "First version of a data flow procedure language," in *Programming Symp.: Proc. Colloque sur la Programmation* (Paris, France, Apr. 1974), B. Robinet, Ed., *Lecture notes in computer science*, vol. 19, Springer-Verlag, New York, 1974, pp. 362–376.

DENN74b   DENNIS, J. B., AND MISUNAS, D. P. "A computer architecture for highly parallel signal processing," in *Proc. 1974 Nat. Computer Conf.*, AFIPS Press, Arlington, Va., 1974, pp. 402–409.

DENN75b   DENNIS, J. B., AND MISUNAS, D. P. "A preliminary architecture for a basic data flow processor," in *Proc. 2nd Int. Symp.*

Computer Architecture (Houston, Tex., Jan. 20–22), IEEE, New York, 1975, pp. 126–132.

DENN79a   DENNIS, J. B., LEUNG, C. K. K., AND MISUNAS, D. P. "A highly parallel processor using a data flow machine language," Tech. Rep. CSG Memo 134-1, Lab. for Computer Science, Massachusetts Institute of Technology, June 1979.

DENN79b   DENNIS, J. B. "The varieties of data flow computers," in *Proc. 1st Int. Conf. Distributed Computing Systems* (Toulouse, France, Oct. 1979), pp. 430–439.

EGAN79   EGAN, G. K. "FLO: A decentralised data-flow system," Dep. Computer Science, Univ. of Manchester, England, Oct. 1979.

ERIK80   ERIKIÖ, L., HEIMONEN, J. HIETALA, P., AND KURKI-SUONIO, R. "PLEXUS II—A data flow system," Tech. Rep. A43, Dep. Mathematical Sciences, Univ. of Tampere, Finland, Apr. 1980.

FARR79   FARRELL, E. P., GHANI, N., AND TRELEAVEN, P. C. "A concurrent computer architecture and a ring based implementation," in *Proc. 6th Int. Symp. Computer Architecture* (April 23-25), IEEE, New York, 1979, pp. 1–11.

FRIE76   FRIEDMAN, D. P., AND WISE, D. S. "CONS should not evaluate its arguments." in *Automata, languages and programming*, S. Michaelson and R. Milner, Eds., Edinburgh Univ. Press, Edinburgh, U. K., 1976, pp. 257–284.

GELL76   GELLY, O., et al. "LAU software system: A high level data driven language for parallel programming," in *Proc. 1976 Int. Conf. Parallel Processing* (Aug. 1976), p. 255.

GOST79a   GOSTELOW, K. P., AND THOMAS, R. E. "A view of dataflow," in *Proc. Nat. Computer Conf.* (New York, N.Y., June 4-7), vol. 48, AFIPS Press, Arlington, Va., 1979, pp. 629–636.

GOST79b   GOSTELOW, K. P., AND THOMAS, R. E. "Performance of a dataflow computer," Tech. Rep. 127a, Dep. Information and Computer Science, Univ. of California, Irvine, Oct. 1979.

GOTO77   GOTO, E., AND IDA, T. "Parallel hashing algorithms." *Inf. Process. Lett.* **6,** 1 (Feb. 1977), pp. 8–13.

HEND76   HENDERSON, P., AND MORRIS, J. M. "A lazy evaluator," in *Proc. 3rd Symp. Principles of Programming Languages* (Atlanta, Ga., Jan. 19-21), ACM, New York, 1976, pp. 95–103.

HOMM79   HOMMES, F., AND SCHLUTTER, H. "Reduction machine system User's guide," Tech. Rep. ISF—Rep. 79, Gesellschaft für Mathematik und Datenverarbeitung MBH Bonn, Dec. 1979.

HOPK79   HOPKINS, R. P., RAUTENBACH, P. W., AND TRELEAVEN, P. C. "A computer supporting data flow, control flow and updateable memory," Tech. Rep. 156, Computing Lab., Univ. Newcastle upon Tyne, Sept. 1979.

JIPD81a   JIPDC. "Preliminary report on study and research on fifth-generation computers 1970–1980," Japan Information Processing Development Center, Tokyo, Japan, 1981.

JIPD81b   JIPDC. "Research reports in Japan," Japan Information Processing Development Center, Tokyo, Japan, Fall 1981.

JIPD81c   JIPDC. in *Proc. Int. Conf. Fifth Generation Computer Systems*, Japan Information Processing Development Center, 1981.

JOHN79   JOHNSON, D., et al. "Automatic partitioning of programs in multiprocessor systems," in *Proc. IEEE COMPCON 80* (Feb. 1980), IEEE, New York, pp. 175–178.

KELL78   KELLER, R. M., PATIL, S., AND LINDSTROM, G. "An architecture for a loosely coupled parallel processor," Tech. Rep. UUCS-78-105, Dep. Computer Science, Univ. of Utah, Oct. 1978.

KELL79   KELLER, R. M., et al. "A loosely coupled applicative multiprocessing system," in *Proc. Nat. Computer Conf.*, AFIPS Press, Arlington, Va., 1978, pp. 861–870.

KLUG79   KLUGE, W. E. "The architecture of a reduction language machine hardware model," Tech. Rep. ISF—Rep. 79.03, Gesellschaft für Mathematik und Datenverarbeitung MBH Bonn, Aug. 1979.

KLUG80   KLUGE, W. E., AND SCHLUTTER, H. "An architecture for the direct execution of reduction languages," in *Proc. Int. Workshop High-Level Language Computer Architecture* (Fort Lauderdale, Fla., May 1980), Univ. of Maryland and Office of Naval Research, pp. 174–180.

LAND64   LANDIN, P. J. "The mechanical evaluation of expressions," *Comput. J.* **6** (Jan. 1964), 308–320.

LECO79   LECOUFFE, M. P. "MAUD: A dynamic single-assignment system," *IEE Comput. Digital Tech.* **2,** 2 (Apr. 1979), 75–79.

MAGO79a   MAGÓ, G. A. "A network of microprocessors to execute reduction languages," *Int. J. Comput. Inform. Sci.* **8,** 5 (1979), 349–385; **8,** 6 (1979), 435–471.

MAGO80   MAGÓ, G. A. "A cellular computer architecture for functional programming," in *Proc. IEEE COMPCON 80* (Feb. 1980), IEEE, New York, pp. 179–187.

McCA62   McCARTHY, J., et al. *LISP 1.5 programmers manual*, M.I.T. Press, Cambridge, Mass., 1962.

MEAD80   MEAD, C. A., AND CONWAY, L. A. *Introduction to VLSI systems*, Addison-Wesley, Reading, Mass., 1980.

MIRA77   MIRANKER, G. S. "Implementation of procedures on a class of data flow processors," in *Proc. 1977 Int. Conf. Parallel Processing* (Aug. 1977), J. L. Baer, Ed., IEEE, New York, pp. 77–86.

ORGA79   ORGANICK, E. I. "New directions in computer system architecture," *Euromicro J.* **5,** 4 (July 1979), 190–202.

PLAS76   PLAS, A., et al. "LAU system architecture: A parallel data driven processor based on single assignment," in *Proc. 1976 Int. Conf. Parallel Processing* (Aug. 1976), pp. 293–302.

RODR69   RODRIGUEZ, J. E. "A graph model for parallel computation," Tech. Rep. ESL-R-398, MAC-TR-64, Lab. for Computer Science, Massachusetts Institute of Technology, Sept. 1969.

RUMB77   RUMBAUGH, J. E. "A data flow multiprocessor," *IEEE Trans. Comput.* **C-26,** 2 (Feb. 1977), 138–146.

SCHO24   SCHONFINKEL, M. "Über die Bausteine der Mathematischen Logik," *Math. Ann.* **92,** 305 (1924).

SEIT79   SEITZ, C. (Ed.) *Proc. Conf. Very Large Scale Integration* (Pasadena, Calif., Jan. 1979).

SHRO77   SHROEDER, M. A., AND MEYER, R. A. "A distributed computer system using a data flow approach," *Proc. 1977 Int. Conf. Parallel Processing* (Aug. 1977), p. 93.

SLEE80   SLEEP, M. R. "Applicative languages, dataflow and pure combinatory code," *Proc. IEEE COMPCON 80* (Feb. 1980), IEEE, New York, pp. 112–115.

SLEE81   SLEEP, M. R., AND BURTON, F. W. "Towards a zero assignment parallel processor," in *Proc. 2nd Int. Conf. Distributed Computing* (Apr. 1981).

SYRE76   SYRE, J. C., et al. "Parallelism, control and synchronization expression in a single assignment language" (abstract), in *Proc. 4th Annu. ACM Computer Science Conf.* (Feb. 1976), ACM, New York.

SYRE77   SYRE, J. C., COMTE, D., AND HIFDI, N. "Pipelining, parallelism and asynchronism in the LAU system," in *Proc. 1977 Int. Conf. Parallel Processing* (Aug. 1977), pp. 87–92.

TESL68   TESLER, L. G., AND ENEA, H. J. "A language design for concurrent processes," in *Proc. Nat. Computer Conf.* (Atlantic City, N.J., April 30–May 2), vol. 32, AFIPS Press, Arlington, Va., 1968, 403–408.

TREL78   TRELEAVEN, P. C. "Principle components of a data flow computer," *Proc. 1978 Euromicro Symp.* (Munich, W. Germany, Oct. 1978), pp. 366–374.

TREL79   TRELEAVEN, P. C. "Exploiting program concurrency in computing systems," *Computer* **12,** 1 (Jan. 1979), 42–49.

TREL80a   TRELEAVEN, P. C., AND MOLE, G. F. "A multi-processor reduction machine for user-defined reduction languages," in *Proc. 7th Int. Symp. Computer Architecture* (May 6–8), IEEE, New York, 1980, pp. 121–130.

TREL80b   TRELEAVEN, P. C. (Ed.) "VLSI: Machine architecture and very high level languages," Tech. Rep. 156, Computing Lab., Univ. of Newcastle upon Tyne, Dec. 1980 (summary in *SIGARCH Comput. Archit. News* 8, 7, 1980).

TREL81a   TRELEAVEN, P. C., AND HOPKINS, R. P. "A recursive (VLSI) computer architecture," Tech. Rep. 161, Computing Lab., Univ. of Newcastle upon Tyne, Mar. 1981.

TREL81b   TRELEAVEN, P. C., AND HOPKINS, R. P. "Decentralised computation," in *Proc. 8th Int. Symp. Computer Architecture* (Minneapolis, Minn., May 12–14), ACM, New York, 1981, pp. 279–290.

TREL82   TRELEAVEN, P. C., HOPKINS, R. P., AND RAUTENBACH, P. W. "Combining data flow and control flow computing," *Comput. J.* **25,** 1 (Feb. 1982).

TURN79a   TURNER, D. A. "A new implementation technique for applicative languages," *Soft. Pract. Exper.* **9** (Sept., 1979), 31–49.

TURN79b   TURNER, D. A. "Another algorithm for bracket abstraction," *J. Symbol. Logic* **44,** 2 (June 1979), 267–270.

VEEN80   VEEN, A. H. "Reconciling data flow machines and conventional languages," Tech. Rep. 1W 146/80, Mathematical Center, Amsterdam, Sept. 1980.

WATS79   WATSON, I., AND GURD, J. "A prototype data flow computer with token labeling," in *Proc. Nat. Computer Conf.* (New York, N.Y., June 4–7), vol. 48, AFIPS Press, Arlington, Va., 1979, pp. 623–628.

WENG75   WENG, K. S. "Stream-oriented computation in recursive data flow schemas," Tech. Rep. TM-68, Lab. for Computer Science, Massachusetts Institute of Technology, Oct. 1975.

WILN80   WILNER, W. "Recursive machines," Intern. Rep., Xerox PARC, Palo Alto, Calif., 1980.

BIBLIOGRAPHY

ADAM68   ADAMS, D. A. "A computation model with data flow sequencing," Tech. Rep. CS 117, Computer Science Dep., Stanford Univ., Stanford, Calif., December 1968.

ARVI77c   ARVIND, GOSTELOW, K. P., AND PLOUFFE, W. "Indeterminacy, monitors and dataflow," in *Proc. 6th ACM Symp. Operating Systems Principles* (Nov. 1977), ACM, New York, pp. 159–169.

BAHR72   BAHRS, A. "Operational patterns: An extensible model of an extensible language," in *Lecture notes in computer science*, vol. 5, Springer-Verlag, New York, 1972, pp. 217–246.

BANA79   BANATRE, J. P., ROUTEAU, J. P., AND TRILLING, L. "An event-driven compiling technique," *Commun. ACM* **22,** 1 (Jan. 1979), 34–42.

BOLE80   BOLEY, H. "A preliminary survey of artificial intelligence machines," Rundbrief der Fachgruppe Künstliche Intelligenz in der Gesellschaft für Informatik, Universität Hamburg, 1980.

BURG75   BURGE, W. H. *Recursive programming techniques*, Addison-Wesley, Reading, Mass., 1975.

CHUR41   CHURCH, A. *"The calculi of lambda-conversion,"* Princeton Univ. Press, Princeton, N.J., 1941.

DARL82   DARLINGTON, J., HENDERSON, P., AND TURNER, A., EDS. *Functional programming and its applications*, Cambridge Univ. Press, in preparation.

DAVI80   DAVIS, A. L., AND DRONGOWSKI, P. J. "Dataflow computers: A tutorial and survey," Tech. Rep. UUCS-80-109, Dep. Computer Science, Univ. of Utah, July 1980.

DAVI81   DAVIS, A. L., AND LOWER, S. A. "A sample management application program in a graphical data-driven programming language," in *Proc. IEEE COMPCON 81* (Feb. 1981), IEEE, New York, pp. 162–165.

DENN75a   DENNIS, J. B. "Packet communication architecture," in *Proc. 1975 Computer Conf. Parallel Processing*, 1975, pp. 224–229.

DENN77   DENNIS, J. B., AND WENG, K.-S. "Application of data flow computation to the weather problem." in *Proc. Symp. High Speed Computer and Algorithm Organisation*, 1977, pp. 143–157.

DENN80   DENNIS, J. B. "Data-flow supercomputers," *Computer* **13,** 11 (Nov. 1980), 48–56.

DOMA81   DOMAN, A. "PARADOCS: A highly parallel dataflow computer and its dataflow language," *Euromicro J.* **7** (1981), 20–31.

FRIE77   FRIEDMAN, D. P., AND WISE, D. S. "Aspects of applicative programming for file systems," *ACM SIGPLAN Not.* **12,** 3 (Mar. 1977), 41–55.

FRIE78   FRIEDMAN, D. P., AND WISE, D. S. "Aspects of applicative programming for parallel processing," *IEEE Trans. Comput.* C-27, 4 (Apr. 1978), 289–296.

GAJS81   GAJSKI, D. D., et al. "Dependence driven computation," in *Proc. IEEE COMPCON 81* (Feb. 1981), IEEE, New York, pp. 156–161.

GURD78   GURD, J., AND WATSON, I. "A multilayered data flow architecture," in *Proc.*
1977 Int. Conf. Parallel Processing (Aug. 1977), p. 94.

HEWI77   HEWITT, C. E., AND BAKER, H. "Actors and continuous functionals," in *Proc. IFIP Working Conf. Formal Description of Programming Concepts* (St. Andrews, N. B., Canada, Aug. 1977), E. J. Neuhold, Ed., Elsevier North-Holland, New York, 1977, pp. 16.1–16.21.

KARP66   KARP, R. M., AND MILLER, R. E. "Properties of a model for parallel computations: Determinacy, termination and queuing," *SIAM J. Appl. Math.* **11,** 6 (Nov. 1966), 1390–1411.

KARP69   KARP, R. M., AND MILLER, R. E. "Parallel program schemata," *J. Comput. Syst. Sci.* **3,** 4 (May 1969), 147–195.

KOSI73a   KOSINSKI, P. R. "A data flow programming language," Tech. Rep. RC 4264, IBM T. J. Watson Research Center, Yorktown Heights, N.Y., Mar. 1973.

KOSI73b   KOSINSKI, P. R. "A data flow language for operating system programming," *ACM SIGPLAN Not.* **8,** 9 (Sept. 1973), 89–94.

KOTO80   KOTOV, V. E. "On basic parallel language," in *Proc. IFIP 80 Congr.* (Tokyo, Japan and Melbourne, Australia), Elsevier North-Holland, New York, 1980.

KOWA79   KOWALSKI, R. "Algorithms = logic + control," *Commun. ACM* **22,** 7 (July 1979), 424–436.

MAGO79b   MAGÓ, G. A. "A cellular, language directed computer architecture," in *Proc. Conf. Very Large Scale Integration* (Pasadena, Calif., Jan. 1979), pp. 447–452.

MAGO81   MAGÓ, G. A., STANAT, D. E., AND KOSTER, A. "Program execution on a cellular computer: Some matrix algorithms," Tech. Rep., Dep. Computer Science, Univ. of North Carolina, Chapel Hill, May 1981.

MANN74   MANNA, Z. *Mathematical theory of computation*, McGraw-Hill, New York, 1974.

MEYE76   MEYER, S. C. "An analytic approach to performance analysis for a class of data flow processors," in *Proc. 1976 Int. Conf. Parallel Processing* (Aug. 1976), pp. 106–115.

MILL72   MILLER, R. E., AND COCKE, J. "Configurable computers: A new class of general purpose machines," in *Lecture notes in computer science*, vol. 5, Springer-Verlag, New York, 1972, pp. 285–298.

MISU75a   MISUNAS, D. P. "Deadlock avoidance in a data-flow architecture," in *Proc. Symp. Automatic Computation and Control* (Milwaukee, Wis., Apr. 1975).

MISU75b   MISUNAS, D. P. "Structure processing in a data flow computer," in *Proc. 1975 Int. Conf. Parallel Processing* (Aug. 1975), pp. 230–234.

Misu76   MISUNAS, D. P.   "Error detection and recovery in a data-flow computer," in *Proc. 1976 Int. Conf. Parallel Processing* (Aug. 1976), pp. 117–122.

Shar80   SHARP, J. A.   "Some thoughts on data flow architectures." *SIGARCH Comput. Archit. News* (ACM) **8,** 4 (June 1980), 11–21.

Shri78   SHRIVER, B. D., AND LANDRY, S.

P.   "An overview of dataflow related research," Tech. Rep. Dep. Computer Science, Univ. of Southwestern Louisiana, 1978.

Weng79   WENG, K. S.   "An abstract implementation for a generalized data flow language," Tech. Rep. TR-228, Lab. for Computer Science, Massachusetts Institute of Technology, May 1979.

Received June 1981; final revision accepted November 1981.

Reprinted from *IEEE Transactions on Computers,* Volume C-23, Number 12, December 1984, pages 1050-1071. Copyright © 1984 by The Institute of Electrical and Electronics Engineers, Inc.

A Survey of Proposed Architectures for the Execution of Functional Languages

STEVEN R. VEGDAHL

Abstract — Functional and imperative programming languages are characterized and compared with regard to *programming style* and *efficiency*. Machine design issues are characterized by interconnection topology, evaluation strategy, program and data representation, process management, and dynamic optimization techniques; short descriptions of a number of "functional" machines are given in terms of these issues. Multiprocessor issues and systems are particularly emphasized. Outstanding problems in the area are reviewed and an overall evaluation of proposed machines is given.

Index Terms — Computer architecture, data-driven architectures, data flow, demand-drive architectures, functional programming, multiprocessing, programming languages.

IN recent years, a number of scientists have advocated the use of functional programming (FP) as a means of increasing programmer productivity, enhancing the clarity of programs, and reducing the difficulty of program verification. A major drawback of using functional languages has been that they are perceived to run slowly on von Neumann computer architectures. This is a survey of architectures that have recently been proposed for executing such languages more efficiently. Also discussed are the major issues involved in designing such architectures, with particular attention given to parallel processing systems.

I. CHARACTERIZATION OF FUNCTIONAL LANGUAGES

The terms *functional language, applicative language, data flow language,* and *reduction language* have been used somewhat interchangeably in the literature to refer to languages that are based on function application and are therefore free of side effects. The term *functional language* is used throughout this paper for the purpose of clarity. This section characterizes functional languages by contrasting them with (traditional) imperative ones.

A. Imperative Languages

Imperative programming languages (e.g., Fortran, Pascal) have tended to be "high-level versions" of the von Neumann computer. Their principal operations involve changing the

Manuscript received January 25, 1984; revised July 16, 1984. This work was supported in part by the Fannie and John Hertz Foundation and in part by the Defense Advanced Research Projects Agency (DOD) ARPA Order 3597, monitored by the Air Force Avionics Laboratory under Contract F33615-78-C-1551.

The author was with Carnegie-Mellon University, Pittsburgh, PA 15213. He is now with the Computer Research Laboratory, Tektronix, Inc., Beaverton, OR 97077.

state of the computation in much the same way a machine-language program does [5].

• Program variables imitate machine words. Programmers think of them as locations in which a value can be saved.

• Control statements imitate jumps. For example *if–then–else* has the semantics: "Test the condition. If true, go and execute the 'then' statements; otherwise go and execute the 'else' statements."

• The assignment statement imitates fetch and store instructions of the underlying machine.

Central to an imperative model of computing is the concept of a *present state,* which encompasses the program counter, the values of all variables, the stack, etc. According to advocates of functional programming, thinking of program execution in terms of a *present state* has a number of undesirable consequences [5], [6].

• Two widely separated pieces of code may reference a common global variable and therefore have an "unanticipated" interaction. A programmer must also be concerned with issues such as aliasing, which can increase program complexity.

• A programmer concentrates on data manipulation, not on the essential algorithm.

• It is difficult to characterize parallel execution when several independent asynchronous processes can have side effects on one another.

• Program proof and transformation are more difficult because the imperative model does not lend itself to easy mathematical characterization. For example, a name in a given context can have different meanings at different times, due to the invocation of an operation that produces a side effect.

On the other hand, it may also be argued that many common computer applications (e.g., updating a database) are inherently imperative in nature, and that imperative programming languages are well suited to such tasks.

B. Functional Languages

Functional programs contain no notion of a *present state, program counter,* or *storage.* Rather, the "program" is a *function* in the true mathematical sense: it is applied to the input of the program, and the resulting value is the program's output. For example, if the "program" *Plus* computes the sum of two numbers, then 3 + 4 can be computed by applying *Plus* to the input ⟨3, 4⟩

$$Plus: \langle 3, 4 \rangle \rightarrow 7.$$

Because a function's argument(s) and output value(s) may be

list structures, a function can define quite complex operations on its input.

Essential to functional programming is the notion of *referential transparency* [8], [46]: the value of an expression depends only on its textual context, *not* on computational history. The value of *Plus*: $\langle 3, 4 \rangle$ is determined only by the static definitions of *Plus*, 3, and 4.

Another way of viewing this is that the *output* is another form of the *function and input;* 7 and *Plus*: $\langle 3, 4 \rangle$ are simply different forms of the same object. The purpose of the computation is to *reduce* an *expression* to an equivalent *constant expression*.

The basic operation, then, in functional programming is function application. Data dependencies exist only as a result of function application, the value of a function being completely determined by its arguments. Notions such as *time dependence*, *side effect*, and *writable memory* do not exist.

Examples of functional languages are pure Lisp, Backus' FP [5], Hope [8], Val [58], Id [2], KRC [85], and ML [26]. Some, like Backus' FP, have no assignment statement. Others, such as Val and Id, are known as *single-assignment languages*, in which an "assignment statement" is simply a notational convenience for binding an expression to an identifier.

As an example of the functional style of programming, consider a functional program for computing the inner product of two vectors using a notation similar to that in [5]

$$IP = (Reduce\ Plus) \circ (Map\ Times) .$$

Map is a functional form that applies an *n*-ary function to *n* vectors of equal length, resulting in a single vector of that length. *Reduce* is identical to the operator of the same name in APL. Thus,

$$IP: \langle\langle 2, 3, -2\rangle, \langle 3, 1, 5\rangle\rangle$$
$$= (Reduce\ Plus) \circ (Map\ Times): \langle\langle 2, 3, -2\rangle, \langle 3, 1, 5\rangle\rangle$$
$$= (Reduce\ Plus): \langle 6, 3, -10\rangle$$
$$= -1 .$$

Similarly, matrix multiplication may be defined as

$$MM = (ApplyToAll(ApplyToAll\ IP)) \circ Pair$$
$$\circ [First, Transpose \circ Second] .$$

ApplyToAll applies a unary function to each element of a vector, resulting in a vector of identical length. *Pair* is a function that creates a matrix of pairs of elements of its two arguments; *First* and *Second* are functions that select the first and second elements of a vector, respectively. Thus, the multiplication of a 2×3 matrix and a 3×2 matrix

$$MM: \langle\langle\langle 0, 3, 2\rangle, \langle 1, -4, 4\rangle\rangle, \langle\langle 1, 0\rangle, \langle 3, -2\rangle, \langle 5, 1\rangle\rangle\rangle$$
$$= (ApplyToAll(ApplyToAll\ IP)) \circ Pair \circ [First, Transpose \circ Second]:$$
$$\langle\langle\langle 0, 3, 2\rangle, \langle 1, -4, 4\rangle\rangle, \langle\langle 1, 0\rangle, \langle 3, -2\rangle, \langle 5, 1\rangle\rangle\rangle$$
$$= (ApplyToAll(ApplyToAll\ IP)) \circ Pair:$$
$$\langle\langle\langle 0, 3, 2\rangle, \langle 1, -4, 4\rangle\rangle, \langle\langle 1, 3, 5\rangle, \langle 0, -2, 1\rangle\rangle\rangle$$
$$= (ApplyToAll(ApplyToAll\ IP)):$$
$$\langle\langle\langle\langle 0, 3, 2\rangle, \langle 1, 3, 5\rangle\rangle, \langle\langle 0, 3, 2\rangle, \langle 0, -2, 1\rangle\rangle\rangle,$$
$$\langle\langle\langle 1, -4, 4\rangle, \langle 1, 3, 5\rangle\rangle, \langle\langle 1, -4, 4\rangle, \langle 0, -2, 1\rangle\rangle\rangle\rangle$$
$$= \langle\langle 19, -4\rangle, \langle 9, 12\rangle\rangle$$

C. Programming in a Functional Language

According to Backus, programs are constructed in an imperative language by writing simple statements — such as the assignment statement — and "gluing them together" with control structures — such as *if–then–else;* programs in a functional language are composed by writing functions, and "gluing them together" with *functional forms*. The major components of his system are [5] the following.

1) A set of *objects*.

2) A set of *functions* that map objects into objects. These functions are analogous to built-in functions and operators in imperative programming languages.

3) A set of *functional forms* that combine existing functions or objects to form new functions. An example of a functional form is the *reduction* operator of APL.[1]

---

[1]Some functional languages [84] allow higher order functions — that is, functions that can be applied to functions — obviating the need for the notion of a *functional form*.

results in a 2×2 matrix.

The functional programming style can thus be characterized as the building of complex functions from simpler ones by using *functional forms;* the notion of the *state* of a computation is absent.

II. THE PROGRAMMER'S PERSPECTIVE

The use of functional languages has been advocated by a number of scientists [5], [24]. Claims have been made that the use of functional programs increases programmer productivity, program lucidity, and ease of verification. Morris *et al.* [61], however, raise the question: "Is applicative programming well-suited to someone who must make a living programming, or is it primarily for 'meta-programmers' who study programming?"

If functional programming is to become commonplace in the "real world," a number of issues must be resolved. Perhaps the most significant issue is whether real applications are suited to functional programming. Can a text editor, operating system, or video game be easily constructed in a functional language? If not, can the domain of its practicality be characterized?

Many argue in favor of functional programming languages by comparing them to conventional languages, such as Fortran or Pascal [5]. Included in such arguments, however, should be other "nonconventional" languages, such as Smalltalk [25], or CLU [53]. It may be the case that most of the high productivity attributed to functional programming is not due to referential transparency, but rather to other properties, such as abstraction, extensibility, higher order functions, and heap-allocated memory.

Finally, there is the question of whether functional languages can be mapped onto computer hardware and executed with reasonable efficiency, a topic that will be discussed in later sections.

A. Advantages of the Functional Programming Style

Proponents of functional programming claim that correct functional programs are easier to produce than equivalent imperative ones. Advantages cited include the following.

• Programs can be written at a higher level; a programmer can get the "big picture" rather than specifying a computation "a word at a time," as is typical in imperative languages [5], [6]. Time can be spent concentrating on the algorithm rather than on the details of its implementation.

• Its compact lucid notation allows more "algorithm" to be expressed per line of code. Evidence suggests that *number of lines of correct code per day* is roughly constant for a given programmer, independent of the language used [91]. A functional language would thus increase productivity because it takes fewer lines of code to express a desired concept in a functional language [84].

• Functional languages are free of side effects. A programmer can construct a program without being concerned about *aliasing* or "unexpected" modifications to variables by other routines. A consequence of this is that the procedure parameter passing mechanisms *call-by-value* and *call-by-name* have the same semantics [6], providing the computation terminates.

• Functional programs are easier to verify because proofs can be based on the rather well-understood concept of a function rather on the more cumbersome notion of a von Neumann computer [5].

• Functional programs often contain a great deal of implicit and easily detected parallelism [24]. Explicitly specifying parallelism on a von Neumann system can be quite difficult [41].

Programming experience seems to indicate that languages with FP features do in fact increase programmer productivity. APL has long been known as a language in which programs can be quickly constructed [54]. Poplar [61], a functional string-processing language, has been used by a number of people to create a report generation system, family budget maintainer, and a purchase order management system. The consensus among programmers was that the use of Poplar significantly decreased programming time. Users and designers of other functional languages have made similar claims about productivity [8], [84].

Although functional languages can be quite powerful, there is nothing "magic" about them. An "imperative" program can be written in a functional language by defining a structure that encodes the values of all variables and passing this structure as a parameter to every function, every function returning a modified version. Such modifications would correspond to changes in the values of variables in the imperative program.

B. Problems with the Functional Programming Style

One of the potential drawbacks of programming in a functional language is the difficulty — or at least the different approach — one encounters when programming an inherently sequential algorithm, such as one that consists largely of I/O operations. Consider an imperative program in which a file is opened and a pointer to it is passed among procedures, each reading a record from the file and then returning to the main program. A functional program, being free of side effects, would be somewhat awkward to write in this (imperative) style. If function A is to read a record from the input file, and function B is to read the next record, functions must be written so that B calls A (either directly or indirectly), and A must return both the *main result* and the *modified versions of all files it uses*. Performing I/O in this manner has much the flavor of simulating a von Neumann machine by "passing the whole machine state around from function to function."

The method of handling I/O that seems to have gained the widest acceptance among function programming advocates is that of using *streams*, which were originally proposed by Landin [51], and were later incorporated into a data flow language by Weng [95]. A stream is a representation of a list structure that is implemented by passing the elements sequentially; the use of streams can allow functional programs to be specified in a natural way, at least for simple input–output behavior. Examples have also been given in which streams can be used to model more complex sequential events in a functional language [4]. The question of whether the stream model is as general and as natural as its proponents claim will likely remain unanswered until a significant number of "real applications" are written in functional languages.

C. Debugging Functional Programs

The debugging of functional programs is another issue that requires further exploration. The experience of several scientists indicates that debugging may actually be easier when using a functional language [8], [61]. Although one cannot examine the state of the computation — there is no state — it certainly seems feasible to trace one or more paths down the "execution tree," examining the inputs and outputs of each function. This type of debugging seems well suited to functional programs since such a tree is a static object for a given input; an imperative program, on the other hand, has a state that changes with time. Debugging a functional program in a traditional way (setting break points, etc.) could be a confusing undertaking if *lazy evaluation* [32] (see Section IV-B-1) is employed because the order of evaluation may be nonintuitive [61].

The *equality assertion* feature of Poplar [61] seems well suited to functional programs and has been shown to be useful in allowing the compiler to aid in debugging. This feature allows the programmer to specify a *test input* for the function along with *values at intermediate points* of the computation and *the output value* for the chosen test input. The assertions act as comments, giving a reader an intuitive feel for what the program is doing. In addition, they are executed by the compiler to ensure that they are consistent with the actual code.

D. Conclusion

There is evidence that functional programs can be used to express a number of algorithms concisely and lucidly, requiring less effort than programming in an imperative language. Additional experience is required before it can be determined how much of the "functional programming advantage" is due to the lack of side effects, and how much is due to other features that are common to many functional languages.

III. EFFICIENCY CONSIDERATIONS

In the previous section, arguments were considered that programming in a functional language is better than programming in an imperative language. In this section, we explore efficiency considerations. Many FP proponents contend that whether or not functional programming increases programmer productivity, it produces programs that are highly suitable for parallel processing. On the other hand, functional programs have gained a reputation for running slowly.

A. Potential for Concurrent Execution

Functional programs often contain a great deal of implicit parallelism, making them attractive candidates for execution on parallel processors. Arguments of a function and distinct elements in a dynamically created structure can all be evaluated concurrently and independently [24]. In addition, a reduction (as in APL) with an associative operator can be evaluated as a tree rather than as a list, decreasing its running time from linear to logarithmic if sufficient processors are available [58], [87]. Finally, if the programmer/system is willing to spend computing time on results that may not be needed, all three clauses of a conditional expression can even be evaluated concurrently [67].

Proponents also argue that functional programs are also attractive for parallel processing because data dependencies are localized; the value of a function depends only on values of its arguments, giving rise to the possibility that communication overhead can be minimized by arranging for the evaluation of a function to occur "near" the evaluation of its arguments (but see Section III-B). Proposals for implementing this typically involve attempting to make the function hierarchy graph correspond roughly to the physical graph of processors.

B. Efficiency Problems

The power of parallel processing may be overshadowed by the apparently inherent inefficiencies of functional programs. Reasons cited for the lack of speed in functional languages have included the following [38], [62], [64], [88].

• The use of linked lists instead of arrays. A random access

to an "array" element takes linear time rather than constant time.

• The high frequency of function calls and the resulting overhead for parameter passing, etc.

• Garbage-collection overhead.

• Lack of destructive updating. To return a modified version of a structure, it is necessary (logically) to return a new copy of the structure with the modification.

• Listful style. Some functional languages encourage the passing of intermediate list structures between composed functions. The use of such structures causes additional storage allocation and dereferencing operations to be performed, and adds to garbage-collection overhead.

Although several of the above points reflect the fact that functional languages are not as "close" to von Neumann computers as are imperative languages, others reflect only that many *implementations* have been inefficient. Fateman [22] points out that one of the reasons functional languages have their reputation for inefficiency is that they have typically been run interpretively rather than compiled. He presents an example in which a good Lisp compiler generates code as efficient as that produced by a Fortran compiler, by performing in-line expansion of common functions such as *car* and *cdr* and by eliminating tail recursion.

Although the use of linked lists is ideal for some operations, it is quite poor for array-like random accesses. It has been suggested that a tree representation of a sequential structure might be a good compromise between a linked list and an array [27], [44]; this would also allow destructive updating to be performed in logarithmic time. In some cases, the use of contiguous arrays is also appropriate.

Another problem is that most FP computations are performed on structures, not scalar values, diminishing the effectiveness of arranging for functions to compute their values "near" the evaluation of their arguments (see Section III-A). When a structure is represented by a pointer, accessing its elements may still require a large number of remote references.

1) The Impact of Programming Style on Efficiency: A more serious issue affecting efficiency is that the functional programming style encourages programmers to operate on large structures rather than "a word at a time." If A and B are arrays, an imperative programmer might write

$$A[i] + B[i]$$

while an APL programmer would likely write

$$(A + B)[i]$$

which, although more concise, causes a completely new array $A + B$ to be created when evaluated in a straightforward manner. Similarly, to compute the third largest element in a list L, an APL programmer might write

$$(Reverse\ Sort\ L)[3]$$

rather than running through a loop and keeping track of the three largest values. The general problem is that the evaluation of functions that operate on large structures can be inefficient. (The use of *lazy evaluation* [32] can lead to substantial improvement in some cases, at the cost of higher space and speed overhead (see Section IV-B-1).)

2) Recomputation of Values: Another potential inefficiency is the performing of the same computation repeatedly. Consider the recursive program to compute the *n*th Fibonacci number

Fib

$= (Leq\ 1) \rightarrow Ident;\ Plus \cdot [Fib \circ (Sub\ 1), Fib \circ (Sub\ 2)].$

Although mathematically concise, this function takes exponential time when executed in the straightforward manner. The recursive program to determine whether a number is prime

$IsPrime = (Reduce\ Or)\ (ApplyToAll\ Divides)\ Distl \cdot$

$[(Filter\ IsPrime)\ Upto \cdot [2, Floor\ Sqrt], Ident]$

also invokes *IsPrime* multiple times for several values.

The fundamental problem seems to be that it can be quite difficult to detect at compile time when a function will be invoked with the same arguments, so that the result can be saved the first time it is computed, and *looked up* during subsequent calls [45]. An imperative program can explicitly save values that are known to be needed later. Keller and Sleep [46] have proposed a mechanism by which an FP programmer can specify when a result is to be cached. A totally automatic caching scheme introduces a number of implementation problems (see Section IV-E-2).

C. Compile Time Techniques for Improving Efficiency

Compiler optimization techniques can be used to solve some of the inefficiency problems of functional programs. Although not the subject of this paper, compiler techniques are a promising area of research, and are sometimes ignored by FP machine designers. Solving an efficiency problem by program transformation should at least be considered before a complex piece of hardware is designed.

Two approaches are being explored in the area of functional program transformation. *Discovery methods* employ a small number of transformations: a heuristic search is performed, applying the transformations in an attempt to improve the efficiency of the program. *Schema methods* employ a larger collection of transformations, but without searching.

Discovery methods [7], [45], [56], [74], [88] are generally variants of an unfolding–folding technique, which coalesces operations and attempts to minimize the number of intermediate list structures. A function is first *unfolded* by expanding some of its functions, replacing each with its definition. The goal is to extract "an atomic step" of a recursive function, and to transform the remainder of the function into an instance of the function itself. Tail recursion may often be eliminated to transform the function into iterative form [77].

Schema methods [48], [69], [87] do not perform heuristic searching; instead, a collection of predefined transformation templates are applied to transform the program. These methods are generally faster than discovery methods — no searching is done — but less general, as all transformations must be predefined.

Schemas have been developed for APL compilers that "understand" certain array manipulation/permutation operations such as transpose and sort, and can optimize such operations as

$$Reverse\ Reverse\ x \rightarrow x$$

and

$$(Sort\ x)[3] \rightarrow `third\ smallest\ element\ in\ x`.$$

Compiler techniques for improving functional programs have generally concentrated on removing overhead such as intermediate list creation. While these techniques clearly improve performance on a von Neumann architecture, there is the possibility that such transformations may reduce the potential for parallelism. If it is necessary to perform a complex operation on each element of a list, performing the operations iteratively so that the list does not have to be physically created may not be the most efficient method on a multiprocessor architecture. The cost of storage management must be weighed against the potential speedup of concurrent evaluation. Such analysis by a compiler will not always be practical.

On the other hand, when an effective well-understood compiler technique is discovered to solve a particular efficiency problem, it should be used rather than building additional hardware to solve the problem. Hardware solutions should be applied only when compiler solutions are inadequate.

D. Conclusion

There is a great deal of inherent parallelism in many functional programs. Because of their freedom from side effects, they are attractive candidates for execution on parallel architectures. Efficiency problems, however, still exist. Some may be classified as "overhead" (e.g., intermediate list construction), while others are more fundamental (e.g., programming style). Whether parallelism and/or compiler techniques can compensate for or solve these problems remains an open research issue.

IV. DESIGN ISSUES FOR FUNCTIONAL PROGRAM MACHINES

This section compares and contrasts design decisions that have been made by architects of various FP machines along the following dimensions.

• The physical interconnection of the processors. These vary from uniprocessor systems to cube-interconnection networks.

• The method used to "drive" the computation.

• The representation of program and data. Most machines use a list or graph structure for both program and data. There are several design issues to consider even if a list structure is chosen.

• How parallelism is invoked and controlled. There are many issues here, including when to invoke parallelism, the mapping of processes to processors, and deadlock avoidance.

• Optimization techniques. Some proposed machines use evaluation strategies that attempt to avoid unnecessary and/or redundant computations.

Specific machines are examined with respect to these issues in Section V.

Not all machines discussed here were intended to execute purely *functional* languages. A number of them, particularly Lisp and APL machines, were designed for the execution of a nonfunctional language that contains a large functional subset; we refer to such languages as *quasi-functional*. Such machines are included to reflect points in the design space that would otherwise be overlooked. Although multiprocessors are the primary emphasis, a number of uniprocessors are included to present a richer view of the design space.

A. Physical Interconnection of Processors

The selection of a processor interconnection scheme in a multiprocessing environment is an important design decision. The subject has been one of great interest for designers of von Neumann multiprocessors [31], and the tradeoffs involved apply to FP multiprocessors as well.

Generally, a richer interconnection offers higher performance and flexibility at a greater hardware expense.[2] A complete interconnection is infeasible, however, because FP machine designers envision systems of hundreds or thousands of processors [9], [13]. At the other end of the spectrum are uniprocessor systems. While some have interesting features with respect to functional program implementation, they are not of particular interest in discussing interconnection strategies.

1) Shared Buses: The concurrent-Lisp processor [78] and Rumbaugh's data flow machine [73] each use a shared bus interconnection. The concurrent-Lisp processor has several memory banks, each attached to a single bus, with each processor directly connected to each memory bus, and processor communication done via the shared memory. Rumbaugh's system has two global memory banks — one for instructions and one for structure values — and local memories in each processor, used for caching. Bandwidth requirements make a shared bus approach feasible only for a small number of processors.

2) Ring: The *ZMOB* multiprocessing system [71] and the TI-data flow machine [39] each use a ring network in which data flow in one direction. Like shared bus architectures, bandwidth can become a bottleneck when the number of processors is large. The communication bandwidth of the 256 processor *ZMOB* network, for example, is only about one bit per microsecond per processor.

3) Tree: A number of designers have proposed tree-structured architectures [14], [43], [55], [65]. For a *reduction machine*, in which the problem can be decomposed into independent parallel subproblems, there is a natural mapping between the hardware (tree) and the software (tree of processes). Unfortunately, it is often necessary to copy data (e.g., parameter values) to each of a number of independent computations, making the bottleneck near the root of the tree a potentially serious problem. Sorting, for example, requires linear time on a tree, but can be performed in $O(\log^2 n)$ on a richer network [86]. Another problem is that the physical tree of processors has a finite depth, so that the resources at a leaf node may be insufficient for solving a large subproblem if the problem decomposes into a structure that is deeper than the physical tree.

A tree architecture may also be used in an SIMD manner, in which the tree is used as an associative memory and as a data shifter [55], [65]; lists may be stored across the leaves of the tree rather than in linked form. When insertion or deletion is required, some of the elements in the list are shifted to their neighbors; a single data shift among leaves of a tree may be performed in logarithmic time [70].

4) Hierarchical: A two-level system has been proposed for the ALICE multiprocessor [13] in which the processors are divided into tightly coupled *clusters*, which are then interconnected as a network. Parallelism unfolds dynamically, requiring the mapping of processes onto processors at runtime. The experience with the Cm* multiprocessor [41], also a clustered system but programmed imperatively, has shown that locality — important for good performance — is not easy to achieve. The performance of such a structure should be no worse than that of a tree, however, because a tree can be viewed as a special case of a hierarchical interconnection.

The U-interpreter [2] also uses a cluster strategy, with the clusters connected in a routing network (see next paragraph). Its designers intend to maintain a high degree of locality by requiring each cluster to work on a very closely coupled portion of the program, such as a single iteration of a loop.

5) Routing Networks: Several data architectures employ a routing network structure for communication between a set of processing elements and a set of memories [19]. The network used for Dennis' data flow project consists of $\log_2 N$ layers of N routers for an N-element system, each receiving packets at two input ports and transmitting them to one of two output ports. Two-way communication between processing elements and memories is achieved using a pair of tree routing networks. Although there is a rather large delay for a single memory access, such architectures are often designed primarily for total throughput. For large systems, however, network contention can easily degrade system throughput by 75 percent [68], although this can be improved by introducing buffering into the network [21].

6) Hypertorus: Hewitt [33] suggests a hypertorus interconnection — each processor being a member of n orthogonal ring networks where n is the dimension of the hypertorus — in which all processors contain local memory and are homogeneous. Attractive features of such a scheme are that the *maximum distance* between any two processors is proportional to the nth root of the number of processors, and that the interconnection structure is quite rich.

7) N-Cube: N-cube interconnections have also been suggested for FP architectures [2], [9], [13]. The connectivity of an n-cube is similar to that of a routing network, but each node contains a processor with memory rather than just a switch. The maximum distance between any two processors is logarithmic in the number of processors.

8) Conclusions: Although functional programs may exhibit a fair amount of locality, it is important for a processor to have reasonably efficient access to any other processor in the system if structures are to be shared. The shared bus, tree, and ring have bottlenecks that make them less desirable candidates. One-way routing networks cannot take advan-

---

[2]Richer interconnections may also give higher reliability, a topic that is beyond the scope of this paper.

tage of any locality, while the *cluster* approach has "arbitrary" locality boundaries with which the system must deal, although it appears to fit in well with the U-interpreter method of process-to-processor mapping. The *n*-cube and hypertorus give "gracefully degrading locality" and a rich interconnection structure, but still require the overhead of dynamic routing.

B. Method of Driving the Computation

Functions in an FP machine may be evaluated either top-down — where a function is evaluated when requested by another function that requires it as an argument — or bottom-

[23]. The infinite list of positive integer perfect squares, for example, may be expressed as

$$SquareList: 1$$

where *SquareList* is defined as

$$SquareList = Square \; \square \; (SquareList \circ (Plus \; 1))$$

where "$\square$" is a right-associative list construction operator (analogous to "cons" in Lisp). If the third element of the list is needed, lazy evaluation can invoke *SquareList* and *Square* until the third element is reduced

$$SquareList: 1 \rightarrow (Square: 1) \; \square \; (SquareList: 2)$$
$$\rightarrow (Square: 1) \; \square \; (Square: 2) \; \square \; (SquareList: 3)$$
$$\rightarrow (Square: 1) \; \square \; (Square: 2) \; \square \; (Square: 3) \; \square \; (SquareList: 4)$$
$$\rightarrow (Square: 1) \; \square \; (Square: 2) \; \square \; 9 \; \square \; (SquareList: 4) \;.$$

up — where a function is evaluated as soon as its arguments are available. The bottom-up approach is known as *data driven* computation, with each function (node) in a data flow graph being scheduled for evaluation as soon as its arguments arrive. Sequential and demand-driven evaluation are top-down — the arguments of function are not evaluated until a request is made that the function itself be evaluated.

1) Demand-Driven Evaluation: The *demand-driven* evaluation strategy makes use of the fact that *call-by-value* and *call-by-name* always return the same value in functional program (with *call-by-name* actually possessing better termination properties). A function's arguments are passed by name, and each is evaluated — again in a demand-driven fashion — the first time its value is needed; subsequent references to the argument use the already-evaluated form. This results in *unreduced* or *partially reduced* structures being passed among functions as arguments, each function application performing only the reductions necessary for its own evaluation. Demand-driven evaluation was used by Abrams [1] in his APL machine, and has been used in a number of implementations since [13], [43], [61]. It is also known as *lazy evaluation* [32] or *call-by-need* [63], [89].

Demand-driven evaluation generally introduces a fair amount of overhead. When a structure element is accessed, it must be determined whether it has already been reduced; if not, additional computation may be required. In a multiprocessor environment, several concurrent processes may simultaneously need the same structure to be reduced, requiring the synchronization and/or blocking [13]. The designers of Poplar note that in the cases where all elements of a structure were eventually required, lazy evaluation slowed programs in their implementation by a factor of about two [61]. In a multiprocessor system, communication and synchronization overhead may cause this factor to be even higher.

The advantages of the demand-driven evaluation include the potential for eliminating a vast amount of computation by evaluating only what is necessary for computing the result and the handling of infinite list structures in a natural way

Whether lazy evaluation may be — or must be — used depends on the semantics of the particular functional language.

2) Data-Driven Evaluation: A data-driven system incurs relatively little time overhead, with each operator node remaining inactive until *fired* — that is to say, when all its inputs have arrived. Parallelism is thus inhibited only by direct data dependencies; it is not inhibited because the result of a computation is not needed, as in demand-driven evaluation. Potential problems that appear in data-driven systems are the following.

• Too much parallelism might be generated. Memory could become swamped with partial results that are not yet used, causing deadlock. Decisions about suspending processes are more difficult because control passes from the bottom up.

• It is not possible to evaluate *structures* in a *lazy* manner because a data flow node only deals with fully evaluated structures; conceptually infinite structures therefore cannot be represented as data entities. Weng [95] applied the *stream* construct [51] to data flow computers, allowing conceptually infinite structures to be produced by sending them through data flow nodes one element at time. This requires the user/compiler to deal with two disjoint representations of the same concept: *structures* which can be manipulated efficiently, and *streams* which must be manipulated serially but can represent infinite objects.

• In a purely data-driven system all three subexpressions of a conditional statement would be evaluated in parallel, causing unnecessary computation to be performed. In practice, *switch* and *merge* nodes are inserted into the data paths of a conditional execution to delay the execution of the *then* or *else* expressions until after the condition is evaluated [19]. This amounts to lazy evaluation at the top level of a conditional expression, demonstrating that lazy evaluation can occur among function arguments — but not for structure elements — in a purely data-driven system.

In the example above, a data-driven system would completely evaluate *SquareList*: 1 before its result is passed to the node that uses the third element, requiring an infinite amount of computation.

3) Sequential Evaluation: The power and efficiency of sequential evaluation (in terms of both overhead and total computation) is closer to data-driven evaluation than to demand-driven. Treleaven *et al.* [82] argue that sequential evaluation is computationally equivalent to data-driven evaluation because both completely evaluate arguments before calling a function. Sequential evaluation does differ from data-driven evaluation in that it is top-down, so parallelism is more easily inhibited. There may be, however, more overhead because control must pass down the "computation graph" before results are passed up; in a data-driven scheme, the data (at the bottom of the computation graph) flow up the graph. Additionally, parallelism is not as natural to express in the sequential model.

4) Summary: Demand-driven evaluation requires more overhead than data-driven evaluation, but allows better control of parallelism, more selective evaluation, and a natural way of handling infinite structures. Data-driven evaluation is more efficient locally, but its "good performance" is limited to a narrower spectrum of computations, namely those which are data intensive and do not "blow up" when maximal parallelism is invoked. Sequential evaluation is similar to data-driven evaluation, but parallelism cannot be expressed as naturally.

C. Representation of Program Structures

Several methods have been proposed for representing programs and data in an FP system, the most common being graph and list structures. The most popular data representation is also a graph/list structure, but the decisions are largely independent.[3]

1) Program Representation and Execution Method: The representation of the program depends largely on the method used for program evaluation.

Sequential execution. In a (traditional) sequential program, code and data are separated, and instructions are executed sequentially; code can be considered an active agent that transforms the passive data. This method of execution is generally used primarily when the source language is quasi-functional.

Data flow. In this case, the data can be considered the active agents, moving through the "code graph" as they are transformed into the final result. The code representation is a data flow graph, possibly augmented by auxiliary data flow graphs that represent user-defined functions.

Reduction. A reduction machine takes the view that the *source-and-input* and *output* are merely two different forms of the same object, the output being the *reduced* form of the original program and input. An *object* in a reduction system is a structure the base elements of which are atoms and functions, a *reduced object* being one in which all base elements are atoms. The reduction process then consists of applying transformations to an object until it is in reduced form. Many

reduction machines use graphs to represent structures and user-defined functions, although strings are sometimes used. Primitive functions — and sometimes even user-defined functions — are generally represented in machine code.

2) Traditional Machine Code: Several *quasi-functional* processors use traditional machine code for machine language [1], [28]. Such machines are usually uniprocessors that are microcoded for improved performance and are not truly functional in that they support global writable variables.

3) Graph-Structured Program Representation: Most of the current and proposed functional machines use some form of graph or list structure to represent the program, normally either list-structured machine code (reduction graph), a combinator graph, or a data flow graph.

Graph-structured machine code, often used in interpretive Lisp systems, is a variation of sequential code in which a graph structure is used to represent the program's structure. The machine executes instructions by traversing the list structure rather than by using a program counter. Reduction machines also use graphs of this form, but the mode of execution differs. In the former case, the environment is kept in a separate structure such as a display or association list, while in the latter case, the data become intermingled with the program as function definitions are inserted during the graph transformation.

A *combinator graph* is a version of the source program in which all variable and function references have been removed by applying combinator transformations [12]. Because there is no distinction between functions and data in a combinator system, function definitions are often *optimized* on the fly [83]. Such an optimization generally occurs when a function is defined in terms of two or more previously defined functions and the definitions are allowed to coalesce.

The combinator reduction proposed by Turner appears to require a large number of transformations, even for a simple program. Hughes [37] extended Turner's method by demonstrating that any function that satisfies two "functional" properties can be defined to be a combinator. Such "supercombinators" may then be compiled, increasing the speed of the object program when compared to Turner's method. Analysis by Jones [42] suggests that even without significant optimization, combinator-reduction outperforms lambda-reduction.

A *data flow graph* is similar to list-structured machine code with its pointers reversed to reflect bottom-up execution. The classical data flow program consists of a static graph that transform data as they pass through, recursive programs not being representable [39]. To allow recursive functions, the U-interpreter [2] replaces a *function node* with a copy of the definition whenever it is invoked, each copy having a *label* to identify it. Watson and Gurd [92] have constructed a machine that employs a similar strategy.

4) Token-String Program Representation: Berkling and Magó [6], [55] have proposed reduction machines that represent an expression by a string. The job of the processor(s) is to recognize patterns that can be reduced, and then to reduce them. Berkling's uniprocessor system evaluates polish prefix expressions using a stack, while Magó's tree-structured machine groups data segments by including parentheses in the token string.

---

[3]The use of list structures as program and data representation was introduced by McCarthy in the Lisp language. Having both program and data structures represented in the same way is considered to be one of Lisp's great strengths [57].

5) Data Representation Issues: The manner in which data are represented and accessed in a machine has a great bearing on the efficiency of a program. For accessing a structure, it is desirable to have the *random access* efficiency that an array representation would provide. On the other hand, data manipulations like concatenation and transposition—generally faster on list-structured data—should also be efficient.

Depending on the representation used, the question of whether to use monolithic data structures or pointers must also be resolved. A policy of always copying whole structures does not appear to be a good idea if large amounts of data are involved.

6) Methods of Representing Data: Traditionally, functional and quasi-functional systems have represented structures as linked linear lists of substructures. Although this has the advantage that many structure-manipulation operations can be done very quickly, *random access* to a structure element takes linear time. Another alternative, typically used in imperative languages, is to represent structures as arrays, allowing fast random access, but having the disadvantages that operations such as insertion take linear time and that memory can become fragmented when data blocks differ in size.

Some systems [28] use both lists and arrays under programmer control, giving the programmer some of the "best of both worlds" at the expense of requiring him to be concerned with another "programming detail." This method still does not solve the problem if a single structure must have both types of operations performed on it.

It has also been suggested that a tree be used to represent linear structures [27], [44], allowing most access and manipulation operations to be performed in logarithmic time. This approach has the disadvantage that the complexity of many simple access and data manipulation operations is increased, especially if the tree is required to remain balanced. Additional advantages of using a tree are that nondestructive updating of a structure can be performed in logarithmic time, and that reductions applying an associative operator can be performed in logarithmic time on a parallel architecture; a list structure requires linear time simply to access the elements in a list.

Some architectures represent all structures as token strings. This has the disadvantage that random access can be efficient only for the lowest-level structures, other data manipulation operations being expensive. An advantage in a multiprocessor system with distributed memory is that storage management can be simplified, as each processor can maintain its own address space.

7) Copying Structures: Tradeoffs exist between *copying pointers* and *copying data* strategies in a multiprocessor systems [66]. Copying large data structures among processors can be expensive in terms of time, bus contention, and memory utilization if only a few elements of a structure are needed. On the other hand, copying data incurs less overhead if all the data are eventually going to be used, and allows storage management to be performed at the individual processor level.

The decision whether to copy data or pointers is an instance of a general problem in FP systems: the program is written at a high enough level that the programmer is freed from—and the system is required to—make the decision. In an imperative program, the copying of data or pointers is generally specified explicitly.

Dennis [17] suggested a variation of the pointer-copying approach in which a pointer is cached in any processor to which it is copied, effectively building a copy of the structure in the remote processor as it is accessed. (Such caching is perfectly safe on a functional machine because a structure is never modified once it is created.) In the case where the remote processor has the only reference to a structure, it gradually migrates toward the remote processor, accessed portions of the structure in the local processor being reclaimed by the storage manager. Dennis suggested that this method might be used as a compromise between the "copy data" and "copy pointers" approaches, and that pointers (or atoms) might be sent in groups rather than singly to reduce communication overhead.

8) Storage Management: When pointers are used to implement structures, it is necessary to reclaim storage that has become unreferenceable. Reference counting may be used if graphs contain no cycles. Otherwise, a strategy such as marking or copying must be employed—possibly in conjunction with reference counting.

Although cycles are not necessary in data graphs—a purely functional language has no destructive operators—the optimization of certain graph representations can introduce cyclic list structures [13], [83]. In such cases the cost of garbage collection overhead must be weighed against the increased efficiency of structure access.

The drawbacks of a reference count strategy are that space is taken for a count field in each structure and that counts must be updated when pointers are copied or deleted. The advantage is that space can be recovered more quickly, and that reference counting is more easily performed asynchronously.

Halstead and Ward [29], [90] suggested a storage management strategy that uses *reference trees,* data structures linking together all references to a particular object in the system. Their approach allows garbage collection to occur on a local processor basis only, while finding global cyclic list structures through a strategy of migrating connected nodes to a common processor.

Magó's machine [55] necessarily approaches storage management in a different manner because there are no pointers; the problem in this case is what to do when the leaves of the tree become full. The method employed to alleviate the problem is to shift computations across the leaves of the tree—possibly quite expensive if large amounts of data are involved. If the entire tree becomes full, some computations are suspended, stored in secondary memory, and restarted at a later time.

D. Parallelism Issues

Design decisions about process communication, load balancing, control of parallelism, and other software issues vary substantially among multiprocessor FP systems. Although many systems are limited by the underlying architecture—a tree machine would not make good use of a global process list because efficient execution on a tree machine depends greatly on locality of reference [43], for example — there are generally many variations to consider.

1) Granularity of Parallelism: Many multiprocessor FP machines have a fine grain of parallelism, with every node in the program graph represented by a process containing small amount of state. A process node in the Dennis data flow machine [18] contains four words: an opcode, two data words, and the name of the successor instruction. Each node in the ALICE reduction machine [13] contains six fields: its name, the function name, argument list pointers, process state information, a reference count, and signal list for blocked processes. On such machines, a process tends to be active for a short period of time, performing a simple transformation.

Other methods of defining granularity include the following.

• Each node acts as a uniprocessor, reducing its own portion of the graph. When parallelism is desired (due to a function needing two operands evaluated, etc.), a new node may be created to perform the collateral evaluation [24].

• Each data item (as well as each operator) acts a process [33], [55].

• Require the user to program parallelism explicitly [78].

• Reducing the overhead of fine-grained parallelism by grouping several reduction nodes together and executing it as a single von Neumann process [47].

Although fine-grained parallelism is conceptually simple, it can lead to a great deal of process management and communication overhead. In particular, as the grain of parallelism becomes finer, less "intelligence" can be applied in making scheduling decisions. Fine-grained parallelism also generally leads to better load balancing [9]; again, this must be weighed against the increased overhead cost.

2) Mapping of Processes onto the Hardware: The mapping of processes onto a machine's processors involves attempting to attain several (sometimes conflicting) goals. On one hand, it is desirable to keep a process close to its data and to keep communicating processes close together. On the other hand, work should be shifted from overloaded processors to underloaded processors. This problem is compounded when the grain of parallelism is fine, and it is therefore not cost-effective to spend much computing time deciding where to execute a process.

Simple strategies at opposite ends of the spectrum are the uniprocessor approach in which all processes and data are kept in the same processor — clearly unacceptable in a multiprocessor system — and keeping a global list of processes from which an idle processor can choose a process to execute. The latter strategy spreads the workload evenly over all processors, but takes no advantage of locality.

Dataflow machines at the Massachusetts Institute of Technology [18] and Manchester [92] use routing networks in which the data (packets) and processors are separated. Locality is not an issue in process mapping on these systems because an instruction travels the same distance, once around the routing network, regardless of which processor it "uses."

Friedman and Wise [24] propose a strategy called *colonel and sergeants* that also uses a global process list. One process, the *colonel,* begins reducing the graph in *normal* order;

that is to say, performing depth-first traversal, visiting the leftmost son first. When the colonel reaches a point where parallelism could be invoked, a *sergeant* (if available) begins the secondary computation. The pending processes that are "close" to the colonel have the highest priority, so locality tends to be maintained in the sense that most processors in the system are working "close to one another."

A compromise between the *global list* and *uniprocessor* approaches involves the use of local lists of processes, either shared by a group of processors or unique to each processor. The *ZAPP* system [9] uses the latter approach, but allows a processor to "steal" a pending process from a neighboring processor when its own process list becomes empty. This strategy encourages processes to migrate to neighboring processors, and allows trees of processes to spread out all over the system while ensuring that no process is more than one processor away from its immediate offspring. The *Rediflow* system [47] uses a similar strategy, employing a "pressure model" to balance processor load among neighbors.

The tree architectures generally map the process tree directly onto the processor tree, resulting in a great deal of process locality. In AMPS [43], each leaf processor has its own list of pending processes, while in Magó's machine [55], each token resides in a unique leaf processor; tokens are mapped onto the sequence of leaf processors in the order in which they occur in the expression.

3) Invoking and Controlling Parallelism: Because functional programs tend to contain a great deal of implicit parallelism, the problem can arise that the system becomes swamped with processes. Another problem with excess concurrency is that it is possible that all memory might become tied up holding intermediate results for computations that are in progress, thereby creating a deadlock situation.

The conservative approach, of course, is never to invoke parallelism; this can be done on reduction machines by performing a *normal-order reduction* order — traversing the reduction tree in a depth-first manner, visiting leftmost son first. A common strategy is to invoke parallelism only on *strict* operators — those operators such as *plus* and *times* that require the evaluation of all their arguments — and to refrain from invoking it for *nonstrict* operators such as *if–then–else* and *cons*.[4] Maximal concurrency, of course, is obtained by evaluating expressions *eagerly* — invoking parallelism even for arguments of nonstrict operators. While such a strategy is optimal given an infinite number of processors, it is likely to cause a great deal of wasted computation, slowing down a system of finite capacity.

Systems that perform *eager evaluation* therefore generally constrain it in some way. The AMPS and ALICE systems [13], [43] allow the programmer to state explicitly whether a nonstrict operator is to be evaluated eagerly. ALICE additionally constrains eagerness by allowing it only when the compiler can determine that the eager computation will terminate [63].

The colonel and sergeants system [24] invokes parallelism

---

[4]Actually, *cons* may or may not be a strict operator, depending upon the semantics of the programming language and whether a *lazy evaluation* strategy is being employed.

whenever there is an idle processor available. This may require that a stray process be purged, in the case where it can be determined that the process is performing an unnecessary or divergent computation.

In the ZAPP [9] and Rediflow [47] systems, the amount of parallelism is determined by the processor load. Breadth-first expansion, which encourages parallelism, is employed when load is light, depth-first when it is heavy. This is implemented in ZAPP on a local basis by maintaining a list of processes, each ordered according to its depth in the computation tree, and giving shallow processes priority over deep ones only when the load is light. The amount of *eager* evaluation is constrained by allowing *unsafe* computations (computations that may never terminate) a limit on the amount of processing that they are allowed to perform [76]. A process may be terminated when it exhausts its "budget," presumably leaving behind a partially reduced graph that becomes subject to garbage collection; alternatively, the budget may be extended if system load is light enough, allowing the unsafe computation to continue, again with a (revised) bound on its computation time.

On data-driven machines, the evaluation of arguments is performed before the operator node is encountered, making it difficult to use properties of the operator in dynamically constraining eager evaluation. A possible solution would be to introduce top-down "demand tokens" [16], allowing parallelism to be controlled more finely at the expense of introducing more overhead.

4) Deadlock Avoidance: The problem of deadlock in FP multiprocessing systems seems to be more easily solved in demand-driven than in data-driven systems because parallelism is more easily constrained. ZAPP's strategy [9] of basing their expansion (depth-first versus breadth-first) on system load is part of its method of deadlock prevention. If the assumption is made that there is always enough memory in any processor to evaluate an expression in *normal order*, this strategy does in fact prevent deadlock by forcing each processor to act as a uniprocessor, evaluating an expression in normal order, when system load becomes extremely high. Such an assumption is valid in cases where the a computation tree remains small.

Another possible approach in concurrent FP systems is to wait until deadlock occurs, and then to free some memory by selecting certain process trees for purging. Because FP computations have no side effects, purging a partially completed computation means only that it may have to be recomputed later. In the extreme case, the computation tree would be pruned to the extent that a single process is active and is performing normal-order reduction.

E. Additional Optimizations

In Section IV-B-1, it was seen that *lazy evaluation* can potentially increase the efficiency of a functional program by reducing the amount of unnecessary computation. This section discusses two other dynamic optimizations that have been suggested. Compile time versions of each are also possible.

1) Avoiding Unnecessary Data Manipulations:

Operations such as transposition, rotation, and slicing can involve a great deal of data manipulation, yet occur frequently in functional programs. In designing his APL machine, Abrams proposed the use of a technique called *beating* [1], in which certain data manipulation operations are implemented by performing transformations on *array descriptors* rather than on arrays themselves. An array transposition might be implemented by exchanging indexes in the array descriptor, for example.

It is not clear that the generalization of this technique to linear list structures would be effective because the effectiveness of *beating* is diminished in the absence of *random access* to structure elements. In systems where arrays (or other structures with efficient random access) are present, optimizations similar to beating may be worthwhile.

2) Avoiding Redundant Computations: A potential source of inefficiency in functional programs is that their straightforward execution often causes the same computation to be performed repeatedly [46]. For example, although most evaluators would evaluate *Transpose*: x only once in

$$[Fcn1, Fcn2] \circ Transpose: x$$

it would probably be necessary for a compiler to discover the common expression in

$$[Fcn1 \circ Transpose, Fcn2 \circ Transpose]: x.$$

Even more difficult is the recognition that [*Fib*: 2] and [*Fib*: 1] (dynamically) occur more than once in

$$Fib: 4 \rightarrow Plus \circ [Fib: 3, Fib: 2]$$
$$Fib: 3 \rightarrow Plus \circ [Fib: 2, Fib: 1]$$
$$Fib: 2 \rightarrow Plus \circ [Fib: 1, Fib: 0]$$

In this particular case, dynamic recognition of common expressions could reduce an exponential algorithm to a linear one.

Most FP systems share the result of the common computation in the first case and could be augmented to do so in the second. Doing so in the third case probably requires some type of result caching, although combinator reductions sometimes recognize these in simple cases (not in *Fib*, however). As a result, the default strategy for result sharing tends be sharing in the first two cases but recomputing in the third.

The policy of saving the result if the common expression is easy to detect, and recomputing it otherwise is not always the most effective. The *Fib* example demonstrates that it is sometimes desirable to detect "difficult" common expressions. Conversely, it may sometimes be desirable to ignore easily detected common expressions. Consider the evaluation of an expression in which a list is traversed in different orders by two functions

$$[Traverses\text{-}forward, Traverses\text{-}backward] \circ$$
$$From\text{-}1\text{-}to\text{-}1\,000\,000$$

the cost of recomputing the common function *From-1-to-1 000 000* may be relatively small, while keeping its value in memory would use a large number (1 000 000) of cells. If *lazy* evaluation and an *appropriate* method of representing structures were used, the necessary number of cells might be reduced to a handful.

The profitability of sharing a computation thus seems to be somewhat independent of the ease of common-expression recognition. The only way of sharing results in a general manner appears to through caching [59], which introduces a number of new issues to consider [46].

• What results should be cached? If the result of every intermediate computation is cached, it seems that memory could be quickly swamped. If not everything is cached, on what basis does one decide what to cache?

• How should the cache directory be structured? How are the cached values mapped onto the processor(s)? How much extra interprocessor traffic will be generated by cache lookup requests? Can cache-lookup be made efficient enough that it does not slow up "fast" operations?

• What replacement algorithm should be used to determine what entries to purge when the cache becomes full? How much overhead does this algorithm introduce? Ideally, one would like to account for factors such as the complexity of the computation, the amount of storage it takes to cache results, the number of "recent" references, and whether there are outstanding computations waiting for the result. It is probably not desirable, however, to spend a great deal of time performing cache management.

• Should *easily detected* common expressions be subject to the same purging strategy as cached ones, so that a function like *From-1-to-1 000 000 does* effectively generate its elements twice if memory becomes scarce?

• Should cache lookup be done in parallel with computation? If this strategy is adopted, the process(es) performing the computation should be aborted if the cache lookup is successful.

The caching issue seems to be another instance of a potential efficiency problem due to the fact that an FP language is higher level than an imperative language. In a typical imperative language, the programmer has explicit control over the decisions about whether a value should be saved or recomputed, basing these decisions on the complexity of the computation, the likelihood of needing to reuse the value, etc. In a functional program, such issues are generally transparent to the user, the system being responsible for deciding whether to save a value. The most practical approach thus far proposed is that the programmer be responsible for specifying which results should be cached [46].

Harbison's analysis [30] of a von Neumann architecture that caches expression values suggest that a moderately sized cache (512 entries) can significantly improve performance. Caching in a functional multiprocessor architecture is likely to be complicated, however, by the cache being distributed over the entire system and by comparisons being performed on structure values rather than scalar values and variable names.

TABLE I
ABRAMS' APL MACHINE

Reference	[1]
Physical interconnection	uniprocessor
Representation of program	machine code
Representation of data	arrays with descriptors
Drive	demand
Avoiding redundant computations	beating (descriptor optimization)
Storage management	reference counts (on array descriptors)
Status	paper design only

V. OVERVIEW OF SPECIFIC ARCHITECTURES

This section is a collection of brief descriptions of a number of architectures for the execution of *functional* or *quasi-functional* languages. The first two sections present architectures with minimal interconnections, namely the uniprocessor and tree machines. The last three sections include *data-driven, demand-driven,* and "other" architectures that have richer interconnections.

A. Uniprocessor Architectures

The architectures in this section are single-processor machines. In many cases, the design goals did not include high performance, but rather demonstration of the feasibility of a particular evaluation strategy.

1) Abrams' APL Machine: Abrams' APL machine, while not a multiprocessor, is important historically because it introduced two important concepts: *beating,* which optimizes array operations, and *dragging,* a type of lazy evaluation. Minter's APL machine [60], which was based on Abrams' work, extended and improved his optimizations.

2) Berkling's Reduction Machine: The uniprocessor designed by Berkling has three stacks, two used for computing and one — the *system stack* — to handle control structure. Execution consists of the application of a handful of simple character-string reduction rules.

Limitations: Characters are the only form of data used, so the machine is quite inefficient when operating on large structures because the data structures must be copied and scanned character-by-character [82]. In addition, a great deal of character scanning is generally required to find instances of reduction rules.

3) Scheme-79: Scheme-79 is a single-chip lexically scoped Lisp machine. Two-level microcode is used to execute programs by traversing list-structured machine code. Interesting features of the architecture include the use of independent register assemblies to enable register parallelism, and the assignment of particular registers to specified hardware functions.

Limitations: The machine is not particularly fast; its compiled code runs at about the same speed as interpreted Lisp on a PDP-10. Its design goals, however, were oriented toward testing a design methodology and bringing up a working

TABLE II
BERKLING'S REDUCTION MACHINE

Reference	[6]
Physical interconnection	uniprocessor
Representation of program	character string
Representation of data	character string
Drive	sequential, with programmer-specified delayed evaluation
Avoiding redundant computations	local variable binding; programmer can specify call-by-name or call-by-value;
Storage management	stack
Status	operational

TABLE III
SCHEME-79

References	[36], [80]
Physical interconnection	uniprocessor
Representation of program	graph/list
Representation of data	graph/list
Drive	sequential
Avoiding redundant computations	Lisp static binding
Storage management	marking garbage collection
Status	operational

TABLE IV
LISP MACHINE

Reference	[28]
Physical interconnection	uniprocessor
Representation of program	machine code
Representation of data	graph/list, array
Drive	sequential
Avoiding redundant computations	Lisp dynamic binding
Storage management	incremental marking garbage collection
Status	operational

TABLE V
TURNER'S COMBINATOR REDUCTION MACHINE

Reference	[83]
Physical interconnection	uniprocessor
Representation of program	combinator graph
Representation of data	combinator graph
Drive	demand
Avoiding redundant computations	common parameter use, combinator optimizations, currying
Storage management	marking garbage collection
Status	operational (software interpreter)

TABLE VI
SKIM

Reference	[10]
Physical interconnection	uniprocessor
Representation of program	combinator graph
Representation of data	combinator graph
Drive	demand
Avoiding redundant computations	common parameter use, combinator optimizations, currying
Storage management	marking garbage collection
Status	operational

machine in a reasonably short period of time. A followup project, *Scheme-81*, is significantly faster [79].

4) Lisp Machine: The Lisp machine is a high-performance personal computer that is microcoded to handle Lisp operations, such as list manipulation and function call, efficiently. Structures may be stored in list or array form, the representation being specified by the programmer. An interesting feature of this machine is the existence of a two-bit *CDR code* for each list cell that saves a word of space in any cell in which the CDR is either *nil* or occupies the subsequent cell.

5) Turner's Combinator Reduction Machine: Turner's machine makes use of combinator logic to translate the functional language SASL into a combinator graph. Execution consists of performing normal-order reductions on the graph until it is completely reduced, except that certain reductions are delayed, causing evaluation to be done in a lazy manner. As implemented, reduction is performed in a destructive

manner; that is to say, when a subgraph is reduced, the memory location that its pointer occupies is overwritten with a pointer to the new structure. Because SASL is a functional language, such a technique is not only correct, but improves the performance of the system, as the reduction is reflected in all structures that (possibly indirectly) reference the reduced cell. The design of a combinator reduction machine (and associated compiler) that is potentially much faster has been reported by Johnsson [40] and Kieburtz [49].

Limitations: Although the design is an elegant one, there may be problems extending the architecture to multiprocessor form. In particular, the combinator expressions used tend to obscure the *true structure* of the program, which could make process scheduling difficult.

6) SKIM: SKIM, a small combinator reduction machine patterned after that of Turner, is a standard uniprocessor architecture with 2K of microcode that performs combinator reductions as well as garbage collection and I/O. Its performance is described as similar to that of an interpretive system on a fairly fast processor.

B. Tree-Structured Machines

The tree machines all suffer from a bottleneck near the root. The first two architectures in this section attempt to alleviate the problem by performing redundant computations in different portions of the tree rather than to communicate results across the tree. The third architecture performs data-driven evaluation on a tree of processors, sending data results among tree elements whenever necessary. The final architecture mentioned, TALCM, uses the tree for performing SIMD operations.

TABLE VII
MAGÓ'S TREE MACHINE

Reference	[55]
Physical interconnection	tree
Representation of program	token string
Representation of data	token string, data copied
Drive	data (effectively)
Granularity of parallelism	one or more processes per reduction
Mapping of processes onto hardware	process tree maps onto physical tree
When to invoke parallelism	always
Avoiding redundant computations	never
Storage management	"shift register" to expand/contract process tree
Status	simulator operational

TABLE VIII
AMPS

Reference	[43]
Physical interconnection	tree
Representation of program	graph/list, array
Representation of data	graph/list, array
Drive	demand
Granularity of parallelism	each expression is a process
Mapping of processes onto hardware	demand list per processor; processors multiplex waiting for data; interior processors (of tree) do load balancing by shifting processes across tree
When to invoke parallelism	strict operators, but programmer can specify more eagerness
Avoiding redundant computations	common parameter use
Storage management	reference count
Status	simulator operational

TABLE IX
DDM 1

References	[14], [15]
Physical interconnection	tree
Representation of program	data flow graph
Representation of data	variable-length character strings
Drive	data
Granularity of parallelism	process per graph node
Mapping of processes onto hardware	recursive division among tree processors
When to invoke parallelism	all strict operators
Avoiding redundant computations	common parameter use
Status	operational

1) Magó's Tree Machine: Magó's tree architecture was one of the first multiprocessors designed for executing functional programs [5]. Both the program and data are represented by token strings, which reside in the leaf cells. Computation consists of reductions, each being performed by one or more interior nodes that transform the leaves. A computation *cycle* consists of an upsweep where data are sent from the leaves to the interior nodes and a downsweep where the leaf nodes are modified. The size of an expression may increase during the reduction process, giving rise to the possibility that an expression may "outgrow" its subtree during execution. When this happens, the *storage manager* shifts expressions among the leaf cells to make room for the growing expression.

Limitations: This architecture may be effective for certain classes of computations, but it has a couple of drawbacks for the general execution of functional programs. The first is the obvious bottleneck near the root of the tree. The second is that the system has no pointers, so all data movement must be performed by copying complete data structures; results are *never* shared, even in the simplest cases.

2) AMPS: AMPS is a reduction tree-machine proposed at the University of Utah in which the interior nodes perform process management and computation is performed in the leaf nodes. Computations are subdivided among the leaf nodes, which act as uniprocessors, each reducing its own portion of the computation. When it is necessary to fetch data from a remote processor, a request is sent across the tree. While waiting for remote data, a processor may choose another process from its process list on which to work. Interior nodes perform load balancing by attempting to keep all subtrees within predetermined load limits, shifting tasks from one subtree to another when necessary. Lazy evaluation is normally performed, but *eager evaluation* may be specified at compile time.

Limitations: Although the machine has the obvious bottlenecks of a tree-structured architecture, the designers claim that a great amount of locality can be maintained. Both the load-balancing scheme and the parameter-passing mechanism, however, promote nonlocality.

3) DDM1: The DDM1 architecture is a data-driven architecture that was developed at the University of Utah. Processing elements are organized into a tree structure, each pair of connected elements communicating via a data queue. Each processing element consists of an *agenda queue*, which contains firable instructions, an *atomic memory*, which provides the program memory, and an *atomic processor*, which performs execution.

Limitations: As with the architecture of Magó, this architecture has a bottleneck at the root of the tree, and does not allow pointers; hence, data must always be copied.

4) TALCM: TALCM is an architecture designed to execute Lisp in an SIMD (single instruction, multiple data) manner. Parallelism is invoked for associative searching and for list structure updates.

Limitations: Although certain operations can be performed faster than in a uniprocessor, such a machine would not take advantage of many of the opportunities available for parallelism in functional programs.

TABLE X
TALCM

Reference	[65]
Physical interconnection	tree
Representation of program	machine code
Representation of data	lists, represented as linear array
Drive	sequential
Granularity of parallelism	SIMD
Mapping of processes onto hardware	SIMD
When to invoke parallelism	during associative search or element shift
Avoiding redundant computations	Lisp dynamic scoping
Storage management	marking garbage collection
Status	simulator operational

TABLE XI
MASSACHUSETTS INSTITUTE OF TECHNOLOGY DATA FLOW PROJECT

References	[18], [20]
Physical interconnection	routing network
Representation of program	data flow graph
Representation of data	atoms (integers, reals, etc.)
Drive	data
Granularity of parallelism	process per graph node
Mapping of processes onto hardware	statically allocated instructions
When to invoke parallelism	except conditional where delay nodes are inserted
Avoiding redundant computations	common parameter use
Status	experimental model operational

TABLE XII
LAU

References	[11], [81]
Physical interconnection	shared/interleaved memory, accessed via switch
Representation of program	data flow graph
Representation of data	fixed-length tokens
Drive	data
Granularity of parallelism	process per graph node
Mapping of processes onto hardware	statically allocated instructions
When to invoke parallelism	all strict operators
Avoiding redundant computations	common parameter use
Status	operational

C. Data-Driven Machines

Data-driven (or data flow) processors have a tremendous potential for parallel processing. The first proposed data flow architectures were connected as routing networks, although more recent ones have different topologies.

1) Massachusetts Institute of Technology Data Flow Project (Dennis): The data flow multiprocessor designed by Dennis *et al.* at the Massachusetts Institute of Technology consists of four components.

• A set of *instruction cells* whose contents collectively represent the data flow program graph being executed.

• One or more *arbitration networks* that move firable instructions (i.e., functions whose operands have all arrived) to processing elements.

• A set of *processing elements* that perform the actual computation. A processing element transforms a firable instruction into one or more *result packets*.

• A *distribution network* that routes each result packet to its destination instruction in an instruction cell.

The execution of a program consists of firable instructions (packets) moving through the arbitration network to processing elements, being transformed into result packets which, in turn, move through the distribution network to update instruction cells, thereby creating more firable instructions.

Processors and memory are connected by a single routing network in which information flows in only one direction; there is therefore no locality. A design was considered in which each processor contained its own memory of instructions, but it was decided that an extremely intelligent compiler would be required to take advantage of the locality [18].

Limitations: The design does not allow recursive functions call of arbitrary depth, or structured data. Like all data-driven schemes, parallel execution occurs automatically, the system having little ability to limit it. Bottlenecking may also be a problem (see Section IV-A-5).

2) LAU: LAU is a data-driven architecture that consists of three major components. The *memory subsystem* is a set of memory banks in which all instructions are stored. The *control subsystem* contains three status bits for each instruction in the memory subsystem, denoting which of its operands have arrived and whether its execution has been completed. The *execution subsystem* consists of a set of processing elements that evaluate instructions that are read from the memory subsystem. Execution consists of an *instruction fetch processor* continuously scanning the control subsystem, placing the names of any firable instructions into a queue. This causes the named instructions to be read and queued up for execution by one of the processors in the execution subsystem, which reads its operands from the memory system, computes the result, and writes its data back into the memory subsystem. Finally, control bits are updated by an *update processor;* this may in turn cause additional instructions to become firable.

Limitations: As with the architecture of Dennis, recursive functions of arbitrary depth are not allowed, and structures are not easily handled because data items are fixed-length tokens. Additionally, communication being performed by a shared memory could lead to difficulty in increasing the size of the system.

3) Rumbaugh's Data Flow Multiprocessor: Rumbaugh's data flow architecture contains three classes of processors and two classes of memory. Three processors perform computing, one performs scheduling, and one, the *structure controller,* handles accesses to nonatomic data structures. *Instruction memory* contains the data flow instructions, and

TABLE XIII
RUMBAUGH'S DATA FLOW MULTIPROCESSOR

References	[72], [73]
Physical interconnection	shared buses (processors separated from memory)
Representation of program	data flow graph
Representation of data	graph/list
Drive	data
Granularity of parallelism	process per user-defined function
Mapping of processes onto hardware	performed by scheduling processor
When to invoke parallelism	except conditional and user-defined function
Avoiding redundant computations	common parameter use
Storage management	reference count
Status	paper design only

TABLE XIV
TEXAS INSTRUMENTS' DATA FLOW MACHINE

Reference	[39]
Physical interconnection	ring (4 processors)
Representation of program	data flow graph
Representation of data	atoms (integers, reals, etc.)
Drive	data
Granularity of parallelism	process per graph node
Mapping of processes onto hardware	all nodes allocated statically
When to invoke parallelism	except on conditionals
Avoiding redundant computations	common parameter use
Status	operational

TABLE XV
MANCHESTER DATA FLOW MACHINE

References	[92], [93]
Physical interconnection	routing network
Representation of program	data flow graph
Representation of data	atoms (integer, real, etc.)
Drive	data
Granularity of parallelism	process per graph node
Mapping of processes onto hardware	processes move through network
When to invoke parallelism	except conditional and functional call
Avoiding redundant computations	common parameter use
Status	20-processor system under construction

structure memory, which is accessed only by the structure controller, contains all data structures. Each *computing processor* is directly connected to the *instruction memory,* the *scheduling processor,* and the *structure processor.*

Each structure is conceptually independent, although substructures are often shared to save computing time and memory space. Because structures in this system are acyclic, reference counts are used for storage management, as well as for structure optimization; modifications to a structure are performed in place whenever the reference count is *one.* Each processor contains a *structure cache,* which contains copies of substructures that are of current interest to the processor. Because functional programs are free of side effects, such caching is not difficult to implement.

Limitations: The processor–memory interconnection structure may make this architecture difficult to extend.

4) Texas Instruments' Data Flow Machine: The data flow machine implemented at Texas Instruments contains four microprogrammed processors in a ring and accepts static program graphs in which all instruction-processor mapping has been performed at compile time. Each processor has four major components.

• An arithmetic unit, which performs standard arithmetic and comparison operations.

• Memory, in which the instructions are stored.

• A hardware queue of pointers to *firable* instructions. The arithmetic unit executes these instructions sequentially.

• An *update controller,* which accepts data from other processors and inserts instruction pointers into the instruction queue.

Programs for this system are written in Fortran. A modified version of an optimizing Fortran compiler is used to create the data flow program graph.

Limitations: The machine does not allow structured data or recursive subroutines, and all subroutines must be expanded at link time. Although the ring could be a bottleneck, such an architecture seems feasible for a small number of processors. The authors [39] do not state how Fortran '66, a language with inherent side-effects (e.g., call-by-reference, common areas), is cleanly executed on a data flow machine.

5) Manchester Data Flow Machine: The Manchester data flow machine is similar to that proposed by Dennis in that it uses a routing networks to send packets between processing units and instruction store. It differs, however, in that there may be more than one logical instantiation of a single-instruction cell, allowing recursive invocations of a function and "unfolded" iterations. To ensure that a result packet arrives at the *correct* instance of an instruction, each instruction instance carries with it a *label,* and each result packet specifies both an instruction *and* a label name, the latter disambiguating among instances of an instruction. This is implemented by placing a *matching store* behind the instruction store; results for instructions with multiple inputs are collected in the matching store and sent to the instruction store as a unit after all results have arrived. A new label is created for each function invocation or loop iteration.

Limitations: Like other routing network data flow machines, parallelism may be difficult to control, and the network interconnection could be a bottleneck. The authors do not mention whether structures are handled, but adding them would not appear to be difficult. Although the matching store could be a bottleneck, there is no reason that multiple matching stores could not, in principle, be added.

6) U-Interpreter: The U-interpreter, a predecessor to Manchester data flow machine, also uses labeled packets to allow multiple instantiations of a single instruction. The major difference is that the U-interpreter uses a cluster architec-

TABLE XVI	
U-INTERPRETER	
References	[2], [3]
Physical interconnection	clusters of processors, connected by routing net
Representation of program	data flow graph
Representation of data	graph/list, stream
Drive	data
Granularity of parallelism	process per graph node
Mapping of processes onto hardware	assignment function
When to invoke parallelism	except conditional, function call
Avoiding redundant computations	common parameter use
Storage management	reference count
Status	under construction

TABLE XVII	
ALICE	
Reference	[13]
Physical interconnection	clusters of processors, each with one memory and ring buffer of processable packets; connection among clusters not decided
Representation of program	graph/list
Representation of data	graph/list
Drive	demand
Granularity of parallelism	process per node
Mapping of processes onto hardware	global (or per-cluster) process list
When to invoke parallelism	always when result is needed; and/or compiler can specify eager evaluation with the constraint that "safeness" is required
Avoiding redundant computations	common parameter use
Storage management	reference count (is considering marking garbage collection)
Status	simulator operational, hardware under construction

ture rather than a routing network. The clusters, each of which contains four processors with local memory, communicate via a routing network. The potential therefore exists for taking advantage of locality to reduce network traffic.

Because data flow programs are executed *bottom up*, a result packet would not necessarily know the location of the instruction instance (dataflow node) to which it is to deliver data. To resolve the problem, an *assignment function*, which computes a hash address from the instruction name and label, is defined that possesses the property that instructions having the same label execute in the same cluster. This gives programs a certain amount of locality, while allowing computation to spread throughout the system when user-defined functions are invoked or when iterations occur.

Limitations: As with all data flow machines, the issue of controlling parallelism remains unresolved. Effectively mapping processes onto hardware, particularly in a dataflow instruction-labeling scheme where two or more result packets must "find" the same destination instruction, could also be a difficult problem because the simplest solutions do not take advantage of locality.

D. Demand-Driven Machines

Demand-driven machines with rich processor interconnection structures show promise for evaluation of functional programs because support for *lazy evaluation* and *interprocessor communication* appear to be important features of a fast FP system. Judgment must be reserved, however, as none of the demand-driven processors has been completely implemented.

1) ALICE: In the ALICE system, several processors are connected via a shared bus to form a *cluster*, with clusters connected in a (yet unspecified) loosely coupled manner. ALICE is truly a *reduction machine:* each node in the original computation is specified by a packet. A packet requiring a subexpression to be reduced sets the *required* flag in the packet representing the subexpression and inserts it into the *packet pool* to be reduced. The parent process is awakened when the subexpression is totally reduced. Although eager evaluation is allowed, it must be specified at compile time,

the programmer/compiler being responsible for ensuring that divergent computations are not eagerly evaluated.

Limitations: The details of execution are given only for a single-cluster system, so process communication and migration, which are critical issues in a multicluster system, are not discussed. The fine granularity of parallelism is likely to create a great deal of process management overhead.

2) ZAPP: Normal mode of operation on the ZAPP system consists of each processor working on independent computation, adding processes to its local process list as it reduces a subgraph. When a processor is underloaded, it steals processes from neighboring processors, resulting in minimal movement of processes across the system when system load is heavy. When system load is light, however, processes tend to spread across the system in a manner similar to many of the tree architectures, but with the advantage that the "tree" in this case has no *a priori* depth, as a binary *n*-cube can be considered a "tree folded upon itself." Additionally, the cost of data communication is reduced (compared to a tree) because there is no bottleneck at the root.

Two other features of the system are noteworthy. The first is that system load determines the order in which computation is performed, reductions being performed depth-first when the system is loaded, and breadth-first otherwise (see Section IV-D-3). The second is the method of evaluating subexpressions that contain a nonstrict operator, and would therefore not necessarily be attempted during a *normal order* reduction because full evaluation of such expressions could cause the computation to diverge. Such an expression is allocated a "renewable budget" — an amount of computing it may apply toward the evaluation of the expression. When it exhausts its "budget," it is required to request additional processor time from the system, which will honor or reject the request, depending on factors such as system load.

TABLE XVIII
ZAPP

References	[9], [76]
Physical interconnection	binary *n*-cube
Representation of program	graph/list
Representation of data	graph/list
Drive	demand
Granularity of parallelism	process per graph node
Mapping of processes onto hardware	local process list on each processor; load balancing by allowing neighbors to steal processes:
When to invoke parallelism	invoked on strict operators, but unsafe nonstrict computations may run if "budgeted" processor load determines whether reductions are performed depth-first or breadth-first
Avoiding redundant computations	common parameter use
Storage management	marking garbage collection
Status	simulator operational

TABLE XIX
REDIFLOW

Reference	[47]
Physical interconnection	Two-dimensional array (or a "richer" connection)
Representation of program	graph/list, array
Representation of data	graph/list, array
Drive	demand, with programmer able to specify functions to be computed sequentially
Granularity of parallelism	one process per path in the computation tree
Mapping of processes onto hardware	local process list on each processor; load balancing by sharing processes with neighbors
When to invoke parallelism	strict operators, but processor load determines whether reductions are performed depth-first or breadth-first
Avoiding redundant computations	common parameter use
Storage management	marking garbage collection
Status	simulator operational

Limitations: Although processes representing connected nodes in the computation graph are usually no more than one processor apart, data structures can exist in remote processors because pointers are used. The question of whether the *n*-cube interconnection is rich enough to support communication also remains unanswered.

3) Rediflow: The Rediflow system is a followup to the AMPS project, differing particularly in processor interconnection, which is richer, and in the grain of parallelism, which is coarser. It is similar to ZAPP [9] in its load balancing strategy, in that a processors is allowed to "steal" processes from overworked neighbors. A "pressure" model is used to determine the flow of processes, in which each processor has an *internal pressure* (the load within the processor) and an *external pressure* (computed as a function of the pressures of

TABLE XX
FRIEDMAN AND WISE'S REDUCTION MACHINE

Reference	[24]
Physical interconnection	unspecified
Representation of program	graph/list
Representation of data	graph/list
Drive	demand
Granularity of parallelism	several reductions per process
Mapping of processes onto hardware	colonel/sergeants scheme
When to invoke parallelism	whenever sergeant processor is available: may have to kill wayward sergeants
Avoiding redundant computations	common parameter use
Storage management	unspecified
Status	paper design only

its neighbors). Load balancing is performed by distributing processes along *pressure gradients*.

The programmer is allowed to group computations into von Neumann processes. If this is done intelligently, a significant amount of fine-grained-parallelism overhead may be eliminated. The method for controlling parallelism is similar to that of ZAPP.

Limitations: As with ZAPP, the sharing of pointers potentially requires a large number of remote accesses; the problem of determining an acceptable interconnection structure is under investigation.

4) Friedman and Wise's Reduction Machine: The proposal of Friedman and Wise is that of an unspecified abstract multiprocessor, their design being primarily concerned with process scheduling. The key idea is that one processor executes a *colonel process* that is always running, and is reducing the program graph in normal order using *lazy evaluation*. All other processors run *sergeant processes*, which evaluate nodes in the graph that have been left suspended by the colonel, the highest priority sergeant processes being the ones that are "near" the colonel. In the event that a sergeant becomes "lost" performing a divergent computation, it is eventually recovered by the storage manager.

Limitations: Although the "nearness" metric is not well defined, it seems clear that only a small amount of computing time should be spent by a sergeant deciding which reduction to perform; otherwise, such time would dominate "useful" computing time, as sergeant tasks tend to be short. The scheduling strategy also does not seem to take advantage of *locality*, but rather tends to have all processors computing "near" one another (i.e., near the colonel); this is likely to cause contention among processors when common data structures are accessed.

E. Miscellaneous Machines

The machines in this section are being designed with artificial intelligence applications in mind. None has functional program execution as a principal goal, but it is expected that each will support one or more functional or quasi-functional languages.

TABLE XXI
CONCURRENT LISP ARCHITECTURE

Reference	[78]
Physical interconnection	shared buses (processors separated from memory)
Representation of program	graph/list
Representation of data	graph/list
Drive	sequential evaluation
Granularity of parallelism	explicitly programmed
Mapping of processes onto hardware	global process list
When to invoke parallelism	explicitly programmed
Avoiding redundant computations	dynamic scoping
Storage management	marking garbage collection
Status	simulator operational, with hardware under construction

TABLE XXII
ZMOB

References	[50], [71]
Physical interconnection	ring (20 MByte/s, 256 processors)
Representation of program	graph/list
Representation of data	graph/list, but copied as ascii strings
Drive	sequential evaluation
Granularity of parallelism	network of course processes
Mapping of processes onto hardware	statically
When to invoke parallelism	implementation-dependent
Avoiding redundant computations	dynamic scoping, common parameter use
Storage management	local marking garbage collection
Status	Several small (16–32 processor) versions are operational

TABLE XXIII
THE ARRAY

References	[33], [34], [52]
Physical interconnection	hypertorus, or any other mesh-connected network
Representation of program	actors
Representation of data	actors
Drive	responsibility of individual actors
Granularity of parallelism	responsibility of individual actors
Mapping of processes onto hardware	dynamic load balancing between neighbors; each processor multiplexes on actors
When to invoke parallelism	normally always, considering limits
Avoiding redundant computations	unspecified
Storage management	marking garbage collection
Status	preliminary version operational on local network; version running on a tightly coupled mesh-connected network under construction [35]

1) Concurrent Lisp Architecture: The concurrent Lisp architecture executes a version of Lisp 1.5 in which several of the destructive list operators have been removed and several parallelism operators added. The *slave processors,* which execute the user program, are scheduled by the *master processor.* There are four dedicated memory banks (process control, list structures, random access, and process stacks), each having a single bus, by which it is connected to each processor. Parallelism is explicitly programmed by the user.

Limitations: Because of the limited number of memory banks, it seems inevitable that system performance will degrade if more than a handful of processors is used.

2) ZMOB: The 256 processors in the ZMOB system are connected via a high-speed ring, so that a processor may communicate with any other in "unit time" where unit time is defined as the time it takes to send data once around the ring. It is intended to support a number of languages, including Lisp and Prolog, although there is no current Lisp effort [94].

Limitations: The coarseness of parallelism is greater than for most applicative architectures. Processors may not share pointers in the current system. While this simplifies garbage collection, it requires literal data to be copied when a (potentially large) structure is to be "shared." The ring architecture,

of course, causes system performance to degrade linearly as processors are added.

3) The Apiary: The Apiary is a multiprocessor actor system on which Lisp and other artificial intelligence languages are expected to run. The fundamental execution entity in the Apiary is the actor, which is an object that contains a small amount of state and can perform a few primitive operations: sending a message, creating another actor, making a decision, and changing its local state. Actors are divided into two classes, *rock bottom* and *scripted.* The actions taken by rock-bottom actors are specified by microcode; those of scripted actors are specified by a script, which is a program in a language such as Lisp. An actor physically runs on a *worker,* which is a collection of processors that define a node in the network. A worker typically consists of a communications processor, a storage management processor, and several *work processors.* Each worker has a *work queue* of actors on behalf of which it performs script-specified actions. If a worker becomes overloaded, it attempts to move some of its actors to neighboring workers.

Limitations: A number of issues relating to the execution of functional languages (e.g., limiting parallelism) have yet to be addressed.

VI. CONCLUSIONS

Can machines be built that will efficiently execute functional programs? Although many architectures have been built or proposed, it has yet to be demonstrated that functional programs can be competitive with von Neumann systems. The Lisp machine [28], which executes a quasi-functional language, is the only architecture considered here that has had widespread use for solving real problems.

A major issue in answering the above question is the high level at which functional programs are written, which may be a blessing during programming, but a curse during execution. The "system" is required to make many decisions that an imperative programmer—or his programming language—

would specify explicitly on a case-by-case basis, including the following.

- Should data be copied or should pointers be used?
- Should results be stored and reused or should they be recomputed?
- How should data be represented?
- When should parallelism be invoked?
- At what granularity should parallelism be invoked?
- How should processes be mapped onto processors?

For a language that is directly executed on hardware, these decisions are likely to be systemwide, and will clearly be "wrong" sometimes. Although it is possible for a compiler to make intelligent decisions in some instances, many questions are yet to be answered in this area as well [88]. Optimizations involving parallelism appear to be particularly difficult for a compiler to perform, as they often involve making use of dynamic information; difficult problems still remain in this area even for imperative languages [75]. On the other hand, other issues, such as synchronizing multiple list traversals, do seem well suited to compile-time analysis.

Allowing a compiler to make decisions about the manner in which data are represented also has ramifications with respect to separate compilation: What happens when two separately compiled programs expect data to be in different forms?

A. Desirable Elements of an FP Machine

What features would an "ideal" FP machine have? Based on the discussion in this paper, the following would be desirable.

- A multiprocessor system with a rich interconnection structure.

A multiprocessor allows the system to take advantage of the inherent concurrency in functional programs. A rich interconnection of processors seems to be essential if there is any hope of spreading work throughout the system, while maintaining moderately efficient access to remote data.

- Representation of list structures by balanced trees, if such does not add too much complexity to the system.

Although a tree is a more complex object than an array or list, the efficiency with which random access, structure manipulation, and destructive updating can be performed makes it an attractive candidate for data representation. This is particularly true if the compiler does not decide the type of data structure to be used.

- Hardware support for demand-driven execution.

Although demand-driven execution can often speed up a computation substantially, it has generated a great deal of overhead on currently built systems; hardware support to decrease this overhead is desirable.

- Hardware support for low-overhead process creation.

It is highly desirable that parallel execution be the norm, not the exception, when a functional program is being evaluated. If the mechanism for invoking parallelism is not efficient, program performance will be unacceptably slow.

- Hardware support for storage management.

The extensive use of structures in functional programs makes hardware support for storage management very attractive. If hardware/firmware support for storage management is not available, system overhead is likely to be markedly higher.

Of the architectures currently proposed, none meets all of the above criteria; most lack a rich interconnection structure or support for demand-driven execution. Of those remaining, ZAPP and Rediflow are the only architectures whose processor interconnections and process-to-processor mapping methodologies are well specified. Other systems such as ALICE and Apiary are worth considering, but are still in need of work in areas of concurrency control and/or interconnection structure.

B. Open Questions

The question of how efficiently functional programs can run on hardware is still largely unanswered. The following are some key issues that have been raised—but not fully answered—in the literature.

Compiler techniques: A major issue, which has not been addressed here, is that of compiler optimization. How much can program transformation and data structure selection improve program performance? Can compiler techniques be as effective when the program is to run on a multiprocessor?

Interconnection structure: What processor interconnections are most effective? N-cube and hypertorus machines have rich interconnection structures, yet have the potential to take advantage of locality. Given that pieces of a structure are likely to be distributed across the system, how much does locality buy? If not much, a routing network—or a routing network of clusters—may be more appropriate.

Controlling parallelism: How should parallelism be controlled? Data-driven architectures seem to be at a disadvantage here, but even those with demand drive have not demonstrated that the problem is solved. The method employed in ZAPP [9] and Rediflow [47] looks promising, but is largely untested.

Granularity of parallelism: Many proposed FP machines have a very fine grain of parallelism. Can hardware be built to support this efficiently, or will process creation and synchronization costs be unacceptably high? Perhaps a somewhat coarser granularity is more appropriate.

Tree representation of lists: Can lists be effectively represented by balanced trees? Are the logarithmic times for operations such as random access and insertion efficient enough that it is not necessary to consider using arrays and lists? How much overhead is involved in keeping trees balanced?

Caching: How big a problem is the recomputation of results? Are the current methods for handling it adequate? If not, can an effective caching scheme be developed?

C. Summary

There is promising evidence that programmer productivity can be increased for some classes of programs by the use of functional programming. Additionally, functional languages seem especially suited to parallel architectures because they lack side effects, giving rise to the possibility that functional programs may run more quickly than their imperative counterparts unless the imperative programmer is willing to program parallelism explicitly.

The efficient execution of functional programs on uniprocessor and multiprocessor systems is currently under active investigation. As of the time of this writing (July 1984), too few FP multiprocessors and compilers have been completely implemented, and hence it is not possible to answer the question until more experimentation is done.

ACKNOWLEDGMENT

The author wishes to thank A. Jones, R. Keller, J. Newcomer, G. Steele, P. Wadler, and W. Wulf for their valuable comments on earlier versions of this paper.

REFERENCES

[1] P. S. Abrams, "An APL machine," Ph.D. dissertation, Stanford Univ., Stanford, CA, Feb. 1970.
[2] Arvind, K. P. Gostelow, and W. Plouffe, "An asynchronous programming language and computing machine," Univ. California, Irvine, CA, Tech. Rep. 114a, Dec. 1978.
[3] Arvind and K. P. Gostelow, "The U-interpreter," IEEE Computer, vol. 15, pp. 42–49, Feb. 1982.
[4] Arvind and J. D. Brock, "Streams and managers," Computation Structure Group, Massachusetts Inst. Technol., Memo 217, June 1982.
[5] J. Backus, "Can programming be liberated from the von Neumann style? A functional style and its algebra of programs," Commun. ACM, vol. 21, pp. 613–641, Aug. 1978.
[6] K. J. Berkling, "Reduction languages for reduction machines," in Proc. IEEE Int. Symp. Comput. Arch., Jan. 1975, pp. 133–140.
[7] R. M. Burstall and J. Darlington, "A transformation system for developing recursive programs," J. ACM, vol. 24, Jan. 1977.
[8] R. M. Burstall, D. B. MacQueen, and D. T. Sannella, "HOPE: An experimental applicative language," in LISP Conf. Rec., Stanford Univ., Stanford, CA, 1980, pp. 136–143.
[9] F. W. Burton and M. R. Sleep, "Executing functional programs on a virtual tree of processors," in Proc. ACM Conf. Functional Programming Lang. Comput. Arch., 1981, pp. 187–194.
[10] T. J. W. Clarke, P. J. S. Gladstone, C. D. MacLean, and A. C. Norman, "SKIM — The S, K, I reduction machine," in LISP Conf. Rec., Stanford Univ., Stanford, CA, 1980, pp. 128–135.
[11] D. Comte and N. Hifde, "LAU multiprocessor: Microfunctional description and technological choices," in Proc. 1st Europ. Conf. Parallel Distrib. Processing, 1979, pp. 8–15.
[12] H. B. Curry and R. Feys, Combinator Logic. Amsterdam, The Netherlands: North-Holland, 1958.
[13] J. Darlington and M. Reeve, "ALICE — A multi-processor reduction machine for the parallel evaluation of applicative languages," in Proc. ACM Conf. Functional Programming Lang. Comput. Arch., 1981, pp. 65–75.
[14] A. L. Davis, "The architecture and system method of DDM1: A recursively structured data driven machine," in Proc. ACM Int. Symp. Comput. Arch., Apr. 1978, pp. 210–215.
[15] ——, "A data flow evaluation system based on the concept of recursive locality," in Proc. AFIPS Nat. Comput. Conf., 1979, vol. 48, pp. 1079–1086.
[16] A. L. Davis and R. M. Keller, "Data flow program graphs," IEEE Computer, vol. 15, pp. 26–41, Feb. 1982.
[17] J. B. Dennis, "First version of a data flow procedure language," in Lecture Notes in Computer Science. New York: Springer-Verlag, 1974, pp. 362–376; see also, Massachusetts Inst. Technol., Cambridge, MA, Tech. Rep. MIT MTMM-61.
[18] ——, "The varieties of data flow computers," in Proc. IEEE Int. Conf. Distrib. Syst., 1979, pp. 430–439.
[19] ——, "Data flow supercomputers," IEEE Computer, vol. 13, pp. 48–56, Nov. 1980.
[20] J. B. Dennis, G.-R. Gao, and K. W. Todd, "Modeling the weather with a data flow supercomputer," IEEE Trans. Comput., vol. C-33, pp. 592–603, July 1984.
[21] D. M. Dias and J. R. Jump, "Analysis and simulation of buffered delta networks," IEEE Trans. Comput., vol. C-30, pp. 273–282, Apr. 1981.
[22] R. J. Fateman, "Reply to an editorial," SigSAM Bull., vol. 25, pp. 9–11, Mar. 1973.
[23] D. P. Friedman and D. S. Wise, "Cons should not evaluate its arguments," in Automata, Languages, and Programming, Michaelson and Milner, Eds. London: Edinburgh University Press, 1976.
[24] ——, "Aspects of applicative programming for parallel processing," IEEE Trans. Comput., vol. C-27, pp. 289–296, Apr. 1978.
[25] A. Goldberg and D. Robson, Smalltalk-80: The Language and Its Implementation. Reading, MA: Addison-Wesley, 1983.
[26] M. Gordon, R. Milner, L. Morris, M. Newey, and C. Wadsworth, "A metalanguage for interactive proof in LCF," in Proc. ACM Symp. Princ. Programming Lang., 1978, pp. 119–130.
[27] K. P. Gostelow and R. E. Thomas, "A view of dataflow," in Proc. AFIPS Nat. Comput. Conf., 1979, vol. 48, pp. 629–636.
[28] R. Greenblatt et al., "LISP machine progress report," Massachusetts Inst. Technol., Cambridge, MA, A. I. Memo. 444, Aug. 1977.
[29] R. H. Halstead, Jr., "Object management on distributed systems," in Proc. Texas Conf. Comput. Syst., Univ. Houston, Houston, TX, 1978, pp. 7-7-7-14.
[30] S. P. Harbison, "A computer architecture for the dynamic optimization of high-level language programs," Ph.D. dissertation, Carnegie-Mellon Univ., Pittsburgh, PA, Sept. 1980.
[31] L. S. Haynes, R. L. Lau, D. P. Siewiorek, and D. W. Mizell, "A survey of highly parallel computing," IEEE Computer, vol. 15, pp. 9–24, Jan. 1982.
[32] P. Henderson and J. H. Morris, "A lazy evaluator," in Proc. ACM Symp. Princ. Programming Lang., 1976, pp. 95–103.
[33] C. Hewitt, "The Apiary network architecture for knowledgeable systems," in LISP Conf. Rec., Stanford Univ., Stanford, CA, 1980.
[34] C. Hewitt and H. Leiberman, "Design issues in parallel architectures for artificial intelligence," in Proc. IEEE COMPCON, Feb. 1984, pp. 418–423.
[35] C. Hewitt, personal communication, 1984.
[36] J. Holloway, G. L. Steele, Jr., G. J. Sussman, and A. Bell, "The SCHEME-79 chip," Massachusetts Inst. Technol., Cambridge, MA, A.I. Memo. 559, Dec. 1979.
[37] R. J. M. Hughes, "Super-combinators: A new implementation method for applicative languages," in Conf. Rec. 1982 ACM Symp. LISP and Functional Programming, Carnegie-Mellon Univ., Pittsburgh, PA, Aug. 1982, pp. 1–10.
[38] R. D. Jenks and J. H. Griesmer, "Editor's comment," SigSAM Bull., vol. 24, pp. 2–3, Oct. 1972.
[39] D. Johnson et al., "Automatic partitioning of programs in multiprocessor systems," in Proc. IEEE COMPCON, 1980, pp. 175–178.
[40] T. Johnsson, "Efficient compilation of lazy evaluation," in Proc. ACM SigPlan Symp. Compiler Construction, June 1984, pp. 58–69.
[41] A. K. Jones, R. J. Chansler, Jr., I. Durham, P. Feiler, D. A. Scelza, K. Schwans, and S. R. Vegdahl, "Programming issues raised by a multiprocessor," Proc. IEEE, vol. 66, pp. 229–237, Feb. 1978.
[42] S. L. P. Jones, "An investigation of the relative efficiencies of combinators and lambda-expressions," in Conf. Rec. 1982 ACM Symp. LISP and Functional Programming, Carnegie-Mellon Univ., Pittsburgh, PA, Aug. 1982, pp. 150–158.
[43] R. M. Keller, G. Lindstrom, and S. Patil, "A loosely-coupled applicative multi-processing system," in Proc. AFIPS Nat. Comput. Conf., 1979, vol. 48, pp. 613–622.
[44] R. M. Keller, "Divide and CONCer: Data structuring in applicative multiprocessing systems," in LISP Conf. Rec., Stanford Univ., Stanford, CA, 1980, pp. 196–202.
[45] R. M. Keller and G. Lindstrom, "Applications of Feedback in functional programming," in Proc. ACM Conf. Functional Programming Lang. Comput. Arch., 1981, pp. 123–130.
[46] R. M. Keller and M. R. Sleep, "Applicative caching," in Proc. ACM Conf. Functional Programming Lang. Comput. Arch., 1981, pp. 131–140.
[47] R. M. Keller, F. C. H. Lin, and J. Tanaka, "Rediflow multiprocessing," in Proc. IEEE COMPCON, Feb. 1984, pp. 410–417.
[48] R. B. Kieburtz and J. Shultis, "Transformations of FP program schemes," in Proc. ACM Conf. Functional Programming Lang. Comput. Arch., 1981, pp. 41–48.
[49] R. B. Kieburtz, "The G-machine: A fast graph-reduction processor," Oregon Grad. Cen., Tech. Rep. 84-003, 1984.
[50] T. Kushner, A. Y. Wu, and A. Rosenfeld, "Image processing in ZMOB," IEEE Trans. Comput., vol. C-31, pp. 943–951, Oct. 1982.
[51] P. J. Landin, "A correspondence between Algol 60 and Church's lambda notation: Part I," Commun. ACM, vol. 8, pp. 89–100, Feb. 1965.
[52] H. Leiberman, "An object-oriented simulator for the Apiary," in Proc. AAAI Nat. Conf. Artificial Intelligence, Aug. 1983, pp. 241–246.
[53] B. Liskov et al., "CLU reference manual," in Lecture Notes in Computer Science, Goos and Hartmanis, Eds. New York: Springer-Verlag, 1981.

[54] E. P. Maclean, "The use of APL for production applications: The concept of throwaway code," in *Proc. ACM-STAPL APL Conf.*, 1976, pp. 303–307.

[55] G. A. Magó, "A cellular computer architecture for functional programming," in *Proc. IEEE COMPCON*, 1980, pp. 179–187.

[56] Z. Manna and R. Waldinger, "Synthesis: Dreams $\Rightarrow$ programs," *IEEE Trans. Software Eng.*, vol. SE-5, no. 4, pp. 157–164, July 1979.

[57] J. McCarthy, "LISP — Notes on its past and future," in *LISP Conf. Rec.*, Stanford Univ., Stanford, CA, 1980, pp. v–viii.

[58] J. R. McGraw, "Data flow computing: Software development," in *Proc. IEEE Int. Conf. Distrib. Syst.*, 1979, pp. 242–251.

[59] D. Michie, "'Memo' functions and machine learning," *Nature*, vol. 218, pp. 19–22, Apr. 1968.

[60] C. R. Minter, "A machine design for efficient implementation of APL," Yale Univ., New Haven, CT, Res. Rep. 81, 1976.

[61] J. H. Morris, E. Schmidt, and P. L. Wadler, "Experience with an applicative string processing language," in *Proc. ACM Symp. Princ. Programming Lang.*, July 1980, pp. 32–46.

[62] J. H. Morris, "Real programming in functional languages," in *Functional Programming and its Applications. An Advanced Course*, Darlington, Henderson, and Turner, Eds. Cambridge, England: Cambridge Univ. Press, 1982.

[63] A. Mycroft, "The theory and practice of transforming call-by-need into call-by-value," in *Proc. 4th Int. Colloq. Programming*, 1980.

[64] ——, "Abstract interpretation and optimising transformations for applicative programs," Ph.D. dissertation, Univ. Edinburgh, Edinburgh, Scotland, 1981.

[65] J. T. O'Donnell, "A systolic associative LISP computer architecture with incremental parallel storage management," Ph.D. dissertation, Univ. Iowa, Iowa City, IA, 1981.

[66] J. K. Ousterhout, "Partitioning and cooperation in a distributed multiprocessor operating system: Medusa," Ph.D. dissertation, Carnegie-Mellon Univ., Pittsburgh, PA, Apr. 1980.

[67] R. L. Page, M. G. Conant, and D. H. Grit, "If-then-else as a concurrency inhibitor in eager beaver evaluation of recursive programs," in *Proc. ACM Conf. Functional Programming Lang. Comput. Arch.*, 1981, pp. 179–186.

[68] J. H. Patel, "Processor-memory interconnections for multiprocessors," in *Proc. IEEE Symp. Comput. Arch.*, 1979, pp. 168–177.

[69] A. J. Perlis, "Steps toward an APL compiler — updated," Yale Univ., New Haven, CT, Tech. Rep. 24, Mar. 1975.

[70] H. A. Presnell and R. P. Pargas, "Communication along shortest paths in a tree machine," in *Proc. ACM Conf. Functional Programming Lang. Comput. Arch.*, 1981, pp. 107–114.

[71] C. Rieger, R. Trigg, and B. Bane, "ZMOB: A new computing engine for AI," in *Proc. IJCAI*, Univ. British Columbia, Vancouver, B.C., Canada, 1981, pp. 955–960.

[72] J. E. Rumbaugh, "A parallel asynchronous computer architecture for data flow programs," Ph.D. dissertation, Massachusetts Inst. Technol., Cambridge, MA, May 1975.

[73] ——, "A data flow multiprocessor," *IEEE Trans. Comput.*, vol. C-26, pp. 138–146, Feb. 1977.

[74] W. L. Scherlis, "Expression procedures and program derivation," Ph.D. dissertation, Stanford Univ., Stanford, CA, Aug. 1980.

[75] K. Schwans, "Tailoring software for multiple processor systems," Ph.D. dissertation, Carnegie-Mellon Univ., Pittsburgh, PA, 1982.

[76] M. R. Sleep, "Applicative languages, dataflow and pure combinatory code," in *Proc. 20th IEEE COMPCON*, Feb. 1980, pp. 112–115.

[77] G. L. Steele, Jr., "Debunking the expensive procedure call myth, or, Procedure call implementations considered harmful, or, LAMBDA: The ultimate goto," in *Proc. ACM Annu. Conf.*, Oct. 1977, pp. 153–162.

[78] S. Sugimoto, T. Koichi, A. Kiyoshi, and Y. Ohno, "Concurrent LISP on a multi-micro-processor system," in *Proc. IJCAI*, Univ. British Columbia, Vancouver, B.C., Canada, 1981, pp. 949–954.

[79] G. J. Sussman, personal communication, 1984.

[80] G. J. Sussman, J. Holloway, G. L. Steele, Jr., and A. Bell, "Scheme-79 — Lisp on a chip," *IEEE Computer*, vol. 14, pp. 10–21, July 1981.

[81] J. C. Syre, D. Comte, and N. Hifdi, "Pipelining, parallelism and asynchronism in the LAU system," in *Proc. Int. Conf. Parallel Processing*, Aug. 1977, pp. 87–92.

[82] P. C. Treleaven, D. R. Brownbridge, and R. P. Hopkins, "Data-driven and demand-driven computer architecture," *ACM Comput. Surveys*, vol. 14, no. 1, pp. 93–143, Mar. 1982.

[83] D. A. Turner, "A new implementation technique for applicative languages," *Software — Practice and Experience*, vol. 9, pp. 31–49, Sept. 1979.

[84] ——, "The semantic elegance of applicative languages," in *Proc. ACM Conf. Functional Programming Lang. Comput. Arch.*, 1981, pp. 85–92.

[85] ——, "Recursion equations as a programming language," in *Functional Programming and its Applications. An Advanced Course*, Darlington, Henderson, and Turner, Eds. Cambridge, England: Cambridge Univ. Press, 1982, pp. 1–28.

[86] J. D. Ullman, "Some thoughts about supercomputer organization," in *Proc. IEEE COMPCON*, Feb. 1984, pp. 424–432.

[87] P. L. Wadler, "Applicative style programming, program transformation, and list operators," in *Proc. ACM Conf. Functional Programming Lang. Comput. Arch.*, 1981, pp. 25–32.

[88] ——, "Listlessness is better than laziness: An algorithm that transforms applicative programs to eliminate intermediate lists," Ph.D. dissertation (draft), Carnegie-Mellon Univ., Pittsburgh, PA, 1983.

[89] C. Wadsworth, "Semantics and pragmatics of lambda-calculus," Ph.D. dissertation, Oxford Univ., Oxford, England, 1971.

[90] S. Ward, "The MuNet: A multiprocessor message-passing system architecture," in *Proc. Texas Conf. Comput. Syst.*, Univ. Houston, Houston, TX, 1978.

[91] A. I. Wasserman and S. Gutz, "The future of programming," *Commun. ACM*, vol. 25, pp. 196–206, Mar. 1982.

[92] I. Watson and J. Gurd, "A prototype data flow computer with token labeling," in *Proc. AFIPS Nat. Comput. Conf.*, 1979, vol. 48, pp. 623–628.

[93] ——, "A practical data flow computer," *IEEE Computer*, vol. 15, pp. 51–57, Feb. 1982.

[94] M. Weiser, personal communication, 1984.

[95] K. S. Weng, "Stream-oriented computation in recursive data flow schemes," Massachusetts Inst. Technol., Cambridge, MA, Tech. Rep. MTMM-68, Oct. 1975.

Steven R. Vegdahl received the B.S. degree in mathematics from Stanford University, Stanford, CA, in 1976, and the Ph.D. degree in computer science from Carnegie-Mellon University, Pittsburgh, PA, in 1983.

He is presently working as a Research Computer Scientist at the Tektronix Computer Research Laboratory, Beaverton, OR. His research interests include algorithm animation, compilers, computer architecture, computational complexity, multiprocessing, object-oriented programming languages, microprogramming, and functional programming languages.

Chapter 2: Dataflow Systems

Background

Data-driven computation and dataflow architectures achieve high-speed computing by (fine-grain) parallelism at instruction execution level. Multiple instructions can be executed simultaneously, depending on the inherent parallelism in an application. There are two abstract models for dataflow computation: static and dynamic. The static models allow only one token per arc in the dataflow graph, whereas the dynamic models allow tagged tokens and thus permit more than one token per arc. The difference between the two is in the way they handle re-entrant code: The static model does not permit recursion, whereas the dynamic model does. The other characteristic of the dataflow architectures is in the way the data structures are represented in architecture. The dataflow systems [10] can also be characterized by the way they handle three basic tasks: accessing the program description, gathering tokens to produce executable packets, and executing the instructions.

The papers in this section represent static and dynamic dataflow models.

Article Summary

Arvind and Culler, in "Dataflow Architectures," describe different types of dataflow systems including the MIT (dynamic) tagged-token dataflow architecture. The paper introduces dataflow graphs and rules that determine when and how the operations are performed. The two main features of the MIT tagged-token dataflow system are that data structures accesses are handled separately from other token activities and there is a two-tiered communication system. The data structures are held in the I-structure store [1], which allows the operations on them to be performed quickly and allows more efficient use of the expensive waiting-matching store. The communication systems relieves the communication switch of excess traffic, providing that the programs have strong locality. The dataflow system is designed around Arvind's language ID [16].

Dennis, in "Dataflow Supercomputers," describes the MIT static dataflow architecture. This represents one of the original ideas on dataflow computation. The static dataflow architectures is more restrictive in terms of programming and less efficient in handling large data structures, thus making it less attractive than those employing the dynamic model. In the practical system, the dataflow tasks are simulated in the processor modules, which are implemented by using conventional microprocessors. However, the size of the system is going to be limited by the size of the interconnection switches.

Gurd et al., in "The Manchester Prototype Dataflow Computer," describe the Manchester University dataflow system, a fully functional tagged dataflow system; analyze results from this study; and describe the limitations and how they can be overcome. The Manchester machine is a single ring implementation, which consists of a token queue, a matching unit, an instruction store, and a bank of arithmetic and logic units (ALU). The matching store is hierarchically organized as a pseudo-associative memory at the top with an overflow memory. The data structures were stored in the matching store, and some special operations were provided to handle the structures in the earlier implementation. The later implementation uses a structure store for storing data structures for efficiency. In contrast to the I-structure store in the MIT tagged-token dataflow system, a single structure store is attached to the network. The programming model is based on the single assignment language SISAL [15].

Yuba et al., in "SIGMA-1: A Dataflow Computer for Scientific Computations," describe the ETL's Sigma-1 system, which is the most ambitious dataflow project. According to their plan, the SIGMA system will have over 200 processing elements with a projected 100 MFLOP performance. The goal of this effort is to lead to a super high speed computer for numerical computation. The architecture is based on the dynamic model and uses a structure store for holding data structures. The system is hierarchically organized where small clusters of processors with their structure memories are connected by a global communication network. This organization falls between the Manchester and the MIT tagged-token dataflow machines.

Additional material can be found in references 1-9, 11-14, and 17-22.

References

[1] Arvind, "I-Structure: An Efficient Data Structure for Functional Languages," *LCS TM-178*, Massachusetts Institute of Technology, Cambridge, Mass., Oct. 1981.

[2] Arvind, Dertouzos, M., and Iannucci, R.A., "A Multiprocessor Emulation Facility," *LCS Technical Re-*

port-302, Massachusetts Institute of Technology, Cambridge, Mass., Oct. 1983.

[3] Bohm, A.P.W., Gurd, J.R., and Sargeant, J., "Hardware and Software Enhancement of the Manchester Dataflow Architecture," *Proc. of COMPCON S'85*, Computer Society of the IEEE Press, Washington, D.C., 1985, pp. 420-423.

[4] Burkowski, F.G., "A Multi-User Dataflow Architecture," *Proc. 8th Ann. Symp. on Computer Architecture*, Computer Society of the IEEE Press, Washington, D.C., 1981, pp. 327-333.

[5] Chambers, F.B., Duce, D.A., and Jones, G.P. (editors), *Distributed Computing*, Academic Press, Inc. (London) Ltd., London, England, 1984.

[6] Cornish, M., "The TI Dataflow Architecture: The Power of Concurrency for Avionics," *Proc. 3rd Conf. Digital Avionics Systems*, Institute of Electrical and Electronics Engineers, Inc., New York, N.Y., Nov. 1979.

[7] Dennis, J.B., Lim, W.Y., and W.B. Ackerman, "The MIT Dataflow Engineering Model," *Proc. IFIPS 1983*, North-Holland Publishing Co., Amsterdam, The Netherlands, 1983, pp. 553-560.

[8] Gurd, J. and Watson, I., "Preliminary Evaluation of a Prototype Dataflow Computer," *Proc. IFIPS 1983*, North-Holland Publishing Co., Amsterdam, The Netherlands, 1983, pp. 545-551.

[9] Gurd, J.R., "The Manchester Dataflow Machine," *Computer Physics Communications*, Vol. 37, 1985, pp. 49-62.

[10] Gurd, J., Barahona, P.M.C.C., Bohm, A.P.W., Kirkham, C.C., Parker, A.J., Sargeant, J., and Watson, I., *Fine Grain Parallel Computing: The Dataflow Approach*, University of Manchester, Manchester, England,

[11] Hiraki, K., Shimada, T., and Nishida, K., "A Hardware Design of the SIGMA-1, A Data Flow Computer for Scientific Computation," *Proc. 1984 Int'l. Conf. on Parallel Processing*, Computer Society of the IEEE Press, Washington, D.C., 1984, pp. 524-531.

[12] Hiraki, K., Nashida, K., Sekigunchi, S., and Shimada, T., "Maintenance Architecture and Its LSI Implementation of a Dataflow Computer with a Large Number of Processors," *Proc. 1986 Int'l. Conf. on Parallel Processing*, Computer Society of the IEEE Press, Washington, D.C., 1986, pp. 584-591.

[13] Kawakami, K. and Gurd, J.R., "A Scalable Dataflow Structure Store," *Proc. 13th Ann. Int'l. Symp. on Computer Architecture*, Computer Society of the IEEE Press, Washington, D.C., 1986, pp. 243-250.

[14] Leler, W., "A Small, High-Speed Dataflow Processor," *Proc. 1983 Int'l. Conf. on Parallel Processing*, Computer Society of the IEEE Press, Washington, D.C., 1983, pp. 341-343.

[15] McGraw, J.R., "SISAL—Streams and Iteration in a Single-Assignment Language," *Language Reference Manual*, Lawrence Livermore National Lab., Livermore, Calif., July 1983.

[16] Nikhil, R.S. and Arvind, "Id/83s," *Lab. for CS Technical Report*, Massachusetts Institute of Technology, Cambridge, Mass., July 1985.

[17] Shimada, T., Sekiguchi, S., Hiraki, K., and Nishida, K., "A New Generation Data Flow Supercomputer," *Proc. Conf. on Algorithms, Architectures, and Futures of Sci. Computation*, University of Texas, Austin, Tx., 1985.

[18] Shimada, T., Hiraki, K., Nishida, K., and Sekiguchi, S., "Evaluation of a Prototype Data Flow Processor of the SIGMA-1 for Scientific Computations," *Proc. 13th Ann. Int'l. Symp. on Computer Architecture*, Computer Society of the IEEE Press, Washington, D.C., 1986, pp. 226-234.

[19] Srini, V.P., "An Architectural Comparison of Dataflow Systems," *Computer*, Vol. 19, No. 3, March 1986, pp. 68-88.

[20] Vedder, R. and Finn, D., "The Hughes DataFlow Multiprocessor," *Proc. 12th Ann. Int'l. Symp. on Computer Architecture, Computer Society of the IEEE Press*, Washington, D.C., 1985, pp. 324-332.

[21] Watson, I. and Gurd, J., "A Prototype Dataflow Computer with Token Labelling," *Proc. of the National Computer Conf.*, AFIPS Press, Reston, Va., 1979, pp. 623-628.

[22] Watson, I. and Gurd, J., "A Practical Data Flow Computer," *Computer*, Vol. 15, No. 2, Feb. 1982, pp. 51-56.

Ann. Rev. Comput. Sci. 1986. 1:225–53
Copyright © 1986 by Annual Reviews Inc. All rights reserved

DATAFLOW ARCHITECTURES

Arvind and David E. Culler

Laboratory for Computer Science, Massachusetts Institute of Technology, 545 Technology Square, Cambridge, Massachusetts 02139

ABSTRACT

Dataflow graphs are described as a machine language for parallel machines. *Static* and *dynamic* dataflow architectures are presented as two implementations of the abstract dataflow model. Static dataflow allows at most one token per arc in dataflow graphs and thus only approximates the abstract model where unbounded token storage per arc is assumed. Dynamic architectures tag each token and keep them in a common pool of storage, thus permitting a better approximation of the abstract model. The relative merits of the two approaches are discussed. Functional data structures and I-structures are presented as two views of data structures that are both compatible with the dataflow model. These views are contrasted and compared in regard to efficiency and exploitation of potential parallelism in programs. A discussion of major dataflow projects and a prognosis for dataflow architectures are also presented.

1. DATAFLOW MODEL

The dataflow model of computation offers a simple, yet powerful, formalism for describing parallel computation. However, a number of subtle issues arise in developing a practical computer based on this model, and dataflow architectures exhibit substantial variation, reflecting different standpoints taken on certain aspects of the model. For example, in the abstract dataflow model, data values are carried on *tokens,* which travel along the arcs connecting various instructions in the program graph, and it is assumed that the arcs are first-in-first-out (FIFO) queues of unbounded capacity (Kahn 1974). This gives rise to two serious, pragmatic concerns: (*a*) How should the tokens on arcs be managed? (*b*) How should data structures, which are essentially composites of many tokens, be represented? The manner in which these concerns are resolved has major impact not only on the machine organization but also on the amount of parallelism that can be exploited in programs. In this review, we examine the major variations in dataflow architectures with regard to token storage mechanisms and data structure storage.

The paper is organized as follows. Section 1 introduces dataflow program graphs and the rules that determine when and how operations are performed. Also, it explains why data structures cannot be viewed as they are in conventional programming languages without seriously compromising the suitability of the dataflow approach for parallel processing. Section 2 examines the two token storage mechanisms adopted in current dataflow architectures. The *static dataflow* approach allows only one token to reside on an arc at any time, while the *tagged-token dataflow* approach allows essentially unbounded queues on the arcs with *no* ordering, but with each token carrying a tag to identify its role in the computation. Section 3 presents two alternatives to the view of data structures embodied in conventional languages. The first alternative treats a data structure as a value that conceptually is carried on a token. "Functional" structure operations, such as *cons,* are provided to create new structures out of old ones. This approach is elegant, but expensive to implement (even if the data structure is actually left behind in storage so that the token carries only a pointer) and restricts parallelism. The second alternative treats a data structure as a collection of slots, each of which can be written only once. Any attempt to read a slot before it is written is deferred until the corresponding write occurs. Section 4 gives an overview of the major dataflow projects. Finally, Section 5 gives our views of future developments in dataflow computers.

1.1 *Acyclic, Conditional, and Loop Program Graphs*

A dataflow program is described by a directed graph where the nodes denote operations, e.g. addition and multiplication, and the arcs denote data dependencies between operations (Dennis 1974). As an example, Figure 1 shows the acyclic dataflow program graph for the following expression.

Let $x = a * b$;
$\quad\quad y = 4 * c$
in $\quad (x + y) * (x - y)/c.$

Any arithmetic or logical expression can be translated into an acyclic dataflow graph in a straightforward manner. Data values are carried on *tokens,* which flow along the arcs. A *node* may *execute* (or fire) when a token is available on

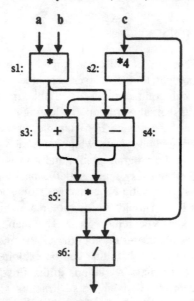

Figure 1 Acyclic dataflow graph.

each input arc. When it fires, a data token is removed from each input arc, a result is computed using these data values, and a token containing the result is produced on each output arc.

Nodes s1 and s2 in Figure 1 are both enabled for execution as soon as tokens are placed on the input arcs a, b, and c. They may fire simultaneously, or one may fire before the other; the results are the same in either case. The result of an operation is purely a function of the input values; there are no implicit interactions between nodes via side effects, for example, through shared memory. This example illustrates two key properties of the dataflow approach: (a) *parallelism,* i.e. nodes may potentially execute in parallel unless there is an explicit data dependence between them, and (b) *determinacy,* i.e. results do not depend on the relative order in which potentially parallel nodes execute.[1] Furthermore, notice that by supplying several sets of input tokens, distinct computations can be pipelined through the graph. In this example, a single wave of tokens on the input arcs produces a single wave of tokens on the output arcs. Graphs that have this property are called *well-behaved.* All acyclic graphs for arithmetic and logical expressions are well-behaved.

In order to build *conditional* and *loop* program graphs, we introduce two control operators: *switch* and *merge.* Unlike the *plus* operator, *switch* and *merge* are not well-behaved in isolation, but yield well-behaved graphs when used in conditional and loop schemas (Dennis et al 1972). Consider first the conditional graph in Figure 2a that represents the expression if $x < y$ then $x + y$ else $x - y$. The initial tokens provide the data input to the *switches* as well as input to the predicate graph. The predicate graph yields a single boolean value that supplies the control input to all the *switches* and *merges.* A *switch* routes its data input to the output arc on the True side or False side, according to the value of the control input. Thus, the wave of input tokens is directed to the True or the False arm of the conditional. As long as the arms of the conditional are well-behaved graphs, a single wave of tokens will eventually arrive at the data input of the appropriate side of the *merge.* The *merge* selects an input token from the True or the False side input arc, according to the value of the control input, and reproduces the data input token on the output arc. To see that the conditional behaves appropriately when waves of inputs are presented to it, consider the tricky case in which the first wave of input tokens is switched to the True side, the second wave to the False side, and the tokens on the False side of the *merge* arrive before the tokens on the True side. The sequence of control tokens at the *merge* restores the proper order among the tokens on the output arcs.

The loop graph shown in Figure 2b computes $\sum_{i=1}^{N} F(i)$. The figure is somewhat stylized in that the dots are used to indicate that the output of the predicate is connected to each of the *switches* and *merges,* and the graph corresponding to function F is indicated by the "blob" containing F. The initial values of i and *sum* enter the loop from the False sides of the *merges* and provide data to the predicate and *switches.* If the predicate evaluates to True, the data values are routed to the loop body. Assuming the body is a well-behaved graph, eventually a single wave of results is produced that provides tokens on the True side of the *merges.* In this way, values circulate through the loop until the predicate turns to False, which causes the final values to be routed out of the loop and restores the initial False values on the control inputs to the *merges.* Note that if many waves of inputs are provided, only one wave at a time is allowed to enter the loop; the second wave enters the loop as soon as the first completes, and so on. Also note that loop values

---

[1]The unbounded FIFO queue model presented in this paper is a generalization of the dataflow model originally formulated by Dennis. His model (Dennis 1974) requires that the output arcs of a node be empty before it fires, implying that at most one token can reside on any arc. Kahn's paper (Kahn 1974) implies that the determinacy of dataflow graphs is preserved even without this restriction. Kahn's result also permits nodes to have internal state, but we do not consider this generalization.

need not circulate in clearly defined waves. Suppose F is a very complicated graph or simply does not fire for a long time. The index variable i may continue to circulate, causing many computations of F to be initiated. This behavior is informally referred to as *dynamic unfolding* of a loop.

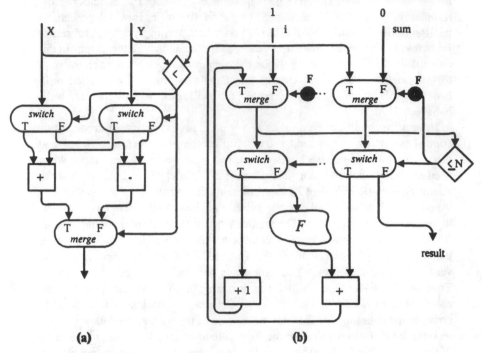

Figure 2   Conditional and loop graphs.

1.2 *Data Structures*

The dataflow model introduced thus far is fully general in a formal computational sense (Jaffe 1979) but has limited practical utility because of the absence of data structures. Suppose we introduce a data structure constructor *cons,* which "glues together" two data values to produce a new value. The components of a pair thus constructed are selected using functions *first* and *rest.* Since these new operators are functions, they fit easily in the dataflow model, provided we assume tokens can carry composite data values. Note that a component of the pair might be a pair, and so on; thus we must allow arbitrarily large structures to be carried on a token. Only in the abstract model do we think of structures as being carried on tokens; in practice, tokens carry pointers to structures that are left behind in storage. The *cons* operation can be extended to a general array operation *append,* which takes an array x, an index i, and an element v, and produces a new array y such that $y[j]$, i.e. the jth element of y, is the same as $x[j]$ for all j not equal to i, and such that $y[i]$ is v.

Even though data structures sit aside in storage, we must be careful not to treat them as we do arrays or records in a conventional language such as Pascal or Fortran. Consider the effect of a conventional store operation that modifies an element of a data structure. In general, there may be many tokens carrying pointers to the structure. Suppose one is destined for a modify operation and another is destined for a *select* operation with the same index. The two operations can potentially execute in parallel because there is no explicit data dependency from one to the other. However, the value produced by the select operation depends upon which operation happens to execute first. This defeats the determinacy of the model: It is no longer true that instructions can execute in any order consistent with the data dependencies and that the results remain unaffected by the order. *Append*, however, does not change the data structure; it produces a new structure that is similar to the old one. Consider the earlier scenario in which a token is destined for a *select* and another carrying a pointer to the same structure is destined for an *append*. The *select* operates on the old structure and hence is not affected by the *append*.

These observations raise a tough question. Is it possible to support data structures efficiently and still maintain the elegance and simplicity of the dataflow model? We return to this question in Section 3.

1.3 *User-Defined Functions*

Another highly desirable property of a computation model is the ability to support user-defined functions. Each of our examples represents a function that, given a set of input values, produces a set of results. Any good high-level language provides a way of *abstracting* variables so that an expression can be turned into a procedure or a function. At the dataflow graph level, a user-defined function is no more than an encapsulation of a graph that allows arguments and results to be transmitted properly. Nonrecursive functions can be handled by graph expansion at compile time. However, to support user-defined functions more generally, we need an *apply* operator that takes as inputs a function value (i.e. the description of an encapsulated dataflow graph) and a set of arguments and that invokes the function on the specified arguments. There are subtle issues involved in the implementation of *apply*. For example, when should the graph corresponding to the function actually be created? After all the arguments have arrived? As soon as a particular argument has arrived? Often the semantics of function application in high-level languages requires the *apply* to be implemented in a particular way. However, all implementations must support dynamic expansion of graphs and a method to route tokens to input arcs of the newly created graph. If a copy of the function graph is to be reused, then a mechanism is required to distinguish tokens belonging to different invocations. In this latter case, the FIFO queueing of tokens on arcs will not suffice. A mechanism for user-defined functions develops naturally out of the tagged-token approach, so we will return to this topic after discussing various implementations.

1.4 *Dataflow Graphs as a Parallel Machine Language*

We can view dataflow graphs as a machine language for a parallel machine where a node in a dataflow graph represents a machine instruction. The instruction format for a dataflow machine is essentially an adjacency list representation of the program graph: Each instruction contains an op-code and a list of destination instruction addresses. Recall that an instruction or node may execute whenever a token is available on each of its input arcs and that when it fires, the input tokens are consumed, a result value is computed, and a result token is produced on each output arc. This dictates the following basic instruction cycle: (*a*) detect when an operation is enabled (this is tantamount to collecting operand values); (*b*) determine the operation to be performed, i.e. fetch the instruction; (*c*) compute results; and (*d*) generate result tokens. This is *the* basic instruction cycle of any dataflow machine; however, there remains tremendous flexibility in the details of how this cycle is performed.

It is interesting to contrast dataflow instructions with those of conventional machines. In a von Neumann machine, instructions specify the addresses of the operands explicitly and the next instruction implicitly via the program counter (except for branch instructions). In a dataflow machine, operands (tokens) carry the address of the instruction for which they are destined, and instructions contain the addresses of the destination instructions. Since the execution of an instruction is dependent upon the arrival of operands, instruction scheduling and management of token storage are intimately related in any dataflow computer.

Dataflow graphs exhibit two kinds of parallelism in instruction execution. The first we might call *spatial* parallelism: Any two nodes can potentially execute concurrently if there is no data dependence between them. The second form of parallelism results from pipelining independent waves of computation through the graph. In the next section we show that it is possible to execute several instances of the same node concurrently, thereby exploiting this *temporal* parallelism.

2. TOKEN STORAGE MECHANISMS

The essential point to keep in mind in considering ways to implement the dataflow model is that tokens imply storage. The token storage mechanism is the key feature of a dataflow architecture. While the dataflow model assumes unbounded FIFO queues on the arcs and FIFO behavior at the nodes, it turns out to be very difficult to implement this model exactly. Two alternative approaches have been researched extensively. The first we call *static dataflow;* it provides a fixed amount of storage per arc. The other approach we call *dynamic* or *tagged-token dataflow;* it provides dynamic allocation of token storage out of a common pool and assumes that tokens carry tags to indicate their logical position on the arcs.

2.1 *Static Dataflow Machine*

The one-token-per-arc restriction can be incorporated in the model by extending the firing rule to require that all output arcs of a node be empty before that node is enabled. With this restriction, storage for tokens can be allocated prior to execution, since the number of arcs is fixed for a given graph. The basic instruction format is expanded to include a slot for each operand. Distributing tokens to destination instructions involves little more than storing data values in the appropriate slots. The slots have *presence flags* to indicate whether or not a value has been stored. Thus, when a token is stored, it can easily be determined if the other inputs are all present. This idea underlies the static dataflow machines proposed by Dennis and his co-workers (Dennis & Misunas 1974; Dennis 1980; Dennis et al 1984a), described in Figure 3.

Instruction templates reside in the *activity store,* and addresses of enabled instructions reside in the *instruction queue*. The *fetch unit* removes the first entry in the instruction queue, fetches the corresponding op-code, data, and destination list from the activity store, forms them into an *operation packet,* forwards the operation packet to an available *operation unit,* and finally clears the operand slots in the template. The operation unit computes a result, generates a *result packet* for each destination, and sends the result packets to the *update unit*. Instructions are identified by their address in the activity store, so the update unit stores each result and checks the presence bits to determine if the corresponding activity is enabled. If that is the case, the address of the instruction is placed in the instruction queue. These units operate concurrently, so instructions are processed in a pipelined fashion.

It is possible to connect many such processors together via a packet communication network. The activity store of each processor can be loaded with a part of a dataflow graph. Notice that large delays in the communication network do not affect the performance, i.e. the number of operations performed per second, as long as enough enabled nodes are present in each processor. This is an important characteristic of dataflow machines; they can use parallelism in programs to hide communication latency between processors.

2.1.1 ENFORCING THE ONE-TOKEN-PER-ARC RESTRICTION   The above description of the static machine skips over a very important and rather subtle point: the one-token-per-arc restriction of Dennis's model. Suppose the units

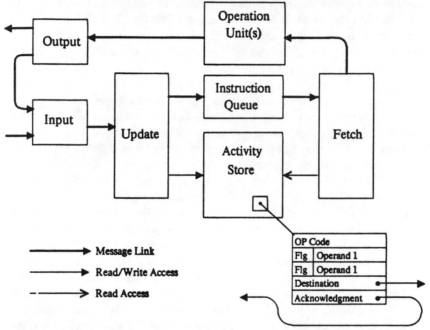

Figure 3   Static dataflow architecture.

communicate with a full send-acknowledge protocol, i.e. a token moves to the next unit only after that unit has signalled that it can accept the token, and the update unit writes into an operand slot only if the slot is empty. Even with these assumptions, multiple tokens belonging to the same arc may coexist in the machine, since there may be buffering in the units and communication network. It is infeasible for the update or fetch units to determine that there is no token in the system for a particular arc. If multiple tokens can coexist on an arc, then the FIFO assumption may be violated because two firings of a node may execute on different operation units within a processing element (PE), and the one that is logically second in the queue may finish first. The communication system will ultimately direct these result tokens to the same destination node, but in the wrong order. To see how the dataflow model malfunctions if tokens on an arc get out of order, consider the example in Figure 2*b* with the *plus* operator replaced by *minus*. The results of F(1) and F(2) can potentially reside on the left input to the *minus* concurrently, but if F(2) is processed before F(1) the answer will be wrong.[2]

If the one-token-per-arc restriction can be enforced, then the problems due

---

[2]Misunas shows (Misunas 1975) that multiple tokens per arc can also cause the machine to deadlock.

to reordering of tokens will not arise. The restriction cannot be enforced at the hardware level, but its effect can be achieved by executing only graphs that have the property whereby no more than one token can reside on any arc at any stage of execution. It is possible to transform any dataflow graph into a dataflow graph with this property. In the simplest transformation, for each arc in the graph, an *acknowledgment arc* is added in the opposite direction. A token on an acknowledgment arc indicates that the corresponding data arc is empty. Initially, a token is placed on each acknowledgment arc. A node is enabled to fire when a token is present on each input arc and each incoming acknowledgment arc. At the hardware level, the only difference between the two kinds of arcs is that the value of a token on an acknowledgment arc is ignored. Instead of the presence bits for operands, a counter is associated with each instruction. The counter is initialized to the number of operands plus the number of incoming acknowledgment arcs and is decremented by the update unit whenever an operand or acknowledgment arrives. The node is enabled when the counter reaches zero. Notice that the generation of acknowledgments must be delayed enough after the operation packet is formed so that there is no way for results of the second firing to overtake the first.

The one-token-per-arc restriction is not entirely satisfactory. Even though many of the acknowledgment arcs in a program graph can be eliminated (Montz 1980), the amount of token traffic increases by a factor of 1.5 to 2, the time between successive firings of a node increases drastically, and most importantly, the amount of parallelism that can be exploited in a program is reduced. In particular, the dynamic unfolding of loops is severely constrained, as shown by the following example. Suppose F in Figure 2b is replaced by the acyclic graph in Figure 1 (perhaps we take the inputs a, b, and c to be i). It should be possible to pipeline four distinct computations through this graph, but, unfortunately, with the static approach the second initiation must wait until the *divide* node fires, clearing the input arc for c. This problem has received substantial attention (Dennis & Gao 1983) and can be partially overcome by introducing extra identity operators to balance the path lengths in a graph. For example, if three identity nodes are added on the right input to the *divide* in Figure 1, the path lengths would be perfectly balanced. The balancing approach assumes that execution times for all operators are the same and that communication delays between operators are constant. Neither assumption is realistic, and balancing becomes computationally intractable without these assumptions.

We note in passing that modeling unbounded-FIFO dataflow graphs by fixed storage dataflow graphs (introduction of acknowledgment arcs is one example of such modeling) changes the "meaning" of a dataflow graph in a subtle way. A graph may be deadlock free in the unbounded case, but its corresponding graph with acknowledgment arcs may deadlock under certain circumstances. These shortcomings, in addition to the inability to handle user-defined functions, motivated work on the more general dynamic dataflow approach discussed below.

2.2 *Dynamic or Tagged-Token Dataflow*

Each token in a static dataflow machine must carry the address of the instruction for which it is destined. This is already a *tag*. Suppose, in addition to specifying the destination node, the tag also specifies a particular firing of the node. Then, two tokens participate in the same firing of a node if and only if their tags are the same. Another way of looking at tags is simply as a means of maintaining the logical FIFO order of each arc, regardless of the physical arrival order of tokens. The token that is supposed to be the ith value to flow along a given arc carries i in its tag. The goal is to give simple tag generation rules for the control operators *switch* and *merge*. Arvind & Gostelow (1977a) have given such rules for Dennis's operators (Dennis 1974). However, if only well-behaved graphs are considered, then it is possible to develop even simpler tag manipulation rules (Arvind & Gostelow 1982). We briefly explain these latter rules as well as the effect of tagging on the dataflow model presented in Section 1.

2.2.1 TAGGING RULES   We associate graphs, called *code blocks,* with each user-defined function. Each graph is either acyclic or a single loop. Thus a function containing nested loops is treated as several code blocks—one corresponding to each loop. A node is identified by a pair: code-block, instruction address. Tags have four parts: invocation ID, iteration ID, code block, and instruction address. The latter two identify the destination instruction and the former two identify a particular firing of that instruction. The iteration ID distinguishes between different iterations of a particular invocation of a loop code-block, while the invocation ID distinguishes between different invocations. All the tokens for one firing of an instruction must have identical tags, and enabled instructions are detected by finding sets of tokens with identical tags. Tokens also carry a port number that specifies the input arc of the destination node on which the token resides; this is not part of the tag and thus does not participate in matching.

Consider first the execution of an acyclic graph such as in Figure 1. A set of tokens whose tags differ only in the instruction address part is placed on the input arcs. When an instruction fires, it generates tags for each result token by using the destination address in the instruction as the instruction address part and copying the rest from the input tag. For conditionals the scenario is similar, but there are two destination lists. A single wave of inputs is steered through one arm or the other. We will ensure, however, that no two waves of inputs carry the same invocation and iteration IDs in their tags. Thus, for any

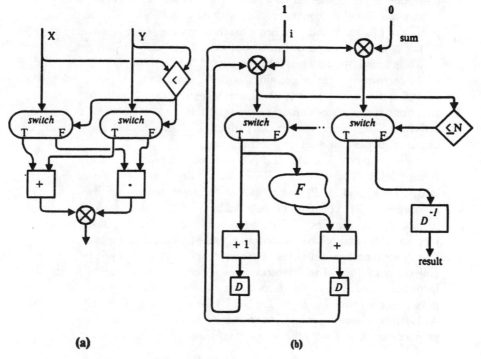

(a)   (b)

Figure 4   Conditional and loop graphs for tagged approach.

given tag, a data item carrying that tag will arrive at most on one side of the *merge*. Since the order of tokens on the arcs is immaterial, there is no need to orchestrate the *merge* via the output of the predicate as in the FIFO model; the streams of tokens produced by the two arms can be merged in an arbitrary fashion. This modified conditional schema is shown in Figure 4*a*. The $\otimes$ is not an operator; it merely denotes that two arcs converge on the same port.

The loop requires a control operator, named D, to increment the iteration ID portion of the tag (see Figure 4*b*). The iteration ID of each initial input to the loop is zero. Like the conditional schema, the *merges* can be eliminated from the loop schema because the tags on the tokens on the True and False sides of a *merge* will be disjoint. The D^{-1} operator is used to reset the iteration ID to zero. To implement nested loops and user-defined functions, an additional operator is required to assign unique invocation IDs. The *apply* operator takes a code-block name and an argument as input and forwards the argument to the designated code-block after assigning it a new invocation ID and setting its iteration ID to zero. The tag for the output arc of the *apply* node is also sent to the invoked graph so that the result can be returned to the destination of the *apply* node, as if it were generated by the *apply* node itself. One may visualize the action of an *apply* as coloring input tokens in such a manner that they do not mix with tokens belonging to other invocations of the same code block. Of course, there must be a complementary operator to restore the original color for the result tokens. The interested reader is referred to Arvind et al (1978) for more detail.

The tagged-token approach eliminates the need to maintain FIFO queues on the arcs (though unbounded storage is still assumed) and consequently offers more parallelism than the abstract model presented in Section 1. In fact, it has been shown that no interpreter can offer more parallelism than the tagged-token approach (Arvind & Gostelow 1977b).

2.2.2 TAGGED-TOKEN DATAFLOW MACHINE A machine proposed by Arvind et al (Arvind et al 1983a) is depicted in Figure 5. It comprises a collection of PEs connected via a packet communications network. Each PE is a complete dataflow computer. The *waiting-matching* store is a key component of this architecture. When a token enters the waiting-matching stage, its tag is compared against the tags of the tokens resident in the store. If a match is found, the matched token is purged from the store and is forwarded to the *instruction fetch* stage, along with the entering token. Otherwise, the incoming token is added to the matching store to await its partner. (Instructions are restricted at most to two operands, so a single match enables an activity.) Tokens that require no partner, i.e. are destined for a monadic operator, bypass the waiting-matching stage.

Once an activity is enabled, it is processed in a pipelined fashion without further delay. The invocation ID in the tag designates a triple of registers (CBR, DBR, and MAP) that contain all the information associated with the invocation. CBR contains the base address of the code block in program memory; DBR contains the base address of a data area that holds values of loop variables that behave as constants, and MAP contains mapping information describing how activities of the invocation are to be distributed over a collection of PEs. The *instruction fetch* stage is thus able to locate the instruction and any required constants. The op-code and data values are passed to the *arithmetic logic unit* (ALU) for processing. In parallel with the ALU, the *compute tag* stage accesses the destination list of the instruction and prepares result tags using the mapping information. Result values and tags are merged into tokens and passed to the network, whereupon they are routed to the appropriate waiting-matching store.

It is important to realize that if the waiting-matching store ever gets full the machine will immediately deadlock; tokens can leave the waiting-matching section only by matching up with incoming tokens. A similar argument can be made to show that if the total storage between the output of the waiting-matching section and the paths leading to its input is bounded, a deadlock can

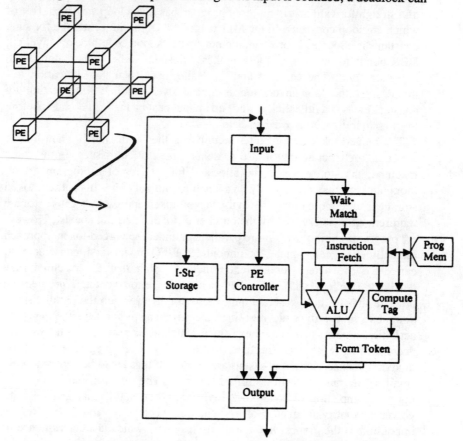

Figure 5 Processing element of the MIT tagged token dataflow machine.

occur (Culler 1985). Therefore, in addition to the functional units described in Figure 5, each PE must have a *token buffer*. This buffer can be placed at a variety of points, including the output stage or the input stage, depending on the relative speeds of the various stages. Both the waiting-matching store and the token buffer have to be large enough to make the probability of overflow acceptably small.

The *apply* operator is implemented as a small graph. The invocation request is passed to a system-wide resource manager so that resources such as a new invocation ID, program memory, etc, can be allocated for the new invocation. A code-block invocation can be placed on essentially any collection of processors. Various instances, i.e. firings, of instructions are assigned to PEs within a collection by "hashing" the tags. A variety of mapping schemes have been developed to distribute efficiently the most frequently encountered program structures. The MAP register assigned to a code-block invocation uses the hashing function for mapping activities of the code block.

Efficient handling of "loop constants" is a fairly low-level optimization, but important enough to deserve mention. In the abstract model, variables that are invariant over all iterations for a particular invocation of a loop, but that vary for different invocations, must be circulated. N in Figure 2b is an example of such a variable. Values of such variables cannot be placed in the instructions without making the graph non-reentrant. To avoid this overhead, most data-flow machines provide a mechanism for efficient handling of loop constants. As an example of the importance of this optimization, note that the inner loop of a straightforward matrix multiply program has seven loop variables, five of which are loop constants. In the MIT tagged-token machine, storage for such constants is allocated in program memory when a loop code-block is invoked; DBR points to this area and allows these constants to be fetched along with the instruction. The constant area is deallocated when the invocation terminates. If the loop invocation is spread over multiple PEs, setting up constant areas is a little tricky, since an image must be made in each PE before the first iteration is allowed to begin.

The tagged-token architecture circumvents the shortcomings identified in the static architecture, but it also presents some difficult issues. In the static machine, the storage has to be allocated for all arcs of a program graph, though tokens may coexist only on a small fraction of them. In contrast, token storage is used more efficiently in the tagged-token approach, because storage requirement is determined by the number of tokens that can coexist. However, programs exhibit much more parallelism under the tagged-token approach (actually even more so than the unbounded-FIFO model) and, consequently, can drive the token storage requirement so high that the machine may deadlock (Culler 1985). This has become a serious enough problem in practice that we now generate only those graphs in which the parallelism is bounded. In the dynamic machine, the mechanism for detecting enabled activities appears more complex, since matching is required as opposed to decrementing a counter. Further, tokens carry more tagging information though no acknowledgment tokens are needed. If tags are to be kept relatively small, there must be facilities for reusing tags. This, in turn, requires detecting the completion of code-block invocations, an action that generally involves a nontrivial amount of computation. This task would be virtually impossible if the graphs were not "self-cleaning," which is a consequence of graphs being well-behaved. Finally, an efficient mechanism is required for allocating resources to new code-block invocations.

2.3 *Tags as Memory Addresses and vice versa*

The performance of a tagged-token machine is crucially dependent upon the rate at which the waiting-matching section can process tokens. Though the size of the waiting-matching store depends upon many factors, based on our preliminary studies we expect that it will be in the range of 10K to 100K tokens. In this size range, a completely associative memory is ruled out, but a hash table possibly augmented with a small associative memory is viable, and the waiting-matching sections of the machines discussed in Section 4 are organized as such. Hashing basically involves calculating the address of a slot in the hash table by applying some "hash" function to the tag of the token. Examples of the hashing functions used in a tagged-machine are given in the references (Hiraki et al 1984).

Gino Maa, a member of our group, has suggested that tags should be viewed as addresses for a virtual memory in which the primitive operation is *store-extract*. Given a data and an address, the *store-extract* operation stores the data in the slot specified by the address if the slot is empty; otherwise, the contents of the slot are read and the slot is considered empty. A page of virtual memory may contain, for example, tokens with identical contexts. It is clear that only a tiny fraction of the virtual address space will be occupied at any given time, and physical storage is required only for this fraction. Thus, the problem of the design of the waiting-matching section becomes the problem of implementing a very large virtual memory (40-bit addresses or larger), where a nonexistent page is allocated automatically upon an attempt to access it and deallocated when all its entries are empty. Caches may be effective in organizing such a memory; there is evidence to suggest that when an incoming token finds its partner, the partner is usually among the most recently arrived tokens (Brobst 1986). The difference between the implementation of a large virtual address space and the hashing approach discussed earlier may be minimal; however, viewing tags as addresses allows us to place many variations of static and dynamic machines on a continuum, in which the address on a token in the static machine becomes the tag on a token in the dynamic machine.

Consider extending the static machine by operators to allocate activity store dynamically, thus allowing procedure calls to be implemented. In all such implementations, a part of the address serves the purpose of the "context" part of the tag in the dynamic machine, and the task of allocating a new context is subsumed by the task of allocating activity storage. A common optimization in such schemes is to separate the operand slots of an instruction from the rest and to allocate a new template containing operand slots for a code block at the time of invocation. To achieve sharing of a code block among several invocations requires relocation registers like CBR, DBR, etc, of the MIT tagged-token machine. Another variation discussed in the literature eliminates the need for acknowledgment arcs by allowing only acyclic graphs (Dennis et al 1984b; Preiss & Hamacher 1985). Since a loop can be modeled as a recursive procedure, this offers a trade-off between the cost of extra procedure calls and the savings gained from the elimination of acknowledgments. As discussed earlier, there are subtle issues associated with the implementation of the *apply* operator, e.g. the time of storage allocation affects the amount of parallelism that can be exploited by the machine.

A variation of the tagged-token machine that has been proposed by David Culler and Gregory Papadopoulos (also of our group) is to replace the waiting-matching section of the tagged-token machine by a token storage that is explicitly allocated at the time of procedure invocation. It is possible to do so if the storage requirement of a code block can be determined prior to invoking it. The type of bounded-loop graphs that we propose to run on the machine have this property.

After examining some of the variations discussed here, the distinction between static and dynamic dataflow becomes somewhat fuzzy. Choosing a good design among the ones proposed (or one yet to be proposed) is an active research topic in this field. The only general statement we can make is that giving the programmer or the compiler a greater control over the management of resources increases his responsibility and burden but may provide significant performance improvements and may simplify the design of the machine.

3. DATA STRUCTURES

Section 1 described how data structures can be incorporated in the dataflow model without sacrificing its elegance or utility for parallel computation. We now illustrate the difficulties in implementing "functional" data structures efficiently and describe an alternative view known as I-structures. This latter approach offers an efficient implementation without sacrificing determinacy and allows more parallelism to be exploited in programs than the "functional" approach.

3.1 *Functional Operations On Data Structures*

The simplest form of "functional" data structures is reflected in the operations *cons, first,* and *rest. Cons* glues two values together to form a pair; *first* and *rest* select values from such pairs. Clearly, we cannot allow arbitrarily large values to be carried on a token, so pairs must be maintained in storage with tokens carrying the addresses of these pairs. To this end, dataflow machines provide *structure storage,* which should be considered as a special operation unit with internal storage. The unit is shared by all PEs and is capable of performing many concurrent structure operations.

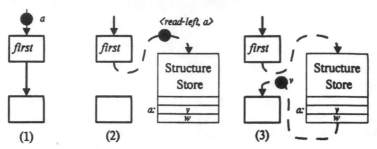

Figure 6   Action of a *first* operation.

To see how the structure store and its associated operations behave, we can step through the execution of a *first* operation. A *first* operation is enabled by the arrival of a token carrying a pointer. Neither the *fetch* unit in the static machine nor the ALU in the tagged-token machine can access the structure storage directly.[3] Thus, a new packet containing the *read* request and the address or tag of the destination node of the *first* operation is sent to the structure storage. Upon receipt of such a request, the structure storage controller produces a token containing the left value of the pair and sends it to the appropriate destination instruction; this is depicted in Figure 6.

Similarly, for the *cons* operator, two input data values together with the destination node address (or tag) are sent to a structure storage unit. The structure controller allocates storage for the pair, writes the elements, and sends a pointer for the newly allocated storage to the destination instruction.

The implementation of large, flat data structures, such as arrays, presents difficult design trade-offs. If arrays are implemented as linked lists using *cons,* selection operations are inefficient. If, instead, array elements are stored contiguously, as a generalization of the pairing operation, the *append* operation becomes costly. This is because *append* involves creating a new array and copying all except one element from the old array. Efficient implementations of arrays have been researched extensively (Ackerman 1978; Guharoy 1985), and two key ideas have emerged to reduce copying. First, if the array descriptor (or pointer) fed to the *append* operator is the only descriptor in existence for the corresponding array, the array can be updated in place without risk of causing a read-write race. Second, if the array is

---

[3]Not providing direct access to a large storage shared by many PEs is certainly a design choice, but a fundamental one. In a machine with many processors and many structure controllers, the time to access a particular memory controller may be very large. If the instruction processing pipeline blocks for structure operations, the performance of the machine will be greatly affected by the latency of the communication system. One advantage of dataflow machines is that they can be made extremely tolerant of latency and thus can sustain high performance with many processors working on a single problem. Detailed arguments concerning these points can be found in Arvind & Iannucci (1983a).

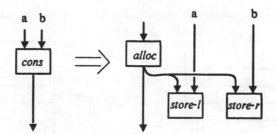

Figure 7 Implementation of nonstrict cons.

represented as a tree, then only the nodes along the path to the appended element need be regenerated; the rest of the tree can be shared. This reduces the amount of allocation and copying but increases the time for selection.

3.2 *I-structures*

The "functional" view of structures imposes unnecessary restrictions on program execution, regardless of how efficiently it is implemented. Consider the simple example *cons*(f(a),g(a)); the *cons* will not be enabled until both f(a) and g(a) have completed. Thus, another part of the program that uses the first element of the pair, but not the second, must wait until both elements have been computed. In programming language jargon, such data structures are called *strict*. In contrast, *cons* can be treated as a *nonstrict* operator (Friedman & Wise 1976), which allows an element of a pair to be used regardless of whether the other element has been produced. The resultant increase in parallelism is far greater than one might naively imagine.

The firing rule for nonstrict *cons* is difficult to implement. One way to circumvent this difficulty is to treat *cons* as a triplet of operations, as shown in Figure 7. The implicit storage allocation of strict *cons* becomes visible as a new type of node in the dataflow graph. The descriptor produced by the *allocate* operator is passed to the two store operations, in addition to the subsequent select operations. This allows consumption of a structure to proceed in parallel with production but also raises an awkward problem: A *first* or *rest* operation may be executed before the corresponding *store*. This seemingly catastrophic situation can be resolved with the help of a smart structure-storage controller. If a *read* request arrives for a storage cell that has not been written, the controller defers the *read* until a write arrives. This is the basic idea behind I-structure storage.

Referring to Figure 8, each storage cell contains status bits to indicate that the cell is in one of three possible states. (*a*) PRESENT: The word contains valid data that can be freely read as in a conventional memory. Any attempt to write it will be signalled as an error. (*b*) ABSENT: Nothing has been written into the cell since it was last allocated. No attempt has been made to read the cell; it may be written as for conventional memory. (*c*) WAITING: Nothing has been written into the cell, but at least one attempt has been made to read it. When it is written, all deferred *reads* must be satisfied. Cells change state in the obvious ways when presented with requests. Destination tags of deferred *read* requests are stored in a part of the I-structure storage specially reserved for that purpose.

While I-structure storage can be used to implement nonstrict *cons*, to exploit the full potential of this form of storage, functional languages can be augmented with explicit allocate and store operations. From a programmer's perspective, an I-structure is an array of slots (Nikhil & Arvind 1985) that are initially empty and that can be written at most once. Regardless of when or

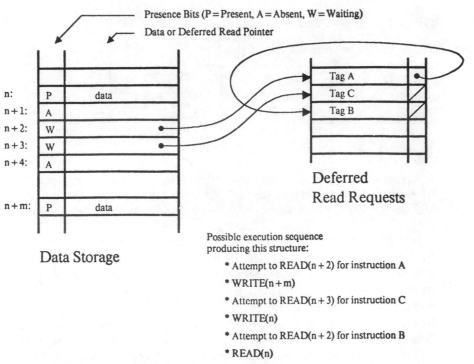

Presence Bits (P = Present, A = Absent, W = Waiting)
Data or Deferred Read Pointer

Tag A
Tag C
Tag B

**Deferred
Read Requests**

Data Storage

Possible execution sequence
producing this structure:

* Attempt to READ(n + 2) for instruction A
* WRITE(n + m)
* Attempt to READ(n + 3) for instruction C
* WRITE(n)
* Attempt to READ(n + 2) for instruction B
* READ(n)

Figure 8 I-structure storage.

how many times a *select* instruction for a particular slot is executed, the value returned is always the same. This preserves the determinacy property of the model. I-structures are not "functional" data structures; they are "monotonic objects" that are constructed incrementally, hence their name.

I-structures provide the kind of synchronization needed for exploiting producer-consumer parallelism without risk of read-write races. I-structure *read* requests for which the data is present require about the same time as conventional *reads,* and with special hardware (Heller 1983) deferred *reads* can be processed quickly. Thus, as long as most *read* requests follow the corresponding *write,* the overhead of I-structure memory is small, and the utility is enormous.

The benefit of nonstrict structures in terms of the amount of parallelism exhibited by programs is surprisingly large. For example, methods in which a large mesh is repeatedly transformed into a new version by performing some calculation for each point are common in numerical computing. Some such methods show tremendous parallelism because all mesh points can be computed simultaneously. However, even when this is not possible because of data dependencies, it is usually possible to overlap the computation of several versions of the mesh. This latter form of parallelism can be exploited only if the mesh is represented as a nonstrict structure.

4. CURRENT DATAFLOW PROJECTS

We now present an overview of some of the more important dataflow projects; we restrict our attention to those that have built or are currently building a dataflow machine. In particular, we do not address how dataflow concepts have influenced high-performance von Neumann computers being designed today.

4.1 *Static Machine Projects*

It is no exaggeration to say that *all* dataflow projects started in the seventies were directly based on seminal work by Dennis (1974). Such projects, besides Dennis's own project, include the LAU project in Toulouse, France (Comte et al 1980), the Texas Instruments dataflow project (Johnson et al 1980), the Hughes dataflow machine (Gaudiot et al 1985), and several projects in Japan (Temma et al 1980; NEC 1985). Even the work on tagged-token machines at the University of Manchester in England and the University of California at Irvine was inspired by Dennis's work.

4.1.1 THE MIT STATIC MACHINE DATAFLOW PROJECT   Dennis's group at MIT has proposed and refined several static dataflow architectures over the years (Dennis & Misunas 1974; Rumbaugh 1977; Dennis et al 1980, 1984a), and has implemented an eight-processor engineering model of the static machine shown in Figure 3 (Dennis et al 1980). The processing elements (PE) were built out of AMD bit-slice microprocessors and were connected by a packet-switched butterfly network composed of 2×2, byte-serial routers with send-acknowledge protocol. The structure controller was not implemented. Dataflow graphs for the machine were compiled from the language VAL (Ackerman & Dennis 1978). A PDP-11 served as a front end. While the machine operated successfully, it was only large enough to run toy programs. Also, because of microcoding, the PEs were far slower than the routers. The Texas Instruments machine (Johnson et al 1980), which was architecturally similar to Dennis's machine, was built by modifying four conventional processors. Even though these machines proved to be too slow to generate commercial interest in dataflow machines, they have had a marked influence on instruction scheduling in high-performance machines intended for scientific computing.

4.1.2 THE NEC DATAFLOW MACHINES   The latest machines that may be classified as static machines are NEC's NEDIPS (Temma et al 1980) and image pipelined processor (IPP) μPD7281 (NEC 1985). NEDIPS is a 32-bit machine that is intended for scientific computation and uses high-speed logic, while the IPP is a single chip processor of similar architecture that is intended as a building block for highly parallel image processing systems. We focus on the latter machine. Generally, image processing involves applying a succession of filters to a stream of image data. Thus, each IPP chip may be loaded with a dataflow program for a specific filter or several filters.

The NEC designers have generalized the machine described in Section 2.1 by allowing multiple tokens per arc. To see how this is done, consider once again the static machine in Figure 3. Instruction templates must be enlarged to include a collection of operand slots. If we assume that the operands of an enabled instruction are immediately removed from the activity store and forwarded to the operation units, then tokens cannot accrue in the slots for both the left and right arcs simultaneously. Thus, both arcs can share the same slots as long as a flag is provided in the instruction template to indicate on which arc (left or right) the current tokens reside. Further, the collection of slots in an instruction are managed as a cyclic buffer, with two pointers marking the head and tail of the queue. When an incoming token is for the same arc as the arc to which the previously arrived tokens in the instruction belong, the update unit adds the data value of the incoming token to the tail of the queue. Otherwise, the data value at the head is removed and placed in the instruction queue, along with incoming token. Notice that it is not necessary for all instruction templates to contain the same number of operand slots.

In the IPP implementation, the three components of the instruction template—op-code, operand slots, and destination list—are placed in three separate memories so that they can be accessed at consecutive stages of the instruction pipeline. Each IPP provides storage for 64 instructions, 128 arcs, and 512 16-bit data elements, which can be partitioned into queues of up to 16 slots per instruction. The IPP also allows regions of the data memory to be used for constants and tables. In addition, special hardware operations are provided for generating, coalescing, splitting, and merging *streams* of tokens. A novel technique is employed to govern the level of activity in the instruction pipeline: Instructions with multiple destinations are queued separately from those with single destinations, so when the pipeline is starved the multiple-destination instruction queue is given priority, and when the instruction pipeline is full the other queue is favored. Buffered input/output ports, which support a full send-acknowledge protocol, are provided and allow up to 14 IPPs to be connected in a ring. The system relies on a host processor to provide input/output, bookkeeping, and operating system support.

IPP does not handle acknowledgments specially and requires that operand storage be allocated statically, i.e. by the programmer or compiler. The programmer must tune the program graph to avoid buffer overflows and to ensure that tokens do not get out of order. As a result, program development for this machine is a tedious task. The buffer overflow problem is much less severe in NEDIPS because it provides much more data memory (64K words) than IPP. Nevertheless, the problem is serious enough to cause the designers to modify NEDIPS so that operand buffers can be extended or shrunk dynamically in 128-word increments. As discussed in Section 2.3, this extension also makes it difficult to classify NEDIPS as a static machine.

NEDIPS and IPP are the first commercially available dataflow processors, and regardless of their commercial success, which only time will tell, they are major milestones in non-von Neumann architectures.

4.2 *Tagged-Token Machine Projects*

The tagged-token dataflow approach was conceived independently by two research groups, one at Manchester University in Manchester, England, and one at the University of California at Irvine. The tagged-token architecture presented in Section 2.2 is based on work by the latter group, which has since moved to the Massachusetts Institute of Technology. The prototype tagged-token machine completed at the University of Manchester in 1981 (Gurd et al 1985) presents some interesting variations on the machine described above. A number of other prototype efforts are in progress in Japan, most notably in Amamiya's group at Nippon Telephone and Telegraph Company (Amamiya et al 1982; Takahashi & Amamiya 1983), and Sigma-1 at the Electrotechnical Laboratory, which is discussed later in this section.

4.2.1 THE MANCHESTER DATAFLOW PROJECT   The Manchester machine is essentially like the instruction processing section shown in Figure 5. It is a single ring consisting of a token queue, a matching unit, an instruction store, and a bank of ALUs. The ALUs are microcoded and fairly slow. It has demonstrated reasonable performance (1.2 MIPS) with this arrangement, although the choice of many slow ALUs has received some criticism because all the ALUs can be easily replaced by a single fast ALU. Tokens are 96 bits wide, including 37 bits for data, 36 for tag, and 22 for destination address.

The matching unit is a two-level store. The first level has a capacity of 1M tokens and uses a parallel hashing scheme to map an incoming tag into a set of eight slots. The contents of the selected slots are associatively matched against the incoming tag. The second-level overflow store uses hashing with linked lists.

The Manchester machine has no structure store per se. Instead, a host of exotic matching operations are provided so that the matching store can function as a structure store as well (Watson & Gurd 1982). The analog of an invocation ID can be treated as an array descriptor, and the iteration ID can function as the index, so a tag can represent an array element. A store operation generates a token that goes to the matching unit and *sticks* there. A read operation generates a token that matches with an element *stuck* in the store, extracts a copy of it, and forwards the copy to the destination of the read operation, but leaves the sticky element in the store. If the read token fails to find a partner in the store, it cycles through the ring, busy-waiting. When the structure is deallocated, its elements must be purged from the store. This approach has not proved very successful. It increases the already large load on the matching unit and communication network, degrades the performance of the matching unit on standard operations, and makes its design much more complex. To resolve these problems, the Manchester group is developing a structure store similar to the I-structure store. Sticky tokens are also used for loop constants (discussed in Section 2.2). The iteration part of the tag is ignored in performing the match, and the sticky token remains in the store even when a match is performed. Cleaning up the matching store when a loop terminates presents difficulties.

The Manchester machine has provided a target for a number of dataflow languages and has run a number of sizable applications. Extensions to multi-ring machines are being studied through simulation. Work continues in areas related to controlling parallelism and instruction set design.

4.2.2 SIGMA-1 AT ELECTROTECHNICAL LABORATORY, JAPAN   Under the auspices of the Japanese National Supercomputer Project, the Electrotechnical Laboratory is developing a machine (Yuba et al 1984) based on the MIT tagged-token architecture. The current proposal is to produce a prototype 32-bit machine capable of 100 Mflops, by the end of 1986. The individual processors are pipelined and operate on a 110-ns clock. The pipeline beat varies from 2 to 16 clock periods and is typically 3 to 4 periods. The network is packet-switched and composed of 10×10 routers. The engineering effort involved in this project is substantial, including the development of a 1-board PE and a 1-board structure memory. Together, these will require eight to ten custom cMOS gate-array chips and a custom VLSI chip. The PE will contain 64K words of program memory, 8K words of token buffering, and 64K words of waiting-matching store; the structure memory will contain 256K words. The machine will have up to 304 boards, divided roughly half and half between the structure memory and ALU boards. A 6-board version of the PE has been operational since November 1984.

A number of interesting design choices have been made in Sigma-1. A short latency two-stage processor pipeline is employed to efficiently execute code with low parallelism. In the first stage, instruction fetch and matching are performed simultaneously. If the match fails, the fetched instruction is discarded. In the second stage, destination tags are generated in parallel with the ALU operation. Tokens are transferred through the network as 80-bit packets. Two cycles are required to receive a packet, but the first stage of the processor pipeline operates on the first 40 bits of the packet (the tag) while the second 40 bits are received. The waiting-matching store is implemented as a chained hash table. The first operand of a pair is inserted in the matching store in 4 cycles; matching the second token of a pair has an expected time of 2.6 cycles. Sticky tokens are employed for loop constants; however, the designers of the ETL machine have intimated that the utility of this approach may not warrant the added complexity in the matching unit. The structure controllers support deferred *reads*. Rather than support a general heap storage model, in which data objects may have arbitrary lifetimes, structures are deleted when the procedure that created the structure terminates. This simplifies storage management and is probably acceptable for writing numerical applications, the intended application area for the machine.

4.2.3 THE MIT TAGGED-TOKEN PROJECT Not surprisingly, the tagged-token machine presented in Section 2.2 reflects the approach of the authors' group at MIT. This machine developed through a sequence of stages (Arvind & Gostelow 1977a; Gostelow & Thomas 1980; Arvind et al 1980, 1983a; Arvind & Kathail 1981; Arvind & Iannucci 1983b) from theoretical work on the U-interpreter model (Arvind & Gostelow 1977b, 1982). The MIT group has focused on developing an entire dataflow system, rather than on hardware development per se. Two soft prototypes have been implemented to serve as vehicles for studying architectures, program development, and resource management. A simulator provides a detailed model of the machine, including internal timings, while a dataflow emulator, which runs on the multiprocessor emulation facility (Arvind et al 1983b) (MEF), supports studying the dynamic behavior of larger applications. The MEF is a collection of 32 Texas Instruments Explorer Lisp machines connected by a high bandwidth packet-switched network. Each Lisp machine emulates a dataflow PE. Both the simulator and emulator execute graphs produced by our compiler from the high-level dataflow language Id (Arvind et al 1978; Nikhil & Arvind 1985). A number of reasonably large benchmarks are being studied on the soft-prototypes of the MIT tagged-token machine, including a complex hydrodynamics and heat conduction code.

5. PROGNOSIS

In this review we have outlined two salient issues in dataflow architectures—token storage mechanisms and data structures. We have also surveyed several dataflow machines. We have not attempted to cover all the current research topics; for the interested reader, these include demand-driven evaluation (Pingali & Arvind 1985), controlled program unfolding and deadlock avoidance (Culler 1985; Ruggiero & Sargeant 1985; Arvind & Culler 1985), efficient procedure invocation, storage reclamation, relationships with parallel reduction architectures (Keller et al 1979; Darlington & Reeve 1981; Keller 1984), network design and topology, and semantics of programming languages with I-structures. However, dataflow architectures are of more than academic interest, so in conclusion we consider their potential in the real world.

Today a vast collection of single-board computers are available and offer roughly 1 MIPS at low cost; these are touted as building blocks for multiprocessors. Can dataflow machines compete? It is not clear if a single dataflow processor can achieve the performance of a von Neumann processor at the same hardware cost. The dataflow instruction-scheduling mechanism is clearly more complex than incrementing a program counter. An engineering effort substantially beyond any of the current dataflow projects is required to make a fair comparison. The Sigma-1 project is an important step in this direction. The question becomes more interesting when we consider machines with multiple processors, where the dataflow scheduling mechanism yields significant benefits. In the basic von Neumann machine the processor issues a memory request and waits for the result to be produced. The memory cycle time is invariably greater than the processor cycle time, so computer architects devote tremendous effort to reduce the amount of waiting. This problem is much more severe in a multiprocessor context because the time to process a memory request is generally much greater than in a single processor and is unpredictable. Furthermore, most traditional techniques for reducing the effects of memory latency do not work well in a multiprocessor setting. The dataflow approach can be viewed as an extreme solution to the memory latency problem: the processor never waits for responses from memory; it continues processing other instructions. Instructions are scheduled based on the availability of data, so memory responses are simply routed along with the tokens produced by processors. Thus, even if individual dataflow processors do not yield the performance per dollar of a conventional processor, we can expect them to be better utilized than a conventional processor in a multiprocessor setting. For large enough collections of processors they should be cost effective and should show absolute performance not achievable by conventional processors. But it is not yet clear where this threshold lies.

The preceding discussion suggests that dataflow machines are likely to be competitive in high-performance range; however, we do not make such a claim lightly. It is unlikely that a large collection of 1 MIPS machines of any ilk will compete with a few very high performance processors, i.e. processors that can perform 10 to 100 MFLOPs each. To compete among supercomputers, it may be necessary to engineer a dataflow machine with the technology and finesse employed in conventional supercomputers. This is a major undertaking, far beyond any of the dataflow projects currently proposed. Most supercomputers include vector accelerators to improve performance on a restricted class of programs. It remains to be seen how effective these will be in a multiprocessor context and the extent to which analogous accelerators will be needed for dataflow machines.

This paper has focused on architectural issues, and accordingly has scarcely touched on the high-level programming model that accompanies dataflow machines. Nonetheless, programmability of parallel machines is critical. Conventional programming languages are imperative and sequential in nature: do this, then do that, etc. Efforts to use these languages for describing parallel computation have been ad hoc and unwieldy, greatly increasing the difficulty of the already onerous programming task. The programmer must determine what synchronization is required to avoid read-write races. Even so, subtle timing bugs are common. A class of languages, called *functional* languages, completely avoid these synchronization problems by disallowing "updatable" variables. Functional languages employ function composition, rather than command sequencing, as the basic concept and can be translated into dataflow graphs easily, thereby exposing parallelism. These languages can be augmented with I-structures to make data structures more efficient, without sacrificing determinacy or parallelism. It is our belief that dataflow architectures together with these new languages will show the programming generality, performance, and cost effectiveness needed to make parallel machines widely applicable.

ACKNOWLEDGMENTS

We gratefully acknowledge Robert Iannucci's drawings of various dataflow architectures, from which we have "borrowed" liberally. Many ideas in this paper derive from the common heritage of the Computation Structures Group at M.I.T. Laboratory for Computer Science, and we are indebted to its members for providing a stimulating research environment. We are grateful to Steven Brobst, Jack Dennis, K. Ekanadham, Bhaskar Guharoy, Gino Maa, Hitoshi Nohmi, Greg Papadopoulos, Natalie Tarbet, and Ken Traub for their valuable comments on drafts of this paper. Of course, we take responsibility for the opinions presented and any remaining errors.

This work was performed at the M.I.T. Laboratory for Computer Science under the Tagged-Token Dataflow project. Funding is provided in part by the Advanced Research Projects Agency of the U.S. Department of Defense, contract N00014-75-C-0661.

Literature Cited

Ackerman, W. B. 1978. A structure processing facility for dataflow computers. *Proc. Int. Conf. Parallel Process.*, pp. 166–72

Ackerman, W. B., Dennis, J. B. 1978. *VAL— A Value-Oriented Algorithmic Language: Preliminary Reference Manual*. Tech. Rep. TR-218, Lab. Comput. Sci., MIT, Cambridge, Mass.

Amamiya, M., Hasegawa, R., Nakamura, O., Mikami, H. 1982. A list-oriented data flow machine architecture. *Proc. Natl. Comput. Conf.*, pp. 143–51

Arvind, Culler, D. E. 1985. Managing resources in a parallel machine. *Proc. IFIP TC-10 Conf. Fifth-Generation Comput. Archit., Manchester, UK*

Arvind, Culler, D. E., Iannucci, R. A., Kathail, V., Pingali, K., Thomas, R. E. 1983a. *The Tagged Token Dataflow Architecture*. Tech. Rep., Lab. Comput. Sci., MIT, Cambridge, Mass. (Prepared for MIT Subject 6.83s)

Arvind, Dertouzos, M. L., Iannucci, R. A. 1983b. *A Multiprocessor Emulation Facility*. Tech. Rep. TR-302, Lab. Comput. Sci., MIT, Cambridge, Mass.

Arvind, Gostelow, K. P. 1977a. A computer capable of exchanging processors for time. *Proc. IFIP Congr. 77, Toronto, Canada,* pp. 849–53

Arvind, Gostelow, K. P. 1977b. Some relationships between asynchronous interpreters of a dataflow language. *Proc. IFIP WG2.2 Conf. Formal Description of Program. Lang., St. Andrews, Canada*

Arvind, Gostelow, K. P. 1982. The U-interpreter. *Computer* 15(2):42–49

Arvind, Gostelow, K. P., Plouffe, W. 1978. *An Asynchronous Programming Language and Computing Machine*. Tech. Rep. 114a, Dep. Inf. Comput. Sci., Univ. Calif., Irvine

Arvind, Iannucci, R. A. 1983a. A critique of multiprocessing von Neumann style. *Proc. 10th Int. Symp. Comput. Archit., Stockholm, Sweden,* pp. 426–36

Arvind, Iannucci, R. A. 1983b. *Instruction Set Definition for a Tagged-token Dataflow Machine*. Tech. Rep. CSG 212-3, Lab. Comput. Sci., MIT, Cambridge, Mass.

Arvind, Kathail, V. 1981. A multiple processor dataflow machine that supports generalized procedures. *Proc. 8th Ann. Symp. Comput. Archit., Minneapolis, Minn.,* pp. 291–302

Arvind, Kathail, V., Pingali, K. 1980. *A Dataflow Architecture with Tagged Tokens*. Tech. Rep. TM-174, Lab. Comput. Sci., MIT, Cambridge, Mass.

Brobst, S. A. 1986. *Token Storage Requirements in a Dataflow Supercomputer*. Tech. Rep., Lab. Comput. Sci., MIT, Cambridge, Mass. Submitted for publication

Comte, D., Hifdi, N., Syre, J. 1980. The data driven LAU multiprocessor system: results and perspectives. *Proc. IFIP Congr. 80, Tokyo, Japan,* pp. 175–80

Culler, D. E. 1985. *Resource Management for the Tagged-Token Dataflow Architecture*. Tech. Rep. TR-332, Lab. Comput. Sci., MIT, Cambridge, Mass.

Darlington, J., Reeve, M. 1981. ALICE: a multi-processor reduction machine for the parallel evaluation of applicative languages. *Proc. Conf. Functional Program. Lang. Comput. Archit., Portsmouth, NH,* pp. 65–76

Dennis, J. B. 1974. First version of a data flow procedure language. *Proceedings of the Colloque sur la Programmation, Vol. 19: Lecture Notes in Computer Science,* pp. 362–76. New York: Springer-Verlag

Dennis, J. B. 1980. Data flow supercomputers. *Computer* 13(11):48–56

Dennis, J. B., Boughton, G. A., Leung, C. K-C. 1980. Building blocks for data flow prototypes. *Proc. 7th Ann. Symp. Comput. Archit., La Boule, France,* pp. 1–8

Dennis, J. B., Fosseen, J., Linderman, J. 1972. Data flow schemas. *Proc. Symp. Theor. Program., Novosibirsk, USSR,* pp. 187–216

Dennis, J. B., Gao, G. R. 1983. Maximum pipelining of array operations on a static dataflow machine. *Proc. Int. Conf. Parallel Process.*

Dennis, J. B., Gao, G. R., Todd, K. 1984a. Modeling the weather with a data flow supercomputer. *IEEE Trans. Comput.* C33(7):592–603

Dennis, J. B., Misunas, D. 1974. *A Preliminary Architecture for a Basic Data Flow Processor.* Tech. Rep. CSG Memo 102, Lab. Comput. Sci., MIT, Cambridge, Mass.

Dennis, J. B., Stoy, J. E., Guharoy, B. 1984b. VIM: an experimental multi-user system supporting functional programming. *Proc. Int. Workshop High-Level Comput. Archit., Los Angeles, Calif.,* pp. 1.1–1.9

Friedman, D. P., Wise, D. S. 1976. CONS should not evaluate its arguments. In *Automata, Languages, and Programming,* ed. Michaelson, Milner. Edinburgh: Univ. Press

Gaudiot, J., Vedder, R., Tucker, G., Finn, D., Campbell, M. 1985. A distributed VLSI architecture for efficient signal and data processing. *IEEE Trans. Comput.* C34(12):1072–87

Gostelow, K. P., Thomas, R. E. 1980. Performance of a simulated dataflow computer. *IEEE Trans. Comput.* C29(10):905–19

Guharoy, B. 1985. *Structure management in a dataflow computer. Master's thesis.* Dep. Elect. Eng. Comput. Sci., MIT, Cambridge, Mass.

Gurd, J. R., Kirkham, C. C., Watson, I. 1985. The Manchester dataflow prototype computer. *Commun. Assoc. Comput. Mach.* 28(1):34–52

Heller, S. K. 1983. *An I-structure memory controller. Master's thesis.* Dep. Elect. Eng. Comput. Sci., MIT, Cambridge, Mass.

Hiraki, K., Nishida, K., Shimada, T. 1984. Evaluation of associative memory using parallel chained hashing. *IEEE Trans. Comput.* C33(9):851–55

Jaffe, J. M. 1979. *The Equivalence of R. E. Programs and Data Flow Schemes.* Tech. Rep. TM-121, Lab. Comput. Sci., MIT, Cambridge, Mass.

Johnson, D., et al. 1980. Automatic partitioning of programs in multiprocessor systems. *Proc. Compcon 80,* pp. 175–78

Kahn, G. 1974. The semantics of a simple language for parallel programming. *Proc. IFIP Cong. 74,* pp. 471–75

Keller, R. 1984. Rediflow multiprocessing. *Proc. Compcon 84*

Keller, R. M., Lindstrom, G., Patil, S. 1979. A loosely-coupled applicative multiprocessing system. *Proc. Natl. Comput. Conf., New York,* pp. 613–22

Misunas, D. 1975. Deadlock avoidance in a data-flow architecture. *Proc. Milwaukee Symp. Autom. Comput. Control*

Montz, L. B. 1980. Safety and Optimization Transformations for Data Flow Programs. *Tech. Rep. TR-240, Lab. Comput. Sci., MIT, Cambridge, Mass.*

NEC. 1985. *Advanced Product Information User's Manual: μPD7281 Image Pipelined Processor*

Nikhil, R., Arvind. 1985. *Id/83s. Tech. Rep., Lab. Comput. Sci., MIT, Cambridge, Mass.* (Prepared for MIT Subject 6.83s)

Pingali, K., Arvind. 1985. Efficient demand-driven evaluation. Pt. I. *ACM TOPLAS* 7(2):311–33

Preiss, B. R., Hamacher, V. C. 1985. Data flow on a queue machine. *Proc. 12th Ann. Int. Symp. Comput. Archit., Boston, Mass.,* pp. 342–51

Ruggiero, J., Sargeant, J. 1985. *Hardware and Software Mechanisms for Control of Parallelism.* Tech. Rep., Comput. Sci. Dep., Univ. Manchester, UK

Rumbaugh, J. A. 1977. Data flow multiprocessor. *IEEE Trans. Comput.* C26(2):138–46

Takahashi, N., Amamiya, M. 1983. A dataflow processor array system: design and analysis. *Proc. 10th Int. Symp. Comput. Archit., Stockholm, Sweden,* pp. 243–50

Temma, T., Hasegawa, S., Hanaki, S. 1980. Dataflow processor for image processing. *Proc. 11th Int. Symp. Mini and Microcomput., Monterey, Calif.,* pp. 52–56

Watson, I., Gurd, J. R. 1982. A practical dataflow computer. *Computer* 15(2):51–57

Yuba, T., Shimada, T., Hiraki, K., Kashiwagi, H. 1984. *Sigma-1: A Dataflow Computer For Scientific Computation.* Tech. Rep., Electrotech. Lab.

*Programmability with increased performance? New strategies to
attain this goal include two approaches to data flow architecture:
data flow multiprocessors and the cell block architecture.*

Data Flow Supercomputers

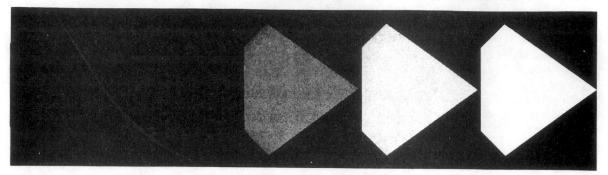

Jack B. Dennis
MIT Laboratory for Computer Science

The architects of supercomputers must meet three
challenges if the next generation of machines is to find
productive large-scale application to the important problems of computational physics. First, they must achieve
high performance at acceptable cost. Instruction execution rates of a billion floating-point operations each second are in demand, whereas current architectures require
intricate programming to attain a fraction of their potential, at best around one tenth of the goal. Brute force approaches to increase the speed of conventional architectures have reached their limit and fail to take advantage of
the major recent advances in semiconductor device technology. Second, they must exploit the potential of LSI
technology. Novel architectures are needed which use
large numbers but only a few different types of parts, each
with a high logic-to-pin ratio. In a supercomputer, most
of these parts must be productive most of the time; hence
the need to exploit concurrency of computation on a massive scale. Third, it must be possible to program supercomputers to exploit their performance potential. This
has proven to be an enormous problem, even in the case of
computations for which reasonably straightforward Fortran programs exist. Thus present supercomputer architectures have exacerbated rather than resolved the software crisis.

It appears that the objectives of improving programmability and increasing performance are in conflict, and
new approaches are necessary. However, any major departure from conventional architectures based on sequential program execution requires that the whole process of
program design, structure, and compilation be redone
along new lines. One architecture under consideration is a
multiprocessor machine made of hundreds of intercom-
municating microcomputer processing elements. This
architecture has attracted wide interest, but has many
drawbacks; even if the processing elements had full float-

ing-point capability and ran at a million instructions per
second, at least one thousand would be required to attain
a billion instructions per second performance. For such a
number of processing elements there is no known way of
permitting access to a shared memory without severe
performance degradation. Similarly, no known way of
arranging conventional microprocessors for synchronization or message passing allows efficient operation while
exploiting fine grain parallelism in an application. And
finally, there is no programming language or methodology that supports mapping application codes onto such a
multiprocessor in a way that achieves high performance.

Language-based computer design can ensure the programmability of a radical architecture. In a language-
based design the computer is a hardware interpreter for a
specific base language, and programs to be run on the system must be expressed in this language.[1] Because future
supercomputers must support massive concurrency to
achieve a significant increase in performance, a base language for supercomputers must allow expression of concurrency of program execution on a large scale. Since conventional languages such as Fortran are based on a global
state model of computer operation, these languages are
unsuitable for the next generation of supercomputers and
will eventually be abandoned for large-scale scientific
computation. At present, functional or applicative programming languages and data flow models of computation are the only known foundation appropriate for a supercomputer base language. Two programming languages have been designed recently in response to the
need for an applicative programming language suitable
for scientific numerical computation: ID, developed at Irvine,[2] and Val, designed at MIT.[3,4]

Data flow architectures offer a possible solution to the
problem of efficiently exploiting concurrency of computation on a large scale, and they are compatible with

modern concepts of program structure. Therefore, they should not suffer so much from the difficulties of programming that have hampered other approaches to highly parallel computation.

The data flow concept is a fundamentally different way of looking at instruction execution in machine-level programs—an alternative to sequential instruction execution. In a data flow computer, an instruction is ready for execution when its operands have arrived. There is no concept of control flow, and data flow computers do not have program location counters. A consequence of data-activated instruction execution is that many instructions of a data flow program may be available for execution at once. Thus, highly concurrent computation is a natural consequence of the data flow concept.

The idea of data-driven computation is old,[5,6] but only in recent years have architectural schemes with attractive anticipated performance and the capability of supporting a general level of user language been developed. Work on data-driven concepts of program structure and on the design of practical data-driven computers is now in progress in at least a dozen laboratories in the US and Europe. Several processors with data-driven instruction execution have been built, and more hardware projects are being planned. Most of this work on architectural concepts for data flow computation is based on a program representation known as data flow program graphs[7] which evolved from work of Rodriguez,[8] Adams,[9] and Karp and Miller.[10] In fact, data flow computers are a form of language-based architecture in which program graphs are the base language. As shown in Figure 1, data flow program graphs serve as a formally specified interface between system architecture on one hand and user programming language on the other. The architect's task is to define and realize a computer system that faithfully implements the formal behavior of program graphs; the language implementer's task is to translate source language programs into their equivalent as program graphs.

The techniques used to translate source language programs into data flow graphs[11] are similar to the methods used in conventional optimizing compilers to analyze the paths of data dependency in source programs. High-level programming languages for data flow computation should be designed so it is easy for the translator to identify data dependence and generate program graphs that expose parallelism. The primary sources of difficulty are unrestricted transfer of control and the "side effects" resulting from assignment to a global variable or input arguments of a procedure. Removal of these sources of difficulty not only makes concurrency easy to identify, it also improves program structure. Programs are more modular, and are easier to understand and verify. The implications of data flow for language designers are discussed by Ackerman.[12]

This article presents two architectures from the variety of schemes devised to support computations expressed as data flow graphs. First we explain data flow graphs by examples, and show how they are represented as collections of activity templates. Next we describe the basic instruction-handling mechanism used in most current projects to build prototype data flow systems. Then we develop the two contrasting architectures and discuss the reasons for their differences—in particular the different approaches to communicating information between parts of a data flow machine.

Data flow programs

A data flow program graph is made up of actors connected by arcs. One kind of actor is the operator shown in Figure 2, drawn as a circle with a function symbol written inside—in this case +, indicating addition. An operator also has input arcs and output arcs which carry tokens bearing values. The arcs define paths over which values from one actor are conveyed by tokens to other actors. Tokens are placed on and removed from the arcs of a program graph according to firing rules, which are illustrated for an operator in Figure 3. To be enabled, tokens must be present on each input arc, and there must be no token on any output arc of the actor. Any enabled actor may be fired. In the case of an operator, this means removing one token from each input arc, applying the specified function to the values carried by those tokens, and placing tokens labeled with the result value on the output arcs.

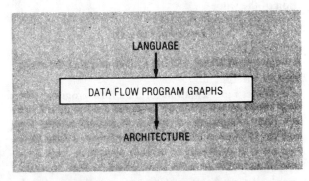

Figure 1. Program graphs as a base language.

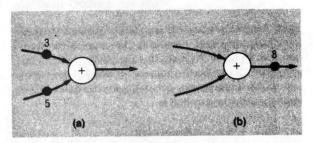

Figure 2. Data flow actor.

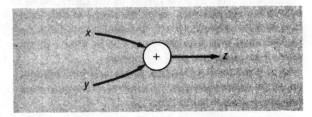

Figure 3. Firing rule: (a) before; (b) after.

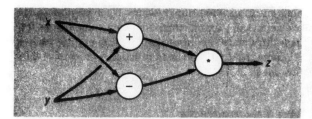

Figure 4. Interconnection of operators.

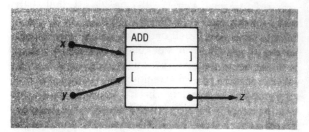

Figure 5. An activity template.

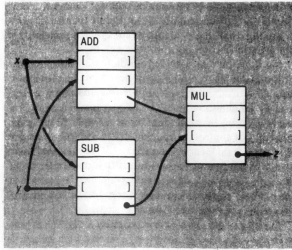

Figure 6. Configuration of activity templates for the program graph of Figure 4.

Operators may be connected as shown in Figure 4 to form program graphs. Here, presenting tokens bearing values for x and y at the two inputs will enable computation of the value

$$z = (x + y) * (x - y)$$

by the program graph, placing a token carrying the result value on output arc z.

Another representation for data flow programs—one much closer to the machine language used in prototype data flow computers—is useful in understanding the working of these machines. In this scheme, a data flow program is a collection of activity templates, each corresponding to one or more actors of a data flow program graph. An activity template corresponding to the plus operator (Figure 2) is shown in Figure 5. There are four fields: an operation code specifying the operation to be performed; two receivers, which are places waiting to be filled in with operand values; and destination fields (in this case one), which specify what is to be done with the result of the operation on the operands.

An instruction of a data flow program is the fixed portion of an activity template. It consists of the operation code and the destinations; that is,

instruction:

< opcode, destinations >

Figure 6 shows how activity templates are joined to represent a program graph, specifically the composition of operators in Figure 4. Each destination field specifies a target receiver by giving the address of some activity template and an input integer specifying which receiver of the template is the target; that is,

destination:

< address, input >

Program structures for conditionals and iteration are illustrated in Figures 7 and 8. These use two new data flow actors, switch and merge, which control the routing of data values. The switch actor sends a data input to its T or F output to match a true or false boolean control input. The merge actor forwards a data value from its T or F input according to its boolean input value. The conditional program graph and implementation in Figure 7 represent computation of

$$y: = (\text{IF } x > 3 \text{ THEN } x + 2 \text{ ELSE } x - 1) * 4$$

and the program graph and implementation in Figure 8 represent the iterative computation

$$\text{WHILE } x > 0 \text{ DO } = x - 3$$

Execution of a machine program consisting of activity templates is viewed as follows. The contents of a template activated by the presence of an operand value in each receiver take the form

operation packet:

< opcode, operands, destinations >

Such a packet specifies one result packet of the form

result packet:

< value, destination >

for each destination field of the template. Generation of a result packet, in turn, causes the value to be placed in the receiver designated by its destination field.

Note that this view of data flow computation does not explicitly honor the rule of program graphs that tokens must be absent from the output arcs of an actor for it to fire. Yet there are situations where it is attractive to use a program graph in pipelined fashion, as illustrated in Figure 9a. Here, one computation by the graph has produced the value 6 on arc z while a new computation represented

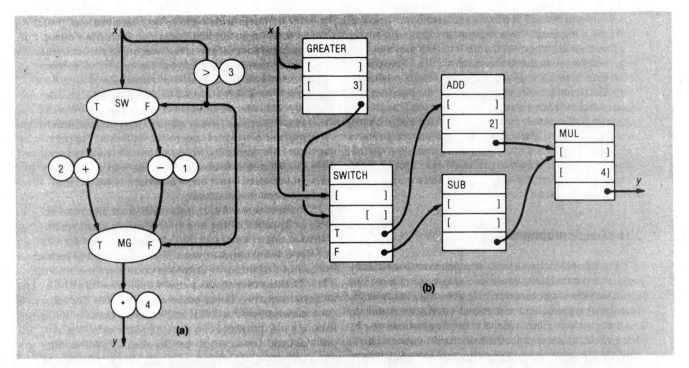

Figure 7. A conditional schema (a) and its implementation (b).

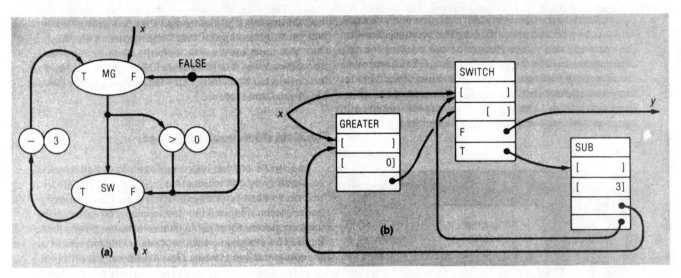

Figure 8. An iterative schema (a) and its implementation (b).

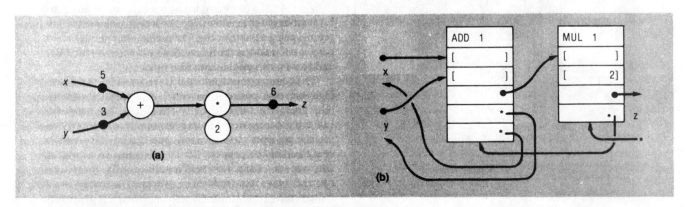

Figure 9. Pipelining in a data flow program (a) and its implementation (b).

by input values 5 and 3 on arcs *x* and *y* is ready to begin. To faithfully implement this computation, the add instruction must not be reactivated until its previous result has been used by the multiply instruction. This constraint is enforced through use of acknowledge signals generated by specially marked designations (∗) in an activity template. Acknowledge signals, in general, are sent to the templates that supply operand values to the activity template in question (Figure 9b). The enabling rule now requires that all receivers contain values, and the required number of acknowledge signals have been received. This number (if nonzero) is written adjacent to the opcode of an activity template.

The basic mechanism

The basic instruction execution mechanism used in several current data flow projects is illustrated in Figure 10. The data flow program describing the computation to be performed is held as a collection of activity templates in the activity store. Each activity template has a unique address which is entered in the instruction queue unit (a FIFO buffer store) when the instruction is ready for execution. The fetch unit takes an instruction address from the instruction queue and reads the activity template from the activity store, forms it into an operation packet, and passes it on to the operation unit. The operation unit performs the operation specified by the operation code on the operand values, generating one result packet for each destination field of the operation packet. The update unit receives result packets and enters the values they carry into operand fields of activity templates as specified by their destination fields. The update unit also tests whether all operand and acknowledge packets required to activate the destination instruction have been received and, if so, enters the instruction address in the instruction queue. During program execution, the number of entries in the instruction queue measures the degree of concurrency present in the program. The basic mechanism of Figure 10 can exploit this potential to a limited but significant degree: once the fetch unit has sent an operation packet off to the operation unit, it may immediately read another entry from the instruction queue without waiting for the instruction previously fetched to be completely processed. Thus a continuous stream of operation packets may flow from the fetch unit to the operation unit so long as the instruction queue is not empty.

This mechanism is aptly called a circular pipeline—activity controlled by the flow of information packets traverses the ring of units leftwise. A number of packets may be flowing simultaneously in different parts of the ring on behalf of different instructions in concurrent execution. Thus the ring operates as a pipeline system with all of its units actively processing packets at once. The degree of concurrency possible is limited by the number of units on the ring and the degree of pipelining within each unit. Additional concurrency may be exploited by splitting any unit in the ring into several units which can be allocated to concurrent activities. Ultimately, the level of concurrency is limited by the capacity of the data paths connecting the units of the ring. This basic mechanism is essentially that implemented in a prototype data flow processing element built by a group at the Texas Instruments Company.[13] The same mechanism, elaborated to handle data flow procedures, was described earlier by Rumbaugh,[14] and a new project at Manchester University uses another variation of the same scheme.[15]

The data flow multiprocessor

The level of concurrency exploited may be increased enormously by connecting many processing elements of the form we have described to form a data flow multiprocessor system. Figure 11a shows many processing elements connected through a communication system, and Figure 11b shows how each processing element relates to the communication system. The data flow program is divided into parts which are distributed over the processing elements. The activity stores of the processing elements collectively realize a single large address space, so the address field of a destination may select uniquely any activity template in the system. Each processing element sends a result packet through the communication network if its destination address specifies a nonlocal activity template, and to its own update unit otherwise.

The communication network is responsible for delivering each result packet received to the processing element that holds the target activity template. This network, called a routing network, transmits each packet arriving at an input port to the output specified by information contained in the packet. The requirements of a routing network for a data flow multiprocessor differ in two important ways from those of a processor/memory switch for a conventional multiprocessor system. First, information flow in a routing network is in one direction—an im-

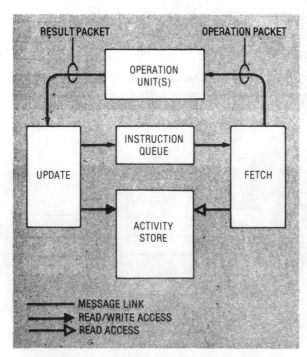

Figure 10. Basic instruction execution mechanism.

mediate reply from the target unit to the originating unit is not required. Second, since each processing element holds many enabled instructions ready for processing, some delay can be tolerated in transmission of result packets without slowing down the overall rate of computation.

The crossbar switch in conventional multiprocessor systems meets requirements for immediate response and small delay by providing for signal paths from any input to any output. These paths are established on request and maintained until a reply completes a processor/memory transaction. This arrangement is needlessly expensive for a data flow multiprocessor, and a number of alternative network structures have been proposed. The ring form of communication network is used in many computer networks, and has been used by Texas Instruments to couple four processing elements in their prototype data flow computer. The drawback of the ring is that delay grows linearly with size, and there is a fixed bound on capacity.

Several groups have proposed tree-structured networks for communicating among processing elements.[16,17,18] Here, the drawback is that traffic density at the root node may be unacceptably high. Advantages of the tree are that the worst case distance between leaves grows only as $\log_2 N$ (for a binary tree), and many pairs of nodes are connected by short paths.

The packet routing network shown in Figure 12 is a structure currently attracting much attention. A routing network with N input and N output ports may be assembled from $(N/2) \log_2(N)$ units, each of which is a 2×2 router. A 2×2 router receives packets at two input ports and transmits each received packet at one of its output ports according to an address bit contained in the packet. Packets are handled first come, first served, and both output ports may be active concurrently. Delay through an $N \times N$ network increases as $\log_2 N$, and capacity rises nearly linearly with N. This form of routing network is described in Leung[19] and Tripathi and Lipovski.[20] Several related structures have been analyzed for capacity and delay.[21]

The cell block architecture

In a data flow multiprocessor (Figure 11), we noted the problem of partitioning the instructions of a program among the processing elements to concentrate communication among instructions held in the same processing element. This is advantageous because the time to transport a result packet to a nonlocal processor through the routing network will be longer (perhaps much longer) than the time to forward a result locally.

At MIT, an architecture has been proposed in response to an opposing view: each instruction is equally accessible to result packets generated by any other instruction, regardless of where they reside in the machine.[22,23] The structure of this machine is shown in Figure 13. The heart of this architecture is a large set of instruction cells, each of which holds one activity template of a data flow program. Result packets arrive at instruction cells from the distribution network. Each instruction cell sends an operation packet to the arbitration network when all operands and signals have been received. The function of the

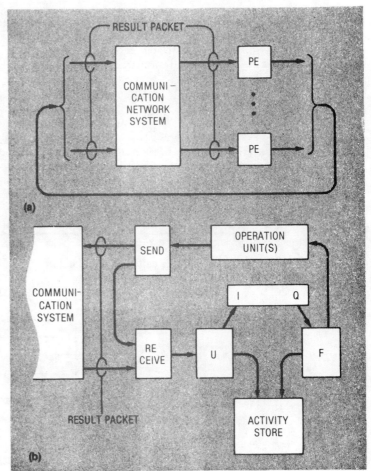

Figure 11. Data flow multiprocessor: (a) connection of many processing elements through a communication system; (b) relationship of each PE to the communication system.

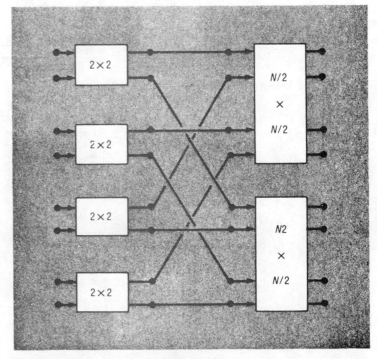

Figure 12. Routing network structure.

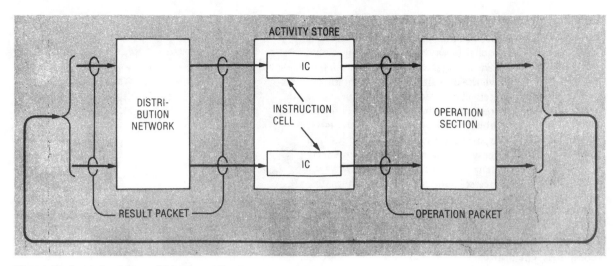

Figure 13. Genesis of the cell block architecture.

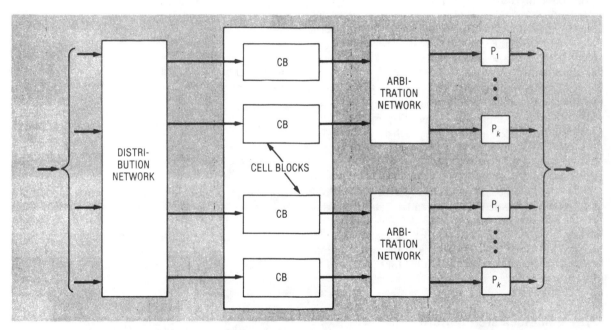

Figure 14. Practical form of the cell block architecture.

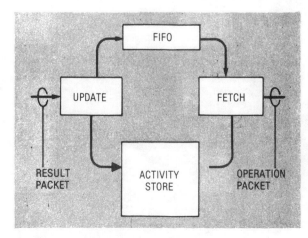

Figure 15. Cell block implementation.

operation section is to execute instructions and to forward result packets to target instructions by way of the distribution network.

The design in Figure 13 is impractical if the instruction cells are fabricated as individual physical units, since the number of devices and interconnections would be enormous. A more attractive structure is obtained if the instruction cells are grouped into blocks and each block realized as a single device. Such an instruction cell block has a single input port for result packets and a single output port for operation packets. Thus one cell block unit replaces many instruction cells and the associated portion of the distribution network. Moreover, a byte-serial format for result and operation packets further reduces the number of interconnections between cell blocks and other units.

The resulting structure is shown in Figure 14. Here, several cell blocks are served by a shared group of functional units $P_i, \ldots, P_k$. The arbitration network in each section of the machine passes each operation packet to the appropriate functional unit according to its opcode. The number of functional unit types in such a machine is likely to be small (four, for example), or just one universal functional unit type might be provided, in which case the arbitration network becomes trivial.

The relationship between the cell block architecture and the basic mechanism described earlier becomes clear when one considers how a cell block unit would be constructed. As shown in Figure 15, a cell block would include storage for activity templates, a buffer store for addresses of enabled instructions, and control units to receive result packets and transmit operation packets. These control units are functionally equivalent to the fetch and update units of the basic mechanism. The cell block differs from the basic data flow processing element in that the cell block contains no functional units, and there is no shortcut for result packets destined for successor instructions held in the same cell block.

Discussion and conclusions

In the cell block architecture, communication of a result packet from one instruction to its successor is equally easy (or equally difficult, depending on your point of view) regardless of how the two instructions are placed within the entire activity store of the machine. Thus the programmer need not be concerned that his program might run slowly due to an unfortunate distribution of instructions in the activity store address space. In fact, a random allocation of instructions may prove to be adequate.

In the data flow multiprocessor, communication between two instructions is much quicker if these instructions are allocated to the same processing element. Thus a program may run much faster if its instructions are clustered to minimize communication traffic between clusters and each cluster is allocated to one processing element. Since it will be handling significantly less packet traffic, the communication network of the data flow multiprocessor will be simpler and less expensive than the distribution network in the cell block architecture. Whether the cost reduction justifies the additional programming effort is a matter of debate, contingent on the area of application, the technology of fabrication, and the time frame under consideration.

Although the routing networks in the two forms of data flow processor have a much more favorable growth of logic complexity ($N \log N$) with increasing size than the switching networks of conventional multiprocessor systems, their growth is still more than linear. Moreover, in all suggested physical structures for $N \times N$ routing networks, the complexity as measured by total wire length grows as $O(N^2)$. This fact shows that interconnection complexity still places limits on the size of practical multi-unit systems which support universal intercommunication. If we need still larger systems, it appears we must settle for arrangements of units that only support com-munication with immediate neighbors.

The advantage data flow architectures have over other approaches to high-performance computation is that the scheduling and synchronization of concurrent activities are built in at the hardware level, enabling each instruction execution to be treated as an independent concurrent action. This allows efficient fine grain parallelism, which is precluded when the synchronization and scheduling functions are realized in software or microcode. Furthermore, there are well-defined rules for translating high-level programs into data flow machine code.

What are the prospects for data flow supercomputers? Machines based on either of the two architectures presented in this paper could be built today. A machine having up to 512 processing elements or cell blocks seems feasible. For example, a 4×4 router for packets, each sent as a series of 8-bit bytes, could be fabricated as a 100-pin LSI device, and fewer than one thousand of these devices could interconnect 512 processing elements or cell blocks. If each processing unit could operate at two million instructions per second, the goal of a billion instructions per second would be achieved.

Yet there are problems to be solved and issues to be addressed. It is difficult to see how data flow computers could support programs written in Fortran without restrictions on and careful tailoring of the code. Study is just beginning on applicative languages like Val and ID.[24,25] These promise solutions to the problems of mapping high-level programs into machine-level programs that effectively utilize machine resources, but much remains to be done. Creative research is needed to handle data structures in a manner consistent with principles of data flow computation. These are among the problems under study in our data flow project at MIT. ∎

Acknowledgment

This paper is based on research supported by the Lawrence Livermore National Laboratory of the University of California under contract 8545403.

References

1. J.B. Dennis, "On the Design and Specification of a Common Base Language," *Proc. Symp. Computers and Automata,* Polytechnic Press, Polytechnic Institute of Brooklyn, Apr. 1971, pp. 47-74.

2. Arvind, K.P. Gostelow, and W. Plouffe, *An Asynchronous Programming Language and Computing Machine,* Dept. of Information and Computer Science, University of California, Irvine, Technical Report 114a, Dec. 1978, 97 pp.

3. W.B. Ackerman and J.B. Dennis, *VAL: A Value Oriented Algorithmic Language, Preliminary Reference Manual,* Laboratory for Computer Science, MIT, Technical Report TR-218, June 1979, 80 pp.

4. J.R. McGraw, *Data Flow Computing: The VAL Language,* submitted for publication.

5. R.R. Seeber and A.B. Lindquist, "Associative Logic for Highly Parallel Systems," *AFIPS Conf. Proc,* 1963, pp. 489-493.

6. R.M. Shapiro, H. Saint, and D.L. Presberg, *Representation of Algorithms as Cyclic Partial Orderings,* Applied Data Research, Wakefield, Mass., Report CA-7112-2711, Dec. 1971.

7. J.B. Dennis, "First Version of a Data Flow Procedure Language," *Lecture Notes in Computer Sci.,* Vol. 19, Springer-Verlag, 1974, pp. 362-376.

8. J.E. Rodriguez, *A Graph Model for Parallel Computation,* Laboratory for Computer Science, MIT, Technical Report TR-64, Sept. 1969, 120 pp.

9. D.A. Adams, *A Computation Model With Data Flow Sequencing,* Computer Science Dept., School of Humanities and Sciences, Stanford University, Technical Report CS 117, Dec. 1968, 130 pp.

10. R.M. Karp and R.E. Miller, "Properties of a Model for Parallel Computations: Determinacy, Termination, Queueing," *SIAM J. Applied Math.,* Vol. 14, Nov. 1966, pp. 1390-1411.

11. J.D. Brock and L.B. Montz, "Translation and Optimization of Data Flow Programs," *Proc. 1979 Int'l Conf. on Parallel Processing,* Bellaire, Mich., Aug. 1979, pp. 46-54.

12. W.B. Ackerman, "Data Flow Languages," *AFIPS Conf. Proc.,* Vol. 48, 1979 NCC, New York, June 1979, pp. 1087-1095.

13. M. Cornish, private communication, Texas Instruments Corp., Austin, Tex.

14. J.E. Rumbaugh, "A Data Flow Multiprocessor," *IEEE Trans. Computers,* Vol. C-26, No. 2, Feb. 1977, pp. 138-146.

15. I. Watson and J. Gurd, "A Prototype Data Flow Computer With Token Labelling," *AFIPS Conf. Proc.,* 1979 NCC, New York, June 1979, pp. 623-628.

16. A. Davis, "A Data Flow Evaluation System Based on the Concept of Recursive Locality," *AFIPS Conf. Proc.,* Vol. 48, 1979 NCC, New York, June 1979, pp. 1079-1086.

17. A. Despain and D. Patterson, "X-Tree: A Tree Structured Multi-Processor Computer Architecture," *Proc. Fifth Annual Symp. Computer Architecture,* Apr. 1978, pp. 144-150.

18. R.M. Keller, G. Lindstrom, and S.S. Patil, "A Loosely-Coupled Applicative Multi-processing System," *AFIPS Conf. Proc.,* 1979 NCC, New York, June 1979, pp. 613-622.

19. C. Leung, *On a Design Methodology for Packet Communication Architectures Based on a Hardware Design Language,* submitted for publication.

20. A.R. Tripathi and G.J. Lopovski, "Packet Switching in Banyan Networks," *Proc. Sixth Annual Symp. Computer Architecture,* Apr. 1979, pp. 160-167.

21. G.A. Boughton, *Routing Networks in Packet Communication Architectures,* MS Thesis, Dept. of Electrical Engineering and Computer Science, MIT, June 1978, 93 pp.

22. J.B. Dennis and D.P. Misunas, "A Preliminary Architecture for a Basic Data-Flow Processor," *Proc. Second Annual Symp. Computer Architecture,* Houston, Tex., Jan. 1975, pp. 126-132.

23. J.B. Dennis, C.K.C. Leung, and D.P. Misunas, *A Highly Parallel Processor Using a Data Flow Machine Language,* Laboratory for Computer Science, MIT, CSG Memo 134-1, June 1979, 33 pp.

24. Arvind and R.E. Bryant, "Design Considerations for a Partial Differential Equation Machine," *Proc. Computer Information Exchange Meeting,* Livermore, Calif., Sept. 1979, pp. 94-102.

25. L. Montz, *Safety and Optimization Transformation for Data Flow Programs,* MS Thesis, MIT, Dept. of Electrical Engineering and Computer Science, Feb. 1980, 77 pp.

Jack B. Dennis, professor of electrical engineering and computer science at MIT, leads the Computation Structures Group of MIT's Laboratory for Computer Science, which is developing language-based computer system architectures that exploit high levels of concurrency through use of data flow principles. Associated with the laboratory since its inception in 1963 as Project MAC, Dennis assisted in the specification of advanced computer hardware for timesharing and was responsible for the development of one of the earliest timeshared computer installations.

Dennis received his DSc degree in electrical engineering from MIT in 1958. He is a member of Eta Kappa Nu, Tau Beta Pi, and Sigma Xi, and is a fellow of the IEEE.

ARTICLES

THE MANCHESTER PROTOTYPE DATAFLOW COMPUTER

The Manchester project has developed a powerful dataflow processor based on dynamic tagging. This processor is large enough to tackle realistic applications and exhibits impressive speedup for programs with sufficient parallelism.

J. R. GURD, C. C. KIRKHAM, and I. WATSON

INTRODUCTION

Since about 1970 there has been a growing and widespread research interest in parallel data-driven computation and dataflow computer architecture. Centers of expertise in dataflow techniques have emerged at MIT in the United States, CERT-ONERA in France, NTT and ETL in Japan, and the authors' establishment in the United Kingdom. This interest has culminated in many designs for data-driven computer systems, several of which have been or are in the process of being implemented in hardware. For example, a machine based on the tagged-token model of dataflow computation has been operational at the University of Manchester since October 1981. This article reviews the architecture and performance of this machine.

Dataflow is a technique for specifying computations in a two-dimensional graphical form: Instructions that are available for concurrent execution are written alongside one another, and instructions that must be executed in sequence are written one under the other. Data dependencies between individual instructions are indicated by directed arcs, as shown for a small program in Figure 1. Instructions do not reference memory, since the data-dependence arcs allow data to be transmitted directly from generating instruction to subsequent instruction. Consequently, instructions can be viewed as pure operations—this perspective is described in the Dataflow Programs section. Each instruction can be activated independently by incoming data values: Execution commences as soon as all required input values for that instruction have arrived (as in the execution sequence of Figure 4).

Dataflow systems implement this abstract graphical model of computation. Individual systems differ mainly in the way they handle reentrant code. Static systems do not permit concurrent reactivation, and so they are restricted to implementing loops and cannot accommodate recursion. Dynamic systems permit recursive reactivation, either by code-copying or by tagging, at every occurrence of reentry. The nature of a system determines the types of language features that can be supported—recursion, for example, *cannot* be handled by static systems. The structure of a dataflow computer follows the model of message-passing multiprocessors. The Manchester project has designed a powerful dataflow processing engine based on dynamic tagging. The system is now running reasonably large user programs at maximum rates of between 1 and 2 MIPS (million instructions per second). Details on the architecture of this system are given in The Manchester Dataflow Processor section.

To date, few details have been published on the performance of operational dataflow hardware—after all, only a few of the larger systems have been active for longer than a year. Skepticism about the potential of dataflow techniques will persist until good performance figures can be demonstrated. First attempts have been made to define the objectives for performance evaluation for dataflow hardware, and some preliminary results from the Manchester prototype system are presented here. The strategy for evaluation is presented in the System Evaluation Strategy section, along with a discussion of program characteristics and their measurement on a dataflow simulator. The Benchmark Process section presents some details of the benchmark pro-

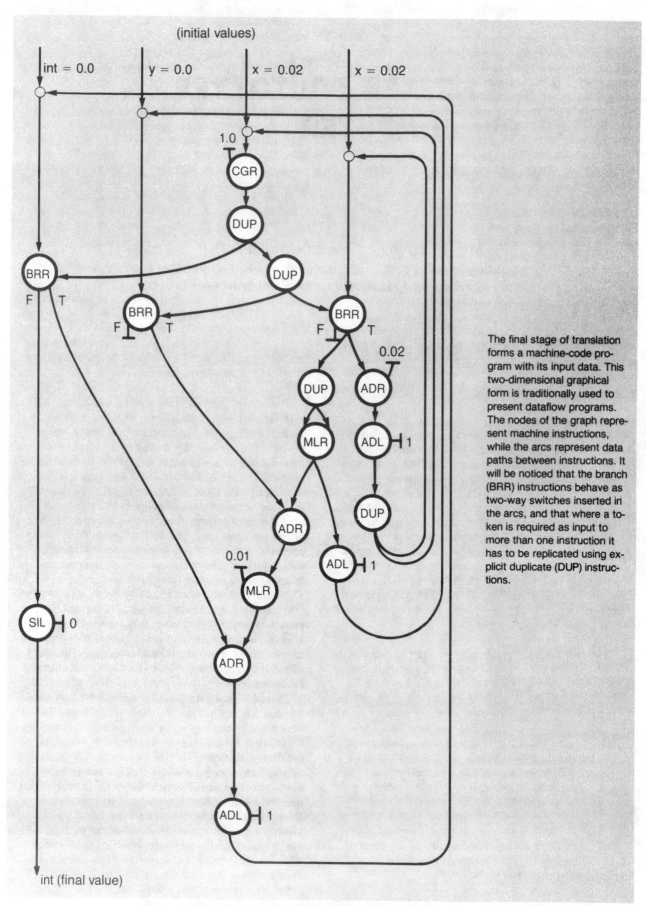

(initial values)

int = 0.0   y = 0.0   x = 0.02   x = 0.02

The final stage of translation forms a machine-code program with its input data. This two-dimensional graphical form is traditionally used to present dataflow programs. The nodes of the graph represent machine instructions, while the arcs represent data paths between instructions. It will be noticed that the branch (BRR) instructions behave as two-way switches inserted in the arcs, and that where a token is required as input to more than one instruction it has to be replicated using explicit duplicate (DUP) instructions.

int (final value)

FIGURE 1. Dataflow Graph for the Integration Program

grams that have been executed, and the Evaluation Results section presents the results obtained when these programs were executed on the prototype hardware.

Programs with large data structures have revealed that there is a need for hardware with specialized structure-storing capabilities. A structure-store unit is being designed to accommodate this need. In the long term, the use of multiple rings opens the possibility of incrementally expandable computing power in a dataflow multiprocessor. The prospects for such extensions to the existing system are discussed in the Future Directions section.

DATAFLOW PROGRAMS

Dataflow programs can be written at a high, an intermediate, or a low level. Figure 2 shows a program for computing the area under the curve $y = x^2$ between $x = 0.0$ and $x = 1.0$. It is written in the high-level single-assignment language SISAL, a typical Pascal-like dataflow language. SISAL's single-assignment property dictates that each variable be assigned only once in a program. This gives the language cleaner-than-usual semantics and makes it easier for the compiler to exploit program parallelism. Of course, parallelism could be extracted from programs written in more conventional languages, but the extraction process would be complex

```
export Integrate

function Integrate (returns real)

for initial
      int := 0.0;
      y   := 0.0;
      x   := 0.02
while
      x < 1.0
repeat
      int := 0.01 * (old y + y);
      y   := old x * old x;
      x   := old x + 0.02
returns
      value of sum int
end for

end function
```

Dataflow applications programs can be written in high-level programming languages in exactly the same way as for conventional computer systems. The most convenient type of language for compiling dataflow code is known as a single-assignment language. This type of language has a syntax similar to that of conventional languages like Pascal but has nonsequential semantics (i.e., it offers concurrent control constructs). An example program written in the single-assignment language SISAL is shown here. The program computes the area under the curve $y = x^2$ between $x = 0.0$ and $x = 1.0$ using a trapezoidal approximation with constant x intervals of 0.02.

FIGURE 2. Integration Program in the High-Level Programming Language SISAL

and would obscure important principles that are naturally apparent in SISAL.

Compilation of the high-level programs first translates the text into an intermediate-level (or compiler target) language roughly equivalent to a conventional macroassembler language. Figure 3 shows an abbreviated form of the intermediate code produced by the SISAL compiler for the program in Figure 2. Here, the template assembler language TASS is used. The main features of the translated program are that the variables (*int*, *y*, *x*, etc.) can be identified with the SISAL program text, whereas the operators (CGR, SIL, BRR, etc.) can be identified with the dataflow instruction set. The abbreviated form of Figure 3 is for the sake of clarity, because the "invented" variables would normally be given unintelligible names and a lot of redundant assembler code would be produced. In essence, Figure 3 shows the form of a program written directly at the intermediate level.

The final step of the compilation is to generate code and data files representing the machine-level program. Manchester machine code is relocatable via a segment table (see the next section) that identifies a base address and limiting offset for each of 64 code segments. Consequently, the code file contains segment table entries as well as the instruction store contents. Each instruction comprises an opcode and a destination address for the instruction output, together with an optional second destination address or a literal operand. The data file contains the initializing values, which represent the program input. Each entry consists of a typed data value and a three-field tag, together with the destination address to which the input should be sent.

Code at any level can be represented graphically, since statements specify paths to be followed by data passing between operators. In particular, it is traditional to represent the machine-level code as a directed graph. Figure 1 shows the machine code generated for the integration program in Figure 3.

The integration program is an example of a reentrant program—that is, one that reuses part of itself. Each separate iteration reuses the same code but with different data. To avoid any confusion of operands from the different iterations, each data value is *tagged* with a unique identifier known as the *iteration level* that indicates its specific iteration. Data are transmitted along the arcs in tagged packets known as *tokens*. Tokens for the same instruction match together and instigate the execution of that instruction only if their tags match.

The idea of tags can be extrapolated to encompass reentrant activation of complete procedures, thereby allowing concurrent executions of the same procedure to share one version of its instruction code. This is achieved by extending the tag with an *activation name*, which must also match. The activation name is also used to implement recursive functions, which need tags to generate a parallel environment analogous to the "stack" environment used in sequential language implementations.

```
(\I "TASS" "TSM");

!    Integration by trapezoidal rule
!    ================================

!    initialize the loop variables
int      = (Data "R 0.0");
y        = (Data "R 0.0");
x        = (Data "R 0.02");

!    merge the initial values with the loop output values
int_mrg  = (Mer int new_int);
y_mrg    = (Mer y new_y);
x_mrg    = (Mer x new_x);

!    test for termination of loop
test     = (CGR "R 1.0" x_mrg);

!    gate the loop variables into new loop instance or direct result to output
gate_int = (BRR int_mrg test);
old_int  = gate_int.R;
old_y    = (BRR y_mrg test).R;
old_x    = (BRR x_mrg test).R;

result   = (SIL gate_int.L "O 0").L;

!    loop body : form new values for loop variables
incr_x   = (ADR old_x "R 0.02");
x_sq     = (MLR old_x old_x);
height_2 = (ADR old_y x_sq);
area     = (MLR "R 0.01" height_2);
cum_area = (ADR old_int area);

!              : increment iteration level for new loop variables
new_int  = (ADL cum_area "I 1").L;
new_y    = (ADL x_sq "I 1").L;
new_x    = (ADL incr_x "I 1").L;

!    output the final value of int
         (OPT result "G 0");

(Finish);
```

Programs written in SISAL are translated into an intermediate language such as TASS. Other high-level languages can be translated into this intermediate form, or programs may be written in TASS directly. For simplicity, the version of the integration program shown here is not a compiled version of the SISAL program in Figure 2, but an assembly-level program for the same task. However, the influence of the high-level version can be seen in the shape of this lower level program. The Manchester dataflow machine code is used in this figure. The Manchester system is an example of a "tagged-token" dataflow machine, which uses tag fields to distinguish reentrant activations of shared code. The "iteration-level" tag field is used to separate loop activations,

using the ADL and SIL instructions. The effect of program "jumps" is achieved by the branch instructions. The remaining instructions are normal arithmetic/logic operations. The following mnemonics have been used:

ADR—add floating-point values
BRR—branch
CGR—compare floating point l.h. > r.h.
ADL—add to iteration level
MLR—multiply floating-point values
OPT—send output to host processor
SIL—set iteration level

FIGURE 3.   Integration Program in the Template Assembly Language TASS

A final cause of reactivation is the reuse of code to process different parts of a data structure, for instance, an array. This is achieved by another extension to the tag, known as the *index.*

The above model of computation is known as tagged-token dataflow. It is the basic model implemented by the prototype Manchester hardware. Note, for example, the use of the tag-manipulating instructions ADL (add

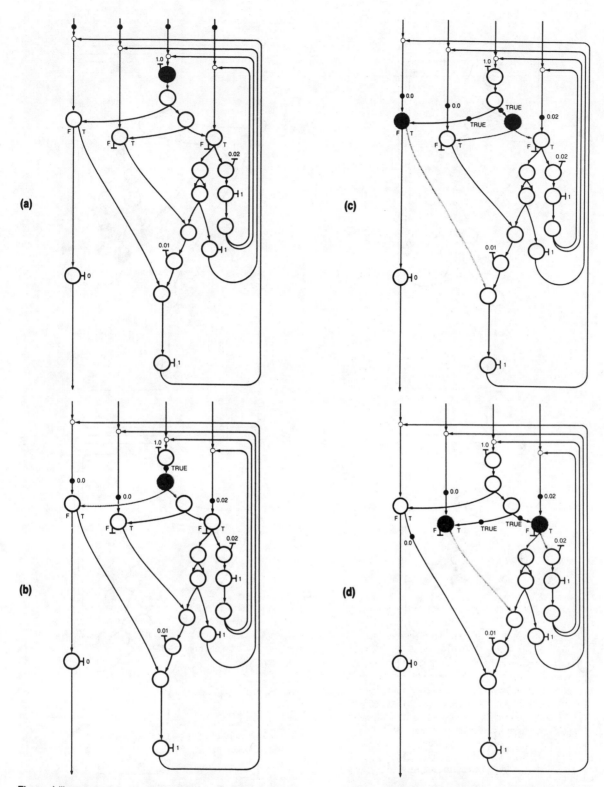

(a)

(b)

(c)

(d)

Figure 4 illustrates the way data appear to flow through the program graph during execution of the machine code. At the start of execution, the input data are presented in the form of data packets, known as tokens, on the input arcs of the graph. Execution then proceeds by transferring each token to the head of the arc on which it lies and executing any instruction that thereby receives a full complement of input tokens. The active arcs in each frame are shown in red, whereas the enabled instructions (i.e., those with a full complement of input tokens) and their output arcs (which will become active in the next frame) are shown in green. The transfer and execute cycle continues as shown until the output data have been sent and there is no further activity in the graph. Each token and instruction is considered in isolation

FIGURE 4. One Possible Execution Sequence for the Dataflow Problem in Figure 1

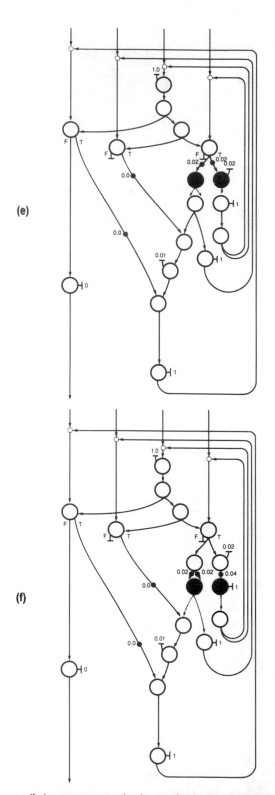

(e)

(f)

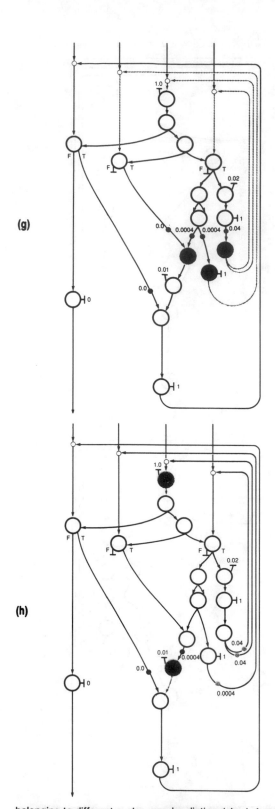

(g)

(h)

so that program execution is completely asynchronous. The required synchronization between communicating instructions is achieved by delaying execution of each instruction until all its input data are available. The process of determining that the input is ready is known as token-matching. At the end of each cycle of the program loop, the ADL instructions increment the iteration-level tag field so that tokens

belonging to different cycles may be distinguished. A useful way of visualizing the effect of this operation is to imagine that each value of iteration level "colors" the tokens uniquely, so that only like-colored tokens can match with one another. This is illustrated by the tokens turning from black to blue as they pass from the first to the second iteration.

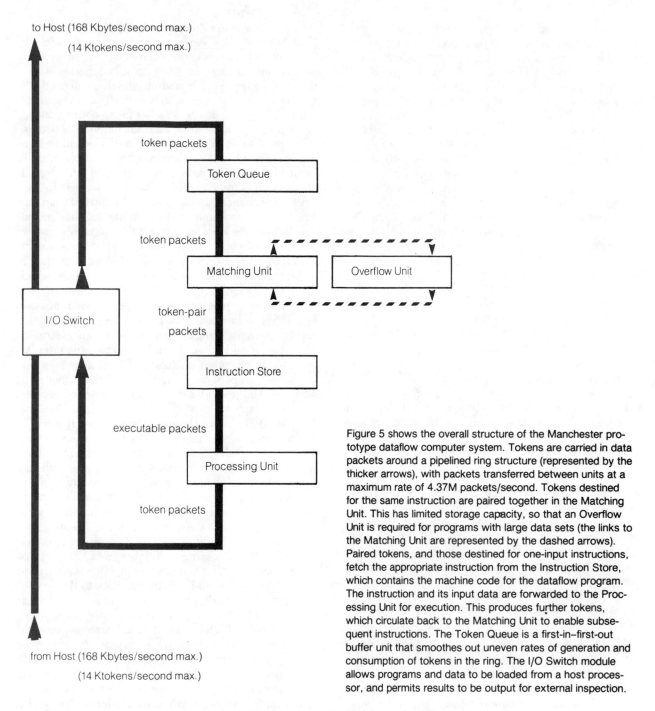

to Host (168 Kbytes/second max.)

(14 Ktokens/second max.)

token packets

Token Queue

token packets

Matching Unit

Overflow Unit

I/O Switch

token-pair
packets

Instruction Store

executable packets

Processing Unit

token packets

from Host (168 Kbytes/second max.)

(14 Ktokens/second max.)

Figure 5 shows the overall structure of the Manchester prototype dataflow computer system. Tokens are carried in data packets around a pipelined ring structure (represented by the thicker arrows), with packets transferred between units at a maximum rate of 4.37M packets/second. Tokens destined for the same instruction are paired together in the Matching Unit. This has limited storage capacity, so that an Overflow Unit is required for programs with large data sets (the links to the Matching Unit are represented by the dashed arrows). Paired tokens, and those destined for one-input instructions, fetch the appropriate instruction from the Instruction Store, which contains the machine code for the dataflow program. The instruction and its input data are forwarded to the Processing Unit for execution. This produces further tokens, which circulate back to the Matching Unit to enable subsequent instructions. The Token Queue is a first-in-first-out buffer unit that smoothes out uneven rates of generation and consumption of tokens in the ring. The I/O Switch module allows programs and data to be loaded from a host processor, and permits results to be output for external inspection.

FIGURE 5. Manchester Dataflow System Structure

to iteration level) and SIL (set iteration level) in Figure 1 to ensure correct queuing of the loop termination control tokens at the inputs to the BRR (branch) instructions. Note also the use of explicit DUP (duplicate) instructions to replicate data required at two or more subsequent instructions. In order to limit the size of instructions, the Manchester system imposes a maximum fan-out from each instruction of two. Chains of duplicates can be used for larger fan-out. In some circumstances it is possible for a subsequent duplicate to

be incorporated into the preceeding instruction (as in Figure 1 for the top-most MLR instruction). The maximum possible number of inputs to an instruction is also two; this has to do with the way tokens traveling to the same instance of an instruction are matched together. Manchester instructions are thus monadic or dyadic only. Certain monadic instructions are formed by dyadic operators with one fixed (literal) input (as also shown in Figure 1).

The BRR (branch) instructions act as "switches" in

the arcs of program graphs and are used to implement conditionals, loops, and recursion. Each branch is controlled by a Boolean control input, which is shown entering the instruction from the side (usually, but not necessarily, the right-hand side). If the value of the token on this input is false, then the other incoming token (on the top input) is sent down the left-hand output (labeled F in Figure 1); otherwise the control is true, and the other input token is sent down the right-hand output (labeled T). Note that branch instructions can be used as "gates" that pass a value or destroy it, according to the Boolean control value, by leaving one of the output arcs unused (as also shown).

The process of executing a machine-level program is started by placing tokens representing the initial data values onto the input arcs of the program graph. Execution then proceeds by repeated application of the following graph execution rules:

1. Tokens travel (at any finite speed) toward the head of the arc on which they lie,
2. any instruction that has tokens ready at the head of all of its input arcs becomes enabled (i.e., ready to execute),
3. any enabled instruction may start execution as soon as there is a free instruction processor, and
4. executing instructions place output on their output arc(s) before terminating and releasing their processor for further executions (outputs from separate processors may be interleaved in any order).

Figure 4, on pages 38–39, illustrates the first steps of one possible execution sequence, based on these rules, for the dataflow program in Figure 1. In this sequence it is assumed that a large number of instruction processors are available so that all possible enabled instructions are executed simultaneously. It is also assumed that each instruction executes in one time step, regardless of the operation being performed. Different assumptions would produce alternative sequences of execution, but the same end results would always be produced. The way data seem to flow through the program graph during execution gives rise to the term "dataflow."

THE MANCHESTER DATAFLOW PROCESSOR

A block diagram of the prototype Manchester dataflow system is shown in Figure 5 on the preceding page. Figure 6a, on page 45, is a photograph of the system. The basic structure is a ring of four modules connected to a host system via an I/O Switch module. The modules operate independently in a pipelined fashion. Tokens are encapsulated in data packets that circulate around the ring. Token packets destined for the same instruction are paired together in the Matching Unit. This unit is organized as a two-tiered hierarchy with a separate Overflow Unit to handle large data sets. Paired tokens, and those destined for one-input instructions, fetch the appropriate instruction from the Instruction Store, which contains the machine-code for the executing program. The instruction is forwarded together with

its input data to the Processing Unit, where it is executed. Output tokens are eventually produced and transmitted back toward the Matching Unit to enable subsequent instructions. The return path passes through the I/O Switch module, which connects the system to a host processor, and to the Token Queue, which is a first-in–first-out buffer for smoothing out uneven rates of generation and consumption of tokens.

The ring modules are independently clocked and are interconnected via asynchronous links capable of transferring large data packets at rates up to 10 million packets per second (represented by the thick arrows in Figure 5). This bandwidth is considerably higher than any that has been required by the modules yet constructed. The links to the Host system and the Overflow Unit are slower by a factor of about 500, although they are to be upgraded in the near future. The I/O Switch module is organized as a simple 2×2 common bus switch, which gives priority to input from the ring and selects the output route by performing a decode of certain marker bits. It has an internal clock period of 50 ns and is capable of transferring up to 5 million tokens/second. This rate is higher than the normal processing rates achieved by the other modules in the ring.

Figure 7, on page 46, illustrates the Token Queue and Matching Unit modules in detail. Figure 6b, on page 45, is a photograph of the Matching Unit module. The Token Queue comprises three pipeline buffer registers and a circular buffer memory. The token packets contained in the registers and store are 96 bits wide. The circular memory has a capacity of 32K tokens with 120 ns access time. The clock period is 37.5 ns, giving a maximum throughput of 2.67 million tokens/second. This is roughly equivalent to the processing rates achieved by the remaining ring modules. The discrepancies between the different module rates are due to the different engineering techniques used.

The Matching Unit contains six pipeline registers, a parallel hash table, and a 16-bit interface to the Overflow Unit. Each hash table board comprises a 64 Ktoken memory plus a 54-bit tag/destination comparator and interface control. There are 16 such boards at present, providing a 1Mtoken capacity, with space for expansion up to 1.25M tokens. Incoming tokens have a 16-bit hash function computed on their tag and destination fields as they are passed to the hash buffer register. The computed value is subsequently used to address the parallel hash table memory banks. Each bank compares its tag and destination contents with those of the incoming token, and a match causes the data field of the matching hash location to be output to the store buffer register along with the incoming token. The resultant token-pair packet is 133 bits wide, as shown in Figure 7. If there is no match between a stored token and the incoming token, the incoming token is written into the first free location accessed by that hash address. Overflows occur when all the accessed locations are occupied, in which case the nonmatching incoming token is sent to the Overflow Unit and indicator flags are set to notify subsequent tokens of this. Tokens that are destined for one-input instructions (such as "DUP" and

Pby	0.00	0.10	0.20	0.30	0.40	0.50	0.60	0.70	0.80	0.90	1.00
Match rate (million matches/ second)	1.11	1.21	1.32	1.46	1.63	1.85	2.14	2.53	3.09	3.97	5.56

"SIL literal 0" in Figure 1) do not need to find partners and therefore bypass the hash memory access. Although bypass tokens do not search for a partner, each is counted as performing a "match" action in determining the processing rate of the Matching Unit.

The Matching Unit clock period is 180 ns, with a memory cycle time of 160 ns, giving "match" rates of 1.11 million matches/second for dyadic operators and 5.56 million bypasses/second for monadic operators. The average match rate thus depends on the proportion of executed instructions that receive only one input token. This proportion is known as the Pby (the proportion of bypass matching operations—see also the Program Characteristics section). Table I lists the maximum average match rates against the Pby (note that, in practice, the Pby is in the range 0.55 to 0.70).

The Overflow Unit is currently emulated by software in a microcomputer attached to the overflow interface. A special-purpose microcoded processor is under construction following the design shown in Figure 7. It will have an initial capacity of 32 Ktokens and will use linked lists accessed by a hash lookup. The target microcycle period is 250 ns, for a processing rate of up to 1 million matches/second.

Figure 8, on page 47, shows the detailed structure of the Instruction Store and Processing Unit modules. Figure 6c, on page 45, is a photograph of a typical board. The Instruction Store comprises two pipeline buffer registers, a segment lookup table, and a random-access instruction store to hold the program. The segment field of the incoming token-pair is used to access a segment descriptor from the segment table. This descriptor contains a base address for the segment and a maximum limit for offsets within the segment. The offset field of the incoming token is added to the base address and, provided the limit is not violated, the resulting address is used to access the instruction from the store. The instruction contents are 70 bits wide, as shown in Figure 8, and are substituted for the destination field of the input token-pair to form a 166-bit executable instruction package. This package is then forwarded for processing. The clock period for the Instruction Store is 40 ns, with a store access time of 150 ns, giving a maximum processing rate of 2 million instruction fetches per second.

The Processing Unit comprises five pipeline buffer registers, a special-purpose preprocessor, and a parallel array of up to 20 homogeneous microcoded function units with local buffer registers and common buses for input and output. The preprocessor executes those few global operations that cannot be distributed among the function units. These occur infrequently compared with the general opcodes, which pass straight through the preprocessor to be distributed to the first available function unit via the distribution bus. Each function unit contains a microcoded bit-slice processor with input and output buffering, 51 internal registers, and 4K words of writable microcode memory. The internal word length is 24 bits, with facilities for microcoding 32-bit floating-point arithmetic. Microinstructions are 48 bits wide. The function units compete to transmit their output onto the arbitration bus and thence out of the module. The Processing Unit clock has a period of 57 ns. The function unit microcycle period is 229 ns. The minimum time required to transmit 96 bits through a function unit is 13 microcycles, and the shortest instruction execution time (for DUP with one output) is 16 microcycles. This leads to a maximum instruction execution rate of 0.27 MIPS per function unit. To date, 14 function units have been used successfully to achieve processing rates of up to 2 MIPS (see the Evaluation Results section). With this complement of function units, the total software parallelism required to keep all the hardware busy is about 35-fold.

It will be noted that the host and overflow systems are much slower than the dataflow ring. This has had two ramifications: Either overflow of the matching store capacity or interaction with the host processor leads to a substantial drop in performance.

At present, the sole measurement that can be made of the system is of the interval between program start and the arrival at the host of the first output token. Programs are loaded in advance of their initial data. The data are then queued in the Token Queue, where reads are disabled until the last input token has been transmitted from the host. At this point Token Queue reads are enabled, and timing commences in the host: It will be halted by the first arrival from the output port of the Switch. Benchmark programs are usually organized to produce a single output token right at the end of their execution. By repeatedly running each program with different numbers of active function units, the speedup efficiency of the system can be assessed, as illustrated in The Benchmark Process section.

SYSTEM EVALUATION STRATEGY

There are three objectives for evaluation of the prototype hardware:

1. to tune the prototype hardware for optimum performance,
2. to determine the nature of software parallelism that

can be effectively exploited by the hardware, and
3. to determine the relative value of dataflow MIPS (compared to conventional MIPS).

The nature of the prototype hardware indicates that a three-phase approach to evaluation might be appropriate. The first phase is to assess performance for those programs that are small enough to execute entirely within the matching store limit (i.e., which do not generate overflow requests). This is the phase reported below. It comprises three subphases:

1. plotting speedup curves,
2. interpreting the results, and
3. rectifying any discovered hardware problems.

The second evaluation phase will involve analysis of programs that generate moderate amounts of overflow. Bottlenecks in the overflow loop will eventually be identified and subsequently rectified, although this cannot be undertaken with the existing overflow processor system. The third phase involves the development of a hierarchical memory to cope with programs that generate enormous quantities of overflow. This is regarded as a longer term objective, which will be addressed initially through the Structure Store Unit discussed in the Future Directions section.

For the evaluation that follows, analysis is restricted to overflow-free programs, although many other characteristics of the codes have been varied. These characteristics were measured by means of a crude software simulator for the dataflow system.

PROGRAM CHARACTERISTICS

In order to measure program characteristics, a dataflow simulator that makes many simplifying assumptions about the system architecture is used. The principal assumptions made are

1. that each instruction executes in the same time (execution therefore proceeds in discrete equal time steps),
2. that an unlimited number of function units can be used during any one time step, and
3. that output from any executed instruction can be transmitted to an enabled successor instruction within the execution time period.

Of course these are somewhat unrealistic assumptions, but they are helpful in making an approximate characterization of each program.

The two fundamental time measurements recorded for each program are S1, the total number of instructions executed (which would be the number of time steps required if only one function unit was available), and Sinf, the number of simulated time steps required (with an unlimited number of function units permanently available). The ratio S1/Sinf = avePara gives a crude measure of the average parallelism available in the program. A more comprehensive trace of the time variance of program parallelism can be obtained if needed.

The simulator also records utilization of the system memories, as follows:

Codesize = the size of the machine-code program (in 9-byte instructions),

maxTQsize = the maximum occupancy of the Token Queue circular buffer store (in 12-byte tokens), and

maxMSsize = the maximum occupancy of the Matching Store hash table (also in 12-byte tokens).

The proportion—the Pby—of executed instructions that bypass the matching store is also recorded. This corresponds to the fraction of one-input instructions executed. An important measure of performance for numerical computation is the execution rate expressed in MFLOPS (million floating-point operations per second). Different machine architectures and programming systems can be compared by measuring their respective MIPS to MFLOPS ratios. Consequently, this ratio is recorded by the simulator.

Looking at one cycle of the integration program in Figure 1, it can be easily seen that S1 = 16. It is not immediately obvious that Sinf = 7, but this can be checked by locating the longest cycle of dependent instructions (i.e., that forming the value of x, which is input to the CGR instruction). Simulation of 50 cycles (i.e., the complete program of Figure 3) gives S1 = 808 and Sinf = 356. Consequently, the average parallelism, avePara, is 2.3. The total Codesize is 17 instructions (153 bytes), maxTQsize is 5 tokens (60 bytes), and maxMSsize is 3 tokens (36 bytes). The Pby is 0.625, and the ratio MIPS/MFLOPS is 2.7 (i.e., 2.7 instructions are executed on average for every useful floating-point operation).

For comparison, the code compiled from the SISAL version of the integration program, shown in Figure 2, produces the following characteristics: S1 = 2455, Sinf = 829, avePara = 3.0, Codesize = 80 (720 bytes), maxTQsize = 11 (132 bytes), maxMSsize = 15 (180 bytes), Pby = 0.628, and the MIPS/MFLOPS ratio = 8.1. This comparison gives a rough indication of the relative efficiencies of compiled and hand-written code. For both programs, DUP (duplicate) accounts for 25 percent of all executed instructions.

THE BENCHMARK PROCESS

A total of 14 benchmark programs with 29 different input data sets has been analyzed for the following performance evaluation. The programs are listed in Table II, along with their characteristics, as measured by a simulator. A variety of problem types is represented, and several source languages have been used. MAD is a single-assignment language like SISAL, and MACRO is an intermediate-level language like TASS. The effect of program parallelism has been assessed for both similar and distinct programs. Parallelism for each particular code was varied by adjustment of the input data values. Many different patterns of time variance of parallelism

TABLE II. Approximate Characterization of the Operational Behavior of Programs

Name	Source	Codesize	S1	Sinf	avePara	Pby	maxTQsize	maxMSsize	MIPS/ FU	MIPS/ MFLOPS
LAPLACEA/1	MACRO	58	290,112	2,167	134	0.70	449	640	0.140	15.9
LAPLACEA/2	MACRO	58	567,200	2,707	210	0.70	701	1,000	0.140	15.6
SUM/1	MAD	107	30	17	2	0.67	6	4	0.165	—
SUM/2	MAD	107	402	79	5	0.62	22	41	0.170	—
SUM/3	MAD	107	1,208	120	10	0.61	56	99	0.171	—
SUM/4	MAD	107	2,820	141	20	0.61	109	220	0.172	—
SUM/5	MAD	107	9,082	182	50	0.61	418	766	0.172	—
SUM/6	MAD	107	20,428	204	100	0.61	824	1,515	0.172	—
SUM/7	MAD	107	44,980	225	200	0.61	1,626	3,293	0.172	—
SUM/8	MAD	107	123,472	247	500	0.61	6,058	11,279	0.172	—
INTEGRATE	MAD	263	2,051	166	12	0.64	41	106	0.158	39.4
FFT/1	MACRO	606	13,989	264	53	0.70	211	794	0.112	11.7
FFT/2	MACRO	606	14,086	264	53	0.70	211	794	0.112	11.7
FFT/3	MACRO	606	15,374	569	27	0.69	152	1,168	0.111	11.1
FFT/4	MACRO	606	32,661	310	105	0.70	419	1,834	0.109	11.3
MATMULT	SISAL	657	100,288	425	236	0.58	6,001	15,074	0.100	50.1
LAPLACEB	SISAL	811	191,984	915	210	0.60	1,987	15,744	0.114	37.0
PLUMBLINE1	MACRO	828	7,531	156	48	0.61	208	262	0.173	—
PLUMBLINE2	MAD	1,462	19,076	908	21	0.56	299	484	0.131	—
GAUSS	SISAL	3,201	215,723	3,620	60	0.57	1,260	18,457	0.106	—
LOGICSIM/1	MACRO	3,819	64,660	1,227	53	0.63	339	905	0.175	—
LOGICSIM/2	MACRO	3,819	348,700	5,067	69	0.63	1,779	3,785	0.175	—
SPLICE	SISAL	6,957	5,031,909	165,647	30	0.69	658	6,921	0.111	—
RSIM/1	SISAL	23,996	189,746	12,611	15	0.61	147	1,894	0.140	—
RSIM/2	SISAL	24,314	1,135,912	62,563	18	0.60	259	3,563	0.137	—
RSIM/3	SISAL	24,477	851,137	50,866	17	0.60	403	2,922	0.139	—
RSIM/4	SISAL	24,850	1,108,104	54,048	20	0.62	691	4,437	0.128	—
SIMPLE	SISAL	26,385	519,501	8,194	63	0.59	1,254	9,635	0.117	39.0
IV/1	SISAL	39,091	126,991	6,571	19	0.62	561	3,711	0.117	—

These data were obtained from software simulation of the Manchester prototype dataflow machine. The simulator imitates sequential execution of programs but also keeps track of the shortest path through the graph, making the assumption that each instruction could be executed in an identical time period. The ratio of the total number of instructions executed (S1) to the length of the shortest path (Sinf) gives a rough measure of the amount of parallelism in the graph (avePara). Store usage is recorded as the maximum simulated store requirement for the Token Queue (maxTQsize) and the Matching Store (maxMSsize), assuming that neither store overflows. The final recorded characteristic is the proportion (Pby) of one-input instructions executed, since these bypass the Matching Unit, which constitutes the major bottleneck in the ring. The variation of parallelism with time is not accounted for since it appears to be unimportant in predicting the speedup obtained when additional parallel resources are used to execute the program. The characteristics of a variety of benchmark programs that have been executed on the prototype Manchester dataflow system are listed. The smaller programs have been written in a macroassembler language, MACRO, which was a forerunner to the template assembler, TASS. The larger programs have been written in the high-level single-assignment languages MAD and SISAL. The final columns record hardware execution characteristics for the benchmark programs. The first of these (MIPS/FU) shows the average processing rate with a single active function unit. This value is related to the average number of microinstructions executed per machine instruction. Low values imply the use of many complex operators, such as the floating-point trigonometric functions. The final column (MIPS/MFLOPS) is recorded for programs that make heavy use of floating-point arithmetic and indicates the average number of instructions executed per "useful" floating-point operation.

were found. In addition, code sizes and store occupancies varied considerably. Note, however, that the Pby is in the range 0.56 to 0.70 for all programs.

As mentioned above, the only measurement that can be made on the prototype hardware is the execution time until the arrival at the host of the first output token with a given number of active function units. For n function units this time is denoted T_n, where n has been varied from 1 to 14. Knowing the simulator-derived characteristics of each program, the following quantities can be derived from the values of T_n:

$P_n = T_1/T_n$:
   the effective number of function units when n is active,

$E_n = 100P_n/n$:
   the percent utilization of n active function units,

FIGURE 6b. The Matching Unit Module

FIGURE 6a. The Manchester Prototype Dataflow Computer

FIGURE 6c. A Typical Board

$Mn = S1/Tn$:
    the actual MIP rate of n active function units, and

$Mn' = nS1/T1$:
    the potential MIP rate of n active function units.

A typical set of measurements (for the SIMPLE program) is shown in Table III.

EVALUATION RESULTS

For each program and data set run together, the values of Tn, Pn, En, Mn, and Mn' were tabulated. To interpret these values as measures of the speedup performance of the system, Pn is plotted against n, as shown in Figure 11 (for the RSIM/1 program). Notice how lines of constant function unit utilization appear on this graph. To compare the results for different kinds of programs, the results are better presented after normalization by a factor $S1/T1 = M1$. This entails plotting Mn against Mn' (actual MIPS versus potential MIPS), as also shown in Figure 9, on page 48.

The shape of the speedup curve is typical of the results obtained when parallelism in a program is limited. There is an initial portion in which speedup is nearly

TABLE III. A Typical Set of Measurements of the Execution Time that Elapses before the First Output Token Arrives at the Host

Function units (n)	Run time (seconds) (Tn)	Speedup (Pn)	Efficiency (En)	Actual MIPS (Mn)	Potential MIPS (Mn')
1	4.4215	1.00	100.0	0.117	0.117
2	2.2106	2.00	100.0	0.235	0.235
3	1.4751	3.00	99.9	0.352	0.352
4	1.1077	3.99	99.8	0.469	0.470
5	0.8886	4.98	99.5	0.585	0.587
6	0.7429	5.95	99.2	0.699	0.705
7	0.6400	6.91	98.7	0.812	0.822
8	0.5643	7.84	97.9	0.921	0.940
9	0.5071	8.72	96.9	1.024	1.057
10	0.4629	9.55	95.5	1.122	1.175
11	0.4301	10.28	93.5	1.208	1.292
12	0.4038	10.95	91.3	1.287	1.410

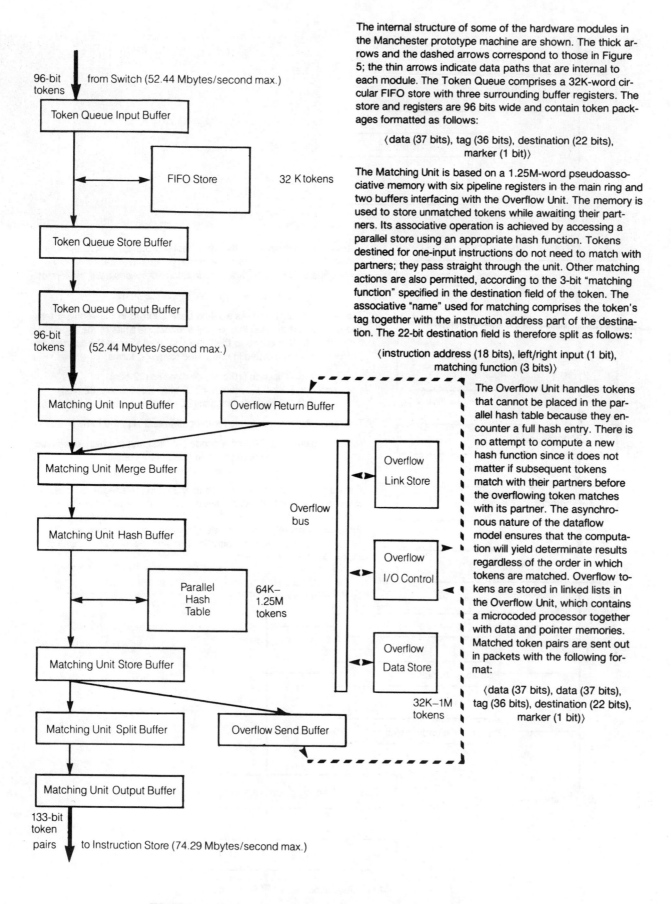

The internal structure of some of the hardware modules in the Manchester prototype machine are shown. The thick arrows and the dashed arrows correspond to those in Figure 5; the thin arrows indicate data paths that are internal to each module. The Token Queue comprises a 32K-word circular FIFO store with three surrounding buffer registers. The store and registers are 96 bits wide and contain token packages formatted as follows:

⟨data (37 bits), tag (36 bits), destination (22 bits), marker (1 bit)⟩

The Matching Unit is based on a 1.25M-word pseudoassociative memory with six pipeline registers in the main ring and two buffers interfacing with the Overflow Unit. The memory is used to store unmatched tokens while awaiting their partners. Its associative operation is achieved by accessing a parallel store using an appropriate hash function. Tokens destined for one-input instructions do not need to match with partners; they pass straight through the unit. Other matching actions are also permitted, according to the 3-bit "matching function" specified in the destination field of the token. The associative "name" used for matching comprises the token's tag together with the instruction address part of the destination. The 22-bit destination field is therefore split as follows:

⟨instruction address (18 bits), left/right input (1 bit), matching function (3 bits)⟩

The Overflow Unit handles tokens that cannot be placed in the parallel hash table because they encounter a full hash entry. There is no attempt to compute a new hash function since it does not matter if subsequent tokens match with their partners before the overflowing token matches with its partner. The asynchronous nature of the dataflow model ensures that the computation will yield determinate results regardless of the order in which tokens are matched. Overflow tokens are stored in linked lists in the Overflow Unit, which contains a microcoded processor together with data and pointer memories. Matched token pairs are sent out in packets with the following format:

⟨data (37 bits), data (37 bits), tag (36 bits), destination (22 bits), marker (1 bit)⟩

FIGURE 7. A Close-Up Look at the Token Queue, Matching Unit, and Overflow Unit

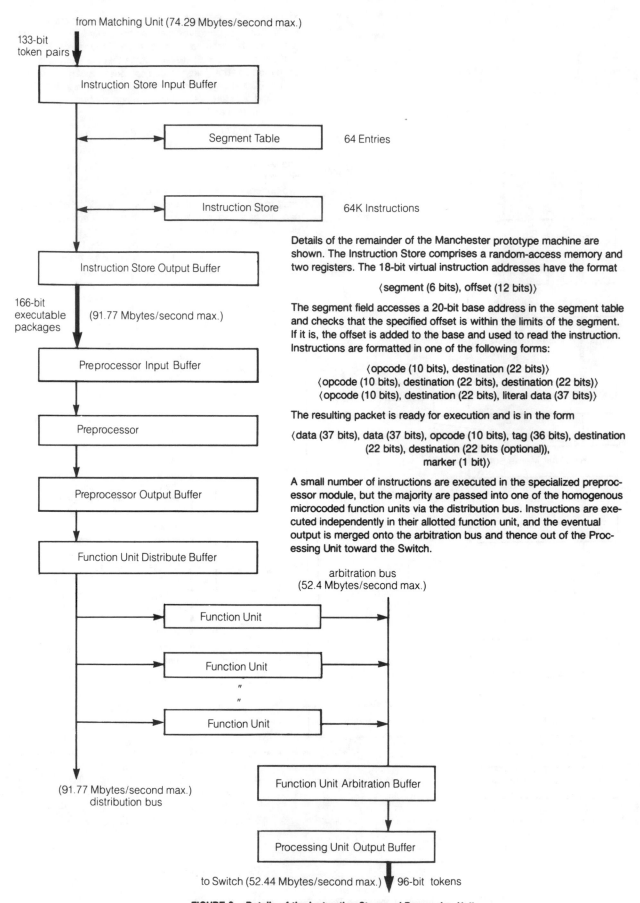

from Matching Unit (74.29 Mbytes/second max.)

133-bit
token pairs

Instruction Store Input Buffer

Segment Table — 64 Entries

Instruction Store — 64K Instructions

Instruction Store Output Buffer

166-bit
executable
packages — (91.77 Mbytes/second max.)

Preprocessor Input Buffer

Preprocessor

Preprocessor Output Buffer

Function Unit Distribute Buffer

arbitration bus
(52.4 Mbytes/second max.)

Function Unit

Function Unit

"
"

Function Unit

(91.77 Mbytes/second max.)
distribution bus

Function Unit Arbitration Buffer

Processing Unit Output Buffer

to Switch (52.44 Mbytes/second max.) 96-bit tokens

Details of the remainder of the Manchester prototype machine are shown. The Instruction Store comprises a random-access memory and two registers. The 18-bit virtual instruction addresses have the format

⟨segment (6 bits), offset (12 bits)⟩

The segment field accesses a 20-bit base address in the segment table and checks that the specified offset is within the limits of the segment. If it is, the offset is added to the base and used to read the instruction. Instructions are formatted in one of the following forms:

⟨opcode (10 bits), destination (22 bits)⟩
⟨opcode (10 bits), destination (22 bits), destination (22 bits)⟩
⟨opcode (10 bits), destination (22 bits), literal data (37 bits)⟩

The resulting packet is ready for execution and is in the form

⟨data (37 bits), data (37 bits), opcode (10 bits), tag (36 bits), destination
(22 bits), destination (22 bits (optional)),
marker (1 bit)⟩

A small number of instructions are executed in the specialized preprocessor module, but the majority are passed into one of the homogenous microcoded function units via the distribution bus. Instructions are executed independently in their allotted function unit, and the eventual output is merged onto the arbitration bus and thence out of the Processing Unit toward the Switch.

FIGURE 8. Details of the Instruction Store and Processing Unit

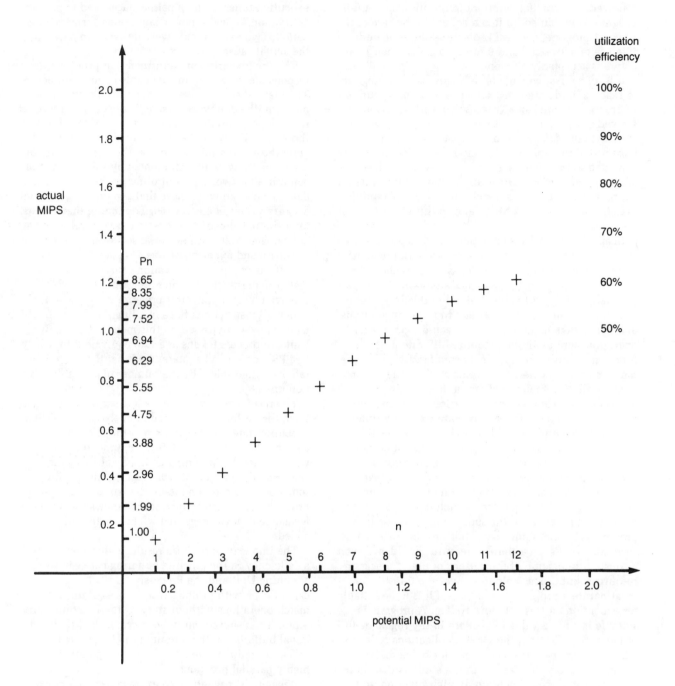

The speedup obtained when additional hardware parallelism is introduced into the prototype ring by allowing extra function units to participate in executing the program RSIM/1 is shown. The curves are obtained by measuring the execution time (Tn) associated with the use of n function units. They can be interpreted in several different ways. First, they show the effective processing rate of n function units (Pn), normal-ized so that $P1 = 1.0$. Second, they demonstrate the effi-ciency of utilization of n function units. This rate should ide-ally be constant at 100 percent to provide linear speedup as extra function units are added, but in practice it decreases as n increases. Third, the curves give the absolute processing rate (in MIPS) achieved by a system with n function units for each program.

FIGURE 9. A Plot of the Speedup Performance of the Prototype

linear in n (and where E_n is thus close to 100 percent), followed by a gradual deterioration in utilization until a program-constrained limit is reached. In the case of the RSIM/1 program, avePara is only 15-fold, so the effective use of between 8 and 9 function units when 12 are active is acceptably efficient.

It is, of course, possible for a highly parallel program to reach a hardware-constrained limit before it runs out of program parallelism. The effect of this behavior, viewed on speedup curves such as in Figure 9, will be similar to the software-limited case described above, except that the limit will be imposed by the match rate achieved in the Matching Unit, as shown in Table I. With the maximum number of function units limited to 14, program runs did not reach the current maximum match rate of around 2 MIPS, and so this effect was not observed.

In another work,[1] we have published superimposed speedup curves for many of the benchmark programs listed in the previous section. These curves show the effects of variable instruction mix and variable program parallelism. It is noticeable that when floating-point instructions (which are microcoded in the function units and hence take much longer to execute than integer operations) are used, the potential MIP rate for each function unit is correspondingly smaller. However, the major pattern to emerge from this study is the importance of the parameter avePara in determining the shape of the speedup curve for various programs. Programs with similar values of avePara exhibit virtually identical speedup curves. The higher the value, the closer the curve is to the 100 percent utilization rate. This seems to indicate that this crude approximation to the overall average parallelism of a code is all that is necessary for an accurate prediction of its speedup curve. This applies regardless of factors such as time variance of parallelism, the source language used, the proportion of one-input instructions executed, etc. It is surprising that such a simple measure should give such a constant indication of the pattern of use of processing resources, but it does help to answer the question of what nature a program has to have if it is to be suitable for execution on this dataflow system. A program is suitable if it has a value of avePara in the region of 40 or more. Significantly, the larger applications codes exhibit the same patterns as the simpler benchmarks.

Another noticeable feature of the study is that there is an unusable area of potentially high function unit utilization above an execution rate of about 1 MIPS. Since this occurs for programs with large values of avePara, it seems unlikely that this performance area has been lost because of a lack of program parallelism, and so other causes have been sought.

One suggestion is that the use of multiple-function units in a pipeline causes contention problems in the Processing Unit arbitrator and thus leads to perform-

ance degradation. Another possibility is that disparate execution times in the pipeline stages lead to pipeline "starvation," a well-known cause of performance degradation. Two experiments were designed to determine the actual cause.

The first experiment confirmed that programs are not responsible for restricting available concurrent activity. The method adopted was to take a well-understood program (the double-recursive SUM code) and force it into a highly parallel form by artificially excluding those parts known to be serial in nature. In this program the serial sections occur at the start and end of each run. They can be eliminated by subtracting the run times for two large, but different, data sets. The data sets chosen were those that generated individual avePara values of 80 and 150. The timing that results is for a simulated code that has an overall avePara value greater than 700, with no serial sections.

The second experiment was designed to eliminate the effects of pipeline starvation caused by unsatisfied match requests in the Matching Unit. This was achieved by running a test program with Pby = 1, in which all instructions have one input and the Matching Unit is always bypassed. In this mode the Matching Unit can process tokens at a rate equivalent to nearly 6 MIPS, and it can be guaranteed that the processing rate is limited solely by the number of available function units.

The results of these experiments show three things. First, the performance degradation above the 1-MIPS execution rate occurs even when the effect of serial code has been eliminated. Second, programs that always bypass the Matching Unit are able to enter the "forbidden" zone. Third, where parallelism is limited solely by software, the totally flat curves exonerate the Processing Unit arbitrator because they show that performance is never degraded when function units are added.

The implication of these results is that there must be a deficiency in the pipeline buffering between the Matching Unit and the Processing Unit. The system cannot cope with prolonged sequences of unsuccessful match operations without starving the function units of input. It has subsequently been established that additional buffering at the output of the Matching Unit significantly reduces the falloff in speedup curves for highly parallel programs.

It is not clear whether an average instruction executed in a dataflow system is more or less powerful than an average conventional instruction. This casts some doubt on the value of the MIPS rates quoted above. Consequently, the relative value of dataflow MIPS has been assessed by studying the MIPS/MFLOPS ratios obtained for various programs. These ratios have been measured for high-speed conventional systems, such as the CDC6600, CDC7600, and Cray-1, by users, such as Lawrence Livermore National Laboratory, who have large floating-point computational requirements. It has been discovered that assembly-language program-

---

[1] Gurd, J. R., and Watson, I. A preliminary evaluation of a prototype dataflow computer. In *Proceedings of the Ninth IFIPS World Computer Congress*, R.E.A. Mason, Ed. Elsevier North-Holland, New York, Sept. 1983.

mers for such systems can achieve between three and four MIPS/MFLOPS, whereas good FORTRAN compilers achieve between five and seven MIPS/MFLOPS. The corresponding ratios for the integration program of Figures 2 and 3 (2.7 for assembler and 8.1 for SISAL) indicate that the measured dataflow MIPS have the potential to match the power of conventional-sequential MIPS. However, ratios for larger SISAL programs are often much bigger than this, ranging from 20 to 50. This indicates that present compilation techniques require considerable improvement.

This opinion is reinforced by a comparison of the dataflow results with the run times achieved for conventional implementations of some of the benchmark programs described above. For example, Table IV compares the dataflow run times for the RSIM family of programs with those obtained for versions written in the C language and executed on a VAX11/780 system. It can be seen that the current SISAL/dataflow system is about five to ten times slower than the C/VAX11/780 system.

More of these direct comparisons are being made between the dataflow system and conventional machines. They involve two categories of competitive run-time measurement for a range of benchmark programs. The first category uses single-source programs, written in SISAL, to evaluate different SISAL implementations. The second allows rewriting of programs, to assess the impact of code optimization in different language systems. The most useful comparisons will be with similar-sized sequential systems, such as the VAX 11/780. The VAX SISAL compiler, expected to be ready in early 1985, will enable comprehensive single-source tests to proceed. Tests in the second category await the translation of more programs from conventional languages into SISAL.

FUTURE DIRECTIONS

For the immediate future, the results presented here should provide ample motivation for improving the efficiency of the generated code for the SISAL/dataflow system. This objective will be pursued with a combination of software and hardware enhancements to tackle inefficiencies in the compiler system and in the machine architecture. It is believed that system performance will exceed that of conventional language systems on the VAX11/780 for a variety of applications within the next year. In the longer term, it should be possible to use the extensible nature of the dataflow hardware to provide much higher computing rates by building a dataflow multiprocessor. We now consider these intended improvements and the benefits we expect them to provide. Implementation of all these various enhancements should significantly improve the SISAL/dataflow system performance reported earlier.

Improvements to the code generation system are being made by letting the SISAL compiler implementation influence the design of the dataflow instruction set. Frequently occurring combinations of instructions are being amalgamated into new "super" instructions, with attendant reduction in S1 and Sinf parameters and improved execution speed. For example, the introduction of the SAZ (set activation name and zero index) instruction reduced Codesize and S1 by about 10 percent for most programs.

Improvements can also be realized through more conventional optimization techniques, such as common subexpression elimination, removal of constants from loops, etc. Researchers at Lawrence Livermore have implemented several such optimizations for an intermediate phase of the SISAL compiler, and these also reduce Codesize and S1 by about 10 percent.

Experience with the larger benchmark programs indicates that the overhead associated with storing data structures in the Matching Unit is excessive. Each stored token carries its tag and destination individually, which leads to replication of information that should be compacted. Two schemes have been proposed to alleviate this waste. The first involves the creation of a matching store hierarchy, using a scheme analogous to a conventional paging system. This is difficult to design unless it proves consistently feasible to identify areas of locality in dataflow programs. With the present state of knowledge, this cannot be guaranteed. Consequently, an alternative scheme involving the construction of a specialized Structure Store Unit has been adopted. This unit will be attached to the processing ring by a second Switch module located between the Processing Unit and the I/O Switch. A prototype implementation should be operational early in 1985.

The effect of a Structure Store Unit on system performance has been studied using an enhanced version of the simulator described in the Program Characteristics section. The programs used were compiled from the SISAL language using a modified compiler. For a typical program, S1 is reduced by about 40 percent. Much of this improvement results from the removal of spurious parallelism, causing the overall parallelism to drop slightly.

Unfortunately, the amounts of Matching Unit and Token Queue store used are high, whether or not the Structure Store Unit is used. It is therefore important to assess matching store usage and to optimize the handling of Matching Unit overflows. Studies in this area are hampered by the slow speed of the current host system and overflow processor interfaces, and so up-

TABLE IV. Comparison of VAX and Dataflow Run Times for RSIM Programs (all run times in seconds)

Program	VAX11/780	Dataflow (1FU)	Dataflow (12FUs)
RSIM/1	0.04	1.36	0.16
RSIM/2	0.10	8.26	0.89
RSIM/3	0.08	6.12	0.68
RSIM/4	0.28	8.67	0.88

graded versions of these are being installed. A longer-term project would involve investigating more general ways of reducing the amount of matching store and Token Queue store required for a computation. This would require the design of an "intelligent" Token Queue that could schedule sections of highly parallel programs in such a way as to minimize these storage requirements. Preliminary studies of recursive divide-and-conquer algorithms indicate that there are enormous potential savings in this area.

It is not feasible to add extra function units to the Processing Unit indefinitely, since the match rate in the Matching Unit will eventually limit the processing rate. An important objective of research into dataflow architecture is thus to establish techniques for constructing and utilizing multiprocessor systems in which the matching process is distributed. In a dataflow multiprocessor, a number of processing rings are connected together via an interconnection network. The network allows any ring to send results to any other ring. The choice of network is critical to large system performance. Some networks have an equal delay for all communications; other networks penalize some transfers more than others. There is also a relationship between the power of each processor and the total size of the network. Some systems emphasize simplicity of processor design and thus require large communications nets. Other systems have powerful processors and therefore need smaller networks to achieve the same overall computing power. The Manchester system falls into the latter category.

There are no present plans to construct a Manchester multiprocessor using the present system design and technology. However, such a system would be attractive if the basic processing ring could be implemented in a higher density VLSI technology. Consequently, simulation of a multiprocessor based on the existing processing ring has been undertaken. Performance results for systems containing up to 64 processing rings have shown respectable speedups for some of the benchmark programs reported above.

The key requirement for high performance in any multiprocessor structure is uniform distribution of work across the processors. This can be achieved at compile/link time, but often requires intervention from the applications programmer and always requires knowledge of the system configuration. It is more desirable to achieve the distribution automatically, whereby the compiler/linker would not need to know the configuration. The fine grain of parallelism in dataflow would facilitate this, although other substantial problems persist. Various load/run-time "split functions" have been investigated to distribute the work load. These use hashing techniques similar to those used in the pseudoassociative Matching Unit.

It should be noted that the ability to use this kind of "randomizing," postcompilation split function constitutes the major advantage of dataflow over more conventional, coarse-grain multiprocessors. In the latter

system it is necessary for the programmer to direct the distribution of code across the processors, since load-time splitting is currently too inefficient and expensive. It may be that future research will uncover automatic coarse-grain split methods, but it is by no means clear that this can be achieved.

CONCLUSIONS

The Manchester project has constructed an operational tagged-token dataflow processor large enough to tackle realistic applications. A small range of benchmark programs has been written and executed on the hardware to provide evaluation data. The preliminary evaluation has returned several important results: First, it has established that a wide variety of programs contains sufficient parallelism to exhibit impressive speedup in relation to the number of active function units in a single-ring system. Second, it has been established that the crude measure, S1/Sinf, of program parallelism is in practice a useful indicator of the suitability of a program for the architecture, regardless of the time variance of the parallelism. Third, a weakness in the present pipeline implementation has been identified, the rectification of which provides better speedup characteristics. Fourth, the effectiveness of the supporting software system has been improved by studying the ratio of instructions executed for each useful floating-point operation in certain large computations. Finally, the need for a Structure Store Unit has been established and specifications for its design have been determined.

It is important, however, to note that this is only an initial attempt at evaluation. In particular, more work is required to determine the behavior of programs that cause matching store overflow. There is also a need to study techniques for parallel algorithm design and transformation and low-level code optimization. In highly parallel programs there is a need to control the amount of active computation by scheduling work within the Token Queue so that matching store requirements are minimized. There also remains the study of multiring systems, in particular the investigatin and evaluation of suitable split functions.

The major long-term interest in dataflow techniques will be in the construction and performance of multiprocessor systems. It is particularly important to know how dataflow systems should be designed for implementation in VLSI, and to be certain that effective software techniques are available for utilizing the hardware. An important advance in this area is the announcement by NEC of a dataflow image-processing chip, the uPD7281 Image Pipeline Processor, which was to be on the market toward the end of 1984.

Acknowledgments. The authors gratefully acknowledge the assistance of their present and former colleagues in the Dataflow Research Group at Manchester, particularly Katsura Kawakami, Adrian Parker, and John Sargeant, who have assisted with the preparation of this paper. Construction of the prototype hardware and software systems has been funded by research grants GR/A/74715, GR/B/40196, and GR/B/74788 from the Science and Engineering Research Council of Great Britain under its Distributed Computing Systems Program. The work has also been supported by an External Research Program grant from Digital Equipment Corporation, the staff of which has written certain of the benchmark programs.

Further Reading. The first four items will serve as useful introductory material for the nonspecialist. On a more specific level, the earliest reference to graphical programming appeared in an obscure internal report within the National Cash Register Corporation in 1958 [5]; a similar idea was published at an MIT Conference in 1962 [6]. The first comprehensive theory for a graphical model of computation, and the most frequently referenced pioneer dataflow paper, was published in 1966 [7]. This was followed by the publication of two influential theses on dataflow computation models at Stanford [8] and MIT [9]. The term "dataflow" was coined in the first of these theses.

There followed a phase of prolific work at MIT by Jack Dennis, who is usually regarded as the instigator of the concepts of dataflow computers as they are now understood. His Computation Structures Group has been responsible for most of the theoretical and development work for static dataflow systems [10–12]. Subsequent static systems have been constructed at CERT-ONERA in Toulouse [13] and Texas Instruments [14].

One of Dennis' early papers [11] suggested the notion of dynamic dataflow. This idea was refined at MIT (in the form of code-copying systems) [15], at Utah by Al Davis [16], and at UCI and MIT by Arvind (in the form of tagged-token systems) [17]. The development of tagged-token dataflow occurred at Manchester simultaneously and independently [18].

The principles of single-assignment programming languages were first published in 1968 [19]. The term "single assignment" was coined by Chamberlin in 1972 [20]. These ideas have subsequently been incorporated into dataflow projects, culminating with the design of the SISAL language in 1983 [21].

REFERENCES

1. IEEE. Special issue on dataflow systems. *IEEE Comput. 15*, 2 (Feb. 1982).
2. Gurd, J.R., Watson, I., Kirkham, C.C., and Glauert, J.R.W. The dataflow approach to parallel computation. In *Distributed Computing*, F.B. Chambers, D.A. Duce, and G.P. Jones, Eds. APIC Studies in Data Processing, vol. 20, Academic Press, New York, Sept. 1984.
3. Glauert, J.R.W. High level languages for dataflow computers. State of the Art Rep. Ser. 10, Number 2, on Programming Technology, Pergamon-Infotech, Maidenhead, U.K., Mar. 1982.
4. Treleaven, P.C., Brownbridge, D.R., and Hopkins, R.P. Data-driven and demand-driven computer architecture. *ACM Comput. Surv. 14*, 1 (Mar. 1982), 93–143.
5. Young, J.W., and Kent, H.K. Abstract formulation of data processing problems. Intern. Rep., Product Specifications Dept., The National Cash Register Company, Hawthorne, Calif., 1958.
6. Brown, G.W. A new concept in programming. In *Computers and the World of the Future*, M. Greenberger, Ed. MIT Press, Cambridge, Mass., 1962.
7. Karp, R.M., and Miller, R.E. Properties of a model for parallel computations: Determinacy, termination and queueing. *SIAM J. Appl. Math. 11*, 6 (Nov. 1966), 1390–1411.
8. Adams, D.A. A computational model with data flow sequencing. Ph.D. thesis, TR/CS-117, Dept. of Computer Science, Stanford Univ., Calif., 1968.
9. Rodriguez, J.E. A graph model for parallel computation. Ph.D. thesis, MIT/LCS/TR-64, Laboratory for Computer Science, MIT, Cambridge, Mass., 1969.
10. Dennis, J.B., Fosseen, J.B., and Linderman, J.P. *Data Flow Schemas*. Lecture Notes in Computer Science, vol. 5. Springer-Verlag, New York, 1974.
11. Dennis, J.B. *First Version of a Data Flow Procedure Language.* Lecture Notes in Computer Science, vol. 19. Springer-Verlag, New York, 1974.
12. Dennis, J.B., and Misunas, D.P. A preliminary architecture for a basic data flow architecture. In *Proceedings of the 2nd Annual Symposium on Computer Architecture.* IEEE Press, New York, Jan. 1975, pp. 126–132.
13. Syre, J.C., et al. LAU system—A parallel data-driven software/hardware system based on single-assignment. In *Parallel Computers—Parallel Mathematics*, M. Feilmeier, Ed. Elsevier North-Holland, New York, 1977.
14. Johnson, D. Automatic partitioning of programs in multiprocessor systems. In *Proceedings of the IEEE COMPCON*, IEEE Press, New York, Apr. 1980.
15. Miranker, G.S. Implementation of procedures on a class of data flow processors. In *Proceedings of the IEEE International Conference on Parallel Processing*, IEEE Press, New York, Aug. 1977.
16. Davis, A.L. The architecture and system method of DDM1: A recursively structured data driven machine. In Proceedings of the 5th ACM Symposium on Computer Architecture. *SIGARCH Newsl. 6*, 7 (Apr. 1978), 210–215.
17. Arvind, Gostelow, K.P., and Plouffe, W. An asynchronous programming language and computing machine. Tech. Rep. TR114a, Dept. of Information and Computer Science, Univ. of California, Irvine, Dec. 1978.
18. Gurd, J.R., Watson, I., and Glauert, J.R.W. A multilayered data flow computer architecture. Intern. Rep., Dept. of Computer Science, Univ. of Manchester, England, Jan. 1978.
19. Tesler, L.G. A language design for concurrent processes. In *Proceedings of AFIPS Spring Joint Computer Conference* (Atlantic City, N.J., Apr. 30–May 2). AFIPS Press, Montvale, N.J., 1968, pp. 403–408.
20. Chamberlin, D.D. The "single-assignment" approach to parallel processing. In *Proceedings of AFIPS Fall Joint Computer Conference* (Las Vegas, Nev., Nov. 16–18). AFIPS Press, Montvale, N.J., 1971, pp. 263–270.
21. McGraw, J., et al. SISAL—Streams and iteration in a single-assignment language. Language Reference Manual (version 1.0), Lawrence Livermore National Laboratory, Livermore, Calif., July 1983.

CR Categories and Subject Descriptors: C.1.3 [Processor Architectures]: Other Architecture Styles; C.4 [Performance of Systems]; D.3.2 [Programming Languages]: Language Classifications
General Terms: Design, Languages, Performance
Additional Key Words and Phrases: tagged-token dataflow, signal-assignment programming, SISAL

Authors' Present Address: J.R. Gurd, C.C. Kirkham, and I. Watson, Dept. of Computer Science, University of Manchester, Oxford Road, Manchester, M13 9PL, England.

Computer Physics Communications 37 (1985) 141–148
North-Holland, Amsterdam

SIGMA-1: A DATAFLOW COMPUTER FOR SCIENTIFIC COMPUTATIONS

Toshitsugu YUBA, Toshio SHIMADA, Kei HIRAKI and Hiroshi KASHIWAGI

Electrotechnical Laboratory, 1-1-4 Umesono, Sakuramura, Niiharigun, Ibaraki 305, Japan

This paper presents an overview of the SIGMA-1, a large-scale dataflow computer being developed at the Electrotechnical Laboratory, Japan. The SIGMA-1 is designed to accommodate about two hundred dataflow processing elements. Its estimated average speed is one hundred MFLOPS for certain numerical computations.

Various aspects of the SIGMA-1, such as the organization of a processing element, the matching memory unit, the structure memory and the communication network, are described. The present status and development plans of the SIGMA-1 project are detailed. It is predicted that the SIGMA-1 will give higher speed over a wide range of applications than conventional von Neumann computers.

1. Introduction

Among parallel computer architectures for large-scale numerical computations, dataflow computer architecture is one of the most promising, since the dataflow concept exploits intrinsic parallelism in programs at the architectural level. In dataflow, execution of an instruction can be performed any time after the arrival of all the operand data. Since this is the only requirement to be satisfied to sequence execution, a high degree of parallelism can be achieved.

Recently attempts have been made to construct computing machines which obey the dataflow concept [2,3,6,9,10]. These small scale dataflow machines show the potential of dataflow computer architecture, but for a more convincing demonstration, it is necessary to construct dataflow machines to execute large, practical programs. However, there are many technical problems to be solved to realize a practical dataflow computer [1]. Feasibility studies are necessary, but have not yet been carried out.

There are three feasibility study levels in novel computer architecture research [11]. The first study level verifies the dataflow concept. This can be carried out by implementing the concept as a software simulator of a virtual machine. At the second study level, it is necessary to design hardware and construct a real machine. Hardware prototyping is indispensible to accurate evaluation of performance and for identifying the engineering problems to be solved. At the third level, the ability to surpass conventional von Neumann computers by a practical dataflow computer is considered. Research results so far obtained have not demonstrated a practical dataflow computer. The current stage of dataflow computer architecture research is at the third feasibility study level. Large size prototypes must be constructed, and the balance of speed and capacity of each resource must be quantitatively evaluated. The prototyping of the SIGMA-1 will facilitate third level feasibility studies.

The goal of the SIGMA-1 project is to identify and establish the basic technology for highly parallel computers with dataflow architecture. This research effort will lead to a super-high speed computer for scientific and technological computations. We are developing a practical-scale prototype with about two hundred processing elements to achieve one hundred MFLOPS speed so that the feasibility of practical application of a dataflow computer for large-scale numerical computation can be studied.

2. Architecture of the SIGMA-1

2.1. Design principles

The design principles of the SIGMA-1 are:
(1) Each functional unit contains a short pipeline.
(2) Each functional unit efficiently balances speed against the amount of hardware.
(3) The total size of a processing element is small and suitable for scaling-up.
(4) The hardware is reliable enough to execute practical programs for numerical computations.
(5) Practical programs written in a high level dataflow language can be executed for evaluation.

The reason a short pipeline scheme has been selected for the functional units is described below. A trade-off is observed between the number of pipeline stages and the clock period of the pipeline, which corresponds to total processing time for, and throughput of, data segments, respectively. A program with a sufficient degree of parallelism for high throughput, i.e. short time slice and long pipeline, directly leads to high speed computing. However, when there is little parallelism in a program, a scheme with short pipeline and long time slice has the advantage. In order to reduce the gap between the maximum and average performances observed in conventional supercomputers, a short pipeline scheme is adopted in the SIGMA-1.

The design principles mentioned above have given rise to the following architectural features of the SIGMA-1 [4,8]:
(1) Two stage pipeline in each processing element.
(2) Chained hashing hardware for the matching memory unit.
(3) Array-oriented structure memory.
(4) A "sticky packet" mechanism for holding loop invariants.
(5) Interrupt handling using a privileged packet.
(6) An hierarchical communication network.

In the following sections, we discuss these features and the hardware specification of the preliminary processing element. Performance evaluation results obtained using a software simulator are presented.

2.2. Global organization

The global organization of the SIGMA-1 is shown in fig. 1. According to the current plan, the SIGMA-1 will be constructed using 210 identical processing elements, divided into thirty groups and connected by a two-level communication network. A processing element group consists of seven processing elements, each containing a structure memory. The hierarchy reflects two levels of parallel processing, i.e., the low and high levels correspond to the parallel execution of iterations and procedure calls, respectively. A partition of a program, such as a loop body (iteration), is allocated to a single group. Therefore, each instruction of an iteration is executed in a group, if it does not include any procedure call. Each procedure also is allocated to a single group. The communication traffic among processing elements in a group is heavier than that between groups.

A multi-stage router network is adopted as the communication network of the SIGMA-1. This is organized as a four-by-four router cell network. A LSI router chip was designed using gate-array technology. Any number of router cells, in four bit increments, can be interconnected to form the communication network. Packets are transferred through the router network in a pipelined fashion. A packet is divided into two packet segments which are transferred in sequence. The eight-by-eight local communication network is constructed using two stages of four-by-four router cells, with some redundant ports.

The host computer, a VAX-11/750, is connected to the global network and works as an I/O processor. Software development and hardware maintenance are carried out via the host computer.

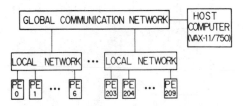

Fig. 1. Global organization of the SIGMA-1.

2.3. The processing element

Fig. 2 illustrates the configuration of a SIGMA-1 processing element [4]. It consists of five functional units, each of which works synchronously as a two stage pipeline. Increasing the number of pipeline stages improves the peak performance, but does not necessarily improve the average performance. The gap between these performances has tended to become wider in recent commercial supercomputers. In the SIGMA-1, the two stage pipeline architecture means that, even in a sequential program, every instruction is executed in at most three basic cycles.

Chained hashing hardware is used for the matching memory unit (see section 3.1). The matching memory unit and the communication network greatly influence the total performance of a dataflow computer. Therefore, ways to speed up the matching memory unit should be researched. The chained hashing hardware scheme is the most efficient for the matching memory unit, since it gives high speed and large capacity as well as hardware simplification.

Access to the instruction fetch unit and the corresponding associative search in the matching memory unit are carried out simultaneously. If the search terminates unsuccessfully, the fetched instruction from the instruction memory is discarded. The execution unit performs logical, integer and floating-point arithmetic. The destina-

tion unit produces an output packet combining the result value of the execution unit together with the destination address sent from the instruction fetch unit. After executing an instruction, the result is sent in packet form to the input buffer memories via the processing element network.

The structure memory unit handles arrays, which are the most important data structure involved in numerical computations. An array is expressed as a named sequence of values called a B-structure [8]. The structure memories within a group are shared by all the processing elements of that group.

Data transfer between processing elements is by fixed length packets. A packet consists of the processing element number (8 bits), the destination identifier (28 bits), the tagged data (40 bits), and miscellaneous control information (12 bits). A packet is divided into two portions, which are transferred in successive basic cycles. The types of packets used are:
(1) Result data of instruction execution.
(2) Procedure calls and returns.
(3) Interrupt handling and system management.
(4) Structure memory unit operation.
(5) System initiation and maintenance.

The minimum length of an instruction is 40 bits. The first 20 bits indicate the operation to be performed, and the next 20 bits indicate the destination address of the result. It is possible to allocate extra destinations to an instruction, up to a maximum of 3. A further 40 bits are required when an instruction contains an immediate (constant) operand.

2.4. Design specifications for the preliminary processing element

Fabrication of the preliminary version of the processing element is now in progress. A processing element consists of six printed circuit boards and one interface board for the host VAX-11/750. There is one board for each of the functional units shown in fig. 2, except the execution unit which has two boards. Each four layer printed circuit board is 40×60 cm^2. Advanced Schottky TTL logic and MOS memories are used, and the total number of ICs is about 1800. The basic cycle is

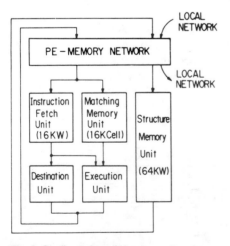

Fig. 2. Configuration of the processing element.

one hundred nanoseconds.

The capacities of the matching memory, the instruction memory and the structure memory are 16 Kwords (80 bits), 16 Kwords (40 bits) and 64 Kwords (40 bits), respectively.

A processing element receives the first 40 bits of a packet and dispatches it to the instruction fetch unit, the matching memory unit or the structure memory unit in the first basic cycle. In the second cycle, the processing element receives the remaining 40 bits containing the data part. The instruction fetch unit completes its operation for the first part by the end of the second basic cycle. The execution unit and the destination unit begin to work at the third basic cycle. The processing for the next packet is started at the fourth, or sometimes third, basic cycle in a pipelined manner.

Since the execution unit causes the maximum pipeline delay of three basic cycles for a floating point non-division arithmetic operation, the average speed of a processing element is estimated to be about three MFLOPS. This performance gives an overall speed of one hundred MFLOPS with a 210 processing element configuration, as explained in section 4.2.

The router cell is a store-and-forward matrix switch with four input and four output ports, each of which sends or receives data in four parallel bits. There are two buffers in each port to transfer a series of data segments successively. The router cell LSI chip is fabricated using a BI-CMOS gate-array, of about 1500 gates, and its transfer rate is 150 ns per data segment.

3. Control mechanisms in SIGMA-1

3.1. Matching memory unit

The performance of the matching memory unit is important in determining the total performance of dataflow computers. After studying several associative search methods such as full-associative memory and open hashing hardware, we decided to adopt chained hashing hardware for implementing the matching memory unit of the SIGMA-1 [5]. The main reasons for this decision are:
(1) Load changing adaptability.

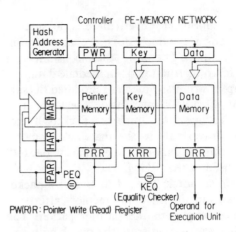

Fig. 3. Organization of the matching memory unit.

(2) Less hardware.
(3) Large capacity.
(4) Easy implementation of the sticky packet mechanism.

Fig. 3 illustrates the organization of the matching memory unit [4]. The hash address generator calculates the address for the first probe. A two stage EXOR gate network is used for the hashing function, since it uses relatively little hardware and gives a reasonably good distribution for a given key. The memory address register (MAR) holds the next probe address, and the HAR and PAR keep the current and previous probe addresses, respectively. The memory read registers, PRR, KRR and DRR, contain the newly read values at every basic cycle. The KEQ and PEQ are equality checkers for key and address comparisons at the time of probing.

The first packet of a two operand instruction can be inserted within four basic cycles, and the second packet can fire the instruction within 2.6 basic cycles after its arrival. This is estimated under the assumption that the load factor of the matching memory is less than 0.7.

One kind of packet contains firing rule information for the matching memory unit. It is used for searching and deleting a partner packet, and handling loop invariants and interruption. There are many constants in ordinary programs. In dataflow computers, constant data will be carried in packet form, which causes heavy overhead in program execution. However, there is no side-effect from constants which do not change during program execution. Therefore, these constants can be placed in an instruction as immediate data.

For loop invariants, which are modified outside a loop but do not change inside the loop, it is possible to reduce the number of packets by retaining loop invariants in the matching memory. To realize this mechanism, the "sticky packet" concept is used in the SIGMA-1.

A loop invariant is treated as a sticky packet which remains in the matching memory after successfully matching with the partner packet. The partner packet is deleted from the matching memory. Therefore, during the execution of a loop containing loop invariants, the sticky packet is retained in the matching memory. An unsticky packet is created for deleting each sticky packet at exit from a loop. The sticky packet mechanism makes it hard to construct the matching memory unit in hardware. However, it helps to improve efficiency since the major part of execution time is consumed in loops during numerical computations.

3.2. Structure memory control

The method of manipulating the array-like data structures involved in numerical computations is important in a dataflow computer. If a data structure is treated as a set of scalar values in the matching memory unit, the problems of read and write synchronization and space management are solved automatically. However, heavy packet traffic causes a serious bottleneck at the matching memory unit, since each element of the structure must be handled separately. Moreover, the matching memory unit generally includes space overhead, caused by key search, and there is a garbage collection problem, due to structure synchronization. These decrease the efficiency of program execution. For these reasons, a structure memory unit is included separately from the matching memory unit.

The B-structure is introduced to manipulate array type data structures efficiently. This is supported by a memory in which each memory element has a waiting queue. The B-structure has the following properties:

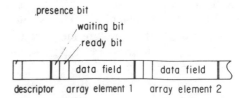

Fig. 4. Format of the B-structure.

(1) Each element can be read an arbitrary number of times, but can be written only once.
(2) When a B-structure is used for passing arguments to a procedure call, the argument values are passed without copying them.
(3) Deletion of a B-structure occurs when the procedure which created it terminates.

These features reduce the necessity for copying array type data structures. The format of a B-structure in the structure memory is shown in fig. 4. It consists of a descriptor field and a contiguous set of array elements. The descriptor includes a presence bit which is set and reset at the times of creation and deletion, respectively. Each element is a 40-bit word, and carries a waiting bit and a ready bit which are used for read and write synchronization.

3.3. Interrupt mechanism

Interruption is the basic control mechanism in both dataflow and conventional von Neumann computers for communication between user and system programs. However, the interrupt mechanism of a dataflow computer is different from that of a conventional computer, since program execution is completely asynchronous; each instruction is carried individually by a packet and its execution is restricted only by data dependency. In a conventional computer, an interrupt passes control to a system program, and all executions except the system program are inhibited. However, in a dataflow computer, execution of system and user programs is concurrent.

Arithmetic errors, data type errors, context field overflow and dynamic loading errors in the SIGMA-1 cause execution to be interrupted. Execution of the instruction is suspended and its operands are inserted into the matching memory

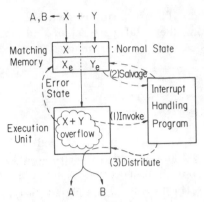

Fig. 5. Interrupt mechanism.

as error state packets. An error state packet is changed into a normal state by a special packet sent by the interrupt handling program (see fig. 5). This interrupt handling program can be written in the dataflow language EMIL (see section 4.1) by a user, therefore various types of handling are available. As a matter of course, the program is executed in a dataflow manner.

The interrupt mechanism of the SIGMA-1 comprises the following steps:
(1) Invoking the interrupt handling program.
(2) Salvaging the instruction which caused the interrupt.
(3) Distributing the result to each destination of the instruction.
(4) Resuming the interrupted program.

A procedure call packet is sent to the interrupt handling program with error information. The interrupt handling program extracts the error state packets from the matching memory by sending a special packet for interrupt handling, and if necessary executing the interrupted instruction.

4. Performance evaluation

4.1. Software simulator

The first step is to construct a sortware simulator to verify the dataflow principle. The required functions and the points at issue are made clear in the process of designing and implementing the virtual machine. A software simulator of the SIGMA-1 has been implemented to evaluate the performance characteristics and to develop system software. The performance of this SIGMA-1 virtual machine is about 100 instructions per second on a DEC-20/60. This decreases to about 5 instructions per second on a VAX-11/750. The description language is LISP, and the size of the program executed on the virtual machine is restricted by memory capacity and address space.

The environments assumed for the simulation study are:
(1) Each functional unit, including communication network stages, operates synchronously.
(2) The delay time of each pipeline stage is three basic cycles.
(3) The execution time of each instruction is one basic cycle.
(4) The matching memory does not overflow.
(5) The allocation of procedures to processing element groups is random.

Livermore Loops are used as benchmark programs, since they are well known representatives of the scientific computing work load [7]. They were proposed at Lawrence Livermore National Laboratory about ten years ago and have been used for comparison of vector computer performance. Livermore Loop 1 (hydro excerpt) and Loop 12 (first difference) are selected to evaluate vector computations. The main parts of these programs are written below in FORTRAN.

Loop 1:   DO 1 J = 1,32
            DO 1 K = 1,40
       1   X(K) = Q + Y(K)*(R*Z(K + 10)
              + T*Z(K + 11))

Loop 12:   DO 12 J = 1,56
            DO 12 K = 1,40
      12   X(K) = Y(K + 1) − Y(K)

The number of loops to be executed is limited by the execution time. Note that the outer loop parameter J represents the number of the trials and reflects parallelism in each program. The benchmark programs are written in the intermediate dataflow language, EMIL, which has the ability to describe dataflow graphs. Each instruction in the EMIL code represents a node of a dataflow graph and the destination list associated with each instruction represents the arcs of the graph.

4.2. Simulation results

The CPU time required increases proportionally with the number of processing elements. The VAX-11/750 CPU time taken to execute Livermore Loop 1 in a 210 processing element simulator is approximately 20000 s. The number of the EMIL instructions executed is approximately 35000 in both benchmark programs.

Fig. 6 shows speed-up curves for Livermore Loops 1 and 12. The horizontal and vertical axes represent the number of processing elements and the performance ratio on logarithmic scales. The performance ratio is given by the quotient of the execution time of a single processing element divided by the execution time of the specified number of processing elements. The straight line shows the ideal case.

Saturation of performance is observed after about 50 processing elements. The main reason for this is limited parallelism, corresponding to the number of iterating loops, in the benchmark programs. Architectural bottlenecks and management and tuning among the communication network, the matching memory unit and the structure memory unit also contribute significantly to this performance. Small modifications improved the performance remarkably.

The performance increased by a factor of 30 to 40 for more than 100 processing elements. From this observation, the total performance of the SIGMA-1 is predicted to average one hundred MFLOPS.

5. Concluding remarks

The SIGMA-1 project financially started at the beginning of 1982 and will be completed in 1987. After carrying out the conceptual design of the SIGMA-1, its software simulator was constructed on DEC-20/60 and VAX-11/750 systems. In 1983, the preliminary version of the SIGMA-1 processing element was designed and its fabrication is almost finished. During 1984, experiments on the preliminary version and some evaluation studies on the prototype were carried out. After confirming the effectiveness of the preliminary version of the processing element, its final version will be designed for fabrication on a single circuit board containing several types of gate-array chips. The basic design of the final version of the processing element was started in the middle of 1984.

In 1987, a full version of the SIGMA-1 with about two hundred processing elements will be in operation at an average speed of one hundred MFLOPS.

There are many problems to be solved for dataflow computer architecture to realize high performance. Until now, research results have not shown the feasibility of dataflow computers for practical computing. More practical sized prototypes must be constructed for experimentation, and the balance of speed and capacity of each device must be quantitatively evaluated.

Acknowledgements

The authors wish to thank the staff of the Computer Architecture Section, Electrotechnical Laboratory, for their fruitful discussions. They are also grateful to the referee for his valuable comments.

This research is supported by the High-speed Computing System for Scientific and Technological Use Project of the Ministry of International Trade and Industry, Japan.

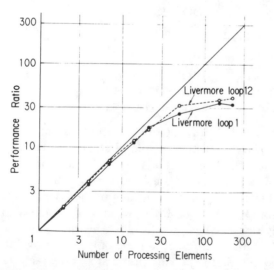

Fig. 6. Speed-up curves for Livermore Loops.

References

[1] Arvind and R.A. Iannucci, Proc. 10th Ann. Intern. Symp. Computer Architecture, IEEE (1983) 426.

[2] J.B. Dennis, W.Y.P. Lim and W.B. Ackerman, The MIT data flow engineering model, Proc. IFIP Congress 83 (1983) 553.

[3] J. Gurd and I. Watson, Data driven system for high speed parallel computing – Part 2: Hardware design, Computer Design 19 (1980) 97.

[4] K. Hiraki, T. Shimada and K. Nishida, Proc. 1984 Intern. Conf. Parallel Processing, IEEE (1984) 524.

[5] K. Hiraki, K. Nishida and T. Shimada, IEEE Trans. C-33 (1984) 851.

[6] M. Kishi, H. Yasuhara and Y. Kawamura, Proc. 10th Ann. Intern. Symp. Computer Architecture, IEEE (1983) 236.

[7] J.P. Riganati and P.B. Schneck, IEEE Computer 17 (1984) 97.

[8] T. Shimada, K. Hiraki and K. Nishida, Proc. COMPCON 84 (Spring), IEEE (1984) 486.

[9] N. Takahashi and M. Amamiya, Proc. 10th Ann. Intern. Symp. Computer Architecture, IEEE (1983) 243.

[10] Y. Yamaguchi, K. Toda, J. Herath and T. Yuba, Proc. Intern. Conf. Fifth Generation Comp. System, ICOT (1984) 524.

[11] T. Yuba, Research and development efforts on dataflow computer architecture in Japan, Recueil des Conf. 1984 Convention Infomatique, SICOB (1984) 48.

Chapter 3: Multiprocessing—Dataflow Solution

Background

Practical dataflow machines now in operation have not yet realized their full potential (namely, linear speedup and ease of parallel programming), but this is only the beginning. Research has just started on these architectures, and the latest technological advances have not yet been applied to them.

But, this should not be a problem, since these architectures are more technology independent than the von Neumann architectures. Because the von Neumann architectures have evolved to such an extent that they have to take advantage of technology to increase performance, architectures are eventually going to run into physical limits of technological advancement.

One alternative for a high performance general-purpose architecture is a parallel von Neumann machine, which is a number of sequential processors tied to a single memory (shared memory) or each with their own memory (distributed memory), because this is a "hardware first" approach, the machines are difficult to program and have problems with scalability.

Another alternative is dataflow and reduction architectures, which seem to be naturally suited to parallel processing and scalability.

The two papers in the section discuss the multiprocessing issues and consider the dataflow solution.

Article Summary

Arvind and Iannucci, in "Two Fundamental Issues in Multiprocessing," discuss the fundamental issues in multiprocessing, describe the limitations of the von Neumann architecture, and show how the dataflow architecture overcomes these limitations. They point out that any parallel system must address two basic issues, which are long memory latencies and waits for synchronization events, and note that from the evolution of high performance computers, one can deduce that the processor idle time induced by memory latency and synchronization waits cannot be simultaneously reduced in von Neumann style multiprocessors. Dataflow architectures are offered as an alternative, because, given enough parallelism in a program, they can reduce both latency and synchronization costs.

Gajski et al., in "A Second Opinion on Data Flow Machines and Languages," express their opinion on dataflow machines and languages and describe their limitations and alternatives. Although this is a dated paper, it does discuss some valid limitations of dataflow architectures. A comparison of compiling dataflow graphs and standard FORTRAN program into parallel code is made. It is argued that compiling FORTRAN programs can produce more efficient code than compiling dataflow graphs for dataflow machines. The issues used in the argument include main memory access, processing speed, input/output systems, diagnosability and maintenance, and dataflow languages.

Additional material can be found in Gajski and Pier [1].

References

[1] Gajski, D.D. and Peir, J.K., "Essential Issues in Multiprocessor Systems," *Computer*, Vol. 18, No. 6, June 1985, pp. 9-28.

Two Fundamental Issues in Multiprocessing

Arvind

Robert A. Iannucci

Laboratory for Computer Science
Massachusetts Institute of Technology
Cambridge, Massachusetts 02139 - USA

Abstract

A general purpose multiprocessor should be scalable, *i.e.*, show higher performance when more
hardware resources are added to the machine. Architects of such multiprocessors must address the
loss in processor efficiency due to two fundamental issues: long memory latencies and waits due
to synchronization events. It is argued that a well designed processor can overcome these losses
provided there is sufficient parallelism in the program being executed. The detrimental effect of
long latency can be reduced by instruction pipelining, however, the restriction of a single thread of
computation in von Neumann processors severely limits their ability to have more than a few
instructions in the pipeline. Furthermore, techniques to reduce the memory latency tend to
increase the cost of task switching. The cost of synchronization events in von Neumann machines
makes decomposing a program into very small tasks counter-productive. Dataflow machines, on
the other hand, treat each instruction as a task, and by paying a small synchronization cost for each
instruction executed, offer the ultimate flexibility in scheduling instructions to reduce processor
idle time.

Key words and phrases: caches, cache coherence, dataflow architectures, hazard resolution,
instruction pipelining, LOAD/STORE architectures, memory latency, multiprocessors, multi-thread
architectures, semaphores, synchronization, von Neumann architecture.

1. Importance of Processor Architecture

Parallel machines having up to several dozen processors are commercially available now. Most of the
designs are based on von Neumann processors operating out of a shared memory. The differences in the
architectures of these machines in terms of processor speed, memory organization and communication
systems, are significant, but they all use relatively conventional von Neumann processors. These
machines represent the general belief that processor architecture is of little importance in designing
parallel machines. We will show the fallacy of this assumption on the basis of two issues: *memory
latency* and *synchronization*. Our argument is based on the following observations:

1. Most von Neumann processors are likely to "idle" during long memory references, and such
   references are unavoidable in parallel machines.

2. Waits for synchronization events often require task switching, which is expensive on von
   Neumann machines. Therefore, only certain types of parallelism can be exploited
   efficiently.

We believe the effect of these issues on performance to be fundamental, and to a large degree, orthogonal to the effect of circuit technology. We will argue that by designing the processor properly, *the detrimental effect of memory latency on performance can be reduced provided there is parallelism in the program.* However, techniques for reducing the effect of latency tend to increase the synchronization cost.

In the rest of this section, we articulate our assumptions regarding general purpose parallel computers. We then discuss the often neglected issue of quantifying the amount of parallelism in programs. Section 2 develops a framework for defining the issues of latency and synchronization. Section 3 examines the methods to reduce the effect of memory latency in von Neumann computers and discusses their limitations. Section 4 similarly examines synchronization methods and their cost. In Section 5, we discuss multi-threaded computers like HEP and the MIT Tagged-Token Dataflow machine, and show how these machines can tolerate latency and synchronization costs provided there is sufficient parallelism in programs. The last section summarizes our conclusions.

1.1. Scalable Multiprocessors

We are primarily interested in *general purpose parallel computers, i.e.,* computers that can exploit parallelism, when present, in any program. Further, we want multiprocessors to be *scalable* in such a manner that adding hardware resources results in higher performance without requiring changes in application programs. The focus of the paper is not on arbitrarily large machines, but machines which range in size from ten to a thousand processors. We expect the processors to be at least as powerful as the current microprocessors and possibly as powerful as the CPU's of the current supercomputers. In particular, the context of the discussion is not machines with millions of one bit ALU's, dozens of which may fit on one chip. The design of such machines will certainly involve fundamental issues in addition to those presented here. Most parallel machines that are available today or likely to be available in the next few years fall within the scope of this paper (*e.g.*, the BBN Butterfly [36], ALICE [13] and now FLAGSHIP, the Cosmic Cube [38] and Intel's iPSC, IBM's RP3 [33], Alliant and CEDAR [26], and GRIP [11]).

If the programming model of a parallel machine reflects the machine configuration, *e.g.*, number of processors and interconnection topology, the machine is not scalable in a practical sense. Changing the machine configuration should not require changes in application programs or system software; updating tables in the resource management system to reflect the new configuration should be sufficient. However, few multiprocessor designs have taken this stance with regard to scaling. In fact, it is not uncommon to find that source code (and in some cases, algorithms) must be modified in order to run on an altered machine configuration. Figure 1 depicts the range of effects of scaling on the software. Obviously, we consider architectures that support the scenario at the right hand end of the scale to be far more desirable than those at the left. It should be noted that if a parallel machine is not scalable, then it will probably not be fault-tolerant; one failed processor would make the whole machine unusable. It is easy to design hardware in which failed components, *e.g.*, processors, may be masked out. However, if the application code must be rewritten, our guess is that most users would wait for the original machine configuration to be restored.

1.2. Quantifying Parallelism in Programs

Ideally, a parallel machine should speed up the execution of a program in proportion to the number of processors in the machine. Suppose $t(n)$ is the time to execute a program on an n-processor machine. The speed-up as a function of n may be defined as follows:[1]

---

[1]Of course, we are assuming that it is possible to run a program on any number of processors of a machine. In reality often this is not the case.

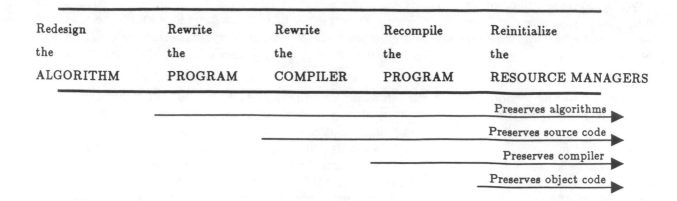

Redesign the ALGORITHM	Rewrite the PROGRAM	Rewrite the COMPILER	Recompile the PROGRAM	Reinitialize the RESOURCE MANAGERS

Preserves algorithms →

Preserves source code →

Preserves compiler →

Preserves object code →

Figure 1: The Effect of Scaling on Software

$$speed\text{-}up(n) = \frac{t(1)}{t(n)}$$

Speed-up is clearly dependent upon the program or programs chosen for the measurement. Naturally, if a program does not have "sufficient" parallelism, no parallel machine can be expected to demonstrate dramatic speedup. Thus, in order to evaluate a parallel machine properly, we need to characterize the inherent or potential parallelism of a program. This presents a difficult problem because the amount of parallelism in the source program that is exposed to the architecture may depend upon the quality of the compiler or programmer annotations. Furthermore, there is no reason to assume that the source program cannot be changed. Undoubtedly, different algorithms for a problem have different amounts of parallelism, and the parallelism of an algorithm can be obscured in coding. The problem is compounded by the fact that most programming languages do not have enough expressive power to show all the possible parallelism of an algorithm in a program. In spite of all these difficulties, we think it is possible to make some useful estimates of the potential parallelism of an algorithm.

It is possible for us to code algorithms in Id [30], a high-level dataflow language, and compile Id programs into dataflow graphs, where the nodes of the graph represent simple operations such as fixed and floating point arithmetic, logicals, equality tests, and memory loads and stores, and where the edges represent only the *essential* data dependencies between the operations. A graph thus generated can be executed on an interpreter (known as GITA) to produce results and the *parallelism profile, pp(t)*, *i.e.*, the number of concurrently executable operators as a function of time on an idealized machine. The idealized machine has unbounded processors and memories, and instantaneous communication. It is further assumed that all operators (instructions) take unit time, and operators are executed as soon as possible. The parallelism profile of a program gives a good estimate of its "inherent parallelism" because it is drawn assuming *the execution of two operators is sequentialized if and only if there is a data dependency between them*. Figure 2 shows the parallelism profile of the SIMPLE code for a representative set of input data. SIMPLE [12], a hydrodynamics and heat flow code kernel, has been extensively studied both analytically [1] and by experimentation.

The solid curve in Figure 2 represents a single outer-loop iteration of SIMPLE on a 20×20 mesh, while a typical simulation run performs 100,000 iterations on 100×100 mesh. Since there is no significant parallelism between the outer-loop iterations of SIMPLE, the parallelism profile for N iterations can be obtained by repeating the profile in the figure N times. Approximately 75% of the instructions executed involve the usual arithmetic, logical and memory operators; the rest are miscellaneous overhead

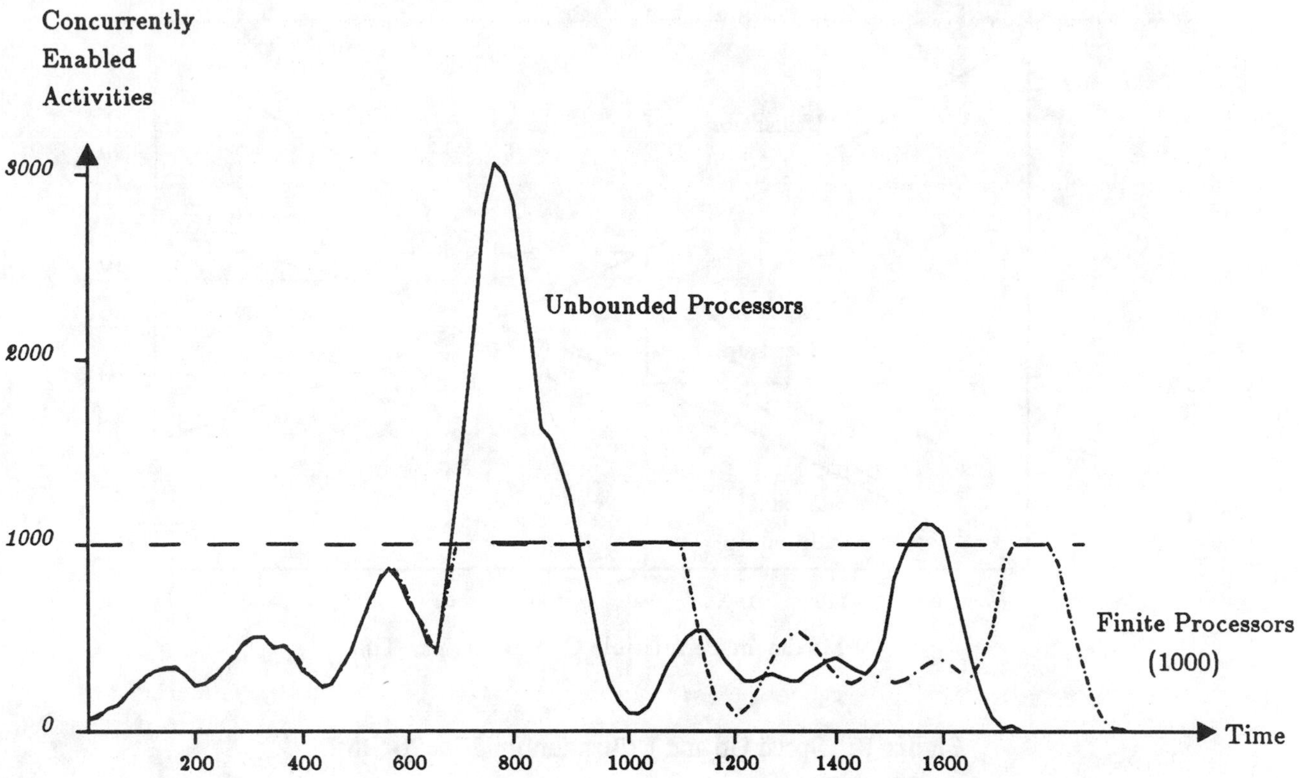

Figure 2: Parallelism Profile of SIMPLE on a 20 × 20 Array

operators, some of them peculiar to dataflow. One can easily deduce the parallelism profile of any set of operators from the raw data that was used to generate the profile in the figure; however, classifying operators as overhead is not easy in all cases.

The reader may visualize the execution on n processors by drawing a horizontal line at n on the parallelism profile and then "pushing" all the instructions which are above the line to the right and below the line. The dashed curve in Figure 2 shows this for SIMPLE on 1000 processors and was generated by our dataflow graph interpreter by executing the program again with the constraint that no more than n operations were to be performed at any step. However, a good estimate for $t(n)$ can be made, very inexpensively, from the ideal parallelism profile as follows. For any τ, if $pp(\tau) \leq n$, we perform all $pp(\tau)$ operations in time step τ. However, if $pp(\tau) > n$, then we assume it will take the least integer greater than $pp(\tau)/n$ steps to perform $pp(\tau)$ operations. Hence,

$$t(n) = \sum_{\tau=1}^{T_{MAX}} \lceil \frac{pp(\tau)}{n} \rceil$$

where T_{MAX} is the number of steps in the ideal parallelism profile. Our estimate of $t(n)$ is conservative because the data dependencies in the program may permit the execution of some instructions from $pp(\tau+1)$ in the last time step in which instructions from $pp(\tau)$ are executed.

In our dataflow graphs the number of instructions executed does not change when the program is executed on a different number of processors. Hence, $t(1)$ is simply the area under the parallelism profile. We can now plot *speed–up(n)*=$t(1)/t(n)$ and *utilization(n)*=$t(1)/n \times t(n)$, for SIMPLE as shown in Figure 3.

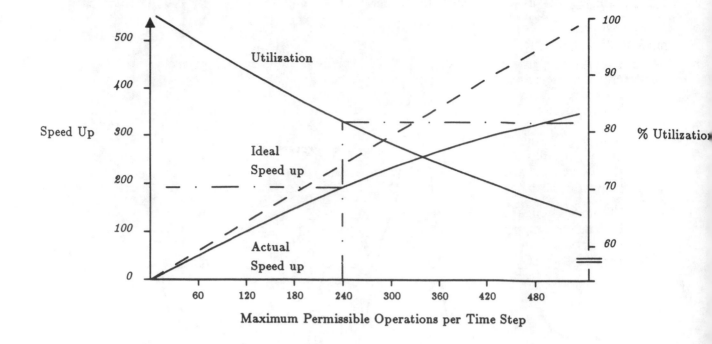

Figure 3: Speed Up and Utilization for 20 × 20 SIMPLE

For example, in the case of 240 processors, *speed–up* is 195, and *utilization* is 81%. One way to understand *utilization*(n) is that a program has n parallel operations for only *utilization*(n) fraction of its total $t(n)$ duration.

It can be argued that this problem does not have enough parallelism to keep, say, 1000 processors fully utilized. On the other hand, if we cannot keep 10 processors fully utilized, we cannot blame the lack of parallelism in the program. Generally, under-utilization of the machine in the presence of massive parallelism stems from aspects of the internal architecture of the processors which preclude exploitation of certain types of parallelism. Machines are seldom designed to exploit inner-loop, outer-loop, as well as instruction-level parallelism simultaneously.

It is noteworthy that the potential parallelism varies tremendously during execution, a behavior which in our experience is typical of even the most highly parallel programs. We believe that any large program that runs for a long time must have sufficient parallelism to keep hundreds of processors utilized; several applications that we have studied support this belief. However, a parallel machine has to be fairly general purpose and programmable for the user to be able to express even the class of partial differential equation-based simulation programs represented by SIMPLE.

2. Latency and Synchronization

We now discuss the issues of latency and synchronization. We believe latency is most strongly a function of the physical decomposition of a multiprocessor, while synchronization is most strongly a function of how programs are logically decomposed.

2.1. Latency: The First Fundamental Issue

Any multiprocessor organization can be thought of as an interconnection of the following three types of modules (see Figure 4):

1. **Processing elements (PE):** Modules which perform arithmetic and logical operations on data. Each processing element has a single *communication port* through which all data values are received. Processing elements interact with other processing elements by sending messages, issuing interrupts or sending and receiving *synchronizing signals* through shared memory. PE's interact with memory elements by issuing LOAD and STORE instructions modified as necessary with atomicity constraints. Processing elements are characterized by the rate at which they can process instructions. As mentioned, we assume the instructions are simple, *e.g.*, fixed and floating point scalar arithmetic. More complex instructions can be counted as multiple instructions for measuring instruction rate.

2. **Memory elements (M):** Modules which store data. Each memory element has a single communication port. Memory elements respond to requests issued by the processing elements by returning data through the communication port, and are characterized by their total capacity and the rate at which they respond to these requests[2].

3. **Communication elements (C):** Modules which transport data. Each nontrivial communication element has at least three communication ports. Communication elements neither originate nor receive synchronizing signals, instructions, or data; rather, they retransmit such information when received on one of the communication ports to one or more of the other communication ports. Communication elements are characterized by the rate of transmission, the time taken per transmission, and the constraints imposed by one transmission on others, *e.g.*, blocking. The maximum amount of data that may be conveyed on a *communication port* per unit time is fixed.

Latency is the time which elapses between making a request and receiving the associated response. The above model implies that *a PE in a multiprocessor system faces larger latency in memory references than in a uniprocessor system* because of the transit time in the communication network between PE's and the memories. The actual interconnection of modules may differ greatly from machine to machine. For example, in the BBN Butterfly machine all memory elements are at an equal distance from all processors, while in IBM's RP3, each processor is closely coupled with a memory element. However, we assume that the average latency in a well designed n-PE machine should be $O(log(n))$. In a von Neumann processor, memory latency determines the time to execute memory reference instructions. Usually, the average memory latency also determines the maximum instruction processing speed. When latency cannot be hidden via overlapped operations, a tangible performance penalty is incurred. We call the cost associated with latency as the total *induced processor idle time* attributable to the latency.

2.2. Synchronization: The Second Fundamental Issue

We will call the basic units of computation into which programs are decomposed for parallel execution *computational tasks* or simply *tasks*. A general model of parallel programming must assume that tasks are created dynamically during a computation and die after having produced and consumed data. Situations in parallel programming which require task synchronization include the following basic operations:

1. *Producer-Consumer*: A task produces a data structure that is read by another task. If producer and consumer tasks are executed in parallel, synchronization is needed to avoid the *read-before-write* race.

---

[2]In many traditional designs, the "memory" subsystem can be simply modeled by one of these M elements. Interleaved memory subsystems are modeled as a collection of M's and C's. Memory subsystems which incorporate processing capability can be modeled with PE's, M's, and C's. Section 4.3 describes one such case.

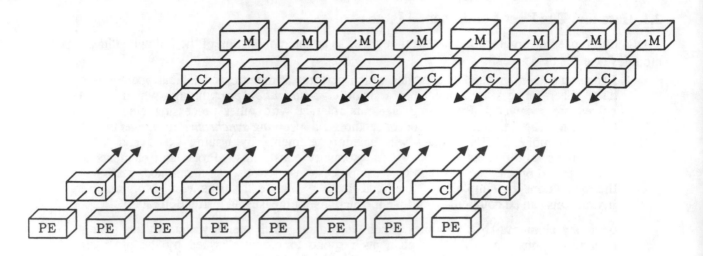

Figure 4: Structural Model of a Multiprocessor

2. *Forks* and *Joins*: The *join* operation forces a synchronization event indicating that two tasks which had been started earlier by some *forking* operation have in fact completed.

3. *Mutual Exclusion*: Non-deterministic events which must be processed one at a time, *e.g.*, serialization in the use of a resource.

The minimal support for synchronization can be provided by including instructions, such as atomic TEST-AND-SET, that operate on variables shared by synchronizing tasks[3]. However, to clarify the true cost of such instructions, we will use the *Operational Model* presented in Figure 5. Tasks in the operational model have resources, such as registers and memory, associated with them and constitute the smallest unit of independently schedulable work on the machine. A task is in one of the three states: *ready-to-execute*, *executing* or *suspended*. Tasks ready for execution may be queued locally or globally. When selected, a task occupies a processor until either it completes or is suspended waiting for a synchronization signal. A task changes from *suspended* to *ready-to-execute* when another task causes the relevant synchronization event. Generally, a suspended task must be set aside to avoid deadlocks[4]. The cost associated with such a synchronization is *the fixed time to execute the synchronization instruction plus the time taken to switch to another task.* The cost of task switching can be high because it usually involves saving the processor state, that is, the *context* associated with the task.

There are several subtle issues in accounting for synchronization costs. An event to enable or dispatch a task needs a *name*, such as that of a register or a memory location, and thus, synchronization cost should also include the instructions that generate, match and reuse identifiers which name synchronization events. It may not be easy to identify the instructions executed for this purpose. Nevertheless, such instructions represent overhead because they would not be present if the program were written to execute on a single sequential processor. The hardware design usually dictates the number of names available for synchronization as well as the cost of their use.

---

[3]While not strictly necessary, atomic operations such as TEST-AND-SET are certainly a convenient base upon which to build synchronization operations. See Section 4.3.

[4]Consider the case of a single processor system which must execute *n* cooperating tasks.

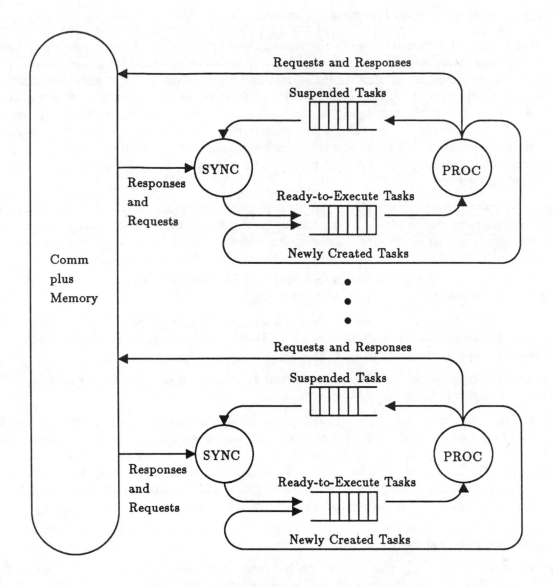

Figure 5: Operational Model of a Multiprocessor

The other subtle issue has to do with the accounting for *intra-task synchronization*. As we shall see in Section 3, most high performance computers overlap the execution of instructions belonging to one task. The techniques used for synchronization of instructions in such a situation (*e.g.*, instruction dispatch and suspension) are often quite different from techniques for inter-task synchronization. It is usually safer and cheaper not to put aside the instruction waiting for a synchronization event, but rather to idle (or, equivalently, to execute NO-OP instructions while waiting). This is usually done under the assumption that the idle time will be on the order of a few instruction cycles. We define the synchronization cost in such situations to be the *induced processor idle time* attributable to waiting for the synchronization event.

3. Processor Architectures to Tolerate Latency

In this section, we describe those changes in von Neumann architectures that have directly reduced the effect of memory latency on performance. Increasing the processor state and instruction pipelining are the two most effective techniques for reducing the latency cost. Using Cray-1 (perhaps the best pipelined machine design to date), we will illustrate that it is difficult to keep more than 4 or 5 instructions in the pipeline of a von Neumann processor. It will be shown that every change in the processor architecture which has permitted overlapped execution of instructions has necessitated introduction of a cheap synchronization mechanism. Often these synchronization mechanisms are hidden from the user and not used for inter-task synchronization. This discussion will further illustrate that reducing latency frequently increases synchronization costs.

Before describing these evolutionary changes to hide latency, we should point out that the memory system in a multiprocessor setting creates more problems than just increased latency. Let us assume that all memory modules in a multiprocessor form one global address space and that any processor can read any word in the global address space. This immediately brings up the following problems:

- The time to fetch an operand may not be constant because some memories may be "closer" than others in the physical organization of the machine.

- No useful bound on the worst case time to fetch an operand may be possible at machine design time because of the scalability assumption. This is at odds with RISC designs which treat memory access time as bounded and fixed.

- If a processor were to issue several (pipelined) memory requests to different remote memory modules, the responses could arrive out of order.

All of these issues are discussed and illustrated in the following sections. A general solution for accepting memory responses out of order requires a synchronization mechanism to match responses with the destination registers (*names* in the task's context) and the instructions waiting on that value. The ill-fated Denelcor HEP [25] is one of the very few architectures which has provided such mechanisms in the von Neumann framework. However, the architecture of the HEP is sufficiently different from von Neumann architectures as to warrant a separate discussion (see Section 5).

3.1. Increasing the Processor State

Figure 6 depicts the modern-day view of the von Neumann computer [9] (*sans* I/O). In the earliest computers, such as EDSAC, the *processor state* consisted solely of an accumulator, a quotient register, and a program counter. Memories were relatively slow compared to the processors, and thus, the time to fetch an instruction and its operands completely dominated the instruction cycle time. Speeding up the Arithmetic Logic Unit was of little use unless the memory access time could also be reduced.

The appearance of multiple "accumulators" reduced the number of operand fetches and stores, and index registers dramatically reduced the number of instructions executed by essentially eliminating the need for self-modifying code. Since the memory traffic was drastically lower, programs executed much faster than before. However, the enlarged processor state did not reduce the time lost during memory references and, consequently, did not contribute to an overall reduction in cycle time; the basic cycle time improved only with improvements in circuit speeds.

3.2. Instruction Prefetching

The time taken by instruction fetch (and perhaps part of instruction decoding time) can be totally hidden if prefetching is done during the execution phase of the previous instruction. If instructions and data are kept in separate memories, it is possible to overlap instruction prefetching and operand fetching also.

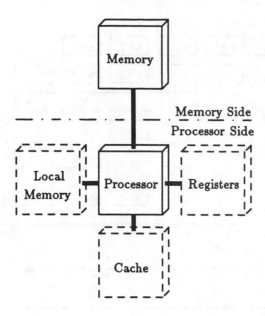

Figure 6: The von Neumann Processor (from Gajski and Peir [20])

(The IBM STRETCH [7] and Univac LARC [16] represent two of the earliest attempts at implementing this idea.) Prefetching can reduce the cycle time of the machine by twenty to thirty percent depending upon the amount of time taken by the first two steps of the instruction cycle with respect to the complete cycle. However, the effective throughput of the machine cannot increase proportionately because overlapped execution is not possible with *all* instructions.

Instruction prefetching works well when the execution of instruction n does not have any effect on either the choice of instructions to fetch (as is the case in a BRANCH) or the content of the fetched instruction (self-modifying code) for instructions $n+1$, $n+2$, ..., $n+k$. The latter case is usually handled by simply outlawing it. However, effective overlapped execution in the presence of BRANCH instructions has remained a problem. Techniques such as prefetching both BRANCH targets have shown little performance/cost benefits. Lately, the concept of *delayed* BRANCH instructions from microprogramming has been incorporated, with success, in LOAD/STORE architectures (see Section 3.4). The idea is to delay the effect of a BRANCH by one instruction. Thus, the instruction at $n+1$ following a BRANCH instruction at n is always executed regardless of which way the BRANCH at n goes. One can always follow a BRANCH instruction with a NO-OP instruction to get the old effect. However, experience has shown that seventy percent of the time a useful instruction can be put in that position.

3.3. Instruction Buffers, Operand Caches and Pipelined Execution

The time to fetch instructions can be further reduced by providing a fast instruction buffer. In machines such as the CDC 6600 [40] and the Cray-1 [37], the instruction buffer is automatically loaded with n instructions in the neighborhood of the referenced instruction (relying on spatial locality in code references), whenever the referenced instruction is found to be missing. To take advantage of instruction buffers, it is also necessary to speed up the operand fetch and execute phases. This is usually done by providing *operand* caches or buffers, and overlapping the operand fetch and execution phases[5]. Of

---

[5]As we will show in Section 4.4, caches in a multiprocessor setting create special problems.

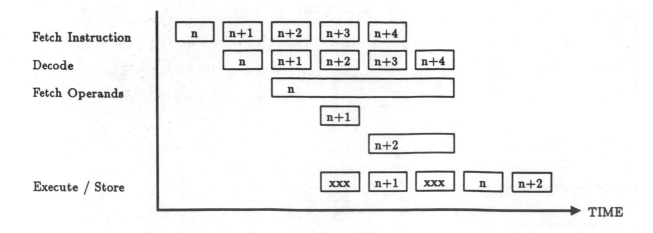

Figure 7: Variable Operand Fetch Time

---

course, balancing the pipeline under these conditions may require further pipelining of the ALU. If successful, these techniques can reduce the machine cycle time to one-fourth or one-fifth the cycle time of an unpipelined machine. However, overlapped execution of four to five instructions in the von Neumann framework presents some serious conceptual difficulties, as discussed next.

Designing a well-balanced pipeline requires that the time taken by various pipeline stages be more or less equal, and that the "things", *i.e.*, instructions, entering the pipe be independent of each other. Obviously, instructions of a program cannot be totally independent except in some special trivial cases. Instructions in a pipe are usually related in one of two ways: Instruction n produces data needed by instruction $n+k$, or only the complete execution of instruction n determines the next instruction to be executed (the aforementioned BRANCH problem).

Limitations on hardware resources can also cause instructions to interfere with one another. Consider the case when both instructions n and $n+1$ require an adder, but there is only one of these in the machine. Obviously, one of the instructions must be deferred until the other is complete. A pipelined machine must be temporarily able to prevent a new instruction from entering the pipeline when there possibility of interference with the instructions already in the pipe. Detecting and quickly resolving these *hazards* is very difficult with ordinary instruction sets, *e.g.*, IBM 370, VAX 11 or Motorola 68000, due to their complexity.

A major complication in pipelining complex instructions is the variable amount of time taken in each stage of instruction processing (refer to Figure 7). Operand fetch in the VAX is one such example: determining the addressing mode for each operand requires a fair amount of decoding, and actual fetching can involve 0 to 2 memory references per operand. Considering all possible addressing mode combinations, an instruction may involve 0 to 6 memory references in addition to the instruction fetch itself! A pipeline design that can effectively tolerate such variations is close to impossible.

3.4. Load/Store Architectures

Seymour Cray, in the sixties, pioneered instruction sets (CDC 6600, Cray-1) which separate instructions into two disjoint classes. In one class are instructions which move data *unchanged* between memory and high speed registers. In the other class are instructions which operate on data in the registers. Instructions of the second class *cannot* access the memory. This rigid distinction simplifies instruction scheduling.

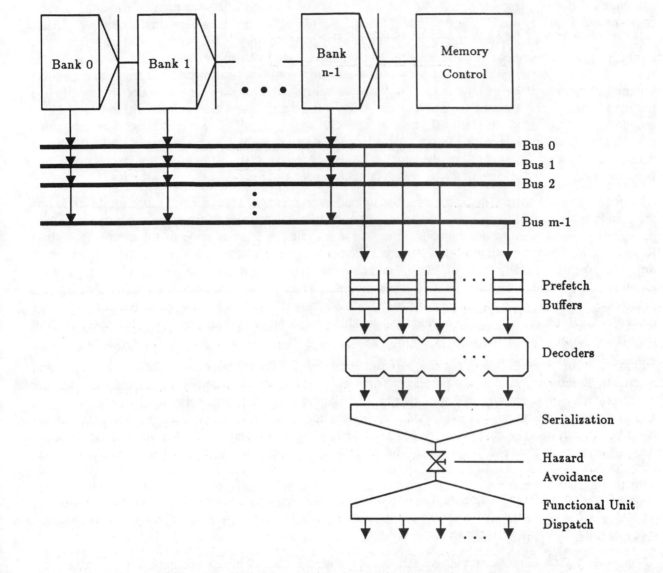

Figure 8: Hazard Avoidance at the Instruction Decode Stage

For each instruction, it is trivial to see if a memory reference will be necessary or not. Moreover, the memory system and the ALU may be viewed as parallel, noninteracting pipelines. An instruction dispatches exactly one unit of work to either one pipe or the other, but never both.

Such architectures have come to be known as LOAD/STORE architectures, and include the machines built by Reduced Instruction Set Computer (RISC) enthusiasts (the IBM 801 [34], Berkeley's RISC [32], and Stanford MIPS [22] are prime examples). LOAD/STORE architectures use the time between instruction decoding and instruction dispatching for hazard detection and resolution (see Figure 8). The design of the instruction pipeline is based on the principle that if an instruction gets past some fixed pipe stage, it should be able to run to completion without incurring any previously unanticipated hazards.

LOAD/STORE architectures are much better at tolerating latencies in memory accesses than other von Neumann architectures. In order to explain this point, we will first discuss a simplified model which detects and avoids hazards in a LOAD/STORE architecture similar to the Cray-1. Assume there is a bit associated with every register to indicate that the contents of the register are undergoing a change. The bit corresponding to register R is set the moment we dispatch an instruction that wants to update R. Following this, instructions are allowed to enter the pipeline only if they don't need to reference or modify register R or other registers reserved in a similar way. Whenever a value is stored in R, the reservation on R is removed, and if an instruction is waiting on R, it is allowed to proceed. This simple scheme works only if we assume that registers whose values are needed by an instruction are read before the next instruction is dispatched, and that the ALU or the multiple functional units within the ALU are pipelined to accept inputs as fast as the decode stage can supply them[6]. The dispatching of an instruction can also be held up because it may require a bus for storing results in a clock cycle when the bus is needed by another instruction in the pipeline. Whenever BRANCH instructions are encountered, the pipeline is effectively held up until the branch target has been decided.

Notice what will happen when an instruction to load the contents of some memory location M into some register R is executed. Suppose that it takes k cycles to fetch something from the memory. It will be possible to execute several instructions during these k cycles as long as none of them refer to register R. In fact, this situation is hardly different from the one in which R is to be loaded from some functional unit that, like the Floating Point multiplier, takes several cycles to produce the result. These gaps in the pipeline can be further reduced if the compiler reorders instructions such that instructions consuming a datum are put as far as possible from instructions producing that datum. Thus, we notice that machines designed for high pipelining of instructions can hide large memory latencies provided there is local parallelism among instructions[7].

From another point of view, latency cost has been reduced by introducing a cheap synchronization mechanism: reservation bits on processor registers. However, the number of *names* available for synchronization, *i.e.*, the size of the task's processor-bound context, is precisely the number of registers, and this restricts the amount of exploitable parallelism and tolerable latency. In order to understand this issue better, consider the case when the compiler decides to use register R to hold two different values at two different instructions say, i_n and i_m. This will require i_n and i_m to be executed sequentially while no such order may have been implied by the source code. *Shadow registers* have been suggested to deal with this class of problems. In fact, shadow registers are an engineering approach to solving a non-engineering problem. The real issue is *naming*. The reason that addition of explicit and implicit registers improves the situation derives from the addition of (explicit and implicit) *names* for synchronization and, hence, a greater opportunity for tolerating latency.

Some LOAD/STORE architectures have eliminated the need for reservation bits on registers by making the compiler responsible for scheduling instructions, such that the result is guaranteed to be available. The compiler can perform hazard resolution only if the time for each operation *e.g.*, ADD, LOAD, is known; it inserts NO-OP instructions wherever necessary. Because the instruction execution times are an intimate part of the object code, *any* change to the machine's structure (scaling, redesign) will at the very least require changes to the compiler and regeneration of the code. This is obviously contrary to our notion of generality, and hinders the portability of software from one generation of machine to the next.

Current LOAD/STORE architectures assume that memory references either take a fixed amount of time (one cycle in most RISC machines) or that they take a variable but predictable amount of time (as in the Cray-1). In RISC machines, this time is derived on the basis of a cache hit. If the operand is found to be missing from the cache, the pipeline stops. Equivalently, one can think of this as a situation where a clock cycle is *stretched* to the time required. This solution works because, in most of these machines,

---

[6]Indeed, in the Cray-1, functional units can accept an input every clock cycle and registers are always read in one clock cycle after an instruction is dispatched from the Decoder.

[7]The ability to reorder two instructions usually means that these instructions can be executed in parallel.

there can be either one or a very small number of memory references in progress at any given time. For example, in the Cray-1, no more than four independent addresses can be generated during a memory cycle. If the generated address causes a bank conflict, the pipeline is stopped. However, any conflict is resolved in at most three cycles.

LOAD/STORE architectures, because of their simpler instructions, often execute 15% to 50% more instructions than machines with more complex instructions [34]. This increase may be regarded as synchronization cost. However, this is easily compensated by improvements in clock speed made possible by simpler control mechanisms.

4. Synchronization Methods for Multiprocessing

4.1. Global Scheduling on Synchronous machines

For a totally synchronous multiprocessor it is possible to envision a master plan which specifies operations for every cycle on every processor. An analogy can be made between programming such a multiprocessor and coding a horizontally microprogrammed machine. Recent advances in compiling [18] have made such code generation feasible and encouraged researchers to propose and build several different synchronous multiprocessors. Cydrome and Multiflow computers, which are based on proposals in [35] and [19], respectively, are examples of such machines. These machines are generally referred to as *very long instruction word*, or VLIW, machines, because each instruction actually contains multiple smaller instructions (one per functional unit or processing element). The strategy is based on maximizing the use of resources and resolving potential run-time conflicts in the use of resources at compile time. Memory references and control transfers are "anticipated" as in RISC architectures, but here, multiple concurrent threads of computation are being scheduled instead of only one. Given the possibility of decoding and initiating many instructions in parallel, such architectures are highly appealing when one realizes that the fastest machines available now still essentially decode and dispatch instructions one at a time.

We believe that this technique is effective in its currently realized context, *i.e.*, Fortran-based computations on a small number (4 to 8) of processors. Compiling for parallelism beyond this level, however, becomes intractable. It is unclear how problems which rely on dynamic storage allocation or require nondeterministic and real-time constraints will play out on such architectures.

4.2. Interrupts and Low-level Context Switching

Almost all von Neumann machines are capable of accepting and handling interrupts. Not surprisingly, multiprocessors based on such machines permit the use of inter-processor interrupts as a means for signalling events. However, interrupts are rather expensive because, in general, the processor state needs to be saved. The state-saving may be forced by the hardware as a direct consequence of allowing the interrupt to occur, or it may occur explicitly, *i.e.*, under the control of the programmer, via a single very complex instruction or a suite of less complex ones. Independent of *how* the state-saving happens, the important thing to note is that each interrupt will generate a significant amount of traffic across the processor - memory interface.

In the previous discussion, we concluded that larger processor state is good because it provided a means for reducing memory latency cost. In trying to solve the problem of low cost synchronization, we have now come across an interaction which, we believe, is more than just coincidental. Specifically, in very fast von Neumann processors, the "obvious" synchronization mechanism (interrupts) will only work well in the trivial case of infrequent synchronization events or when the amount of processor state which must be saved is *very small*. Said another way, reducing the cost of synchronization by making interrupts cheap would generally entail increasing the cost of memory latency.

Uniprocessors such as the Xerox Alto [42], the Xerox Dorado [27], and the Symbolics 3600 family [29] have used a technique which may be called *microcode-level context switching* to allow sharing of the CPU resource by the I/O device adapters. This is accomplished by duplicating programmer-visible registers, in other words, the processor state. Thus, in one microinstruction the processor can be switched to a new task without causing any memory references to save the processor state[8]. This dramatically reduces the cost of processing certain types of events that cause frequent interrupts. As far as we know, nobody has adapted the idea of keeping multiple contexts in a multiprocessor setting (with the possible exception of the HEP, to be discussed in Section 5) although it should reduce synchronization cost over processors which can hold only a single context. It may be worth thinking about adopting this scheme to reduce the latency cost of a nonlocal memory references as well.

The limitations of this approach are obvious. High performance processors may have a small programmer-visible state (number of registers) but a much larger implicit state (caches). Low-level task switching does not necessarily take care of the overhead of flushing caches[9]. Further, one can only have a small number of independent contexts without completely overshadowing the cost of ALU hardware.

4.3. Semaphores and the Ultracomputer

Next to interrupts, the most commonly supported feature for synchronization is an *atomic operation* to test and set the value of a memory location. A processor can signal another processor by writing into a location which the other processor keeps reading to sense a change. Even though, theoretically, it is possible to perform such synchronization with ordinary read and write memory operations, the task is much simpler with an atomic TEST-AND-SET instruction. TEST-AND-SET is powerful enough to implement all types of synchronization paradigms mentioned earlier. However, the synchronization cost of using such an instruction can be very high. Essentially, the processor that executes it goes into a *busy-wait* cycle. Not only does the processor get blocked, it generates extra memory references at every instruction cycle until the TEST-AND-SET instruction is executed successfully. Implementations of TEST-AND-SET that permit non-busy waiting imply context switching in the processor and thus are not necessarily cheap either.

It is possible to improve upon the TEST-AND-SET instruction in a multiprocessor setting, as suggested by the NYU Ultracomputer group [17]. Their technique can be illustrated by the atomic FETCH-AND-<OP> instruction (an evolution of the REPLACE-ADD instruction). The instruction requires an address and a value, and works as follows: suppose two processors, i and j, simultaneously execute FETCH-AND-ADD instructions with arguments (A,v_i) and (A,v_j) respectively. After one instruction cycle, the contents of A will become $(A)+v_i+v_j$. Processors i and j will receive, respectively, either (A) and $(A)+v_i$, or $(A)+v_j$ and (A) as results. Indeterminacy is a direct consequence of the race to update memory cell A.

An architect must choose between a wide variety of implementations for FETCH-AND-<OP>. One possibility is that the processor may interpret the instruction with a series of more primitive instructions. While possible, such a solution does not find much favor because it will cause considerable memory traffic. A second scheme implements FETCH-AND-<OP> in the memory controller (this is the alternative chosen by the CEDAR project [28]). This typically results in a significant reduction of network traffic because atomicity of memory transactions from the memory's controller happens by default. The scheme suggested by the NYU Ultracomputer group implements the instruction *in the switching nodes of the network*.

---

[8]The Berkeley RISC idea of providing "register windows" to speed up procedure calls is very similar to multiple contexts.

[9]However, solutions such as multicontext caches and multicontext address translation buffers have been used to advantage in reducing this task switching overhead, (*c.f.*, the STO stack mechanism in the IBM 370/168).

This implementation calls for a *combining* packet communication network which connects n processors to an n-port memory. If two packets collide, say FETCH-AND-ADD(A,v_i) and FETCH-AND-ADD(A,v_j), the switch extracts the values v_i and v_j, forms a new packet (FETCH-AND-ADD(A,v_i+v_j)), forwards it to the memory, and stores the value of v_i temporarily. When the memory returns the old value of location A, the switch returns two values $((A)$ and $(A)+v_i)$. The main improvement is that some synchronization situations which would have taken $O(n)$ time can be done in $O(logn)$ time. It should be noted, however, that one memory reference may involve as many as $log_2 n$ additions, and implies substantial hardware complexity. Further, the issue of processor idle time due to latency has not been addressed at all. In the worst case, the complexity of hardware may actually increase the latency of going through the switch and thus completely overshadow the advantage of "combining" over other simpler implementations.

The simulation results reported by NYU [17] show quasi-linear speedup on the Ultracomputer (a shared memory machine with ordinary von Neumann processors, employing FETCH-AND-ADD synchronization) for a large variety of scientific applications. We are not sure how to interpret these results without knowing many more details of their simulation model. Two possible interpretations are the following:

1. Parallel branches of a computation hardly share any data, thus, the costly *mutual exclusion* synchronization is rarely needed in real applications.

2. The synchronization cost of using shared data can be acceptably brought down by judicious use of cachable/non cachable annotations in the source program.

The second point may become clearer after reading the next section.

4.4. Cache Coherence Mechanisms

While highly successful for reducing memory latency in uniprocessors, caches in a multiprocessor setting introduce a serious synchronization problem called *cache coherence*. Censier and Feautrier [10] define the problem as follows: *"A memory scheme is coherent if the value returned on a LOAD instruction is always the value given by the latest STORE instruction with the same address."*. It is easy to see that this may be difficult to achieve in multiprocessing.

Suppose we have a two-processor system tightly coupled through a single main memory. Each processor has its own cache to which it has exclusive access. Suppose further that two tasks are running, one on each processor, and we know that the tasks are designed to communicate through one or more shared memory cells. In the absence of caches, this scheme can be made to work. However, if it happens that the shared address is present in both caches, the individual processors can read and write the address and *never* see any changes caused by the other processor. Using a store-through design instead of a store-in design does not solve the problem either. What is logically required is a mechanism which, upon the occurrence of a STORE to location x, invalidates copies of location x in caches of other processors, and guarantees that subsequent LOADs will get the most recent (cached) value. This can incur significant overhead in terms of decreased memory bandwidth.

All solutions to the cache coherence problem center around reducing the cost of detecting rather than avoiding the possibility of cache incoherence. Generally, *state* information indicating whether the cached data is private or shared, read-only or read-write, etc., is associated with each cache entry. However, this state somehow has to be updated after each memory reference. Implementations of this idea are generally intractable except possibly in the domain of bus-oriented multiprocessors. The so-called *snoopy bus* solution uses the broadcasting capability of buses and purges entry x from all caches when a processor attempts a STORE to x. In such a system, at most one STORE operation can go on at a time in the whole system and, therefore, system performance is going to be a strong function of the snoopy bus' ability to handle the coherence-maintaining traffic.

It is possible to improve upon the above solution if some additional state information is kept with each cache entry. Suppose entries are marked "shared" or "non-shared". A processor can freely read shared entries, but an attempt to STORE into a shared entry immediately causes that address to appear on the snoopy bus. That entry is then deleted from all the other caches and is marked "non-shared" in the processor that had attempted the STORE. Similar action takes place when the word to be written is missing from the cache. Of course, the main memory must be updated before purging the private copy from any cache. When the word to be read is missing from the cache, the snoopy bus may have to first reclaim the copy privately held by some other cache before giving it to the requesting cache. The status of such an entry will be marked as shared in both caches. The advantage of keeping shared/non-shared information with every cache entry is that the snoopy bus comes into action only on cache misses and STOREs to shared locations, as opposed to all LOADs and STOREs. Even if these solutions work satisfactorily, bus-oriented multiprocessors are not of much interest to us because of their obvious limitations in scaling.

As far as we can tell, there are no known solutions to cache coherence for non-bussed machines. It would seem reasonable that one needs to make caches partially visible to the programmer by allowing him to mark data (actually addresses) as shared or not shared. In addition, instructions to flush an entry or a block of entries from a cache have to be provided. Cache management on such machines is possible only if the concept of shared data is well integrated in the high-level language or the programming model. Schemes have also been proposed explicitly to interlock a location for writing or to bypass the cache (and flush it if necessary) on a STORE; in either case, the performance goes down rapidly as the machine is scaled. Ironically, in solving the latency problem via multiple caches, we have introduced the synchronization problem of keeping caches coherent.

It is worth noting that, while not obvious, a direct trade-off often exists between decreasing the parallelism and increasing the cachable or non-shared data.

5. Multi-Threaded Architectures

In order to reduce memory latency cost, it is essential that a processor be capable of issuing multiple, overlapped memory requests. The processor must view the memory/communication subsystems as a logical pipeline. As latency increases, keeping the pipeline full implies that more memory references will have to be in the pipeline. We note that memory systems of current von Neumann architectures have very little capability for pipelining, with the exception of array references in vector machines. The reasons behind this limitation are fundamental:

1. von Neumann processors must observe instruction sequencing constraints, and

2. since memory references can get out of order in the pipeline, a large number of identifiers to distinguish memory responses must be provided.

One way to overcome the first deficiency is to interleave many threads of sequential computations (as we saw in the very long instruction word architectures of Section 4.1). The second deficiency can be overcome by providing a large register set with suitable reservation bits. It should be noted that these requirements are somewhat in conflict. The situation is further complicated by the need of tasks to communicate with each other. Support for cheap synchronization calls for the processor to switch tasks quickly and to have a non-empty queue of tasks which are ready to run. One way to achieve this is again by interleaving multiple threads of computation and providing some intelligent scheduling mechanism to avoid busy-waits. Machines supporting multiple threads and fancy scheduling of instructions or processes look less and less like von Neumann machines as the number of threads increases.

In this section, we first discuss the erstwhile Denelcor HEP [25, 39]. The HEP was the first commercially available multi-threaded computer. After that we briefly discuss dataflow machines, which may be regarded as an extreme example of machines with multiple threads; machines in which each instruction constitutes an independent thread and only non-suspended threads are scheduled to be executed.

5.1. The Denelcor HEP: A Step Beyond von Neumann Architectures

The basic structure of the HEP processor is shown in Figure 9. The processor's data path is built as an eight step pipeline. In parallel with the data path is a control loop which circulates process status words (PSW's) of the processes whose threads are to be interleaved for execution. The delay around the control loop varies with the queue size, but is never shorter than eight pipe steps. This minimum value is intentional to allow the PSW at the head of the queue to initiate an instruction but not return again to the head of the queue until the instruction has completed. If at least eight PSW's, representing eight processes, can be kept in the queue, the processor's pipeline will remain full. This scheme is much like traditional pipelining of instructions, but with an important difference. The inter-instruction dependencies are likely to be weaker here because adjacent instructions in the pipe are always from *different processes*.

There are 2048 registers in each processor; each process has an index offset into the register array. Inter-process, *i.e.*, inter-thread, communication is possible via these registers by overlapping register allocations. The HEP provides FULL/EMPTY/RESERVED bits on each register and FULL/EMPTY bits on each word in the data memory. An instruction encountering EMPTY or RESERVED registers behaves like a NO-OP instruction; the program counter of the process, *i.e.*, PSW, which initiated the instruction is not incremented. The process effectively *busy-waits* but without blocking the processor. When a process issues a LOAD or STORE instruction, it is removed from the control loop and is queued separately in the Scheduler Function Unit (SFU) which also issues the memory request. Requests which are not satisfied because of improper FULL/EMPTY status result in recirculation of the PSW within the SFU's loop and also in reissuance of the request. The SFU matches up memory responses with queued PSW's, updates registers as necessary and reinserts the PSW's in the control loop.

Thus, the HEP is capable up to a point of using parallelism in programs to hide memory and communication latency. At the same time it provides efficient, low-level synchronization mechanisms in the form of presence-bits in registers and main memory. However, the HEP approach does not go far enough because there is a limit of *one* outstanding memory request per process, and the cost of synchronization through shared registers can be high because of the loss of processor time due to *busy-waiting*. A serious impediment to the software development on HEP was the limit of 64 PSW's in each processor. Though only 8 PSW's may be required to keep the process pipeline full, a much larger number is needed to name all concurrent tasks of a program.

5.2. Dataflow Architectures

Dataflow architectures [2, 15, 21, 23] represent a radical alternative to von Neumann architectures because they use dataflow graphs as their machine language [4, 14]. Dataflow graphs, as opposed to conventional machine languages, specify only a partial order for the execution of instructions and thus provide opportunities for parallel and pipelined execution at the level of individual instructions. For example, the dataflow graph for the expression a*b + c*d only specifies that both multiplications be executed before the addition; however, the multiplications can be executed in any order or even in parallel. The advantage of this flexibility becomes apparent when we consider that the order in which a, b, c and d will become available may not be known at compile time. For example, computations for operands a and b may take longer than computations for c and d or *vice versa*. Another possibility is that the time to fetch different operands may vary due to scheduling and hardware characteristics of the machine. Dataflow graphs do not force unnecessary sequentialization and dataflow processors schedule instructions according to the availability of the operands.

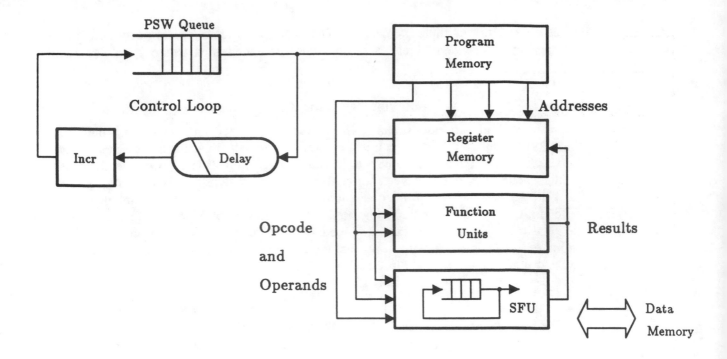

Figure 9: Latency Toleration and Synchronization in the HEP

The instruction execution mechanism of a dataflow processor is fundamentally different from that of a von Neumann processor. We will briefly illustrate this using the MIT Tagged-Token architecture (see Figure 10). Rather than following a *Program Counter* for the next instruction to be executed and then fetching operands for that instruction, a dataflow machine provides a low-level synchronization mechanism in the form of *Waiting-Matching* section which dispatches only those instructions for which data are already available. This mechanism relies on *tagging* each datum with the address of the instruction to which it belongs and the context in which the instruction is being executed. One can think of the instruction address as replacing the program counter, and the context identifier replacing the frame base register in traditional von Neumann architecture. It is the machine's job to match up data with the same tag and then to execute the denoted instruction. In so doing, new data will be produced, with a new tag indicating the successor instruction(s). Thus, each instruction represents a synchronization operation. Note that the number of synchronization names is limited by the size of the tag, which can easily be made much larger than the size of the register array in a von Neumann machine. Note also that the processor pipeline is non-blocking: given that the operands for an instruction are available, the corresponding instruction can be executed without further synchronization.

In addition to the waiting-matching section which is used primarily for dynamic scheduling of instructions, the MIT Tagged-Token machine provides a second synchronization mechanism called *I-Structure Storage*. Each word of I-structure storage has 2 bits associated with it to indicate whether the word is empty, full or has pending read-requests. This greatly facilitates overlapped execution of a producer of a data structure with the consumer of that data structure. There are three instructions at the graph level to manipulate I-structure storage. These are *allocate* - to allocate *n* empty words of storage, *select* - to fetch the contents of the ith word of an array and *store* - to store a value in a specified word. Generally software concerns dictate that a word be written into only once before it is deallocated. The dataflow processor treats all I-structure operations as *split-phase*. For example, when the *select*

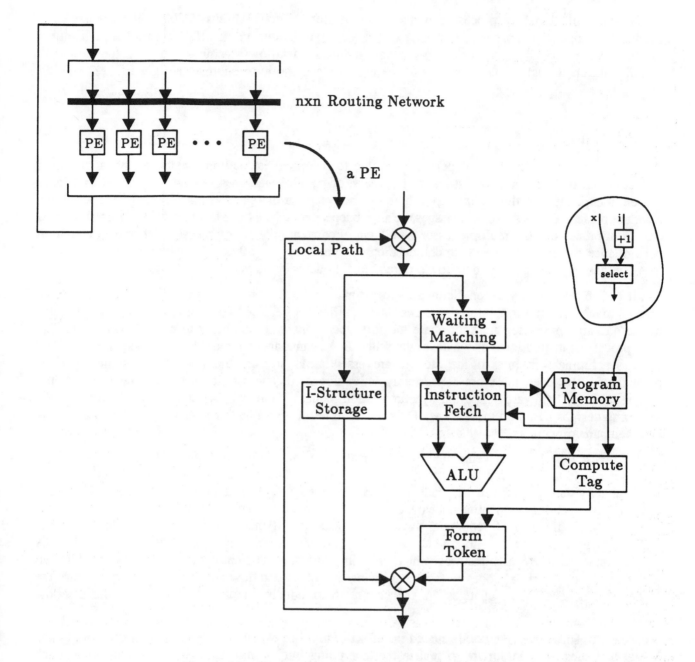

Figure 10: The MIT Tagged-Token Dataflow Machine

instruction is executed, a packet containing the tag of the destination instruction of the select instruction is forwarded to the proper address, possibly in a distant I-structure storage module. The actual memory operation may require waiting if the data is not present and thus the result may be returned many instruction times later. The key is that the instruction pipeline need not be suspended during this time. Rather, processing of other instructions may continue immediately after *initiation* of the operation. Matching of memory responses with waiting instructions is done via tags in the waiting-matching section.

One advantage of tagging each datum is that data from different contexts can be mixed freely in the instruction execution pipeline. Thus, instruction-level parallelism of dataflow graphs can effectively absorb the communication latency and minimize the losses due to synchronization waits. We hope it is clear from the prior discussion that even the most highly pipelined von Neumann processor cannot match the flexibility of a dataflow processor in this regard. A more complete discussion of dataflow machines is beyond the scope of this paper. An overview of executing programs on the MIT Tagged-Token Dataflow machine can be found in [6]. A deeper understanding of dataflow machines can be gotten from [2]. Additional, albeit slightly dated, details of the machine and the instruction set are given in [3] and [5], respectively.

6. Conclusions

We have presented the loss of performance due to increased latency and waits for synchronization events as the two fundamental issues in the design of parallel machines. These issues are, to a large degree, independent of the technology differences between various parallel machines. Even though we have not presented it as such, these issues are also independent of the high-level programming model used on a multiprocessor. If a multiprocessor is built out of conventional microprocessors, then degradation in performance due to latency and synchronization will show up regardless of whether a shared-memory, message-passing, reduction or dataflow programming model is employed.

Is it possible to modify a von Neumann processor to make it more suitable as a building block for a parallel machine? In our opinion the answer is a qualified "yes". The two most important characteristics of the dataflow processor are split-phase memory operations and the ability to put aside computations (*i.e.*, processes, instructions, or whatever the scheduling quanta are) without blocking the processor. We think synchronization bits in the storage are essential to support the producer-consumer type of parallelism. However, the more concurrently active threads of computation we have, the greater is the requirement for hardware-supported synchronization names. Iannucci [24] and others [8] are actively exploring designs based on these ideas. Only time will tell if it will be fair to classify such processors as von Neumann processors.

The biggest appeal of von Neumann processors is that they are widely available and familiar. There is a tendency to extrapolate these facts into a belief that von Neumann processors are "simple" and efficient. A technically sound case can be made that well designed von Neumann processors are indeed very efficient in executing sequential codes and require less memory bandwidth than dataflow processors. However, the efficiency of sequential threads disappears fast if there are too many interruptions or if idling of the processor due to latency or data-dependent hazards increases. Papadopoulos [31] is investigating dataflow architectures which will improve the efficiency of the MIT Tagged-Token architecture on sequential codes without sacrificing any of its dataflow advantages. We can assure the reader that none of these changes are tantamount to introducing a program counter in the dataflow architecture.

For lack of space we have not discussed the effect of multi-threaded architectures on the compiling and language issues. It is important to realize that compiling into primitive dataflow operators is a much simpler task than compiling into cooperating sequential threads. Since the cost of inter-process communication in a von Neumann setting is much greater than the cost of communication within a process, there is a preferred process or "grain" size on a given architecture. Furthermore, placement of synchronization instructions in a sequential code requires careful planning because an instruction to wait for a synchronization event may experience very different waiting periods in different locations in the program. Thus, even for a given grain size, it is difficult to decompose a program optimally. Dataflow graphs, on the other hand, provide a uniform view of inter- and intra-procedural synchronization and communication, and as noted earlier, only specify a partial order to enforce data dependencies among the instructions of a program. Though it is very difficult to offer a quantitative measure, we believe that an Id Nouveau compiler to generate code for a multi-threaded von Neumann computer will be significantly more complex than the current compiler [41] which generates fine grain dataflow graphs for the MIT

Tagged-Token dataflow machine. Thus dataflow computers, in addition to providing solutions to the fundamental hardware issues raised in this paper, also have compiler technology to exploit their full potential.

Acknowledgment

The authors wish to thank David Culler for valuable discussions on much of the subject matter of this paper, particularly Load/Store architectures and the structure of the Cray machines. Members of the Computation Structures Group have developed many tools, without which the analysis of the Simple code would have been impossible. In particular, we would like to thank Ken Traub for the ID Compiler and David Culler and Dinarte Morais for GITA. This paper has benefited from numerous discussions with people both inside and outside MIT. We wish to thank Natalie Tarbet, Ken Traub, David Culler, Vinod Kathail and Rishiyur Nikhil for suggestions to improve this manuscript.

Research Credit

This report describes research done at the Laboratory for Computer Science of the Massachusetts Institute of Technology. Funding for the Laboratory is provided in part by the Advanced Research Projects Agency of the Department of Defense under Office of Naval Research contracts N00014-83-K-0125 and N00014-84-K-0099. The second author is employed by the International Business Machines Corporation.

References

1. Arvind and R. E. Bryant. Design Considerations for a Partial Equation Machine. Proceedings of Scientific Computer Information Exchange Meeting, Lawrence Livermore Laboratory, Livermore, CA, September, 1979, pp. 94-102.

2. Arvind and D. E. Culler. "Dataflow Architectures". *Annual Reviews of Computer Science 1* (1986), 225-253.

3. Arvind, D. E. Culler, R. A. Iannucci, V. Kathail, K. Pingali, and R. E. Thomas. The Tagged Token Dataflow Architecture. Internal report. (including architectural revisions of October, 1983).

4. Arvind and K. P. Gostelow. "The U-Interpreter". *Computer 15*, 2 (February 1982), 42-49.

5. Arvind and R. A. Iannucci. Instruction Set Definition for a Tagged-Token Data Flow Machine. Computation Structures Group Memo 212-3, Laboratory for Computer Science, MIT, Cambridge, Mass., Cambridge, MA 02139, December, 1981.

6. Arvind and R. S. Nikhil. Executing a Program on the MIT Tagged-Token Dataflow Architecture. Proc. PARLE, (Parallel Architectures and Languages Europe), Eindhoven, The Netherlands, June, 1987.

7. Block, E. The Engineering Design of the STRETCH Computer. Proceedings of the EJCC, 1959, pp. 48-59.

8. Buehrer, R. and K. Ekanadham. Dataflow Principles in Multi-processor Systems. ETH, Zurich, and Research Division, Yorktown Heights, IBM Corporation, July, 1986.

9. Burks, A., H. H. Goldstine, and J. von Neumann. "Preliminary Discussion of the Logical Design of an Electronic Instrument, Part 2". *Datamation 8*, 10 (October 1962), 36-41.

10. Censier, L. M. and P. Feautrier. "A New Solution to the Coherence Problems in Multicache Systems". *IEEE Transactions on Computers C-27*, 12 (December 1978), 1112-1118.

11. Clack, C. and Peyton-Jones, S. L. The Four-Stroke Reduction Engine. Proceedings of the 1986 ACM Conference on Lisp and Functional Programming, Association for Computing Machinery, August, 1986, pp. 220-232.

12. Crowley, W. P., C. P. Hendrickson, and T. E. Rudy. The SIMPLE Code. Internal Report UCID-17715, Lawrence Livermore Laboratory, Livermore, CA, February, 1978.

13. Darlington, J. and M. Reeve. ALICE: A Multi-Processor Reduction Machine for the Parallel Evaluation of Applicative Languages. Proceedings of the 1981 Conference on Functional Programming Languages and Computer Architecture, Portsmouth, NH, 1981, pp. 65-76.

14. Dennis, J. B. *Lecture Notes in Computer Science*. Volume 19: First Version of a Data Flow Procedure Language. In *Programming Symposium: Proceedings, Colloque sur la Programmation*, B. Robinet, Ed., Springer-Verlag, 1974, pp. 362-376.

15. Dennis, J. B. "Data Flow Supercomputers". *Computer 13*, 11 (November 1980), 48-56.

16. Eckert, J. P., J. C. Chu, A. B. Tonik & W. F. Schmitt. Design of UNIVAC - LARC System: 1. Proceedings of the EJCC, 1959, pp. 59-65.

17. Edler, J., A. Gottlieb, C. P. Kruskal, K. P. McAuliffe, L. Rudolph, M. Snir, P. J. Teller & J. Wilson. Issues Related to MIMD Shared-Memory Computers: The NYU Ultracomputer Approach. Proceedings of the 12th Annual International Symposium On Computer Architecture, Boston, June, 1985, pp. 126-135.

18. Ellis, J. R.. *Bulldog: a Compiler for VLIW Architectures*. The MIT Press, 1986.

19. Fisher, J. A. Very Long Instruction Word Architectures and the ELI-512. Proc. of the 10th, International Symposium on Computer Architecture, IEEE Computer Society, June, 1983.

20. Gajski, D. D. & J-K. Peir. "Essential Issues in Multiprocessor Systems". *Computer 18*, 6 (June 1985), 9-27.

21. Gurd, J. R., C. C. Kirkham, and I. Watson. "The Manchester Prototype Dataflow Computer". *Communications of ACM 28*, 1 (January 1985), 34-52.

22. Hennessey, J. L. "VLSI Processor Architecture". *IEEE Transactions on Computers C-33*, 12 (December 1984), 1221-1246.

23. Hiraki, K., S. Sekiguchi, and T. Shimada. System Architecture of a Dataflow Supercomputer. Computer Systems Division, Electrotechnical Laboratory, Japan, 1987.

24. Iannucci, R. A. *A Dataflow / von Neuamnn Hybrid Architecture*. Ph.D. Th., Dept. of Electrical Engineering and Computer Science, MIT, Cambridge, Mass., (in preparation) 1987.

25. Jordan, H. F. Performance Measurement on HEP - A Pipelined MIMD Computer. Proceedings of the 10th Annual International Symposium On Computer Architecture, Stockholm, Sweden, June, 1983, pp. 207-212.

26. Kuck, D., E. Davidson, D. Lawrie, and A. Sameh. "Parallel Supercomputing Today and the Cedar Approach". *Science Magazine 231* (February 1986), 967-974.

27. Lampson, B. W. and K. A. Pier. A Processor for a High-Performance Personal Computer. Xerox Palo Alto Research Center, January, 1981.

28. Li, Z. and W. Abu-Sufah. A Technique for Reducing Synchronization Overhead in Large Scale Multiprocessors. Proc. of the 12th, International Symposium on Computer Architecture, June, 1985, pp. 284-291.

29. Moon, D. A. Architecture of the Symbolics 3600. Proceedings of the 12th Annual International Symposium On Computer Architecture, Boston, June, 1985, pp. 76-83.

30. Nikhil, R. S., K. Pingali, and Arvind. Id Nouveau. Computation Structures Group Memo 265, Laboratory for Computer Science, MIT, Cambridge, Mass., Cambridge, MA 02139, July, 1986.

31. Papadopoulos, G. M. *Implementation of a General Purpose Dataflow Multiprocessor*. Ph.D. Th., Dept. of Electrical Engineering and Computer Science, MIT, Cambridge, Mass., (in preparation) 1987.

32. Patterson, D. A. "Reduced Instruction Set Computers". *Communications of ACM 28*, 1 (January 1985), 8-21.

33. Pfister, G. F., W. C. Brantley, D. A. George, S. L. Harvey, W. J. Kleinfelder, K. P. McAuliffe, E. A. Melton, V. A. Norton, and J. Weiss. The IBM Research Parallel Processor Prototype (RP3): Introduction and Architecture. Proceedings of the 1985 International Conference on Parallel Processing, Institute of Electrical and Electronics Engineers, Piscataway, N. J., 08854, August, 1985, pp. 764-771.

34. Radin, G. The 801 Minicomputer. Proceedings of the Symposium on Architectural Support for Programming Languages and Operating Systems, ACM, March, 1982.

35. Rau, B., D. Glaeser, and E. Greenwalt. Architectural Support for the Efficient Generation of Code for Horizontal Architectures. Proceedings of the Symposium on Architectural Support for Programming Languages and Operating Systems, March, 1982. Same as Computer Architecture News 10,2 and SIGPLAN Notices 17,4.

36. Rettberg, R., C. Wyman, D. Hunt, M. Hoffman, P. Carvey, B. Hyde, W. Clark, and M. Kraley. Development of a Voice Funnel System: Design Report. 4098, Bolt Beranek and Newman Inc., August, 1979.

37. Russell, R. M. "The CRAY-1 Computer System". *Communications of ACM 21*, 1 (January 1978), 63-72.

38. Seitz, C. M. "The Cosmic Cube". *Communications of ACM 28*, 1 (January 1985), 22-33.

39. Smith, B. J. A Pipelined, Shared Resource MIMD Computer. Proceedings of the 1978 International Conference on Parallel Processing, 1978, pp. 6-8.

40. Thornton, J. E. Parallel Operations in the Control Data 6600. Proceedings of the SJCC, 1964, pp. 33-39.

41. Traub, K. R. A Compiler for the MIT Tagged-Token Dataflow Architecture - S.M. Thesis. Technical Report 370, Laboratory for Computer Science, MIT, Cambridge, Mass., Cambridge, MA 02139, AUGUST, 1986.

42. *ALTO: A Personal Computer System - Hardware Manual.* Xerox Palo Alto Research Center, Palo Alto, California, 94304, 1979.

*Due to their simplicity and strong appeal to intuition,
data flow techniques attract a great deal of attention.
Other alternatives, however, offer more hope for the future.*

A Second Opinion on Data Flow Machines and Languages

Reprinted from *Computer*, February 1982, pages 58-69. Copyright © 1982
by The Institute of Electrical and Electronics Engineers, Inc.

D. D. Gajski, D. A. Padua, and D. J. Kuck
University of Illinois

R. H. Kuhn
Northwestern University

Simultaneity is a key to high-speed computation. Assuming hardware components of a given speed, it is the only remaining consideration in achieving raw speed. Simultaneity can be shackled by dependences, however, and years of hardware and software work have been devoted to understanding the types of dependences and how they can be obeyed or removed from a computation.

Dependence types. There are three types of dependence[1]: data, control, and resource. The first two arise in programs and the third in machines. Therefore, exact definitions depend on the type of language and machine under consideration, although many nearly universal dependences exist.

We will discuss three types of *data dependence*[1] (see Kuck et al.[2] for a fourth type): flow dependence, output dependence, and antidependence. *Flow dependence* exists from the computation to the use of a variable. *Output dependence* exists between two subsequent computations of the same variable. *Antidependence* exists from the use of a variable to its next computation. These three types ensure that the intended values are, in fact, used in a computation.

Control dependence types vary from language to language. For example, loop dependences exist from a loop header to each statement inside the loop, conditional dependences exist from an IF to its THEN and ELSE parts, and GOTO dependences exist from a GOTO to its destination.

Resource dependences arise when programs are compiled for and executed on a particular machine. For example, the existence of an adder and a multiplier that can be sequenced simultaneously by the control unit allows these two (but no more) arithmetic operations to be executed at once. A four-way interleaved memory allows simultaneous access to four words, but no more. A single program counter, a single arithmetic unit, and a single memory led to the so-called von Neumann machine, and these resource dependences were reflected in the definition of Fortran and other high-level programming languages.

Dependence observation. Given a problem to solve on some machine, it is useful to observe dependences at five points in the selection, preparation, and execution of an algorithm. These are in (1) algorithm choice, (2) programming, (3) compiling, (4) instruction processing (control unit), and (5) instruction execution (processor, memory, interconnection).

A given algorithm has certain built-in data dependences. For example, in certain iterative computations, an iterate must be computed before it can be used. However, other algorithms that solve the same problem might have less sequential dependence. For example, many highly concurrent algorithms to solve linear recurrences are known,[1] and the use of any of these relaxes the sequentiality between iterations.

Once an algorithm has been selected, the programming language and programming style used to express the algorithm can introduce additional dependences, as well as encode its inherent dependences. For example, a complex expression could be computed once, then stored, and subsequently used in several other expressions. This introduces flow dependences. Usually, programmers are not concerned with the number or type of dependences they introduce. Some languages or styles prevent or try to avoid certain types of dependences in programs. For example, the single-assignment approach advocated in data flow languages avoids output and antidependences.

Compilers can remove and/or introduce dependences. For example, a block of assignment statements in any language can easily be compiled into a form that obeys the single-assignment rule. In fact, all three types of data dependences can be removed automatically to produce a completely independent set of assignment statements[2]; statement substitution is used to remove flow dependences. On the other hand, two array variables must not have a dependence, but a compiler that examines only array names and not subscripts will introduce a spurious dependence. For example, if $1 \leq I \leq n$, there is no dependence between $A[2I]$ and $A[2I-1]$. This will be missed if the check is only for the array name A.

Consider the instruction processing carried out by a control unit. Assumptions about data, control, and resource dependence are always built into the hardware of a control unit. For example, the traditional von Neumann machine assumes that machine instructions are processed one at a time, with some simultaneity possible in multiple address instruction formats. Multifunction machines such as the CDC 6600 have look-ahead control units that examine two or more instructions and check dependences at runtime. If data and control dependences in the instruction stream allow and resources are available, the control unit can sequence several instructions at once.

More recent machines (e.g., the CDC Cyber 205 and the Burroughs BSP) have machine instructions that can express array operations such as vector add or recurrence operations such as inner product. If the compiler recognizes such an operation (because it is, for example, programmed sequentially or expressed in a vector extension to a sequential language), it can generate a single machine instruction that carries it out by using a fast, highly parallel algorithm. In parallel or pipeline machines, the control unit must access chunks of the operands, process them, and store chunks of the result until the operation is finished. In the case of recurrence operations, the control unit must carry out a sequence of steps. These might correspond to a complex dependence graph in which simultaneity was maximized when the machine was designed. For example, a vectorized inner product could be a vector multiply followed by a summation tree. Thus, an entire small loop from a sequential program has all of its dependences mapped onto the control-unit hardware for fast runtime sequencing.

The line between instruction processing and instruction execution is somewhat blurred across various types of computers. In machines with array instruction sets, the control unit knows, by virtue of the way in which its array instructions were implemented, exactly how to sequence its memory, processor, and interconnection network parts to carry out an operation. In other types of machines, the control unit decodes instructions, processes addresses, and decides that an instruction can be issued. The individual steps, however, are not executed until all of the dependences of the instructions are satisfied. This principle is used in the Scoreboard of the CDC 6600,[3] the Tomasulo algorithm of the IBM 360/91,[4]

and in current data flow proposals. The point is that the processor, memory, and interconnection networks themselves can ensure satisfaction of all dependences. For example, if there is a great deal of randomness in a program arising, perhaps, from conditional statements or irregular subscripts, the intuitive notion is that little can be preplanned and that execution time-dependence handling is, in fact, necessary for fast computation.

Article overview. In this article we undertake two tasks. The first is to sketch the principles and practices of data flow computation and to point out a number of shortcomings of this approach to high-speed computation. The second is to sketch an alternative that leads to high-speed computation through higher-level use of dependence graphs.

The data flow approach and our alternative are roughly characterized in Figure 1. The data flow approach usually begins with a special programming language, which researchers hope can be easily compiled into a dependence graph. (Ordinary languages can also be used.) The problem then becomes one of efficiently mapping this onto a machine that has decentralized control hardware. Often, this machine is capable of exploiting substantially less parallelism than exists in the program because it lacks the hardware to cause the dependence graph constraints to be followed as quickly as possible at runtime. That is, queues of partially completed computations are relied upon to keep the machine busy, and the queue lengths absorb some of the parallelism of the program.

Our approach can begin with either a data flow language or an ordinary programming language. A program is first put into a standard form (normalized). Next, a dependence graph is generated by, for example, analysis of array subscripts. Then some arcs are removed by program transformation, and some nodes and arcs are abstracted* because they represent high-level constructs for

---

*Abstraction here refers to the process of reducing a subgraph to a higher-level node.

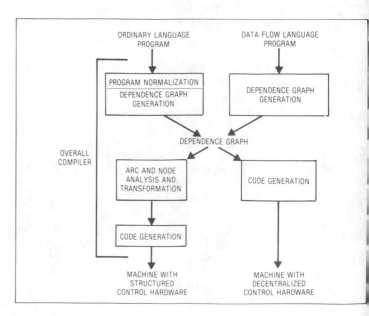

Figure 1. Comparison of methods.

which special algorithms (instructions) can be used. Finally, code generation produces high-level machine instructions that contain much of the dependence structure of the original program, but transformed for high-speed evaluation. The machine that executes the generated code can have a degree of simultaneity that is matched to the program and still execute it efficiently, because most dependence testing need not be done at runtime. However, this approach relies on compilation techniques more powerful than those usually assumed by data flow people.

Other sections of this article investigate the principles of data flow architecture and proposed data flow languages.

Data flow principles

In contrast to the sequential, one-instruction-at-a-time, memory cell semantics of the von Neumann model, the data flow model of computation is based on two principles:

(1) *Asynchrony*. All operations executed when and only when the required operands are available.

(2) *Functionality*. All operations are functions; that is, there are no side effects.

The first denotes an execution mechanism in which data values pass through data flow graphs as tokens and an operation is triggered whenever all input tokens are present at a node in the graph. The second principle implies that any two enabled operations can be executed in either order or concurrently.

Dynamic parallelism. Even when there is data dependence between operations of the same iteration of a loop, there is nothing to stop further iterations from proceeding, even though one iteration is not totally completed. This causes tokens to accumulate on certain arcs of the data flow graph. It is then no longer possible to declare a node executable by the presence of any two tokens on its input, as they might belong to totally different parts of the computation. There are five possible solutions to this problem:

(1) *The use of a re-entrant graph is prohibited.* That is, each stage of the iteration must be described by a separate graph. This solution obviously requires large amounts of program storage. It also requires dynamic code generation if the loop's iteration depth is only known at runtime. Both of these deficiencies can result in significant overhead in practical systems.

(2) *The use of a re-entrant graph is allowed, but an iteration is not allowed to start before the previous one has finished.* This approach does not allow for parallelism between iterations and requires extra instructions or hardware to test the completion of an iteration. It is used in the LAU system.[5]

(3) *The use of a data flow graph is limited by allowing only one token to reside on each arc of the graph at any time.* This is accomplished by allowing an operation to be executable only when all its input tokens are present and no tokens exist on its output arc. This approach, which implies sequential but pipelined use of the data flow graph, allows exploitation of more parallelism than do the previous two solutions. Pipelining is implemented through the use of acknowledge signals, which are returned to the nodes in the graph that generated those values by the nodes that consumed the values.[6,7] These acknowledge signals approximately double the number of arcs in the corresponding data flow graph, and therefore double the traffic through the data flow machine.

(4) *The tokens are assumed to carry their index and iteration level as a label.* This label is usually called *color*. A node is executable only if all input tokens have the same color. The labeling method permits the use of pure static code and enables maximum use of any parallelism that exists in the problem specification. This is clearly at the cost of the extra information that must be carried by each token and the extra nodes (instructions) for labeling and delabeling.[8,9] The penalty of this approach is obviously extra time for calculating labels, or extra hardware (silicon area) if calculation is concurrent.

(5) *The tokens are queued on arcs in order of their arrival.* This solution can deliver as much parallelism as the labeling approach, but requires large queues, which are very costly.

To compare the performance of data flow machines that use these five approaches, consider the program in Figure 2a. Assume that division takes three time units, multiplication two, and addition one. The hypothetical data flow machine has four processing units, each capable of executing any operation. We idealize the machine by assuming that memory and interconnection delays are zero.

Our example program dictates a certain order of execution, which is determined by the simplified data flow program in Figure 2b. Obviously, the critical path is $a_1, b_1, c_1, c_2, \ldots, c_8$, which results in a lower bound on execution of 13 time units.

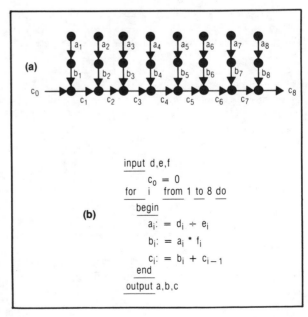

Figure 2. A nonsense example: (a) program; (b) simplified data flow graph.

Since there is one division, one multiplication, and one addition in each iteration of the loop, it will take $6 \times 8 = 48$ time units (Figure 3a) to execute the complete loop when using the one-iteration-at-a-time strategy described in approach (2), above. This is basically a sequential execution, and one processor would suffice. In practice, the computation is distributed over all four processors, but the utilization of processors remains at $12/48 = 0.25$.

The one-token-per-arc strategy (3) practically turns into pipelining of the block of assignment statements inside the loop, as shown in Figure 3b. Execution time is determined by the longest operation (division) in the loop. Thus, $3 \times 8 + 3 = 27$ time units are necessary, with utilization at $12/27 = 0.44$. Approaches (1), (4), and (5) are similar. They achieve the best performance and utilization, as shown in Figure 3c. They need only 14 time units, with utilization equal to $12/14 = 0.86$. However, a random-scheduling strategy (followed in many data flow architecture proposals) can result in less than optimal execution, as shown in Figure 3d, where 18 time units were needed to finish the computation. The detection of possible critical paths and scheduling along these paths is a problem that none of the proposed data flow machines have solved.

For comparison, a possible execution on a vector machine with a vectorizing compiler is shown in Figure 3e. A mediocre vectorizing compiler would detect that the first and second statements in the loop can be vectorized. The execution time is 18 and the utilization $12/18 = 0.66$. A good vectorizing compiler would detect the recurrence in the third statement, substitute a different algorithm, and lower the execution time to 14 with a utilization of one, as shown in Figure 3f. Note that recurrences arise frequently in ordinary programs.[10]

It is obvious from this simple example that the sequential machine offers the worst performance and the data flow machine with labeled tokens the best. Pipelined and vector machines are somewhere between those extremes, although the vector machine with a good optimizing compiler was competitive with the data flow machine in our example. Remember, however, that our models are gross oversimplifications of real machines. Since there are no hard facts on performance of data flow machines, it remains to be seen whether the overhead in token labeling, data storage, and instruction communication will lower their theoretical upper bound on performance.

Performance under a low degree of parallelism. The data flow graph can be considered the machine language of a data flow machine. Each node of the graph represents an instruction, and the arcs pointing from each node can be thought of as the addresses of instructions receiving the

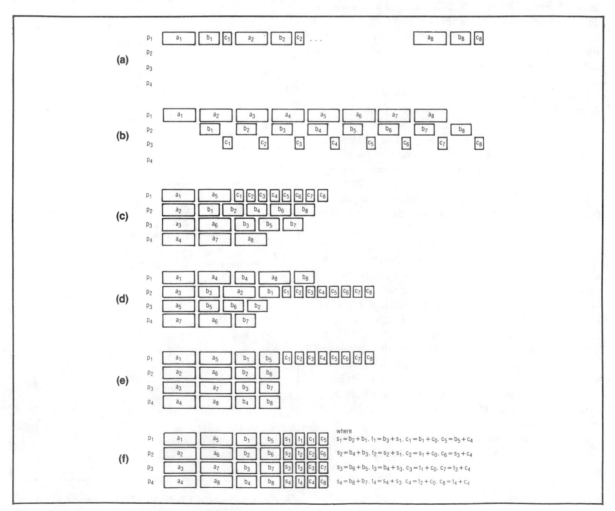

Figure 3. Comparison of data flow strategies (a) through (f).

result. Roughly speaking, a data flow machine consists of four components: an instruction memory that contains all instructions in the data flow graph, a set of processing units that perform the operations specified by each instruction, an arbitration network that carries instruction packets to appropriate processing units, and a distribution network that carries the result packets back to the instruction memory. Obviously, the instruction memory can be partitioned into several modules, to match the bandwidth of the processing units and communication networks. We assume also that one unit of time is needed to pass through each of the four components of our data flow model.

In contrast to the data flow model, the von Neumann model consists of a central processing unit and a memory. The central processing unit has a general-purpose register file and an arithmetic-logic unit. Each register-to-register operation takes one unit of time, as do fetch and store from memory.

To crudely compare the performance and the program size of these two models, we considered several programs that, like the one given by Arvind, Kathail, and Pingali,[11] integrate function f from a to b over n intervals of size h by the trapezoidal rule. We concluded that the data flow model apparently requires more instructions than the von Neumann model. This code inefficiency stems from two principles of the data flow model:

(1) *Distributed control.* Each datum (or path in the graph) is controlled individually. There are several separate SWITCH instructions (at least one for each variable assignment inside the body of a loop) that correspond to one BRANCH instruction in the von Neumann model. Similarly, several independent MERGE instructions substitute for one JUMP instruction.

(2) *No explicit storage.* Since only values are passed from one instruction to the other, values that do not change during the computation from one iteration to the other must circulate in one way or another through the system.

These redundancies lower the expected performance when the degree of parallelism (the number of operations executable in parallel) is equal to or greater than the ideal rate (the maximum possible number of operations executed concurrently).

In terms of raw speed on small programs, the von Neumann model requires less time. This performance advantage is the consequence of two things:

(1) *Instruction pipelining.* In von Neumann computers, the fetch, decode address generation, and execution phases of an instruction are allowed to overlap. Thus, each instruction averages only one time unit in a reasonably sequential code. On the other hand, the data flow model does not allow pipelining on the critical path. That is, each instruction must complete before the new one—which uses the result from the previous one—can start.

(2) *Local storage.* A data flow machine is basically a memory-to-memory machine, since there is no concept of storage. It usually helps to keep all the input parameters to a subroutine in high-speed, general-purpose registers, as in our examples. This lack of locality severely degrades the performance of the data flow machines on programs with a low degree of parallelism.

One might argue that although the data flow processor is slower in raw speed, it is faster overall because it contains many overlapped processing units operating in parallel. Still, the degree of parallelism must be taken into account. In a crude approximation appropriate to this case, the data flow machine can be thought of as a long pipeline. To keep the pipeline saturated, the degree of parallelism must be larger than the number of stages in the pipeline. Under low parallelism, the pipeline is not saturated for a long period of time and serious degradation of performance occurs. For comparison, Cray-1 computers have functional unit pipelines with five to eight stages in which register fetches are included. Data flow machines have pipelines many times longer. They include functional units, communication networks, and instruction memory. Therefore, we can expect them to perform poorly under low parallelism. If features for parallelism exploitation such as token labeling and array management are added, the performance under low parallelism becomes even worse.

Data flow machines require a parallelism of several hundred independent instructions to saturate the pipeline. Arvind et al.[11] have computed, for example, that for a data flow machine with 100-microsecond interprocessor communication time and 64 processing units, each of which performs a floating-point operation in 10 microseconds, the degree of parallelism to keep the machine saturated is 640. To date, the only programs with such a high degree of parallelism are computationally intensive numerical calculations that operate on large arrays of data. Unfortunately, data flow machines do not handle arrays of data very efficiently because of their emphasis on fine-grain, operation-level concurrency.

Structures storage. If tokens are allowed to carry vectors, arrays, and other structures in general, the result is a large transmission and storage overhead. This is particularly the case when operators modify only a small part (possibly only one element) of the whole structure. For this reason, Dennis[6] suggested that all structures be represented by a finite, acyclic, directed graph having one or more root nodes arranged so that each node can be reached over some directed path from some root node (that is, a forest of trees with possibly common nodes).

Arrays are stored as trees, with array elements at the leaves. For example, an array $A = [a_{i,j}]$, $1 \leq i,j \leq 3$ can be stored as a ternary tree. Obviously, trees of any order can be used for storing arrays.

According to the functionality principle of the data flow model, a data structure must be free of any side-effects. An easy way to accomplish this is to forbid any sharing or overlapping of structures. Since every structure would have its own private area of memory, there would be no side effects. However, this is prohibitively expensive since it requires each structure to be completely copied whenever its value is duplicated. The solution proposed by Dennis is to share the structures whenever possible and use the reference count technique. Each node of a structure has a reference count, which is the total number of pointers to that node from other nodes and tokens in the data flow program. For example, if a copy B of the array A is created, the pointer for B points to the same root node as the pointer for A (Figure 4a).

When an APPEND operator is used, it is necessary to copy all nodes with a reference count greater than one, as well as their successors, on the directed path from the root to the selected node. For example, if an array B' is obtained from B by setting $a_{23} = 0$, the structure in Figure 4b will be generated. Similarly, B'' can be obtained from B' by setting $a_{33} = 0$ (Figure 4c). The above two operations, setting $a_{23} = 0$ and $a_{33} = 0$, are completely independent of each other but cannot be executed concurrently; by the asynchrony principle of the data flow model, concurrent execution could result in two different structures, B' and B''' (Figure 4d), from which it is very difficult to obtain B''.

Here we see that a simple operation, such as setting a row or a column in a matrix to zero, requires sequential execution, which in turn significantly degrades performance for large structures. The performance degradation can come from two independent mechanisms used in this scheme. The first mechanism uses the reference count to share data. Therefore, there will be many unnecessary accesses to the memory in order to change the reference count without using data. This occurs for all operations that create or destroy pointers. For example, when a SWITCH operator destroys a token, the count must be decreased. The second mechanism uses tree structures to store arrays. If the order of the tree is small, large arrays will be stored as trees of considerable depth and therefore many memory references will be needed to access an array element. On the other hand, there is an unnecessary data transmission and wasted space due to excessively large memory blocks when the order is large.

To avoid the excessive storage demand and slow access time due to the functional semantics of the data structure operations, Arvind and Thomas[12] proposed I-structures, array-like data structures whose storage is allocated before expressions to produce them are invoked. Since an I-structure construction is not strictly ordered (to improve parallelism), it is possible that part of a program might attempt to read an element before that element's creation. Therefore, a presence bit is associated with every element, and an attempt to read an empty location causes deferral of the read operation. Unfortunately, when the element is finally created all deferred reads must be executed. Checking for those deferred reads on every write slows down the access of I-structures in comparison with the simple von Neumann model and a language based on it, in which the programmer has some control over storage.

Basically, two observations can be made:

(1) Instead of sending data in only one direction—from place of creation to place of consumption—a request (address in the von Neumann model) must be sent in one direction, with the I-structure value (data) returning in the other direction. This unnecessarily increases traffic through the system.

(2) Since memory is allocated before it is used, the problem of optimally distributing I-structures over many processors to minimize traffic through the networks has been introduced. This problem, well known as the *memory contention problem*, has plagued designers of vector machines and multiprocessors for years.

In summary, the proposed I-structures, although expected to solve data storage and access problems more efficiently, are a small step back toward the von Neumann model.

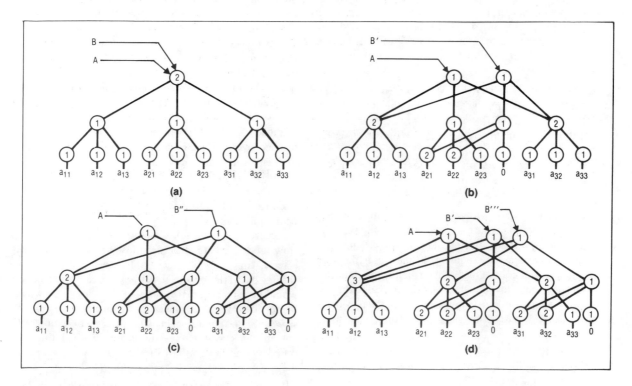

Figure 4. Storage scheme for a 3 × 3 array.

Data flow languages

The success of any computer, data flow or otherwise, depends on the quality of its programming languages. Data flow machines demand high-level languages, since graphs, their machine language, are not an appropriate programming medium; they are error-prone and hard to manipulate.

Three high-level language classes have been considered by data flow researchers. The first is the *imperative* class. For instance, the Texas Instruments group considered the use of a modified ASC Fortran compiler for their data flow machine.[13] Compiler techniques for the translation of imperative high-level languages into data flow graphic languages have also been studied at Iowa State University.[14] The second is the *functional* class. By functional languages, we mean those resembling pure Lisp, which is based on Church's lambda calculus, and Backus' FP, which is based on Curry's combinatory logic. This second class is now being studied in a data flow context at the University of Utah.[15]

The third class—our focus here—consists of the so-called *data flow languages,* which are designed with data flow machines in mind. The most notable examples are Id,[9,12] LAU,[5] and Val.[16] The syntax of these languages is essentially that of imperative languages. For example, all data flow languages include IF and LOOP statements. On the other hand, their semantics are basically that of functional languages.

Below, focus on the two characteristics that set data flow languages apart: the functional semantics of the language and the implicit expression of parallelism. Data flow languages have many other characteristics, which are not unique. For example, the freedom from side effects and the locality of effects have been mentioned as being of paramount importance,[17] and we agree. However, some imperative languages possess these characteristics.

Functional semantics. A consequence of this first characteristic is that in data flow languages variables stand for values and not for memory locations. Imperative languages like Fortran, PL/I, and Pascal allow programmers to be aware of and have some control over the primary memory allocation for both programs and data. Thus, in PL/I we can classify variables as static or dynamic, and memory can be explicitly requested and freed.

In data flow and functional languages, on the other hand, programmers deal only with values. These languages do not allow the explicit control of memory allocation, relying instead on mechanisms like garbage collection to keep memory utilization at a reasonable level.

Functional semantics offers parallel processing the advantage of a simplified translation process. Thus, data flow languages are free of side effects. This makes it possible to translate subroutines separately, without unnecessarily constraining parallelism. Again, freedom from side effects is not unique to data flow languages; imperative languages can also be side-effect free.

Another welcome consequence of functional semantics is the single assignment rule.[18] Thanks to this rule,

parallelism is less constrained by anti dependences and output dependences than it is in conventional imperative languages. Consider, for example, the following Fortran program:

$$
\begin{array}{ll}
1 & A = D + 1 \\
2 & B = A + 1 \\
3 & A = 0.
\end{array}
$$

It is easy to see that statement 3 cannot be executed until statement 2 fetches $A;$ that is, statement 3 is antidependent on statement 2. In a data flow language, the use of A in statement 3 is not valid; a different variable must be used in place of A to allow execution of statements 1 and 2 to be concurrent with statement 3.

On the other hand, a compiler can very easily rid imperative language programs of antidependences and output dependences by using the simple transformation techniques of renaming and expansion. Renaming, as its name indicates, changes variable names to avoid antidependences and output dependences. This transformation would replace A in statement 3 with some other variable. To understand expansion, consider the following Fortran loop:

$$
\begin{array}{lll}
DO & 10 & I = 1, N \\
 & & X = A(I) + 1 \\
10 & & B(I) = X^{**}2
\end{array}
$$

The different iterations of this loop cannot be executed in parallel, since there is only one memory location corresponding to X and because N locations would be needed for all iterations to proceed in parallel. After expansion, the scalar variable X would be replaced by a vector of N elements, and the occurrences of X would be replaced by $X(I)$. This would allow parallelism, at the expense of using more memory. We have found these techniques, as implemented in the Parafrase system,[2] to be successful almost all the time.

Some data flow researchers have been unaware of this fact. This has led them to believe that functional semantics makes a big difference in terms of efficient parallel object code, but this does not seem to be true.

Consider the following quotation from Arvind.[19]

A straightforward Fortran program would do this in the following way.

```
C   X IS AN ARRAY OF N + 2 ELEMENTS
C   X(1) AND X(N + 2) REMAIN CONSTANT
    N1    = N + 1
    DO   20 K  = 1, KMAX
    DO   10 I  = 2, N1
    Y(I) = (X(I − 1) + (X(I) + X(I + 1))/3
10  CONTINUE
    DO   15 I  = 2, N1
    X(I) = Y(I)
15  CONTINUE
20  CONTINUE                                    (1)
```

A compiler can easily generate good code for a multiple processor machine from the above program. Even if a programmer is clever, and avoids copying array Y into X by switching back and forth between X and Y, a vectorizing compiler will be able to deal with it effectively. However, if array X is large, and a programmer decides to avoid using another array Y altogether, the following program may result:

```
N1  =  N+1
DO   20 K  =1, KMAX
T1  =  X(1)
T2  =  X(2)
DO   10 I  =2, N1
X(I) = , (T1 + T2 + X(I + 1))/3.
T1  =  T2
T2  =  X(I + 1)
10  CONTINUE
20  CONTINUE                              (2)
```

It would be extremely difficult for a compiler to detect a transformation in which all the elements of array X are relaxed simultaneously.

When the last Fortran program is transformed by Parafrase, the simple expansion technique leads to the following program. It can be effectively executed in parallel (loops 2, 3, and 4 are detected by Parafrase as vector operations).

```
N1  =  N+1
DO   1     I  =1, KMAX
      T1(I)  =  X(1)
      T2(I)  =  X(2)
      DO  2  J  =1, N1
2           T2(J + 1)  =  X(J + 2)
      DO  3  J  =1, N1
3           T1(J + 1)  =  T2(J)
      DO  4  J  =1, N1
            X(J + 1)  =  (T1(J) + T2(J) + X(J + 2))/3
4   CONTINUE
```

The functional semantics might have advantages besides those related to parallel processing. For example, data flow languages might help produce programs that are easier to verify and understand than those in imperative languages. But so far, no scientific evidence has been produced to either confirm or deny such advantages.

Our main objection to functional semantics is that it denies the programmer direct control of memory allocation. Thus, the success of data flow languages depends on how efficiently garbage collection can be implemented and on the specific compiler algorithms used to control memory allocation.

Implicit parallelism. The second characteristic is that parallelism is often implicit in data flow languages. Thus, a data flow language compiler must compute the flow dependences and use them to generate parallel machine code. Implicit parallelism is a worthy goal; it can save the programmer tedious, error-prone tasks. However, we would like to make some observations on compiler techniques and on the need for explicit parallelism.

Compiler techniques. The algorithms used by a data flow compiler determine how much implicit parallelism can be exploited. Therefore, implicit parallelism and compilers must be discussed together. The data flow literature discusses two compiler techniques: flow dependence computation and loop unraveling.[9] These techniques must be developed further if data flow compilers are to successfully exploit implicit parallelism.

Flow dependence is computed by using variable names only. It is very important, however, to look at subscripts, as well. Consider, for example, the Fortran program in Figure 5a. A compiler that ignores the subscripts will not detect the parallelism in this program. Furthermore, the application of loop unraveling when the target machine is a data flow multiprocessor requires some study. Now consider the Fortran program in Figure 5b. If the different iterations of the inner loop are distributed across the data flow processors, a speed-up on the order of N could be obtained. However, if the distribution is done on the basis of the outer loop, and M is much smaller than the number of processors, the speed-up will be substantially smaller.

There are other important techniques that are not discussed in the data flow literature. These include techniques for handling memory allocation and deallocation for code and data (see "functional semantics," above) and techniques that define the storage layout of arrays when the target machine is a multiprocessor.

Explicit vs. implicit parallelism. Implicit parallelism is not sufficient for a powerful programming language, for at least two reasons. The first is the spurious flow dependences mentioned above, and the second is the need to express in summary form the parallel evaluation of recurrences.

Spurious flow dependences are due to the limitations of the compiler. Some can be removed by improving the compiler algorithms; others might be impossible to remove. The discussion of Figure 5a, above, provides an example of how to remove limitations by improving the compiler algorithm. An example in which the limitations cannot be removed is shown in Figure 5c. The Fortran program in this figure is the same as the one in Figure 5a, except that 1 is replaced by $W(K)$. Since $W(K)$ is not known at compile time, it is not possible to determine how or even if this program can be executed in parallel.

Parallel execution is possible in cases like the program in Figure 5c, but only through explicit parallelism. The programmer might know that $W(K)$ is always less than some small value and therefore know that the wavefront algorithm[20] can be applied successfully. In the LAU language and in Val, the programmer could handle this by using the FORALL construct or the EXPAND constructs. However, it is not possible to handle this problem in Id, which has no form of explicit parallelism.

```
(a)     DO   11   I = 1, N
          DO   11   J = 1, N
                A(I,J) = A(I-1,J) + A(I,J-1)

(b)     DO   12   I = 1, M
          DO   12   J = 1, N
                A(I,J) = A(I-1,J) + 1

(c)     DO   13   I = 1, N
          DO   13   J = 1, N
                A(I,J) = A(I-W(K),J) + A(I,J-W(K))
```

Figure 5. Fortran programs: (a) requiring subscript analysis for parallelism detection; (b) with inner loop parallel and outer loop sequential; (c) with parallelism that cannot be detected by a compiler.

It should be clear from the previous example that data flow languages need better ways to express general forms of parallelism. It is not clear what those constructs must be, and it is not clear that these constructs can be nicely incorporated in a data flow language.

Only the designers of Val have recognized the need to express recurrences. However, they provide only reduction-type recurrences such as sums and minimums. Other types of recurrences arise often enough to require their inclusion in a parallel programming language.[10] Examples include general arithmetic recurrences and boolean recurrences originating from IF statements inside loops.

Comments. It has been claimed that data flow languages have some advantages over imperative languages for parallel processing and programming in general. Functional semantics, however, is not a real advantage, since well-known compiler techniques applied to a good imperative language allow equal exploitation of parallelism. Also, implicit parallelism requires translation techniques as complicated as those used to extract parallelism from imperative languages. In fact, most of the techniques used in Parafrase[2,21] to translate Fortran programs into parallel programs can be used without change in data flow compilers.

Certainly, data flow languages have nice features, such as freedom from side effects, which are very advantageous for the compiler writer and programmer. However, these do not justify the effort required for the introduction of a totally new class of programming languages. Clearly, imperative languages with these characteristics can be designed.

The immensity of introducing a new language class becomes clear when we consider all the work required before data flow languages stand a chance of becoming common tools. This work must start with syntax; data flow languages are verbose. This verbosity might be a consequence of the syntactic similarity between data flow and imperative languages. The language designers, striving to make the semantic difference clear, introduced unnecessary keywords like NEW in Id, and cumbersome expressions like $Y[I:X(I)]$ in Val to denote an array Y with the Ith element replaced by $X(I)$.

Work is also necessary in the area of explicit parallelism. Data flow languages need constructs to specify parallelism in a general form and to specify general forms of recurrences. Finally, the functional semantics could be a source of difficulty, since it implies that memory allocation is not a concern of the programmer.

Conclusion

In all high-speed computer systems, it is important to achieve two goals:

(1) the discovery of as much potential simultaneity as possible in the computations to be performed; and

(2) the delivery at runtime of as much of the potential simultaneity as possible.

We have discussed various aspects of these points and argued that data flow researchers have done little to further our understanding of the first. It would appear that their contributions have been more concentrated on the second point, but there are a number of shortcomings in data flow ideas in this regard. It is possible to design much better machines than those available today—supersystems, in fact—but by following a bottom-up approach, the data flow people have made it difficult to reach their goal. Data flow notions are quite appealing at the scalar level, but array, recurrence, and other high-level operations become difficult to manage.

In pursuit of the first goal, data flow researchers have introduced the concept of value instead of location into high-level languages. In principle, this was a praiseworthy move. From the compiler point of view, however, there is little improvement over imperative languages. Explicit parallelism and nontrivial compiler techniques are still needed, mostly because of array variables. I-structures represent an attempt to free data flow languages from these two concerns.[12] They essentially allow the flow dependences between array element operations to be automatically satisfied at runtime. It is unlikely, however, that such a mechanism will efficiently solve many of the problems associated with flow dependence between arrays.

We question whether programming language design, as practiced by data flow researchers, is germane to the task of high-speed computer design. We are not prepared to make a pronouncement on programming languages for parallel processing; both applicative and imperative languages have advantages and drawbacks. We do, however, have some questions. First, are data flow languages marketable? To date, the high-speed computer market has been dominated by conservatism and software compatibility. Can data flow languages, as currently proposed, overcome this conservatism? Second, will data flow languages enhance programmer productivity? (The emphasis in imperative programming language design has also been toward increasing programmer productivity.) Although data flow researchers have made some claims to this effect, they remain, to our knowledge, unsubstantiated.

An alternative approach. A much better approach to successful high-speed machine design begins by acknowledging that the programming interface to a high-speed machine requires more latitude than is allowed by current data flow architectures. The following alternative incorporates that latitude. We define *compound functions* with the following properties:

- They represent computational tasks for which good speed-up can be achieved (in most cases) by using multiple processors.
- The compound operations that implement them allow simple control of a substantial amount of hardware in parallel.
- Fast compiler algorithms for deriving them from programs can be written in ordinary sequential programming languages.

Six such compound functions are discussed in Gajski et al.[22]: array operations, linear recurrences, FORALL loops, pipeline loops, blocks of assignment statements, and compound conditional expressions.

We can view a program as a dependence graph connecting compound function nodes. A function dispatch unit must schedule the execution of the compound function nodes. Since the times required by the nodes can be determined at runtime, the function dispatch unit might be considered a data flow machine. We call this a *dependence-driven computation* because several types of data and control dependence are used in determining the execution sequence.

As we return to the second goal of high-speed computer systems—the delivery of simultaneity at runtime—our criticisms of data flow processing should be put in perspective. High-speed computer architecture, in general, has many flaws and weaknesses: Pipeline processors often suffer from long start-up times, and parallel or multiprocessors can waste processor cycles because of mismatches between machine size and problem size. It is very difficult to design a multipurpose machine that is well-matched to a wide range of computations.

The scope of the problem is such that an appeal to engineering intuition should be made at this point. Such an appeal yields three observations:

(1) Dependences should be attacked on all fronts, subject to system design constraints.

(2) Designers should be guided by previously successful designs, when such designs are consistent with the overall constraints.

(3) Deterministic analysis and system operation should be favored over probabilistic analysis and system operation.

With regard to point 1, some data flow researchers have ignored explicit parallelism, and most have considered compiling techniques only superficially. With regard to point 2, data flow researchers often claim that an entirely new approach to high-speed computation is needed. The frequent occurrence of such constructs as array and recurrence operations, however, justifies the exploitation of well-known designs for conflict-free memory access and centrally synchronized global instructions. Adherence to point 3 can guarantee rather than maximize the likelihood of good system performance. In regard to all these aspects, data flow researchers tend not to exploit the global regularity in the problem because the focus is on a small granularity.

Summary of arguments. The following is a brief summary of the arguments against the data flow approach with respect to the principal architectural components in a high-speed computer system.

First, consider main memory array access, which is by far the biggest bandwidth load in many computations. Well-known methods can achieve conflict-free array access[23]; they have been demonstrated in the Burroughs BSP.[24] While data flow people claim to be trying to eliminate the von Neumann bottleneck[25] between CPU and memory, they have created several new bottlenecks of their own. Array access conflicts arise due to asynchrony, shared data cannot be accessed in parallel, unnecessary memory accesses can arise, and tree-like storage of arrays can lead to multiple accesses per array element. Furthermore, data flow programs tend to waste memory space for programs and arrays.

In the area of interconnection networks, data flow machines with nontrivial parallelism (only four-processor machines have been built) will have the same types of problems found in other architectures. No interesting new results in this area have come from data flow researchers; the problem remains an important one.

With respect to processing speeds, data flow architectures seem to inherently deliver less than maximum speedups. Control unit pipelining and instruction look-ahead cannot be exploited to the degree they are in other architectures. Furthermore, since data paths contain very long pipelines, data flow machines suffer from the same long pipeline-filling problems as other pipelined processors, and one must settle for less than maximum speedup. Thus, the performance is weak for programs with low parallelism.

Several practical aspects of data flow machines are worrisome. To date, no one has proposed a way to handle input/output operations, although they seem to be solvable, and debugging data flow programs could be difficult. We have already remarked on the questionable marketability of a data flow processor. As far as we know, there is no difference between the ability to implement a highly parallel data flow processor (with its global arbitration and distribution networks) using present VLSI technology, and the ability to implement a more conventional machine. Finally, there has been no discussion of the diagnosability and maintainability of data flow machines. These could be difficult areas for machines without program counters or deterministic behavior.

We have tried to level pointed criticism directly at data flow principles or at least at a majority of data flow systems. Our task was complicated by several factors. The design of a computing system from language to machine covers a lot of ground, and some researchers gloss over some aspects of the problem. Several groups have independently interpreted data flow principles with different design goals, and these goals are not always spelled out. Finally, a paper design is rarely as good as a practical implementation. Hence, we have had a difficult time discerning exactly what the data flow principles are.

Although we have attempted to point out weaknesses, we should add that data flow does have a good deal of potential. In small-scale parallel systems, data flow principles have been successfully demonstrated. When simultaneity is low, irregular, and runtime-dependent, data flow might be the architecture of choice. In very large-scale parallel systems, data flow principles still show some potential for high-level control. When several compound functions are to be executed in parallel, data flow offers some software engineering benefits, such as elimination of side effects.

It is in medium-scale parallel systems that data flow has little chance of success. Pipelined, parallel, and multiprocessor systems are all effective in this range. For data flow processing to become established here, its inherent inefficiencies must be overcome.

Most data flow researchers are engaged at too low a level of abstraction in dealing with dependence graphs and their relations to machines. They have placed much importance on language design issues that are not always inherently tied to their architecture. While they sometimes imply a radically new approach to high-speed computation, they are plagued by its standard problems. ∎

Acknowledgment

We are in debt to Arvind, who provided help in many ways during the writing of this article. Furthermore, we want to acknowledge Burton J. Smith and the anonymous referees whose constructive comments greatly improved the article. Finally, we thank Vivian Alsip for the high-quality job of typing and retyping the manuscript.

This work was supported in part by the National Science Foundation under Grants US NSF MCS76-81686 and MCS80-01561 and the US Department of Energy under Grant US DOE DE-AC02-81ER10822.

References

1. D. J. Kuck, *The Structure of Computers and Computations,* Vol. I, John Wiley & Sons, New York, 1978.

2. D. J. Kuck, R. H. Kuhn, D. A. Padua, B. Leasure, and M. Wolfe, "Dependence Graphs and Compiler Optimizations," *Proc. 8th ACM Symp Principles Programming Languages,* Jan. 1981, pp. 207-218.

3. J. E. Thornton, *Design of a Computer, The Control Data 6600,* Scott, Foresman and Co., Glenview, Ill., 1970.

4. R. M. Tomasulo, "An Efficient Algorithm for Exploiting Multiple Arithmetic Units," *IBM J. Research and Development,* Vol. 11, No. 1, Jan. 1967, pp. 25-33.

5. D. Conte, N. Hifdi, and J. C. Syre, "The Data Driven LAU Multiprocessor System: Results and Perspectives," *Proc. IFIP Congress,* 1980.

6. J. B. Dennis, "First Version of a Data Flow Procedure Language," *Lecture Notes in Computer Science,* Vol. 19, Springer-Verlag, 1974, pp. 362-376.

7. J. B. Dennis, "Data Flow Supercomputers," *Computer,* Vol. 13, No. 11, Nov. 1980, pp. 48-56.

8. I. Watson and J. Gurd, "A Practical Data Flow Computer," *Computer,* this issue.

9. Arvind, K. P. Gostelow, and W. E. Plouffe, *An Asynchronous Programming Language and Computing Machine,* Dept. of Information and Computer Science Report TR 114a, University of California, Irvine, Dec. 1978.

10. D. J. Kuck, "Parallel Processing of Ordinary Programs," in *Advances in Computers,* Vol. 15, M. Rubinoff and M. C. Yovits, eds., Academic Press, New York, 1976, pp. 119-179.

11. Arvind, V. Kathail, and K. Pingali, *A Data Flow Architecture with Tagged Tokens,* Laboratory for Computer Science, Technical Memo 174, MIT, Cambridge, Mass., Sept. 1980.

12. Arvind and R. H. Thomas, *I-Structures: An Efficient Data Type for Functional Languages,* Laboratory for Computer Science, Technical Memo 178, MIT, Cambridge, Mass., Sept. 1980.

13. J. C. Jensen, "Basic Program Representation in the Texas Instruments Data Flow Test Bed Compiler," unpublished memo, Texas Instruments, Inc., Jan. 1980.

14. S. J. Allan and A. E. Oldehoeft, "A Flow Analysis Procedure for the Translation of High Level Languages to a Data Flow Language", *Proc. Int'l Conf. Parallel Processing,* Aug. 1979, pp. 26-34.

15. R. M. Keller, B. Jayaraman, D. Rose, and G. Lindstrom, *FGL Programmer's Guide,* Dept. of Computer Science AMPS Technical Memo 1, University of Utah, Salt Lake City, Utah, July 1980.

16. W. B. Ackerman and J. B. Dennis, *VAL—A Value-Oriented Algorithmic Language, Preliminary Reference Manual,* Laboratory for Computer Science Technical Report 218, MIT, Cambridge, Mass., June 1979.

17. W. B. Ackerman, "Data Flow Languages," *Computer,* this issue.

18. L. G. Tesler and H. J. Enea, "A Language Design for Concurrent Processes," *AFIPS Conf. Proc.,* Vol. 32, 1968 SJCC, pp. 403-408.

19. Arvind, "Decomposing a Program for Multiple Processor Systems," *Proc. Int'l Conf. Parallel Processing,* Aug. 1980, pp. 7-16.

20. R. H. Kuhn, *Optimization and Interconnection Complexity for: Parallel Processors, Single-Stage Networks, and Decision Trees,* PhD thesis, Dept. of Computer Science Report 80-1009, University of Illinois, Urbana-Champaign, Ill., Feb. 1980.

21. D. A. Padua, D. J. Kuck, and D. H. Lawrie, "High-Speed Multiprocessors and Compilation Techniques," *IEEE Trans. Computers,* Vol. C-29, No. 9, Sept. 1980, pp. 763-776.

22. D. D. Gajski, D. J. Kuck, and D. A. Padua, "Dependence Driven Computation," *Proc. Compcon Spring,* Feb. 1981, pp. 168-172.

23. P. P. Budnik and D. J. Kuck, "The Organization and Use of Parallel Memories," *IEEE Trans. Computers,* Vol. C-20, No. 12, Dec. 1971, pp. 1566-1569.

24. D. Lawrie and C. Vora, "The Prime Memory System for Array Access," submitted for publication, 1980.

25. J. Backus, "Can Programming be Liberated from the von Neumann Style? A Functional Style and Its Algebra of Programs," *Comm. ACM,* Vol. 21, No. 8, Aug. 1978, pp. 613-641.

Daniel D. Gajski is an associate professor in the Department of Computer Science at the University of Illinois, Urbana-Champaign. Before joining the university in 1978, he had 10 years of industrial experience in digital circuits, switching systems, supercomputer design, and VLSI structures. His research interests are in computer system design, algorithm design for supercomputers, hardware and silicon compilers, and design automation. He received the Dipl. Ing. and MS degrees in electrical engineering from the University of Zagreb, Yugoslavia, and the PhD in computer and information sciences from the University of Pennsylvania.

David A. Padua is Professor Agregado at the Universidad Simón Bolívar in Venezuela. From 1979 to 1981, he was a visiting assistant professor at the University of Illinois.

He received the degree of Licenciado en Computación from the Universidad Central de Venezuela in 1973 and a PhD in computer science from the University of Illinois in 1979.

David J. Kuck is a professor in the Department of Computer Science at the University of Illinois, Urbana-Champaign. He joined the department in 1965. Currently, his research interests are in the coherent design of hardware and software systems. This includes the development of the Parafrase system, a program transformation facility for array and multiprocessor machines.

Kuck has served as an editor for a number of professional journals; among his publications is *The Structure of Computers and Computations, Vol. 1*. He has also consulted with many computer manufacturers and users and is the founder and president of Kuck and Associates, Inc., an architecture and optimizing compiler company.

Kuck received the BSEE degree from the University of Michigan, Ann Arbor, in 1959, and the MS and PhD degrees from Northwestern University in 1960 and 1963.

Robert H. Kuhn is an assistant professor at Northwestern University in the Department of Electrical Engineering and Computer Science. His interests are in machine organization and VLSI design. He is currently on the editorial board of *Computer* and is a member of the ACM and IEEE.

Kuhn obtained his PhD in computer science at the University of Illinois in 1980 and received a master's degree in computer science from the University of Connecticut in 1976. At Illinois, he worked with D. J. Kuck on vectorizing compilers for pipelined machines and parallel computer organization.

February 1982

Chapter 4: Dataflow Programming Languages

Background

Most von Neumann architectures use an imperative language model. A program forms a sequence of control instructions that determine the order in which values are extracted from memory locations; computations using these values are then performed, and the resulting values are replaced in the memory. It is the ability to reassign values to variables that imposes constraints on the sequencing of instructions and inhibits concurrent computations. The dataflow computation model allows the simultaneous execution of several instructions purely on the availability of data, provided there is enough concurrency in the application and there are sufficient resources available. Thus, the dataflow computers allow fine grain concurrency at the instruction level.

The imperative language model is not suited to the fine grain parallelism, since it provides a set of instructions that have to be evaluated in a predetermined sequence. Newer imperative languages, such as Ada, MODULA, and OCCAM, provide a parallel construct that allows a programmer to specify the tasks to be executed concurrently. This allows explicit specification of parallelism, which becomes unmanageable when the architecture is scaled beyond a small number of processors. These languages are mostly suited for large grain parallelism applications, where chunks of sequential instructions can be executed concurrently. Restructing sequential programs for parallel execution at compilation time is difficult and limited.

Most dataflow systems use single-assignment languages (SAL), which do not require the programmer to specify information to sequence the evaluation of a program. To avoid the ambiguities that may arise from reassigning values to the variables, the languages allow each variable to be assigned just once in the program. The order of statements that appear in a SAL program is not used to determine the order in which the programs are executed. Instead, a variable may be assigned a value as soon as all of the statements producing the variables on which it depends have been executed. By implication, statements assigning variables that do not depend on each other may be evaluated concurrently. As a result of the close relationship between the use of variables in SAL and the dataflow computation model, these languages provide an ideal textual syntax for dataflow graphs.

Article Summary

Ackerman explains the important properties of languages for dataflow computation and compares them with imperative languages such as FORTRAN in "Data Flow Languages." These properties examine freedom of side effects, locality of effects, equivalence of instruction scheduling constraints with data dependencies, single assignment convention, and the iteration notation. Two languages, VAL [6] and ID [7], are used in the discussion.

Davis and Keller, in "Data Flow Program Graphs," describe two basic approaches to using graphs to represent data flow programs: the token-stream model and the structure model. In the token-stream model, data are always viewed as flowing on arcs from one node to another in a stream of discrete tokens. Tokens are considered carriers or instantiations of data objects. In structure models, a single data structure is constructed on each arc. The structure may be interpreted as a stream of tokens or as a scalar value. The paper also discusses the utility of graphs as a programming media.

Arvind and Gostelow, in "The U-Interpreter," provide a description of how computations represented by cyclic data flow graphs can be automatically unfolded to expose all parallelism to the underlying hardware. They introduce the notion of tagging tokens (values) that are dynamically generated during program execution, which allows the disadvantages of the static dataflow model of computation to be overcome. The result of this work led to the construction of the MIT tagged-token dataflow machine.

Additional material on dataflow languages including SISAL, LUCID, ID, and DFC can be found in references 1-18.

References

[1] Ackerman, W.B., "Efficient Implementation of Applicative Languages," *LCS Technical Report 323*, Massachusetts Institute of Technology, Cambridge, Mass., March 1984.

[2] Allan, S.J. and Oldehoeft, R.R., "HEP SISAL: Parallel Functional Programming," *Parallel MIMD Computation: HEP Supercomputer and Its Application*, Massachusetts Institute of Technology Press, Cambridge, Mass., 1985.

[3] Ashcroft, E.A. and Wadge, W.W., "The Syntax and Semantics of Lucid," *Technical Report CSL 146*, SRI, Int'l., Menlo Park, Calif., March 1985.

[4] Chambers, F.B., Duce, D.A., and Jones, G.P. (editors), *Distributed Computing*, Academic Press, Inc. (London) Ltd., London, England, 1984.

[5] Glauert, J., "High-Level Languages for Dataflow Computers," *Pergamon-Infotech State of Art Report on Programming Technology*, Pergamon-Infotech Ltd., Maidenhead, England, March 1982, pp. 173-193.

[6] McGraw, J.R., "The VAL Language," *ACM Transactions on Programming Languages and Systems*, Vol. 4, No. 1, Jan. 1982, pp. 44-82.

[7] Nikhil, R.S. and Arvind, "Id/83s," *Lab. for CS Technical Report*, Massachusetts Institute of Technology, Cambridge, Mass., July 1985.

[8] Shimada, T., Sekiguchi, S., Hiraki, K., and Nishida, K., "A New Generation Data Flow Supercomputer," *Proc. Conf. on Algorithms, Architectures, and Futures of Sci. Computation*, University of Texas, Austin, Tx., 1985.

In a data flow language, locality of effect is easily achieved.
But obtaining freedom from side effects requires a fundamental
alteration in the execution model of the language.

Data Flow Languages

Reprinted from *Computer*, February 1982, pages 15-24. Copyright © 1982
by The Institute of Electrical and Electronics Engineers, Inc.

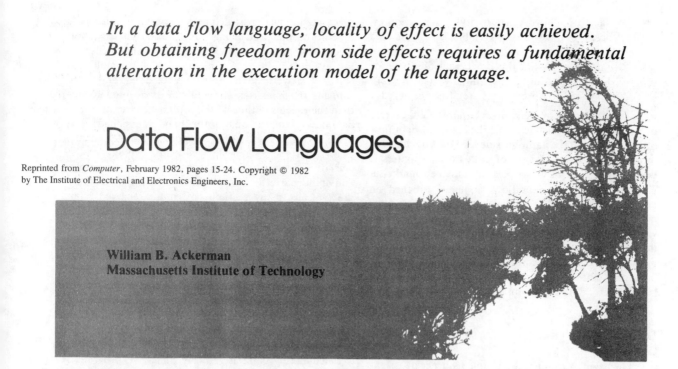

William B. Ackerman
Massachusetts Institute of Technology

The exploitation of parallelism is a primary goal for the architects of multiprocessor, vector machine, and array processor computer systems. Over the years, attempts have been made to design compilers that optimize programs written in conventional languages (e.g., "vectorizing" compilers for Fortran). There have also been various language designs developed to facilitate the use of these systems, such as concurrent Pascal for multiprocessors.[1] In order to utilize the features of the systems directly, researchers have even developed highly specialized languages like Glypnir for the Illiac IV array processor[2] and the various "vector" dialects of Fortran.[3] These languages almost always make the multiprocessor, vector, or array properties of the computer visible to the programmer, that is, they are actually vehicles that the programmer can use to help the compiler uncover parallelism. Many of these languages or dialects are "unnatural" in the sense that they closely reflect the behavior of the systems for which they were designed, rather than the manner in which programmers normally think about problem solving.

Data flow computer design also seeks to take advantage of parallelism. The parallelism in a data flow computer is both microscopic (much more so than in a multiprocessor) and all-encompassing (much more so than in a vector processor). Like other forms of parallel computers, data flow computers are best programmed in special languages: most data flow designs would be extremely inefficient if programmed in conventional languages such as Fortran or PL/1. However, languages suitable for data flow computers can be very elegant. The language properties that a data flow computer requires are beneficial in and of themselves and are very similar to some of the properties (e.g., disciplined control structures and orderly module interactions) that are known to facilitate understandable and maintainable software. In fact,

languages with many of these properties existed long before data flow computers were conceived. When discussing data flow, some of the relevant properties to keep in mind are:

(1) Freedom from side effects. This property is all-important. The (pure) Lisp language[4-6] is perhaps the best known example of a language without side effects. "Functional" languages such as FP[7] also fit in this category.* The connection between freedom from side effects and efficient parallel computation has been known for many years.[8]

(2) Locality of effect. Data flow languages generally exhibit considerable locality.

(3) Equivalence of instruction scheduling constraints with data dependencies. This means that all of the information needed to execute a program is contained in its "data flow graph." Since the data flow graph is, in effect, the machine code for a data flow computer, this property is what makes a language suitable for such a computer.

(4) A "single assignment" convention. A variable may appear on the left side of an assignment only once within the area of the program in which it is active. This is a notational convention that is widely accepted.

(5) A somewhat unusual notation for iterations, necessitated by (1) and (4).

---

* The term "functional" is often used, along with "applicative," to describe a language that operates by application of functions to values. This implies freedom from side effects. There is also a narrower meaning of the term in which "functional language" denotes a language such as FP, where all control structures are replaced by combining operators that manipulate functions directly, without ever appearing to explicitly manipulate data. The difference between such a language and the data flow languages discussed in this article is simply a difference in the notation used to route data through functions. The languages in this article are "functional" in the first sense only.

EH0260-0/87/0000/0179$01.00 © 1982 IEEE

(6) A lack of "history sensitivity" in procedures. Procedures have no state variables that retain data from one invocation to the next, so they cannot "remember." While this is generally observed for ordinary procedures (as required by (1) and (2)), history-sensitive procedures are often permitted.

To see why data flow computers require languages free of side effects, we must examine the nature of data flow computation and the nature of side effects. A detailed description of the mechanism of data flow computers is beyond the scope of this article but may be found elsewhere,[9-15] The two data flow languages touched on here, Val[16] and Id,[10] were developed by the data flow projects at the MIT and the University of California at Irvine, respectively. Lucid[17] and FP[7] were developed for their attractive mathematical properties and their amenability to program verification, rather than for programming data flow computers, but are nevertheless suitable languages for data flow computation.

Data flow analysis

Let us begin by examining a simple sequence of assignment statements written in a conventional language such as Fortran:

```
1  P = X + Y
2  Q = P/Y
3  R = X * P
4  S = R - Q
5  T = R * P
6  RESULT = S/T
```

A straightforward analysis of this program will show that many of these instructions can be executed concurrently, as long as certain constraints are met. These constraints can be represented by a graph in which nodes represent instructions and an arrow from one instruction to another means that the second may not be executed until the first has been completed. So the permissible computation sequences include, among others, (1,3,5,2,4,6), (1,2,3,5,4,6), and (1,[2 and 3 simultaneously],[4 and 5 simultaneously],6).

This type of analysis (commonly called data flow analysis, a term which long predates data flow computers) is frequently performed at runtime in the arithmetic processing units of high-performance conventional computers such as the IBM 360/91 and at compile time in optimizing compilers. In optimizing compilers, data flow analysis yields improved utilization of temporary memory locations. For example, on a computer with high-speed general-purpose or floating-point registers, this program can be compiled to use the registers instead of main memory for P, Q, R, S, and T, if it can be determined that they will not be used again. (This determination is very difficult, principally because of GOTOs, which is one of the reasons why it is very difficult to write optimizing compilers for languages such as Fortran.)

In the graph representation, an instruction can be executed as soon as all the instructions with arrows pointing into it have completed. On a multiprocessor system, we would allocate a processor for each instruction, with ap-

propriate instructions (such as semaphore operations[18]) to enforce the sequencing constraints, but execution would be hopelessly inefficient because the parallelism of this example is far too "fine grained" for a multiprocessor. The overhead in the process scheduling and in the *wait* and *signal* instructions would be many times greater than the execution time of the arithmetic operations. A data flow computer, on the other hand, is designed to execute algorithms with such a fine grain of parallelism efficiently. In these machines, parallelism is exploited at the level of individual instructions, as in the above example, and at all coarser levels as well. In most programs there are typically many sections, often far removed from each other, at which computations may proceed simultaneously.

To exploit parallelism at all levels, the instruction sequencing constraints must be deducible from the program itself. The sequencing constraints in Figure 1a are given by arrows. It is not difficult to see that these arrows coincide with data transmission from one instruction to its successor through variables. In fact, the graph could be redrawn with the arrows labeled by the variables that they represent (Figure 1b).

In a data flow computer, the machine-level program is essentially represented as a graph with pointers between nodes, the pointers representing both the flow of data and the sequencing constraints. The status of each instruction is kept in a special memory that is capable of "firing" (executing) the instruction when all of the necessary data values have arrived, and using the result to update the status of the destination instructions.* The programming language for a data flow computer must therefore satisfy two criteria: it must be possible to deduce the data dependencies of the program operations; and the sequencing constraints must always be exactly the same as the data dependencies, so that the instruction firing rule can be based simply on the availability of data.** A language can meet these criteria if it utilizes the general properties of locality of effect and freedom from side effects.

Locality of effect

Locality of effect means that instructions do not have unnecessary far-reaching data dependencies. For example, the Fortran program fragment given previously appears to use variables P, Q, R, S, and T only as temporaries. A similar fragment appearing elsewhere in the program might use the same temporaries for some unrelated computation, and the logic of the program might allow the two fragments to be executed concurrently were it not for this duplication of names. (Unfortunately,

---

* Although the language concepts presented in this article assume that the computer exploits parallelism at a microscopic level, not all data flow or data-driven computers do so. Designs of data flow computers that exploit parallelism only at the subroutine level may be found in Davis[19] and Rumbaugh.[20]

** Not all designs for data flow computers accept the second of these criteria or its consequences. The LAU language[21] is intended for execution on a data flow computer, but it was designed to support conventional forms of data-base updating and retrieval, so it has side effects on certain operations. The sequencing of these operations must therefore be constrained by means other than data dependencies, and so it does not satisfy the second criterion. The extra constraints in LAU are specified by path expressions[22] written into the source program.

many conventional languages encourage this style of programming in the name of "saving space.") Any attempt to execute the fragments concurrently would be impossible because of the apparent data dependencies arising from the duplication of these temporaries, unless the compiler can deduce that the conflict is not real and remove it by using different sets of temporaries.

In languages such as Fortran and PL/1, this deduction is not an easy one to make. A reference to a variable in one part of the program does not necessarily imply dependence on the value computed in another part: the variable might be overwritten before it is next read. Careful analysis is required to determine whether a variable is actually transmitting data or is "dead." This analysis is made much more difficult if unrestricted GOTOs or other undisciplined control structures are allowed. Of course, existing optimizing compilers can do a very good job of analyzing the various types of dependencies in reasonably well-structured programs,[23] but the languages being proposed in this article make that unnecessary.

The problem can be simplified by assigning every variable a definite "scope," or region of the program in which it is active, and carefully restricting the entry to and exit from the blocks that constitute scopes. It is also helpful to deny procedures access to any data items that are not transmitted as arguments, though this is not really necessary if global variables are avoided and procedure definitions are carefully block structured as in Pascal.

Side effects

Freedom from side effects is necessary to ensure that the data dependencies are the same as the sequencing constraints. It is much more difficult to achieve than locality of effect because locality only requires superficial restrictions on the language, whereas freedom from side effects requires fundamental changes in the way the language's "virtual machine" processes data. Side effects come in many forms—the most well-known examples arise in procedures that modify variables in the calling program, as in this Pascal example:

procedure GETRS(X, Y: real) ;
begin RS : = X * X + Y * Y
      (* RS is declared in an outer block *)
end ;

Absence of global or "common" variables and careful control of the scopes of variables make it possible for a compiler to prohibit this sort of thing, but a data flow computer imposes much stricter prohibitions against side effects: a procedure may not even modify its own arguments. In a sense nothing may ever be modified at all.

If we prohibit global variables and modification of arguments, simple side effect problems such as the above can be cured, but problems will remain that could interfere with concurrent computation. These more serious side effects do not arise in the manipulation of simple (scalar) data, but only from the processing of data structures such as arrays and records. More precisely, they arise from the way data structures are manipulated in conventional languages. The solution is to manipulate data structures in the same way scalars are manipulated.

Consider the following procedure, which modifies its arguments by a conventional "call by reference" mechanism. SORT2 is a procedure to sort two elements, the *J*th and the *J* + 1st, of array A into ascending order by exchanging them if necessary.

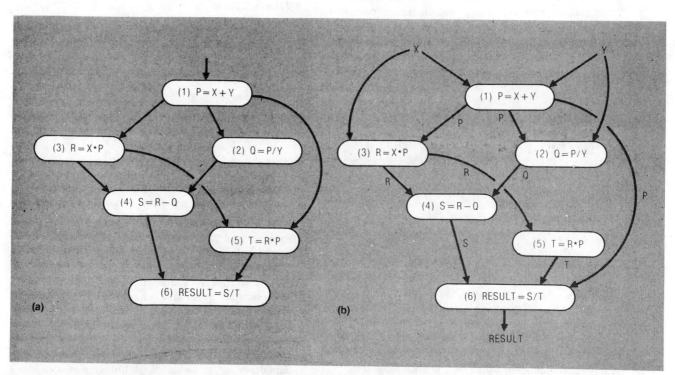

Figure 1. (a) Sequencing constraints in Fortran assignment statements; (b) constraints with variables represented.

```
procedure SORT2(var A: array[1 . .10] of real ;
    J: integer) ;
var T: real ;
begin if A[J] > A[J + 1] begin
        T : = A[J] ;
        A[J] : = A[J + 1] ;
        A[J + 1] : = T ;
        end
    end ;
(1)  SORT2(AA, J) ;
(2)  SORT2(AA, K) ;
(3)  P : = AA[L] ;
```

Statements 1 and 2 might interfere with each other and with statement 3. Since the values of J, K, and L are not known to the compiler, it must assume that the statements will conflict, and execute them in the exact order specified. Any attempt at parallel execution might result in the incorrect results, depending on J, K, L, and unpredictable fluctuations in timing.

A phenomenon known as "aliasing" makes the problem even more difficut. This occurs when different formal parameters to a procedure refer to the same actual parameter, that is, they are "aliases" of each other:

```
procedure REVERSE(var A, B: array[1 . .10] of real);
begin for J : = 1 to 10 do
        B[J] : = A[11 – J] ;
    end ;
```

In this program it would appear that since A and B are different arrays, all 10 assignments could proceed concurrently or in any order. However, if this were part of a larger program and REVERSE were invoked in the statement "REVERSE(Q, Q) ;" arrays A and B would actually be the same, and the assignments would seriously interfere with each other. Languages such as Fortran and PL/1, in which external procedures are not available to the compiler when the calling program is being compiled, make the problem harder still. Facilities for manipulating data structures by pointers, such as the pointer data type in PL/1 and Pascal, make it possible for all of these problems to arise without using procedures—the "call by reference" mechanism is not at fault here. Even if proce-

dures and pointers are not used, the sequencing constraints may be far from clear, as in

```
(1) A[J] : = 3 ;
(2) X : = A[K] ;
```

If the convention is adopted that any statement modifying any element of an array constitutes a "writing" of the array, statement 1 clearly passes array A to statement 2. But then a statement such as the assignment in

```
for J : = 1 to 10 do
    A[J + 1] : = A[J] + 1 ;
```

depends on itself!

All of this leads to one inescapable conclusion: if arrays and records exist as global objects in memory and are manipulated by statements and passed as pointers or procedure parameters, it is virtually impossible to tell, at the time an array element is modified, what effects that modification may have elsewhere in the program.

One way to solve some of these problems is to use "call by value" instead of the more common "call by reference." This solves the aliasing problem and the problem of procedures modifying their arguments. In a "call by value" scheme, a procedure copies its arguments (even if they are arrays). Thus it can never modify the actual argument in the calling program. Call by reference has traditionally been use instead of call by value because it is a more faithful way of modeling computation, and is more efficient, on von Neumann computers.

Applicative languages

A scheme is used for data flow languages which goes far beyond call by value: all arrays are values rather than objects and are treated as such at all times, not just when being passed as procedure arguments. Arrays are not modified by subscripted assignment statements such as "A[J] : = S;" but are processed by operators which create new array values. The simplest operator to perform the applicative equivalent of modifying an array takes three arguments: an array, an index, and a new data value. The result of the operation is a new array, containing the given data value at the given index, and the same data as the original array at all other indices. In the Val language this elementary operator appears as "A [J:S]", while in the Id language it is "A + [J] S". This operation does not modify its argument. Hence, in this Val program,

```
(1) B  :=  A [J:S] ;
(2) C  :=  A [K: T] ;
(3) P  :=  A[L] ;
(4) Q  :=  B[M] ;
(5) R  :=  C[N] ;
```

statements 1 and 2 do not interfere with each other or with array A. Statement 3 may be executed immediately, whether 1 and/or 2 have completed or not, since they would have no effect on statement 3 anyway. Statement 4 can be executed as soon as statement 1 completes, whether statement 2 has completed or not. In fact, the sequencing constraints are those shown in Figure 2. This situation is similar to the one in our first simple Fortan example: the sequencing constraints are exactly the same as the data dependencies, which is the property we seek for

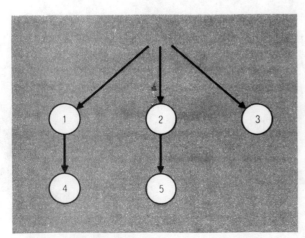

Figure 2. Sequencing constraints in a Val program.

COMPUTER

data flow. Note that an assignment like "A : = A [J: S]" makes no sense conceptually, and the single assignment rule will in fact forbid it.

An operator-based handling of arrays and records automatically accomplishes call by value. In a call by value scheme, a routine such as the SORT2 given previously would not accomplish its purpose. SORT2 must return the new array as its value. It would be written in simplified Val as

```
function SORT 2(A, J)
    if A[J] < A[J + 1] then A
    else ( A[J: A[J + 1]] ) [J + 1: A[J]]
                % No temporary variable needed
                % during this exchange because
                % A is not modified.
        end
    end
```

Note that the array construction operator may be composed with itself and with other operators in the same way as arithmetic operators.

In conventional languages, procedures do most, if not all, of their work through side effects: a procedure might be designed to alter dozens of variables in the calling program. Functions, on the other hand, typically return a single value, which is usually not an array or record. To make functions as powerful and flexible as the procedures of conventional languages, applicative languages often allow functions to return several values, entire records or arrays, or both. If a function returns several values, its invocation can be used in a "multiple assignment" such as

$$X, Y, Z := FUNC(P, Q, R) \quad \% FUNC \text{ returns 3 values}$$

Perhaps the most profound difference in the way people must think when writing programs in data flow languages as opposed to conventional languages lies in regarding arrays and records as values instead of objects. The customary view of arrays as objects residing in static locations of memory and being manipulated by statements that are executed in some sequence is incompatible with detection of parallelism among the statements. Viewing arrays and records as values manipulated by operations (as scalar values are) allows the parallelism among the operators to be deduced from the data dependencies, again as is the case with scalar values.

The value-oriented approach to arrays is, at first, confusing to some, but it need not be. An integer array can be thought of as a string of integers, just as an integer can be thought of as a string of digits. If J has the value 31416, the statement "K : = J − 400 ;" leaves K equal to 31016; no programmer would expect the value of J to be affected. If A is an array with elements [3, 1, 4, 1, 6], the statement "B : = A [3: 0]" is completely analogous; it leaves B with elements [3, 1, 0, 1, 6] and does not change A.

Languages that perform all processing by means of operators applied to values are called applicative languages, and are thus the natural langues for data flow computation. Lisp is the earliest well-known applicative language to be implemented on a computer. (It is applicative only if RPLACA, RPLACD, and all other functions with side effects are avoided; this subset of the language is often called "pure" Lisp.) The connection between applicative languages and the detection of parallelism has been reported by Tesler and Enea[8] and more recently by Friedman and Wise.[24] The Tesler/Enea paper, and the development of Lisp and other applicative languages, all predate the data flow computer concept by several years. In even more "historical" terms, the concept of computation by applicative evaluation of expressions actually goes back to the invention of the lambda calculus in 1941.[25]

Definitional languages and the single assignment rule

Having accepted an applicative programming style and a value-oriented rather than object-oriented execution model, let us examine the implications of this style as they relate to the meaning of assignment statements. Except in iterations (which will be discussed later), an assignment statement has no effect except to provide a value and bind that value to the name appearing on its left side. The result of the assignment is accessible only in later expressions in which that name appears. If the language uses blocks in which all variables are local to the block for which they are declared, the places where a variable is used can be determined by inspection. If the expression on the right side of an assignment is substituted for the variable on the left side everywhere within the block, the resultant program will be completely equivalent. (Note in the example below that the program on the left is clearly more efficient, requiring only two additions instead of four. I am not proposing the substitution be made in practice.)

$$
\begin{aligned}
S &:= X + Y; \\
D &:= 3 * S; \\
E &:= S/2 + F(S);
\end{aligned}
$$

is equivalent to

$$
\begin{aligned}
D &:= 3 * (X + Y); \\
E &:= (X + Y)/2 + F(X + Y);
\end{aligned}
$$

Now this situation is the same as a system of mathematical equations. If a system of equations contains "S = X + Y", it is clear that $3 * S$ and $3 * (X + Y)$ are equivalent. Hence the statement "S : = X + Y ;" means the same thing in the program that the equation "S = X + Y" means in a system of equations, namely that within the scope of these variables S is the sum of X and Y. The correspondence can be thought of as holding for all time; it is not necessary to consider the statements as being executed at particular instants. (In fact, perhaps the word "variable" is an appropriate term.) Of course, the addition of X and Y to form S must take place before any of the operations that use S can be performed, but the programmer does not need to be directly concerned with this.

In short, the statement "S: = X + Y" should be thought of as a *definition*, not an assignment. Languages which use this interpretation of assignments are called *definitional languages* as opposed to conventional imperative languages. Definitional languages are well suited to program verification because the assertions made in proving correctness are exactly the same as the definitions appearing in the program itself. In conventional languages one must follow the flow of control to determine where in the program text assertions such as "S = X + Y" are true, because the variables S, X, and Y can be changed many times, and assertions must therefore be associated with points in the program. In a definitional language, however, the situation is extremely simple. If a program block contains the statement "S: = X + Y;" then the assertion "S = X + Y" is true. Of course, care must be taken to prevent a system of circular definitions such as

$$X := Y;$$
$$Y := X + 3;$$

Such circular definitions can easily be checked by the compiler. The simplest way is to require that every name be defined (appear on the left side of a definition) before it appears on the right side of any definition, and that it be defined only once. So the actual proof rule is: if a program block contains the statement "S: = X + Y;" and the program compiles correctly, then "S = X + Y" is true. Strictly speaking, it is true only in statements after the one defining S, but since S could not have appeared in earlier statements, the assertion can be treated as being true throughout the block.

The power of definitional languages for program verification is well-known outside the data flow field. Lucid[17] is an example of an applicative definitional language designed expressly for ease of program verification. A language proposed by Kessels[26] would allow a program to be a mixture of modules, some imperative and some definitional.

There is one problem that could ruin the elegance of definitional languages: multiple definition of the same name. Definitional languages almost invariably obey the single assignment rule, which prevents program constructs which imply mathematical abominations such as "J : = J + 1;". Since the appearance of J on the right side precedes the actual definition of J, it implies an inconsistent statement sequence that the compiler would diagnose. The prevention of such abominations is necessary if the definitions in the program are to be carried directly into assertions used to prove correctness, since the assertion "J = J + 1" is absurd.

But it is not actually necessary for a data flow language to conform to the single assignment rule. A data flow language could be designed with multiple assignments in which the scope of a variable extends only from one definition to the next, which, in effect, introduces a new variable that simply happens to have the same name. A program written this way can easily be transformed into one obeying the single assignment rule by simply choosing a new name for any redefined variable, and changing all subsequent references to the new name. However, the advantages of single assignment languages, namely, clarity and ease of verification, generally outweigh the "convenience" of reusing the same name.

Iterations

In spite of the previous discussions, one area remains in which statements in conventional languages, such as

$$I := I - 1;$$

or

$$A := A[J: X + Y];$$

seem to be explicitly or implicitly necessary, and that is in iterations. The technique of renaming variables to make a program conform to the single assignment rule works only for straight-line programs. If a statement appears in a loop, renaming its variables will not preserve the programmer's intentions. For example:

$$\text{for } I := 1 \text{ to } 10 \text{ do}$$
$$J := J + 1;$$

cannot be transformed to

$$\text{for } I := 1 \text{ to } 10 \text{ do}$$
$$J1 := J + 1;$$

If the language allows general GOTOs, with the resulting possibility of complex and unstructured loops, the problem becomes difficult indeed. But data flow languages have no GOTO statement, and require loops to be created only by specific program structures (such as the "while . . . do . . . " and similar statements found in PL/1 and Pascal). This makes the problem easy to solve, and allows for simple and straightforward iterations.

To develop the data flow equivalent of a "while . . . do . . . " type of iteration, we must consider what the "do" part of such a structure contains. Since there are no side effects, the only state information in an iteration is in the bindings of the loop variables, and the only activity that can take place is the redefinition of those variables through functional operators. An iteration therefore consists of

(1) definitions of the initial values of the loop variables,
(2) a test to determine, for any given values of the loop variables, whether the loop is to terminate or to cycle again,
(3) if it is to terminate, some expression giving the value(s) to be returned (these values typically depend on the current values of the loop variables), and
(4) if it is to cycle again, some expressions giving the new values to be assigned to the loop variables. These also typically depend on the current values of the loop variables.

An iteration to compute the factorial of N could be written in simplified Val as follows:

```
for J, K : = N, 1;   % Give loop variables J and K initial
                     % values N and 1, respectively. J will
                     % count downward. K will keep the
                     % accumulated product.

do if J = 0          % Decide whether to terminate.
     then K          % Yes, final result is current K.
   else iter J, K : = J − 1, K ∗ J ;
                     % No, compute new values of J and K,
     end             % and cycle again.
end
```

It could be written in Id (with a similar representation in Lucid) as

```
(initial J ← N ; K ← 1
while J ≠ 0 do
    new J ← J − 1 ;
    new K ← K * J ;
return K)
```

Although the values of the loop variables do change, they change only between one iteration cycle and the next. The single assignment rule, with its prohibition against things like "J = J − 1", is still in force within any one cycle. All redefinitions take place precisely at the boundary between iteration cycles (though they need not actually occur simultaneously). This is enforced in Val by allowing redefinitions only after the word *iter,* which is the command to begin a new iteration cycle. In Id and Lucid, the "new" values become the "current" values at the boundary between cycles.

Since the single assignment rule is obeyed and names have single values, the mathematical simplicity of assertions about values still exists within any single iteration cycle. The assertions typically take the form "In any cycle, $S = X + Y$" and assertions used in proving correctness of an iteration are usually proved inductively. Because the assertions take a simple form, such proofs are usually simpler than in conventional languages. For example, the assertion "$J \geq 0$ and $K * (J!) = N!$" is the "invariant" used to prove correctness of the factorial program. Note that a loop invariant is not something that is true only at certain places in the loop (e.g., at its beginning), but is true throughout the body of the loop. An invariant has a different interpretation during different iteration cycles because the values of the iteration variables change from one cycle to another. It must be proved for each cycle, typically by induction from the preceding cycle.

In the factorial program, the basis of the induction is that the invariant is true for the initial values $J = N$ (assuming $N \geq 0$) and $K = 1$. The induction step is that, if another cycle is started with the values $J - 1$ and $K * J$ substituted for J and K, respectively, these values will obey the assertion, that is, "$J - 1 \geq 0$ and $(K * J) * ((J-1)!) = N!$". This is clearly true if we observe that a new cycle will only be started if $J > 0$ and, hence, $J - 1 \geq 0$. The next step is to examine the value returned when and if the iteration terminates. Since $J = 0$ at that time, we will have $K * (0!) = N!$, or $K = N!$ Since K is the value returned, it is N!. Finally, we must show that the iteration will terminate, meaning that within a finite number of steps the termination condition will be satisfied—that condition is $J = 0$, which is clearly satisfied after N cycles.

Parallelism demands that sequential computations be held to a minimum. The iteration constructs just described seem to imply a sequential execution of the various cycles. If the values of the iteration variables in one cycle depend on those in the previous cycles (as they do in the factorial example), nothing can be done, although a data flow computer can often execute part of a cycle before the previous one has completed. If the values in one cycle do not depend on those of the previous cycles, the cycles can be performed in parallel. In Val this is done with a FORALL program construct that does not allow

one cycle to depend on another and directs the computer to perform all cycles simultaneously. In Id the same effect is achieved when the cycles do not depend on each other by an automatic "unfolding" of the iteration that permits the cycles to be performed simultaneously.

Errors and exceptional conditions

Locality of effect requires that errors such as arithmetic overflow be handled by error values rather than by program interruptions or manipulation of global status flags. If an error occurs in an operation, that fact must be transmitted only to the destinations of that operation. This can easily be accomplished by enlarging the set of values to include error values such as overflow, underflow, or zero-divide.

If the intent is to abort the computation when an error occurs, it can be achieved by making the error values propagate: if an argument to an arithmetic operation is an error, the result is an error. When an error propagates to the end of an iteration body, that iteration always terminates rather than cycling again. In this way the entire computation will quickly come to a stop, yielding an error value as its result. If the computer keeps a record of every error generation and propagation, that record will tell us when and where the error occurred, and what iterations and procedures were active.

If the intent is to correct an error when it occurs (perhaps keeping a list of such errors in some array), that can be accomplished through operations that test for errors. For example, a program to set Z to the quotient of X and Y, or to zero when an error occurs, could be written in Val as follows:

```
ZZ : = X/Y ;
Z : = if is_error (ZZ) then 0 else ZZ end ;
```

History sensitive computation

While the mechanism described thus far is universal in a theoretical sense, it exhibits a glaring shortcoming in performing real-time computation. Consider the problem of printing the cumulative totals of a series of input values.

Inputs:	1	3	−2	7	5
Outputs:	1	4	2	9	14

It is, of course, easy to write a function that transforms the input as an array to the output array shown above, but this will not work if each output value needs to be seen immediately after the corresponding input value is entered. If each output depended only on the corresponding input instead of on the corresponding input and all earlier inputs, the problem would be trivial—trivial because the same function could be repeatedly invoked, once per input, and the result of each invocation then printed. This is the normal mode of operation of an abstract interactive system, such as the read/eval/print loop of Lisp.

The problem can therefore be seen as one of providing a history-sensitive function: a function that "remembers" its past inputs. In the cumulative sum example, the function would have to keep the sum of its past inputs and add to that sum each input when it arrives. Another way to view the problem is to think of the function as operating on a stream of values.[10,27-29] A stream is like an array handled so that its values can be transmitted in real time. Of course, any function that operates on streams instead of arrays must obey certain restrictions to avoid obvious violations of causality. For example, an output value, once written, may not be erased. Programs that manipulate streams may be written in a recursive style[27,29] in which a stream is treated like a list in Lisp, or in an iterative style[10] in which the rebinding of an iteration variable denoting a stream causes that stream to advance to the next element. Either method enforces the causality constraint if certain rules are followed regarding the permissible recursions or iterations.

The cumulative sum function could be written (in an iterative style) in Id as

```
(initial SUM ← 0
for each T in INPUT_DATA do
        !INPUT_DATA is the incoming stream
    new SUM ← SUM + T
return all SUM)
                ! Produce each cumulative sum as a stream item
```

This approach can be used to solve general data-base query and update problems. In such an application, the entire data base would be one or more loop variables that are redefined in response to items in the input stream.

In addition to history sensitivity, functions that manipulate streams have another property that makes them indispensable for real-time input/output operation: they can emit more (or fewer) outputs than their inputs. A typical example would be a function to remove all <newline> characters from its input or to insert a <newline> after every 80 characters. Operations of this sort are commonly performed by coroutines. A data flow program using streams is a network of parallel communicating processes, a computational model that has been of some theoretical interest in the last few years.[30-32]

Methods of achieving high speed

When programs written in applicative languages are to be run on data flow computers or other supercomputers, care must be taken to exploit the maximum amount of parallelism whenever arrays are involved. The problem is that there is an apparent data dependency, and therefore a scheduling constraint, between any array-construction operation and any fetch operation that uses the resultant array, even if the element it fetches is not the one that was added. In a program written in a conventional language that allows concurrency and nondeterminacy (concurrent Pascal, for example), a knowledgeable programmer might be able to explicitly specify parallelism, and make the program run more efficiently than in the applicative system. Consider the conventional program

$$
\begin{array}{ll}
(1) & A[J] := S \ ; \\
(2) & A[K] := T \ ; \\
(3) & P := A[M] \ ; \\
(4) & Q := A[N] \ ;
\end{array}
$$

If the programmer knows that J and M will always be even, and K and N always odd, then statements 1 and 3 interact only with each other, as do 2 and 4. Statements 1 and 2 could be executed simultaneously, 3 need only follow 1, and 4 would only need to follow 2. If the programmer has the ability to control parallelism explicitly, he could exactly specify those constraints. This would produce a program that would appear (to the compiler) to be nondeterminate, although the programmer would know that it is determinate. Such an explicit specification of scheduling constraints in disagreement with the apparent data dependencies is not possible in a data flow language, but simultaneous execution could still be realized by writing the program as follows (using the programmer's knowledge that J and M are even while K and N are odd):

$$
\begin{array}{lll}
B0 := A0 [J:S] \ ; & \% & A0 \text{ and } B0 \text{ are constructed} \\
B1 := A1 [K:T] \ ; & \% & \text{with the even elements,} \\
P := B0[M] \ ; & \% & A1 \text{ and } B1 \text{ with the} \\
Q := B1[N] \ ; & \% & \text{odd ones.}
\end{array}
$$

This exploits the parallelism exactly.

Lenient Cons. The data dependency problem also arises in a much more general context. If function "F" creates an array value by filling the array one element at a time and then passes the array to "G," which reads the elements one at a time, G cannot begin until F completes. In many instances this delay is unnecessary, and a number of techniques have been proposed for eliminating it without departing from the principle that the sequencing constraints are exactly the data dependencies. These techniques are variously called lenient Cons[24] or I-structures.[33] The array-construction operation "computes" its result as soon as the array argument is available, even if the index and data arguments are not. It fills the unknown array positions with a special code indicating that the datum at that position is not yet available. The computation of each datum proceeds concurrently, and, when it completes, that datum goes into the array, replacing the special code. Any attempt to read an array position containing such a code waits until the actual datum is available. Using lenient Cons, when the function F is to fill an array, the array comes back almost instantly, whether or not it contains useful data. From this point on, when function G attempts to use an element of the array, it only needs to wait for that element to be computed. (Note that a computer with lenient Cons automatically takes care of the problem in the previous example.)

The lenient Cons principle is somewhat similar to a computational principle called lazy evaluation.[34] Under lazy evaluation, an operation is not performed until its result is actually demanded by another operation, so there is a flow of "demands" upward through the data flow graphs as well as a flow of data downward. With this method, even infinite arrays can be "created," such as an array containing all prime numbers. Whenever a reference to an element is made, its prime number is computed. A form of lenient Cons and lazy evaluation is used in a data flow computer proposed by Keller, Lindstrom, and Patil.[14]

Streams. The ability of a stream to act as an array that is fragmented in time makes streams suitable for the data dependency problem. The output of F and the input of G could be a stream. G would receive each element as soon as F created it, and G would be processing the Nth element while F computes the $N+1$st, resulting in parallel pipelined computation of F and G. The same language constraints that prevent streams from violating causality will force G to process the elements in the order in which they were produced by F, and will generally prevent random access to streams.

Conclusion

There have recently been calls to realize the enormous potential of VLSI technology[7] by abandoning traditional von Neumann computer architecture. There has also been widespread recognition of the fact that proper language design is essential if the high cost of software is to be brought under control, and that most existing languages are seriously deficient in this area.

Fortunately, the implications of these two trends for language design are similar: languages must avoid an execution model (the von Neumann model) that involves a global memory whose state is manipulated by the sequential execution of commands. Such a global memory makes realization of the potential of VLSI technology difficult because it creates a bottleneck between the computer's control unit and its memory. Languages that use a global memory in their execution model also exacerbate the software problem by allowing program modules to interact with each other in ways that are difficult to understand, rather than through simple transmission of argument and result values. Language designs based on concepts of applicative programming should be able to help control the high cost of software and meet the needs of future computer designs. ∎

Acknowledgment

This research was supported in part by the Lawrence Livermore National Laboratory of the University of California under contract no. 8545403, in part by the National Science Foundation under research grant DCR75-04060, and in part by the Advanced Research Projects Agency of the Department of Defense under Office of Naval Research contract no. N00014-75-C-0661.

References

1. P. Brinch Hansen, "The Programming Language Concurrent Pascal," *IEEE Trans. Software Eng.,* Vol. SE-1, No. 2, June 1975, pp. 199-207.

2. D. H. Lawrie, T. Layman, D. Baer, and J. M. Randal, "Glypnir—A Programming Language for Illiac IV," *Comm. ACM,* Vol. 18, No. 3, Mar. 1975, pp. 157-164.

3. J. T. Martin, R. G. Zwakenberg, and S. V. Solbeck, "LRLTRAN Language Used with the CHAT and STAR Compilers," Livermore Time-Sharing System Manual, Chapter 207, Lawrence Livermore National Laboratory, edition 4, Dec. 11, 1974.

4. J. McCarthy, "Recursive Functions of Symbolic Expressions and their Computation by Machine," *Comm. ACM,* Vol. 3, No. 4, Apr. 1960, pp. 185-195.

5. J. McCarthy et al., "LISP 1.5 Programmer's Manual," MIT Press, 1966.

6. P. H. Winston and B. K. P. Horn, *LISP,* Addison-Wesley, Reading, Mass., 1981.

7. J. Backus, "Can Programming Be Liberated from the von Neumann Style? A Functional Style and Its Algebra of Programs," *Comm. ACM,* Vol. 21, No. 8, Aug. 1978, pp. 613-641.

8. L. G. Tesler and H. J. Enea, "A Language Design for Concurrent Processes," *AFIPS Conf. Proc.,* Vol. 32, 1968 SJCC, pp. 403-408.

9. Arvind and K. P. Gostelow, "Dataflow Computer Architecture: Research and Goals," Department of Information and Computer Science Technical Report TR-113, University of California, Irvine, Feb. 1978.

10. Arvind, K. P. Gostelow, and W. Plouffe, "An Asynchronous Programming Language and Computing Machine," Department of Information and Computer Science Technical Report 114a, University of California, Irvine, Dec. 1978.

11. J. B. Dennis, "Data Flow Supercomputers," *Computer,* Vol. 13, No. 11, Nov. 1980, pp. 48-56.

12. J. B. Dennis, D. P. Misunas, and C. K. C. Leung, "A Highly Parallel Processor Using a Data Flow Machine Language," Computation Structures Group Memo 134, Laboratory for Computer Science, MIT, Cambridge, Mass., Jan. 1977.

13. J. Gurd, I. Watson, and J. Glauert, "A Multilayered Data Flow Computer Architecture," Department of Computer Science, University of Manchester, Manchester, England, July 1978.

14. R. M. Keller, G. Lindstrom, and S. Patil, "A Loosely-Coupled Applicative Multi-Processing System," *AFIPS Conf. Proc.,* Vol. 48, 1979 NCC, pp. 613-622.

15. A. Plas, D. Comte, O. Gelly, and J. C. Syre, "LAU System Architecture: A Parallel Data Driven Processor Based on Single Assignment," *Proc. 1976 Int'l Conf. Parallel Processing,* Aug. 1976, pp. 293-302.

16. W. B. Ackerman and J. B. Dennis, "VAL—A Value-Oriented Algorithmic Language: Preliminary Reference Manual," MIT Laboratory for Computer Science Technical Report TR-218, MIT, Cambridge, Mass., June 1979.

17. E. A. Ashcroft and W. W. Wadge, "Lucid, a Nonprocedural Language with Iteration," *Comm. ACM,* Vol. 20, No. 7, July 1977, pp. 519-526.

18. E. W. Dijkstra, "Cooperating Sequential Processes," *Programming Languages,* F. Genuys, ed., Academic Press, New York, 1968.

19. A. L. Davis, "The Architecture and System Method of DDM1: A Recursively Structured Data Driven Machine," *Proc. Fifth Ann. Symp. Computer Architecture,* Apr. 1978, pp. 210-215.

20. J. E. Rumbaugh, "A Data Flow Multiprocessor," *IEEE Trans. Computers,* Vol. C-26, No. 2, Feb. 1977, pp. 138-146.

21. D. Comte, G. Durrieu, O. Gelly, A. Plas, and J. C. Syre, "Parallelism, Control and Synchronization Expressions in a Single Assignment Language," *Sigplan Notices,* Vol. 13, No. 1, Jan. 1978, pp. 25-33.

22. R. H. Campbell, "Path Expressions: A Technique for Specifying Process Synchronization," Department of Computer Science Report UIUCDCS-R-77-863, University of Illinois at Urbana-Champaign, Urbana, Ill., 1977.

23. D. J. Kuck et al., "Dependence Graphs and Compiler Optimizations." *Conf. Record Eighth ACM Symp. Principles of Programming Languages,* Jan. 1981, pp. 207-218.

24. D. P. Friedman and D. S. Wise, "The Impact of Applicative Programming on Multiprocessing," *Proc. 1976 Int'l Conf. Parallel Processing,* Aug. 1976, pp. 263-272.

25. A. Church, "The Calculi of Lambda-Conversion," *Ann. Math. Studies,* Vol. 6, Princeton University Press, Princeton, N.J., 1941.

26. J. L. W. Kessels, "A Conceptual Framework for a Nonprocedural Programming Language," *Comm. ACM,* Vol. 20, No. 12, Dec. 1977, pp. 906-913.

27. J. B. Dennis, "A Language Design for Structured Concurrency," *Design and Implementation of Programming Languages: Proceedings of a DoD Sponsored Workshop,* J. H. Williams and D. A. Fisher, eds., *Lecture Notes in Computer Science,* Vol. 54, Oct. 1976; also in Computation Structures Group Note 28-1, Feb. 1977, Laboratory for Computer Science, MIT, Cambridge, Mass.

28. J. B. Dennis and K-S. Weng, "An Abstract Implementation for Concurrent Computation with Streams," *Proc. 1979 Int'l Conf. Parallel Processing,* Aug. 1979, pp. 35-45; also in Computation Structures Group Memo 180, Laboratory for Computer Science, MIT, Cambridge, Mass., July 1979.

29. K-S. Weng, "Stream-Oriented Computation in Recursive Data Flow Schemas," Laboratory for Computer Science Technical Manual TM-68, MIT, Cambridge, Mass., Oct. 1975.

30. C. A. R. Hoare, "Communicating Sequential Processes," *Comm. ACM,* Vol. 21, No. 8, Aug. 1978, pp. 666-677.

31. G. Kahn, "The Semantics of a Simple Language for Parallel Programming," *Proc. IFIP Congress 74,* pp. 471-475.

32. G. Kahn and D. MacQueen, "Coroutines and Networks of Parallel Processes," *Proc. IFIP Congress 77,* pp. 993-998.

33. Arvind and R. E. Thomas, "I-Structures: An Efficient Data Type for Functional Languages," MIT Laboratory for Computer Science Technical Manual TM-178, MIT, Cambridge, Mass., Sept. 1980.

34. P. Henderson and J. Morris, Jr., "A Lazy Evaluator," *Conf. Record Third ACM Symp. Principles of Programming Languages,* Jan. 1976, pp. 95-103.

William B. Ackerman is a graduate student in the Department of Electrical Engineering and Computer Science at MIT. He has been associated with the data flow project at MIT since 1977, and is one of the designers of the Val language. His current research interests include machine architecture and compiler design. He received the BS degree in mathematics and the MS in electrical engineering at MIT.

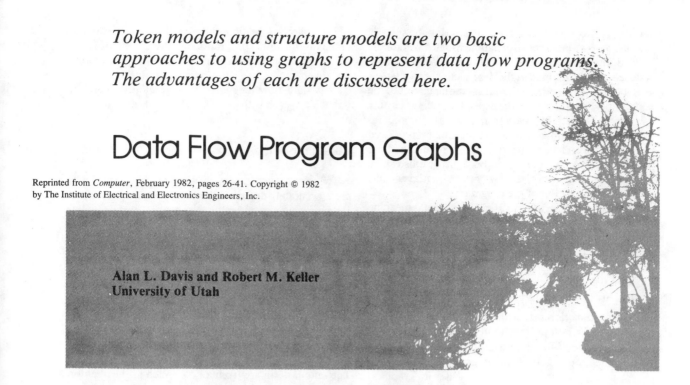

Token models and structure models are two basic approaches to using graphs to represent data flow programs. The advantages of each are discussed here.

Data Flow Program Graphs

Reprinted from *Computer*, February 1982, pages 26-41. Copyright © 1982 by The Institute of Electrical and Electronics Engineers, Inc.

Alan L. Davis and Robert M. Keller
University of Utah

Data flow languages form a subclass of the languages which are based primarily upon function application (i.e., applicative languages). By *data flow language* we mean any applicative language based entirely upon the notion of data flowing from one function entity to another or any language that directly supports such flowing. This flow concept gives data flow languages the advantage of allowing program definitions to be represented exclusively by graphs. Graphical representations and their applications are the subject of this article.

Applicative languages provide the benefits of extreme modularity, in that the function of each of several subprograms that execute concurrently can be understood *in vacuo.* Therefore, the programmer need not assimilate a great deal of information about the environment of the subprogram in order to understand it. In these languages, there is no way to express constructs that produce global side-effects. This decoupling of the meaning of individual subprograms also makes possible a similar decoupling of their execution. Thus, when represented graphically, subprograms that look independent can be executed independently and, therefore, concurrently.

By contrast, concurrent programs written in more conventional assignment-based languages cannot always be understood *in vacuo,* since it is often necessary to understand complex sequences of interactions between a subprogram and its environment in order to understand the meaning of the subprogram itself. This is not to say that data flow subprograms cannot interact with their environments in specialized ways, but that it is possible to define a subprogram's meaning without appealing to those interactions.

There are many reasons for describing data flow languages in graphical representations, including the following:

(1) Data flow languages sequence program actions by a simple *data availability firing rule:* When a node's arguments are available, it is said to be firable. The function associated with a firable node can be fired, i.e., applied to is arguments, which are thereby absorbed. After firing, the node's results are sent to other functions, which need these results as their arguments.

A mental image of this behavior is suggested by representing the program as a directed graph in which each node represents a function and each (directed) arc a conceptual medium over which data items flow. Phantom nodes, drawn with dashed lines, indicate points at which the program communicates with its environment by either receiving data from it or sending data to it.

(2) Data flow programs are easily *composable* into larger programs. A phantom node representing output of one program can be spliced to a phantom node representing input to another. The phantom nodes can then be deleted, as shown in Figure 1.

There are two distinct differences between this type of composability and the splicing of two flowcharts. First, spliced data flow graphs represent *all* information needed at the interface. With flowcharts, the connectivity among variables is not represented by splicing. Second, flowchart splicing represents a one-time passing of control from one component to the next. With data flow graphs, splicing can indicate information that crosses from one component to the next; this motion is distributed over the entire lifetime of the computation.

(3) Data flow programs avoid prescribing the specific execution order inherent to assignment-based programs. Instead, they prescribe only essential data *dependencies*. A dependency is defined as the dependence of the data at an output arc of a node on the data at the input arcs of the node. (For some functions, the dependency might be only apparent.) The lack of a path from one arc to another indicates that data flowing on those arcs can be produced independently. Hence, the functions producing those data can be executed concurrently. Thus, graphs can be used to present an intuitive view of the potential concurrency in the execution of the program.

(4) Graphs can be used to attribute a formal meaning to a program. This meaning can take the form of an *operational* definition or a *functional* one. The former defines a permissible sequence of operations that take place when the program is executed. The latter describes a single function represented by the program and is independent of any particular execution model.

This article explores the utility of graphical representations for data flow programs, including the possibility and advantages of dispensing entirely with the text and viewing the graph itself as the program. This suggests a programming style in which the user deals with graphs as the primary representation in programming, editing, and execution. In this context, human engineering rather than concurrent execution becomes the motivation for investigating data flow program graphs.

The following section elaborates on the meaning of graphs as functional programs. The discussion focuses on the two prevailing models for data flow representation: the token model and the structure model. The terms classify data flow languages that developed along different lines, each with certain implementation subtleties.

Token models

The term *token* is a shortening of *token-stream,* which more accurately describes the behavior of these models. Data is always viewed as flowing on arcs from one node to another in a stream of discrete tokens. Tokens are considered carriers or instantiations of data objects. Each object is representable by a finite encoding.

When a node is labeled with a scalar function, such as + or *, it is understood that the function is repeated as tokens arrive at its inputs. Each repetition produces a token at its output. For example, suppose that we use a token model to interpret the graph in Figure 2. This graph defines a repeated computation of the polynomial function of X: $X^2 - 2*X + 3$ for a sequence of values of X. The fanout of an arc from a node, such as the phantom node X, denotes the conceptual replication of tokens leaving that node. A node marked with a constant value is assumed to regenerate that value as often as it is needed by nodes to which it is input.

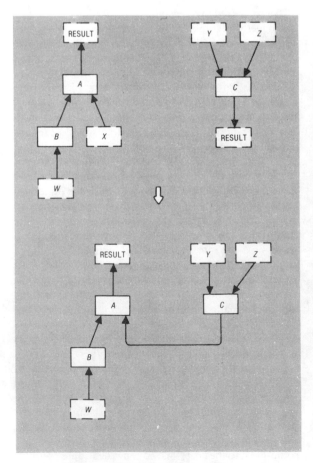

Figure 1. Splicing of two data flow graphs.

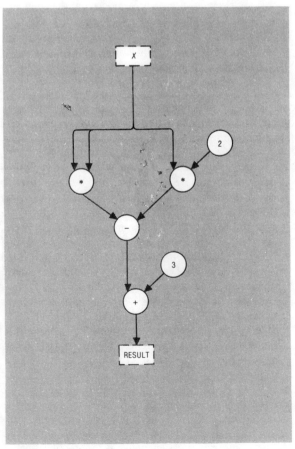

Figure 2. Data flow graph for $X^2 - 2*X + 3$.

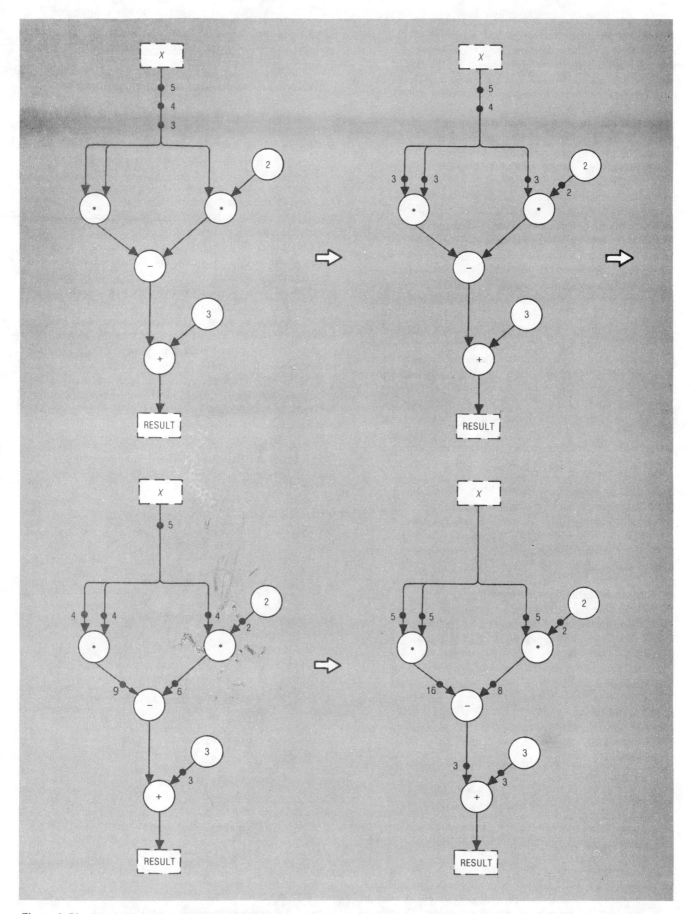

Figure 3. Pipelined graph computation.

The results of node operations correspond to the inputs in first-in-first-out order. The operation is usually, but not necessarily, performed on those inputs in the same order. Furthermore, each node corresponds to a function, and no fan-in of arcs is allowed—there is no opportunity for tokens to be interleaved arbitrarily at an arc. It follows, therefore, that data flow graphs ensure *determinate* execution. That is, the output of any program or subprogram for a given input is guaranteed to be well defined and independent of system timing. This has been clearly demonstrated for several data flow models.[1-5]

Determinacy also imples an absence of side-effects, which are apt to be present in conventional read and write operations. Such operations often require extra concurrency-reducing synchronization to prevent time-dependent errors. By contrast, the only errors possible in data flow programs are those due to an improper functional formulation of the solution to a problem; these are always reproducible, due to the feature of determinacy. A more thorough discussion of data flow errors is given elsewhere.[6]

In Figure 2, no arc connects the two * operators. This implies that there is no data dependency between the two nodes; that is, the node functions can be computed concurrently. The lack of data dependency between the multiply operators in Figure 2 is sometimes called *horizontal,* or *spatial,* concurrency. This contrasts with *temporal* concurrency, or pipelining, which exists among computations corresponding to several generations of input tokens. A brief scenario of both types of concurrency is illustrated by the sequence of snapshots in Figure 3.

Conditional constructions in data flow programs achieve selective routing of data tokens among nodes. Boolean or index-valued tokens can be produced by a node that performs some decision function. Figure 4 shows the *selector* and the *distributor,* two nodes used in conditional constructs. In the case of a selector, a token is first absorbed from the horizontal input. The value of that token, either true or false, determines from which of the two vertical inputs the next token will be absorbed; any token on the other input remains there until selected. The firing of a selector is a two-phase process, since the value at the horizontal input must be known before the corresponding vertical input can be selected. In the case of the distributor, a token is absorbed from the vertical input and passed to one of the vertical ouputs. Again, the choice of output depends on the value of the token at the horizontal input.

Generalizations of the selector and distributor are easily devised:

- selection (or distribution) is based on a set of integer or other scalar values instead of on booleans, or
- the vertical arcs are replaced by bundles of arcs so that tokens pass through in parallel.

Iteration can be achieved through cyclic data flow graphs. The body of the iteration is initially activated by a token that arrives on the input of the graph. The body subgraph produces a new token, which is cycled back on a feedback path until a certain condition is satisfied. An example of an iterative graph is shown in Figure 5, which illustrates Newton's method to find the roots of a function.

Node *f* could be replaced by the graph shown in **Figure 2.** A similar graph could replace node *f′* to compute the derivative $2*X-2$. An execution scenario for **Figure 5** is as follows:

(1) The program is started by introducing a real-number token at the output of phantom node X.

(2) The selector is now firable, as a *true* token exists on its horizontal input in the initial state shown. When the selector fires, the token from X passes to the two $-$ operators and to the boxes that calculate $f(x)$ and $f′(x)$.

(3) Neither of the $-$ operations can fire yet, as their right-operand tokens are not available. Nodes $f(x)$ and $f′(x)$ can fire concurrently to produce their output values and absorb their input values. At this point, the $\div$, $-$, abs, and $<$ operations fire, in that order.

(4) The ouput of the $<$ node is a boolean value that indicates whether or not the new and old approximations have converged sufficiently. If they have, a *true* token is produced by $<$. This causes the feedback-in value to be distributed and the approximation to be passed through as the result of the iteration. At this point, a *true* token has been regenerated at the horizontal input to the selector, putting the graph in its original state. Thus, the program is reusable for a subsequent input token.

(5) If the $<$ node produces *false,* the feedback-in token is passed through the distributor and selector and becomes the next feedback-out token, to be used in the next iteration.

In the example in Figure 5, very little pipelining can take place because of the use of the selector function at the input. This selector requires each set of iterations to be com-

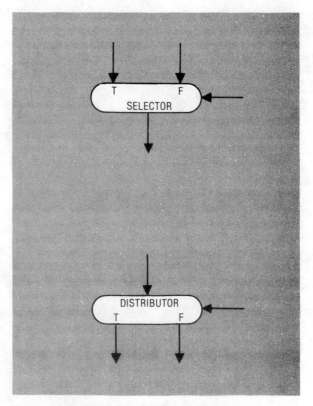

Figure 4. Selector and distributor functions.

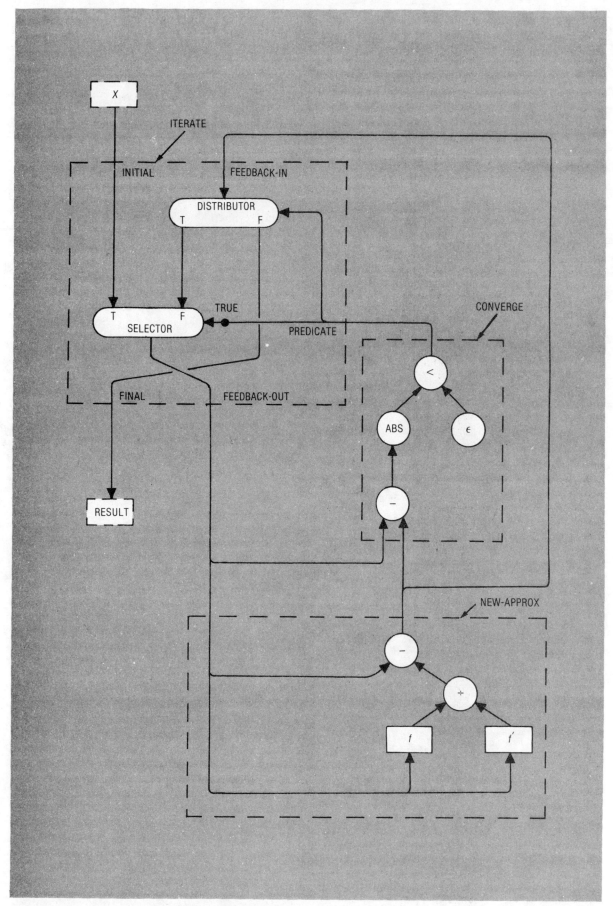

Figure 5. A graph for Newton's method.

plete (i.e., the horizontal input to be true) before the next token can be absorbed into the graph. However, the horizontal input is repeatedly false during any given set of iterations. Thus, an alternative formulation is necessary for concurrent processing of several input tokens.

Program structuring

It is cumbersome to deal with graphical programs consisting of single very large graphs. Just as subroutines and procedures are used to structure conventional programs, macrofunctions can be used to structure graphical ones. This idea appeals to intuition: A macrofunction is defined by specifying a name and associating it with a graph, called the *consequent* of that name. A node in a program graph labeled with that name is, in effect, replaced by its consequent; the arcs are spliced together in place of the phantom nodes. In the diagrams in this article, the orientation of the arcs in the consequent is assumed to match that of the node the consequent replaces. This replacement is called *macroexpansion,* in analogy to the similar concept used in conventional languages. It is valid to view data flow languages as performing macroexpansion dur-

ing execution rather than during compilation. A macroexpansion is shown in Figure 6.

Macrofunctions often aid in understanding and developing graphical programs. For example, one might wish to encapsulate the iterate subgraph in Figure 5 into a node type called Iterate. *Atomic* functions are those that are not macrofunctions. In some systems, a node such as Iterate could be either atomic or a macro available from a library.

Recursion is easy to visualize in data flow graphs. As mentioned above, a node labeled with a macrofunction can be thought of as replaced by its consequent. This rule can be adopted for recursively specified functions, such as those in which a series of macroexpansions from a node labeled G can result in a subgraph containing a node labeled G.

For example, Figure 7 shows a recursive specification of the example given in Figure 6. Unlike its predecessor, this version can be understood without appealing to the definition of the complicated Iterate subgraph. Although a graph with recursive macrofunction can, in concept, be expanded to an infinite graph, either distributors or the underlying implementation must ensure that expansion takes place incrementally as needed. Since copies of

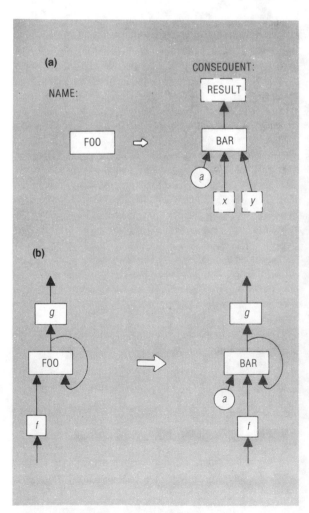

Figure 6. Example of graphical macroexpansion: (a) definition; (b) expansion.

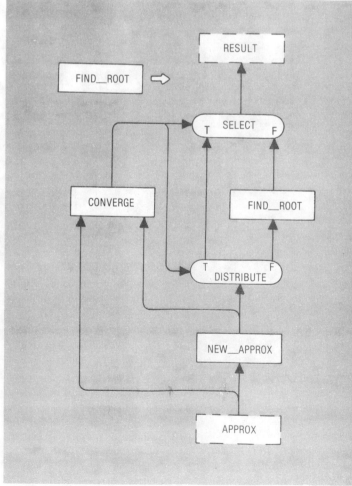

Figure 7. Recursive Newton graph.

find_root can be instantiated for different generations of input tokens, this graph permits pipelined concurrency in contrast to Figure 6.

Data structuring

Graph programs, like conventional programs, are amenable to incorporation of various data structuring features. Examples thus far have had numbers and boolean values as tokens. But succinct expression of solutions to complicated problems requires structuring operations that build tokens containing complex data objects from more primitive tokens. Data structuring also provides a way of exploiting concurrency; operations that deal with large structures, such as adding two vectors, can often perform many subfunctions concurrently. Such concurrency is frequently of a much higher degree than that resulting from a lack of visible data dependencies among nodes.

Tuples. The tuple is an important example of a complex token. A tuple is simply a grouping of objects into a single object. A tuple can flow as a single token, and the original objects can be recovered from it. The objects are ordered within the tuple so that recovery of one of the original objects occurs by supplying both the tuple and an ordinal index to an indexing function. In other words, a tuple is similar to a one-dimensional array in conventional programming, except that there is no notion of assignment in regard to the components of a tuple. Instead, a tuple is created by specifying the application of a constructor function to specified components.

Suppose the tuple-creating function is denoted by brackets. Let

$$t = [c_1, c_2, \ldots, c_n]$$

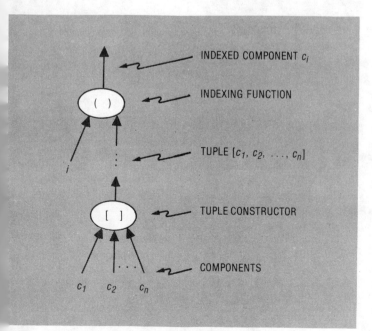

be the tuple with components $c_1, c_2, \ldots, c_n$. Parentheses denote the indexing function, so $t(i)$ will be c_i. This notation is often used for application of a function to its argument. Indeed, one might consider a tuple to be a function applicable to its range of indices.

We can now extend our basic data flow graphs to permit the tuple constructors and indexing function to be operators at a node, as shown in Figure 8. It is possible to view computations involving tuple tokens and operators as if the entire tuple flows from one node to another on an arc. However, the entire object need not flow in a particular implementation; more economical approaches are possible.

In addition to constructing tuples by using the [. . .] operator, other operations, such as *concatenation,* can be defined on tuples, that is

$$\text{conc}([c_1, c_2, \ldots, c_n], [d_1, d_2, \ldots, d_m]) = [c_1, c_2, \ldots, c_n, d_1, d_2, \ldots, d_m]$$

Conc can similarly be extended to more than two arguments.

The tuple concept leads to the construction of strings (tuples of characters), lists, etc. Tuples can have tuples as components to any number of levels of nesting.

Files. The sequential processing of files fits naturally into the data flow framework. One approach is to treat an input file as a stream of tokens, which is introduced into a graph at one of its inputs. Such a stream can then be processed with the types of operators introduced above or by using first/rest operators. *First* gives the first token in the stream, while *rest* passes all of the stream but the first token. Sequential files are often created by using *fby* (followed by), a two-argument function that builds a stream by using its first argument as the first component of the stream and its second argument—a stream—as the rest of the stream. Often, the rest has not been constructed at the time fby is applied. Instead, there is a *promise* to construct it in the future, as represented by some function that gives the rest as output.

Figure 9 illustrates a simple recursive definition for file processing. It produces an output stream by deleting all carriage-return characters in the input stream. Files can also be treated as single tuples, in which case they can be accessed nonsequentially. Such files can be created by using conc.

The utility of viewing sequential input and output as if it were a file coming directly from or going directly to a device has been observed and exploited in such systems as the pipe concept[7] of Unix.* Data-structuring operations that support streams provide one of the most compelling arguments for data flow programming and, particularly, viewing programs as graphs. Each module of such a program can be viewed as a function that operates on streams of data and is activated by the presence of data. The behavior of a module over its lifetime can be captured in one function definition, and low-level details of the protocol for information transmission can be suppressed. The system of interconnected modules can be specified by

Figure 8. Tuple formation and component selection.

*Unix is a trademark of Bell Laboratories.

COMPUTER

a graph, which might even be constructed dynamically through use of macroexpansion. Contrast this with conventional assignment-based programs, which require explicitly set-up processes. Furthermore, communication of these processes is based on shared variables or explicit interchange of messages. Although characterizing the behavior of such a process for any single interaction requires only sequential program analysis techniques, it is generally difficult to succinctly characterize the long-term behavior.

Functions as values. Data objects that can represent functions and be applied to other objects by a primitive operator *apply* can enhance the power of data flow programming considerably. In one approach, a constant-producing node N can contain a graph, which is conceived as the value of a token flowing from N. The graph generally flows through conditionals, etc. When and if it enters the first input arc of an apply node, its phantom nodes serve a role similar to that of a macrofunction definition: Input/output phantom nodes are spliced to the input arcs of the apply node, and the graph effectively replaces the apply node. More generally, it is possible for arcs to enter the node N and be connected to the graph inside of it. These arcs are called *imports* to the graph. The same tokens flow on them, regardless of where the graph itself might flow. Since a graph-valued node can be present within the consequent of any macrofunction, many versions of the encapsulated graph can be generated, each customized by different import values. The concept forms a graphical equivalent to the notion of *closures*[8] or *funargs*.[9] A simple example is given in Figure 10. Further examples are in the literature.[5,10]

Data typing. The notion of data type is playing an increasingly important role in modern programming language design. Data flow graphs lend themselves to the support and exhibition of typing. It is quite natural to indicate, on each arc of a data flow graph, the type of data object that flows there. Hence, most developments concerned with typing are applicable in the domain of graphical programs.

Structure models

As we have seen, a token model views each node as processing a single stream of tokens over its entire lifetime. Each node produces tokens on output arcs in response to tokens absorbed on input arcs. Each operator is expressed in terms of what it does token-by-token. In structure models, a single data structure is constructed on each arc. The construction can, possibly, spread out over the lifetime of the graph. The structure might be interpretable as a stream of tokens, but it might be a tuple, a tree (formed, for example, by nested tuples), or just a scalar value. Within a structure model, each argument of an operator is one structure on which the operator operates to produce a new structure. A nontrivial structure model allows tuples or some equivalent structure to be conceptually infinite. That is, while a tuple always has a definite first component, it might not have a last component. If it does, it

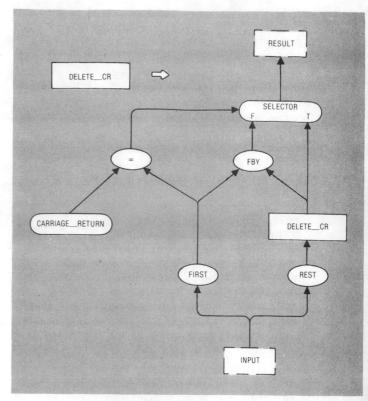

Figure 9. Graphical program for a file-processing problem.

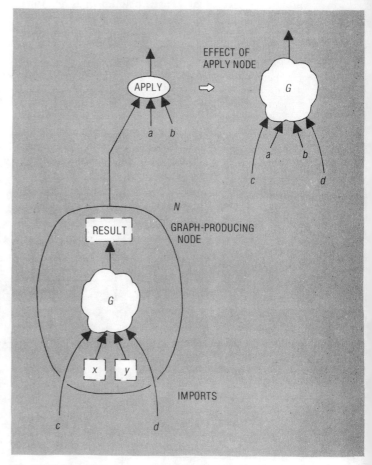

Figure 10. The apply function and use of imports.

might be infeasible to even attempt to know the extent of the tuple, since this would be tantamount to reading the entire input into a buffer before processing, a step quite contrary to desirable interactive I/O modes. Thus, an open-ended stream of characters is representable by the tuple $[c_1, c_2, c_3, \ldots]$, where three dots indicate possible continuation ad infinitum.

Values on arcs in a structure model are single structures. Therefore, structures (e.g., an entire stream) can be selected by a conditional, used as an argument, etc. It is not necessary to deal with a structure's tokens individually.

It is also possible to randomly access a stream by exploiting the fact that an entire structure is built on an arc. For example, the tuple indexing function described above could be used for ths purpose. In a structure model, if we are to think of a node in a data flow graph as firing, we must be willing to accept this firing as generally incremental. It is physically infeasible for a node to instantaneously produce an infinite object.

One can distinguish a structure model from a token model by examining the atomic operators. Token models always operate on streams of tokens and not on other single objects; if this is not the case, we have a structure

model. A structure model achieves the effects of stream processing by means of macrofunctions. In the case of Figure 2, this could be done in two ways: by defining a stream-procesing version of each of the arithmetic operators, or by creating a function (the graph shown) and applying it to each component of an input stream. Likewise, some of the functions (such as switching streams) of structure models can be emulated in some token models by macrofunctions.

We have alluded to the fact that the behavior of a data flow program over its lifetime can be captured as a single function. Perhaps the most important distinction between structure and token models is that in the former this behavior is expressible as a recursive function within the model, while the latter requires a more encompassing language to capture the behavior. For a token model, the long-term behavior is captured as a function on histories of token streams.[11] In a structure model, the notion of history degenerates since each arc carries exactly one object.

To maintain certain aspects of the history of a stream in a token model program, special provisions must be coded to save relevant components as they pass through a function. In structure models, for reasons cited above, it is easy to maintain the equivalent of the history of all or part of a token stream, as the entire stream is accessible as a single object.

Token model interpreters usually process tokens in sequence. This causes asynchrony and concurrency to be less than the maximum possible.[12] In structure models, there is no implied order for processing structure components. Thus, these componets can be processed out of sequence without use of a more specialized interpreter.

Some functions are easily expressed in structure models but more difficult to express in token models. An example is the generalized indexing function, or gen_index, which operates on two finite or infinite tuples, stream $= [s_1, s_2, s_3, \ldots]$ and indices $= [i_1, i_2, i_3, \ldots]$, to produce $[s_{i_1}, s_{i_2}, s_{i_3}, \ldots]$. This function can be expressed by the graph in Figure 11 or by the textual expression below.

```
gen_index(stream, indices) =
        if indices = [ ]
            then [ ]
            else fby(stream(first(indices)),
                    gen_index(stream, rest(indices)))
```

This is obviously a recursive definition. The condition eventually becomes true when indices is finite. When the indices or tuples are not empty, the result is the tuple obtained by indexing the component of the stream that corresponds to the first index (using the parenthesis notation for indexing given above). This is followed by the result of the gen_index function on the remainder of the tuple.

This example illustrates a correspondence between a graphical and a textual notation. It is possible to design a language so that each program graph has an exact textual equivalent, and vice-versa.[13] This permits use of graphical programming concepts even when there is no graphical input device, as well as the use of hybrid representations, which help suppress uninteresting graphical detail.[14]

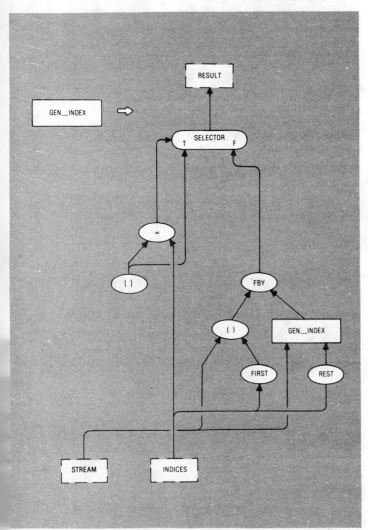

Figure 11. A generalized indexing function.

Structure models can perform the functions of token models. Is the opposite also true? A relaxation of our definition, to allow tokens to be infinite objects, would make it possible. This, however, seems contrary to the notion of a token as an object that can flow in a single step. Another means is to introduce *pointer,* or *reference,* tokens. The infinite objects then become homomorphic images of a network of tokens involving pointers. Although necessary to perform correctness proofs of a structure model,[15] the introduction of such objects into a programming language should be avoided where possible because they make the language less machine-independent. Introducing infinite objects into token models[16] is counter to the interests of conceptual economy. One could use, instead, a structure model, which does not necessarily require token streams yet allows representation of stream-like behavior by using the appropriate structures. Furthermore, a great many applications cannot exploit the repetitive stream-processing capability of a token model. For these applications, a token-model language amounts to overkill.

Why would one ever choose a token model (with only finite tokens, as defined herein) instead of a structure model, given the flexibility of the latter? The answer lies in the trade-off of execution efficiency vs. ease in programming. The token-by-token processing of token models often results in efficient storage-management. Since structure models use structures to emulate all stream-processing functions of token models (which are often macrofunctions involving recursion) token-by-token processing is difficult to detect. Therefore, structure models typically use fully general storage management, which recycles storage in a more costly manner than do the more specialized token models. Compiler optimization and special execution techniques that improve the efficiency of structure model execution without sacrificing generality are topics of active research.

Machine representation and execution of graphical programs

Program storage. It is possible to compile graphical programs into conventional machine languages. However, if the main goal is the execution of such programs, there are advantages in directly encoding the graphs themselves as the machine program for a specially constructed processor. Alternatively, such an encoding can be interpreted on a conventional processor as virtual machine code. The advantages of the special-processor and virtual-machine approaches include direct exploitation of the concurrency implicit in the graphical formulation and a clearer connection between a higher-level graphical language and its machine representation.

A survey of the numerous possible encodings of graph programs is beyond the present scope. The discussion below is a qualitative look at one version for a token model. The first task is to establish an encoding for a program graph, which consists of nodes labeled with function names and arcs connecting the nodes. The orientation of the arcs entering the nodes is, of course, relevant. We represent the entire graph as a set of contiguous memory locations, each corresponding to one node of the graph. Thus, relative addressing can be used to identify any particular node. Our use of relative addressing should not be interpreted as the use of a single memory module. Use of one address space to address a multitude of physical memories is a common way to avoid memory contention. In practice, addressing might take place on two levels: short addresses within the consequent of each macrofunction, and long addresses for the global interconnection of such functions.[17]

For simplicity, assume that each node has a single output arc. As long as nodes represent functions, nodes with more than one output arc can always be decomposed into one function for each arc, and thus represented as several nodes with fanout from the same input arcs (Figure 12). This allows association of a node with its only output arc, and vice-versa.

Having identified a location for each node, we can discuss the encoding of the relevant information for each node. Obviously, there must be a field in each location to indicate an encoding of that node's label, since the label determines the function to be executed. There is an ordered listing of each node's input arcs, but since each of these arcs is identified as the output of some node, we can use that node's location to represent the arc. Similarly, we include an ordered listing of the destinations of each node's output arc. Figure 13 illustrates the encoding of a graphical program as a contiguous set of locations, called a *code block.*

Data-driven execution. Let us now consider data-driven execution in the context of our representational model. For simplicity, assume that one token, at most, is present on any arc at a given time. This is an invariant property maintained by the execution model. To simplify further, we treat only node functions that are *strict,* i.e., require tokens on all arcs in order to fire. A slight modification is necessary for other cases, such as selector nodes.

In addition to the code block that specifies a data flow graph (discussed above) we provide a second *data block*

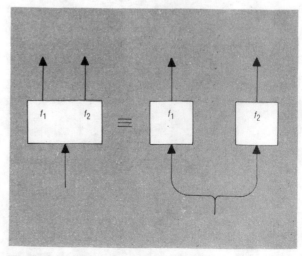

Figure 12. Replacing multiple-output-arc with single-output-arc nodes by means of fanout.

of contiguous locations. It contains the data tokens that are to flow on the arcs of the graph. These locations exactly parallel those representing the graph itself. That is, if location i in the graph encoding represents a particular node (and, by convention, its output arc), then location i in the data block represents the token value on that arc.

Initially, an arc is empty. To indicate this, its corresponding location is marked with a special bit pattern. It is convenient, but not absolutely essential, to include with this bit pattern a *shortage count* that indicates how many remaining input arcs must get tokens before the corresponding node can fire. As an arc gets a token, the shortage counts of nodes to which that arc is input are each decreased by one. This act is called *notification,* as if one node notifies another that data is ready. When the shortage count is zero, the node is firable. Shortage counts are initialized from values stored in the code block.

Suppose that a node has become firable, as indicated by its zero shortage count. The processor can then compute the function specified for that node. It does so by fetching the values in the node's input arcs (as indicated by the encoding in the code block location) and then storing the result value of the function in the corresponding data location. The nodes needing the stored value are then notified. The shortage count of one or more of these nodes might be decreased to zero, indicating that the node is firable. The process then repeats.

Any number of firable nodes can be processed concurrently. For any system state, the set of nodes that need attention (e.g., are firable) can be recorded on a *task list* of their addresses. This list need not be centralized; it can be distributed over many physical processing units.

To start things off, we need only put data in locations corresponding to the phantom input nodes of the graph. Then we add to the task list the nodes to which the input nodes are connected. The firing of nodes continues in a chain reaction until no firable nodes are left. By this time, all results have been produced. That is, the output values are either resident on selected output locations or have been moved to some output device.

We have not discussed the *recycling* of data locations. Most token model implementations suggest that some form of reset signal be used to return a location to its initialized state. An alternative approach, in which data blocks are "thrown away," is presented by Keller, Lindstrom, and Patil.[17]

Representation of complex tokens. The use of complex data objects, such as tuples and functions, as tokens that can conceptually flow on arcs has been described above. It is possible, in the case of finite objects, to send packets consisting of the complete objects.[18] This, however, presents difficulties in storage management, as the size of an object might be unknown before it arrives. Another difficulty is that this approach can involve much unnecessary copying, as an object can be sent to a number of nodes, each of which selects only a small portion for its use. It might be more efficient to introduce, at the implementation level, pointers to take the place of objects that exceed a certain size.

For example, a tuple might be constructed of objects, one or more of which is itself a tuple. In this case, we want to build the outer tuple by using pointers to the inner tuples, rather than by copying the inner tuples themselves. Of course, this type of representation is essential in dealing with conceptually infinite objects; in such a case, the outermost tuple could never be completely constructed. The same is true for recursively defined function objects. Thus, while the conceptualization of program graphs supports the flow of arbitrarily complex objects on arcs, pointers might be required to efficiently implement this conceptual flow. Techniques from Lisp and its variants are especially relevant.[9,19,20]

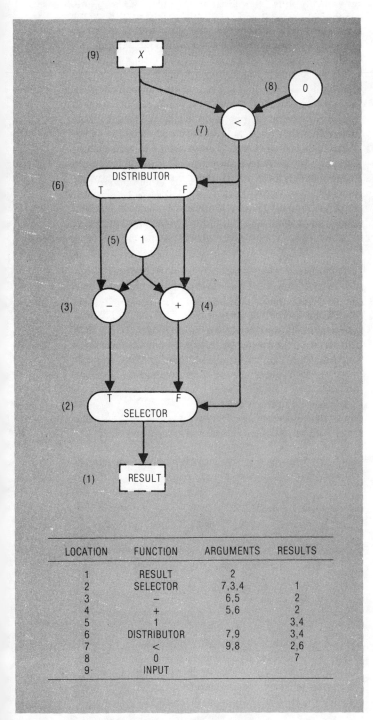

LOCATION	FUNCTION	ARGUMENTS	RESULTS
1	RESULT	2	
2	SELECTOR	7,3,4	1
3	–	6,5	2
4	+	5,6	2
5	1		3,4
6	DISTRIBUTOR	7,9	3,4
7	<	9,8	2,6
8	0		7
9	INPUT		

Figure 13. Internal encoding of a data flow graph.

Demand-driven execution. The mode of execution described in the previous section can be termed *data-driven* because it involves the following (possibly overlapping) phases of the execution of a function node within its environment (the rest of the graph to which the node is connected):

(1) A node receives data from its environment via its input arcs.

(2) A node sends data to its environment via its output arc.

An alternative is the *demand-driven* evaluation mode. It has a more extensive set of phases, which can also be overlapping:

(1) A node's environment requests data from it at its output arc.

(2) A node requests data from its environment at its input arcs, if necessary.

(3) The environment sends data to a node via its input arcs, if requested.

(4) A node sends data to its environment via its output arc.

This suggests that a data-driven execution is like a demand-driven execution in which all data has already been requested.

Suppose that sufficient input data has been made available at the input arc in a demand-driven execution situation. Nothing would happen until a demand is made at the output arc. Although we need not implement it as such, we can think of this demand as being represented by a *demand token* that flows against the direction of the arcs. When a demand token enters a node at an output arc, it might cause the generation of demand tokens at selected input arcs of that node. As this flow of demands continues, data tokens are produced that satisfy the demand. At that point, computation takes place much as it does in the data-driven case. Demands and data can flow concurrently in different parts of the graph.

In demand-driven execution of a graph, a node becomes firable when its shortage count becomes zero *and* it has been demanded. An extra bit in the data location can be used to indicate whether or not the corresponding datum has been demanded. If destination addresses are set dynamically, the presence of at least one of them can indicate demand. Initially, certain nodes (usually those connected to output arcs of the graph) are marked as demanded. The processor attempts those nodes that are so marked and have shortage counts of zero.

The advantages of the demand-driven approach include the elimination of distributor nodes that, on the basis of test outcomes, prevent certain nodes from firing. This advantage accrues because only needed data values are ever demanded. Thus, demand-driven execution does not require the distributor shown in Figure 7 and can be simplified as shown in Figure 14.

Although token models can have either data- or demand-driven execution models, *structure* models seem to require a demand-driven one. Otherwise, the data-driven elaboration of infinite structures tends to usurp system resources unnecessarily. The prime disadvantage of demand-driven execution is the extra delay required to propagate demand. In part, this is balanced by the lack of distributor functions present in the data driven approach. It is as if the selector and distributor operations are folded into a single selector in the demand-driven approach. It is also possible to optimize the demand-driven execution model to statically propagate demand at compile time and recover some of the efficiency of data-driven execution.

A certain minimum overhead is required in both demand- and data-driven execution but appears in different forms. When a computing system is integrated into an asynchronous external environment, an appropriate regulatory protocol must exist at any interface. It is impossible to have the environment dump arbitrarily large quantities of data into the system without having this process punctuated by handshaking signals from the system to the environment. Similarly, we don't normally wish to have the system dump large quantities of data into the environment without regulation. For example, when observing output on a CRT terminal, scrolling should stop when the screen is full and proceed at the viewer's command. Thus, every implementation, data-driven or demand-driven, must have a means of controlling the flow of data by sending signals in a direction that opposes the flow. This requirement exists within the system as well, in the form of controlling the flow of data from one subsystem to another. Propagation of demand before the flow

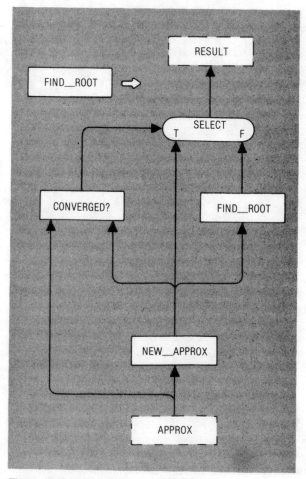

Figure 14. Demand-driven conditional graph.

of data is often balanced by reset signals, which occur after the flow of data and indicate that the location can be reused. These signals present overhead comparable to the flow of demands.

Input-output interfacing. We can interface the fby function to an output device so that individual components of an infinite stream can be constructed within a graph program and directed to that device. Interfacing these types of functions to external devices is much simpler than it might appear. All we need are primitives to input/output single atomic components; recursion at the graph program level does the rest. For example, Figure 15 shows the expression of a pseudofunction that sequentially prints the components of a stream ad infinitum, given a primitive pseudofunction *print* that prints one stream component. Assuming demand-driven mode, print causes its argument to be printed whenever its result is demanded. The function *seq* simply demands its arguments in sequence, the second being demanded only after the first has yielded its result. Of course, tests for end-of-stream atoms can be added to functions such as print_stream. Such I/O functions have been successfully implemented[13]

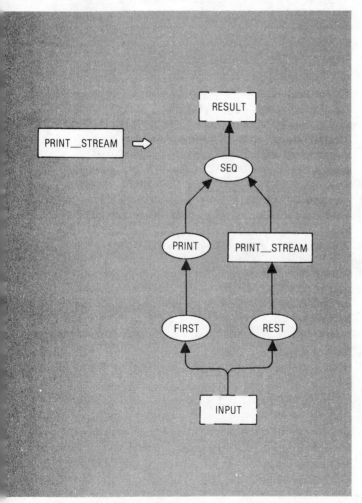

Figure 15. Pseudofunction for printing a stream in demand-driven mode.

Historical background

Many of the concepts presented in graphical representations have appeared in earlier work. Dynamo was an early language with a graphical representation.[21] Although used only to perform synchronous simulation, it is a true data flow language, since the ordering of its statement executions is governed by data dependencies rather than syntax. The integration of Dynamo-like functions into a general-purpose data flow language is discussed by Keller and Lindstrom.[22]

The literature of engineering sciences, particularly electrical engineering and control theory, describes many uses of graphical models for function-based systems. Zadeh, for example, discusses determinacy for general systems.[23] In the related area of digital signal processing, digital filters are often represented graphically.[24] However, most literature in that area presents algorithmic results by translating them to Fortran programs rather than employing a data flow language that can directly represent signal-processing structures. This is one area where graphical data flow programming has much to contribute.

The use of modules that communicate via streams as a structuring device appeared in Conway's definition of a *coroutine:* ". . . an autonomous program which communicates with adjacent modules as if they were input or output subroutines."[25] Conway's paper also included the observation that such coroutines could execute simultaneously on parallel processors. Since then, the coroutine notion seems to have become rather more implementation-oriented. Kahn and MacQueen argue for a return to the elegance of the original definition,[26] which is consistent with the type of programming advocated here.

Brown prophesies the use of applicative languages for the exploitation of parallel processing capability.[27] Patil discusses parallel evaluation in a graphical lambda calulus model.[3] Many others have published important related references on applicative languages.[8,9,28-34] Other aspects of structure models have also been reported.[4,5,19,35-38] Many modern methods for presenting semantics of most any language rely on the presentation of functional expressions for the primitives of the language.[39,40]

Fitzwater and Schweppe offered an early suggestion for data-driven computation.[41] After Karp and Miller's[1] discussion of determinancy in the data flow model, many graphical token models for data-flow have appeared.[2,6,42-47]

Although the firing-rule notion for data flow graphs is thought by some to derive from Petri nets,[48,49] this appears to be a matter of transferred terminology rather than historical dependence. In the Petri-net model, tokens are valueless. Therefore it does not directly represent data, as do data flow models. The basic Petri-net model includes ways to introduce indeterminate behavior; these are not present in basic data flow models.

Finally, an important topic is the incorporation of indeterminate operators into graphical and functional models. This must be considered if such models are to be able to represent operating systems and related programs in which tokens can be merged according to order of arrival from an external environment. Some preliminary discussions of semantic problems, syntax, etc., have appeared.[50-54]

Future developments

Researchers attempting to make data flow program graphs the basis for a practical programming language face several major problems. Some of these problems involve human engineering and the need to create a reasonably priced terminal system to support graphical programming.

Physical implementation decisions. To date, most data flow program graph models have been used as either *just models* or *intermediate languages* for data flow programs. Two exceptions are FGL[14] (based on a structure model) and GPL[55] (based on a token model), in which the models are used as high-level languages. These allow the programmer to draw the program and execute its graphical form.

Impediments to direct use of graphs as data flow programming languages include the expense of graphical terminals, the added cost of graphical software, and the increased workload imposed on execution resources due to interactive display and editing. The evolution of personal computers packaged with powerful microprocessors, bit-mapped displays, disk storage, etc., is beginning to change this equipment-based deficiency. Ongoing experiments indicate that graphical resolution of $4K \times 4K$ pixels or greater might be desirable. Ironically, this is due mainly to the display of the text (comments, node names, etc.) that accompanies a program module of reasonable size. When adequate hardware is available, it will only be a matter of time before researchers develop the additional tools to make graphical programming practicable.

Graphical representations are widely used in nonprogramming disciplines because they provide a more intuitive view of system structure. It seems reasonable to investigate the possibility that such representations could do the same for programming. We suggest that tools for debugging, statistical monitoring, and resource management be coupled with data flow program graphs to allow a programmer to produce programs more productively than is currently possible.

The use of graphical tools for software development seems to be gaining momentum.[56-59] When similar tools are used in the context of a data flow language, an additional advantage accrues: the graphs have a well defined functional meaning, rather than just the ability to represent procedure nesting, loop nesting, calling sequences, etc. This meaning is a specification of the system under development.

The programmer education problem. For graphical data flow methods to succeed in a practical sense, they must have an acceptable link to the 30 prior years of software and hardware development, which present a legacy of considerable inertia. The design of a clean interface between functional programs and existing assignment-based programs (e.g., data-base systems and operating systems) is one aspect of the problem. Several solutions are being pursued.

Professional programmers with years of experience in writing Fortran code have become very good at writing Fortran-like solutions to problems. The change to Algol, Cobol, Pascal, etc., is not a large conceptual step, in that the structural styles of these languages are not radically different from Fortran's. However, data flow languages require and support very different styles. Programmers trained only in conventional languages might be unwilling to try problem-solving techniques based on graphical or even functional program structures. Therefore, the potential gains of such techniques must be made apparent to programming management. ■

Acknowledgments

We wish to thank Arvind, Tilak Agerwala, Paul Drongowski, Chu-Shik Jhon, Gary Lindstrom, and Elliott Organick for numerous comments that helped improve the article. We also thank Kathy Burgi for drafting the figures.

This material is based upon work supported by a grant from the Burroughs Corporation and by National Science Foundation grant MCS 81-06177.

References

1. R. M. Karp and R. E. Miller, "Properties of a Model for Parallel Computations: Determinacy, Termination, Queueing," *SIAM J. Applied Mathematics,* Vol. 14, No. 6, Nov. 1966, pp. 1390-1141.

2. D. A. Adams, *A Computational Model with Data Flow Sequencing,* Technical Report CS117, Computer Science Dept., Stanford University, Palo Alto, Calif., 1968.

3. S. Patil, *Parallel Evaluation of Lambda-Expressions,* MS thesis, MIT Dept. of EE, Jan. 1967.

4. G. Kahn, "The Semantics of a Simple Language for Parallel Programming," *Information Processing 74,* IFIP, North-Holland, Amsterdam, 1974, pp. 471-475.

5. R. M. Keller, *Semantics and Applications of Function Graphs,* Technical Report UUCS-80-112, Computer Science Dept., University of Utah, Salt Lake City, Utah, 1980.

6. A. L. Davis, *Data-Driven Nets: A Maximally Concurrent, Procedural, Parallel Process Representation for Distributed Control Systems,* Technical Report UUCS-78-108, Computer Science Dept., University of Utah, Salt Lake City, Utah, 1978.

7. D. M. Ritchie and K. Thompson, "The Unix Time-Sharing System," *Comm. ACM,* Vol. 17, No. 7, July 1974, pp. 365-381.

8. P. J. Landin, "The Mechanical Evaluation of Expressions," *Computer J.,* Vol. 6, No. 4, Jan. 1964, pp. 308-320.

9. J. McCarthy et al., *Lisp 1.5 Programmers Manual,* MIT Press, Cambridge, Mass., 1965.

10. J. Rumbaugh, "A Data Flow Multiprocessor," *IEEE Trans. Computers,* Vol. C-26, No. 2, Feb. 1977, pp. 138-146.

11. S. Patil, "Closure Properties of Interconnections of Determinate Systems," *Proc. Project MAC Conf. Concurrent Systems and Parallel Computation,* June 1970, pp. 107-116.

12. Arvind and K. P. Gostelow, "Some Relationships Between Asynchronous Interpreters of a Dataflow Language," in *Formal Description of Programming Concepts*, E. J. Neuhold, ed., North-Holland, Amsterdam, 1978, pp. 95-119.

13. R. M. Keller, B. Jayaraman, D. Rose, and G. Lindstrom, *FGL (Function Graph Language) Programmers' Guide*, AMPS Technical Memorandum No. 1, Computer Science Dept., University of Utah, Salt Lake City, Utah, 1980.

14. R. M. Keller and W-C. J. Yen, "A Graphical Approach to Software Development Using Function Graphs," *Digest of Papers Compcon Spring 81*, Feb. 1981, pp. 156-161.

15. R. M. Keller and G. Lindstrom, "Hierarchical Analysis of a Distributed Evaluator," *Proc. Int'l Conf. Parallel Processing*, Aug. 1980, pp. 299-310.

16. K-S. Weng, *An Abstract Implementation for a Generalized Data Flow Language*, PhD thesis, MIT, Cambridge, Mass., May 1979.

17. R. M. Keller, G. Lindstrom, and S. Patil, "A Loosely-Coupled Applicative Multi-Processing System," *AFIPS Conf. Proc.*, Vol. 40, 1979 NCC, June 1979, pp. 613-622.

18. A. L. Davis, "The Architecture and System Method of DDM-1: A Recursively-Structured Data Driven Machine," *Proc. Fifth Ann. Symp. Computer Architecture*, 1978.

19. D. P. Friedman and D. S. Wise, "CONS Should Not Evaluate Its Arguments," in *Automata, Languages, and Programming*, S. Michaelson and R. Milner, eds., Edinburgh University Press, Edinburgh, Scotland, 1976, pp. 257-284.

20. R. M. Keller, "Divide and CONCer: Data Structuring for Applicative Multiprocessing," *Proc. Lisp Conf.*, Aug. 1980, pp. 196-202.

21. J. W. Forrester, *Industrial Dynamics*, MIT Press, Cambridge, Mass., 1961.

22. R. M. Keller and G. Lindstrom, "Applications of Feedback in Functional Programming," *Proc. ACM Conf. Functional Languages and Computer Architecture*, Oct. 1981, pp. 123-130.

23. L. A. Zadeh and C. A. Desoer, *Linear System Theory*, McGraw-Hill, New York, 1963.

24. L. R. Rabiner and C. M. Rader, *Digital Signal Processing*, IEEE Press, New York, 1972.

25. M. E. Conway, "Design of a Separable Transition-Diagram Compiler," *Comm. ACM*, Vol. 6, No. 7, July 1963, pp. 396-408.

26. G. Kahn and D. MacQueen, "Coroutines and Networks of Parallel Processes," *Proc. IFIP Congress 77*, Aug. 1977, pp. 993-998.

27. G. Brown, "A New Concept in Programming," in *Management and the Computer of the Future*, M. Greenberger, ed., John Wiley & Sons, 1962.

28. A. Church, *The Calculi of Lambda-Conversion*, Princeton University Press, Princeton, N.J., 1941.

29. A. Evans, Jr., "PAL—A Language Designed for Teaching Programming Linguistics," *Proc. ACM Nat'l Conf.*, 1968, pp. 395-403.

30. C. P. Wadsworth, *Semantics and Pragmatics of the Lambda-Calculus*, PhD thesis, University of Oxford, Oxford, England, 1971.

31. E. A. Ashcroft and W. W. Wadge, "Lucid, A Nonprocedural Language with Iteration," *Comm. ACM*, Vol. 20, No. 7, July 1977, pp. 519-526.

32. M. O'Donnell, "Subtree Replacement Systems: A Unifying Theory for Recursive Equations, Lisp, Lucid, and Combinatory Logic," *Proc. Ninth Ann. Symp. Theory of Computing*, May 1977, pp. 295-305.

33. D. P. Friedman and D. S. Wise, "The Impact of Applicative Programming on Multiprocessing," *IEEE Trans. Computers*, Vol. C-27, No. 4, Apr. 1978, pp. 289-296.

34. D. A. Turner, "A New Implementation Technique for Applicative Languages," *Software—Practice & Experience*, Vol. 9, No. 1, 1979, pp. 31-49.

35. W. H. Burge, *Recursive Programming Techniques*, Addison-Wesley, Reading, Mass., 1975.

36. P. Henderson and J. H. Morris, Jr., "A Lazy Evaluator," *Proc. Third ACM Conf. Principles Programming Languages*, 1976, pp. 95-103.

37. R. M. Keller, *Semantics of Parallel Program Graphs*, Technical Report UUCS-77-110, Computer Science, Dept., University of Utah, Salt Lake City, Utah, July, 1977.

38. P. Henderson, *Functional Programming*, Prentice-Hall, Englewood Cliffs, N.J., 1980.

39. R. Milne and C. Strachey, *A Theory of Programming Language Semantics*, Champman and Hall, London, 1976.

40. J. Stoy, *The Scott-Strachey Approach to the Mathematical Semantics of Programming Languages*, MIT Press, Cambridge, Mass., 1977.

41. D. R. Fitzwater and E. J. Schweppe, "Consequent Procedures in Conventional Computers," *AFIPS Conf. Proc.*, Vol. 26, Part II, 1964 FJCC, pp. 465-476.

42. J. B. Dennis, "Programming Generality, Parallelism, and Computer Architecture," *Proc. IFIP Congress*, 1969, pp. 484-492.

43. J. D. Rodriguez, *A Graph Model for Parallel Computation*, Technical Report TR-64, Project MAC, MIT, Cambridge, Mass., 1969.

44. D. Seror, *DCPL: A Distributed Control Programming Language*, Technical Report UTEC-CSc-70-108, Computer Science Dept., University of Utah, Salt Lake City, Utah, Dec. 1970.

45. J. B. Dennis, J. B. Fosseen, and J. P. Linderman, "Dataflow Schemas," in *Theoretical Programming*, Springer-Verlag, Berlin, 1972, pp. 187-216.

46. K-S. Weng, *Stream-Oriented Computation in Recursive Data Flow Schemas*, Master's thesis, MIT, Cambridge, Mass., Oct. 1975.

47. Arvind, K. P. Gostelow, and W. Plouffe, *An Asynchronous Programming Language and Computing Machine*, Technical Report TR 114a, University of California, Irvine, Calif., Dec. 1980.

48. C. A. Petri, "Fundamentals of a Theory of Asnychronous Information Flow," *Information Processing 62*, IFIP, North-Holland, 1962, pp. 386-391.

49. J. L. Peterson, *Petri Net Theory and the Modeling of Systems*, Prentice-Hall, Englewood Cliffs, N.J., 1981.

50. Arvind, K. P. Gostelow, and W. Plouffe, "Indeterminacy, Monitors, and Dataflow," *Operating Systems Rev.*, Vol. 11, No. 5, Nov. 1977, pp. 159-169.

51. R. M. Keller, "Denotational Models for Parallel Programs with Indeterminate Opeators," in *Formal Discription of Programming Concepts*, E. J. Neuhold, ed., North-Holland, Amsterdam, 1978, pp. 337-366.

52. P. R. Kosinski, "A Straightforward Denotational Semantics for Non-Determinate Data Flow Programs," *Proc. Fifth Ann. ACM Symp. Principles Programming Languages*, Jan. 1978, pp. 214-221.

53. D. P. Friedman and D. S. Wise, "An Approach to Fair Applicative Multiprogramming," in *Semantics of Concurrent Computation*, G. Kahn, ed., Springer-Verlag, Berlin, 1979, pp. 203-225.

54. B. Jayaraman and R. M. Keller, "Resource Control in a Demand-Driven Data-Flow Model," *Proc. Int'l Conf. Parallel Processing,* 1980, pp. 118-127.

55. A. L. Davis and S. A. Lowder, "A Sample Management Application Program in a Graphical Data-Driven Programming Language," *Digest of Papers Compcon Spring 81,* Feb. 1981, pp. 162-167.

56. D. T. Ross, "Structured Analysis (SA): A Language for Communicating Ideas," *IEEE Trans. Software Eng.,* Vol. SE-6, No. 1, Jan. 1977, pp. 16-33.

57. V. Weinberg, *Structured Analysis,* Prentice-Hall, Englewood Cliffs, N.J., 1978.

58. E. Yourdon and L. L. Constantine, *Structured Design,* Prentice-Hall, Englewood cliffs, N.J., 1979.

59. P. G. Hebalkar and S. N. Zilles, *Graphical Representations and Analysis of Information Systems Design,* IBM Research Report RJ 2465, Poughkeepsie, N.Y., Jan. 1979.

Alan L. Davis is an associate professor of computer science at the University of Utah. His current research interests include distributed architecture, graphically concurrent programming languages, parallel program schemata, device integration, asynchronous circuits, and self-timed systems. He has been a National Academy of Science exchange visitor and a visiting scholar in the Soviet Union, as well as a guest research fellow at the Gesellschaft fuer Matematik und Datenverarbeitung in West Germany.

Davis received a BS degree in electrical engineering from MIT in 1969 and a PhD in computer science from the University of Utah in 1972.

Robert M. Keller is a professor of computer science at the University of Utah. From 1970-1976 he was an assistant professor of electrical engineering at Princeton University. His primary interests are in asynchronous distributed systems, including their theory, implementation, verification, programming, and applications. Currently, these interests are manifest in the FGL/AMPS project, which entails research in construction of a usable general-purpose applicative language and in its support on a distributed multiprocessing system.

Keller received the MSEE from Washington University in St. Louis and the PhD from the University of California, Berkeley.

*By giving a unique name to every activity generated
during a computation, the U-interpreter can provide
greater concurrency in the interpretation of data flow graphs.*

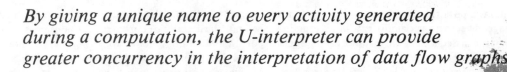

The U-Interpreter

Reprinted from *Computer*, February 1982, pages 42-49. Copyright © 1982
by The Institute of Electrical and Electronics Engineers, Inc.

Arvind
MIT

Kim P. Gostelow
General Electric

The usual method of interpreting data flow graphs
assumes a finite token capacity (usually one) on each arc.
This unnecessarily limits the amount of parallelism that
can be easily exploited in a program. The U-interpreter is
a method for assigning labels to each computational activity as it is dynamically generated during program execution. The U-interpreter assigns and manipulates labels
in a totally distributed manner, thus avoiding a sequential
controller, which can be a bottleneck in the design of large
multiple-processor machines.

Motivation

Suppose we want to integrate a function $f(x)$ from
$x = a$ to $x = b$. If the interval from a to b is divided into n
equal parts of size $h = (b - a)/n$, then according to the
trapezoidal rule the integral is

$$\sum_{i=1}^{n} (f(x_i) + f(x_{i-1})) * h/2$$

$$= ((f(x_0) + f(x_n))/2 + \sum_{i=1}^{n-1} f(x_i)) * h$$

where $x_i = a + i * h$.

On a multiple-processor machine we would like to
evaluate concurrently as many f's as the number of processors in the machine permits. There are several ways of
exposing parallelism in a problem, and in the following
paragraphs we discuss some of these methods briefly.

The most common method for exposing parallelism is
to write the program in a conventional language like For-

tran and then detect the opportunities for parallel execution by a compiler. Such a compiler can be quite complex
because it has to check against side effects permitted by
the language. In the trapezoidal rule example, if function
f is (textually) large and uses common storage for parameters, the compiler may fail to detect that all f's can be executed concurrently. Generally, clever coding of an algorithm for a sequential computer obscures the inherent
parallelism of a problem. The greatest advantage of using
Fortran is that existing programs only have to be recom-
piled for new high-performance architectures. This has
been the most popular approach in the past. State-of-the-
art analytical techniques for detecting parallelism and
compiling suitable code are represented by the Parafrase
system of Kuck.[1]

Another method for exposing parallelism is to extend
an existing programming language with explicit parallel
constructs: vector operators, and constructs such as
DOALL are examples of extensions suggested in the past
(e.g., Fortran for Burrough's scientific processor).[2-4] The
theoretical weakness of this approach is that programs
with parallel constructs are not necessarily well formed; a
program may show unintended nondeterministic behavior and thus produce wrong results. Detection of such errors complicates the compiler considerably, and this approach, though quite old, has not been widely practiced.
(Languages such as Concurrent Pascal are intended to express *nondeterministic* behavior of concurrent processes,
and thus are not relevant to the discussion of expressing
parallelism in deterministic computation.)

It has been pointed out many times during the last 15
years that it is easier to detect parallelism in functional
languages than in imperative languages.[5-7] Parallelism in
functional programs can be detected without a global
analysis of programs.[8,9] Function f in the trapezoid rule

example remains a pure function when coded in a functional language. Therefore, a compiler, without examining the body of f, can deduce that all instances of f are permitted to execute concurrently.

One way to execute functional languages is to translate them into data flow graphs suitable for execution on a multiple-processor machine.[10,11] Some functional languages (e.g., Val)[12] have also incorporated parallel constructs such as FORALL to provide further opportunities for optimization. (The FORALL construct in Val does not destroy the determinacy property of its programs.) Functional languages, in addition to expressing parallelism, seem to offer opportunities for writing more modular, reliable, and verifiable programs. Interest in functional languages has increased dramatically in recent years. However, their acceptance has been slow because of incompatibility with existing systems and a lack of good implementations.

In this article we present a different approach to exploiting parallelism in functional language programs. It does not involve special compile time analysis, nor does it rely on special constructs to specify parallelism explicitly. We interpret programs in such a way that during execution any two computations not dependent on each other for data are automatically eligible for concurrent execution. The U-interpreter has this property and can be used for any functional language that can be compiled into the usual data flow graphs. Such a compiler for the high-level language Id (Irvine data flow) is already in use.

An efficient implementation of the U-Interpreter requires special hardware structures. In fact, the original motivation for developing the U-interpreter was to define some appropriate basis for a highly parallel multiple-processor machine.[13] Results of the simulation of a U-interpreter machine have been reported by Gostelow and Thomas,[14] and a multiple-processor machine that implements the U-interpreter is being designed at the MIT Laboratory for Computer Science.[15]

Assigning labels to computational activities

Consider the following Id program that integrates function f by the trapezoidal rule:

```
(initial s←(f(a)+f(b))/2;
        x←a+h;
    for i from 1 to n−1 do
      new s←s+f(x);
      new x←x+h;
    return s)*h
```

A translation of this program into a data flow graph appears in Figure 1. In order of understand the translation, note that a token is replicated when it encounters a fork, and a SWITCH operator switches the data input token to one of the output arcs according to the boolean value of the control input token.[10] For the moment, treat operators L, L^{-1}, D, and D^{-1} as identity operators. Now, if we assume that each arc in the graph has a capacity to hold only one token, then the output arc of an operator must be empty before each firing of that operator. In the graph of Figure 1 this assumption severely limits the amount of concurrency that is possible. Suppose that function f, relative to $+$, takes a long time to execute. Then f will soon block the firing of the middle switch, which in turn will block the firing of the loop predicate. Essentially, not much will happen until f completes its first execution.

Now assume that arcs in the graph have unbounded token capacity. This will not change the outcome of the program and will greatly improve execution speed, but it will require very different hardware structures for implementation. Consider again the movement of tokens on the graph of Figure 1. Since the loop predicate $i \le n-1$ does not depend on $f(x)$, the production of the $n-1$ values for x over the range $a+h$ to b proceeds relatively quickly. Hence it is possible that even before f completes its first execution, the next $n-2$ input values for f pile up on the input arc to f. Under such circumstances, $n-2$ *true* tokens followed by one *false* token will accumulate on the control input of the leftmost switch, and a single token will sit on the first input arc of the $+$ operator. Every time f produces an output, one token from the control input of the switch will be removed. However, the U-interpreter will actually start $n-1$ executions of f by dynamically assigning a different label to each instance of f. (In data flow graphs an operator or a function does not have internal memory; hence, theoretically, several may execute concurrently as long as all inputs are available.) A computation activity with a label can execute (proceed) as soon as its inputs are available.

Note that when concurrent invocations of f are permitted, the correctness of results must be ensured even if the second instance of f completes before the first. In our particular example this issue is of no consequence—if one assumes that $+$ is an associative operator. However, in order to make the U-interpreter completely general, we don't assign any specific interpretation to noncontrol operators; whether an operator is arithmetic or relational, commutative or associative is immaterial to the U-interpreter. Each operator is assumed to produce exactly one output token for each set of input tokens and is considered "strict" in all its inputs. (A function f is said to be strict with respect to input x if divergence, or nontermination, of the computation of x implies divergence of f.) Thus, in the trapezoidal program, the U-interpreter adds the outputs of f in the correct order even if the second instance completes before the first.

An *activity* is a single execution of an operator. The U-interpreter gives a unique name to every activity generated during a computation, and each token (value) in the machine carries the name of its destination activity. An activity accepts all, but only, those tokens that carry its destination *activity name*. An activity name comprises four fields: u, c, s, and i.

- u is the context field, which uniquely identifies the context in which a code block is invoked. The context field is itself an activity name, so the definition is recursive.
- c is the code block name. In Id, every procedure and loop is given a unique code block name by the compiler.

- *s* is the instruction number within the code block.
- *i* is the initiation number, which identifies the loop iteration in which this activity occurs. (This field is 1 if the activity occurs outside a loop.)

Since the destination operator may require more than one input, each token also carries the number of its destination port. In the following we represent a token by $<u.c.s.i,$ data $>_p$ where p is the port number. (We often omit the port number when there is no ambiguity.) Note that fields c, s, and p of an activity name specify that the token is moving along an arc of the program graph connected to input port p of the operator in instruction s of code block c. This implies, of course, that the operator that produced the token is a predecessor of instruction s in code block c consistent with the static structure of the program. Fields u and i, on the other hand, must be consistent with the dynamics of program execution. For example, a token that has been generated during the ith iteration of a loop carries value i in its initiation number field.

Rules for manipulating activity names

Generating unique activity names for each computational activity is easy if one does not insist on performing this task in a distributed manner. A trivial scheme uses an integer counter that is read and incremented every time a new activity name is needed. This scheme will generate activity names sequentially, requiring only simple coordination among activities that generate tokens for the same destination activity.

The scheme employed by the U-interpreter generates new activity names based solely on the activity names carried by input tokens and a description of the code block. Thus no centralized name generator need be involved. At this point we describe the activity-name generation mechanism for a set of base language operators sufficient to implement a language with conditional, loop, and recursive procedure constructs.

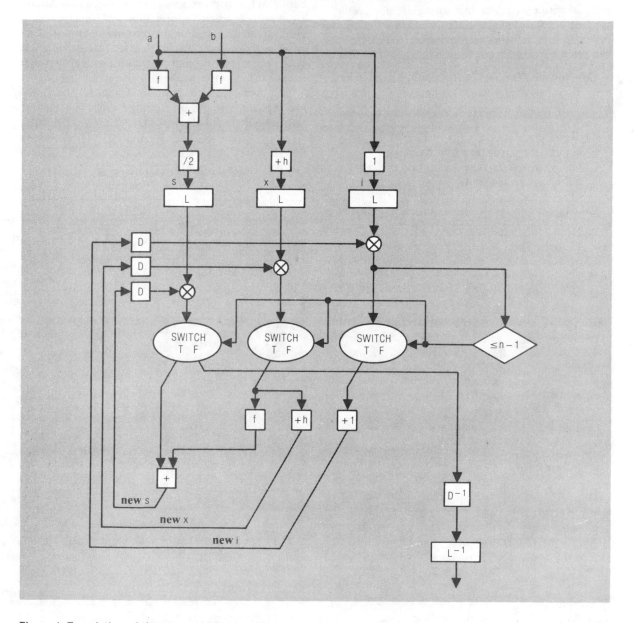

Figure 1. Translation of the trapezoidal program.

COMPUTER

Functions and predicates. This class of operators includes all arithmetic, boolean, and relational operators, as well as select and append operations on data structures. If the operator in instruction s of code block c performs the (binary) function f, and if instruction t is the destination of s, then we have

$$\text{input token set} \quad = \quad \{<u.c.s.i, x>_1, <u.s.c.i, y>_2\}$$
$$\text{output token set} \quad = \quad \{<u.c.t.i, f(x,y)>_p\}$$

If an output of s forks to n distinct inputs, then the output part of s will produce n distinct tokens, one for each input. Note that an acyclic base-language program (i.e., an Id block expression) composed of any number of interconnected function and predicate operators has the property that the ith set of input tokens produces the ith set of output tokens. This is true for any expression in the base language that is formed by composition of blocks, conditionals, loops, and procedure schemas. The activity-name generation rule given here does not require multiple initiations of a block to initiate or terminate in any particular order. In fact, activities corresponding to each initiation can execute independently of each other.

Conditionals. The SWITCH operator needed to implement the conditonal schema (Figure 2) may be described by

$$\text{input} = \{<u.c.s.i, x>_{\text{data}}, <u.c.s.i, b>_{\text{control}}\}$$
$$\text{output} = \textbf{if } b = \textbf{true then } \{<u.c.s_{\text{T}}.i, x>\}$$
$$\textbf{else if } b = \textbf{false then } \{<u.c.s_{\text{F}}.i, x>\}$$
$$\textbf{else undefined}$$

Exactly one of the successor instructions s_{T} or s_{F} receives a token. The total number of successors need not be the same on both sides of the switch. Since the iteration counts of the tokens going into f and g will be mutually exclusive for valid f and g, the iteration counts of the tokens on the output arcs of f and g will also be mutually exclusive. Hence, merging of outputs of f and g using $\otimes$ will not cause any activity names to be duplicated. Note that an *if*-expression behaves as a function box from input to output; the ith set of input tokens produces the ith set of output tokens.

Loops. A simplified loop schema is shown in Figure 3, for which the corresponding Id expression is

$$(\textbf{while } p(x) \textbf{ do}$$
$$\quad \textbf{new } x \leftarrow f(x)$$
$$\textbf{return } x)$$

A loop uses operators D, D^{-1}, L, and L^{-1}, as well as SWITCH. None of these operators affect the data portion of the tokens passing through. An execution of a loop expression can receive information only from tokens explicitly input to it because Id loops have no memory (i.e., no leftover tokens). Thus, in the case of nested loops it is quite possible that the input tokens for several instantiations of an inner loop may be available at the same time. It is the L operator (in conjunction with the L^{-1} operator) that capitalizes on this by creating a new context u' for each instantiation of a loop. An L operator is described by

$$\text{input} = \{<u.c.s.i, x>\}$$
$$\text{output} = \{<u'.c'.t'.1, x>\}$$

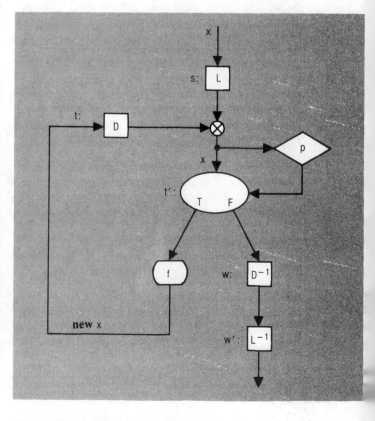

Figure 2. Translation of the if *p(x)* then *f(x)* else *g(x)*.

Figure 3. A loop schema.

where $u' = (u.c.s,i)$ and c' is the code block name of the invoked loop.

The initiation number of a token in a loop must be incremented every time a token goes around the loop. Corresponding to every **new** x-type variable in a loop, a D operator accomplishes this as follows:

$$\text{input} = \{<u'.c'.t.j, x>\}$$
$$\text{output} = \{<u'.c'.t'.j+1, x>\}$$

If after $n-1$ iterations the loop predicate p becomes false, the switch sends the last token with initiation number n to the D^{-1} operator, which changes the initiation number n to 1:

$$\text{input} = \{<u'.c'.w.n, x>\}$$
$$\text{output} = \{<u'.c'.w'.1, x>\}$$

The L^{-1} operator sends its input token to an activity whose context and initiation number are identical to those of the activity that initiated this loop:

$$\text{input} = \{<u'.c'.w'.1, x>\}$$
$$\text{output} = \{<u.c.s'.i, x>\}$$

where $c.s'$ is the successor of instruction $c'.w'$ (i.e., the L^{-1} operator) and $u' = (u.c.s.i)$.

Note that the L operator generates exactly one set of input tokens (with initiation number 1) for a loop expression in a given context ($u' = (u.c.s.i)$). Therefore, the input arcs of f, D, p, and SWITCH receive tokens with unique activity names, provided f is a valid expression. Clearly the D^{-1} operator never receives more than one token; hence L^{-1} also receives and produces exactly one token on each line. The L^{-1} operator unstacks the context part stacked by the corresponding L operator, so the tokens produced by L^{-1} have an iteration number equal to that of the input to the L operator. Thus, a loop expression also behaves like a function box in the sense that the ith set of input tokens produces the ith set of output tokens.

All activities belonging to a particular instantiation of a loop are said to constitute a *loop domain* and can proceed independent of activities outside the loop domain, including those of nested loops. It is interesting to note that tokens need not go around a loop in any particular order unless constrained by the need for intermediate results. This situation was illustrated by the program in Figure 1 where several initiations of f could execute concurrently. Even if the $j+1$st execution of f terminates before the jth execution, the activities of the $+$ operator will not be affected. However, in Figure 1, the $j+1$st activity of the $+$ can take place only after its jth activity has completed because of the data dependency of s on **new** s. Hence the $j+1$st output of f has been produced and absorbed by the jth activity of the $+$. Automatic unraveling of loops, constrained only by data dependencies that are actually present, greatly increases the concurrency within programs, many of which would otherwise be considered completely sequential.

We have analyzed the behavior of the graph in Figure 1 assuming that f took considerable time to compute

relative to a $+$. In passing we note that if f were some trivial operation and took only as long as the $+$ operator, probably no effective unfolding of this loop program would take place. In other words, the programmer need not know the relative timing of operators in order to write a parallel program. The fewer the data dependencies implied in a program, the more concurrent activities will be generated by the U-interpreter.

Procedure application. A procedure application is implemented using two operators: A and A^{-1}. As shown in Figure 4, each procedure is prefixed by a BEGIN operator and suffixed by an END operator. The A operator must create a new context u' within which the procedure whose code block name arrives on arc q may execute, and it must pass the argument value on line a to that context. The A operator is described by:

$$\text{input token set} = \{<u.c.s_A.i, q>_{\text{proc}}, <u.c.s_A.i, a>_{\text{arg}}\}$$
$$\text{output token set} = \{<u'.c_q.\text{begin}.1, a>\}$$

where $u' = (u.c.s_T.i)$ and s_T is the number of the A^{-1} operator corresponding to the A operator in s_A.

That is, the "return address" $u.c.s_T.i$ is stacked, and u' becomes the new context in which procedure q is executed. The output of A goes to the BEGIN operator, which simply replicates tokens for each fork in its output line. The END operator is more complex. It returns the result to the caller by unstacking the return address:

$$\text{input token set} = \{<u'.c_q.\text{end}.1, b>\}$$

$$\text{where } u' = (u.c.s_T.i)$$

$$\text{output token set} = \{<u.c.s_T.i, b>\}$$

Finally, the A^{-1} operator is straightforward, since, just like the BEGIN operator, it also serves only to replicate its output for its successors.

Maximum parallelism in a program

The U-interpreter is free of implementation details and is therefore quite amenable to formal analysis. We have shown that the U-interpreter does provide more concurrency than the usual way of interpreting data flow graphs.[16] To compare the relative parallelism of two interpreters, we choose a model that is independent of timing assumptions. Consider a program P involving two computations, x and y. We call interpreter I1 more parallel than interpreter I2 if results produced by I1 and I2 never differ, and if the execution of P on I2 implies that x must be computed before y while the execution of P on I1 does not imply any such constraint. Thus, in general, I1 has more parallelism than I2 if for all programs I1 implies no more execution constraints than I2. In fact, we have also shown that the U-interpreter finds maximum parallelism in an uninterpreted graph[16] (i.e., a graph in which operators other than control operators SWITCH, D, D^{-1}, L, L^{-1}, A, and A^{-1} are not assigned any meaning). It should be noted that the U-interpreter cannot improve on the graph itself; any unnecessary data dependencies will remain even if the graph is executed using the

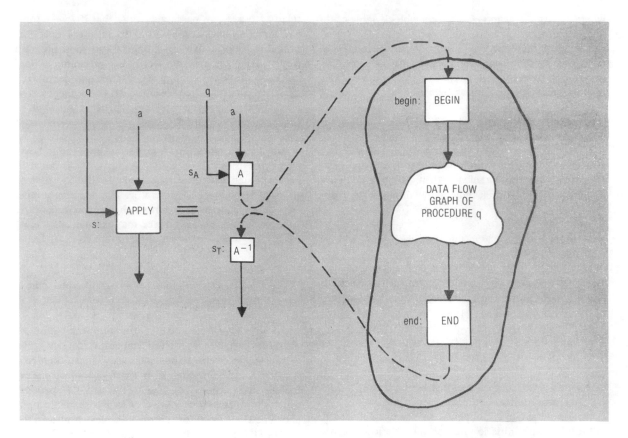

Figure 4. Application and execution of procedure *q*.

U-interpreter. The most common situation involving extraneous data dependencies arises in data structure operations. For example, the computation $a + x[2]$ depends on a and the 2nd element of x. However, the semantics of the particular high-level language may require the compiler to generate data flow graphs that cause all elements of x to be computed before $x[2]$ can be used.[8]

A formal definition of termination is often needed to resolve questions about how fast the final results will be produced. Program termination under the U-interpreter can be defined as the situation in which no activity is enabled or executing. The graphs produced for Id are "self-cleaning": on termination no tokens remain in the graph except on the output arcs. Our definition of termination is, in some sense, at odds with the notion of termination of a sequential program. In a sequential program the production of results and program termination occur simultaneously. On the other hand, if the "results" of a parallel program are the history of tokens on the output arcs, then results may be produced long before a program terminates. Thus, until the data flow program terminates, there is a possibility of producing more results. There is, however, no possibility of changing results that have already been produced. (The history of an arc is *monotonic*.) It should be noted that in order to assert that all output tokens that will be produced actually *are* produced, even if the computation does not terminate, one has to assume only a *fair* scheduling of activities: no enabled activity waits indefinitely.[16]

If function f in the trapezoidal rule example is some trivial function, not much is gained by unfolding the loop

for concurrent execution. As we pointed out earlier, the U-interpreter would automatically avoid unfolding the loop in that case. However, if each instance of f requires a lot of computation, then too much unfolding may take place. This would pose the practical problem of managing limited processing and memory resources.

We have described labeling of activities for graphs of deterministic computations. The U-interpreter is easily extended to deal with nonstrict as well as nondeterministic operators. The Id language has *resource managers,* which can be used to describe the nondeterministic interaction between processes that share objects. The labeling scheme for these constructs has been discussed elsewhere.[10] We believe the U-interpreter that incorporates nondeterministic and nonstrict operators, and that treats conventional sequential programs as primitive nodes of a graph, may help in structuring distributed systems.

Implications for computer architecture

Dynamic and explicit labeling of activities by an interpreter can increase the asynchrony and parallelism of any functional language. However, it seems that the practical benefits of dynamic labeling can best be exploited only by building special hardware structures. The benefits of the U-interpreter have been measured on a simulated machine and reported by Gostelow and Thomas.[14] A prototype for a thousand-processor machine based on the U-interpreter is currently being designed at MIT.[15]

A group at the University of Manchester in England independently discovered the idea of explicitly labeling computational activities for parallel execution. An experimental computer in which tokens carry long labels (56 bits) is currently under construction at Manchester.[17,18] In this machine a number of mechanisms for manipulating labels are provided for the language designer, without imposing *a priori* a specific set of label manipulation rules. Since the U-interpreter is an abstract model for interpreting data flow programs, it can probably be implemented on the Manchester machine, which is also capable of supporting the nondeterministic constructs of Id.[19]

A machine to implement the U-interpreter must provide an efficient mechanism for matching tokens with identical labels. In the Manchester machine, one waiting-matching store with 16K token capacity is provided. The matching is done by hashing and searching.[18] The tagged-token data flow machine under construction at MIT provides one small (32- or 64-token) waiting-matching store per processing element. The processing element is selected by hashing part of the label on the token,[14,15] and then the waiting-matching section is searched accordingly. This machine has a much smaller waiting-matching store because, unlike the Manchester machine, tokens for data-structure storage operations do not go through the waiting-matching section.

Logically, activity names can become arbitrarily long because the context field is recursive. For terminating computations, names can be kept within bounds by proper encoding of the information. One proposed scheme[15] works as follows: Suppose processing elements of a machine are (logically) partitioned into groups of various sizes called *physical domains*. Given the size of a processing element and a physical domain, there must be a maximum number (n) of loop and procedure invocation (i.e., *logical domains*) that can be concurrently executed. (One may draw analogy with an elevator that has a maximum capacity of 10 people or 2000 lbs.) We assign n "tickets" to such a physical domain. A new loop or procedure invocation is started in a physical domain only if a ticket is available. For example, an L operator will have to get a ticket from a finite ticket pool for the new context $u' = (u.c.s.i)$ and then send the current context associated with this ticket on a special dummy token directly to the corresponding L^{-1} operator. With the help of the dummy token, the L^{-1} operator will be able to generate the proper activity names for the output tokens and release the ticket for further use. If all the tickets are in use, then execution of an L operator will be delayed until a ticket is freed. Similar behavior holds for A and A^{-1} operators. This scheme does imply a degree of sequentiality in securing a ticket. It remains to be shown that disadvantages of this type of sequentiality are more than compensated for by an even distribution of activities on processing elements. A complete discussion of this and other architectural issues is beyond the scope of this paper.

The notion of labeling computational activities as used in the U-interpreter, coupled with an understanding of the rules for manipulating the activity names, should help to enhance the parallelism of programs written in any functional language. This implies the need to build special hardware structures to exploit the practical benefits of the method. ∎

Acknowledgment

This research was done by the authors at the University of California, Irvine, and was partially supported by NSF grant MCS76-12460.

References

1. D. J. Kuck, R. H. Kuhn, D. A. Padua, B. Leasure, and M. Wolfe, "Dependence Graphs and Compiler Optimizations," *Proc. ACM Symp. Principles of Programming Languages,* Jan. 1981, pp. 207-218.

2. N. E. Abel, et al., "TRANQUIL: A Language for an Array Processing Computer," *AFIPS Conf. Proc.,* Vol. 34, 1969 SJCC, pp. 57-73.

3. D. H. Lawrie, T. Layman, D. Baer, and J. M. Randel, "GLYPNIR—A Programming Language for Illiac IV," *Comm. ACM,* Vol. 18, No. 3, Mar. 1975, pp. 157-164.

4. R. E. Millstein, "Control Structures in Illiac IV Fortran," *Comm. ACM,* Vol. 6, No. 10, Oct. 1973, pp. 621-627.

5. L. G. Tesler and H. J. Enea, "A Language Design for Concurrent Processes," *AFIPS Conf. Proc.,* Vol. 32, 1968 SJCC, pp. 403-408.

6. J. B. Dennis, "First Version of a Data Flow Procedure Language," (in) *Lecture Notes in Computer Science, Volume 19: Programming Symp.: Proc. Colloque sur la Programmation,* B. Robinet (ed.), Springer-Verlag, 1974, pp. 362-376.

7. J. Backus, "Can Programming be Liberated from the von Neumann Style? A Functional Style and its Algebra of Programs," *Comm. ACM,* Vol. 21, No. 8, Aug. 1978, pp. 613-641.

8. W. B. Ackerman, "Data Flow Languages," *Computer,* this issue.

9. A. L. Davis and R. M. Keller, "Data Flow Program Graphs," *Computer,* Vol. 15, No. 2, Feb. 1982, pp. 26-41.

10. Arvind, K. P. Gostelow, and W. Plouffe, "An Asynchronous Programming Language and Computing Machine," Tech. Report TR114a, Department of Information and Computer Science, University of California, Irvine, Dec. 1978.

11. R. M. Keller, G. Lindstrom, and S. S. Patil, "A Loosely-Coupled Applicative Multiprocessing System," *AFIPS Conf. Proc.,* Vol. 48, 1979 NCC, pp. 613-622.

12. W. B. Ackerman and J. B. Dennis, "VAL—A Value-Oriented Algorithmic Language: Preliminary Reference Manual," Tech. Report TR-218, Laboratory for Computer Science, MIT, Cambridge, Mass., June 1979.

13. Arvind and K. P. Gostelow, "A Computer Capable of Exchanging Processors for Time," *Proc. IFIP Congress 77,* Aug. 1977, pp. 849-853.

14. K. P. Gostelow and R. E. Thomas, "Performance of a Simulated Dataflow Computer," *IEEE Trans. Computers,* Vol. C-29, No. 10, Oct. 1980, pp. 905-919.

15. Arvind and V. Kathail, "A Multiple Processor Dataflow Machine That Supports Generalized Procedures," *8th Ann. Symp. Computer Architecture,* May 1981, pp. 291-302.

16. Arvind and K. P. Gostelow, "Some Relationships Between Asynchronous Interpreters of a Dataflow Language," (in) E. J. Neuhold (ed.), *Formal Description of Programming Languages,* North-Holland Publ. Co., New York, 1977.

17. J. Gurd and I. Watson, "Data Driven System for High Speed Parallel Computing—Part 2: Hardware Design," *Computer Design,* Vol. 19, No. 7, July 1980, pp. 97-106.

18. I. Watson and J. R. Gurd, "A Practical Data Flow Computer," *Computer,* Vol. 15, No. 2, Feb. 1982, pp. 51-57.

19. A. J. Catto and J. R. Gurd, "Resource Management in Dataflow," *Proc. Conf. Functional Programming Languages and Computer Architecture,* Portsmouth, NH, Oct. 1981, pp. 77-84.

Kim P. Gostelow is currently with the General Electric Research and Development Center in Schenectady, New York. His interests include operating systems, machine architecture, and the semantics of programming languages. From 1972 to 1974 he did work on network modeling at the Stichting Academisch Rekencentrum Amsterdam, The Netherlands. From 1974 to 1980 he was assistant, and then associate professor of information and computer science at the University of California, Irvine. He received the BS and MS degrees in engineering and the PhD in computer science from the University of California, Los Angeles, in 1966, 1968, and 1971, respectively.

Arvind is a guest editor of this issue of *Computer*. His biography appears on p. 13.

Chapter 5: Functional Programming Languages

Background

Functional languages are based on the mathematics of functional algebra and have no concepts of storage state and assignment. The main concept is the *definition* and application of mathematical functions.

The assignment in the single assignment languages (SAL) is superfluous, and, thus SAL can be regarded as being similar to functional languages. There is no sequencing mechanism in functional languages, and they are free from side effects like SAL. However, functional algebra has more powerful programming constructs than SAL because functional algebra permits construction of higher order functions and abstract data structures.

The functional programming languages allow functional aspects of the programs to be separated from the operational aspects, which makes them well suited for parallel computation since their declarative nature does not place artificial constraints on the order of evaluation of expression. The *Church-Rosser Property* guarantees determinancy regardless of the execution order that happens to occur. The programmer does not have to be concerned with specification of the order of execution. The model for evaluation of an expression is to apply continually the functions involved in its definition until the expression is reduced to its simplest form. The opportunity for exploiting parallelism arises from the concurrent evaluation of arguments of a function.

Article Summary

Backus, in "Can Programming Be Liberated from the von Neumann Style? A Functional Style and Its Algebra of Programs," describes the limitation of von Neumann architectures and imperative programming languages and how functional programming languages overcome these limitations. He explains that the limitation of the conventional architectures is caused by the von Neumann bottleneck, which he describes as the path from processor to memory. The task of the program is to change the contents of the memory in some way that must be performed by moving the words back and forth through this bottleneck. Thus, conventional programming languages just allow planning and detailing the traffic through this bottleneck. He also introduces the notion of functional programming languages and why they are superior to imperative languages in terms of software development. These languages are based on func-tional algebra and thus provide useful properties for reasoning about programs. More importantly, he describes how they overcome the von Neumann bottleneck.

Turner describes a variable free representation for programs, in functional languages, which contain bound variables, in his article "A New Implementation Technique for Applicative Languages." Turner introduces combinatory logic and combinators that serve the role of bound variables in a program. The compilation into combinators removes the bound variables from the program. He also describes a graph reduction machine that can efficiently execute the resulting code and compares this with a conventional interpreter.

Kenneway and Sleep, in "The Language First Approach," address the problem with von Neumann multiprocessor systems and consider why declarative (equational) languages provide a better alternative for multiprocessor architectures. It is a language first approach; design the architecture for efficient execution of these languages. Evaluation models for these languages are categorized and their implementation is studied.

Additional material can be found in references 1-15.

References

[1] Arvind, Kathail, V., and Pengali, K., "Sharing of Computation in Functional Language Implementations," *Lab. for CS Technical Report*, Massachusetts Institute of Technology, Cambridge, Mass., July 1984.

[2] Arvind and Brock, J.D., "Resource Managers in Functional Programming," *Journal of Parallel and Distributed Computing*, Vol. 1, 1984, pp. 5-21.

[3] Ashcroft, E. and Wadge, W., *LUCID, the Dataflow Programming Language*, Academic Press, Orlando, Fla., 1985.

[4] Bailey, R., "A HOPE Tutorial," *Byte*, Vol. 10, No. 8, Aug. 1985, pp. 235-258.

[5] Burstall, R.M., McQueen, D.B., and Sannella, D.N., "Hope: An Experimental Applicative Language," *Proc. ACM LISP Conf.*, Association for Computing Machinery, Inc., New York, N.Y., 1980, pp. 136-143.

[6] Chambers, F.B., Duce, D.A., and Jones, G.P. (editors), *Distributed Computing*, Academic Press, Inc. (London) Ltd., London, England, 1984.

[7] Darlington, J., Henderson, P., and Turner, D., *Functional Programming Application and Implementation*, Cambridge University Press, Cambridge, England, 1980.

[8] Darlington, J., "Program Transformation," *Byte*, Vol. 10, No. 8, Aug. 1985, pp. 201-216.

[9] Eisenbach, S. and Sadler, C., "Declarative Languages: An Overview," *Byte*, Vol. 10, No. 8, Aug. 1985, pp. 181-192.

[10] Harrison, P.G. and Khoshnevisan, H., "Functional Programming Using FP," *Byte*, Vol. 10, No. 8, Aug. 1985, pp. 219-232.

[11] Jayaraman, B. and Leller, R.M., "Resource Expressions for Applicative Languages," *Proc. of the 1982 Int'l. Conf. on Parallel Processing*, Computer Society of the IEEE Press, Washington, D.C., 1982, pp. 160-167.

[12] Johnsson, T., "The G-Machine: An Abstract Machine for Graph Reduction," *Proc. of the Declarative Prog. Workshop*, University College of London, London, England, 1983.

[13] Keller, R.M. and Sleep, M.R., "Applicative Caching," *ACM Transactions on Programming Languages and Systems*, Vol. 8, No. 1, Jan. 1986, pp. 89-108.

[14] Mauny, M. and Suarez, A., "Implementing Functional Languages in the Categorical Abstract Machine," *Proc. ACM LISP and Functional Programming Conf.*, Association for Computing Machinery, Inc., New York, N.Y., Aug. 1986, pp. 266-278.

[15] Milner, R., "A Proposal for Standard ML," *Proc. ACM LISP and Functional Programming Languages Conf.*, Association for Computing Machinery, Inc., New York, N.Y., 1984, pp. 184-197.

The 1977 ACM Turing Award was presented to John Backus at the ACM Annual Conference in Seattle, October 17. In introducing the recipient, Jean E. Sammet, Chairman of the Awards Committee, made the following comments and read a portion of the final citation. The full announcement is in the September 1977 issue of *Communications,* page 681.

"Probably there is nobody in the room who has not heard of Fortran and most of you have probably used it at least once, or at least looked over the shoulder of someone who was writing a Fortran program. There are probably almost as many people who have heard the letters BNF but don't necessarily know what they stand for. Well, the B is for Backus, and the other letters are explained in the formal citation. These two contributions, in my opinion, are among the half dozen most important technical contributions to the computer field and both were made by John Backus (which in the Fortran case also involved some colleagues). It is for these contributions that he is receiving this year's Turing award.

The short form of his citation is for 'profound, influential, and lasting contributions to the design of practical high-level programming systems, notably through his work on Fortran, and for seminal publication of formal procedures for the specifications of programming languages.'

The most significant part of the full citation is as follows:

'. . . Backus headed a small IBM group in New York City during the early 1950s. The earliest product of this group's efforts was a high-level language for scientific and technical computations called Fortran. This same group designed the first system to translate Fortran programs into machine language. They employed novel optimizing techniques to generate fast machine-language programs. Many other compilers for the language were developed, first on IBM machines, and later on virtually every make of computer. Fortran was adopted as a U.S. national standard in 1966.

During the latter part of the 1950s, Backus served on the international committees which developed Algol 58 and a later version, Algol 60. The language Algol, and its derivative compilers, received broad acceptance in Europe as a means for developing programs and as a formal means of publishing the algorithms on which the programs are based.

In 1959, Backus presented a paper at the UNESCO conference in Paris on the syntax and semantics of a proposed international algebraic language. In this paper, he was the first to employ a formal technique for specifying the syntax of programming languages. The formal notation became known as BNF—standing for "Backus Normal Form," or "Backus Naur Form" to recognize the further contributions by Peter Naur of Denmark.

Thus, Backus has contributed strongly both to the pragmatic world of problem-solving on computers and to the theoretical world existing at the interface between artificial languages and computational linguistics. Fortran remains one of the most widely used programming languages in the world. Almost all programming languages are now described with some type of formal syntactic definition.'"

Can Programming Be Liberated from the von Neumann Style? A Functional Style and Its Algebra of Programs

John Backus
IBM Research Laboratory, San Jose

"Can Programming Be Liberated from the von Neumann Style? A Functional Style and Its Algebra of Programs" by J. Backus from *Communications of the ACM*, August 1978, pages 613-641. Copyright 1978, Association for Computing Machinery, Inc.

Author's address: 91 Saint Germain Ave., San Francisco, CA 94114.

Conventional programming languages are growing ever more enormous, but not stronger. Inherent defects at the most basic level cause them to be both fat and weak: their primitive word-at-a-time style of programming inherited from their common ancestor—the von Neumann computer, their close coupling of semantics to state transitions, their division of programming into a world of expressions and a world of statements, their inability to effectively use powerful combining forms for building new programs from existing ones, and their lack of useful mathematical properties for reasoning about programs.

An alternative functional style of programming is founded on the use of combining forms for creating programs. Functional programs deal with structured data, are often nonrepetitive and nonrecursive, are hierarchically constructed, do not name their arguments, and do not require the complex machinery of procedure declarations to become generally applicable. Combining forms can use high level programs to build still higher level ones in a style not possible in conventional languages.

Associated with the functional style of programming is an algebra of programs whose variables range over programs and whose operations are combining forms. This algebra can be used to transform programs and to solve equations whose "unknowns" are programs in much the same way one transforms equations in high school algebra. These transformations are given by algebraic laws and are carried out in the same language in which programs are written. Combining forms are chosen not only for their programming power but also for the power of their associated algebraic laws. General theorems of the algebra give the detailed behavior and termination conditions for large classes of programs.

A new class of computing systems uses the functional programming style both in its programming language and in its state transition rules. Unlike von Neumann languages, these systems have semantics loosely coupled to states—only one state transition occurs per major computation.

Key Words and Phrases: functional programming, algebra of programs, combining forms, functional forms, programming languages, von Neumann computers, von Neumann languages, models of computing systems, applicative computing systems, applicative state transition systems, program transformation, program correctness, program termination, metacomposition

CR Categories: 4.20, 4.29, 5.20, 5.24, 5.26

Introduction

I deeply appreciate the honor of the ACM invitation to give the 1977 Turing Lecture and to publish this account of it with the details promised in the lecture. Readers wishing to see a summary of this paper should turn to Section 16, the last section.

1. Conventional Programming Languages: Fat and Flabby

Programming languages appear to be in trouble. Each successive language incorporates, with a little cleaning up, all the features of its predecessors plus a few more. Some languages have manuals exceeding 500 pages; others cram a complex description into shorter manuals by using dense formalisms. The Department of Defense has current plans for a committee-designed language standard that could require a manual as long as 1,000 pages. Each new language claims new and fashionable features, such as strong typing or structured control statements, but the plain fact is that few languages make programming sufficiently cheaper or more reliable to justify the cost of producing and learning to use them.

Since large increases in size bring only small increases in power, smaller, more elegant languages such as Pascal continue to be popular. But there is a desperate need for a powerful methodology to help us think about pro-

grams, and no conventional language even begins to meet that need. In fact, conventional languages create unnecessary confusion in the way we think about programs.

For twenty years programming languages have been steadily progressing toward their present condition of obesity; as a result, the study and invention of programming languages has lost much of its excitement. Instead, it is now the province of those who prefer to work with thick compendia of details rather than wrestle with new ideas. Discussions about programming languages often resemble medieval debates about the number of angels that can dance on the head of a pin instead of exciting contests between fundamentally differing concepts.

Many creative computer scientists have retreated from inventing languages to inventing tools for describing them. Unfortunately, they have been largely content to apply their elegant new tools to studying the warts and moles of existing languages. After examining the appalling type structure of conventional languages, using the elegant tools developed by Dana Scott, it is surprising that so many of us remain passively content with that structure instead of energetically searching for new ones.

The purpose of this article is twofold; first, to suggest that basic defects in the framework of conventional languages make their expressive weakness and their cancerous growth inevitable, and second, to suggest some alternate avenues of exploration toward the design of new kinds of languages.

2. Models of Computing Systems

Underlying every programming language is a model of a computing system that its programs control. Some models are pure abstractions, some are represented by hardware, and others by compiling or interpretive programs. Before we examine conventional languages more closely, it is useful to make a brief survey of existing models as an introduction to the current universe of alternatives. Existing models may be crudely classified by the criteria outlined below.

2.1 Criteria for Models
2.1.1 Foundations. Is there an elegant and concise mathematical description of the model? Is it useful in proving helpful facts about the behavior of the model? Or is the model so complex that its description is bulky and of little mathematical use?

2.1.2 History sensitivity. Does the model include a notion of storage, so that one program can save information that can affect the behavior of a later program? That is, is the model history sensitive?

2.1.3 Type of semantics. Does a program successively transform states (which are not programs) until a terminal state is reached (state-transition semantics)? Are states simple or complex? Or can a "program" be successively reduced to simpler "programs" to yield a final "normal form program," which is the result (reduction semantics)?

2.1.4 Clarity and conceptual usefulness of programs. Are programs of the model clear expressions of a process or computation? Do they embody concepts that help us to formulate and reason about processes?

2.2 Classification of Models

Using the above criteria we can crudely characterize three classes of models for computing systems—simple operational models, applicative models, and von Neumann models.

2.2.1 Simple operational models. Examples: Turing machines, various automata. *Foundations*: concise and useful. *History sensitivity*: have storage, are history sensitive. *Semantics*: state transition with very simple states. *Program clarity*: programs unclear and conceptually not helpful.

2.2.2 Applicative models. Examples: Church's lambda calculus [5], Curry's system of combinators [6], pure Lisp [17], functional programming systems described in this paper. *Foundations*: concise and useful. *History sensitivity*: no storage, not history sensitive. *Semantics*: reduction semantics, no states. *Program clarity*: programs can be clear and conceptually useful.

2.2.3 Von Neumann models. Examples: von Neumann computers, conventional programming languages. *Foundations*: complex, bulky, not useful. *History sensitivity*: have storage, are history sensitive. *Semantics*: state transition with complex states. *Program clarity*: programs can be moderately clear, are not very useful conceptually.

The above classification is admittedly crude and debatable. Some recent models may not fit easily into any of these categories. For example, the data-flow languages developed by Arvind and Gostelow [1], Dennis [7], Kosinski [13], and others partly fit the class of simple operational models, but their programs are clearer than those of earlier models in the class and it is perhaps possible to argue that some have reduction semantics. In any event, this classification will serve as a crude map of the territory to be discussed. We shall be concerned only with applicative and von Neumann models.

3. Von Neumann Computers

In order to understand the problems of conventional programming languages, we must first examine their intellectual parent, the von Neumann computer. What is a von Neumann computer? When von Neumann and others conceived it over thirty years ago, it was an elegant, practical, and unifying idea that simplified a number of engineering and programming problems that existed then. Although the conditions that produced its architecture have changed radically, we nevertheless still identify the notion of "computer" with this thirty year old concept.

In its simplest form a von Neumann computer has three parts: a central processing unit (or CPU), a store, and a connecting tube that can transmit a single word between the CPU and the store (and send an address to the store). I propose to call this tube the *von Neumann bottleneck*. The task of a program is to change the contents of the store in some major way; when one considers that this task must be accomplished entirely by pumping single words back and forth through the von Neumann bottleneck, the reason for its name becomes clear.

Ironically, a large part of the traffic in the bottleneck is not useful data but merely names of data, as well as operations and data used only to compute such names. Before a word can be sent through the tube its address must be in the CPU; hence it must either be sent through the tube from the store or be generated by some CPU operation. If the address is sent from the store, then *its* address must either have been sent from the store or generated in the CPU, and so on. If, on the other hand, the address is generated in the CPU, it must be generated either by a fixed rule (e.g., "add 1 to the program counter") or by an instruction that was sent through the tube, in which case *its* address must have been sent . . . and so on.

Surely there must be a less primitive way of making big changes in the store than by pushing vast numbers of words back and forth through the von Neumann bottleneck. Not only is this tube a literal bottleneck for the data traffic of a problem, but, more importantly, it is an intellectual bottleneck that has kept us tied to word-at-a-time thinking instead of encouraging us to think in terms of the larger conceptual units of the task at hand. Thus programming is basically planning and detailing the enormous traffic of words through the von Neumann bottleneck, and much of that traffic concerns not significant data itself but where to find it.

4. Von Neumann Languages

Conventional programming languages are basically high level, complex versions of the von Neumann computer. Our thirty year old belief that there is only one kind of computer is the basis of our belief that there is only one kind of programming language, the conventional—von Neumann—language. The differences between Fortran and Algol 68, although considerable, are less significant than the fact that both are based on the programming style of the von Neumann computer. Although I refer to conventional languages as "von Neumann languages" to take note of their origin and style, I do not, of course, blame the great mathematician for their complexity. In fact, some might say that I bear some responsibility for that problem.

Von Neumann programming languages use variables to imitate the computer's storage cells; control statements elaborate its jump and test instructions; and assignment statements imitate its fetching, storing, and arithmetic.

The assignment statement is the von Neumann bottle-neck of programming languages and keeps us thinking in word-at-a-time terms in much the same way the computer's bottleneck does.

Consider a typical program; at its center are a number of assignment statements containing some subscripted variables. Each assignment statement produces a one-word result. The program must cause these statements to be executed many times, while altering subscript values, in order to make the desired overall change in the store, since it must be done one word at a time. The programmer is thus concerned with the flow of words through the assignment bottleneck as he designs the nest of control statements to cause the necessary repetitions.

Moreover, the assignment statement splits programming into two worlds. The first world comprises the right sides of assignment statements. This is an orderly world of expressions, a world that has useful algebraic properties (except that those properties are often destroyed by side effects). It is the world in which most useful computation takes place.

The second world of conventional programming languages is the world of statements. The primary statement in that world is the assignment statement itself. All the other statements of the language exist in order to make it possible to perform a computation that must be based on this primitive construct: the assignment statement.

This world of statements is a disorderly one, with few useful mathematical properties. Structured programming can be seen as a modest effort to introduce some order into this chaotic world, but it accomplishes little in attacking the fundamental problems created by the word-at-a-time von Neumann style of programming, with its primitive use of loops, subscripts, and branching flow of control.

Our fixation on von Neumann languages has continued the primacy of the von Neumann computer, and our dependency on *it* has made non-von Neumann languages uneconomical and has limited their development. The absence of full scale, effective programming styles founded on non-von Neumann principles has deprived designers of an intellectual foundation for new computer architectures. (For a brief discussion of that topic, see Section 15.)

Applicative computing systems' lack of storage and history sensitivity is the basic reason they have not provided a foundation for computer design. Moreover, most applicative systems employ the substitution operation of the lambda calculus as their basic operation. This operation is one of virtually unlimited power, but its complete and efficient realization presents great difficulties to the machine designer. Furthermore, in an effort to introduce storage and to improve their efficiency on von Neumann computers, applicative systems have tended to become engulfed in a large von Neumann system. For example, pure Lisp is often buried in large extensions with many von Neumann features. The resulting complex systems offer little guidance to the machine designer.

5. Comparison of von Neumann and Functional Programs

To get a more detailed picture of some of the defects of von Neumann languages, let us compare a conventional program for inner product with a functional one written in a simple language to be detailed further on.

5.1 A von Neumann Program for Inner Product

```
c := 0
for i := 1 step 1 until n do
    c := c + a[i]×b[i]
```

Several properties of this program are worth noting:

a) Its statements operate on an invisible "state" according to complex rules.

b) It is not hierarchical. Except for the right side of the assignment statement, it does not construct complex entities from simpler ones. (Larger programs, however, often do.)

c) It is dynamic and repetitive. One must mentally execute it to understand it.

d) It computes word-at-a-time by repetition (of the assignment) and by modification (of variable i).

e) Part of the data, n, is in the program; thus it lacks generality and works only for vectors of length n.

f) It names its arguments; it can only be used for vectors a and b. To become general, it requires a procedure declaration. These involve complex issues (e.g., call-by-name versus call-by-value).

g) Its "housekeeping" operations are represented by symbols in scattered places (in the **for** statement and the subscripts in the assignment). This makes it impossible to consolidate housekeeping operations, the most common of all, into single, powerful, widely useful operators. Thus in programming those operations one must always start again at square one, writing "**for** i := ..." and "**for** j := ..." followed by assignment statements sprinkled with i's and j's.

5.2 A Functional Program for Inner Product

Def Innerproduct
$$\equiv (\text{Insert} +)\circ(\text{ApplyToAll} \times)\circ\text{Transpose}$$

Or, in abbreviated form:

Def IP $\equiv (/+)\circ(\alpha\times)\circ\text{Trans.}$

Composition (∘), Insert (/), and ApplyToAll (α) are *functional forms* that combine existing functions to form new ones. Thus $f\circ g$ is the function obtained by applying first g and then f, and αf is the function obtained by applying f to every *member* of the argument. If we write $f:x$ for the result of applying f to the object x, then we can explain each step in evaluating Innerproduct applied to the pair of vectors $<<1, 2, 3>, <6, 5, 4>>$ as follows:

IP:$<<1,2,3>, <6,5,4>> =$

Definition of IP	$\Rightarrow (/+)\circ(\alpha\times)\circ\text{Trans:} <<1,2,3>, <6,5,4>>$
Effect of composition, ∘	$\Rightarrow (/+):((\alpha\times):(\text{Trans:}$
	$<<1,2,3>, <6,5,4>>))$

218

Applying Transpose	$\Rightarrow (/+){:}((\alpha\times){:} <<1,6>, <2,5>, <3,4>>)$
Effect of ApplyToAll, α	$\Rightarrow (/+){:} <\times{:} <1,6>, \times{:} <2,5>, \times{:} <3,4>>$
Applying $\times$	$\Rightarrow (/+){:} <6,10,12>$
Effect of Insert, /	$\Rightarrow +{:} <6, +{:} <10,12>>$
Applying +	$\Rightarrow +{:} <6,22>$
Applying + again	$\Rightarrow 28$

Let us compare the properties of this program with those of the von Neumann program.

a) It operates only on its arguments. There are no hidden states or complex transition rules. There are only two kinds of rules, one for applying a function to its argument, the other for obtaining the function denoted by a functional form such as composition, $f{\circ}g$, or ApplyToAll, αf, when one knows the functions f and g, the *parameters* of the forms.

b) It is hierarchical, being built from three simpler functions ($+$, $\times$, Trans) and three functional forms $f{\circ}g$, αf, and $/f$.

c) It is static and nonrepetitive, in the sense that its structure is helpful in understanding it without mentally executing it. For example, if one understands the action of the forms $f{\circ}g$ and αf, and of the functions $\times$ and Trans, then one understands the action of $\alpha\times$ and of $(\alpha\times){\circ}$Trans, and so on.

d) It operates on whole conceptual units, not words; it has three steps; no step is repeated.

e) It incorporates no data; it is completely general; it works for any pair of conformable vectors.

f) It does not name its arguments; it can be applied to any pair of vectors without any procedure declaration or complex substitution rules.

g) It employs housekeeping forms and functions that are generally useful in many other programs; in fact, only $+$ and $\times$ are not concerned with housekeeping. These forms and functions can combine with others to create higher level housekeeping operators.

Section 14 sketches a kind of system designed to make the above functional style of programming available in a history-sensitive system with a simple framework, but much work remains to be done before the above applicative style can become the basis for elegant and practical programming languages. For the present, the above comparison exhibits a number of serious flaws in von Neumann programming languages and can serve as a starting point in an effort to account for their present fat and flabby condition.

6. Language Frameworks versus Changeable Parts

Let us distinguish two parts of a programming language. First, its *framework* which gives the overall rules of the system, and second, its *changeable parts,* whose existence is anticipated by the framework but whose particular behavior is not specified by it. For example, the **for** statement, and almost all other statements, are part of Algol's framework but library functions and user-defined procedures are changeable parts. Thus the framework of a language describes its fixed features and provides a general environment for its changeable features.

Now suppose a language had a small framework which could accommodate a great variety of powerful features entirely as changeable parts. Then such a framework could support many different features and styles without being changed itself. In contrast to this pleasant possibility, von Neumann languages always seem to have an immense framework and very limited changeable parts. What causes this to happen? The answer concerns two problems of von Neumann languages.

The first problem results from the von Neumann style of word-at-a-time programming, which requires that words flow back and forth to the state, just like the flow through the von Neumann bottleneck. Thus a von Neumann language must have a semantics closely coupled to the state, in which every detail of a computation changes the state. The consequence of this semantics closely coupled to states is that every detail of every feature must be built into the state and its transition rules.

Thus every feature of a von Neumann language must be spelled out in stupefying detail in its framework. Furthermore, many complex features are needed to prop up the basically weak word-at-a-time style. The result is the inevitable rigid and enormous framework of a von Neumann language.

7. Changeable Parts and Combining Forms

The second problem of von Neumann languages is that their changeable parts have so little expressive power. Their gargantuan size is eloquent proof of this; after all, if the designer knew that all those complicated features, which he now builds into the framework, could be added later on as changeable parts, he would not be so eager to build them into the framework.

Perhaps the most important element in providing powerful changeable parts in a language is the availability of combining forms that can be generally used to build new procedures from old ones. Von Neumann languages provide only primitive combining forms, and the von Neumann framework presents obstacles to their full use.

One obstacle to the use of combining forms is the split between the expression world and the statement world in von Neumann languages. Functional forms naturally belong to the world of expressions; but no matter how powerful they are they can only build expressions that produce a one-word result. And it is in the statement world that these one-word results must be combined into the overall result. Combining single words is not what we really should be thinking about, but it is a large part of programming any task in von Neumann languages. To help assemble the overall result from single words these languages provide some primitive combining forms in the statement world—the **for, while,** and **if-then-else** statements—but the split between the two worlds prevents the combining forms in either world from attaining the full power they can achieve in an undivided world.

A second obstacle to the use of combining forms in von Neumann languages is their use of elaborate naming conventions, which are further complicated by the substitution rules required in calling procedures. Each of these requires a complex mechanism to be built into the framework so that variables, subscripted variables, pointers, file names, procedure names, call-by-value formal parameters, call-by-name formal parameters, and so on, can all be properly interpreted. All these names, conventions, and rules interfere with the use of simple combining forms.

8. APL versus Word-at-a-Time Programming

Since I have said so much about word-at-a-time programming, I must now say something about APL [12]. We owe a great debt to Kenneth Iverson for showing us that there are programs that are neither word-at-a-time nor dependent on lambda expressions, and for introducing us to the use of new functional forms. And since APL assignment statements can store arrays, the effect of its functional forms is extended beyond a single assignment.

Unfortunately, however, APL still splits programming into a world of expressions and a world of statements. Thus the effort to write one-line programs is partly motivated by the desire to stay in the more orderly world of expressions. APL has exactly three functional forms, called inner product, outer product, and reduction. These are sometimes difficult to use, there are not enough of them, and their use is confined to the world of expressions.

Finally, APL semantics is still too closely coupled to states. Consequently, despite the greater simplicity and power of the language, its framework has the complexity and rigidity characteristic of von Neumann languages.

9. Von Neumann Languages Lack Useful Mathematical Properties

So far we have discussed the gross size and inflexibility of von Neumann languages; another important defect is their lack of useful mathematical properties and the obstacles they present to reasoning about programs. Although a great amount of excellent work has been published on proving facts about programs, von Neumann languages have almost no properties that are helpful in this direction and have many properties that are obstacles (e.g., side effects, aliasing).

Denotational semantics [23] and its foundations [20, 21] provide an extremely helpful mathematical understanding of the domain and function spaces implicit in programs. When applied to an applicative language (such as that of the "recursive programs" of [16]), its foundations provide powerful tools for describing the language and for proving properties of programs. When applied to a von Neumann language, on the other hand, it provides a precise semantic description and is helpful in identifying trouble spots in the language. But the complexity of the language is mirrored in the complexity of the description, which is a bewildering collection of productions, domains, functions, and equations that is only slightly more helpful in proving facts about programs than the reference manual of the language, since it is less ambiguous.

Axiomatic semantics [11] precisely restates the inelegant properties of von Neumann programs (i.e., transformations on states) as transformations on predicates. The word-at-a-time, repetitive game is not thereby changed, merely the playing field. The complexity of this axiomatic game of proving facts about von Neumann programs makes the successes of its practitioners all the more admirable. Their success rests on two factors in addition to their ingenuity: First, the game is restricted to small, weak subsets of full von Neumann languages that have states vastly simpler than real ones. Second, the new playing field (predicates and their transformations) is richer, more orderly and effective than the old (states and their transformations). But restricting the game and transferring it to a more effective domain does not enable it to handle real programs (with the necessary complexities of procedure calls and aliasing), nor does it eliminate the clumsy properties of the basic von Neumann style. As axiomatic semantics is extended to cover more of a typical von Neumann language, it begins to lose its effectiveness with the increasing complexity that is required.

Thus denotational and axiomatic semantics are descriptive formalisms whose foundations embody elegant and powerful concepts; but using them to describe a von Neumann language can not produce an elegant and powerful language any more than the use of elegant and modern machines to build an Edsel can produce an elegant and modern car.

In any case, proofs about programs use the language of logic, not the language of programming. Proofs talk *about* programs but cannot involve them directly since the axioms of von Neumann languages are so unusable. In contrast, many ordinary proofs are derived by algebraic methods. These methods require a language that has certain algebraic properties. Algebraic laws can then be used in a rather mechanical way to transform a problem into its solution. For example, to solve the equation

$$ax + bx = a + b$$

for x (given that $a+b \neq 0$), we mechanically apply the distributive, identity, and cancellation laws, in succession, to obtain

$$(a + b)x = a + b$$
$$(a + b)x = (a + b)1$$
$$x = 1.$$

Thus we have proved that x = 1 without leaving the "language" of algebra. Von Neumann languages, with their grotesque syntax, offer few such possibilities for transforming programs.

As we shall see later, programs can be expressed in a language that has an associated algebra. This algebra can be used to transform programs and to solve some equations whose "unknowns" are programs, in much the same way one solves equations in high school algebra. Algebraic transformations and proofs use the language of the programs themselves, rather than the language of logic, which talks about programs.

10. What Are the Alternatives to von Neumann Languages?

Before discussing alternatives to von Neumann languages, let me remark that I regret the need for the above negative and not very precise discussion of these languages. But the complacent acceptance most of us give to these enormous, weak languages has puzzled and disturbed me for a long time. I am disturbed because that acceptance has consumed a vast effort toward making von Neumann languages fatter that might have been better spent in looking for new structures. For this reason I have tried to analyze some of the basic defects of conventional languages and show that those defects cannot be resolved unless we discover a new kind of language framework.

In seeking an alternative to conventional languages we must first recognize that a system cannot be history sensitive (permit execution of one program to affect the behavior of a subsequent one) unless the system has some kind of state (which the first program can change and the second can access). Thus a history-sensitive model of a computing system must have a state-transition semantics, at least in this weak sense. But this does *not* mean that every computation must depend heavily on a complex state, with many state changes required for each small part of the computation (as in von Neumann languages).

To illustrate some alternatives to von Neumann languages, I propose to sketch a class of history-sensitive computing systems, where each system: a) has a loosely coupled state-transition semantics in which a state transition occurs only once in a major computation; b) has a simply structured state and simple transition rules; c) depends heavily on an underlying applicative system both to provide the basic programming language of the system and to describe its state transitions.

These systems, which I call applicative state transition (or AST) systems, are described in Section 14. These simple systems avoid many of the complexities and weaknesses of von Neumann languages and provide for a powerful and extensive set of changeable parts. However, they are sketched only as crude examples of a vast area of non-von Neumann systems with various attractive properties. I have been studying this area for the

past three or four years and have not yet found a satisfying solution to the many conflicting requirements that a good language must resolve. But I believe this search has indicated a useful approach to designing non-von Neumann languages.

This approach involves four elements, which can be summarized as follows.

a) *A functional style of programming without variables.* A simple, informal functional programming (FP) system is described. It is based on the use of combining forms for building programs. Several programs are given to illustrate functional programming.

b) *An algebra of functional programs.* An algebra is described whose variables denote FP functional programs and whose "operations" are FP functional forms, the combining forms of FP programs. Some laws of the algebra are given. Theorems and examples are given that show how certain function expressions may be transformed into equivalent infinite expansions that explain the behavior of the function. The FP algebra is compared with algebras associated with the classical applicative systems of Church and Curry.

c) *A formal functional programming system.* A formal (FFP) system is described that extends the capabilities of the above informal FP systems. An FFP system is thus a precisely defined system that provides the ability to use the functional programming style of FP systems and their algebra of programs. FFP systems can be used as the basis for applicative state transition systems.

d) *Applicative state transition systems.* As discussed above. The rest of the paper describes these four elements, gives some brief remarks on computer design, and ends with a summary of the paper.

11. Functional Programming Systems (FP Systems)

11.1 Introduction

In this section we give an informal description of a class of simple applicative programming systems called functional programming (FP) systems, in which "programs" are simply functions without variables. The description is followed by some examples and by a discussion of various properties of FP systems.

An FP system is founded on the use of a fixed set of combining forms called functional forms. These, plus simple definitions, are the only means of building new functions from existing ones; they use no variables or substitution rules, and they become the operations of an associated algebra of programs. All the functions of an FP system are of one type: they map objects into objects and always take a single argument.

In contrast, a lambda-calculus based system is founded on the use of the lambda expression, with an associated set of substitution rules for variables, for building new functions. The lambda expression (with its substitution rules) is capable of defining all possible computable functions of all possible types and of any number of arguments. This freedom and power has its disadvantages as well as its obvious advantages. It is analogous to the power of unrestricted control statements in conventional languages: with unrestricted freedom comes chaos. If one constantly invents new combining forms to suit the occasion, as one can in the lambda calculus, one will not become familiar with the style or useful properties of the few combining forms that are adequate for all purposes. Just as structured programming eschews many control statements to obtain programs with simpler structure, better properties, and uniform methods for understanding their behavior, so functional programming eschews the lambda expression, substitution, and multiple function types. It thereby achieves programs built with familiar functional forms with known useful properties. These programs are so structured that their behavior can often be understood and proven by mechanical use of algebraic techniques similar to those used in solving high school algebra problems.

Functional forms, unlike most programming constructs, need not be chosen on an ad hoc basis. Since they are the operations of an associated algebra, one chooses only those functional forms that not only provide powerful programming constructs, but that also have attractive algebraic properties: one chooses them to maximize the strength and utility of the algebraic laws that relate them to other functional forms of the system.

In the following description we shall be imprecise in not distinguishing between (a) a function symbol or expression and (b) the function it denotes. We shall indicate the symbols and expressions used to denote functions by example and usage. Section 13 describes a formal extension of FP systems (FFP systems); they can serve to clarify any ambiguities about FP systems.

11.2 Description

An FP system comprises the following:

1) a set O of *objects*;

2) a set F of *functions* f that map objects into objects;

3) an operation, *application*;

4) a set F of *functional forms*; these are used to combine existing functions, or objects, to form new functions in F;

5) a set D of *definitions* that define some functions in F and assign a name to each.

What follows is an informal description of each of the above entities with examples.

11.2.1 Objects, O. An *object* x is either an *atom*, a *sequence* $<x_1, \ldots, x_n>$ whose *elements* x_i are objects, or $\perp$ ("bottom" or "undefined"). Thus the choice of a set A of atoms determines the set of objects. We shall take A to be the set of nonnull strings of capital letters, digits, and special symbols not used by the notation of the FP system. Some of these strings belong to the class of atoms called "numbers." The atom ϕ is used to denote the empty sequence and is the only object which is both an atom and a sequence. The atoms T and F are used to denote "true" and "false."

There is one important constraint in the construction of objects: if x is a sequence with $\perp$ as an element, then $x = \perp$. That is, the "sequence constructor" is "$\perp$-preserving." Thus no proper sequence has $\perp$ as an element.

Examples of objects

$\perp \quad 1.5 \quad \phi \quad AB3 \quad <AB, 1, 2.3>$
$<A, <<B>, C>, D> \quad <A, \perp> = \perp$

11.2.2 Application. An FP system has a single operation, application. If f is a function and x is an object, then $f:x$ is an *application* and denotes the object which is the result of applying f to x. f is the *operator* of the application and x is the *operand*.

Examples of applications

$+:<1,2> = 3 \quad \text{tl}:<A,B,C> = <B,C>$
$1:<A,B,C> = A \quad 2:<A,B,C> = B$

11.2.3 Functions, F. All functions f in F map objects into objects and are *bottom-preserving*: $f:\perp = \perp$, for all f in F. Every function in F is either *primitive*, that is, supplied with the system, or it is *defined* (see below), or it is a *functional form* (see below).

It is sometimes useful to distinguish between two cases in which $f:x=\perp$. If the computation for $f:x$ terminates and yields the object $\perp$, we say f is *undefined* at x, that is, f terminates but has no meaningful value at x. Otherwise we say f is *nonterminating* at x.

Examples of primitive functions

Our intention is to provide FP systems with widely useful and powerful primitive functions rather than weak ones that could then be used to define useful ones. The following examples define some typical primitive functions, many of which are used in later examples of programs. In the following definitions we use a variant of McCarthy's conditional expressions [17]; thus we write

$$p_1 \rightarrow e_1; \ldots; p_n \rightarrow e_n; e_{n+1}$$

instead of McCarthy's expression

$$(p_1 \rightarrow e_1, \ldots, p_n \rightarrow e_n, T \rightarrow e_{n+1}).$$

The following definitions are to hold for all objects x, x_i, y, y_i, z, z_i:

Selector functions

$1:x \equiv x=<x_1, \ldots, x_n> \rightarrow x_1; \perp$

and for any positive integer s

$s:x \equiv x = <x_1, \ldots, x_n> \text{ \& } n \geq s \rightarrow x_s; \perp$

Thus, for example, $3:<A,B,C> = C$ and $2:<A> = \perp$. Note that the function symbols 1, 2, etc. are distinct from the atoms *1*, *2*, etc.

Tail

$\text{tl}:x \equiv x=<x_1> \rightarrow \phi;$
$\qquad\qquad x=<x_1, \ldots, x_n> \text{ \& } n \geq 2 \rightarrow <x_2, \ldots, x_n>; \perp$

Identity

$\text{id}:x \equiv x$

Atom
$atom : x \equiv x$ is an atom $\rightarrow T; x \neq \bot \rightarrow F; \bot$

Equals
$eq : x \equiv x = <y,z>$ & $y=z \rightarrow T; x = <y,z>$ & $y \neq z \rightarrow F; \bot$

Null
$null : x \equiv x = \phi \rightarrow T; x \neq \bot \rightarrow F; \bot$

Reverse
$reverse : x \equiv x = \phi \rightarrow \phi;$
$$x = <x_1, \dots, x_n> \rightarrow <x_n, \dots, x_1>; \bot$$

Distribute from left; distribute from right
$distl : x \equiv x = <y,\phi> \rightarrow \phi;$
$$x = <y,<z_1, \dots, z_n>> \rightarrow <<y,z_1>, \dots, <y,z_n>>; \bot$$
$distr : x \equiv x = <\phi,y> \rightarrow \phi;$
$$x = <<y_1, \dots, y_n>,z> \rightarrow <<y_1,z>, \dots, <y_n,z>>; \bot$$

Length
$length : x \equiv x = <x_1, \dots, x_n> \rightarrow n; x = \phi \rightarrow 0; \bot$

Add, subtract, multiply, and divide
$+ : x \equiv x = <y,z>$ & y,z are numbers $\rightarrow y+z; \bot$
$- : x \equiv x = <y,z>$ & y,z are numbers $\rightarrow y-z; \bot$
$\times : x \equiv x = <y,z>$ & y,z are numbers $\rightarrow y \times z; \bot$
$\div : x \equiv x = <y,z>$ & y,z are numbers $\rightarrow y \div z; \bot$
$$\text{(where } y \div 0 = \bot)$$

Transpose
$trans : x \equiv x = <\phi, \dots, \phi> \rightarrow \phi;$
$$x = <x_1, \dots, x_n> \rightarrow <y_1, \dots, y_m>; \bot$$
where
$x_i = <x_{i1}, \dots, x_{im}>$ and
$$y_j = <x_{1j}, \dots, x_{nj}>, 1 \leq i \leq n, 1 \leq j \leq m.$$

And, or, not
$and : x \equiv x = <T,T> \rightarrow T;$
$$x = <T,F> \lor x = <F,T> \lor x = <F,F> \rightarrow F; \bot$$
etc.

Append left; append right
$apndl : x \equiv x = <y,\phi> \rightarrow <y>;$
$$x = <y,<z_1, \dots, z_n>> \rightarrow <y,z_1, \dots, z_n>; \bot$$
$apndr : x \equiv x = <\phi,z> \rightarrow <z>;$
$$x = <<y_1, \dots, y_n>,z> \rightarrow <y_1, \dots, y_n,z>; \bot$$

Right selectors; Right tail
$1r : x \equiv x = <x_1, \dots, x_n> \rightarrow x_n; \bot$
$2r : x \equiv x = <x_1, \dots, x_n>$ & $n \geq 2 \rightarrow x_{n-1}; \bot$
etc.
$tlr : x \equiv x = <x_1> \rightarrow \phi;$
$$x = <x_1, \dots, x_n> \text{ & } n \geq 2 \rightarrow <x_1, \dots, x_{n-1}>; \bot$$

Rotate left; rotate right
$rotl : x \equiv x = \phi \rightarrow \phi; x = <x_1> \rightarrow <x_1>;$
$$x = <x_1, \dots, x_n> \text{ & } n \geq 2 \rightarrow <x_2, \dots, x_n,x_1>; \bot$$
etc.

11.2.4 Functional forms, F. A functional form is an expression denoting a function; that function depends on the functions or objects which are the *parameters* of the expression. Thus, for example, if f and g are any functions, then $f \circ g$ is a functional form, the *composition* of f

and g, f and g are its parameters, and it denotes the function such that, for any object x,

$$(f \circ g) : x = f : (g : x).$$

Some functional forms may have objects as parameters. For example, for any object x, $\bar{x}$ is a functional form, the *constant* function of x, so that for any object y

$$\bar{x} : y \equiv y = \bot \rightarrow \bot; x.$$

In particular, $\bar{\bot}$ is the everywhere-$\bot$ function.

Below we give some functional forms, many of which are used later in this paper. We use $p, f,$ and g with and without subscripts to denote arbitrary functions; and $x, x_1, \dots, x_n, y$ as arbitrary objects. Square brackets [...] are used to indicate the functional form for *construction*, which denotes a function, whereas pointed brackets <...> denote sequences, which are objects. Parentheses are used both in particular functional forms (e.g., in *condition*) and generally to indicate grouping.

Composition
$$(f \circ g) : x \equiv f : (g : x)$$

Construction
$[f_1, \dots, f_n] : x \equiv <f_1 : x, \dots, f_n : x>$ (Recall that since $<\dots, \bot, \dots> = \bot$ and all functions are $\bot$-preserving, so is $[f_1, \dots, f_n].$)

Condition
$$(p \rightarrow f; g) : x \equiv (p : x) = T \rightarrow f : x; \quad (p : x) = F \rightarrow g : x; \bot$$

Conditional *expressions* (used outside of FP systems to describe their functions) and the *functional form* condition are both identified by "$\rightarrow$". They are quite different although closely related, as shown in the above definitions. But no confusion should arise, since the elements of a conditional expression all denote values, whereas the elements of the functional form condition all denote functions, never values. When no ambiguity arises we omit right-associated parentheses; we write, for example, $p_1 \rightarrow f_1; p_2 \rightarrow f_2; g$ for $(p_1 \rightarrow f_1; (p_2 \rightarrow f_2; g))$.

Constant (Here x is an object parameter.)
$$\bar{x} : y \equiv y = \bot \rightarrow \bot; x$$

Insert
$/f : x \equiv x = <x_1> \rightarrow x_1; x = <x_1, \dots, x_n >$ & $n \geq 2$
$$\rightarrow f : <x_1, /f : <x_2, \dots, x_n>>; \bot$$

If f has a unique right unit $u_f \neq \bot$, where $f : <x,u_f> \in \{x, \bot\}$ for all objects x, then the above definition is extended: $/f : \phi = u_f$. Thus

$$/+ : <4,5,6> = + : <4, + : <5, /+ : <6>>>$$
$$= + : <4, + : <5,6>> = 15$$
$/+ : \phi = 0$

Apply to all
$\alpha f : x \equiv x = \phi \rightarrow \phi;$
$$x = <x_1, \dots, x_n> \rightarrow <f : x_1, \dots, f : x_n>; \bot$$

Binary to unary (x is an object parameter)

(bu f x):$y \equiv f$:$<x,y>$

Thus

(bu $+$ 1):$x = 1+x$

While

(while p f):$x \equiv p$:$x=T \to$ (while p f):$(f$:$x)$;
$$p$:$x=F \to x; \perp$$

The above functional forms provide an effective method for computing the values of the functions they denote (if they terminate) provided one can effectively apply their function parameters.

11.2.5 Definitions. A *definition* in an FP system is an expression of the form

Def $l \equiv r$

where the left side l is an unused function symbol and the right side r is a functional form (which may depend on l). It expresses the fact that the symbol l is to denote the function given by r. Thus the definition **Def** last1 $\equiv$ 1∘reverse defines the function last1 that produces the last element of a sequence (or $\perp$). Similarly,

Def last $\equiv$ null∘tl $\to$ 1; last∘tl

defines the function last, which is the same as last1. Here in detail is how the definition would be used to compute last:$<1,2>$:

last:$<1,2>$ =
definition of last $\Rightarrow$ (null∘tl $\to$ 1; last∘tl):$<1,2>$
action of the form $(p \to f; g)$ $\Rightarrow$ last∘tl:$<1,2>$
  since null∘tl:$<1,2>$ = null:$<2>$
  $= F$
action of the form $f \circ g$ $\Rightarrow$ last:(tl:$<1,2>$)
definition of primitive tail $\Rightarrow$ last:$<2>$
definition of last $\Rightarrow$ (null∘tl $\to$ 1; last∘tl):$<2>$
action of the form $(p \to f; g)$ $\Rightarrow$ 1:$<2>$
  since null∘tl:$<2>$ = null:$\phi = T$
definition of selector 1 $\Rightarrow$ 2

The above illustrates the simple rule: to apply a defined symbol, replace it by the right side of its definition. Of course, some definitions may define nonterminating functions. A set D of definitions is *well formed* if no two left sides are the same.

11.2.6 Semantics. It can be seen from the above that an FP system is determined by choice of the following sets: (a) The set of atoms A (which determines the set of objects). (b) The set of primitive functions P. (c) The set of functional forms F. (d) A well formed set of definitions D. To understand the semantics of such a system one needs to know how to compute f:x for any function f and any object x of the system. There are exactly four possibilities for f:

(1) f is a primitive function;
(2) f is a functional form;
(3) there is one definition in D, **Def** $f \equiv r$; and
(4) none of the above.

If f is a primitive function, then one has its description

and knows how to apply it. If f is a functional form, then the description of the form tells how to compute f:x in terms of the parameters of the form, which can be done by further use of these rules. If f is defined, **Def** $f \equiv r$, as in (3), then to find f:x one computes r:x, which can be done by further use of these rules. If none of these, then f:$x \equiv \perp$. Of course, the use of these rules may not terminate for some f and some x, in which case we assign the value f:$x \equiv \perp$.

11.3 Examples of Functional Programs

The following examples illustrate the functional programming style. Since this style is unfamiliar to most readers, it may cause confusion at first; the important point to remember is that no part of a function definition is a result itself. Instead, each part is a *function* that must be applied to an argument to obtain a result.

11.3.1 Factorial.

Def ! $\equiv$ eq0 $\to$ $\bar{1}$; $\times$∘[id, !∘sub1]

where

Def eq0 $\equiv$ eq∘[id, $\bar{0}$]
Def sub1 $\equiv$ $-$∘[id, $\bar{1}$]

Here are some of the intermediate expressions an FP system would obtain in evaluating !:2:

!:$2 \Rightarrow$ (eq0 $\to$ $\bar{1}$; $\times$∘[id, !∘sub1]):2
  $\Rightarrow \times$∘[id, !∘sub1]:2
$\Rightarrow \times$:$<$id:2, !∘sub1:$2> \Rightarrow \times$:<2, !:$1>$
  $\Rightarrow \times$:<2, $\times$:<1, !:$0>>$
$\Rightarrow \times$:<2, $\times$:$<1,\bar{1}$:$0>> \Rightarrow \times$:<2, $\times$:$<1,1>>$
  $\Rightarrow \times$:$<2,1> \Rightarrow 2$.

In Section 12 we shall see how theorems of the algebra of FP programs can be used to prove that ! is the factorial function.

11.3.2 Inner product. We have seen earlier how this definition works.

Def   IP $\equiv$ (/+)∘($\alpha\times$)∘trans

11.3.3 Matrix multiply. This matrix multiplication program yields the product of any pair $<m,n>$ of conformable matrices, where each matrix m is represented as the sequence of its rows:

$m = <m_1, \dots, m_r>$
  where $m_i = <m_{i1}, \dots, m_{is}>$ for i = 1, $\dots$, r.
Def MM $\equiv$ ($\alpha\alpha$IP)∘(αdistl)∘distr∘[1, trans∘2]

The program MM has four steps, reading from right to left; each is applied in turn, beginning with [1, trans∘2], to the result of its predecessor. If the argument is $<m,n>$, then the first step yields $<m,n'>$ where $n' =$ trans:n. The second step yields $<<m_1,n'>, \dots, <m_r,n'>>$, where the m_i are the rows of m. The third step, αdistl, yields

$<$distl:$<m_1,n'>, \dots,$ distl:$<m_r,n'>> = <p_1, \dots, p_r>$

where

$$p_i = \text{distl}:<m_i,n'> = <<m_i,n_1'>, \ldots , <m_i,n_s'>>$$
$$\text{for } i = 1, \ldots , r$$

and n_j' is the jth column of n (the jth row of n'). Thus p_i, a sequence of row and column pairs, corresponds to the i-th product row. The operator $\alpha\alpha\text{IP}$, or $\alpha(\alpha\text{IP})$, causes αIP to be applied to each p_i, which in turn causes IP to be applied to each row and column pair in each p_i. The result of the last step is therefore the sequence of rows comprising the product matrix. If either matrix is not rectangular, or if the length of a row of m differs from that of a column of n, or if any element of m or n is not a number, the result is $\perp$.

This program MM does not name its arguments or any intermediate results; contains no variables, no loops, no control statements nor procedure declarations; has no initialization instructions; is not word-at-a-time in nature; is hierarchically constructed from simpler components; uses generally applicable housekeeping forms and operators (e.g., αf, distl, distr, trans); is perfectly general; yields $\perp$ whenever its argument is inappropriate in any way; does not constrain the order of evaluation unnecessarily (all applications of IP to row and column pairs can be done in parallel or in any order); and, using algebraic laws (see below), can be transformed into more "efficient" or into more "explanatory" programs (e.g., one that is recursively defined). None of these properties hold for the typical von Neumann matrix multiplication program.

Although it has an unfamiliar and hence puzzling form, the program MM describes the essential operations of matrix multiplication without overdetermining the process or obscuring parts of it, as most programs do; hence many straightforward programs for the operation can be obtained from it by formal transformations. It is an inherently inefficient program for von Neumann computers (with regard to the use of space), but efficient ones can be derived from it and realizations of FP systems can be imagined that could execute MM without the prodigal use of space it implies. Efficiency questions are beyond the scope of this paper; let me suggest only that since the language is so simple and does not dictate any binding of lambda-type variables to data, there may be better opportunities for the system to do some kind of "lazy" evaluation [9, 10] and to control data management more efficiently than is possible in lambda-calculus based systems.

11.4 Remarks About FP Systems

11.4.1 FP systems as programming languages.

FP systems are so minimal that some readers may find it difficult to view them as programming languages. Viewed as such, a function f is a program, an object x is the contents of the store, and $f:x$ is the contents of the store after program f is activated with x in the store. The set of definitions is the program library. The primitive functions and the functional forms provided by the system are the basic statements of a particular programming language. Thus, depending on the choice of prim-

itive functions and functional forms, the FP framework provides for a large class of languages with various styles and capabilities. The algebra of programs associated with each of these depends on its particular set of functional forms. The primitive functions, functional forms, and programs given in this paper comprise an effort to develop just one of these possible styles.

11.4.2 Limitations of FP systems.

FP systems have a number of limitations. For example, a given FP system is a fixed language; it is not history sensitive: no program can alter the library of programs. It can treat input and output only in the sense that x is an input and $f:x$ is the output. If the set of primitive functions and functional forms is weak, it may not be able to express every computable function.

An FP system cannot compute a program since function expressions are not objects. Nor can one define new functional forms within an FP system. (Both of these limitations are removed in formal functional programming (FFP) systems in which objects "represent" functions.) Thus no FP system can have a function, apply, such that

$$\text{apply}:<x,y> \equiv x:y$$

because, on the left, x is an object, and, on the right, x is a function. (Note that we have been careful to keep the set of function symbols and the set of objects distinct: thus 1 is a function symbol, and 1 is an object.)

The primary limitation of FP systems is that they are not history sensitive. Therefore they must be extended somehow before they can become practically useful. For discussion of such extensions, see the sections on FFP and AST systems (Sections 13 and 14).

11.4.3 Expressive power of FP systems.

Suppose two FP systems, FP_1 and FP_2, both have the same set of objects and the same set of primitive functions, but the set of functional forms of FP_1 properly includes that of FP_2. Suppose also that both systems can express all computable functions on objects. Nevertheless, we can say that FP_1 is more expressive than FP_2, since every function expression in FP_2 can be duplicated in FP_1, but by using a functional form not belonging to FP_2, FP_1 can express some functions more directly and easily than FP_2.

I believe the above observation could be developed into a theory of the expressive power of languages in which a language A would be *more expressive* than language B under the following roughly stated conditions. First, form all possible functions of all types in A by applying all existing functions to objects and to each other in all possible ways until no new function of any type can be formed. (The set of objects is a type; the set of continuous functions [T→U] from type T to type U is a type. If $f\in[T\rightarrow U]$ and $t\in T$, then ft in U can be formed by applying f to t.) Do the same in language B. Next, compare each type in A to the corresponding type in B. If, for every type, A's type includes B's corresponding type, then A is more expressive than B (or equally expressive). If some type of A's functions is incomparable to B's, then A and B are not comparable in expressive power.

11.4.4 Advantages of FP systems. The main reason FP systems are considerably simpler than either conventional languages or lambda-calculus-based languages is that they use only the most elementary fixed naming system (naming a function in a definition) with a simple fixed rule of substituting a function for its name. Thus they avoid the complexities both of the naming systems of conventional languages and of the substitution rules of the lambda calculus. FP systems permit the definition of different naming systems (see Sections 13.3.4 and 14.7) for various purposes. These need not be complex, since many programs can do without them completely. Most importantly, they treat names as functions that can be combined with other functions without special treatment.

FP systems offer an escape from conventional word-at-a-time programming to a degree greater even than APL [12] (the most successful attack on the problem to date within the von Neumann framework) because they provide a more powerful set of functional forms within a unified world of expressions. They offer the opportunity to develop higher level techniques for thinking about, manipulating, and writing programs.

12. The Algebra of Programs for FP Systems

12.1 Introduction

The algebra of the programs described below is the work of an amateur in algebra, and I want to show that it is a game amateurs can profitably play and enjoy, a game that does not require a deep understanding of logic and mathematics. In spite of its simplicity, it can help one to understand and prove things about programs in a systematic, rather mechanical way.

So far, proving a program correct requires knowledge of some moderately heavy topics in mathematics and logic: properties of complete partially ordered sets, continuous functions, least fixed points of functionals, the first-order predicate calculus, predicate transformers, weakest preconditions, to mention a few topics in a few approaches to proving programs correct. These topics have been very useful for professionals who make it their business to devise proof techniques; they have published a lot of beautiful work on this subject, starting with the work of McCarthy and Floyd, and, more recently, that of Burstall, Dijkstra, Manna and his associates, Milner, Morris, Reynolds, and many others. Much of this work is based on the foundations laid down by Dana Scott (denotational semantics) and C. A. R. Hoare (axiomatic semantics). But its theoretical level places it beyond the scope of most amateurs who work outside of this specialized field.

If the average programmer is to prove his programs

correct, he will need much simpler techniques than those the professionals have so far put forward. The algebra of programs below may be one starting point for such a proof discipline and, coupled with current work on algebraic manipulation, it may also help provide a basis for automating some of that discipline.

One advantage of this algebra over other proof techniques is that the programmer can use his programming language as the language for deriving proofs, rather than having to state proofs in a separate logical system that merely talks *about* his programs.

At the heart of the algebra of programs are laws and theorems that state that one function expression is the same as another. Thus the law $[f,g] \circ h \equiv [f \circ h, g \circ h]$ says that the construction of f and g (composed with h) is the same function as the construction of (f composed with h) and (g composed with h) no matter what the functions f, g, and h are. Such laws are easy to understand, easy to justify, and easy and powerful to use. However, we also wish to use such laws to solve equations in which an "unknown" function appears on both sides of the equation. The problem is that if f satisfies some such equation, it will often happen that some extension f' of f will also satisfy the same equation. Thus, to give a unique meaning to solutions of such equations, we shall require a foundation for the algebra of programs (which uses Scott's notion of least fixed points of continuous functionals) to assure us that solutions obtained by algebraic manipulation are indeed least, and hence unique, solutions.

Our goal is to develop a foundation for the algebra of programs that disposes of the theoretical issues, so that a programmer can use simple algebraic laws and one or two theorems from the foundations to solve problems and create proofs in the same mechanical style we use to solve high-school algebra problems, and so that he can do so without knowing anything about least fixed points or predicate transformers.

One particular foundational problem arises: given equations of the form

$$f \equiv p_0 \rightarrow q_0; \dots ; p_i \rightarrow q_i; E_i(f), \tag{1}$$

where the p_i's and q_i's are functions not involving f and $E_i(f)$ is a function expression involving f, the laws of the algebra will often permit the formal "extension" of this equation by one more "clause" by deriving

$$E_i(f) \equiv p_{i+1} \rightarrow q_{i+1}; E_{i+1}(f) \tag{2}$$

which, by replacing $E_i(f)$ in (1) by the right side of (2), yields

$$f \equiv p_0 \rightarrow q_0; \dots ; p_{i+1} \rightarrow q_{i+1}; E_{i+1}(f). \tag{3}$$

This formal extension may go on without limit. One question the foundations must then answer is: when can the least f satisfying (1) be represented by the infinite expansion

$$f \equiv p_0 \rightarrow q_0; \dots ; p_n \rightarrow q_n; \dots \tag{4}$$

in which the final clause involving f has been dropped,

so that we now have a solution whose right side is free of f's? Such solutions are helpful in two ways: first, they give proofs of "termination" in the sense that (4) means that $f:x$ is defined if and only if there is an n such that, for every i less than n, $p_i:x = F$ and $p_n:x = T$ and $q_n:x$ is defined. Second, (4) gives a case-by-case description of f that can often clarify its behavior.

The foundations for the algebra given in a subsequent section are a modest start toward the goal stated above. For a limited class of equations its "linear expansion theorem" gives a useful answer as to when one can go from indefinitely extendable equations like (1) to infinite expansions like (4). For a larger class of equations, a more general "expansion theorem" gives a less helpful answer to similar questions. Hopefully, more powerful theorems covering additional classes of equations can be found. But for the present, one need only know the conclusions of these two simple foundational theorems in order to follow the theorems and examples appearing in this section.

The results of the foundations subsection are summarized in a separate, earlier subsection titled "expansion theorems," without reference to fixed point concepts. The foundations subsection itself is placed later where it can be skipped by readers who do not want to go into that subject.

12.2 Some Laws of the Algebra of Programs

In the algebra of programs for an FP system variables range over the set of functions of the system. The "operations" of the algebra are the functional forms of the system. Thus, for example, $[f,g]\circ h$ is an expression of the algebra for the FP system described above, in which f, g, and h are variables denoting arbitrary functions of that system. And

$$[f,g]\circ h \equiv [f\circ h, g\circ h]$$

is a law of the algebra which says that, whatever functions one chooses for f, g, and h, the function on the left is the same as that on the right. Thus this algebraic law is merely a restatement of the following proposition about any FP system that includes the functional forms $[f,g]$ and $f\circ g$:

PROPOSITION: For all functions f, g, and h and all objects x, $([f,g]\circ h):x \equiv [f\circ h, g\circ h]:x$.
PROOF:
$([f,g]\circ h):x = [f,g]:(h:x)$
     by definition of composition
$= \langle f:(h:x), g:(h:x)\rangle$
     by definition of construction
$= \langle (f\circ h):x, (g\circ h):x\rangle$
     by definition of composition
$= [f\circ h, g\circ h]:x$
     by definition of construction □

Some laws have a domain smaller than the domain of all objects. Thus $1\circ[f,g] \equiv f$ does not hold for objects x such that $g:x = \bot$. We write

$$\text{defined}\circ g \longrightarrow\rightarrow 1\circ[f,g] \equiv f$$

to indicate that the law (or theorem) on the right holds within the domain of objects x for which $\text{defined}\circ g:x = T$. Where

Def $\text{defined} \equiv \bar{T}$

i.e. $\text{defined}:x \equiv x=\bot \rightarrow \bot; T$. In general we shall write a *qualified functional equation*:

$$p \longrightarrow\rightarrow f \equiv g$$

to mean that, for any object x, whenever $p:x = T$, then $f:x = g:x$.

Ordinary algebra concerns itself with two operations, addition and multiplication; it needs few laws. The algebra of programs is concerned with more operations (functional forms) and therefore needs more laws.

Each of the following laws requires a corresponding proposition to validate it. The interested reader will find most proofs of such propositions easy (two are given below). We first define the usual ordering on functions and equivalence in terms of this ordering:

DEFINITION $f \leq g$ iff for all objects x, either $f:x = \bot$, or $f:x = g:x$.
DEFINITION $f \equiv g$ iff $f \leq g$ and $g \leq f$.

It is easy to verify that $\leq$ is a partial ordering, that $f \leq g$ means g is an extension of f, and that $f \equiv g$ iff $f:x = g:x$ for all objects x. We now give a list of algebraic laws organized by the two principal functional forms involved.

I Composition and construction
I.1 $[f_1, \ldots, f_n]\circ g \equiv [f_1\circ g, \ldots, f_n\circ g]$
I.2 $\alpha f \circ [g_1, \ldots, g_n] \equiv [f\circ g_1, \ldots, f\circ g_n]$
I.3 $/f\circ[g_1, \ldots, g_n]$
   $\equiv f\circ[g_1, /f\circ[g_2, \ldots, g_n]]$ when $n\geq 2$
   $\equiv f\circ[g_1, f\circ[g_2, \ldots, f\circ[g_{n-1}, g_n]\ldots]]$
  $/f\circ[g] \equiv g$
I.4 $f\circ[\bar{x},g] \equiv (\text{bu } f\, x)\circ g$
I.5 $1\circ[f_1, \ldots, f_n] \leq f_1$
  $s\circ[f_1, \ldots, f_s, \ldots, f_n] \leq f_s$ for any selector s, $s\leq n$
  $\text{defined}\circ f_i$ (for all $i\neq s$, $1\leq i\leq n$) $\rightarrow\rightarrow$
          $s\circ[f_1, \ldots, f_n] \equiv f_s$
I.5.1 $[f_1\circ 1, \ldots, f_n\circ n]\circ[g_1, \ldots, g_n] \equiv [f_1\circ g_1, \ldots, f_n\circ g_n]$
I.6 $\text{tl}\circ[f_1] \leq \bar{\phi}$ and
     $\text{tl}\circ[f_1, \ldots, f_n] \leq [f_2, \ldots, f_n]$ for $n\geq 2$
  $\text{defined}\circ f_1 \rightarrow\rightarrow \text{tl}\circ[f_1] \equiv \bar{\phi}$
  and $\text{tl}\circ[f_1, \ldots, f_n] \equiv [f_2, \ldots, f_n]$ for $n\geq 2$
I.7 $\text{distl}\circ[f, [g_1, \ldots, g_n]] \equiv [[f,g_1], \ldots, [f,g_n]]$
  $\text{defined}\circ f \rightarrow\rightarrow \text{distl}\circ[f,\bar{\phi}] \equiv \bar{\phi}$
  The analogous law holds for distr.
I.8 $\text{apndl}\circ[f, [g_1, \ldots, g_n]] \equiv [f,g_1, \ldots, g_n]$
  $\text{null}\circ g \rightarrow\rightarrow \text{apndl}\circ[f,g] \equiv [f]$
And so on for apndr, reverse, rotl, etc.
I.9 $[\ldots, \bar{\bot}, \ldots] \equiv \bar{\bot}$
I.10 $\text{apndl}\circ[f\circ g, \alpha f\circ h] \equiv \alpha f\circ \text{apndl}\circ[g,h]$
I.11 $\text{pair \& not}\circ\text{null}\circ 1 \longrightarrow\rightarrow$
   $\text{apndl}\circ[[1\circ 1,2], \text{distr}\circ[\text{tl}\circ 1,2]] \equiv \text{distr}$

Where $f \& g \equiv$ and$\circ[f,g]$;
$$\text{pair} \equiv \text{atom} \rightarrow \bar{F}; \text{eq}\circ[\text{length},\bar{2}]$$

II Composition and condition (right associated parentheses omitted) (Law II.2 is noted in Manna et al. [16], p. 493.)

II.1 $(p \rightarrow f; g)\circ h \equiv p\circ h \rightarrow f\circ h; g\circ h$

II.2 $h\circ(p \rightarrow f; g) \equiv p \rightarrow h\circ f; h\circ g$

II.3   or$\circ[q,\text{not}\circ q] \longrightarrow$ and$\circ[p,q] \rightarrow f$;
     and$\circ[p,\text{not}\circ q] \rightarrow g$; $h \equiv p \rightarrow (q \rightarrow f; g)$; h

II.3.1 $p \rightarrow (p \rightarrow f; g)$; $h \equiv p \rightarrow f$; h

III Composition and miscellaneous

III.1 $\bar{x}\circ f \leq \bar{x}$
     defined$\circ f \longrightarrow \bar{x}\circ f \equiv \bar{x}$

III.1.1 $\bar{\bot}\circ f \equiv f\circ \bar{\bot} \equiv \bar{\bot}$

III.2 $f\circ \text{id} \equiv \text{id}\circ f \equiv f$

III.3   pair $\longrightarrow 1\circ\text{distr} \equiv [1\circ 1, 2]$ also:
$$\text{pair} \longrightarrow 1\circ\text{tl} \equiv 2 \quad \text{etc.}$$

III.4 $\alpha(f\circ g) \equiv \alpha f \circ \alpha g$

III.5   null$\circ g \longrightarrow \alpha f\circ g \equiv \bar{\phi}$

IV Condition and construction

IV.1 $[f_1, \dots, (p \rightarrow g; h), \dots, f_n]$
$$\equiv p \rightarrow [f_1, \dots, g, \dots, f_n]; [f_1, \dots, h, \dots, f_n]$$

IV.1.1 $[f_1, \dots, (p_1 \rightarrow g_1; \dots; p_n \rightarrow g_n; h), \dots, f_m]$
$$\equiv p_1 \rightarrow [f_1, \dots, g_1, \dots, f_m];$$
$$\dots; p_n \rightarrow [f_1, \dots, g_n, \dots, f_m]; [f_1, \dots, h, \dots, f_m]$$

This concludes the present list of algebraic laws; it is by no means exhaustive, there are many others.

Proof of two laws

We give the proofs of validating propositions for laws I.10 and I.11, which are slightly more involved than most of the others.

PROPOSITION 1

apndl $\circ$ $[f\circ g, \alpha f\circ h] \equiv \alpha f \circ$ apndl $\circ [g,h]$

PROOF. We show that, for every object x, both of the above functions yield the same result.

CASE 1. $h{:}x$ is neither a sequence nor ϕ.
Then both sides yield $\bot$ when applied to x.

CASE 2. $h{:}x = \phi$. Then

apndl$\circ[f\circ g, \alpha f\circ h]{:} x$
    $=$ apndl: $<f\circ g{:}x, \phi> = <f{:}(g{:}x)>$

$\alpha f\circ$apndl$\circ[g,h]{:} x$
    $= \alpha f\circ$apndl: $<g{:}x, \phi> = \alpha f{:}<g{:}x>$
    $= <f{:}(g{:}x)>$

CASE 3. $h{:}x = <y_1, \dots, y_n>$. Then

apndl$\circ[f\circ g, \alpha f\circ h]{:} x$
    $=$ apndl: $<f\circ g{:}x, \alpha f{:} <y_1, \dots, y_n>>$
    $= <f{:}(g{:}x), f{:}y_1, \dots, f{:}y_n>$

$\alpha f\circ$apndl$\circ[g,h]{:} x$
    $= \alpha f\circ$apndl: $<g{:}x, <y_1, \dots, y_n>>$
                   $= \alpha f{:}<g{:}x, y_1, \dots, y_n>$
    $= <f{:}(g{:}x), f{:}y_1, \dots, f{:}y_n>$ $\square$

PROPOSITION 2

Pair & not$\circ$null$\circ 1 \longrightarrow$
$$\text{apndl}\circ[[1^2, 2], \text{distr}\circ[\text{tl}\circ 1, 2]] \equiv \text{distr}$$

where $f \& g$ is the function: and$\circ[f, g]$, and $f^2 \equiv f\circ f$.

PROOF. We show that both sides produce the same result when applied to any pair $<x,y>$, where $x \neq \phi$, as per the stated qualification.

CASE 1. x is an atom or $\bot$. Then distr: $<x,y> = \bot$, since $x \neq \phi$. The left side also yields $\bot$ when applied to $<x,y>$, since tl$\circ 1{:}<x,y> = \bot$ and all functions are $\bot$-preserving.

CASE 2. $x = <x_1, \dots, x_n>$. Then

apndl$\circ[[1^2, 2], \text{distr}\circ[\text{tl}\circ 1, 2]]{:}<x, y>$
   $=$ apndl: $<<1{:}x, y>, \text{distr}{:} <\text{tl}{:}x, y>>$
   $=$ apndl: $<<x_1,y>, \phi> = <<x_1,y>>$ if tl$\circ x = \phi$
   $=$ apndl: $<<x_1,y>, <<x_2,y>, \dots, <x_n,y>>>$
                       if tl$\circ x \neq \phi$
    $= <<x_1,y>, \dots, <x_n,y>>$
   $=$ distr: $<x,y>$ $\square$

12.3 Example: Equivalence of Two Matrix Multiplication Programs

We have seen earlier the matrix multiplication program:

Def MM $\equiv \alpha\alpha$IP $\circ$ αdistl $\circ$ distr $\circ$ [1, trans$\circ$2].

We shall now show that its initial segment, MM$'$, where

Def MM$' \equiv \alpha\alpha$IP $\circ$ αdistl $\circ$ distr,

can be defined recursively. (MM$'$ "multiplies" a pair of matrices after the second matrix has been transposed. Note that MM$'$, unlike MM, gives $\bot$ for all arguments that are not pairs.) That is, we shall show that MM$'$ satisfies the following equation which recursively defines the same function (on pairs):

$f \equiv$ null$\circ 1 \rightarrow \bar{\phi}$; apndl$\circ[\alpha$IP$\circ$distl$\circ[1\circ 1, 2], f\circ[\text{tl}\circ 1, 2]]$.

Our proof will take the form of showing that the following function, R,

Def R $\equiv$ null$\circ 1 \rightarrow \bar{\phi}$;
$$\text{apndl}\circ[\alpha\text{IP}\circ\text{distl}\circ[1\circ 1, 2], \text{MM}'\circ[\text{tl}\circ 1, 2]]$$

is, for all pairs $<x,y>$, the same function as MM$'$. R "multiplies" two matrices, when the first has more than zero rows, by computing the first row of the "product" (with αIP$\circ$distl$\circ[1\circ 1, 2]$) and adjoining it to the "product" of the tail of the first matrix and the second matrix. Thus the theorem we want is

pair $\longrightarrow$ MM$' \equiv$ R,

from which the following is immediate:

MM $\equiv$ MM$' \circ$ [1, trans$\circ$2] $\equiv$ R $\circ$ [1, trans$\circ$2];

where

Def pair $\equiv$ atom $\rightarrow \bar{F}$; eq$\circ$[length, $\bar{2}$].

THEOREM: pair $\longrightarrow$ MM$' \equiv$ R
where

Def $MM' \equiv \alpha\alpha IP \circ \alpha distl \circ distr$
Def $R \equiv null \circ 1 \to \bar{\phi};$
$$apndl \circ [\alpha IP \circ distl \circ [1^2, 2], MM' \circ [tl \circ 1, 2]]$$

PROOF.

CASE 1. pair & $null \circ 1 \longrightarrow MM' \equiv R$.

pair & $null \circ 1 \longrightarrow R \equiv \bar{\phi}$ by def of R
pair & $null \circ 1 \longrightarrow MM' \equiv \bar{\phi}$
since distr: $<\phi, x> = \phi$ by def of distr
and $\alpha f : \phi = \phi$ by def of Apply to all.
And so: $\alpha\alpha IP \circ \alpha distl \circ distr : <\phi, x> = \phi$.
Thus pair & $null \circ 1 \longrightarrow MM' \equiv R$.

CASE 2. pair & $not \circ null \circ 1 \longrightarrow MM' \equiv R$.

pair & $not \circ null \circ 1 \longrightarrow R \equiv R'$, (1)

by def of R and R', where

Def $R' \equiv apndl \circ [\alpha IP \circ distl \circ [1^2, 2], MM' \circ [tl \circ 1, 2]]$.

We note that

$R' \equiv apndl \circ [f \circ g, \alpha f \circ h]$

where

$f \equiv \alpha IP \circ distl$
$g \equiv [1^2, 2]$
$h \equiv distr \circ [tl \circ 1, 2]$
$\alpha f \equiv \alpha(\alpha IP \circ distl) \equiv \alpha\alpha IP \circ \alpha distl$ (by III.4). (2)

Thus, by I.10,

$R' \equiv \alpha f \circ apndl \circ [g, h]$. (3)

Now $apndl \circ [g, h] \equiv apndl \circ [[1^2, 2], distr \circ [tl \circ 1, 2]]$,
thus, by I.11,

pair & $not \circ null \circ 1 \longrightarrow apndl \circ [g, h] \equiv distr$. (4)

And so we have, by (1), (2), (3) and (4),

pair & $not \circ null \circ 1 \longrightarrow R \equiv R'$
$\equiv \alpha f \circ distr \equiv \alpha\alpha IP \circ \alpha distl \circ distr \equiv MM'$.

Case 1 and Case 2 together prove the theorem. $\square$

12.4 Expansion Theorems

In the following subsections we shall be "solving" some simple equations (where by a "solution" we shall mean the "least" function which satisfies an equation). To do so we shall need the following notions and results drawn from the later subsection on foundations of the algebra, where their proofs appear.

12.4.1 Expansion. Suppose we have an equation of the form

$f \equiv E(f)$ (E1)

where $E(f)$ is an expression involving f. Suppose further that there is an infinite sequence of functions f_i for $i = 0, 1, 2, \ldots$, each having the following form:

$f_0 \equiv \bar{\perp}$
$f_{i+1} \equiv p_0 \to q_0; \ldots ; p_i \to q_i; \bar{\perp}$ (E2)

where the p_i's and q_i's are particular functions, so that E has the property:

$E(f_i) \equiv f_{i+1}$ for $i = 0, 1, 2, \ldots$ (E3)

Then we say that E is *expansive* and has the f_i's as *approximating functions.*

If E is expansive and has approximating functions as in (E2), and if f is the solution of (E1), then f can be written as the infinite expansion

$f \equiv p_0 \to q_0; \ldots ; p_n \to q_n; \ldots$ (E4)

meaning that, for any x, $f : x \neq \perp$ iff there is an $n \geq 0$ such that (a) $p_i : x = F$ for all $i < n$, and (b) $p_n : x = T$, and (c) $q_n : x \neq \perp$. When $f : x \neq \perp$, then $f : x = q_n : x$ for this n. (The foregoing is a consequence of the "expansion theorem".)

12.4.2 Linear expansion. A more helpful tool for solving some equations applies when, for any function h,

$E(h) \equiv p_0 \to q_0; E_1(h)$ (LE1)

and there exist p_i and q_i such that

$E_1(p_i \to q_i; h) \equiv p_{i+1} \to q_{i+1}; E_1(h)$
for $i = 0, 1, 2, \ldots$ (LE2)

and

$E_1(\bar{\perp}) \equiv \bar{\perp}$. (LE3)

Under the above conditions E is said to be *linearly expansive.* If so, and f is the solution of

$f \equiv E(f)$ (LE4)

then E is expansive and f can again be written as the infinite expansion

$f \equiv p_0 \to q_0; \ldots ; p_n \to q_n; \ldots$ (LE5)

using the p_i's and q_i's generated by (LE1) and (LE2).

Although the p_i's and q_i's of (E4) or (LE5) are not unique for a given function, it may be possible to find additional constraints which would make them so, in which case the expansion (LE5) would comprise a canonical form for a function. Even without uniqueness these expansions often permit one to prove the equivalence of two different function expressions, and they often clarify a function's behavior.

12.5 A Recursion Theorem

Using three of the above laws and linear expansion, one can prove the following theorem of moderate generality that gives a clarifying expansion for many recursively defined functions.

RECURSION THEOREM: Let f be a solution of

$f \equiv p \to g; Q(f)$ (1)

where

$Q(k) \equiv h \circ [i, k \circ j]$ for any function k (2)

and p, g, h, i, j are any given functions, then

$f \equiv p \to g; p \circ j \to Q(g); \dots ; p \circ j^n \to Q^n(g); \dots$ (3)

(where $Q^n(g)$ is $h \circ [i, Q^{n-1}(g) \circ j]$, and j^n is $j \circ j^{n-1}$ for $n \geq 2$) and

$$Q^n(g) \equiv /h \circ [i, i \circ j, \dots , i \circ j^{n-1}, g \circ j^n]. \quad (4)$$

PROOF. We verify that $p \to g; Q(f)$ is linearly expansive. Let p_n, q_n and k be any functions. Then

$Q(p_n \to q_n; k)$
  $\equiv h \circ [i, (p_n \to q_n; k) \circ j]$ by (2)
  $\equiv h \circ [i, (p_n \circ j \to q_n \circ j; k \circ j)]$ by II.1
  $\equiv h \circ (p_n \circ j \to [i, q_n \circ j]; [i, k \circ j])$ by IV.1
  $\equiv p_n \circ j \to h \circ [i, q_n \circ j]; h \circ [i, k \circ j]$ by II.2
  $\equiv p_n \circ j \to Q(q_n); Q(k)$ by (2)   (5)

Thus if $p_0 \equiv p$ and $q_0 \equiv g$, then (5) gives $p_1 \equiv p \circ j$ and $q_1 = Q(g)$ and in general gives the following functions satisfying (LE2)

$$p_n \equiv p \circ j^n \quad \text{and} \quad q_n \equiv Q^n(g). \quad (6)$$

Finally,

$Q(\bar{\perp}) \equiv h \circ [i, \bar{\perp} \circ j]$
  $\equiv h \circ [i, \bar{\perp}]$ by III.1.1
  $\equiv h \circ \bar{\perp}$ by I.9
  $\equiv \bar{\perp}$ by III.1.1.   (7)

Thus (5) and (6) verify (LE2) and (7) verifies (LE3), with $E_1 \equiv Q$. If we let $E(f) \equiv p \to g; Q(f)$, then we have (LE1); thus E is linearly expansive. Since f is a solution of $f \equiv E(f)$, conclusion (3) follows from (6) and (LE5). Now

$Q^n(g) \equiv h \circ [i, Q^{n-1}(g) \circ j]$
  $\equiv h \circ [i, h \circ [i \circ j, \dots , h \circ [i \circ j^{n-1}, g \circ j^n] \dots]]$

             by I.1, repeatedly

  $\equiv /h \circ [i, i \circ j, \dots , i \circ j^{n-1}, g \circ j^n]$ by I.3   (8)

Result (8) is the second conclusion (4).   □

12.5.1 Example: correctness proof of a recursive factorial function. Let f be a solution of

$$f \equiv \text{eq}0 \to \bar{I}; \times \circ [\text{id}, f \circ s]$$

where

Def $s \equiv - \circ [\text{id}, \bar{I}]$ (subtract 1).

Then f satisfies the hypothesis of the recursion theorem with $p \equiv \text{eq}0$, $g \equiv \bar{I}$, $h \equiv \times$, $i \equiv \text{id}$, and $j \equiv s$. Therefore

$$f \equiv \text{eq}0 \to \bar{I}; \dots ; \text{eq}0 \circ s^n \to Q^n(\bar{I}); \dots$$

and

$$Q^n(\bar{I}) \equiv /\times \circ [\text{id}, \text{id} \circ s, \dots , \text{id} \circ s^{n-1}, \bar{I} \circ s^n].$$

Now $\text{id} \circ s^k \equiv s^k$ by III.2 and $\text{eq}0 \circ s^n \longrightarrow \bar{I} \circ s^n \equiv \bar{I}$ by III.1, since $\text{eq}0 \circ s^n{:}x$ implies $\text{defined} \circ s^n{:}x$; and also $\text{eq}0 \circ s^n{:}x \equiv \text{eq}0{:} (x - n) \equiv x{=}n$. Thus if $\text{eq}0 \circ s^n{:} x = T$, then $x = n$ and

$Q^n(\bar{I}){:} n = n \times (n - 1) \times \dots \times (n - (n - 1))$
                     $\times (\bar{I}{:} (n - n)) = n!.$

Using these results for $\bar{I} \circ s^n$, $\text{eq}0 \circ s^n$, and $Q^n(\bar{I})$ in the previous expansion for f, we obtain

$f{:}x \equiv x{=}0 \to 1; \dots ; x{=}n$
              $\to n \times (n - 1) \times \dots \times 1 \times 1; \dots$

Thus we have proved that f terminates on precisely the set of nonnegative integers and that it is the factorial function thereon.

12.6 An Iteration Theorem

    This is really a corollary of the recursion theorem. It gives a simple expansion for many iterative programs.

ITERATION THEOREM: Let f be the solution (i.e., the least solution) of

$$f \equiv p \to g; h \circ f \circ k$$

then

$$f \equiv p \to g; p \circ k \to h \circ g \circ k; \dots ; p \circ k^n \to h^n \circ g \circ k^n; \dots$$

PROOF. Let $h' \equiv h \circ 2$, $i' \equiv \text{id}$, $j' \equiv k$, then

$$f \equiv p \to g; h' \circ [i', f \circ j']$$

since $h \circ 2 \circ [\text{id}, f \circ k] \equiv h \circ f \circ k$ by I.5 (id is defined except for $\perp$, and the equation holds for $\perp$). Thus the recursion theorem gives

$$f \equiv p \to g; \dots ; p \circ k^n \to Q^n(g); \dots$$

where

$Q^n(g) \equiv h \circ 2 \circ [\text{id}, Q^{n-1}(g) \circ k]$
    $\equiv h \circ Q^{n-1}(g) \circ k \equiv h^n \circ g \circ k^n$

by I.5   □

12.6.1 Example: Correctness proof for an iterative factorial function. Let f be the solution of

$$f \equiv \text{eq}0 \circ 1 \to 2; f \circ [s \circ 1, \times]$$

where **Def** $s \equiv - \circ [\text{id}, \bar{I}]$ (substract 1). We want to prove that $f{:}{<}x, 1{>} = x!$ iff x is a nonnegative integer. Let $p \equiv \text{eq}0 \circ 1$, $g \equiv 2$, $h \equiv \text{id}$, $k \equiv [s \circ 1, \times]$. Then

$$f \equiv p \to g; h \circ f \circ k$$

and so

$$f \equiv p \to g; \dots ; p \circ k^n \to g \circ k^n; \dots \quad (1)$$

by the iteration theorem, since $h^n \equiv \text{id}$. We want to show that

$$\text{pair} \longrightarrow k^n \equiv [a_n, b_n] \quad (2)$$

holds for every $n \geq 1$, where

$a_n \equiv s^n \circ 1$ (3)
$b_n \equiv /\times \circ [s^{n-1} \circ 1, \dots , s \circ 1, 1, 2]$ (4)

Now (2) holds for $n = 1$ by definition of k. We assume it holds for some $n \geq 1$ and prove it then holds for $n + 1$. Now

$$\text{pair} \longrightarrow k^{n+1} \equiv k \circ k^n \equiv [s \circ 1, \times] \circ [a_n, b_n] \quad (5)$$

since (2) holds for n. And so

pair $\longrightarrow k^{n+1} \equiv [s \circ a_n, \times \circ [a_n, b_n]]$ by I.1 and I.5   (6)

To pass from (5) to (6) we must check that whenever a_n or b_n yield $\perp$ in (5), so will the right side of (6). Now

$$s \circ a_n \equiv s^{n+1} \circ 1 \equiv a_{n+1} \tag{7}$$
$$\times \circ [a_n, b_n] \equiv /\times \circ [s^n \circ 1, s^{n-1} \circ 1, \ldots, s \circ 1, 1, 2]$$
$$\equiv b_{n+1} \text{ by I.3.} \tag{8}$$

Combining (6), (7), and (8) gives

$$\text{pair} \longrightarrow k^{n+1} \equiv [a_{n+1}, b_{n+1}]. \tag{9}$$

Thus (2) holds for n = 1 and holds for n + 1 whenever it holds for n, therefore, by induction, it holds for every n ≥ 1. Now (2) gives, for pairs:

$$\text{defined} \circ k^n \longrightarrow p \circ k^n \equiv eq0 \circ 1 \circ [a_n, b_n]$$
$$\equiv eq0 \circ a_n \equiv eq0 \circ s^n \circ 1 \tag{10}$$
$$\text{defined} \circ k^n \longrightarrow g \circ k^n$$
$$\equiv 2 \circ [a_n, b_n] \equiv /\times \circ [s^{n-1} \circ 1, \ldots, s \circ 1, 1, 2] \tag{11}$$

(both use I.5). Now (1) tells us that $f:<x,1>$ is defined iff there is an n such that $p \circ k^i:<x,1> = F$ for all i < n, and $p \circ k^n:<x,1> = T$, that is, by (10), $eq0 \circ s^n:x = T$, i.e., $x = n$; and $g \circ k^n:<x,1>$ is defined, in which case, by (11),

$$f:<x,1> = /\times:<1, 2, \ldots, x-1, x, 1> = n!,$$

which is what we set out to prove.

12.6.2 Example: proof of equivalence of two iterative programs.
In this example we want to prove that two iteratively defined programs, f and g, are the same function. Let f be the solution of

$$f \equiv p \circ 1 \to 2; h \circ f \circ [k \circ 1, 2]. \tag{1}$$

Let g be the solution of

$$g \equiv p \circ 1 \to 2; g \circ [k \circ 1, h \circ 2]. \tag{2}$$

Then, by the iteration theorem:

$$f \equiv p_0 \to q_0; \ldots ; p_n \to q_n; \ldots \tag{3}$$
$$g \equiv p'_0 \to q'_0; \ldots ; p'_n \to q'_n; \ldots \tag{4}$$

where (letting $r^0 \equiv id$ for any r), for n = 0, 1, …

$$p_n \equiv p \circ 1 \circ [k \circ 1, 2]^n \equiv p \circ 1 \circ [k^n \circ 1, 2] \quad \text{by I.5.1} \tag{5}$$
$$q_n \equiv h^n \circ 2 \circ [k \circ 1, 2]^n \equiv h^n \circ 2 \circ [k^n \circ 1, 2] \quad \text{by I.5.1} \tag{6}$$
$$p'_n \equiv p \circ 1 \circ [k \circ 1, h \circ 2]^n \equiv p \circ 1 \circ [k^n \circ 1, h^n \circ 2] \quad \text{by I.5.1} \tag{7}$$
$$q'_n \equiv 2 \circ [k \circ 1, h \circ 2]^n \equiv 2 \circ [k^n \circ 1, h^n \circ 2] \quad \text{by I.5.1.} \tag{8}$$

Now, from the above, using I.5,

$$\text{defined} \circ 2 \longrightarrow p_n \equiv p \circ k^n \circ 1 \tag{9}$$
$$\text{defined} \circ h^n \circ 2 \longrightarrow p'_n \equiv p \circ k^n \circ 1 \tag{10}$$
$$\text{defined} \circ k^n \circ 1 \longrightarrow q_n \equiv q'_n \equiv h^n \circ 2 \tag{11}$$

Thus

$$\text{defined} \circ h^n \circ 2 \longrightarrow \text{defined} \circ 2 \equiv \bar{T} \tag{12}$$
$$\text{defined} \circ h^n \circ 2, \longrightarrow p_n \equiv p'_n \tag{13}$$

and

$$f \equiv p_0 \to q_0; \ldots ; p_n \to h^n \circ 2; \ldots \tag{14}$$
$$g \equiv p'_0 \to q'_0; \ldots ; p'_n \to h^n \circ 2; \ldots \tag{15}$$

since p_n and p'_n provide the qualification needed for $q_n \equiv q'_n \equiv h^n \circ 2$.

Now suppose there is an x such that $f:x \not\equiv g:x$. Then there is an n such that $p_i:x = p'_i:x = F$ for i < n, and $p_n:x \not\equiv p'_n:x$. From (12) and (13) this can only happen when $h^n \circ 2:x = \perp$. But since h is $\perp$-preserving, $h^m \circ 2:x = \perp$ for all m ≥ n. Hence $f:x = g:x = \perp$ by (14) and (15). This contradicts the assumption that there is an x for which $f:x \not\equiv g:x$. Hence $f \equiv g$.

This example (by J. H. Morris, Jr.) is treated more elegantly in [16] on p. 498. However, some may find that the above treatment is more constructive, leads one more mechanically to the key questions, and provides more insight into the behavior of the two functions.

12.7 Nonlinear Equations
The preceding examples have concerned "linear" equations (in which the "unknown" function does not have an argument involving itself). The question of the existence of simple expansions that "solve" "quadratic" and higher order equations remains open.

The earlier examples concerned solutions of $f \equiv E(f)$, where E is linearly expansive. The following example involves an $E(f)$ that is quadratic and expansive (but not linearly expansive).

12.7.1 Example: proof of idempotency ([16] p. 497).
Let f be the solution of

$$f \equiv E(f) \equiv p \to id; f^2 \circ h. \tag{1}$$

We wish to prove that $f \equiv f^2$. We verify that E is expansive (Section 12.4.1) with the following approximating functions:

$$f_0 \equiv \bar{\perp} \tag{2a}$$
$$f_n \equiv p \to id; \ldots ; p \circ h^{n-1} \to h^{n-1}; \bar{\perp} \quad \text{for n > 0} \tag{2b}$$

First we note that $p \longrightarrow f_n \equiv id$ and so

$$p \circ h^i \longrightarrow f_n \circ h^i \equiv h^i. \tag{3}$$

Now $E(f_0) \equiv p \to id; \bar{\perp}^2 \circ h \equiv f_1,$ (4)

and

$E(f_n)$
$$\equiv p \to id; f_n \circ (p \to id; \ldots ; p \circ h^{n-1} \to h^{n-1}; \bar{\perp}) \circ h$$
$$\equiv p \to id; f_n \circ (p \circ h \to h; \ldots ; p \circ h^n \to h^n; \bar{\perp} \circ h)$$
$$\equiv p \to id; p \circ h \to f_n \circ h; \ldots ; p \circ h^n \to f_n \circ h^n; f_n \circ \bar{\perp}$$
$$\equiv p \to id; p \circ h \to h; \ldots ; p \circ h^n \to h^n; \bar{\perp} \quad \text{by (3)}$$
$$\equiv f_{n+1}. \tag{5}$$

Thus E is expansive by (4) and (5); so by (2) and Section 12.4.1 (E4)

$$f \equiv p \to id; \ldots ; p \circ h^n \to h^n; \ldots . \tag{6}$$

But (6), by the iteration theorem, gives

$$f \equiv p \to id; f \circ h. \tag{7}$$

Now, if $p:x = T$, then $f:x = x = f^2:x$, by (1). If $p:x = F$, then

$$f:x = f^2 \circ h:x \quad \text{by (1)}$$

231

$$= f:(f \circ h:x) = f:(f:x) \quad \text{by (7)}$$
$$= f^2:x.$$

If $p:x$ is neither T nor F, then $f:x = \bot = f^2:x$. Thus $f \equiv f^2$.

12.8 Foundations for the Algebra of Programs

Our purpose in this section is to establish the validity of the results stated in Section 12.4. Subsequent sections do not depend on this one, hence it can be skipped by readers who wish to do so. We use the standard concepts and results from [16], but the notation used for objects and functions, etc., will be that of this paper.

We take as the domain (and range) for all functions the set O of objects (which includes $\bot$) of a given FP system. We take F to be the set of functions, and $\mathbf{F}$ to be the set of functional forms of that FP system. We write $E(f)$ for any function expression involving functional forms, primitive and defined functions, and the function symbol f; and we regard E as a functional that maps a function f into the corresponding function $E(f)$. We assume that all $f \in F$ are $\bot$-preserving and that all functional forms in $\mathbf{F}$ correspond to continuous functionals in every variable (e.g., $[f, g]$ is continuous in both f and g). (All primitive functions of the FP system given earlier are $\bot$-preserving, and all its functional forms are continuous.)

DEFINITIONS. Let $E(f)$ be a function expression. Let

$$f_0 \equiv \bot$$
$$f_{i+1} \equiv p_0 \to q_0; \dots ; p_i \to q_i; \bot \quad \text{for } i = 0, 1, \dots$$

where $p_i, q_i \in F$. Let E have the property that

$$E(f_i) \equiv f_{i+1} \quad \text{for } i = 0, 1, \dots .$$

Then E is said to be *expansive* with the *approximating functions* f_i. We write

$$f \equiv p_0 \to q_0; \dots ; p_n \to q_n; \dots$$

to mean that $f \equiv \lim_i\{f_i\}$, where the f_i have the form above. We call the right side an *infinite expansion* of f. We take $f:x$ to be defined iff there is an $n \geq 0$ such that (a) $p_i:x = F$ for all $i < n$, and (b) $p_n:x = T$, and (c) $q_n:x$ is defined, in which case $f:x = q_n:x$.

EXPANSION THEOREM: Let $E(f)$ be expansive with approximating functions as above. Let f be the least function satisfying

$$f \equiv E(f).$$

Then

$$f \equiv p_0 \to q_0; \dots ; p_n \to q_n; \dots$$

PROOF. Since E is the composition of continuous functionals (from $\mathbf{F}$) involving only monotonic functions ($\bot$-preserving functions from F) as constant terms, E is continuous ([16] p. 493). Therefore its least fixed point f is $\lim_i\{E^i(\bot)\} \equiv \lim_i\{f_i\}$ ([16] p. 494), which by definition is the above infinite expansion for f. $\square$

DEFINITION. Let $E(f)$ be a function expression satisfying the following:

$$E(h) \equiv p_0 \to q_0; E_1(h) \quad \text{for all } h \in F \tag{LE1}$$

where $p_i \in F$ and $q_i \in F$ exist such that

$$E_1(p_i \to q_i; h) \equiv p_{i+1} \to q_{i+1}; E_1(h)$$
$$\text{for all } h \in F \text{ and } i = 0, 1, \dots \tag{LE2}$$

and

$$E_1(\bot) \equiv \bot. \tag{LE3}$$

Then E is said to be *linearly expansive* with respect to these p_i's and q_i's.

LINEAR EXPANSION THEOREM: Let E be linearly expansive with respect to p_i and q_i, $i = 0, 1, \dots$. Then E is expansive with approximating functions

$$f_0 \equiv \bot \tag{1}$$
$$f_{i+1} \equiv p_0 \to q_0; \dots ; p_i \to q_i; \bot. \tag{2}$$

PROOF. We want to show that $E(f_i) \equiv f_{i+1}$ for any $i \geq 0$. Now

$$E(f_0) \equiv p_0 \to q_0; E_1(\bot) \equiv p_0 \to q_0; \bot \equiv f_1 \tag{3}$$
$$\text{by (LE1) (LE3) (1).}$$

Let $i > 0$ be fixed and let

$$f_i \equiv p_0 \to q_0; w_1 \tag{4a}$$
$$w_1 \equiv p_1 \to q_1; w_2 \tag{4b}$$
etc.
$$w_{i-1} \equiv p_{i-1} \to q_{i-1}; \bot. \tag{4-}$$

Then, for this $i > 0$

$$\begin{aligned} E(f_i) &\equiv p_0 \to q_0; E_1(f_i) \quad \text{by (LE1)} \\ E_1(f_i) &\equiv p_1 \to q_1; E_1(w_1) \quad \text{by (LE2) and (4a)} \\ E_1(w_1) &\equiv p_2 \to q_2; E_1(w_2) \quad \text{by (LE2) and (4b)} \end{aligned}$$
etc.
$$\begin{aligned} E_1(w_{i-1}) &\equiv p_i \to q_i; E_1(\bot) \quad \text{by (LE2) and (4-)} \\ &\equiv p_i \to q_i; \bot \quad \text{by (LE3)} \end{aligned}$$

Combining the above gives

$$E(f_i) \equiv f_{i+1} \quad \text{for arbitrary } i > 0, \text{ by (2).} \tag{5}$$

By (3), (5) also holds for $i = 0$; thus it holds for all $i \geq 0$. Therefore E is expansive and has the required approximating functions. $\square$

COROLLARY. If E is linearly expansive with respect to p_i and q_i, $i = 0, 1, \dots$, and f is the least function satisfying

$$f \equiv E(f) \tag{LE4}$$

then

$$f \equiv p_0 \to q_0; \dots ; p_n \to q_n; \dots . \tag{LE5}$$

12.9 The Algebra of Programs for the Lambda Calculus and for Combinators

Because Church's lambda calculus [5] and the system of combinators developed by Schönfinkel and Curry [6]

232

are the primary mathematical systems for representing the notion of application of functions, and because they are more powerful than FP systems, it is natural to enquire what an algebra of programs based on those systems would look like.

The lambda calculus and combinator equivalents of FP composition, $f \circ g$, are

$$\lambda fgx.(f(gx)) \equiv B$$

where B is a simple combinator defined by Curry. There is no direct equivalent for the FP object $<x,y>$ in the Church or Curry systems proper; however, following Landin [14] and Burge [4], one can use the primitive functions prefix, head, tail, null, and atomic to introduce the notion of list structures that correspond to FP sequences. Then, using FP notation for lists, the lambda calculus equivalent for construction is $\lambda fgx.<fx,gx>$. A combinatory equivalent is an expression involving prefix, the null list, and two or more basic combinators. It is so complex that I shall not attempt to give it.

If one uses the lambda calculus or combinatory expressions for the functional forms $f \circ g$ and $[f,g]$ to express the law I.1 in the FP algebra, $[f,g] \circ h \equiv [f \circ h, g \circ h]$, the result is an expression so complex that the sense of the law is obscured. The only way to make that sense clear in either system is to name the two functionals: composition $\equiv B$, and construction $\equiv A$, so that $Bfg \equiv f \circ g$, and $Afg \equiv [f,g]$. Then I.1 becomes

$$B(Afg)h \equiv A(Bfh)(Bgh),$$

which is still not as perspicuous as the FP law.

The point of the above is that if one wishes to state clear laws like those of the FP algebra in either Church's or Curry's system, one finds it necessary to select certain functionals (e.g., composition and construction) as the basic operations of the algebra and to either give them short names or, preferably, represent them by some special notation as in FP. If one does this and provides primitives, objects, lists, etc., the result is an FP-like system in which the usual lambda expressions or combinators do not appear. Even then these Church or Curry versions of FP systems, being less restricted, have some problems that FP systems do not have:

a) The Church and Curry versions accommodate functions of many types and can define functions that do not exist in FP systems. Thus, Bf is a function that has no counterpart in FP systems. This added power carries with it problems of type compatibility. For example, in $f \circ g$, is the range of g included in the domain of f? In FP systems all functions have the same domain and range.

b) The semantics of Church's lambda calculus depends on substitution rules that are simply stated but whose implications are very difficult to fully comprehend. The true complexity of these rules is not widely recognized but is evidenced by the succession of able logicians who have published "proofs" of the Church-Rosser theorem that failed to account for one or another

of these complexities. (The Church-Rosser theorem, or Scott's proof of the existence of a model [22], is required to show that the lambda calculus has a consistent semantics.) The definition of pure Lisp contained a related error for a considerable period (the "funarg" problem). Analogous problems attach to Curry's system as well.

In contrast, the formal (FFP) version of FP systems (described in the next section) has no variables and only an elementary substitution rule (a function for its name), and it can be shown to have a consistent semantics by a relatively simple fixed-point argument along the lines developed by Dana Scott and by Manna et al [16]. For such a proof see McJones [18].

12.10 Remarks

The algebra of programs outlined above needs much work to provide expansions for larger classes of equations and to extend its laws and theorems beyond the elementary ones given here. It would be interesting to explore the algebra for an FP-like system whose sequence constructor is not $\perp$-preserving (law I.5 is strengthened, but IV.1 is lost). Other interesting problems are: (a) Find rules that make expansions unique, giving canonical forms for functions; (b) find algorithms for expanding and analyzing the behavior of functions for various classes of arguments; and (c) explore ways of using the laws and theorems of the algebra as the basic rules either of a formal, preexecution "lazy evaluation" scheme [9, 10], or of one which operates during execution. Such schemes would, for example, make use of the law $1 \circ [f,g] \leq f$ to avoid evaluating $g{:}x$.

13. Formal Systems for Functional Programming (FFP Systems)

13.1 Introduction

As we have seen, an FP system has a set of functions that depends on its set of primitive functions, its set of functional forms, and its set of definitions. In particular, its set of functional forms is fixed once and for all, and this set determines the power of the system in a major way. For example, if its set of functional forms is empty, then its entire set of functions is just the set of primitive functions. In FFP systems one can create new functional forms. Functional forms are represented by object sequences; the first element of a sequence determines which form it represents, while the remaining elements are the parameters of the form.

The ability to define new functional forms in FFP systems is one consequence of the principal difference between them and FP systems: in FFP systems objects are used to "represent" functions in a systematic way. Otherwise FFP systems mirror FP systems closely. They are similar to, but simpler than, the Reduction (Red) languages of an earlier paper [2].

We shall first give the simple syntax of FFP systems, then discuss their semantics informally, giving examples, and finally give their formal semantics.

13.2 Syntax

We describe the set O of objects and the set E of expressions of an FFP system. These depend on the choice of some set A of *atoms*, which we take as given. We assume that T (true), F (false), ϕ (the empty sequence), and $\#$ (default) belong to A, as well as "numbers" of various kinds, etc.

1) Bottom, $\perp$, is an *object* but not an atom.

2) Every atom is an *object*.

3) Every object is an *expression*.

4) If $x_1, \ldots, x_n$ are objects [expressions], then $<x_1, \ldots, x_n>$ is an *object* [resp., *expression*] called a *sequence* (of *length* n) for $n \geq 1$. The object [expression] x_i for $1 \leq i \leq n$, is the ith *element* of the sequence $<x_1, \ldots, x_i, \ldots, x_n>$. ($\phi$ is both a sequence and an atom; its length is 0.)

5) If x and y are expressions, then $(x:y)$ is an *expression* called an *application*. x is its *operator* and y is its *operand*. Both are *elements* of the expression.

6) If $x = <x_1, \ldots, x_n>$ and if one of the elements of x is $\perp$, then $x = \perp$. That is, $<\ldots, \perp, \ldots> = \perp$.

7) All objects and expressions are formed by finite use of the above rules.

A *subexpression* of an expression x is either x itself or a subexpression of an element of x. An FFP object is an expression that has no application as a subexpression. Given the same set of atoms, FFP and FP objects are the same.

13.3 Informal Remarks About FFP Semantics

13.3.1 The meaning of expressions; the semantic function μ. Every FFP expression e has a *meaning*, μe, which is always an object; μe is found by repeatedly replacing each innermost application in e by its meaning. If this process is nonterminating, the meaning of e is $\perp$. The meaning of an innermost application $(x:y)$ (since it is innermost, x and y must be objects) is the result of applying the function *represented* by x to y, just as in FP systems, except that in FFP systems functions are represented by objects, rather than by function expressions, with atoms (instead of function symbols) representing primitive and defined functions, and with sequences representing the FP functions denoted by functional forms.

The association between objects and the functions they represent is given by the *representation function*, ρ, of the FFP system. (Both ρ and μ belong to the description of the system, not the system itself.) Thus if the atom *NULL* represents the FP function null, then $\rho NULL$ = null and the meaning of $(NULL:A)$ is $\mu(NULL:A) = (\rho NULL):A = \text{null}:A = F$. From here on, as above, we use the colon in two senses. When it is between two objects, as in $(NULL:A)$, it identifies an FFP application that denotes only itself; when it comes between a *function* and an object, as in $(\rho NULL):A$ or null:A, it identifies an FP-like application that denotes the *result* of applying the function to the object.

The fact that FFP operators are objects makes pos-

sible a function, apply, which is meaningless in FP systems:

$$\text{apply}:<x,y> = (x:y).$$

The result of apply:$<x,y>$, namely $(x:y)$, is meaningless in FP systems on two levels. First, $(x:y)$ is not itself an object; it illustrates another difference between FP and FFP systems: some FFP functions, like apply, map objects into expressions, not directly into objects as FP functions do. However, the *meaning* of apply:$<x,y>$ is an object (see below). Second, $(x:y)$ could not be even an intermediate result in an FP system; it is meaningless in FP systems since x is an object, not a function and FP systems do not associate functions with objects. Now if *APPLY* represents apply, then the meaning of $(APPLY:<NULL,A>)$ is

$$\begin{aligned}
\mu(APPLY&:<NULL,A>) \\
&= \mu((\rho APPLY):<NULL,A>) \\
&= \mu(\text{apply}:<NULL,A>) \\
&= \mu(NULL:A) = \mu((\rho NULL):A) \\
&= \mu(\text{null}:A) = \mu F = F.
\end{aligned}$$

The last step follows from the fact that every object is its own meaning. Since the meaning function μ eventually evaluates all applications, one can think of apply:$<NULL,A>$ as yielding F even though the actual result is $(NULL:A)$.

13.3.2 How objects represent functions; the representation function ρ. As we have seen, some atoms (*primitive* atoms) will represent the primitive functions of the system. Other atoms can represent defined functions just as symbols can in FP systems. If an atom is neither primitive nor defined, it represents $\bar{\perp}$, the function which is $\perp$ everywhere.

Sequences also represent functions and are analogous to the functional forms of FP. The function represented by a sequence is given (recursively) by the following rule.

Metacomposition rule

$$(\rho<x_1, \ldots, x_n>):y = (\rho x_1):<<x_1, \ldots, x_n>, y>,$$

where the x_i's and y are objects. Here ρx_1 determines what functional form $<x_1, \ldots, x_n>$ represents, and $x_2, \ldots, x_n$ are the parameters of the form (in FFP, x_1 itself can also serve as a parameter). Thus, for example, let **Def** $\rho CONST \equiv 2\circ 1$; then $<CONST,x>$ in FFP represents the FP functional form $\bar{x}$, since, by the metacomposition rule, if $y \neq \perp$,

$$\begin{aligned}
(\rho<CONST,x>):y &= (\rho CONST):<<CONST,x>,y> \\
&= 2\circ 1:<<CONST,x>,y> = x.
\end{aligned}$$

Here we can see that the first, controlling, operator of a sequence or form, *CONST* in this case, always has as its operand, after metacomposition, a pair whose first element is the sequence itself and whose second element is the original operand of the sequence, y in this case. The controlling operator can then rearrange and reapply the elements of the sequence and original operand in a great variety of ways. The significant point about metacomposition is that it permits the definition of new functional forms, in effect, merely by defining new functions. It also permits one to write recursive functions without a definition.

We give one more example of a controlling function for a functional form: **Def** $\rho CONS \equiv \alpha apply \circ tl \circ distr$. This definition results in $<CONS, f_1, \ldots, f_n>$—where the f_i are objects—representing the same function as $[\rho f_1, \ldots, \rho f_n]$. The following shows this.

$$(\rho<CONS, f_1, \ldots, f_n>):x$$
$$= (\rho CONS):<<CONS, f_1, \ldots, f_n>, x>$$
by metacomposition

$$= \alpha apply \circ tl \circ distr:<<CONS, f_1, \ldots, f_n>, x>$$
by def of $\rho CONS$

$$= \alpha apply:<<f_1, x>, \ldots, <f_n, x>>$$
by def of tl and distr and $\circ$

$$= <apply:<f_1, x>, \ldots, apply:<f_n, x>>$$
by def of α

$$= <(f_1:x), \ldots, (f_n:x)> \quad \text{by def of apply.}$$

In evaluating the last expression, the meaning function μ will produce the meaning of each application, giving $\rho f_i : x$ as the ith element.

Usually, in describing the function represented by a sequence, we shall give its overall effect rather than show how its controlling operator achieves that effect. Thus we would simply write

$$(\rho<CONS, f_1, \ldots, f_n>):x = <(f_1:x), \ldots, (f_n:x)>$$

instead of the more detailed account above.

We need a controlling operator, *COMP*, to give us sequences representing the functional form composition. We take $\rho COMP$ to be a primitive function such that, for all objects x,

$$(\rho<COMP, f_1, \ldots, f_n>):x$$
$$= (f_1:(f_2:(\ldots:(f_n:x)\ldots))) \quad \text{for n} \geq 1.$$

(I am indebted to Paul McJones for his observation that ordinary composition could be achieved by this primitive function rather than by using two composition rules in the basic semantics, as was done in an earlier paper [2].)

Although FFP systems permit the definition and investigation of new functional forms, it is to be expected that most programming would use a fixed set of forms (whose controlling operators are primitives), as in FP, so that the algebraic laws for those forms could be employed, and so that a structured programming style could be used based on those forms.

In addition to its use in defining functional forms, metacomposition can be used to create recursive functions directly without the use of recursive definitions of the form **Def** $f \equiv E(f)$. For example, if $\rho MLAST \equiv$ null$\circ$tl$\circ 2 \rightarrow 1 \circ 2$; apply$\circ[1, tl \circ 2]$, then $\rho<MLAST> \equiv$ last, where last: $x \equiv x = <x_1, \ldots, x_n> \rightarrow x_n; \perp$. Thus the operator $<MLAST>$ works as follows:

$$\mu(<MLAST>:<A,B>)$$

$$= \mu(\rho MLAST:<<MLAST>, <A,B>>)$$
by metacomposition

$$= \mu(apply \circ [1, tl \circ 2]:<<MLAST>, <A,B>>)$$
$$= \mu(apply:<<MLAST>, <B>>)$$
$$= \mu(<MLAST>:<B>)$$
$$= \mu(\rho MLAST:<<MLAST>, <B>>)$$
$$= \mu(1 \circ 2:<<MLAST>, <B>>)$$
$$= B.$$

13.3.3 Summary of the properties of ρ and μ. So far we have shown how ρ maps atoms and sequences into functions and how those functions map objects into expressions. Actually, ρ and all FFP functions can be extended so that they are defined for all expressions. With such extensions the properties of ρ and μ can be summarized as follows:

1) $\mu \in$ [expressions $\rightarrow$ objects].
2) If x is an object, $\mu x = x$.
3) If e is an expression and $e = <e_1, \ldots, e_n>$, then $\mu e = <\mu e_1, \ldots, \mu e_n>$.
4) $\rho \in$ [expressions $\rightarrow$ [expressions $\rightarrow$ expressions]].
5) For any expression e, $\rho e = \rho(\mu e)$.
6) If x is an object and e an expression, then $\rho x:e = \rho x:(\mu e)$.
7) If x and y are objects, then $\mu(x:y) = \mu(\rho x:y)$. In words: the meaning of an FFP application $(x:y)$ is found by applying ρx, the function represented by x, to y and then finding the meaning of the resulting expression (which is *usually* an object and is then its own meaning).

13.3.4 Cells, fetching, and storing. For a number of reasons it is convenient to create functions which serve as names. In particular, we shall need this facility in describing the semantics of definitions in FFP systems. To introduce naming functions, that is, the ability to *fetch* the contents of a cell with a given name from a store (a sequence of cells) and to *store* a cell with given name and contents in such a sequence, we introduce objects called *cells* and two new functional forms, *fetch* and *store*.

Cells

A *cell* is a triple $<CELL, name, contents>$. We use this form instead of the pair $<name, contents>$ so that cells can be distinguished from ordinary pairs.

Fetch

The functional form *fetch* takes an object n as its parameter (n is customarily an atom serving as a name); it is written $\uparrow n$ (read "fetch n"). Its definition for objects n and x is

$$\uparrow n:x \equiv x = \phi \rightarrow \#; \text{atom}:x \rightarrow \perp;$$
$$(1:x) = <CELL, n, c> \rightarrow c; \uparrow n \circ tl:x,$$

where $\#$ is the atom "default." Thus $\uparrow n$ (fetch n) applied to a sequence gives the contents of the first cell in the sequence whose name is n; If there is no cell named n, the result is default, $\#$. Thus $\uparrow n$ is the name function for the name n. (We assume that $\rho FETCH$ is the primitive function such that $\rho<FETCH, n> \equiv \uparrow n$. Note that $\uparrow n$ simply passes over elements in its operand that are not cells.)

Store and push, pop, purge

Like fetch, *store* takes an object n as its parameter; it is written $\downarrow n$ ("store n"). When applied to a pair $<x,y>$, where y is a sequence, $\downarrow n$ removes the first cell named n from y, if any, then creates a new cell named n with contents x and appends it to y. Before defining $\downarrow n$ (store n) we shall specify four auxiliary functional forms. (These can be used in combination with fetch n and store n to obtain multiple, named, LIFO stacks within a storage sequence.) Two of these auxiliary forms are specified by recursive functional equations; each takes an object n as its parameter.

(cellname n) $\equiv$ atom $\rightarrow \bar{F}$;
$\qquad$ eq$\circ$[length, $\bar{3}$] $\rightarrow$ eq$\circ$[[$\overline{CELL}$, $\bar{n}$], [1, 2]]; $\bar{F}$
(push n) $\equiv$ pair $\rightarrow$ apndl$\circ$[[$\overline{CELL}$, $\bar{n}$, 1], 2]; $\perp$
(pop n) $\equiv$ null $\rightarrow \bar{\phi}$;
$\qquad$ (cellname n)$\circ$1 $\rightarrow$ tl; apndl$\circ$[1, (pop n)$\circ$tl]
(purge n) $\equiv$ null $\rightarrow \bar{\phi}$; (cellname n)$\circ$1 $\rightarrow$ (purge n)$\circ$tl;
$\qquad\qquad$ apndl$\circ$[1, (purge n)$\circ$tl]
$\downarrow n \equiv$ pair $\rightarrow$ (push n)$\circ$[1, (pop n)$\circ$2]; $\perp$

The above functional forms work as follows. For $x \neq \perp$, (cellname n):x is T if x is a cell named n, otherwise it is F. (pop n):y removes the first cell named n from a sequence y; (purge n):y removes all cells named n from y. (push n):$<x,y>$ puts a cell named n with contents x at the head of sequence y; $\downarrow n$:$<x,y>$ is (push n):$<x$, (pop n):$y>$.

(Thus (push n):$<x,y> = y'$ pushes x onto the top of a "stack" named n in y'; x can be read by $\uparrow n$:$y' = x$ and can be removed by (pop n):y'; thus $\uparrow n \circ$(pop n):y' is the element below x in the stack n, provided there is more than one cell named n in y'.)

13.3.5 Definitions in FFP systems. The semantics of an FFP system depends on a fixed set of definitions D (a sequence of cells), just as an FP system depends on its informally given set of definitions. Thus the semantic function μ depends on D; altering D gives a new μ' that reflects the altered definitions. We have represented D as an *object* because in AST systems (Section 14) we shall want to transform D by applying functions to it and to fetch data from it—in addition to using it as the source of function definitions in FFP semantics.

If $<CELL,n,c>$ is the first cell named n in the sequence D (and n is an atom) then it has the same effect as the FP definition **Def** $n \equiv \rho c$, that is, the meaning of $(n$:$x)$ will be the same as that of ρc:x. Thus for example, if $<CELL,CONST,<COMP,2,1>>$ is the first cell in D named $CONST$, then it has the same effect as **Def** $CONST \equiv 2 \circ 1$, and the FFP system with that D would find

$$\mu(CONST:<<x,y>,z>) = y$$

and consequently

$$\mu(<CONST,A>:B) = A.$$

In general, in an FFP system with definitions D, the meaning of an application of the form $(atom$:$x)$ is de-

pendent on D; if $\uparrow atom$:D $\neq \#$ (that is, *atom* is defined in D) then its meaning is $\mu(c$:$x)$, where $c = \uparrow atom$:D, the contents of the first cell in D named *atom*. If $\uparrow atom$:D $= \#$, then *atom* is not defined in D and either *atom* is primitive, i.e. the system knows how to compute $\rho atom$:x, and $\mu(atom$:$x) = \mu(\rho atom$:$x)$, otherwise $\mu(atom$:$x) = \perp$.

13.4 Formal Semantics for FFP Systems

We assume that a set A of atoms, a set D of definitions, a set P $\subset$ A of primitive atoms and the primitive functions they represent have all been chosen. We assume that ρa is the primitive function represented by a if a belongs to P, and that $\rho a = \perp$ if a belongs to Q, the set of atoms in A-P that are not defined in D. Although ρ is defined for all expressions (see 13.3.3), the formal semantics uses its definition only on P and Q. The functions that ρ assigns to other expressions x are implicitly determined and applied in the following semantic rules for evaluating $\mu(x$:$y)$. The above choices of A and D, and of P and the associated primitive functions determine the objects, expressions, and the semantic function μ_D for an FFP system. (We regard D as fixed and write μ for μ_D.) We assume D is a sequence and that $\uparrow y$:D can be computed (by the function $\uparrow y$ as given in Section 13.3.4) for any atom y. With these assumptions we define μ as the least fixed point of the functional τ, where the function $\tau\mu$ is defined as follows for any function μ (for all expressions x, x_i, y, y_i, z, and w):

$(\tau\mu)x \equiv x \in A \rightarrow x$;
$\qquad x = <x_1, ... , x_n> \rightarrow <\mu x_1, ... , \mu x_n>$;
$\qquad x = (y$:$z) \rightarrow$
$\qquad\qquad (y \in A$ & $(\uparrow y$:D$) = \# \rightarrow \mu((\rho y)(\mu z))$;
$\qquad\qquad y \in A$ & $(\uparrow y$:D$) = w \rightarrow \mu(w$:$z)$;
$\qquad\qquad y = <y_1, ... , y_n> \rightarrow \mu(y_1$:$<y,z>)$; $\mu(\mu y$:$z)$); $\perp$

The above description of μ expands the operator of an application by definitions and by metacomposition before evaluating the operand. It is assumed that predicates like "$x \in A$" in the above definition of $\tau\mu$ are $\perp$-preserving (e.g., "$\perp \in A$" has the value $\perp$) and that the conditional expression itself is also $\perp$-preserving. Thus $(\tau\mu)\perp \equiv \perp$ and $(\tau\mu)(\perp$:$z) \equiv \perp$. This concludes the semantics of FFP systems.

14. Applicative State Transition Systems (AST Systems)

14.1 Introduction

This section sketches a class of systems mentioned earlier as alternatives to von Neumann systems. It must be emphasized again that these applicative state transition systems are put forward not as practical programming systems in their present form, but as examples of a class in which applicative style programming is made available in a history sensitive, but non-von Neumann system. These systems are loosely coupled to states and depend on an underlying applicative system for both their programming language and the description of their state transitions. The underlying applicative system of the AST system described below is an FFP system, but other applicative systems could also be used.

To understand the reasons for the structure of AST systems, it is helpful first to review the basic structure of a von Neumann system, Algol, observe its limitations, and compare it with the structure of AST systems. After that review a minimal AST system is described; a small, top-down, self-protecting system program for file maintenance and running user programs is given, with directions for installing it in the AST system and for running an example user program. The system program uses "name functions" instead of conventional names and the user may do so too. The section concludes with subsections discussing variants of AST systems, their general properties, and naming systems.

14.2 The Structure of Algol Compared to That of AST Systems

An Algol program is a sequence of statements, each representing a transformation of the Algol state, which is a complex repository of information about the status of various stacks, pointers, and variable mappings of identifiers onto values, etc. Each statement communicates with this constantly changing state by means of complicated protocols peculiar to itself and even to its different parts (e.g., the protocol associated with the variable x depends on its occurrence on the left or right of an assignment, in a declaration, as a parameter, etc.).

It is as if the Algol state were a complex "store" that communicates with the Algol program through an enormous "cable" of many specialized wires. The complex communications protocols of this cable are fixed and include those for every statement type. The "meaning" of an Algol program must be given in terms of the total effect of a vast number of communications with the state via the cable and its protocols (plus a means for identifying the output and inserting the input into the state). By comparison with this massive cable to the Algol state/store, the cable that is the von Neumann bottleneck of a computer is a simple, elegant concept.

Thus Algol statements are not expressions representing state-to-state functions that are built up by the use of orderly combining forms from simpler state-to-state functions. Instead they are complex *messages* with context-dependent parts that nibble away at the state. Each part transmits information to and from the state over the cable by its own protocols. There is no provision for applying general functions to the *whole* state and thereby making large changes in it. The possibility of large, powerful transformations of the state S by function application, $S \rightarrow f{:}S$, is in fact inconceivable in the von Neumann—cable and protocol—context: there could be no assurance that the new state $f{:}S$ would match the cable and its fixed protocols unless f is restricted to the tiny changes allowed by the cable in the first place.

We want a computing system whose semantics does not depend on a host of baroque protocols for communicating with the state, and we want to be able to make large transformations in the state by the application of general functions. AST systems provide one way of achieving these goals. Their semantics has two protocols for getting information from the state: (1) get from it the definition of a function to be applied, and (2) get the whole state itself. There is one protocol for changing the state: compute the new state by function application. Besides these communications with the state, AST semantics is applicative (i.e. FFP). It does not depend on state changes because the state does not change at all during a computation. Instead, the result of a computation is output *and* a new state. The structure of an AST state is slightly restricted by one of its protocols: It must be possible to identify a definition (i.e. cell) in it. Its structure—it is a sequence—is far simpler than that of the Algol state.

Thus the structure of AST systems avoids the complexity and restrictions of the von Neumann state (with its communications protocols) while achieving greater power and freedom in a radically different and simpler framework.

14.3 Structure of an AST System

An AST system is made up of three elements:

1) An *applicative subsystem* (such as an FFP system).

2) A *state* D that is the set of definitions of the applicative subsystem.

3) A set of *transition rules* that describe how inputs are transformed into outputs and how the state D is changed.

The programming language of an AST system is just that of its applicative subsystem. (From here on we shall assume that the latter is an FFP system.) Thus AST systems can use the FP programming style we have discussed. The applicative subsystem cannot change the state D and it does not change during the evaluation of an expression. A new state is computed along with output and replaces the old state when output is issued. (Recall that a set of definitions D is a sequence of cells; a cell name is the name of a defined function and its contents is the defining expression. Here, however, some cells may name data rather than functions; a data name n will be used in $\uparrow n$ (fetch n) whereas a function name will be used as an operator itself.)

We give below the transition rules for the elementary AST system we shall use for examples of programs. These are perhaps the simplest of many possible transition rules that could determine the behavior of a great variety of AST systems.

14.3.1 Transition rules for an elementary AST system. When the system receives an input x, it forms the application $(SYSTEM{:}x)$ and then proceeds to obtain its meaning in the FFP subsystem, using the current state D as the set of definitions. $SYSTEM$ is the distinguished name of a function defined in D (i.e. it is the "system program"). Normally the result is a pair

$\mu(SYSTEM:x) = <o,d>$

where o is the system output that results from input x and d becomes the new state D for the system's next input. Usually d will be a copy or partly changed copy of the old state. If $\mu(SYSTEM:x)$ is not a pair, the output is an error message and the state remains unchanged.

14.3.2 Transition rules: exception conditions and startup. Once an input has been accepted, our system will not accept another (except $<RESET,x>$, see below) until an output has been issued and the new state, if any, installed. The system will accept the input $<RESET,x>$ at any time. There are two cases: (a) If $SYSTEM$ is defined in the current state D, then the system aborts its current computation without altering D and treats x as a new normal input; (b) if $SYSTEM$ is not defined in D, then x is appended to D as its first element. (This ends the complete description of the transition rules for our elementary AST system.)

If $SYSTEM$ is defined in D it can always prevent any change in its own definition. If it is not defined, an ordinary input x will produce $\mu(SYSTEM:x) = \perp$ and the transition rules yield an error message and an unchanged state; on the other hand, the input $<RESET, <CELL,SYSTEM,s>>$ will define $SYSTEM$ to be s.

14.3.3 Program access to the state; the function $\rho\,DEFS$. Our FFP subsystem is required to have one new primitive function, defs, named $DEFS$ such that for any object $x \neq \perp$,

defs:$x = \rho DEFS:x = $ D

where D is the current state and set of definitions of the AST system. This function allows programs access to the whole state for any purpose, including the essential one of computing the successor state.

14.4 An Example of a System Program

The above description of our elementary AST system, plus the FFP subsystem and the FP primitives and functional forms of earlier sections, specify a complete history-sensitive computing system. Its input and output behavior is limited by its simple transition rules, but otherwise it is a powerful system once it is equipped with a suitable set of definitions. As an example of its use we shall describe a small system program, its installation, and operation.

Our example system program will handle queries and updates for a file it maintains, evaluate FFP expressions, run general user programs that do not damage the file or the state, and allow authorized users to change the set of definitions and the system program itself. All inputs it accepts will be of the form $<key,input>$ where key is a code that determines both the input class (*system-change, expression, program, query, update*) and also the identity of the user and his authority to use the system for the given input class. We shall not specify a format for key. *Input* is the input itself, of the class given by key.

14.4.1 General plan of the system program. The state D of our AST system will contain the definitions of all nonprimitive functions needed for the system program and for users' programs. (Each definition is in a cell of the sequence D.) In addition, there will be a cell in D named *FILE* with contents *file*, which the system maintains. We shall give FP definitions of functions and later show how to get them into the system in their FFP form. The transition rules make the input the operand of *SYSTEM*, but our plan is to use name-functions to refer to data, so the first thing we shall do with the input is to create two cells named *KEY* and *INPUT* with contents *key* and *input* and append these to D. This sequence of cells has one each for *key*, *input*, and *file*; it will be the operand of our main function called subsystem. Subsystem can then obtain *key* by applying $\uparrow KEY$ to its operand, etc. Thus the definition

Def system $\equiv$ pair $\to$ subsystem$\circ f$; $[\overline{NONPAIR}, \text{defs}]$

where

$f \equiv \downarrow INPUT \circ [2, \downarrow KEY \circ [1, \text{defs}]]$

causes the system to output *NONPAIR* and leave the state unchanged if the input is not a pair. Otherwise, if it is $<key,input>$, then

$f:<key,input> = <<CELL,INPUT,input>,$
$<CELL,KEY,key>, d_1, \dots, d_n>$

where D $= <d_1, \dots, d_n>$. (We might have constructed a different operand than the one above, one with just three cells, for *key*, *input*, and *file*. We did not do so because real programs, unlike subsystem, would contain many name functions referring to data in the state, and this "standard" construction of the operand would suffice then as well.)

14.4.2 The "subsystem" function. We now give the FP definition of the function subsystem, followed by brief explanations of its six cases and auxiliary functions.

Def subsystem $\equiv$
is-system-change$\circ\uparrow KEY \to$ [report-change, apply]$\circ[\uparrow INPUT, \text{defs}]$;
is-expression$\circ\uparrow KEY \to [\uparrow INPUT, \text{defs}]$;
is-program$\circ\uparrow KEY \to$ system-check$\circ$apply$\circ[\uparrow INPUT, \text{defs}]$;
is-query$\circ\uparrow KEY \to$ [query-response$\circ[\uparrow INPUT, \uparrow FILE]$, defs];
is-update$\circ\uparrow KEY \to$
[report-update, $\downarrow FILE\circ$[update, defs]]
$\circ[\uparrow INPUT, \uparrow FILE]$;
[report-error$\circ[\uparrow KEY,\uparrow INPUT]$, defs].

This subsystem has five "$p \to f$;" clauses and a final default function, for a total of six classes of inputs; the treatment of each class is given below. Recall that the *operand* of subsystem is a sequence of cells containing *key*, *input*, and *file* as well as all the defined functions of D, and that subsystem:*operand* $= <output,newstate>$.

Default inputs. In this case the result is given by the last (default) function of the definition when *key* does not satisfy any of the preceding clauses. The output is report-error: $<key,input>$. The state is unchanged since it is given by defs:*operand* $=$ D. (We leave to the reader's imagination what the function report-error will generate from its operand.)

System-change inputs. When

$$\text{is-system-change} \circ \uparrow KEY\text{:}operand =$$
$$\text{is-system-change:}key = T,$$

key specifies that the user is authorized to make a system change and that $input = \uparrow INPUT\text{:}operand$ represents a function f that is to be applied to D to produce the new state $f\text{:}D$. (Of course $f\text{:}D$ can be a useless new state; no constraints are placed on it.) The output is a report, namely report-change:$<input,\text{D}>$.

Expression inputs. When is-expression:$key = T$, the system understands that the output is to be the meaning of the FFP expression *input*; $\uparrow INPUT\text{:}operand$ produces it and it is evaluated, as are all expressions. The state is unchanged.

Program inputs and system self-protection. When is-program:$key = T$, both the output and new state are given by $(\rho input)\text{:}D = <output,newstate>$. If *newstate* contains *file* in suitable condition and the definitions of system and other protected functions, then
system-check: $<output,newstate> = <output,newstate>$.
Otherwise, system-check:$<output,newstate>$
$$= <error\text{-}report,\text{D}>.$$

Although *program* inputs can make major, possibly disastrous changes in the state when it produces *newstate*, system-check can use any criteria to either allow it to become the actual new state or to keep the old. A more sophisticated system-check might correct only prohibited changes in the state. Functions of this sort are possible because they can always access the old state for comparison with the new state-to-be and control what state transition will finally be allowed.

File query inputs. If is-query:$key = T$, the function query-response is designed to produce the output = answer to the query *input* from its operand $<input,file>$.

File update inputs. If is-update:$key = T$, *input* specifies a file transaction understood by the function update, which computes *updated-file* = update:$<input,file>$. Thus $\downarrow FILE$ has $<updated\text{-}file,\text{D}>$ as its operand and thus stores the updated file in the cell *FILE* in the new state. The rest of the state is unchanged. The function report-update generates the output from its operand $<input,file>$.

14.4.3 Installing the system program. We have described the function called system by some FP definitions (using auxiliary functions whose behavior is only indicated). Let us suppose that we have FP definitions for all the nonprimitive functions required. Then each definition can be converted to give the name and contents of a cell in D (of course this conversion itself would be done by a better system). The conversion is accomplished by changing each FP function name to its equivalent atom (e.g., update becomes *UPDATE*) and by replacing functional forms by sequences whose first member is the controlling function for the particular form. Thus $\downarrow FILE \circ [\text{update, defs}]$ is converted to

$$<COMP,<STORE,FILE>,$$
$$<CONS,UPDATE,DEFS>>,$$

and the FP function is the same as that represented by the FFP object, provided that update $\equiv \rho UPDATE$ and *COMP, STORE*, and *CONS* represent the controlling functions for composition, store, and construction.

All FP definitions needed for our system can be converted to cells as indicated above, giving a sequence D_0. We assume that the AST system has an empty state to start with, hence *SYSTEM* is not defined. We want to define *SYSTEM* initially so that it will install its next input as the state; having done so we can then input D_0 and all our definitions will be installed, including our program—system—itself. To accomplish this we enter our first input
$$<RESET, <CELL,SYSTEM,loader>>$$
where $loader \equiv <CONS, <CONST,DONE>,ID>$.
Then, by the transition rule for *RESET* when *SYSTEM* is undefined in D, the cell in our input is put at the head of $D = \phi$, thus defining $\rho SYSTEM \equiv \rho loader \equiv [\overline{DONE}, \text{id}]$. Our second input is D_0, the set of definitions we wish to become the state. The regular transition rule causes the AST system to evaluate
$\mu(SYSTEM\text{:}D_0) = [\overline{DONE}, \text{id}]\text{:}D_0 = <DONE,D_0>$. Thus the output from our second input is *DONE*, the new state is D_0, and $\rho SYSTEM$ is now our system program (which only accepts inputs of the form $<key,input>$).

Our next task is to load the file (we are given an initial value *file*). To load it we input a *program* into the newly installed system that contains *file* as a constant and stores it in the state; the input is
$<program\text{-}key, [\overline{DONE},store\text{-}file]>$ where

$$\rho store\text{-}file \equiv \downarrow FILE \circ [\overline{file}, \text{id}].$$

Program-key identifies $[\overline{DONE}, store\text{-}file]$ as a program to be applied to the state D_0 to give the output and new state D_1, which is:

$$\rho store\text{-}file\text{:}D_0 = \downarrow FILE \circ [\overline{file}, \text{id}]\text{:}D_0,$$

or D_0 with a cell containing *file* at its head. The output is $\overline{DONE}\text{:}D_0 = DONE$. We assume that system-check will pass $<DONE,D_1>$ unchanged. FP expressions have been used in the above in place of the FFP objects they denote, e.g. $\overline{DONE}$ for $<CONST,DONE>$.

14.4.4 Using the system. We have not said how the system's file, queries or updates are structured, so we cannot give a detailed example of file operations. However, the structure of subsystem shows clearly how the system's response to queries and updates depends on the functions query-response, update, and report-update.

Let us suppose that matrices m, n named M, and N are stored in D and that the function MM described earlier is defined in D. Then the input

$$<expression\text{-}key, (MM \circ [\uparrow M, \uparrow N] \circ DEFS\text{:}\#)>$$

would give the product of the two matrices as output and an unchanged state. *Expression-key* identifies the application as an expression to be evaluated and since defs:$\# = D$ and $[\uparrow M, \uparrow N]\text{:}D = <m,n>$, the value of the expression is the result MM:$<m,n>$, which is the output.

Our miniature system program has no provision for giving control to a user's program to process many inputs, but it would not be difficult to give it that capability while still monitoring the user's program with the option of taking control back.

14.5 Variants of AST Systems

A major extension of the AST systems suggested above would provide combining forms, "system forms," for building a new AST system from simpler, component AST systems. That is, a system form would take AST systems as parameters and generate a new AST system, just as a functional form takes functions as parameters and generates new functions. These system forms would have properties like those of functional forms and would become the "operations" of a useful "algebra of systems" in much the same way that functional forms are the "operations" of the algebra of programs. However, the problem of finding useful system forms is much more difficult, since they must handle *RESETS*, match inputs and outputs, and combine history-sensitive systems rather than fixed functions.

Moreover, the usefulness or need for system forms is less clear than that for functional forms. The latter are essential for building a great variety of functions from an initial primitive set, whereas, even without system forms, the facilities for building AST systems are already so rich that one could build virtually any system (with the general input and output properties allowed by the given AST scheme). Perhaps system forms would be useful for building systems with complex input and output arrangements.

14.6 Remarks About AST Systems

As I have tried to indicate above, there can be innumerable variations in the ingredients of an AST system—how it operates, how it deals with input and output, how and when it produces new states, and so on. In any case, a number of remarks apply to any reasonable AST system:

a) A state transition occurs once per major computation and can have useful mathematical properties. State transitions are not involved in the tiniest details of a computation as in conventional languages; thus the linguistic von Neumann bottleneck has been eliminated. No complex "cable" or protocols are needed to communicate with the state.

b) Programs are written in an applicative language that can accommodate a great range of changeable parts, parts whose power and flexibility exceed that of any von Neumann language so far. The word-at-a-time style is replaced by an applicative style; there is no division of programming into a world of expressions and a world of statements. Programs can be analyzed and optimized by an algebra of programs.

c) Since the state cannot change during the computation of system:x, there are no side effects. Thus independent applications can be evaluated in parallel.

d) By defining appropriate functions one can, I believe, introduce major new features at any time, using the same framework. Such features must be built into the framework of a von Neumann language. I have in mind such features as: "stores" with a great variety of naming systems, types and type checking, communicating parallel processes, nondeterminacy and Dijkstra's "guarded command" constructs [8], and improved methods for structured programming.

e) The framework of an AST system comprises the syntax and semantics of the underlying applicative system plus the system framework sketched above. By current standards, this is a tiny framework for a language and is the only fixed part of the system.

14.7 Naming Systems in AST and von Neumann Models

In an AST system, naming is accomplished by functions as indicated in Section 13.3.3. Many useful functions for altering and accessing a store can be defined (e.g. push, pop, purge, typed fetch, etc.). All these definitions and their associated naming systems can be introduced without altering the AST framework. Different kinds of "stores" (e.g., with "typed cells") with individual naming systems can be used in one program. A cell in one store may contain another entire store.

The important point about AST naming systems is that they utilize the functional nature of names (Reynolds' GEDANKEN [19] also does so to some extent within a von Neumann framework). Thus name functions can be composed and combined with other functions by functional forms. In contrast, functions and names in von Neumann languages are usually disjoint concepts and the function-like nature of names is almost totally concealed and useless, because a) names cannot be applied as functions; b) there are no general means to combine names with other names and functions; c) the objects to which name functions apply (stores) are not accessible as objects.

The failure of von Neumann languages to treat names as functions may be one of their more important weaknesses. In any case, the ability to use names as functions and stores as objects may turn out to be a useful and important programming concept, one which should be thoroughly explored.

15. Remarks About Computer Design

The dominance of von Neumann languages has left designers with few intellectual models for practical computer designs beyond variations of the von Neumann computer. Data flow models [1] [7] [13] are one alternative class of history-sensitive models. The substitution rules of lambda-calculus based languages present serious problems for the machine designer. Berkling [3] has developed a modified lambda calculus that has three kinds of applications and that makes renaming of variables unnecessary. He has developed a machine to evaluate expressions of this language. Further experience is needed to show how sound a basis this language is for an effective programming style and how efficient his machine can be.

Magó [15] has developed a novel applicative machine built from identical components (of two kinds). It evaluates, directly, FP-like and other applicative expressions from the bottom up. It has no von Neumann store and no address register, hence no bottleneck; it is capable of evaluating many applications in parallel; its built-in operations resemble FP operators more than von Neumann computer operations. It is the farthest departure from the von Neumann computer that I have seen.

There are numerous indications that the applicative style of programming can become more powerful than the von Neumann style. Therefore it is important for programmers to develop a new class of history-sensitive models of computing systems that embody such a style and avoid the inherent efficiency problems that seem to attach to lambda-calculus based systems. Only when these models and their applicative languages have proved their superiority over conventional languages will we have the economic basis to develop the new kind of computer that can best implement them. Only then, perhaps, will we be able to fully utilize large-scale integrated circuits in a computer design not limited by the von Neumann bottleneck.

16. Summary

The fifteen preceding sections of this paper can be summarized as follows.

Section 1. Conventional programming languages are large, complex, and inflexible. Their limited expressive power is inadequate to justify their size and cost.

Section 2. The models of computing systems that underlie programming languages fall roughly into three classes: (a) simple operational models (e.g., Turing machines), (b) applicative models (e.g., the lambda calculus), and (c) von Neumann models (e.g., conventional computers and programming languages). Each class of models has an important difficulty: The programs of class (a) are inscrutable; class (b) models cannot save information from one program to the next; class (c) models have unusable foundations and programs that are conceptually unhelpful.

Section 3. Von Neumann computers are built around a bottleneck: the word-at-a-time tube connecting the CPU and the store. Since a program must make its overall change in the store by pumping vast numbers of words back and forth through the von Neumann bottleneck, we have grown up with a style of programming that concerns itself with this word-at-a-time traffic through the bottleneck rather than with the larger conceptual units of our problems.

Section 4. Conventional languages are based on the programming style of the von Neumann computer. Thus variables = storage cells; assignment statements = fetching, storing, and arithmetic; control statements = jump and test instructions. The symbol ":=" is the linguistic von Neumann bottleneck. Programming in a conventional—von Neumann—language still concerns itself with the word-at-a-time traffic through this slightly more sophisticated bottleneck. Von Neumann languages also split programming into a world of expressions and a world of statements; the first of these is an orderly world, the second is a disorderly one, a world that structured programming has simplified somewhat, but without attacking the basic problems of the split itself and of the word-at-a-time style of conventional languages.

Section 5. This section compares a von Neumann program and a functional program for inner product. It illustrates a number of problems of the former and advantages of the latter: e.g., the von Neumann program is repetitive and word-at-a-time, works only for two vectors named a and b of a given length n, and can only be made general by use of a procedure declaration, which has complex semantics. The functional program is nonrepetitive, deals with vectors as units, is more hierarchically constructed, is completely general, and creates "housekeeping" operations by composing high-level housekeeping operators. It does not name its arguments, hence it requires no procedure declaration.

Section 6. A programming language comprises a framework plus some changeable parts. The framework of a von Neumann language requires that most features must be built into it; it can accommodate only limited changeable parts (e.g., user-defined procedures) because there must be detailed provisions in the "state" and its transition rules for all the needs of the changeable parts, as well as for all the features built into the framework. The reason the von Neumann framework is so inflexible is that its semantics is too closely coupled to the state: every detail of a computation changes the state.

Section 7. The changeable parts of von Neumann languages have little expressive power; this is why most of the language must be built into the framework. The lack of expressive power results from the inability of von Neumann languages to effectively use combining forms for building programs, which in turn results from the split between expressions and statements. Combining forms are at their best in expressions, but in von Neumann languages an expression can only produce a single word; hence expressive power in the world of expressions is mostly lost. A further obstacle to the use of combining forms is the elaborate use of naming conventions.

Section 8. APL is the first language not based on the lambda calculus that is not word-at-a-time and uses functional combining forms. But it still retains many of the problems of von Neumann languages.

Section 9. Von Neumann languages do not have useful properties for reasoning about programs. Axiomatic and denotational semantics are precise tools for describing and understanding conventional programs, but they only talk about them and cannot alter their ungainly properties. Unlike von Neumann languages, the language of ordinary algebra is suitable both for stating its laws and for transforming an equation into its solution, all within the "language."

Section 10. In a history-sensitive language, a program can affect the behavior of a subsequent one by changing some store which is saved by the system. Any such language requires some kind of state transition semantics. But it does not need semantics closely coupled to states in which the state changes with every detail of the computation. "Applicative state transition" (AST) systems are proposed as history-sensitive alternatives to von Neumann systems. These have: (a) loosely coupled state-transition semantics in which a transition occurs once per major computation; (b) simple states and transition rules; (c) an underlying applicative system with simple "reduction" semantics; and (d) a programming language and state transition rules both based on the underlying applicative system and its semantics. The next four sections describe the elements of this approach to non-von Neumann language and system design.

Section 11. A class of informal functional programming (FP) systems is described which use no variables. Each system is built from objects, functions, functional forms, and definitions. Functions map objects into objects. Functional forms combine existing functions to form new ones. This section lists examples of primitive functions and functional forms and gives sample programs. It discusses the limitations and advantages of FP systems.

Section 12. An "algebra of programs" is described whose variables range over the functions of an FP system and whose "operations" are the functional forms of the system. A list of some twenty-four laws of the algebra is followed by an example proving the equivalence of a nonrepetitive matrix multiplication program and a recursive one. The next subsection states the results of two "expansion theorems" that "solve" two classes of equations. These solutions express the "unknown" function in such equations as an infinite conditional expansion that constitutes a case-by-case description of its behavior and immediately gives the necessary and sufficient conditions for termination. These results are used to derive a "recursion theorem" and an "iteration theorem," which provide ready-made expansions for some moderately general and useful classes of "linear" equations. Examples of the use of these theorems treat: (a) correctness proofs for recursive and iterative factorial functions, and (b) a proof of equivalence of two iterative programs. A final example deals with a "quadratic" equation and proves that its solution is an idempotent function. The next subsection gives the proofs of the two expansion theorems.

The algebra associated with FP systems is compared with the corresponding algebras for the lambda calculus and other applicative systems. The comparison shows some advantages to be drawn from the severely restricted FP systems, as compared with the much more powerful classical systems. Questions are suggested about algorithmic reduction of functions to infinite expansions and about the use of the algebra in various "lazy evaluation" schemes.

Section 13. This section describes formal functional programming (FFP) systems that extend and make precise the behavior of FP systems. Their semantics are simpler than that of classical systems and can be shown to be consistent by a simple fixed-point argument.

Section 14. This section compares the structure of Algol with that of applicative state transition (AST) systems. It describes an AST system using an FFP system as its applicative subsystem. It describes the simple state and the transition rules for the system. A small self-protecting system program for the AST system is described, and how it can be installed and used for file maintenance and for running user programs. The section briefly discusses variants of AST systems and functional naming systems that can be defined and used within an AST system.

Section 15. This section briefly discusses work on applicative computer designs and the need to develop and test more practical models of applicative systems as the future basis for such designs.

Acknowledgments. In earlier work relating to this paper I have received much valuable help and many suggestions from Paul R. McJones and Barry K. Rosen. I have had a great deal of valuable help and feedback in preparing this paper. James N. Gray was exceedingly generous with his time and knowledge in reviewing the first draft. Stephen N. Zilles also gave it a careful reading. Both made many valuable suggestions and criticisms at this difficult stage. It is a pleasure to acknowledge my debt to them. I also had helpful discussions about the first draft with Ronald Fagin, Paul R. McJones, and James H. Morris, Jr. Fagin suggested a number of improvements in the proofs of theorems.

Since a large portion of the paper contains technical material, I asked two distinguished computer scientists to referee the third draft. David J. Gries and John C. Reynolds were kind enough to accept this burdensome task. Both gave me large, detailed sets of corrections and overall comments that resulted in many improvements, large and small, in this final version (which they have not had an opportunity to review). I am truly grateful for the generous time and care they devoted to reviewing this paper.

Finally, I also sent copies of the third draft to Gyula A. Magó, Peter Naur, and John H. Williams. They were kind enough to respond with a number of extremely helpful comments and corrections. Geoffrey A. Frank and Dave Tolle at the University of North Carolina reviewed Magó's copy and pointed out an important error in the definition of the semantic function of FFP systems. My grateful thanks go to all these kind people for their help.

References

1. Arvind, and Gostelow, K.P. A new interpreter for data flow schemas and its implications for computer architecture. Tech. Rep. No. 72, Dept. Comptr. Sci., U. of California, Irvine, Oct. 1975.
2. Backus, J. Programming language semantics and closed applicative languages. Conf. Record ACM Symp. on Principles of Programming Languages, Boston, Oct. 1973, 71–86.
3. Berkling, K.J. Reduction languages for reduction machines. Interner Bericht ISF-76-8, Gesellschaft für Mathematik und Datenverarbeitung MBH, Bonn, Sept. 1976.
4. Burge, W.H. *Recursive Programming Techniques.* Addison-Wesley, Reading, Mass., 1975.
5. Church, A. *The Calculi of Lambda-Conversion.* Princeton U. Press, Princeton, N.J., 1941.
6. Curry, H.B., and Feys, R. *Combinatory Logic, Vol. 1.* North-Holland Pub. Co., Amsterdam, 1958.
7. Dennis, J.B. First version of a data flow procedure language. Tech. Mem. No. 61, Lab. for Comptr. Sci., M.I.T., Cambridge, Mass., May 1973.
8. Dijkstra, E.W. *A Discipline of Programming.* Prentice-Hall, Englewood Cliffs, N.J., 1976.
9. Friedman, D.P., and Wise, D.S. CONS should not evaluate its arguments. In *Automata, Languages and Programming,* S. Michaelson and R. Milner, Eds., Edinburgh U. Press, Edinburgh, 1976, pp. 257–284.
10. Henderson, P., and Morris, J.H. Jr. A lazy evaluator. Conf. Record Third ACM Symp. on Principles of Programming Languages, Atlanta, Ga., Jan. 1976, pp. 95–103.
11. Hoare, C.A.R. An axiomatic basis for computer programming. *Comm. ACM 12,* 10 (Oct. 1969), 576–583.
12. Iverson, K. *A Programming Language.* Wiley, New York, 1962.
13. Kosinski, P. A data flow programming language. Rep. RC 4264, IBM T.J. Watson Research Ctr., Yorktown Heights, N.Y., March 1973.
14. Landin, P.J. The mechanical evaluation of expressions. *Computer J. 6,* 4 (1964), 308–320.
15. Magó, G.A. A network of microprocessors to execute reduction languages. To appear in *Int. J. Comptr. and Inform. Sci.*
16. Manna, Z., Ness, S., and Vuillemin, J. Inductive methods for proving properties of programs. *Comm. ACM 16,* 8 (Aug. 1973) 491–502.
17. McCarthy, J. Recursive functions of symbolic expressions and their computation by machine, Pt. 1. *Comm. ACM 3,* 4 (April 1960), 184–195.
18. McJones, P. A Church-Rosser property of closed applicative languages. Rep. RJ 1589, IBM Res. Lab., San Jose, Calif., May 1975.
19. Reynolds, J.C. GEDANKEN—a simple typeless language based on the principle of completeness and the reference concept. *Comm. ACM 13,* 5 (May 1970), 308–318.
20. Reynolds, J.C. Notes on a lattice-theoretic approach to the theory of computation. Dept. Syst. and Inform. Sci., Syracuse U., Syracuse, N.Y., 1972.
21. Scott, D. Outline of a mathematical theory of computation. Proc. 4th Princeton Conf. on Inform. Sci. and Syst., 1970.
22. Scott, D. Lattice-theoretic models for various type-free calculi. Proc. Fourth Int. Congress for Logic, Methodology, and the Philosophy of Science, Bucharest, 1972.
23. Scott, D., and Strachey, C. Towards a mathematical semantics for computer languages. Proc. Symp. on Comptrs. and Automata, Polytechnic Inst. of Brooklyn, 1971.

SOFTWARE—PRACTICE AND EXPERIENCE, VOL. 9, 31–49 (1979)

A New Implementation Technique for Applicative Languages

D. A. TURNER

Computer Laboratory, University of Kent, Canterbury CT2 7NF

SUMMARY

It is shown how by using results from combinatory logic an applicative language, such as LISP, can be translated into a form from which all bound variables have been removed. A machine is described which can efficiently execute the resulting code. This implementation is compared with a conventional interpreter and found to have a number of advantages. Of these the most important is that programs which exploit higher order functions to achieve great compactness of expression are executed much more efficiently.

KEY WORDS   Applicative languages   Combinators   Bracket abstraction   Normal graph reduction   Lazy evaluation   Substitution machine

INTRODUCTION

A ubiquitous feature of applicative languages is the presence of *bound variables*. These include formal parameters, like the n in the following definition of the factorial function

$$\mathbf{def}\ fac\ n =$$

$$n = 0 \to 1; \quad n \times fac\ (n-1)$$

and more simply local variables like the x in the following expression

$$(x+1) \times (x-1) \quad \mathbf{where}\ x = 7$$

(These and subsequent examples of applicative notation are written in SASL,[1] a more readable alternative to LISP used by the author for teaching purposes. The notation hopefully requires no explanation other than to remark that the construction '$A \to B; C$' means '**if** A **then** B **else** C'.)

Each bound variable has associated with it a region of text called its *scope* and within its scope the variable can be consistently replaced by any other variable, up to some rules about avoiding name clashes, without altering the meaning. Of course the use of bound variables is not confined to applicative languages but is a feature also of high level imperative languages with their procedures and block structure, though here we have the added complication that variables denote not values but locations whose contents can be altered by assignment statements.

As is well known the behaviour of bound variables can be explicated by associating with each region of the program text an *environment*[2] that is a function whose domain consists of the variables currently in scope and which associates with each such variable its current value (or in the case of an imperative language a location containing its current value). On entering a scope the environment is extended to include the variable bindings local to that scope, on leaving a scope the old environment is restored.

0038–0644/79/0109–0031$01.00

© 1979 by John Wiley & Sons, Ltd.

Received 5 December 1977

Aside from its use in defining the semantics of languages with bound variables, the 'environments' model can fairly be considered the basis of all the conventional methods of implementing this language feature. The apparently wide divergences between one implementation technique and another are largely due to the choice of different concrete data structures to represent the abstract data type 'environment'. The representation of the environment generally used in interpreters is a linked list of name-value pairs (an 'association list'), see for example Landin's SECD machine[2] and of course the standard LISP interpreter.[3] Another strategy, used by most Algol compilers, is to keep variables on the stack and represent the environment by a small data structure, the 'display',[4] which gives access to various reference points on the stack. These are the two commonest strategies though other variations occur.

A radically different method of dealing with bound variables is possible, however, at least for purely applicative languages (those without assignment or side effects) and it is this that we describe here. It does not derive from the 'environments' model at all but rather from a curious result in logic which shows that variables, as they are used in logic and ordinary mathematics are not strictly necessary.[5] Given a modest number of extra constants, called *combinators*, we can systematically translate whatever we have to say into a notation in which bound variables do not occur. This process of removing variables can be thought of as a kind of compilation and the resulting variable-free notation as a kind of object code. Although it is quite unreadable by human beings this code can be efficiently 'executed' by a machine of a very simple character. The author has found that it is possible along these lines to produce a viable implementation of an applicative language such as pure LISP (in fact SASL was used). It was found to be broadly comparable in speed and space utilization to a conventional interpreter using association lists but to have certain advantages.

A number of recent authors[10-12] have advocated that the semantics of applicative languages should be redefined so as to permit *non-strict functions*. (A non-strict function is one that can return an answer even if one of its arguments is undefined.) In a conventional implementation the necessary changes are found to bring about a slowdown in execution speed of up to an order of magnitude. The implementation technique described here, however, provides this behaviour quite naturally and without any extra cost. The second principal advantage is that the combinatory 'code' turns out to have some remarkable self-optimizing properties including that constant calculations are automatically moved outside loops and that the overhead cost of calling a user-defined function falls to zero after the first occasion of its use.

The remainder of the paper is organized as follows. In the first section we discuss the algorithm used for removing bound variables from the source text ('compiling'). In the second section we outline the strategy of the machine which executes the resulting code. Finally, in the third section we give some preliminary performance figures and discuss the properties of this kind of implementation. In order to make the article self-contained absolutely no technical knowledge of combinatory logic on the part of the reader has been assumed. The results developed in the first section are in fact well known and can be found in the standard text.[6]

REMOVING VARIABLES FROM THE SOURCE TEXT

We start by introducing a notion crucial to the whole plan—that of a higher order function. An ordinary function, say *sin*, returns for its result a number or similar simple object. But it is possible to conceive of a function which returns for its result another function.

The 'differentiate' operation of school calculus is a function of this kind, for example we might write

$$D \; sin = cos$$

showing that the (higher order) function D when applied to the argument sin returns for its result the function cos. Note the convention here that the application of a function to its argument is denoted simply by juxtaposition—we do not insist on enclosing the argument in brackets. We will further assume that juxtaposition associates to the left, so we can write, say

$$D \; sin \; 0 = 1$$

meaning

$$(D \; sin) \; 0 = 1, \quad \text{i.e. } cos \; 0 = 1$$

As an additional example of a higher order function consider the following definition of a function $plus$

$$plus \; x \; y = x + y$$

meaning that $plus$ can be applied to an argument, x say, and returns a function which when applied to an argument, y say, returns the sum of x and y. So

$$plus \; 2 \; 3 = 5$$

but it is read as '($plus$ 2) 3'. And '$plus$ 2' has a meaning in its own right—it is the function that adds two to things. (This device for reducing a first order function of several arguments to a higher order function of one argument is called *currying* after the logician H. B. Curry. Thus we would say that $plus$ is here a curried version of the $+$ operation.)

The basic algorithm

We are now ready to begin removing variables from the source text. The source is in the form of a series of messages from the user to the SASL system (the system is interactive). Each message is either an expression to be evaluated, in which case its value is printed immediately, or else it is a definition to be stored for latter use, like

$$\textbf{def} \; pi = 3 \cdot 141592$$

or like the definition of factorial given earlier.

To begin with a very simple example take the following definition of the successor function

$$\textbf{def} \; suc \; x = x + 1 \tag{1}$$

The aim is to eliminate the variable x obtaining a definition of the form

$$\textbf{def} \; suc = \ldots$$

where the right hand side is an expression containing only constants. The first step is to rewrite equation (1) using a curried version of the $+$ operator

$$\textbf{def} \; suc \; x = \textbf{plus} \; 1 \; x \tag{2}$$

Now we can remove x from both sides of the equation obtaining

$$\textbf{def} \; suc = \textbf{plus} \; 1 \tag{3}$$

which is an acceptable solution. (A good question is, why can we 'cancel' x in this way? The anwer is, because of the *principle of extensionality* which states that two functions f and g say, are equal if and only if: $f \; x = g \; x$ for all x.)

The step from equation (2) to equation (3) was very easy in this case because the variable to be removed from the body of the function occurred only once, at the extreme right. To handle the general case we need to borrow some technical results from combinatory logic. We take as the typical definition

$$\textbf{def}\, f\, x = \ldots \tag{4}$$

where ... is an expression built up from constants and the variable x using various operators. For a first step we replace all the operators by their curried versions, giving

$$\textbf{def}\, f\, x = E \tag{5}$$

where E is an expression in which functional application is the only operation (such an expression is called a *combination*). We can now write the solution as

$$\textbf{def}\, f = [x]\, E \tag{6}$$

where $[x]\, E$ denotes the result of a textual operation to be defined shortly, pronounced 'abstract x from E' and which removes all occurrences of x. For equation (6) to be a correct solution we require that

$$([x]\, E)\, x = E \quad \text{(law of abstraction)}$$

i.e. that abstraction be an exact inverse of application. We introduce three combinators, **S**, **K** and **I**, defined by the equations

$$\textbf{S}\, f\, g\, x = f\, x\, (g\, x) \tag{S}$$

$$\textbf{K}\, x\, y = x \tag{K}$$

$$\textbf{I}\, x = x \tag{I}$$

and define the abstraction operation as follows

$$[x]\, (E_1\, E_2) \Rightarrow \textbf{S}\, ([x]\, E_1)\, ([x]\, E_2)$$
$$[x]\, x \Rightarrow \textbf{I}$$
$$[x]\, y \Rightarrow \textbf{K}\, y$$

where y is a constant or a variable other than x. That abstraction thus defined obeys the law of abstraction given above can be proved by an induction on the size of the combination E—we leave this as an exercise for the interested reader.

This is the basic algorithm for removing variables but if used without modification it tends to produce rather long-winded 'code'. For the successor function we get

$$\textbf{def}\, suc = [x]\, (\textbf{plus}\, 1\, x)$$
$$\Rightarrow \textbf{S}\, ([x]\, (\textbf{plus}\, 1))\, ([x]\, x)$$
$$\Rightarrow \textbf{S}\, (\textbf{S}\, (\textbf{K}\, \textbf{plus})\, (\textbf{K}\, 1))\, \textbf{I}$$

which while perfectly correct (as the reader may confirm by applying the above expression to an arbitrary x and checking that the result simplifies, by the use of the equations (S), (K) and (I), to '**plus** $1\, x$') is much less compact than the '**plus** 1' which we obtained earlier.

To give one more example, from the definition of factorial given at the very beginning of this paper the basic algorithm yields the solution

$$\textbf{def}\, fac = \textbf{S}\, (\textbf{S}\, (\textbf{S}\, (\textbf{K}\, \textbf{cond})\, (\textbf{S}\, (\textbf{S}\, (\textbf{K}\, \textbf{eq})\, (\textbf{K}\, 0))\, \textbf{I}))$$
$$(\textbf{K}\, 1))\, (\textbf{S}\, (\textbf{S}\, (\textbf{K}\, \textbf{times})\, \textbf{I})\, (\textbf{S}\, (\textbf{K}\, fac)$$
$$(\textbf{S}\, (\textbf{S}\, (\textbf{K}\, \textbf{minus})\, \textbf{I})\, (\textbf{K}\, 1))))$$

where the constants **cond, eq, times** and **minus** are the curried versions of the conditional, $=$, $\times$ and $-$ operators respectively.

Improving the algorithm

To improve the performance of the algorithm we introduce the extra combinators **B** and **C**, defined by

$$\mathbf{B}\,f\,g\,x = f\,(g\,x)$$

$$\mathbf{C}\,f\,g\,x = f\,x\,g$$

and the optimizations (E_1 and E_2 stand for arbitrary combinations):

$$\mathbf{S}\,(\mathbf{K}\,E_1)\,(\mathbf{K}\,E_2) \Rightarrow \mathbf{K}\,(E_1\,E_2)$$

$$\mathbf{S}\,(\mathbf{K}\,E_1)\,\mathbf{I} \Rightarrow E_1$$

$$\mathbf{S}\,(\mathbf{K}\,E_1)\,E_2 \Rightarrow \mathbf{B}\,E_1\,E_2 \quad \text{if no earlier rule applies}$$

$$\mathbf{S}\,E_1\,(\mathbf{K}\,E_2) \Rightarrow \mathbf{C}\,E_1\,E_2 \quad \text{if no earlier rule applies}$$

(The interested reader can satisfy himself that the left and right hand sides of each of these rules are always equal by applying both sides to an arbitrary x and simplifying.)

The above rules recognize various special cases where the variable being abstracted is absent from one or more subexpressions. This brings about a considerable improvement in the quality of the code produced. The code above for *suc* reduces to **plus** 1 under the above rules and for *fac* we get the much shortened version

$$\mathbf{def}\,fac = \mathbf{S}\,(\mathbf{C}\,(\mathbf{B}\,\mathbf{cond}\,(\mathbf{eq}\,0))\,1)\,(\mathbf{S}\,\mathbf{times}\,(\mathbf{B}\,fac\,(\mathbf{C}\,\mathbf{minus}\,1)))$$

In the author's compiler these optimizations are incorporated as an integral part of the abstraction algorithm and the long-winded form of the code never comes into existence.

Up to now we have been assuming that we have to deal only with definitions of functions of one argument and with no local definitions in the body of the function. In fact the abstraction algorithm can be applied repeatedly to cope with more complex situations. In SASL functions of several arguments are normally defined as curried functions, for example

$$\mathbf{def}\,f\,x\,y = E$$

which would compile to

$$\mathbf{def}\,f = [x]\,([y]\,E)$$

where the inner abstraction must of course be performed first.

Local variables, introduced by a **where** clause as in

$$E_1 \quad \mathbf{where}\,x = E_2$$

are removed by transforming an expression of the above form to

$$([x]\,E_1)\,E_2$$

So for example the expression

$$(x+1)\times(x-1) \quad \mathbf{where}\,x = 7$$

would compile to

$$\mathbf{S}\,(\mathbf{B}\,\mathbf{times}\,(\mathbf{C}\,\mathbf{plus}\,1))\,(\mathbf{C}\,\mathbf{minus}\,1)\,7$$

This transformation is applied repeatedly to handle arbitrary nestings of **where** inside **where** and inside function bodies—as always inner abstractions are performed first.

Functions can be defined in **where** clauses also but this presents no new difficulties. For example

$$\ldots f \ldots \quad \textbf{where } f\, x = E$$

would compile to

$$([f]\ (\ldots f \ldots))\ ([x]\ E)$$

Data structures

Like LISP, SASL has only one method of data structuring namely a pairing operation. We represent this by an infix colon, thus

$$x : y$$

is the data structure whose head is x and whose tail is y; in LISP it would be written '(*cons x y*)'. As usual this operation can be cascaded to the right to form a linked list and a syntactic sugaring is provided for this. So, for example, a three list is written

$$a,\, b,\, c$$

which is taken as shorthand for

$$a : (b : (c : \textbf{nil}))$$

We introduce the combinator **P** as a curried version of the pairing operation and so the above expression compiles to

$$\textbf{P}\ a\ (\textbf{P}\ b\ (\textbf{P}\ c\ \textbf{nil}))$$

In SASL the explicit use of the selectors **hd** and **tl** is generally avoided by using colons and commas on the left of definitions instead. For example it is permitted to write

$$\textbf{def}\ a : b = x$$

The compiler treats this as equivalent to

$$\textbf{def}\ a = \textbf{hd}\ x$$

$$\textbf{def}\ b = \textbf{tl}\ x$$

It is permitted to write arbitrarily complicated 'templates' on the left of a definition in this way. Such templates can also occur on the left of **where** clauses and in formal parameter positions. To compile such constructions the author has introduced the new combinator **U** (for 'uncurry') defined by the equation

$$\textbf{U}\ f\ (x : y) = f\ x\ y$$

and has generalized the abstraction algorithm to permit abstraction with respect to a template. We define

$$[x : y]\ E$$

to mean

$$\textbf{U}\ ([x]\ ([y]\ E))$$

By recursive application of the above rule we can abstract with respect to an arbitrary template (we leave it to the reader to check that this extended definition of abstraction satisfies a suitably generalized version of the law of abstraction). So for example

$$E_1 \quad \textbf{where } a : b = E_2$$

compiles to

$$([a : b] \; E_1) \; E_2 \Rightarrow \mathbf{U} \; ([a] \; ([b] \; E_1)) \; E_2$$

and

$$\mathbf{def} \, f \, (x, \, y, \, z) = E$$

compiles to

$$\mathbf{def} \, f = [x, \, y, \, z] \; E$$
$$\Rightarrow [x : (y : (z : \mathbf{nil}))] \; E$$
$$\Rightarrow \mathbf{U} \; ([x] \; (\mathbf{U} \; ([y] \; (\mathbf{U} \; ([z] \; (\mathbf{K} \; E))))))$$

(A detail—in the actual implementation rather than **K** we would here use a combinator with a similar action but which checks that its second argument does in fact take the value **nil**.)

Assembling the code

Using the foregoing rules then, the compiler is able to transform each incoming expression into a pure combination and each incoming **def** definition into one or more definitions of the form

def *name* = *combination*

The combinations are stored as binary trees, with the nodes representing functional applications. At the leaves of the tree there will be constants (like 1 or **plus** or **S**). When an unbound variable occurs it is replaced by the combination with which it has been associated by a **def** definition, or it is so replaced as soon as such a definition is encountered. That is, outer level names (i.e. those defined by **def**) are handled by substituting their definitions as subtrees into the trees in which they occur. Subtrees are included by pointing not by copying, so combinations can share subtrees (since we have no assignment this is perfectly safe). A recursive definition will compile to a cyclic graph. For example, the definition of the factorial function given in the introduction will result in the name *fac* being associated with the graph shown in Figure 1. A subsequent request to evaluate, say *fac* 3, will compile to a tree whose left subtree is the structure shown in Figure 1 and whose right subtree is 3.

(This seems a suitable place to make a comment on the conventions used in diagrams such as that in Figure 1. Letters and numbers will sometimes be drawn inside cells as here and sometimes drawn outside with a pointer to them shown originating from a field of the cell. There is absolutely no logical significance in our using sometimes the one convention and sometimes the other—it is dictated purely by what is topologically convenient when drawing the diagram. Whether, say, numbers are actually stored immediately or stored elsewhere and pointed to, is a low level implementation detail depending on, for example, the word length of the computer, with which this article is not concerned.)

Local recursion

There is one further complication which the compiler must be able to handle—local recursion, as in

$$E_1 \quad \mathbf{where} \; x = \dots x \dots$$

This is transformed to

$$([x] \; E_1) \; (\mathbf{Y} \; ([x] \; (\dots x \dots)))$$

where **Y** is the fixpoint combinator, defined by the equation

$$\mathbf{Y} \, f = f \, (\mathbf{Y} \, f)$$

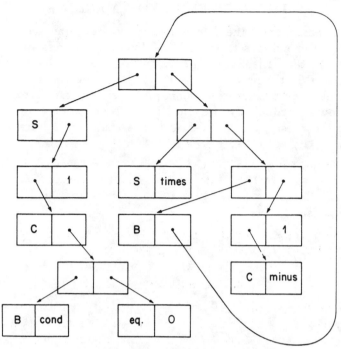

Figure 1. The code compiled for factorial

That is, for any function f, $\mathbf{Y} f$ is a fixed point of f. (See Burge[7] for further explanation of the use of $\mathbf{Y}$ in eliminating recursion.)

Mutual recursion following a **where** is handled by combining all the definitions following the **where** into a single definition with a complex left hand side and then proceeding as above. So for example

$$E_1 \quad \textbf{where } f\, x = \ldots g \ldots$$
$$g\, y = \ldots f \ldots$$

is first transformed to

$$E_1 \quad \textbf{where } f = [x]\, (\ldots g \ldots)$$
$$g = [y]\, (\ldots f \ldots)$$

eliminating the variables x and y. Now the mutually recursive pair of definitions can be converted into a single recursive definition as follows

$$E_1 \quad \textbf{where } (f,g) = ([x]\, (\ldots g \ldots), [y]\, (\ldots f \ldots))$$

which can be compiled as

$$([f,\, g]\, E_1)\, (\mathbf{Y}\, ([f,g]\, ([x]\, (\ldots g \ldots),\, [y]\, (\ldots f \ldots))))$$

using the rules already given.

In handling a moderately complicated definition then it is quite possible for the compiler to get a dozen or so levels deep in abstraction operations. In order that the code produced should continue to be reasonably compact under these circumstances it was found to be necessary to introduce some further optimizations into the abstraction algorithm. These take account of the way successive abstractions interact to bring about a considerable increase in the efficiency of nested abstraction. We omit the details here as they are fully described elsewhere.[8]

THE S–K REDUCTION MACHINE

Having described the action of the compiler we now pass to an account of the run time system. When the user submits to the SASL system an expression to be evaluated the compiler removes all the variables and passes to the run time system a binary graphical structure as described in the previous section. The run time system consists of a machine (currently implemented in software) which progressively transforms this structure by applying the following reduction rules until it has been reduced to a number or other printable object. (In these rules lower case letters stand for arbitrary structures unless otherwise specified.)

$$\mathbf{S}\, f\, g\, x \Rightarrow f\, x\, (g\, x)$$

$$\mathbf{K}\, x\, y \Rightarrow x$$

$$\mathbf{Y}\, h \Rightarrow \text{(see Figure 3)}$$

$$\mathbf{C}\, f\, g\, x \Rightarrow (f\, x)\, g$$

$$\mathbf{B}\, f\, g\, x \Rightarrow f\, (g\, x)$$

$$\mathbf{I}\, x \Rightarrow x$$

$$\mathbf{U}\, f\, (\mathbf{P}\, x\, y) \Rightarrow f\, x\, y$$

$$\mathbf{cond\ true}\, x\, y \Rightarrow x$$

$$\mathbf{cond\ false}\, x\, y \Rightarrow y$$

$$\mathbf{plus}\, m\, n \Rightarrow m+n \quad \text{where } m, n \text{ must already have been reduced to numbers.}$$

And similarly for **times**, **minus**, **divide**, etc. The name of the machine is taken from the first two rules.

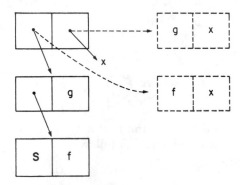

*Figure 2. The effect of an **S**-reduction. The dotted lines show the state after the reduction has been performed*

It should be understood that these reduction rules are implemented as graph-transformation rules, that is to say that a node which matches the left hand side of a rule is overwritten with the corresponding right hand side. By way of illustration the effect of the rule for **S** is shown in Figure 2.

One rule in particular, that for **Y**, takes advantage of the graphical representation in an essential way. The reduction rule for **Y** given in the textbooks is

$$\mathbf{Y}\, h \Rightarrow h\, (\mathbf{Y}\, h)$$

Applying this rule again to the **Y** in the resulting expression we get *h* (*h* (**Y** *h*)) and one can imagine obtaining after an infinite number of steps the infinite expression

$$h (h (h (\ldots)))$$

whose finite representation as a cyclic graph is shown in Figure 3. Our reduction rule for **Y** produces this form directly in one step, with a considerable gain in efficiency. (Note then that a recursive definition whether local or global always results in the construction of a cyclic graph.)

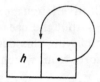

Figure 3. The result of reducing **Y** *h*

Before going on to discuss further details of the working of the machine it may be helpful to follow right through the processing of a simple example. Suppose the user types on his console as an expression to be evaluated

$$suc\ 2 \quad \textbf{where}\ suc\ x = 1 + x$$

First of all the compiler transforms this to

$$([suc]\ (suc\ 2))\ ([x]\ (1 + x))$$

thereby producing the code

$$\textbf{C I}\ 2\ (\textbf{plus}\ 1)$$

The reduction machine progressively transforms this to

I (**plus** 1) 2   using the **C**-rule

plus 1 2   using the **I**-rule

3   using the **plus**-rule

and the number 3 is then printed as the system's response to the user's request. The form of the compiled code and the first step in its reduction are shown in Figure 4.

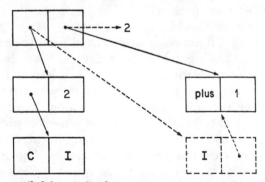

Figure 4. The code compiled for suc 2 **where** *suc x* = 1 + *x and the first step in its reduction*

Quite apart from the use of combinators this machine is unconventional in that its operation consists in the progressive transformation of the compiled code. This is a very different mode of operation from that of a conventional 'fixed program' machine in which the code is not normally altered once it has been compiled. In contrast we can call the kind of machine considered here a 'substitution machine' because it carries out literal substitutions on the compiled program. What is usually considered the principal objection to self-modifying code, namely that it is not re-entrant (i.e. cannot be shared between different uses) does not apply here because the transformations consist always in the replacement of an expression by another to which it is mathematically equivalent (for example, '**plus** 1 2' by '5').

Such a machine can be considered as a kind of *simplifier*, analogous to an algebraic simplifier. The program, in an applicative language, is an expression, which can be read as a mathematical description of the output the user desires to produce. The action of the machine consists in progressively simplifying this description, by applying rules known to preserve meaning, until it reaches a form from which the output can be printed directly.

Normal graph reduction

A major policy decision not yet touched on is the order in which the machine carries out the reductions, for in general more than one redex (redex = instance of the lhs of a rule) will be present at any given stage. We know on theoretical grounds that the final outcome of a reduction sequence is independent of the order in which the reduction rules are applied. One reduction sequence will differ from another, however, in the number of steps taken to reach the final outcome, including for certain initial expressions the possibility that one sequence will terminate while another fails to do so (for example, by getting stuck in a loop).

The ordering rule actually used is that at each stage we carry out reduction of the *leftmost* redex present. This is so called 'normal order reduction', which aside from being very simple and convenient to administer, as we shall see shortly, has the advantage that it is known to bring about termination whenever termination is possible. The other widely studied reduction regime is 'applicative order reduction' in which no redex is reduced until all redexes internal to it have been dealt with. To see that this terminates less often, suppose that a function which discards its argument and returns a constant answer (for example '**K** 2') is applied to a non-terminating sub-expression. Here evaluation will terminate under normal order but not under applicative order, where it will be attempted, in vain, to reduce the sub-expression completely before discarding it (i.e. normal order supports non-strict functions while applicative order does not).

Normal order reduction, it should be noted, means that in general an argument is substituted into the body of a function in unevaluated form (because initially the redexes inside the argument are to the right of other redexes). Mechanisms of this sort have a reputation for being inefficient on the grounds that they lead to repeated re-evaluation of the argument (cf Algol call by name). Here it is necessary to stress the importance of the fact that we are working with graphs. After the substitution all occurrences of the argument in the body of the function will be pointers to a shared sub-expression and all simultaneously 'feel the benefits' of any reductions carried out on the argument. So normal *graph* reduction, which is what we have here, combines the safety advantage of normal order (arguments are not evaluated needlessly) with the efficiency advantage of applicative order (arguments are evaluated at most once). See Wadsworth[9] for a fuller discussion of the properties of normal order reduction on graphs.

(It should be mentioned in passing that another possible reduction regime, with the same termination properties as normal order but a potentially enormous gain in speed, is at each stage to perform all available reductions *in parallel*. Foreseeable developments in computer hardware might make this or some suitable variant an attractive possibility, but we shall not pursue this possibility here.)

Controlling the sequence of reductions

To schedule the sequence of reductions in normal order we use a 'left ancestors stack' which initially contains only (a pointer to) the expression to be evaluated. So long as the expression at the front of the stack is an application we keep taking its *left* subtree (the function of the function–argument pair) and pushing that onto the stack also. Eventually we shall get an atom at the front of the stack. If it is a combinator we apply the appropriate reduction rule, using the pointers in the stack to gain efficient access to its arguments (the *n*th argument of the combinator will be the right subtree of the object *n* places behind it on the stack). In Figure 5 we show the state of the stack before and after applying the **C**-rule

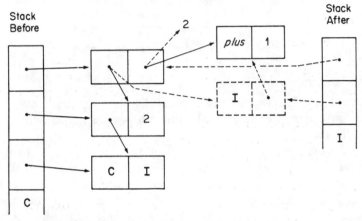

Figure 5. Behaviour of the stack during a reduction

of Figure 4 (stacks are drawn growing downwards). After applying a rule we resume stacking left components until we reach another atom. If the object at stack front is an arithmetic operator, say **plus**, we must call the reduction procedure recursively to reduce its arguments to numbers and then apply the appropriate rule. Note that the rules for **U** and **cond** also require reduction of one of their arguments before they can be used.

The sequence of reductions continues in this way, being controlled at each stage by the form of the expression at stack front, until eventually we have only one item left in the stack and that is a number or some other printable object. For brevity we have omitted from this account the possibility of an error arising such as that a combinator is found to have too few arguments or that an operator has arguments of the wrong type or that a non-function turns up as the leftmost item of a combination. Unless the compiler includes complete type-checking of the input text, which the author's currently does not, it is necessary to arrange to be able to detect such situations at run time and give appropriate error reports.

The user may submit for evaluation an expression whose value is a data structure (a list or a list of lists or whatever) instead of a number or a truthvalue or similar simple object. In this case the reduction algorithm will leave residing on the stack a representation of the data structure in which the components will not yet have been reduced. The printing routine prints the data structure from right to left, calling up the reduction algorithm to simplify each component before it is printed (and in case the component is itself a data structure this process will be recursive). So the whole process of normal graph reduction can be thought of as being driven by the need to print—nothing is evaluated until the printer requires to know its value.

Among the intriguing possibilities to which this gives rise is that the user can submit an infinite list to be printed, for example the list of all prime numbers as defined by the SASL expression shown in Figure 6. For a fuller discussion of this and other properties of normal order implementations of applicative languages see Turner.[12]

$$\textit{sieve (from 2)}$$
$$\textbf{where}$$
$$\textit{from } n = n\colon \textit{from } (n+1)$$
$$\textit{sieve } (p : x) = p\colon \textit{sieve (filter } x)$$
$$\qquad\qquad\textbf{where}$$
$$\qquad\textit{filter } (n : x) =$$
$$\qquad\qquad n \ \textbf{rem} \ p = 0 \to \textit{filter } x;$$
$$\qquad\qquad n\colon \textit{filter } x$$

Figure 6. The list of all the prime numbers

Storage allocation and indirection nodes

All the structures manipulated by the run-time system are built out of two-field cells which makes it convenient to use a LISP-style storage allocation scheme with markbits and a garbage collector.

Whenever a reduction rule is applied, it will be recalled, the node to which the rule is being applied is *overwritten* with the result. A problem arises if the result of applying the rule is either at atom or an already existing expression rather than a new node, as occurs for example when applying the rule for **K**. In the first case we have a problem because we have to overwrite a two-field cell with an object that can only occupy one field; in the second case we have a problem because if we overwrite the subject node with a copy of the top node of the result we shall destroy the sharing properties on which the efficiency of normal graph reduction depends.

The solution in both cases is to make the node into an *indirection node* with the identity combinator **I** in its left field and the result in question (an atom or a pointer to an existing expression) in its right field. On the stack of course we can leave the result itself rather than a pointer to the indirection node. Figure 7 shows by way of example the reduction of a redex of the form **K** x y.

In order to save space and time, pointers via indirection nodes are elided whenever they are encountered during processing. That is to say whenever we come across a field containing a pointer to a node of the form **I** x we overwrite the field with x. When all references to the indirection node have been bypassed in this way the space it occupies will of course be reclaimed by the garbage collector. It would also be possible to include a search for and elision of all pointers via indirection nodes during the mark phase of garbage collection.

As a final point on storage allocation it should be noted that the use of mark-scan garbage collection rather than a reference count technique is necessitated by the fact that the graphs which constitute the code are in general cyclic, because of the way we handle recursion. The occurrence of cycles could be avoided if all recursion (global as well as local) were done via the use of **Y** and if the reduction rule use for **Y** were

$$\mathbf{Y} \ h = h \ (\mathbf{Y} \ h)$$

rather than the 'knot-tying' rule shown in Figure 3. The graphs would then be and remain acyclic, permitting the use of reference count techniques of storage allocation. This would be, however, at the cost of a considerable loss of efficiency, especially in the implementation of global recursions.

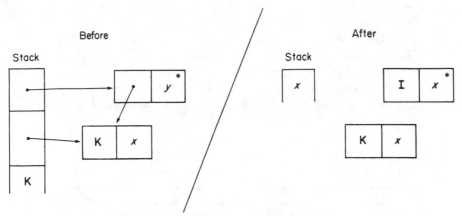

Figure 7. **K**-*reduction, note that the cell marked * becomes an indirection node*

RESULTS AND CONCLUSIONS

The compiler and the reduction machine described above have been implemented by the author and some measurements of performance taken, which we present in this section. An earlier implementation of the SASL language by means of a conventional interpreter using association lists was available for comparison.[13] The two implementations are written in different languages for different machines so there are a number of incidental differences between them. Any inferences from the relative performance of the implementations to the relative merits of the techniques are therefore tentative.

The first comparison made was in the compactness of the object code produced by the two compilers. The earlier implementation consists of an SECD machine together with a compiler for generating a suitable SECD machine-code. By way of illustration the code generated for the body of the factorial function (as defined in the introduction) is shown in Figure 8. Anyone familiar with SECD machines should find the code in Figure 8 self-explanatory—for details see Reference 13. Comparing this with the combinatory code shown for the same function in Figure 1 we see that the latter occupies 13 cells while the SECD code needs 24 cells, not counting the space occupied by the names '*n*' and '*fac*'.

This ratio seems fairly typical—the author finds that in general the combinatory form is about twice as compact as the SECD code, not counting the latter's extra storage require-ment for bound variables. Over several hundred lines of source the SECD compiler averaged 14 cells of object code per line of source, the combinatory compiler six cells per line (not counting space occupied by names in either case). It should be stressed that the optimizations for multiple abstraction described in Reference 9 proved essential to main-taining this degree of compactness.

Execution speed

The second comparison made was in the relative speeds of execution of the two object codes. A direct measurement of elapsed times would have been meaningless because of incidental differences between the implementations that would have greatly affected the

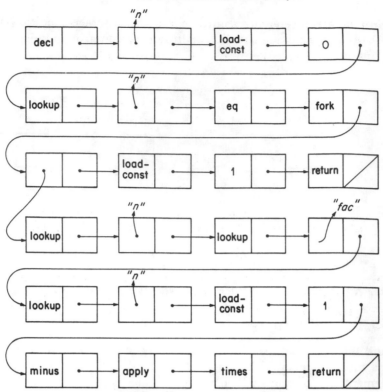

Figure 8. The SECD machine code for the body of factorial

(a) *hanoi 5 'a' 'b' 'c'*
     where
     hanoi n a b c =
         *n = 0 → **nil**;*
         hanoi (n−1) a c b,
         "move a disc from", a, "to", b, "\n",
         hanoi (n−1) c b a

(b) *for 1 10 line*
     where
     line n = "factorial", n, "is", fac n, "\n"
     for a b f =
         *a > b → **nil**;*
         f a: for (a+1) b f
     fac n =
         n = 0 → 1;
         n × fac (n−1)

(c) *twice twice twice suc 0*
     where
     twice f x = f (f x)
     suc x = x+1

Figure 9. Three test programs

timings, not least that they were running on different computers under different operating systems. One possible approximation to a machine independent measure of elapsed time is to count the number of 'steps' taken—i.e. SECD instructions in the one case and reductions performed in the other. Three sample programs are shown in Figure 9—(a) solves the

'Towers of Hanoi' problem with five disks, (b) prints a table of factorials and (c) is a calculation to test the use of higher order functions. Table I compares the number of steps in the execution of these test programs under the two implementations.

Table I. Number of steps

Program	SECD m/c	Reduction m/c
(a) Hanoi	1,488	3,067
(b) Factorials	975	1,280
(c) Twice	158	92

In general it seems to take the reduction machine rather more 'steps' to perform the same task, though this might be felt only to reflect the fact that the concept of a 'step' is here somewhat smaller.

Since both machines compose all their structures from two-field cells an arguably more comparable measure of 'work done' would be to count in each case the cumulative total of cells claimed from the store manager during execution (i.e. in LISP terms we are counting the total number of times CONS is called at run-time). The results for the same three test programs are shown in Table II.

Table II. Number of cells claimed during execution

Program	SECD m/c	Reduction m/c
(a) Hanoi	1,488	3,131
(b) Factorial	470	975
(c) Twice	128	65

In fact this measure can be seen to yield essentially the same results as those obtained by counting 'steps'. Notice that the relative cost of program (c), which is very dense in function calls, is much lower for the combinatory implementation—a point to which we shall return shortly.

We conclude then that the execution cost of programs is somewhat higher (perhaps by a factor of two) for the reduction machine than for the SECD machine (but for code dense in function calls the position is reversed).

A reservation must be made, however, on this comparison of execution costs. The reduction machine gives a *normal order* implementation, while the SECD machine gives an *applicative order* one. This means that the former implements a much more powerful version of the SASL language than the latter, for example in the ability to handle infinite data-structures. The SECD machine can be modified so that it also evaluates in (graphical) normal order. This is done by altering the parameter passing mechanism so that an actual parameter is passed as an unevaluated form (a 'suspension' containing pointers to the actual parameter expression and to the environment in which it is to be evaluated) and only later overwritten with its value if required.

Such a machine has been called 'procrastinating'[7] or 'lazy'.[10] We show in Table III the results of repeating the measurements of Table II on a 'lazy' version of the SECD machine coded by the author. We see that this modification slows the SECD machine down by *an order of magnitude*. Compared with a 'lazy' fixed program machine then, the **S K**-reduction machine is much superior in execution speed.

Table III. Number of cells claimed during execution

Program	SECD m/c	LAZY SECD m/c
(a) Hanoi	1,488	10,428
(b) Factorial	470	5,565
(c) Twice	128	1,206

Self-optimizing properties

In contrast to programs in a conventional 'fixed program' machine, programs in the **S K**-reduction machine exhibit a number of important self-optimizing properties. First consider the case of a function whose body contains a sub-expression not involving any parameters or local variables of the function. During the first call of the function which requires this sub-expression to be evaluated it will be *replaced* by its value. That is to say the code for the function is permanently modified to that which would have been compiled if the user had written a constant in place of this sub-expression. As a consequence a constant calculation inside a loop is performed only once, regardless of how many times the body of the loop is executed.

A second aspect of this self-optimization concerns the cost of introducing extra levels of functional abstraction into a program. Take the following definition of a function to sum the elements of a list

$$\textbf{def } sum\ x =$$
$$x = \textbf{nil} \to 0;\ \textbf{hd } x + sum\ (\textbf{tl } x)$$

This represents a commonly occurring pattern of recursion which can be captured in the following definition of a generic function for 'folding a list to the right'

$$\textbf{def } foldr\ op\ a = f$$
$$\textbf{where}$$
$$f\ x =$$
$$x = \textbf{nil} \to a;$$
$$op\ (\textbf{hd } x)\ (f\ (\textbf{tl } x))$$

Now *sum* can be defined succinctly as

$$\textbf{def } sum = foldr\ \textbf{plus}\ 0$$

and many other functions now lend themselves to compact definitions in terms of *foldr*, for example

$$\textbf{def } product = foldr\ \textbf{times}\ 1$$
$$\textbf{def } all = foldr\ \textbf{and true}$$
$$\textbf{def } some = foldr\ \textbf{or false}$$

It will readily be appreciated that a systematic policy of defining and using generic functions like *foldr* whenever there is a commonly occurring pattern of recursion leads to

4

a programming style of great compactness and elegance—see for example Burge.[7] Such a 'combinatory' programming style involves of course a combinatorial increase in the number of function calls implied during the execution of the program. For a typical function instead of being defined directly is expressed as the application of a generic function to some previously defined functions, all of which may themselves have 'combinatory' definitions and so on to perhaps a considerable depth.

Under a conventional implementation the overhead of all the extra function calls places a definite limit on the extent to which such techniques can be exploited without intolerable slowdown. With the implementation technique described here, however, the overhead disappears entirely. To take the example in question, the first time *sum* is called the expression for sum, namely *foldr* **plus** 0 is replaced by the code associated with *f* in the body of *foldr*, with **plus** and 0 substituted for *op* and *a*. That is it is replaced by exactly the same code as would have been compiled from the direct definition of *sum*. So for the second and subsequent calls of *sum* the overhead associated with the programmer's introduction of the extra abstraction *foldr* simply disappears.

This property of the new implementation means that the programmer can freely introduce extra layers of abstraction whenever they contribute to modularity or to conciseness of expression without any loss in speed of execution. Such abstractions simply 'expand themselves out' the first time they are used.

Such behaviour is not peculiar to the **S K**-reduction machine—it would be shown by any *substitution* (as opposed to *fixed-program*) machine. For example, we could simply desugar our functional notation to λ-calculus at the compilation stage and have a machine which performed beta-reductions on the resulting λ-expressions (see Wadsworth[9] for a normal graph reducer for the λ-calculus). This would display the same self-optimizing behaviour. The advantage special to the use of combinators is that the associated reduction rules are much simpler and can be performed much faster than beta-reductions.

Some drawbacks

Under some circumstances the use of a substitution machine can have undesirable consequences for space utilization. It can be that the 'expanded out' form of an expression is so large that it would be preferable (or even essential) to lose it after each use and take the time to recreate it afresh from the original expression if it is needed again. (This is of course what always happens in a fixed-program machine.) It would be possible to give the programmer some special syntax for marking areas of the source text where this behaviour was wanted. Such a machine-oriented feature, however, would sit most oddly in an otherwise very clean high level language.

John Hammond, of the University of Kent, has suggested to the author that this problem could be solved by having the machine automatically discard expanded out versions in favour of original code whenever it runs out of space, rather after the manner of throw-away compiling.[14] Such a machine could display a continuum of possible behaviours ranging from full self-optimization to conventional fixed-program, depending on the amount of space available. Clearly further investigation of this matter is required.

The other main difficulty with the present implementation is that run-time error reports are very opaque. Descriptions of the run-time state in terms of the configuration of combinators on the stack are quite unintelligible to users. The system keeps a record, however, of the association of user-coined names with combinations of combinators as established by the user's **def** definitions. By using this 'dictionary' backwards, it should be possible to translate the information on the stack back into intelligible high level language expressions.

Here also further investigation is obviously needed. In fact the requirement for good run-time diagnostics will become less pressing in the future, since it is intended to introduce complete compile time type checking of the SASL source. Almost all programs that now cause run-time errors will then draw compile time diagnostics.

ACKNOWLEDGEMENTS

The author would like to thank Peter Welch and John Hammond of the University of Kent for many valuable suggestions made during frequent discussions during the course of the above work, Peter Collinson of the University of Kent for invaluable assistance in negotiating the interface with the host operating system, and Anthony Davie and Michael Weatherill of the University of St. Andrews for taking measurements on the earlier implementations of SASL.

REFERENCES

1. D. A. Turner, *SASL Language Manual*, University of St. Andrews, 1976.
2. P. J. Landin, 'The mechanical evaluation of expressions', *Comput. J.* **6**, 308 (1963–4).
3. J. McCarthy *et al.*, *LISP 1.5 Programmers Manual*, M.I.T. Press, 1962.
4. B. Randell and L. J. Russell, *The Implementation of Algol 60*, Academic Press, 1964.
5. M. Schonfinkel, 'Uber die Bausteine der mathematischen Logik', *Math. Annalen*, **92**, 305 (1924).
6. H. B. Curry and R. Feys, *Combinatory Logic*, Vol. I, North Holland, 1958.
7. W. H. Burge, *Recursive Programming Techniques*, Addison–Wesley, 1975.
8. D. A. Turner, 'Another algorithm for bracket abstraction', to appear in *Journal of Symbolic Logic*.
9. C. P. Wadsworth, *Semantics and Pragmatics of the λ-calculus*, Chapter 4, Oxford University; *DPhil. Thesis*, 1971.
10. P. Henderson and J. M. Morris, *A lazy evaluator*, 3rd Symposium on Principles of Programming Languages, Altanta, 1976.
11. D. P. Friedman and D. S. Wise, *CONS should not evaluate its arguments*, 3rd int. colloq. Automata Languages and Programming, Edinburgh, 1976.
12. D. A. Turner, *Programming without Assignment* (to appear).
13. D. A. Turner, *An Implementation of SASL*, University of St. Andrews, Dept. of Comp. Science, Report TR/75/4.
14. P. J. Brown, 'Throw-away compiling', *Software—Practice and Experience*, **6**, 423–434 (1976).

7 The 'Language First' Approach

J. R. Kennaway and M. R. Sleep

7.1 MOTIVATION FOR CHANGE

Technology has advanced considerably since the first computers were built. Very Large Scale Integration (VLSI) techniques make it possible to produce huge numbers of single chip computers at low cost. In spite of such advances, the basic organizational principles on which computer design is based have remained largely static, with the following key features:

(1) sequential, centralized control of computation via a unique sequence control register.

(2) a centralized random access memory.

These 'von Neumann' features have served us well for over 30 years, particularly with the use of clever engineering ideas like pipelining, virtual memory, and Single Instruction Multiple Data (SIMD) extensions. These ideas, when carefully integrated and realized using the most advanced technology, have led to very powerful computers like the Cray and the ICL DAP. Before considering more novel forms of architecture, an obvious first question is: why not stick with von Neumann architectures?

The clearest motivation for re-examining the basic principles is sheer speed. Given VLSI technology, we can produce cheaply huge armies of chips to attack problems in parallel. Provided we can work out some way of organizing these chips to do the work required, we can 'buy speed' from VLSI. But - particularly if we wish to exploit a Multiple Instruction Multiple Data (MIMD) approach to parallelism - new organizational principles are needed.

A less obvious motivation is the software crisis. We want to produce high-quality software at reasonable cost. Backus [1] has argued that conventional languages are unnecessarily difficult to program in, and that many of the difficulties stem from a 'von Neumann' orientation of the languages concerned. The underlying concern of a conventional programmer is to guide a single locus of control through a cunningly designed maze of assignment, conditional and repetitive statements (ie the program). At each step the programmer has (perhaps quite unconsciously) as a major concern the details of *how* things are done rather than getting right *what* is done.

Because much of our civilization manages to stagger along using programs developed in this imperative style, it may be judged reasonably successful - at least for programming von Neumann machines with a single locus of control. Even here, however, the software crisis indicates there is something wrong with conventional languages and suggests we should examine alternatives. When 5th generation architectures [2] with perhaps thousands of chips working in parallel are considered, the prospect of programming each chip individually becomes unthinkable, and the case for a new approach which does not require the programmer to consider individual control loci in detail becomes overwhelming.

In this chapter and the next we present one view of the growing body of work on novel architectures for declarative languages. Such work is motivated by the following beliefs:

(1) Architecture should be language oriented.

(2) The most harmful feature of conventional languages after the *goto* statement is destructive assignment.

Reprinted from *Distributed Computing*, edited by F.R. Chambers, D.A. Duce, and G.P. Jones, 1984, pages 111-124. Copyright © 1984 by Academic Press, Inc. (London Ltd.)

(3) Declarative (zero assignment) languages not only facilitate the reading and writing of programs by people, but also enable automatic program transformation techniques [3].

(4) Banishing destructive assignment from the programmers vocabulary has the interesting side effect of making declarative programs naturally amenable to parallel execution. In particular, sub-expressions can be evaluated safely in parallel.

7.2 THE 'LANGUAGE-FIRST' APPROACH

Although the following quote from Dijkstra [4] is taken out of context, it neatly summarizes the general approach of novel architects: *It used to be the program's purpose to instruct our computers; it became the computer's purpose to execute our programs.*

The architects' starting point is now the language rather than some fiendishly clever engineering idea which takes no account of programmability. A possible disadvantage of this approach is that each language may lead to a quite individual architecture which is unsuited to other languages. In the event, just two families of declarative languages have been considered seriously by novel architects, the *lambda-based* languages, for example Burge's language [5], HOPE [6], SASL [7], FFP [1], ML [8] and VAL [9]; and the *logic-based* languages, for example Prolog [10]. Operationally, lambda-based languages require only simple (non-backtracking) pattern matching facilities and are therefore easier to support. Perhaps for this reason, and the fact that logic languages are fairly recent, the bulk of the work so far on novel architectures has focussed on lambda-based languages.

There are now signs that logic and lambda languages (and perhaps process-oriented languages too) can be integrated in a natural manner. While this does not simplify the problem, it does suggest that work on lambda-oriented architectures provides useful guidelines for parallel architectures which support more advanced languages.

7.2.1 An Example of Declarative Programming

Both logic and lambda languages are *declarative*. The most striking feature of these languages for a conventional programmer is the total absence of assignments as well as goto statements. Programming in a declarative language is much closer to writing a set of mathematical equations than conventional programming. Earlier chapters present excellent introductions to lambda and logic languages. Here we give only a simple example intended to highlight operational and architectural issues. We use SASL rather than HOPE because it illustrates nicely the lazy evaluation issue.

The problem we consider is a simplified form of the Hamming problem discussed in [4]. We want to generate and print in ascending order integers of the form $(2^i)*(3^j)$ where i and j range from 0 upwards.

Our basic approach is to write equations which define the required infinite list, which we will call ans. There are many equations which have the desired solution. Because we want to feed the equations to some machine which we expect to produce the answer, we must be careful to make sure our equations have a workable *procedural* (machine oriented) reading as well as the *declarative* (equational) reading.

In lambda languages, the procedural interpretation of equations is to regard them as rewrite rules which permit the machine to replace elements of an expression which match the left hand side of an equation with the corresponding right hand side.

For example, in order to define a function which accepts a (possibly infinite) list of integers, and returns a new list in which every element has been doubled, we may write in SASL:

```
DEF DoubleAll ( ) = ( )
    DoubleAll (h:t) = (2*h):(DoubleAll t)
```

The first equation says that given an empty list the result is also an empty list. The second equation deals with the more general case of a list with head h and a tail called t, using the infix ':' operator to represent the LISP constructor CONS. In procedural terms, the equation says that we can produce a doubled version of a list by doubling the first element and then applying the function DoubleAll to the tail. Given the list (1:(2:( ))) we can ask a SASL system to print a doubled version by typing:

DoubleAll (1:(2:( ))) ?

First, the SASL machine will see that the form as input cannot be printed because it is a function application. It now searches the 'database' of equations, and recognizes that the second equation can be used as a rewrite rule, matching h with 1 and t with the list (2:( )). This produces the revised form:

2:(DoubleAll (2:( )))

Because this is (in LISP terms) a CONS, the machine now attempts to print the head, and succeeds immediately because it is the integer 2, which is directly printable. The machine will now process the tail, whose form is currently:

(DoubleAll (2:( )))

After further deductions like those illustrated above, the system will print the required result and then stop. Notice that although the equations were written in terms of infinite lists, this does not present a problem because of the printer-driven nature of the SASL machine. It is perfectly possible (and very useful) to write equations which define real infinite objects in SASL. For example,

DEF PosInts = (from 1) WHERE from n = n:(from(n + 1))

defines the list of natural numbers. SASL progams written using this infinite list will of course use only part of it if they terminate.

Although we have interpreted the equations procedurally as rewrite rules, each operational step represents a change of *form* in keeping with the equations. Each change preserves the meaning. Because of this fact, unlike programmers, architectures for declarative languages may actually overwrite old forms with equivalent ones, using destructive assignment. This is the basis for *graph reduction* described in more detail below.

Returning to our problem, we can also define a function called TrebleAll which is similar to DoubleAll except that it uses 3 as a multiplier instead of 2. We can now write:

DoubleAns = DoubleAll(ans)
TrebleAns = TrebleAll(ans)

and observe that if we merge DoubleAns with TrebleAns we obtain (with some repetitions) ans with the first element (1) missing. This is the critical observation which allows us to solve the problem and write:

DEF ans = 1:(RemoveDups(Merge(DoubleAll(ans)),(TrebleAll(ans)))))
    WHERE
        DoubleAll ( ) = ( )
        DoubleAll (h:t) = (2*h):(DoubleAll(t))
        TrebleAll ( ) = ( )
        TrebleAll (h:t) = (3*h):(TrebleAll(t))
        Merge (( ),( )) = ( )
        Merge (x ,( )) = x
        Merge (( ), x) = x
        Merge (x , y) = IF head(x)<head(y)
            THEN head(x):(Merge((tail(x)),y))
            ELSE head(y):(Merge(x,(tail(y))))
            FI
        RemoveDups ( ) = ( )
        RemoveDups (h:(h:t)) = RemoveDups (h:t)
        RemoveDups (h:t) = h:(RemoveDups(t))

Having input these equations to a SASL system, we can ask for the whole (infinite) sequence to be printed, or select some finite portion using an appropriate function.

Note the use of pattern matching to define the auxiliary functions Merge and RemoveDups. The ordering of the equations for the different cases is significant, because the machine will try the cases in the order presented. In the interests of clarity, we have deviated slightly from real SASL syntax by using the IF.....FI form of conditional, and using the selectors head and tail which should really be hd and tl in runnable SASL.

The major points to note from this example are:

(1) Running a declarative program changes its *form* but never its *meaning*.

(2) The declarative programmer must have a good understanding of the procedural interpretation of the equations he writes if he is to produce good programs.

(3) The basic idea in declarative programming is to conceive of the result as some complex data structure, and then to devise defining equations which, besides their mathematical interpretation also have a machine oriented (procedural) interpretation.

(4) Printer-driven control of the use of equations as rewrite rules. This makes it possible to write equations involving infinite objects without necessarily producing non-termination.

Not all declarative languages have the final property, which perhaps emphasizes the fact that declarative languages, like conventional languages, require the programmer to think operationally. But the declarative framework constrains the programmer to a world in which *form* but not *meaning* can change. This means that if the equations are right, a wrong answer will never be produced, although termination may be affected. This property makes declarative programming much more like writing specifications than conventional programming. Resulting programs are much easier to read, write and prove. The new approach adds new problems, however. In particular, updating a single element of a huge data structure requires in principle a complete copy of the whole object, and clever implementation techniques are needed to deal with this.

7.2.2 The Design Process

For a given language, an idealized machine can be designed which defines operationally the semantics of the language. This *computational model* usually makes unrealistic assumptions - for example an idealized Algol machine supports arrays of unbounded size and no real computer can deal with this. The job of the computer architect is to devise a *physical model* which, within its limitations, behaves exactly like the computational model. The process of designing a language oriented architecture starts with the rather high level computational model and progressively refines it until it becomes physically realisable at which point it is a physical model. By the time this stage is reached, the set of programs which the model will deal with satisfactorily will be considerably smaller than the set of programs which the idealized computational model supports. Finally, the physical model is mapped onto existing technology using all the clever engineering ideas around to yield a *real machine*.

Given a single computational model, a huge number of differing physical models may be derived using the top-down methodology. The physical models may be distinguished both in performance terms (sheer speed) and also in terms of the restrictions placed on the programmer. A good physical model leads to real machines which run fast, and perhaps more important, do not unduly force the user to 'program round' their limitations.

No real architect uses a pure top-down methodology. In practice, there is a strong temptation to let 'efficient' instructions on the real machine find their way into a language implementation, often changing the language semantics dramatically. Thus 'real' LISPs support destructive assignment, and most language implementations provide 'hooks' which allow the user to get at a relatively naked form of the raw machine.

Novel architects are not immune from this bottom-up influence, especially if they support an active user community. But the novel architect feels guilty when he succumbs to such pressures, and asks the language designer for help.

7.3 DESIGN ISSUES FOR LAMBDA MACHINES

Because functional languages such as HOPE and SASL are based on the lambda calculus, the starting point for a 'top down' architect is the lambda calculus core of such languages. From this core we now develop some of the central architectural issues.

7.3.1 The Lambda Calculus

The following remarkably simple syntax captures the essence of all the classical functional languages:

$$E ::= \text{identifier}$$
$$\lambda \text{ identifier . E}$$
$$@ \ E \ E$$

The first production allows us to introduce names for objects, the second production gives the power of abstraction, and the third production expresses the application of one function to another. The (usually invisible) symbol @ is read APPLY. This very sparse notation is in fact very general, but we will follow [11] and use a richer notation which allows atoms representing constructors, integers, integer operations etc. in what follows. We will also use the conditional form of expression.

In most conventional languages, the function which triples its argument is (give or take minor syntactical details) written in the following form:

$$f(x) = x*3$$

In lambda languages, we write instead:

$$f = \lambda x. (x*3)$$

or without the infix sugar:

$$f = \lambda x. @ (@ * x) 3$$

This allows us to talk about f without worrying about naming its arguments. In particular, we can now write equations defining functions in which just one identifier appears on the left hand side. We 'call' functions in the lambda calculus by applying them to an argument, eg

$$@ f 5$$

will 'send' 5 to f, to produce the result 15 which - because it is exactly equivalent to the original expression - can replace it.

At first sight the lambda calculus with an explicit symbol for application looks rather horrid; for example $f(x) = 2*x + x/3$ turns into

$$\lambda x. (@ (@ + (@ (@ * 2) x) (@ (@ / x) 3)))$$

However, the unsugared (machine) form has advantages: in particular, functions which both accept and return functions may be defined. (@ * 2) is the function which doubles its argument. In general, the 'equal civil rights' property of the lambda calculus is a powerful mechanism for developing - in conventional terms - program forming programs, the advantages of which have been amply illustrated elsewhere [12].

Usable ('sugared') lambda languages allow the user to adopt conventional infix notation, to pre-name values of expressions using LET, and to post-name values using WHERE. Structured data types can be made available by adding a few built-in functions and constants. Programming in a pure lambda-based language can be done in a purely descriptive fashion: we imagine the output (presumably some complex data structure) and describe it in terms of the input, as illustrated in section **7.2.1**. Aside from the capability to write 'program forming programs' (which takes some practice), the most notable feature of programming in a lambda-based notation is the total absence of the assignment statement. This means, for example, that the usual 'loop counting' variables must be replaced by recursive calls. The reward is *referential transparency*: within its scope, any mention of an identifier denotes the same value *throughout the run of the program*. This key property makes life easier for both the human reader and the machine reader (e.g. some architecture expected to run the program).

7.3.2 From Semantics to Architectural Issues

The basic formal rule for evaluating lambda expressions is *beta-conversion*:

$$@ \, (\lambda x. \, E) \, F \;\; \rightarrow \;\; [x \leftarrow F] \, E$$

where the right hand side means (a copy of) the expression E with all free occurrences of x replaced by (a copy of) the expression F, possibly with name changes to avoid free variables in F being captured by abstractions in E. This rule appears simple to state, is incredibly powerful, but is very difficult to implement efficiently. It is also very ambiguous: in particular, given a large expression containing many reducible sub-expressions, *no evaluation order is specified*.

All usable lambda languages considerably extend the core syntax, for example by allowing arithmetic operators and numeric atoms. Although such extensions lead to many new reduction rules (e.g. $3*4 \rightarrow 12$) besides beta-conversion, there are two central issues in developing lambda-oriented architectures:

(1)   What evaluation order should we use?

(2)   How should beta conversion be done?

Very roughly, in conventional terms the questions are: (1) when should we evaluate parameters? and (2) how should parameters be passed? In the sections which follow we illustrate and discuss both issues.

7.3.2.1 Evaluation Order

In conventional (control flow) languages, the order in which statements are executed usually has a dramatic effect on the outcome. A major result of the lambda calculus (see e.g [5]) states (roughly) that the choice of order makes no difference to the value, although it may affect termination. Evaluation of a lambda expression proceeds by identifying one or more reducible sub-expressions (or *redexes*), and replacing them with equivalent, but simpler expressions using the reduction rules. This *reduction* process is repeated until there are no more redexes, when the expression is in *normal form*. For example, $((3*4)+(5*6))$ contains 2 redexes: $(3*4)$ and $(5*6)$. These may be reduced in any order (or in parallel) to 12 and 30 respectively. The original expression has now been reduced to the form $(12+30)$ which may be further reduced to the normal form 42. Essentially, *computation is viewed as controlled deduction* rather than a sequence of apparently meaningless state changes. This change of viewpoint is perhaps the most fundamental aspect of 'novel architecture' work.

It looks at first sight as if exploiting parallelism gains speed and loses nothing. Why not 'data drive' the computation so that all redexes are reduced in parallel? Unfortunately, an injudicious choice of evaluation order may have undesirable consequences:

(1)   it may lead to non-termination, most obviously when the two arms of a conditional statement are evaluated in parallel. Most interesting computations depend on conditional statements to prevent fruitless (and possibly infinite) computation.

(2)   however many chips are used, any real machine has a finite capacity for realizing parallelism. Once this limit is reached, further attempts to exploit parallelism simply clog up the system queues.

(3)   in a distributed architecture, the communication costs involved in distributing sub-expressions to other processing elements may outweigh the time saved.

Thus the choice of evaluation order affects performance in a marked manner, and the issues noted above provide a useful checklist for evaluating novel architectures. One attractive solution is to pass the buck to the user by introducing annotations to the language which he may use to specify the evaluation order, and perhaps the form (ranging from string to pointer) in which arguments are passed. This is reminiscent of pre virtual-memory days when every programmer worth his salt had his optimal overlay scheme for memory management. The alternative approach is to make the architecture take the decisions in a dynamic manner. This is the ideal approach, but it is much harder. At present, we cannot be sure that the distributed equivalent of virtual memory 'magic' will appear, and certainly annotations are useful in the short term.

7.3.2.2 Beta-conversion

Methods of implementing beta-conversion can be divided into several classes.

(i) String Reduction

Whenever a function is applied to an argument, a copy is made of the function body with a copy of the argument substituted for each occurrence of the formal parameter. Using an 'outermost first' evaluation order, the following expression:

$$
\text{f(sqrt(4)) WHERE f(x)} \quad = \qquad
\begin{aligned}
&\text{IF } x = 1\\
&\text{THEN h(x)}\\
&\text{ELSE g(x*5)}\\
&\text{FI}
\end{aligned}
$$

is beta-convertible to:

$$\text{IF sqrt(4)} = 1 \text{ THEN h(sqrt(4)) ELSE g(sqrt(4)*5) FI}$$

Here we have used *string reduction* to realize beta-conversion, making 3 complete copies of the argument. Because the new form is a conditional, and the argument occurs in both arms, one of the copies will certainly be thrown away. Further, because of the evaluation order, two evaluations of sqrt(4) are involved assuming both h and g force evaluation of their arguments.

For this reason, systems using string reduction generally evaluate expressions in applicative order, reducing arguments to normal form before supplying them to functions. This loses the software engineering advantages of being able to handle infinite data structures in a uniform way. It is interesting to note that HOPE [6] though having predominantly applicative order semantics, includes a non-strict list-constructor for precisely this purpose. Furthermore, some functions - such as conditional, mentioned above - should not be evaluated with applicative order.

(ii) Graph Reduction

We can save much of the unnecessary work of string reduction by copying *pointers* to sub-expressions rather than the full text. This *graph-reduction* approach is described in detail for the pure lambda-calculus in [13]. The basic idea is that the current form of the expression being evaluated is stored not as a string or a parse-tree, but as a graph, in which common subexpressions may be shared. As an example, the expression

$$\text{IF sqrt(4)} = 1 \text{ THEN h(sqrt(4)) ELSE g(sqrt(4)*5) FI}$$

might be represented in graphical form as in **Figure 7-1**, where the subexpression sqrt(4), which occurs three times in the linear representation, occurs but once in the graph, with three references to it.

To perform the beta reduction of an expression @ (λx.f) g (where f and g are expression graphs) we make a new copy of f in which all occurrences of the formal parameter x are replaced, not by copies of g, but by pointers to g. Notice that we cannot simply substitute pointers to g for x in f itself, as there may be other references to f. We must 'peel off' a new copy to make the substitution in.

The great advantage of this method is that when g is eventually evaluated, every reference to g will have the benefit of the work performed. g will be evaluated at most once, however many times its value is needed. And if we perform reductions in normal order, then if the value of g is never needed it will never be evaluated at all. Thus we obtain normal order semantics without the overhead of multiple evaluation which we saw for string reduction.

This method may still require some unnecessary copying. Whenever a function is applied, we must peel off a copy of its body. Some of this can be avoided. Any subexpressions of the body in which the formal parameter does not occur need not be copied, but can be shared between the original and all peeled off copies. It is not clear, however, that the cost of storing the information necessary to recognize these subexpressions does not outweigh the benefits gained. Another possibility is that if there are no references to the function body other than through one particular application of it (and a reference counting scheme could be used to recognize this) then substitution for the formal parameter can be done in the original, without copying. But in general there may be substan-

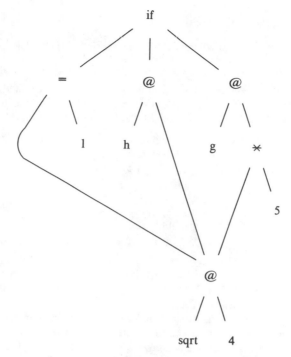

Figure 7-1

tial parts of the function body which a graph reducer cannot avoid copying, and which (because they lie on unselected arms of conditionals) may be thrown away.

(iii) Environmental Schemes

Moving from string to graph reduction involves being progressively lazier about making copies, in the sense that we copy pointers instead of strings of arbitrary length. The standard *environmental* scheme for realizing beta-substitution takes this process to its logical conclusion by doing no copying at all. Instead, beta-substitution is simply 'remembered' by adding an (identifier,expression) pair to an *environment*. In the example above, the pair would be (x,sqrt(4)). When the identifier x is needed for further evaluation, (e.g. in the conditional test x=1) it is looked up in the environment, and future lookups can share the benefit of forced evaluation if we take some care in the implementation.

At first sight, the environmental scheme wins hands down because copying is never done unless it is needed. In this sense, it is a purely *demand-driven* scheme. On closer examination, however, the picture is not so clear:

(1) The basic drawback of the environmental mechanism is that in order to understand an expression fully the environment in which it was created must be consulted. In a correct implementation which supports functions which can accept and return functions, this means that each expression must contain at least a reference to the environment in which it was created. In a simple-minded environmental scheme, in which every beta-conversion is remembered, a considerable amount of excess baggage may be accumulated in the form of environmental entries which will never be consulted. Schemes which minimize excess baggage tend to destroy the basic point of the environmental approach by complicating the remembering process.

(2) Even if the excess baggage problem can be cured, efficient lookup mechanisms are needed. The larger the environment, the higher the cost of entry and lookup. In an expression with a huge environment and many free occurrences of a variable x, it might be cheaper to perform the lookup once and distribute copies (possibly as pointers) rather than do many lookups.

(3) In a highly parallel machine access to the environment acts as a bottleneck.

270

(iv) Lazy Graph Reduction and Combinators

The newest approach to beta-substitution is to use *lazy* graph reduction. In Wadsworth's original scheme [13] every beta substitution involved a 'full peel' of a copy of the original graph. It would be better to only do the copying in response to the demands of the rest of the computation. One method of achieving this is to introduce environments, though in a way rather different to the previous section. When we encounter a beta-redex @ (λx.f) g, we merely replace it with the pair (f,{x=g}), where {x=g} is the environment which associates x with g. Such a pair is called a *closure*. We then continue by attempting to evaluate f. If we discover further redexes, we reduce them. But if we find an occurrence of x whose value we need before proceeding further, then we 'push' the environment {x=g} down through f to that occurrence of x, peeling off a copy only of the path traversed. At the end of the path we substitute for x a pointer to g, and continue looking for the next redex to reduce. In general, when we find a redex we reduce it; when we find a variable we look for the closure where it is defined and peel off a copy of the path from that closure down to the variable.

The evaluation method we have just described can be programmed directly. Another way of obtaining lazy graph copying is by the use of *director strings* [14]. We examine the program at compile time and translate it into a variable-free form which replaces a tree consisting of interior nodes and leaf nodes which mention variables by a tree of interior *director* nodes which will switch incoming arguments to exactly the places specified by the variables. The 'switches' encode the information in the variables, which may now be replaced by anonymous holes which notionally wait to be filled by the switching process.

For example, the expression:

f(5) WHERE f(x) = 2*x + x*(3*4)

may be replaced by the tree shown in **Figure 7-2**.

The *distribution sub-tree* for x has been marked with double lines: it indicates that in order to evaluate the expression, the argument 5 may (in this case will) have to be sent both left and right at the uppermost + node in the tree, and that this + node should distribute copies both right and left. Copies (string or pointer) now arrive at the * nodes in the diagram, to be further distributed right (by the leftmost * node) and left (by the rightmost * node). Intuitively, we imagine the incoming value for x being distributed to

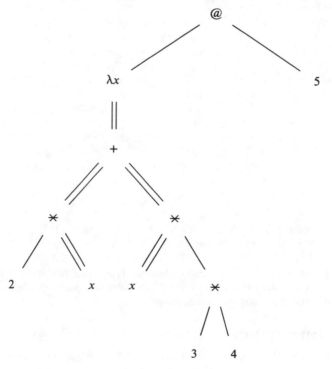

Figure 7-2

just the places it is needed in the expression via the distribution sub-tree. An obvious encoding for distribution sub-trees is to tag each *apply* with a *director* from the set $(\wedge, \backslash, /)$ representing the distribution instructions 'send both ways, send right, send left' respectively. Multiple abstractions produce strings of directors. Using this idea, **Figure 7-2** translates to the variable-free form shown in **Figure 7-3**, where the boxes represent 'holes' for the missing argument values. The directors guide an argument to just the places required in an expression, in a number of small steps *which may be realized concurrently* when 'both-ways' directors are involved. Conditional expressions effectively represent directors which are determined dynamically, switching an argument left or right depending on whether the condition is true or false. Director strings provide a simpler means of obtaining lazy graph copying than the environmental scheme, but at the cost of some loss of flexibility of reduction order.

The practicability of this technique was first suggested by Turner [7] who introduced the S1, B1, and C1 *combinators* (switches) which closely correspond to the three directors. A fuller description of the director approach is available in [14, 15].

7.3.2.3 Choice of computational model

It would be nice if the architect could select a preferred evaluation order and a scheme for beta-substitution in the secure knowledge that the decisions are independent. Unfortunately, this is not the case. For example, selection of outermost (lazy) evaluation favours some pointer scheme (graph reduction, lazy graph reduction or environment) as against string reduction to reduce the amount of copying. In general, string reduction is only practicable for innermost (eager) evaluators.

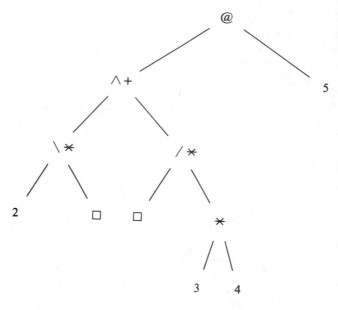

Figure 7-3

To complicate matters further, use of 'lazy' evaluation [16] (which corresponds to outermost evaluation) extends significantly the class of programs which terminate: in particular, the programmer can define his output using functions which operate on 'folded up' versions of infinite lists. Because this is an extremely useful tool in the programmer's kit, the expressive power of the language adds another dimension to the problem of choosing a computational model.

7.4 THE IMPORTANCE OF THEORY

In the last section, we saw that the choice of evaluation order and method for beta substitution are not independent. This suggests that we may be working at too high a level.

Lazy beta substitution breaks a single potentially large beta substitution into a number of bounded operations, and allows the evaluator to order these so as to optimize some measure of performance.

Although some theoretical results have emerged from recent U.K. work in this area, notably on the space complexity of translation to combinator form [17, 18] a powerful theoretical handle on the basic pragmatic issues is needed.

The recent work of Staples may provide such a handle. In a series of papers [19, 20, 21] Staples develops a general theory of optimal reduction orders in graph rewriting systems, of which lambda calculus with beta reduction, combinators, and directors are examples. In particular he develops a key requirement of the 'basic reductions' provided by a machine which ensures that there exists a simple optimal reduction order. For 'pure' combinators and directors (i.e. without any built-in operators such as addition, multiplication, etc.) this optimal order is just the leftmost-outermost ordering. When arithmetic operators are added this algorithm only has to be augmented with 'demand forking' at such operators. In [22] he develops a form of lambda-calculus in which beta-reduction is broken down into small steps in a way similar to the environmental scheme of section 7.3.2.2(iii). For this system too, leftmost-outermost reduction is optimal.

Because Staples' work applies to any 'reduction' machine, it provides important clues to the designers of novel architectures. More generally, it illustrates the importance of theory in a new and exciting area.

7.5 REFERENCES

1. J. Backus, "Can Programming be liberated from the von Neumann style?," *Comm. ACM* **21**(8) (1978).

2. Uchida, "Towards A New Generation Computer Architecture," ICOT report TR/A-001, Tokyo (July 1982).

3. R.M. Burstall and J. Darlington, "A transformation system for developing recursive programs," *JACM* **24**(1) (Jan.1977).

4. E.W. Dijkstra, *A Discipline of Programming.*, Prentice-Hall. (1976).

5. W.H. Burge, *Recursive Programming Techniques,* Addison-Wesley (1975).

6. R.M. Burstall, D.B. MacQueen, and D.T. Sannella, "HOPE: An Experimental Applicative Language," Internal Report CSR-62-80, University of Edinburgh, Department of Computer Science (1980).

7. D.A. Turner, "A New Implementation Technique for Applicative Languages," *Software, Practice and Experience* **9**(1) (1979).

8. M.J. Gordon, A.J. Milner, and C.P. Wadsworth, "Edinburgh LCF.," *Lecture Notes in Computer Science*, Springer-Verlag. (1979).

9. W.B. Ackerman and J.B. Dennis, "VAL - Preliminary Reference Manual," Report TR-218., MIT Lab. for Computer Science (1979).

10. W.F. Clocksin and C.S. Mellish, *Programming in Prolog,* Springer Verlag (1981).

11. P.J. Landin, "The next 700 programming languages.," *Comm.ACM* **9**(3, 157-166) (1966).

12. D.A. Turner, "The Semantic Elegance of Applicative Languages.," *Proc. ACM Conf. on Functional Programming Languages and Computer Architectures*, New Hampshire (Oct. 1981).

13. C.P. Wadsworth, *Semantics and Pragmatics of the Lambda Calculus; D.Phil. thesis,* Univ. of Oxford (1971).

14. J.R. Kennaway and M.R. Sleep, *Director Strings as Combinators.,* University of East Anglia. (1982).

15. E.W. Dijkstra, "A Mild Variant of Combinatory Logic.," EWD735. (1980).

16. P. Henderson and J.M. Morris, "A Lazy Evaluator.," *3rd. Symp. on the Principles of Programming Languages*, Atlanta (Jan. 1976).

17. F.W. Burton, "A linear space translation of functional programs to Turner combinators," *Inf. Proc. Letters* **14**(5), pp.201-204 (1982).

18. J.R. Kennaway and M.R. Sleep, *Efficiency of counting director strings,* University of East Anglia (1983).

19. J. Staples, "Optimal reductions in replacement systems," *Bull. Austral. Math. Soc.* **16**, pp.341-349 (1977).

20. J. Staples, "Computation on graph-like expressions," *Th. Comp. Sci.* **10**, pp.171-185 (1980).

21. J. Staples, "Optimal evaluations of graph-like expressions," *Th. Comp. Sci.* **11**, pp.39-47 (1980).

22. J. Staples, "A graph-like lambda calculus for which leftmost-outermost reduction is optimal," *Lecture Notes in Computer Science* **73**, Springer-Verlag (1978).

Chapter 6: Sequential Reduction Machines

Background

Conventional computer languages and conventional computer architectures have grown up side by side and are more suited to one another than functional languages and conventional architectures. There has been no similar development of computer architectures for evaluating functional language programs. Attempts to bridge this gap with software have produced functional language programs that use a computer's resources inefficiently, and fail to realize the level of performance that should be possible for an application. The papers in this chapter show that execution of functional programming languages can be made efficient if appropriate support is provided. These simple sequential processors for functional programming provide an evolutionary path from von Neumann architectures to parallel dataflow and reduction architectures of the future. Both of the papers in this chapter show that hardware implementation of these processors is considerably simpler than that of conventional architectures, and increase in execution speed is possible. This kind of architecture model closely resembles the conventional reduced instruction set computers. The nature of computation makes it possible to extend these architectures for parallel computation.

Article Summary

Stoye describes SKIM II, an efficient implementation of Turner's combinator reduction machine. SKIM I was the first graph reduction machine built that performed combinator reduction as described by Turner in Chapter 5. SKIM I is also described in Chapter 1 by Treleaven et al. The combinators are microcoded. Execution is performed by traversing down the leftmost branch of the program tree to find an operator at the leaf. During the traversal, the pointers are reversed so that they lead from leaf to root. When the operator is reached, it is executed, and pointers are then used to access the arguments to the operator. SKIM II overcomes some of the inefficiencies of SKIM I and explores implementation issues for recursion, garbage collection, equating equal structures, and compiling complex operation into microcode.

Kieburtz, in "The G-Machine," describes an implementation of the architecture of a reduction machine that uses supercombinators (programmable combinators) [8]. The *G-machine* is an abstract model for evaluating functional language programs. The abstract model was defined by Johnsson and Augustsson [2,9] as an evaluation model for a compiler for a dialect of ML [13] (a functional programming language) called Lazy ML (LML). The abstract model represents an expression as a graph and through successive transformations, or *reductions*, modifies the graph until its form is that of a fully evaluated result. Hence, the model is called *graph-reduction*, and the architecture is called the G-machine (graph-reduction machine). This G-machine implementation is a pipelined von Neumann architecture that provides support for evaluation of functional language programs by programmed graph reduction that is specified by a sequence of instructions derived by compiling an applicative expression. This is different from *combinator reduction* [17], where control is derived dynamically from the expression graph.

Additional material can be found in references 1, 3-7, 10-12, 14-16.

References

[1] Athas, W.C., "A VLSI Combinator Reduction Engine," *CS Dept. Document No. 5086: Technical Report 83*, California Institute of Technology, Pasadena, Calif., June 1983.

[2] Augustsson, L., "A Compiler for Lazy ML," *Proc. ACM Symp. on LISP and Functional Programming*, Association for Computing Machinery, Inc., New York, N.Y., Aug. 1984, pp. 218-227.

[3] Berkling, K., "Experiences with Integrating Parts of the GMD Reduction Language Machine," *VLSI Architecture*, Prentice-Hall, Old Tappan, N.J., 1983, pp. 381-394.

[4] Berkling, K., "Epsilon-Reduction: Another View of Unification," *Fifth Generation Computer Architectures*, edited by J.V. Woods, Elsevier Science Publishers B.V., Amsterdam, The Netherlands, 1986, pp. 163-176.

[5] Cardelli, L., "The Amber Machine," *Combinator and Functional Programming Languages*, Springer-Verlag, New York, N.Y., 1985, pp. 48-70.

[6] Clarke, T., Gladstone, P.J.S., Maclean, C.D., and Norman, A.C., "SKIM—The S,K,I Reduction Machine," *Proc. ACM Symp. on LISP and Functional*

Programming, Association for Computing Machinery, Inc., New York, N.Y., 1980, pp. 128-135.

[7] Cousineau, G., Curien, P.L., and Mauny, M., "The Categorical Abstract Machine," *IFIP Conference on Functional Programming Lang. and Computer Arch.*, North-Holland Publishing Co., Amsterdam, The Netherlands, Sept. 1985, pp. 50-64.

[8] Hughes, R.J.M., "Super-Combinators," *Proc. ACM Symp. on LISP and Functional Programming*, Association for Computing Machinery, Inc., New York, N.Y., 1982, pp. 1-10.

[9] Johnsson, T., "Efficient Compilation of Lazy Evaluation," *Proc. of 1984 ACM SIGPLAN Notices Conf. on Compiler Constr.*, Association for Computing Machinery, Inc., New York, N.Y., June 1984, pp. 58-69.

[10] Jones, S.L.P., "An Investigation of the Relative Efficiencies of Combinators and Lamda Expressions," *Proc. ACM Symp. on LISP and Functional Programming*, Association for Computing Machinery, Inc., New York, N.Y., 1982, pp. 150-158.

[11] Jones, N.D. and Muchnick, S.S., "A Fixed Program Machine for Combinator Expression Evaluation," *Proc. ACM Symp. on LISP and Functional Programming*, Association for Computing Machinery, Inc., New York, N.Y., Aug. 1982, pp. 11-20.

[12] Knight, T., "An Architecture for Mostly Functional Languages," *Proc. ACM Symp. on LISP and Functional Programming*, Association for Computing Machinery, Inc., New York, N.Y., Aug. 1986, pp. 105-112.

[13] Milner, R., "A Proposal for Standard ML," *Proc. ACM Symp. on LISP and Functional Programming*, Association for Computing Machinery, Inc., New York, N.Y., 1984, pp. 184-197.

[14] Ramsdell, J.R., "The Curry Chip," *Proc. ACM Symp. on LISP and Functional Programming*, Association for Computing Machinery, Inc., New York, N.Y., 1986, pp. 122-131.

[15] Scheevel, M., "NORMA: A Graph Reduction Processor," *Proc. ACM Symp. on LISP and Functional Programming*, Association for Computing Machinery, Inc., New York, N.Y., 1986, pp. 212-219.

[16] Thakkar, S.S. and Hostmann, W.B., "An Instruction Fetch Unit for Graph Reduction Machine," *Proc. 13th Ann. Int'l. Symp. on Computer Architecture*, Computer Society of the IEEE Press, Washington, D.C., 1986, pp. 82-91.

[17] Turner, D.A., "A New Implementation Technique for Applicative Languages," *Software Experience and Practice*, Vol. 9, 1979, pp. 31-49.

Some Practical Methods for Rapid Combinator Reduction

W. R. Stoye, T. J. W. Clarke and A. C. Norman

University of Cambridge Computer Laboratory

Abstract

The SKIM II processor is a microcoded hardware machine for the rapid evaluation of functional languages. This paper gives details of some of the more novel methods employed by SKIM II, and resulting performance measurements. The authors conclude that combinator reduction can still form the basis for the efficient implementation of a functional language.

Introduction

The SKIM I processor was designed and built here at Cambridge several years ago [Clarke 80]. It is a microcoded machine for the reduction of combinators [Turner 79], and it has been a great success as such.

A successor to it, SKIM II, has now been constructed. At first SKIM II was microcoded to reduce combinators in much the same way as SKIM I, but since then its speed of computation has been improved by about fifty percent by careful remicrocoding. This involved several new methods and algorithms, which are the subject of this paper.

The authors' conclusion is that there is still considerable room for improvement in the implementation of functional languages, because they are sufficiently far removed from a hardware-dominated model of computation that the implementor has great freedom in the choice of evaluation methods.

The following subjects will be covered:
the elimination of recursion in the evaluator
one bit reference counts on the heap
equating identical structures transparently
compilation of complex operations into microcode

Little will be said about SKIM II's hardware except that it is a simple, microcoded machine fairly similar to SKIM I. A description can be found in [Stoye 83]. The main improvements are a larger address space, the allocation of more tag bits to each word, and microcode in RAM. SKIM I was an experimental hardware device, SKIM II is in contrast a stable basis for software experimentation.

The Elimination of Recursion

A new scheme is presented for the elimination of recursion from a combinator evaluator when dealing with strict functions.

Turner's original scheme for combinator reduction is that expressions should be represented as graphs, with function application denoted by head linked lists of binary cells. For example, the expression

plus a b

would be represented as shown in diagram 1. Note that the 'application' pointers shown in this diagram are distinguishable from data pointers, so that a cell containing a and b represents 'b applied to a' rather than 'a pair with a on the left and b on the right'. Fundamental functions like 'plus' are represented by objects known as combinators. Turner's algorithm for evaluating this object was to follow the chain of application pointers in the head sides of cells, pushing onto a stack the addresses of cells past. When a combinator object (like plus) is reached at the extreme left hand end, a jump is performed in the reducer to code specific to that combinator.

"Some Practical Methods for Rapid Combinator Reduction" by W.R. Stoye, T.J.W. Clarke, and A.C. Norman from *Conference Record of the 1984 ACM LISP and Functional Programming Languages*, August 6-8, 1984, pages 159-166. Copyright 1984, Association for Computing Machinery, Inc.

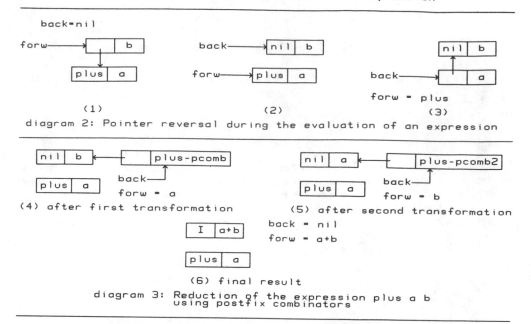

plus a b

diagram 1: graph representation of an expression

diagram 2: Pointer reversal during the evaluation of an expression

(1)

(2)

(3)

forw = plus

(4) after first transformation

back
forw = a

(5) after second transformation

back
forw = b

back = nil
forw = a+b

(6) final result

diagram 3: Reduction of the expression plus a b using postfix combinators

The code for plus, to continue this example, would check on the stack that it had two arguments, call the evaluator recursively on each of its arguments (they should both evaluate to be integer objects in this case), add their values together and overwrite the top cell in the diagram with the new value. This overwriting has to occur because there might be other application pointers to this fragment of the graph, and it is an important principle of lazy evaluation that no computation should be performed twice.

Note that plus is a 'strict' combinator in that it has to evaluate its arguments. Other combinators (like S and K) do not have to do this, but in practice many of the combinators evaluated are strict ones.

There are two uses for a stack in this process, one to record the sequence of cells passed when traversing the left hand sides and another associated with the need to evaluate the arguments of some functions before performing the function itself. Both version of SKIM use pointer reversal to cope with the first of these. Two registers are used when evaluating called 'forw' and 'back', to hold the expression being evaluated and the list of reversed pointers. To evaluate an expression forw is initialised to point to the graph representing the expression and a null value is placed in back. Evaluation proceeds as shown in diagram 2.

At this point evaluation continues at the code specific to the plus combinator. The combinator has to re-reverse the pointers in order to find its arguments, and so that the tree is left in a tidy state after the reduction. On SKIM II pointer reversing performance is enhanced through the use of read-modify-write memory access cycles so that fetching the forward pointer and writing the backward pointer occur in one memory cycle.

SKIM I uses a stack for the implementation of strict combinators, when the evaluator is called recursively to evaluate the arguments. This stack is implemented as a list of cells on the heap, mainly because there is no hardware support for anything else.

SKIM II extends the idea of pointer reversal to deal with strict arguments. This is reminiscent of the pointer reversal in Deutch-Schorr-Waite garbage collection [Schorr 67], where both left and right subtrees of a cell must be marked without using any extra storage. We continue the pointer reversal process when evaluating the arguments a and b, leaving a special marker in the back chain saying where to continue computation of the suspended 'plus' operation. The first part of the code for plus reforms the graph to look like state (4), shown in diagram 3. The (plus a) cell has to be left unchanged, in case there are other pointers to it. A new cell has been generated, which sits on the back chain and contains a special marker which is designated plus-pcomb in the diagram.

This marker is called a postfix-combinator or pcomb and it contains an entrypoint to the reducer, just like a normal combinator. Evaluation now continues, and the argument a becomes fully evaluated.

When the **forw** register contains an object that is fully evaluated, the reducer looks at the backward pointer. If it contains the null value, evaluation is complete. If not, the chain of pointers that it represents will be re-reversed until a cell is found with a postfix-combinator in its tail. A jump will occur in the reducer to the code represented by this pcomb.

In this way the first argument has been 'recursively' evaluated with a minimum of state-saving in the evaluator. There is now no data structure involved in evaluation except the expression graph itself, which fits in well with the reduction paradigm that SKIM is designed to support. The further evaluation of plus in fact involves a second pcomb, because the evaluator has to be 'reentered' again for the evaluation of b, but this is merely a repetition of the above process.

There have been two main benefits from the implementation of this algorithm, the first being a performance improvement of about ten percent overall due to reduced state-saving in evaluating strict combinators. The second is that the reducer has a very small amount of internal state, and is in fact simpler than the first version of the microcode, which used a stack. This proved a great advantage when adapting SKIM's microcode to provide a multi-tasking model of parallel reduction [Stoye 84]. The combinator expression graph in SKIM's main memory is reduced at many places 'simultaneously', to simulate the operation of a machine with many processors, and it is very important that this should not cause incorrect interactions when several processes try to reduce the same expression graph at the same time. Keeping all state information as part of a single graph structure has helped us concentrate on the interlocks that are required. The effect of having multiple physical processors involved in this operation has not yet been considered by us in detail.

It might be argued that better performance would be obtained from SKIM by the addition of a separate hardware stack, which could be used to remember the arguments of any suspended operations. But this would add substantially to the complexity of SKIM's hardware, and would have made multi-tasking more complicated, while better performance improvements could probably be gained by a simple associative cache on the main memory.

One Bit Reference Counts

One problem with combinator reduction is that the use of heap storage seems profligate. The process of reduction involves the continuous use of heap cells, and although SKIM's memory structure is carefully optimised to allow rapid marking during garbage collection it was found to be spending more than half of its time in the garbage collector when memory was only one third full. Most cells are only in use for a very short time, and then discarded.

Reference counting is often suggested as a replacement for or an addition to garbage collection, but the bookkeeping overheads concerned with doing it for very small scale objects are considerable. Every time a pointer to an object is copied the object has to be accessed and its reference count incremented and written back. As it is necessary to cope with increment overflow this can be an absurdly complex operation, so that although most storage may be reclaimed computation would proceed overall at a slower rate.

SKIM uses reference counts in a way that speeds up computation even for calculations that do not provoke garbage collection, as well as reducing garbage collection. This is done by maintaining one bit reference counts <u>in pointers</u> rather than in objects.

The method is that any application pointer is identifiable as being either a 'multiple application pointer' or a 'unique application pointer' (**mappl** and **uappl**). Use of a **mappl** is synonymous with the conventional meaning of an application pointer, but use of a **uappl** has the additional meaning that 'there are no other pointers to this cell'. Thus, if a **uappl** pointer is being discarded then the cell that it designates is known to be free and can be given back to the memory allocator (ie placed at the head of the freechain).

If an object is being copied, there is no need to access it under this scheme. If the copied object is a **uappl** then it must be changed to a **mappl**, but this is a very simple operation and does not take very long. It is not useful to have more than two states, because the increment operation would have to change all other pointers to the object and that is clearly not possible.

This can speed up computation when reducing combinators, because new cells are frequently needed just as old ones become available, so that overheads associated with freechain maintenance are reduced. As an example, consider the S combinator which performs the following action:

$$S\ a\ b\ c = a\ c\ (b\ c)$$

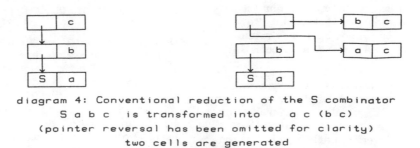

diagram 4: Conventional reduction of the S combinator
S a b c   is transformed into   a c (b c)
(pointer reversal has been omitted for clarity)
two cells are generated

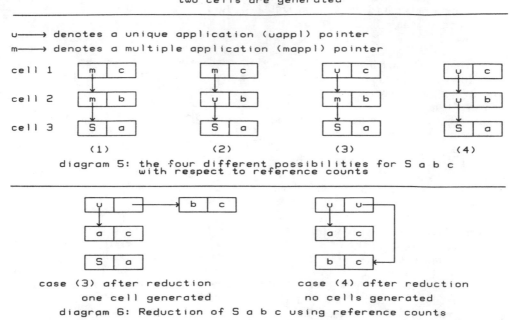

u———▶ denotes a unique application (uappl) pointer

m———▶ denotes a multiple application (mappl) pointer

cell 1   cell 2   cell 3

(1)   (2)   (3)   (4)

diagram 5: the four different possibilities for S a b c
with respect to reference counts

case (3) after reduction
one cell generated

case (4) after reduction
no cells generated

diagram 6: Reduction of S a b c using reference counts

In terms of graph structures this is represented by the transformation shown in diagram 4. Note that the original cells have to be left, <u>in case</u> there are other pointers to the middle of this structure. Two new cells have been generated, and the value 'c' copied without being evaluated.

In terms of uappls and mappls, there are four forms in which this expression may appear, depending on the two pointers in it. These are shown in diagram 5.

When cases one and two are encountered, the reduction method is unchanged. In case 3, cell 2 will not be accessible after the reduction and so can be reused. In case 4, cells 2 and 3 can both be reused, which is very convenient as we were just about to generate two new cells. By not giving the inaccessible cells back to the space allocator, but reusing them straight away, the reduction of this combinator will proceed faster. After the reduction, cases (3) and (4) will appear as shown in diagram 6.

Deciding which of these cases to use happens while picking up the arguments, and works very neatly. Although the amount of microcode for each combinator is increased because of the number of different cases to prepare for, in practice <u>most</u>

reductions salvage some space in this way. The S combinator has an additional complication in that it duplicates its third argument, so if 'c' is a uappl it must be changed to a mappl. Some other combinators (like plus) have free cells that they cannot immediately use, these are placed on the freechain.

The results of applying this technique have been spectacular - on average, about seventy percent of wasted cells are immediately reclaimed. Detailed timings were made for two small computations. The first is defined by

tak x y z =   If   y >= x
              Then z
              Else   tak (tak (x - 1, y, z),
                          tak (y - 1, z, x),
                          tak (z - 1, x, y));

tak 18 12 6
   (the answer should be 7)

This test is called Takeuchi's function and has been used on a number of Lisp systems as a crude benchmark. The second computation is the sorting of 2000 numbers, using a very simple minded sort program that divides its input into two lists of

test name	free memory (K nodes)	microcode version 1		microcode version 2		microcode version 3	
		secs	GC's	secs	GC's	secs	GC's
tak	125	16	12	15	5	13	4
	105	16	13	15	6	14	6
	75	18	14	17	9	14	7
	45	29	32	20	15	19	12
	15	82	96	38	41	36	38
sort	125	23	18	21	6	17	5
	105	25	22	21	7	18	6
	75	32	32	23	9	19	8
	45	48	58	27	17	23	15

table 1: Speed improvements for reference counts and recursion removal

equal length, recursively sorts the two sublists and then does a binary merge. The time spent is almost independent of what the numbers are. The results are shown in table 1.

The table shows measurements for three different versions of microcode, running with varying amounts of free memory. The machine has a total of about 130,000 cells of heap. For each run the total time t in seconds and the number g of garbage collections was recorded. Version 1 microcode did no reference counting and used recursion to evaluate strict functions, version 2 microcode did reference counting, version 3 also used pointer reversal instead of recursion for strict functions. As the figures show, performance degredation with memory full is dramatically reduced when using reference counts.

It is important to note that the wasted cells saved by this technique form a different set to those saved by eliminating redundant laziness [Mycroft 81]. Compiled code using this technique is slightly more complex (but not unmanageably so) and would benefit considerably.

At the moment this technique has only been implemented on application pairs, but there is no reason why it should not be used on data pairs too. Indeed, it could be useful in any heap storage system.

Equating Equal Structures

One frequently used combinator compares two data structures recursively for equality and returns a boolean value, like the Lisp function EQUAL. The implementation on SKIM has a secret side effect, that if the objects are equal their space is commoned up. This not only saves space, it speeds up future comparisons of the same objects.

This would not be possible in a Lisp system, because future use of RPLACA and RPLACD would cause chaos. There is also the more subtle possibility that future use of EQ would generate a misleading reply. Optimisations like this can be performed safely on a functional machine because there are no side effects to consider, and because there are no functions whose semantics are based on the conventional view of computer memory. It would be perfectly legitimate to common up equal objects or expressions wherever they are found, and this has a number of possibilities for further optimisation.

In idle time there is no reason why the machine should not scan over the heap and common up any equal structures that it finds. Although no measurements have been done, we estimate that combinator expressions could be reduced to about half their previous size by commoning up equal parts. This is becuase of the very small number of distinct combinators. It would be very interesting to implement Hashcons [Goto 74] on SKIM, as many of the conventional arguments against it for Lisp systems do not apply, but this has not yet been done. The saving of space would provide a considerable performance boost, and structure comparison would always be instantaneous.

Another operation that could be performed in any idle time is the reduction of any combinators that have enough arguments to be reduced, and whose reduction would not increase the size of the resulting expression. This limitation, or perhaps a less severe one, is needed to prevent store being filled with unwanted expansions of expressions.

```
combinators
    length              7000 per second
    reverse             7000 per second
    append              7000 per second
    equal               1650 per second
    nfib benchmark      8000 per second

hand compiled
    length            220000 per second   (*30 speedup)
    reverse           120000 per second   (*18 speedup)
    append             30000 per second   (* 6 speedup)
    equal              20000 per second   (*13 speedup)
    tak               tak 18 12 6 in 1.5 seconds
    nfib               90000 per second
```

table 2: Speed improvements for microcode compilation

Compilation into Microcode

The lack of fast implementations for functional languages is frequently bemoaned, as being a serious stumbling block in the examination of large software systems written in a functional style. We have chosen to deal with this problem by constructing special hardware to implement existing techniques of evaluation (ie combinator reduction), but many other groups are attempting to develop new techniques for the evaluation of functional languages.

In particular, a great deal of work is being done on the design of sophisticated compilers targeted towards conventional machines, and theoretical and practical knowledge in this field is increasing all the time. Work in Cambridge [Fairbairn 82] parallelling the SKIM development has produced a compiler from a pure functional language into code for a 68000 microprocessor [Motorola 82]. This compiler's code is orders of magnitude faster than interpreted combinator reduction on a 68000, and it would be highly beneficial if SKIM could make use of advances of this kind.

Microcode is usually viewed as a small control program sitting in fast, expensive RAM: it is part of the main processor, as an engineer's implementation mechanism for complex hardware. Even on machines with microcode in RAM such as the DEC VAX and the Xerox Dorado, most microcode is hand written by experts as part of systems implementation.

SKIM is better viewed as a machine with separate data and program memory, with the structure of each optimised for its intended use. The program memory is only microcode in as much as it is viewed as being static. It is implemented using cheap 150 nanosecond static RAMs organised into 40 bit words, with a 250 nanosecond cycle time. There is a 16 bit microcode address bus, so that the processor could support up to 64K*40 bit

words of microcode. Using 8K*8 static RAMs, which should be cheap and common within the next year, this occupies one Extended Double Eurocard.

Thus there is no reason why SKIM microcode should not be generated by compiler, from a functional language. As the same language is used to generate combinators, compilation into microcode would not require functional programs to be rewritten, merely submitted to a different version of the compiler. This would allow the programmer to boost the performance of important or frequently used functions while retaining the flexibility of combinators for less critical ones.

Some small functions have been 'compiled by hand' for SKIM, which are nevertheless more complex operations than what is generally viewed as being a 'combinator'. The microcode instruction set was found to be no more difficult to work with than the machine code of a conventional machine. The functions compiled so far have included the recursive structure comparison EQUAL, and reverse and append for lists. The results are shown in table 2, and demonstrate a speedup by a considerable factor over combinator evaluation. The measurements are crudely expressed in terms of cells per second of action on a linear list. Reverse and equal are completely strict and compile into microcode loops, while append does not. Garbage collection time is included. A compiler's code would not be quite as fast as this, but should be close.

The best strategy for compilation appears to be to remove laziness wherever possible, as laziness means the generation and reduction of more graph structures. It is clear that some functions are more susceptible to this than others, and so while some functions (e.g. simple recursive numerical computations like factorial) would speed up far more than this, others (complex manipulation of high level functions) will hardly speed up at all. We do not have any evidence yet about the overall effect of compilation on large programs.

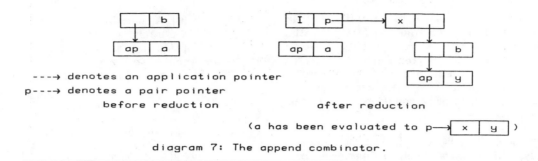

---→ denotes an application pointer
p---→ denotes a pair pointer

before reduction   after reduction

(a has been evaluated to p---→ [x | y])

diagram 7: The append combinator.

The best 'grain' at which to work appears to be that of 'supercombinators' [Hughes 82]. For instance, the append combinator performs the following operation shown in diagram 7. The argument **a** must be evaluated and examined. If it evaluates to a data pair then the head and tail halves are fetched and a new structure built as in (2). Otherwise, the result is **b**. Three new cells are needed, although in practice the reference counting mechanism will collect up the two superfluous ones.

We do not yet have any practical experience of how large programs written in a functional language will perform when compiled, but (as an example) current compilation techniques [Mycroft 81] will not reduce the number of new cells used in the append example above. Even when compilers become common for functional languages, SKIM should still provide competitive performance.

Results and Conclusions

Details have been given of various optimisations to Turner's combinator reduction method. Many of these methods are not at all obvious, and there may be many more similar ideas waiting to be discovered. They have resulted in considerable performance improvements for SKIM.

It is important to note that all of these improvements are transparent to the high level, functional programmer. They have been possible becuase the combinator model of computation is not tied to any one hardware scheme. By resisting the temptation to bend the high level programming model towards what is efficient to implement, as I believe has happened to many Lisp and Prolog systems, the implementor keeps future options open as well as ensuring software compatability. Although current implementations of functional languages may not rival more serious implementations of Lisp, future improvements in implementation expertise are likely to narrow this gap over the next few years.

Are all of these optimisations dependent on special hardware? Implementors of functional languages on conventional machines may conclude that the methods described here are of no interest, becuase they rely on the particular strengths of the SKIM processor. To address this issue it is worth examining the motivation for the SKIM project. There are two main reasons why we felt that it was worth building specialised hardware to execute functional languages.

By having a moderately powerful test implementation more substantial test programs will get tried. Although we do not provide detailed measurements here, considerably larger programs than simple sorting routines (e.g. a screen editor, a small compiler) have already been run on SKIM, and we are confident that over the next year more system software will get written. A simulator or an interpreter running on already available hardware may appear to provide greater flexibility in trying new implementation techniques, but will not lead to such meaningful tests of the true usefulness of the result.

We argue that 'conventional' machines are specialised to the running of stack-based languages such as Pascal, and that in fact SKIM is a <u>less</u> specialised hardware device. Efforts to implement functional languages efficiently on conventional machines are dominated by the benefits gained from transforming the language to conform with the conventional stack-based model of computation. We consider it more interesting to study how to do graph reduction better, rather than how to remove graph reduction from the program. The result is a very different perspective on what strategies are productive, and (we hope) better insight into how future implementations should be constructed.

Note that the use of multiple processors to increase performance is orthogonal to our work, although it appears that our techniques map onto multiple processors more easily than other approaches that take advantage of more conventional architectures.

The developments discussed here are also orthogonal to improvements in techniques for generating combinators (e.g. work by M. S. Joy at the Universiy of East Anglia, and S. L. Peyton-Jones at University College London). Current methods for generating combinators are still far from satisfactory, but when improvements happen SKIM should be able to make use of them.

Although such things are difficult to measure absolutely, SKIM appears to deliver a performance in solving common problems that is about one-quarter of that of a conventional compiled language on hardware of similar cost. The machine used for this comparison had a 68000 CPU running at 8-MHz, running BCPL and Algol68C as representative high level languages. Programming is far simpler, being in a functional language, and our future research is in the organisation of large programs and system software on such a machine.

References

[Clarke 80]: T. J. W. Clarke, P. J. S. Gladstone,
    C. D. MacLean and A. C. Norman,
    SKIM - the S, K, I Reduction Machine,
    Proceedings of the 1980 ACM Lisp Conference,
    pp 128 - 135, August 1980.

[Motorola 82]:
    MC68000 16-bit Microprocessor User's Manual,
    Prentice-Hall,
    1982.

[ACM 82]:
    Conference record of the
    1982 ACM Symposium on Lisp and
      Functional Programming,
    August 15-18, 1982,
    ACM order no 552820

[Hughes 82]: R. J. M. Hughes, Oxford University,
    Super Combinators:
    A New Implementation Method
    for Applicative Languages,
    [ACM 82].

[Fairbairn 82]: J. Fairbairn,
    Ponder and its Type System,
    Cambridge University Computer Laboratory
    Technical Note, 1982.

[Turner 79]: D. A. Turner,
    A New Implementation Technique
    for Applicative Languages,
    Software Practice and Experience,
    Volume 19, pp31-34, 1979.

[Mycroft 81]: A. Mycroft,
    Abstract Interpretation
    and Optimising Transformations
    for Applicative Programs,
    University of Edinburgh Dept. of Comp. Science,
    1981.

[Goto 74]: E. Goto,
    Monocopy and Associative Algorithms
    in an Extended Lisp,
    University of Tokyo, Japan,
    May 1974.

[Schorr 67]: H. Schorr and W. Waite,
    An efficient Machine-independent Procedure for
    Garbage Collection in Various List Structures,
    Comm ACM 10, 8, pp 501-506,
    August 1967.

[Stoye 83]: W. R. Stoye,
    The SKIM II Microprogrammer's Guide,
    Cambridge University Computer Laboratory
    Technical Note, 1983.

[Stoye 84]: W. R. Stoye,
    An Operating System written
    in a Purely Functional Language,
    document in preparation.

The G-machine: A fast, graph-reduction evaluator

Richard B. Kieburtz
Oregon Graduate Center
Beaverton, Oregon USA

Abstract

The G-machine is an abstract architecture for evaluating functional-language programs by programmed graph reduction. Unlike combinator reduction, in which control is derived dynamically from the expression graph itself, control in programmed graph reduction is specified by a sequence of instructions derived by compiling an applicative expression.

The G-machine architecture was defined by Thomas Johnsson and Lennart Augustsson (Gothenburg) as the evaluation model for a compiler for a dialect of ML with lazy evaluation rules. This paper describes a sequential evaluator based upon that abstract architecture. It discusses performance issues affecting reduction architectures, then describes the organization of a hardware design to address these issues. The interplay between compilation strategies and the computational engine is exploited in this design.

Principal features of the design are (i) hardware support for graph traversal, (ii) a vertically microcoded, pipelined internal architecture, (iii) an instruction fetch and translation unit with very low latency, and (iv) a new memory architecture, one specifically suited to graph reduction and which can be extended to very large memories.

1. Reduction systems

A reduction architecture evaluates an expression by transforming it through a series of intermediate forms until it cannot be further transformed, under a set of rewrite rules. The expression is then said to be in normal form, which is the value attributed to the original expression.

To be deemed useful for evaluating functional-language programs, a reduction system must be consistent with the mathematical semantics of applicative expressions. It should also have the Church-Rosser property, which assures the uniqueness of a normal form independent of the particular reduction sequence by which it is produced. These, however, are the only constraints placed upon reduction systems, and a great variety of elegant and imaginative schemes are possible.

Church's lambda-calculus and Curry's combinatory calculus are the best known examples of reduction systems, and have served as abstract models for experimental computing engines [Ber75, Cla80, SCN84, Sch85]. There are other systems as well. A string-reduction system implementing the semantics of Backus' metalanguage FFP has been used as the basis for an architecture allowing massive parallelism [Mag79]. String reduction is essentially like combinator reduction except that the value of an expression is not shared among multiple references; the expression is multiply evaluated.

Architectures based upon β-reduction (lambda-calculus), combinator reduction, or string reduction all have in common the property that *control* -- the selection of the next reduction step -- is dynamically derived from the current expression form at each stage in a reduction sequence. We call systems with this property *pure reduction* systems.

As an alternative to pure reduction systems, we may also consider *programmed* reduction. In a programmed reduction system, the steps of computation are still transformations of an expression form by application of reduction rules, just as in a pure reduction system. However, control is derived from the original expression form by static analysis -- compilation of a program. This derived control is manifested as a stream of instructions just as in a conventional von Neumann computer. A programmed reduction system is not so elegant an idea as a pure reduction system, but it offers the advantage that we can make use of technology developed over the last 35 years to implement it by a von Neumann computer architecture.

The research reported in this paper has been partially supported by the National Science Foundation under grant No. DCR-8405247.

1.1. Graph reduction

In a β-reduction step, each occurrence of a bound variable is eliminated by substitution of the corresponding argument expression found in an application. In the GMD reduction machine [Ber75] β-reduction has been implemented by recopying the matrix of a redex, during which (possibly multiple) copies of the argument expression are substituted for the variable being eliminated. This is a costly operation, whose asymptotic complexity is proportional to the square of the length of a redex.

Multiple copies of an argument expression are required only if expressions are represented as strings. Using a slightly more complex representation of expressions as graphs allows multiple references to a common subexpression to be realized by multiple arcs incident upon the root of a common subgraph. This form of representation allows us to make fuller use of the architectural primitive of addressable memory. *Graph reduction* then refers to a reduction process in which expressions are represented as graphs, rather than as strings, and there may be shared subgraphs. Sharing is extremely important to the performance of a sequential evaluator, because it allows redundant re-evaluations of copies of a common expression to be avoided. It can, however, inhibit fully parallel evaluation to some degree.

1.2. Combinator reduction

The combinator reduction architecture proposed by Turner [Tur79] is a pure reduction system based upon Curry's combinatory calculus, and employing graph reduction. Prior to Turner's experiments, the combinatory calculus had not been seriously studied as a model for practical computation. Among those in computing who knew of the model, the extreme simplicity of the combinators was thought to make their use hopelessly impractical, akin to computing with a Turing machine. Turner found that if the combinators S, K, and I, sufficient to form a primitive basis, were augmented by a few additional dependent combinators that much better performance was obtained from an evaluator when applied to expressions occurring in typical programs. As an expression undergoes reduction, the intermediate expressions generated tend not to display the combinatorial growth in size that is typical when using only the S,K and I combinators. This has been referred to as a "self-optimizing" property of combinator reduction, and seems to occur as the set of judiciously chosen dependent combinators reaches a critical size.

Following this lead, Hughes [Hug82] explored the idea that one could abandon the restriction to a fixed number of combinators, creating instead customized combinators derived from the expression to be reduced. The representation of an applicative expression using customized combinators may be much more compact and its evaluation can require fewer reduction steps. Of course, the set of reduction rules must be expanded and tailored to the customized combinators. This idea, which Hughes called super-combinators, led to the concept of programmed reduction architectures.

1.3. Programmed graph reduction

In a graph-reduction architecture, the reducer walks through the graph of an applicative expression to locate a redex, chosen according to the computation rule (normal-order or applicative-order) being followed. As it walks the graph, it caches a trail of unreduced application nodes leading to the redex. We show this cache as a stack of pointers in the diagram of Fig. 1a. In a pure combinator reducer, the function symbol $f^{(2)}$ at the lower left corner of the graph is one of a fixed set of combinators. The machine interprets this combinator to rewrite the left corner redex of the graph, as shown in Fig. 1b. In this particular example, the combinator $f^{(2)}$ takes only two arguments and the entire expression graph is not reduced to normal form in a single step.

In a programmed graph-reduction architecture, the symbol f can be any defined function symbol. To reduce the application of that function, the reducer executes a program compiled from the definition of the function. The architecture does not restrict the arity of the function to some previously restricted number of arguments; if argument values are needed to compute the application, the program will direct the reducer to access the needed arguments from the stack of application pointers.

Realizing that this is the use to be made of the application pointers, we can change the configuration of the traversal stack so that its contents point directly to the graphs of argument expressions. In addition, the stack holds a pointer to the principal application that is to be reduced, for it is that node that will be replaced to complete the reduction. This configuration is illustrated in Fig. 1c.

Furthermore, in case the graph we have been considering is the direct translation of an expression from the source program text (rather than a dynamically constructed intermediate expression), and this expression is to be evaluated immediately, then many steps of constructing an application graph can be avoided. Graphs for the argument expressions $x_1, \ldots x_n$ must be constructed, but then the compiled code can simply configure the stack to point at the appropriate subgraphs, without building a connecting spine of application nodes, as shown in

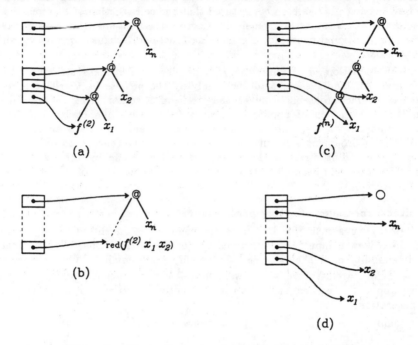

(a)

(c)

(b)

(d)

Figure 1 -- illustrating several possible traversal stacks

Fig. 1d. The function to be applied is known (by the compiler) to consume exactly n arguments, so that only the principal application node needs to be accessible. This is shown by an open circle in Fig. 1d. Avoiding the construction of redundant graph nodes when possible achieves a considerable economy in computation.

The G-machine described in this paper is a design for a programmed, graph-reduction machine, based upon an abstract architecture defined by Thomas Johnsson and Lennart Augustsson [Joh84, Aug84]. The abstract architecture was used to define an evaluation model for a functional-language compiler which compiles code for a conventional computer. We have refined it slightly with a view toward hardware implementation.

1.4. Non-reduction evaluators

In spite of the fact that the lambda-calculus has been the conceptual model for most applicative languages, until recently evaluators have not used a reduction model. Evaluators have been influenced more strongly by conventional computer architectures than by the language model that they implement. This influence has not been restricted to the idea of using programmed control, but extends to the mode of representation and the use of addressable memory.

In conventional evaluators, such as the SECD machine [Lan63] or a LISP interpreter, *values* are distinguished from *expressions*. Values are given a direct representation but expressions are not. This implies that it is rather cumbersome to deal with unevaluated expressions as data, and has dictated that most evaluators perform applicative-order evaluation (almost) exclusively. A function value is represented by a *closure* object[1], which is a

---

[1]We shall comment only upon models that correctly implement the lambda calculus.

pair consisting of a program text and an environment. An environment is a mapping of identifiers to their values, and the environment component in a closure must bind all of the free (i.e. non-local) identifiers in a function definition.

There are several technical schemes for representing a closure object. In each, reference to the value of a non-local variable involves at least one additional level of address indexing or indirect reference, beyond that required to access a local variable. Furthermore, an environment is represented by a data structure that must be constructed in memory. If an environment is not static, then its representation must be built during execution of a programmed evaluation. It has been conjectured that the construction of environment representations and the extra indirection required to access the contents of a closure are principal sources of computational overhead in evaluating functional language programs with conventional evaluators.

In graph reduction, it is unnecessary to provide explicit data structures to represent environments. All bindings are made uniformly by the process of rewriting a redex of the graph at each reduction step. However, the overhead of constructing closure objects is mirrored in the construction of application graphs (when that cannot be avoided). Indirect access to arguments via the contents of a stack of argument pointers is analogous to indirect access via the environment structure of a closure. We have chosen to reduce that level of indirection by providing direct hardware support in the G-machine for a stack of argument pointers. The stack has been given the performance characteristic of a register file in a conventional machine.

2. Architectural issues affecting performance

Any abstract evaluation model can be mapped onto a conventional computing system by programming. New computer architectures are justified if they offer improved performance, increased reliability or if they significantly simplify programming. The primary motivation for the G-machine architecture is that we believe it can significantly improve performance in evaluating applicative expressions. A secondary motivation is ease of programming (i.e. ease of code generation).

The dominant factor limiting the performance of any computer system is the overhead of moving data. The metric of distance used to analyze systems is the time required to access data that reside on one functional unit when they are needed by another. Indirect access via a pointer stored in memory may double the cost of access to a datum by requiring two memory fetches instead of one. Cache memories can reduce average access cost by dynamically establishing address neighborhoods. Pipelined operation reduces cost by providing a bounded degree of parallel data movement.

The largest overheads in conventional applicative-language evaluators can be attributed to five factors (not necessarily given in order of importance):

1) Indirect reference to variables via data structures that implement environment mappings;

2) Construction of closure frames, with attendant movement of data between processor and memory;

3) Saving and restoring contexts when evaluating function applications;

4) Dynamic memory management;

5) Extensive use of list structures, which implies sequential access paths to data.

A graph-reduction architecture alters the balance of importance of these five factors, and thus provides opportunities to address performance issues with somewhat different mechanisms.

1') Non-local variables are eliminated during compilation of a functional-language program for evaluation by graph reduction. Local variables are eliminated at the onset of evaluation of a function application, by binding the corresponding argument expressions in place of local variables. In an expression graph, subexpressions are referred to directly by arcs of the graph itself, rather than indirectly through an environment. Since the graph is transformed by update-in-place during evaluation, it is never necessary to employ a run-time data structure to represent an environment.

2') In performing graph reduction, closures are not explicitly constructed, although when normal-order (lazy) evaluation is performed or function values are returned, *suspensions* (application graphs) must be constructed.

3') The G-machine makes use of internal register queues, and therefore machine state must be preserved while evaluating nested function applications. The machine state consists of its register contents and a control pointer. However, state-saving can be supported largely by hardware, almost eliminating the penalty for a "context switch" when a nested application is evaluated.

4') In graph reduction, dynamic memory management is required. Graphs derived from recursive definitions can be cyclic, and therefore simple reference-counting is not an adequate memory management strategy. Furthermore, memory allocations may be more frequent than with conventional, applicative-order evaluation since expressions, as well as values, are directly represented as data. We propose a new, incremental collection strategy based upon a modified reference counting scheme. It can be supported by a parallel processor and should not impose any significant in-line burden upon the reduction processor.

5') The use of arrays in preference to list structures would allow evaluation to benefit from the indexed-address computation hardware available in conventional computers. However, the implementation of a hybrid memory model, combining "flat" addressable segments with list-structure memory, adds another increment of complexity to a design. We have not attempted to implement arrays.

On the other hand, in a programmed machine, software and hardware can cooperate to program the use of machine registers so that many list-structure constructions can be avoided entirely. The registers of the G-machine are organized as a pair of indexed stacks, which simplifies the task of compiling code to use the registers effectively.

3. The G-machine

The G-machine is a programmable graph-reduction engine that can perform either applicative-order or normal-order evaluations. It employs a tagged, dynamically allocatable list-structure memory (G) in which to store an expression graph undergoing reduction, and a byte-addressable control store (C). The processor consists of an instruction fetch and translation unit (IFTU) that fetches G-code from the control store, translates it to microcode, and delivers a stream of micro-instructions to a processor control unit (PCU). A separate data and address bus (G-bus) connects the G-memory with a stack (P) that holds graph pointers, an arithmetic-logical unit (ALU) which also has an associated register stack (V), and a small number of special registers. The top segment of the P-stack is supported by hardware registers in the G-machine processor, and some fixed number of cells adjacent to the stack top can be directly accessed by stack operation instructions. The remainder of the P-stack overflows into fast memory.

G-code [Joh84] is a predominately zero-address machine code. When instructions do have operands they are either control addresses in control-transfer instructions, indices for bit-shift instructions, literal data, pointers to constants stored in G-memory, or indices relative to the top of the P- or V-stack. Operation codes are represented in one byte. The mean instruction length gotten by averaging over the code compiled for 35 small programs is 2.18 bytes. Although the mean instruction length is a simplistic measure, it indicates that the code efficiency of the G-machine is probably somewhat better than that of most current generation, general-purpose von-Neumann architectures.

3.1. Organization

The G-machine processor will operate as a slave to a host processor which shares access to its control memory and to the graph memory (see Fig. 2). The host processor will be responsible for sending the G-processor an initialization signal, for loading the control and graph memories, and for signalling the G-processor to begin evaluation. During an evaluation, the G-processor can signal its host, interrupting it to request service. To make a service request the G-processor deposits the address of a node in G-memory onto the G-bus, from which it will be read by the host processor. Details of the service request are communicated as a graph in G-memory, whose root is pointed to by the address deposited on the G-bus when the request is signalled.

This arrangement allows the G-processor to run free of interrupts. Upon initialization and following a signal of a service request, the G-processor enters a wait state, awaiting a continuation signal from its host. The host is to be realized by a conventional microprocessor. It will supply all necessary operating system services, as well as memory-management functions not directly supported by specialized hardware. Access to the G-bus is arbitrated by fixed priorities that give the G-processor preference over the host.

The G-machine is designed to provide hardware support for the following aspects of evaluation:

Graph traversal, and access to arguments during evaluation of an applicative expression. The P-stack is loaded during traversal of an application graph, and subsequently holds

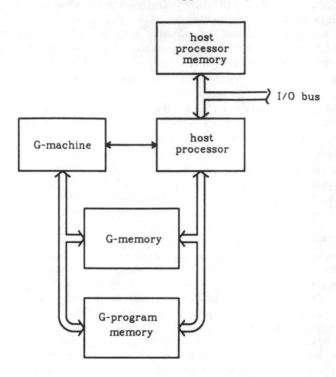

Figure 2 -- block diagram of the G-machine and its host processor

---

pointers to the arguments needed during evaluation of the application. The current design of the G-processor holds the topmost 24 cells of the P-stack in a register queue within the processor. Any of these 24 cells can be brought to the stack top by an instruction executable in a single internal clock cycle, a fraction of the time needed to fetch a datum from the G-memory. The contents of the topmost segment of the P-stack are the addresses of a "working set" of graph nodes used in reducing a given function application.

Functional simulation of the G-machine shows that stack-manipulation instructions account for 20-25 per cent of all G-code issued. These instructions are:

PUSH	--	moves a 32-bit datum from the G-bus to the top of the P-stack
POP	--	removes the top of the P-stack onto the G-bus
COPY *index*	--	copies the contents of the indexed stack cell to the top of the P-stack
MOVE *index*	--	removes the cell at the top of the stack and overwrites the indexed cell

ROT   *index*   --   removes the indexed cell from the
interior of the stack and places
it at the stack top

Instruction fetch. The relatively high incidence of rapidly executed stack instructions imposes fairly severe stress on the instruction fetch unit. A burst of stack instructions can be consumed by the control unit at a faster rate than instructions can be continuously fetched from a conventional control memory. To buffer the bursts of rapid consumption of stack instructions, the IFTU and PCU are designed to function as a buffered pipeline with high throughput and extremely short latency. During expansion of more complex G-code instructions into a sequence of micro-instructions, considerable pre-fetching of G-code can occur.

Context switching. A context switch saves or restores the processor state (program counter, P-stack register contents). Since there are no non-local control transfers, contexts are saved and restored according to a LIFO discipline. Context switches can be accomplished at almost no overhead by a hardware implementation that allows the hardware register queue holding the top segment of the P-stack to overflow into fast memory. In such an implementation, the inline overhead of a context switch consists in saving (or restoring) a program counter value on the P-stack.

Context switching by sequentially storing or fetching the contents of the P-stack under programmed control has been estimated from simulations to account for 8-12 per cent of total execution time. This overhead is virtually eliminated by the automatic register-queue overflow mechanism.

Dynamic, list-structured memory. Graph-reduction places heavy demands upon dynamic memory allocation because expressions, as well as list-structured data, are represented as graphs. Dynamically allocatable memory is considered an architectural primitive, to be supported by hardware. ALLOC (allocate a node of G-memory) is a primitive instruction to G-memory, just as is READ or WRITE. Furthermore, collection of inaccessible graph nodes has been made the task of the memory manager, rather than the G-processor. The obligation of the processor is limited to signalling the memory manager i) whenever a reference pointer is written as data into a graph node, so that a reference count can be incremented, ii) whenever a reference pointer in a node is overwritten, so that a reference count can be decremented, and iii) when a function call or return occurs. The first kind of signal accompanies writes to memory and incurs no in-line overhead. The second kind of signal is also associated with some writes, but precedes the write itself in order that write operations are not encumbered with delay. This kind of signal will require an additional memory cycle. The third kind of signal is independent of any direct memory access by the G-processor, and will consume one memory cycle. The memory management scheme is described in a later section.

These, then are the aspects of a reduction architecture that have seemed to deserve hardware-supported implementation. Several of the components, the P-stack and parts of the IFTU in particular, will benefit from VLSI realizations, for they buffer data movements by using moderately sized, dynamic storage structures with a high degree of regularity.

Beyond the aspects of programmed graph-reduction that can be effectively supported by hardware or by microprogramming, there still remains great potential for performance improvement by improving the compilation schemes. When it is safe to perform, applicative-order evaluation will be less costly than normal-order evaluation. An application graph does not have to be explicitly constructed to do applicative-order evaluation. Thus, performance can be improved by a compiler that does strictness analysis to find cases in which applications that would nominally require normal-order evaluation can be safely done in applicative order.

A compiler can further improve performance if it can discover cases in which a node of G-memory can safely be re-used, in preference to allocating a fresh node and leaving the old one to be reclaimed by the memory manager. This will save ALLOC instructions, reduce the rate of memory allocations and relieve load on the dynamic memory manager.

Additional improvement can be obtained if a compiler creates "wrapped" and "unwrapped" code for many functions. A wrapped version of the code text will obtain its arguments from the graph in G-memory, and will deposit the results there. In many cases the result of a function is a tuple of two, three, or more values which is represented as a short list in G-memory. An unwrapped version of the same function will simply leave its results in the P- and V-stacks of the G-processor. This corresponds to the practice of passing arguments in registers in conventional multi-register machines. A wrapped version of a function can be obtained from an unwrapped version by appending to its code body a suffix to perform the list construction before returning. In evaluating an application of a recursively-defined function, the advantage of executing the code of an unwrapped version is obvious.

3.2. Processor design

The G-processor itself is organized as shown in Fig. 3. The internal data/address bus (G-bus) connects the major functional units of the processor with one another and to the G-memory. The ALU implements integer addition, add-with-carry, and complementation on signed 32-bit data. It also provides shift operations, byte insertion, and constant zero. There are condition codes for zero, negative, carry generation and overflow generation.

The processor controller (PCU) is responsible for dispatch and distribution of control signals extracted from fields of 20-bit micro-instructions. Its actual decoding function is not much more complicated than that of the Berkeley RISC architecture [PaS82]. Unlike the Berkeley RISC, however, the G-processor is not completely synchronous, and micro-instruction dispatch is subject to the availability of the resources required by the instruction. In particular, this allows the processor to have a much shorter instruction cycle time, not tied to the speed of the memory. Instruction dispatch may await the availability of G-memory, of the next micro-instruction or literal from the G-code stream, or of completion of an ALU operation. This will accommodate alternative hardware implementation strategies, and it

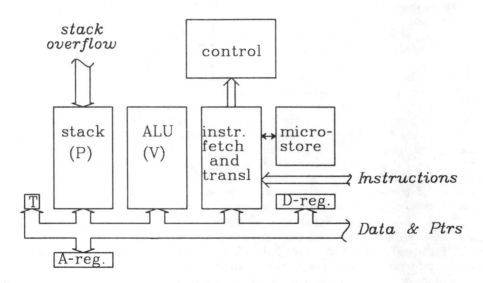

Figure 3 -- functional units of the G-processor

'lows some degree of overlap in actual micro-instruction execution. For instance, an ALU operation can begin before a preceding READ or WRITE to G-memory has completed.

The D-register shown in Fig. 3 is an anachronism from an earlier design in which a context switch caused the contents of the P-stack to be saved on a memory dump under program control. Although this is now handled automatically by the P-stack overflow mechanism, the D-register has been preserved to provide diagnostic support. While the hardware is being debugged, stack contents can be explicitly dumped for inspection.

The A-register holds a G-memory address for a READ or WRITE operation. The T-register holds current values of the relevant data tags, "is_evaluated" and "contains pointer" (see Figure 5).

3.2.1. Instruction fetch and translation

The IFTU fetches G-code from the control memory and translates instructions into sequences of 20-bit wide vertical microcode. Several G-code instructions, such as the stack manipulation operations, translate directly into micro-instructions, whereas others, such as EVAL (evaluate a graph) translate into rather complex sequences which themselves contain control flow instructions.

G-code can contain literal data, G-memory addresses, and jump instructions specifying addresses in control memory. These data are all removed by the IFTU. Literals and G-memory address constants are routed to a literals queue, from whence they can subsequently be moved to the G-bus. Jump addresses are interpreted directly by the IFTU to initialize its code buffers. Thus unconditional jumps are never translated into microcode at all, they simply reinitialize a code buffer into which G-code is fetched [Wil83].

Conditional jump and case-switch instructions are also partially interpreted by the IFTU. A conditional jump specifies a possible alternative code stream to the one currently being fetched. The IFTU maintains multiple instruction buffers (four in the current design) and a new buffer is enabled and given the target address of the conditional jump from which to begin fetching a code stream. The IFTU uses nondeterministic prediction of the path to be taken at the jump, and attempts to fill all enabled code buffers by multiplexed fetches. Case-switch instructions may specify wider than two-way branch alternatives. The multiple code-buffers scheme will accommodate up to four-way case switches.

This scheme's effectiveness will be limited by the available bandwidth to the control memory. Each G-code instruction expands into a sequence of micro-instructions. The expansion ratio is highly variable over different G-code sequences, but seems to have a dynamic average in the range of 5-7 as observed in simulations. Thus we expect there to be some excess memory bandwidth over that required to support a single stream of G-code instructions.

Only a single level of nondeterministic jump prediction is supported. When a second conditional jump instruction is encountered in translating a G-code stream, translation stops until execution of the already-translated microcode stream resolves the previous jump.

Conditional jump instructions are translated into micro-instructions that specify the index of one of the enabled code buffers. (See Fig. 4.) When a conditional jump is taken, the IFTU must flush the queue of translated but not yet executed micro-instructions, for they were produced on the assumption that the jump would not be taken. It must abort translation of the G-code instruction currently in the translation unit, restart translation from the indexed code buffer, and disable all other code buffers. Most of these operations can be done simultaneously, in a single internal clock cycle. Restarting the translation process will require at least two additional cycles before the first micro-instruction can be produced. Fetch of new G-code instructions into the single code buffer that remains enabled after a jump has been taken will be accelerated by the absence of competition.

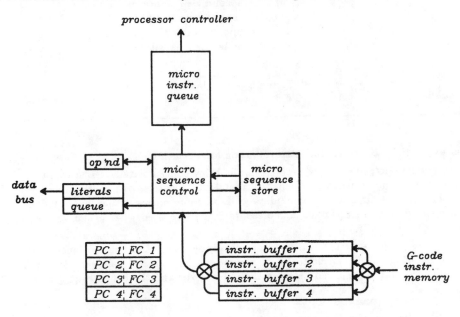

Figure 4 -- instruction fetch and translation unit

When a conditional jump is not taken, the action required of the IFTU is much simpler; it needs only to disable all but the currently active code buffer. No interruption of the micro-code stream occurs.

Although this activity sounds complicated, it is in fact quite straightforward to support with hardware. It can have a considerable advantage if programs exhibit loops with conditional exit, as is the case when tail-recursive function definitions are compiled. The translation unit unwinds the code loop as if it were straight-line code, punctuated occasionally by conditional jump instructions. The only taken jump will be the one that finally terminates execution of the loop.

3.3. G-memory

A node of G-memory consists of a pair of 32-bit data cells, plus six tag bits and 18 bits of reference-count fields used in memory management. The layout of a node is shown in Figure 5. The G-memory controller performs most functions of dynamic memory management automatically, with very limited cooperation required of the G-processor. The controller is implemented partly by special hardware, and partly by software running on the host processor.

An address selects a node, and the low-order bit of a node address further selects the first or second data cell. When a cell is fetched or written, certain of the node tags are also fetched or written.

Graph-reduction requires a tagged memory architecture. A graph component may be shared, and can be reduced by the first reference that demands its value. Thus any reference to a graph component may either find it unevaluated or find that it has been evaluated by a previous reference. To allow this, each node of G-memory carries a tag bit called

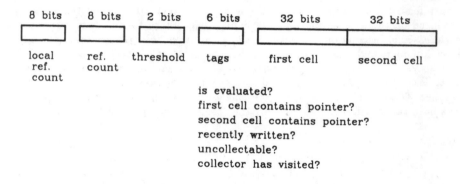

is evaluated?
first cell contains pointer?
second cell contains pointer?
recently written?
uncollectable?
collector has visited?

Figure 5 -- a node of G-memory

"is_evaluated" to tell whether its evaluation has occurred.

When a tagged memory architecture is being contemplated, it is useful to consider other tags that might be useful. We find it useful to allocate a pair of tag bits to designate the contents of the first and second data cells as representing either basic values or pointers. This allows more compact data representations to be used when basic values occur as components of lists or tuples.

The "recently-written" bit is automatically set each time the reference count of the node is modified. This bit can be tested or cleared by the memory manager. It provides the explicit synchronization required between the G-processor and the concurrent garbage collector.

3.4. Memory management

The strategy behind G-memory is to provide a storage structure that behaves as a dynamically allocatable, list-structure memory. The basic operations on such a memory are to allocate a new node and to read or write to a designated cell of an addressed node. The G-processor which uses this memory is (almost) completely unconcerned with its management.

To implement such a memory, its free nodes are linked together in a linear list. Several elements of the head of this list are pre-allocated, having been unlinked from the list and given initial settings of their tag fields and reference counts. Pointers to pre-allocated nodes are stored in a hardware-supported FIFO queue, so that they are immediately available in response to an allocation request by the G-processor. The memory manager maintains for its own use a separate record of the set of nodes allocated but not yet examined for collection.

Reference counts are maintained by the memory manager whenever a node of G-memory is written. Reference counts only need to be decremented when a node is overwritten by the UPDATE of an application by its value, or when an ancestor in the graph is collected. Only the former action is initiated by the G-processor, and it is signalled by a TRASH-node memory reference. This is the only explicit in-line overhead of the reference counting scheme. Each WRITE instruction in which the datum is a pointer (indicated by the is-pointer bit) causes incrementation of the reference count of the node pointed to.

Collection is triggered when the G-processor signals return from the code of a function application. At that time, the collector removes from the record of nodes previously allocated, the set of nodes allocated since execution of the function call began, and at its leisure, examines each such node for collectability. Any node whose reference count is zero is immediately collectable. As collection proceeds, nodes pointed to by a collected node have their reference counts decremented and are added to the list of eligibles. Any node whose reference count has ever overflowed is forever uncollectable. Other nodes with non-zero reference counts are subjected to a local graph traversal to determine whether the reference count can be accounted for solely by pointers from within the subgraph, forming cycles. If this is true of every node in the subgraph, and no such node has had its reference count modified (by action of the G-processor) during the collector's examination of the subgraph, then the subgraph is collectable.

This is a somewhat simplified summary of a modified reference-count scheme invented by Ashoke Deb [Deb84]. Its advantages are that it is incremental, imposes no additional overhead on the management of acyclic graphs, requires only the simplest of synchronization for concurrent implementation, maintains comparable locality of reference to that of the G-processor, and does not suffer performance degradation when the ratio of occupied to free memory nodes is high. These are considerable advantages. In addition, simulations show the computational overhead of this collection scheme to be considerably lower than that of conventional mark-sweep collection, even when memory occupancy is quite low.

4. Present state of the project

As of this writing, the architecture of the G-machine is complete and an early version has undergone functional simulation. The results of this simulation [Sar84] showed that stack manipulation instructions occur more frequently than any other type, and provided some statistics on the use of memory and the dynamic occurrence of jump instructions. These results reinforced our decisions to provide direct hardware support for the P-stack, and a fast, low-latency, pipelined IFTU. They indicated that context switching by unloading of the processor's stacks under programmed control would be a large source of overhead, and led to the decision to implement automatic overflow management of the P-stack.

A micro-architecture has also been fully designed and an initial edition of the microcode written. A full simulation is currently being constructed. We expect to obtain significant performance data from this simulation.

A VLSI implementation of the P-stack has also been designed and simulated, and is currently being tested. Work continues on detailed design of the G-memory and memory manager.

Acknowledgements

The author wishes to thank Thomas Johnsson and Lennart Augustsson for many stimulating discussions on functional language implementation; Shreekant Thakkar for pointing out some pitfalls to be avoided in planning a hardware implementation, and Ananda Sarangi, Linda Rankin, Mark Foster, Richard Vireday and Shyue-Ling Kuo for their contributions to design and simulation of the G-machine.

References

[Aug84] Augustsson, L., A compiler for Lazy ML, *Proc. of 1984 ACM Conf. on Lisp and Funct. Prog.*, August, 1984, pp. 218-227.

[Ber75] Berkling, K., Reduction languages for reduction machines, *Proc. IEEE Int. Sympos. on Computer Arch.*, pp. 133-140, Jan. 1975.

[Cla80] Clarke, T.J.W., Gladstone, P.J.S., MacLean, C.D. and Norman, A.C., SKIM - the S, K, I reduction machine, *Proc. of 1980 ACM Lisp Conf.*, pp. 128-135, August, 1980.

[Deb84] Deb, A., An efficient garbage collector for graph machines, Oregon Graduate Center, Tech. Rept. No. CS/E-84-003, August, 1984.

[Hug82] Hughes, J., Supercombinators: a new implementation method for applicative languages, *Proc. of 1982 ACM Conf. on Lisp and Funct. Prog.*, August, 1982, pp. 1-10.

[Joh84] Johnsson, T., Efficient compilation of lazy evaluation, *Proc. of 1984 ACM SIGPLAN Conf. on Compiler Constr.*, June, 1984

[LMO84] Lampson, B.W., McDaniel, G. and Ornstein, S.M., An instruction fetch unit for a high-performance personal computer, *IEEE Trans. on Computers C-33*, No. 8 (Aug. 1984), pp. 712-730.

[Lan63] Landin, P.J., The mechanical evaluation of expressions, *Comp. J. 6*, (1963-4) p. 308.

[Mag79] Mago, G.A., A network of microprocessors to execute reduction languages - Parts I and II, *Int. J. of Comp. & Inf. Sci. 8*, No. 5 (Oct. 1979), pp. 349-385, No. 6 (Dec. 1979), pp. 435-471.

[PaS82] Patterson, D.A. and Sequin, C., A VLSI RISC, *Computer 15*, No. 9 (Sept. 1982), pp. 8-21.

[Sar84] Sarangi, A.G., Simulation and performance evaluation of a graph reduction machine architecture, M.S. thesis, Oregon Graduate Center, July, 1984.

[Sch85] Scheevel, M., NORMA, a normal-order combinator reduction machine, colloquium presented at Oregon Graduate Center, January, 1985.

[SCN84] Stoye, W.R., Clarke, T.J.W. and Norman, A.C., Some practical methods for rapid combinator reduction, *Proc. of 1984 ACM Conf. on Lisp and Functional Prog.*, pp. 159-166, August, 1984.

[Tur79] Turner, D.A., New implementation techniques for applicative languages, *Software - Prac. & Exper. 9*, No. 1 (Jan. 1979), pp. 31-49.

[Wil83] Wilkes, M.V., Keeping jump instructions out of the pipeline of a RISC-like computer, *Computer Arch. News 11*, No. 5 (Dec. 1983), pp. 5-7.

Chapter 7: Parallel Reduction Machines

Background

The von Neumann architecture has evolved with dramatic changes in the hardware technology, which has brought about a decrease in clock speed and an increase in the integration at chip and board levels. However, we are reaching the physical limit imposed by the laws of physics. The other factors in the evolution are an increase in granularity of instructions, pipelining, and parallel computation. Increase in granularity of instruction (namely vectorization) only speeds up some numeric data intensive applications and is harder to exploit. Vectorizing constructs and compiler directives are used to express parallel execution. Pipelining is a more general technique that takes advantage of locality of computation. However, this work can be lost when a context change occurs in the instruction stream. Parallel computation, using a network of von Neumann processors, is increasingly becoming possible because more commercial parallel systems are becoming available. These systems fall into two categories, shared (e.g., Sequent's Balance) and distributed memory systems (e.g., Intel's iPSC). The shared memory model is easier to program because of the memory model, while the distributed memory model is much harder to program [10]. The parallel computation model is based on a process (tasks) model [7] and tends to favor large grain parallelism because of the overheads of the tasking mechanism. In this model, the tasks are forked from a single thread program and executed concurrently on multiple processors. The programmer has to be intimately familiar with operational aspects of the hardware architecture, and this makes it difficult to manage when hundreds of processors are employed. Load balancing and scheduling become impossible activities for most applications. Imperative (conventional) languages are inherently sequential, as mentioned in Chapter 5. Functional languages are free from side effects and have the property that will generate the same results no matter how the program is executed. Thus, functional languages contain a great deal of implicit parallelism that is easy to detect [5]. Researchers [9, 14] are now exploring the implementation of functional languages for parallel von Neumann architectures. The advantage they have over imperative language implementation is that they may be able to achieve better speedups for applications, be easier to program, and be consistent over different parallel architectures. However, as was mentioned before, imperative languages enjoy a lot of support from von Neumann architectures and functional languages may suffer because of a lack of any support.

The alternative for functional languages is parallel non-von Neumann architectures. These architectures depart from the von Neumann principles of each instruction appointing its unique successor and an assumption of large address space (not true for some distributed memory von Neumann parallel systems). Kennaway and Sleep [13] developed a general mode of non-von Neumann architecture that consists of a (scalable) number of processing elements and two *task pools* (Figure 7.1).

Consider the expression

$$f(x) * g(y)$$

where f(x) and g(y) are two independent functions and thus can be evaluated concurrently. Each expression (task) describes the computation and a destination of where to place the evaluated result. For the original expression, the destination will be the output device, whereas original expressions are held in *the waiting pool*.

The processing elements pick tasks to examine if the task requires a sub-expression to be evaluated. If it is required, then the sub-expression is extracted and added to the *selected pool*. The original task, which now has holes in it, is added to the waiting pool. These holes are filled by returning results. If the original task does not require any further

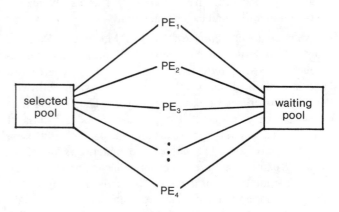

Figure 7.1

EH0260-0/87/0000/0297$01.00 © 1987 IEEE   297

evaluation, then it is evaluated, and the result is used to fill the hole in some expression or output device. Filling in the holes in a waiting task moves it to the selected pool.

Thus the program counter in the von Neumann architecture is now replaced by a set of tasks selected for execution at each time step. The computation model specifies a scheme for *beta substitution*. There are two alternatives for implementing beta substitution, use of pointers or making copies of expression. Copying requires more time and requires more space but may overcome bottlenecks in accessing pools.

Kenneway and Sleep categorizes the new architectures as follows: pipelined ring architectures (e.g., Manchester Dataflow and MIT Static Dataflow machines), packet circulation ring architectures (e.g., early ALICE implementation), physical tree architectures (e.g., FFP machine, AMPS [11], DDM1 [4]), virtual tree architectures [1], shared distributed memory architecture (e.g., GRIP), and sequential reduction machines (e.g., SKIM, G-machine).

Article Summary

Cripps et al., in "The Design and Implementation of ALICE: A Parallel Graph Reduction Machine," describe ALICE (Applicative Language Idealized Computing Engine). The machine architecture fits the general model as described above. The waiting pool and the selected pool are both a part of a pool of rewritable packets surrounded by a pool of rewrite agents. The behavior of the machine is the same as for the general model. The agents dip into the pool to pick up a packet to rewrite and reduce it according to rewrite rules, and finally return the package back to the pool. ALICE is implemented by using INMOS Transputer [20] chips, which serve as the rewrite agents, and a multi-stage network, which connects the rewrite pool (memory) to rewrite agents (processor). The memory is physically distributed though globally accessible through the network. An earlier version used a packet circulation ring instead of multi-stage network. The machine performs lazy evaluation and compiler directed eager evaluation.

Mago and Middleton, in "The FFP Machine: A Progress Report," describe an ambitious VLSI project that implements a tree string reduction machine. No pointers are used, and it is claimed that parallelism in the system will overcome the overhead of excessive copying. The FFP machine is a cellular machine that executes Backus' FP class of languages and automatically exploits the parallelism present in the FP programs. The nature of computation is fine grain. The FP expressions are stored in a linear array of *lcells*, which are the leaves of the tree. The lcells are composed of the processor and memory and are connected to their neighbors. The interior nodes of the tree are called *tcells*, which

corporate with their neighbors in an asynchronous manner to achieve distributed reduction. Computation is achieved by waves sweeping from the root node to the leaves and back.

Clack and Peyton Jones, in "The Four-Stroke Reduction Engine," describe another parallel graph reduction machine that supports transparent management of parallel tasks with no explicit communication between processors. The graph reduction algorithm is represented as a finite state machine replicated across the 120 processing nodes. The GRIP (Graph Reduction in Parallel) machine is being implemented as a bus-based shared memory multiprocessor by using the IEEE Future bus. The memory is composed of 30 intelligent memory units that hide all the low-level administration of nodes in a graph from the processing elements. Currently, the machine only exists as a simulator model form. Note that this project has ambitious goals to overcome the bus-bandwidth limitation that plagues expansion of bus-based shared-memory von Neumann multiprocessor architectures. The assumption is that the behavior of a graph reduction computation model is significantly different.

Additional material can be found in references 1-3, 6, 8, 11, 12, 15-19, and 21.

References

[1] Burton, F.W. and Sleep, M.R., "Executing Functional Programs on a Virtual Tree of Processors," *Proc. ACM Conf. on Functional Programming Languages and Computer Architecture*, Association for Computing Machinery, Inc., New York, N.Y., Oct. 1981, pp. 187-194.

[2] Burton, F.W., "Annotations to Control Parallelism and Reduction Order in the Distributed Evaluation of Functional Programs," *ACM Transactions on Programming Languages and Systems*, Vol. 6, No. 2, April 1984, pp. 160-174.

[3] Darlington, J. and Reeve M., "ALICE—A Multiprocessor Reduction Machine for Parallel Evaluation of Applicative Languages," *Proc. ACM Conf. on Functional Programming Languages and Architecture*, Association for Computing Machinery, Inc., New York, N.Y., Oct. 1981, pp. 65-75.

[4] Davis, A.L., "The Architecture and System Method of DDM1: A Recursively Structured Data Driven Machine," *Proc. 5th Ann. Symp. on Computer Architecture*, Computer Society of the IEEE Press, Washington, D.C., 1978, pp. 210-215.

[5] Friedman, D.P. and Wise, D.S., "Aspects of Applicative Programming for Parallel Processing," *IEEE Transactions on Computers*, Vol. C-27, No. 4, April 1978, pp. 289-296.

[6] Hankin, C.L., Osmon, P.E., and Shute, M.J., "COWEB—A Combinator Reduction Architecture," *Proc. ACM Conf. on Functional Programming Languages and Architecture*, Association for Computing Machinery, Inc., New York, N.Y., Sept. 1985, pp. 99-112.

[7] Hoare, C.A.R., "Communicating Sequential Processors," *Communications of the ACM*, Vol. 21, No. 8, Aug. 1978, pp. 666-677.

[8] Hudak, P. and Keller, R.M., "Garbage Collection and Task Deletion in Distributed Applicative Processing Systems," *Proc. ACM Symp. on LISP and Functional Programming*, Association for Computing Machinery, Inc., New York, N.Y., Aug. 1982, pp. 168-178.

[9] Hudak, P., "Para-Functional Programming," *Computer*, Vol. 19, No. 8, Aug. 1986, pp. 60-69.

[10] Kallstrom, M. and Thakkar, S., "Experiences with Three Parallel Programming Systems," *Proc. COMPCON S'87*, Computer Society of the IEEE Press, Washington, D.C., 1987, pp. 344-349.

[11] Keller, R.M., Lindstrom, G., and Patil, S., "A Loosely-Coupled Applicative Multiprocessing System," *Proc. AFIPS 1979 National Computer Conf.*, 1979, pp. 613-622.

[12] Keller, R.M., "Divide and CONCer: Data Structuring for Applicative Multiprocessing," *Proc. 1980 LISP Conf.*, Association for Computing Machinery, Inc., New York, N.Y., Aug. 1980, pp. 196-202.

[13] Kennaway, J.M. and Sleep, M.R., "Towards a Successor to von Neumann," *Distributed Computing*, edited by F.B. Chambers, D.A. Duce, and G.P. Jones, Academic Press, Inc. (London) Ltd., London, England, 1984, pp. 125-138.

[14] Kieburtz, R.B., Private discussion, 1986.

[15] Lemaitre, M., Castan, M., Durand, M., Durrieu, G., and Lecussan, B., "Mechanisms for Efficient Multiprocessor Combinator Reduction," *Proc. ACM Symp. on LISP and Functional Programming*, Aug. 1986, pp. 113-121.

[16] Mago, G., "A Network of Microprocessors to Execute Reduction Languages—I," *Int'l. J. of Comp. and Info. Sci.*, Vol. 8, No. 5, Oct. 1979, pp. 349-385.

[17] Mago, G., "A Network of Microprocessors to Execute Reduction Languages—II," *Int'l. J. of Comp. and Info. Sci.*, Vol. 8, No. 6, Dec. 1979, pp. 435-471.

[18] Mago, G., "Data Sharing in an FFP Machine," *Proc. ACM Symp. on LISP and Functional Programming*, Association for Computing Machinery, Inc., New York, N.Y., Aug., 1982, pp. 201-207.

[19] Mago, G.A., "Making Parallel Computation Simple: The FFP Machine," *Proc. COMPCON S'85*, Computer Society of the IEEE Press, Washington, D.C., 1985, pp. 424-428.

[20] Whitby-Strevens, C.W., "The Transputer," *Proc. 12th Ann. Int'l. Symp. on Computer Architecture*, Computer Society of the IEEE Press, Washington, D.C., 1985, pp. 292-300.

[21] Traub, T.R., "An Abstract Parallel Graph Reduction Machine," *Proc. 12th Ann. Int'l. Symp. on Computer Architecture*, Computer Society of the IEEE Press, Washington, D.C., 1985, pp. 333-341.

THE DESIGN AND IMPLEMENTATION OF ALICE: A PARALLEL GRAPH REDUCTION MACHINE

M.D. Cripps, J. Darlington, A.J. Field, P. G. Harrison and M. J. Reeve
Department of Computing
Imperial College of Science and Technology
London SW7 2BZ

Abstract

Traditionally the design of programming languages has been compromised in order to exploit the most efficient machine architecture available, which has usually been of the von Neumann type. However, we believe that *functional languages* provide the most effective means for producing software and that the right approach is to develop a *customised architecture* for the implementation of the most suitable computational model for these languages.

In this paper we adopt *graph reduction* as the most natural computational model for functional languages and show how to represent it in a packet-based abstract computer architecture, ALICE. This architecture is highly parallel in nature, with a collection of processing agents performing redex reductions concurrently and asynchronously on the one hand, and the packets that represent the nodes in a function expression graph being distributed over several memory segments on the other. We suggest how a concrete parallel machine can be built to realise this abstract architecture, and describe the design of an experimental prototype machine. This prototype is a hardware emulator of the ideal concrete architecture which is to be built in customised VLSI, and is constructed using the INMOS Transputer as the basic building block. The design utilised a performance model to assist in choosing the optimal organisation of machine components, such as the ratio of processor to memory boards, and the model's predictions for the performance of various configurations of the machine are presented, along with some preliminary measurements made on the prototype. Finally, we make some suggestions for future design enhancements based on our experiences to date.

1.   Introduction

We advocate the design of a machine tailored to executing programs written in *functional languages*. This contrasts with the historical approach where programming language design has been constrained by the von Neumann computer architecture. A natural computational model for the evaluation of functional expressions is *graph reduction*, in which the graph representing an expression is repeatedly reduced, by transforming subgraphs which represent *redexes* (reducible expressions). At each stage there may be one or more redexes which can be reduced, the choice of the next redex or redexes being determined by the evaluation order (computation rule). Thus we may adopt for our customised architecture a parallel evaluator in which the tasks to be computed simultaneously are identified with the redex rewrites which occur in the graph reduction computational model. In this way the architecture can exploit the parallelism inherent in functional languages, and formal transformation offers the prospect of providing techniques to find equivalent functions for which parallelism can be exploited to a greater extent.

In the next section we explain the concept of graph reduction in the context of the functional language HOPE [BM80], and show how a packet-based machine architecture can be used to realise this computational model. This leads to an outline, at the abstract level, of the ALICE architecture, [DR81]. In section 3 we describe the design of the transputer-based prototype machine, before discussing its parameterisation, which employed an analytical model, in section 4. Performance issues and current status are addressed in section 5 before the paper concludes with an outline for future research and a summary in section 6.

2.   A packet-based abstract architecture for graph reduction

2.1   Evaluation of first-order expressions

Graph reduction, corresponding to the evaluation of first-order functional expressions, proceeds by transforming the graph representing an expression with respect to some *redex* node which represents a function application (β-reduction in the case of λ-expressions). The node is then *overwritten* with the sub-graph which represents the result of the application. There are three cases to consider:

(i)   If the associated function is primitive, and all of its required argument sub-graphs have been evaluated, i.e. cannot be further reduced, then the application is evaluated and the redex node is replaced by the root-node of its result. In the case of a primitive arithmetic function, for example, all the arguments must be evaluated, and the result-sub-graph consists of the single root-node which contains an item of atomic data. But in the case of the conditional function, only the predicate must be evaluated, and the result is the appropriate argument-sub-graph.

(ii)   If the associated function is primitive, but not all of the arguments it requires have been evaluated, evaluation of the next required argument (specified in the delta rules of the primitive function) is initiated.

(iii)   If the associated function is programmer-defined, the redex node is replaced by the sub-graph formed from that representing the function's body (i.e. its defining expression), but with each arc that is connected to a node representing a formal parameter redirected to the corresponding sub-graph representing the actual argument. In other words, the body is essentially copied with its formal parameters instantiated by argument expressions in the usual way.

In fact (iii) is a little more complex if the reduction machine performs *pattern matching*, as is the case with ALICE. Pattern matching requires that certain arguments have been evaluated at least far enough to permit comparison with the patterns. When they have not, analogues of the delta rules of primitive functions initiate such evaluation prior to reduction.

The selection of the next redex to reduce corresponds to the evaluation order (or computation rule), for example Normal Order Reduction (which is semantically safe) or Parallel Reduction. We will return to this point later in this section, but it should be noted that Parallel Reduction gives Normal Order Semantics (apart from the problems of halting unwanted non-terminating computations, if such are initiated).

We now give an example of a functional program, written in HOPE, which will be used to illustrate the operation of the ALICE machine and then show how an expression-graph can be represented as a collection of packets in the memory of an abstract architecture. Consider the data type "tree", and suppose we wish to write a function, "size", which takes a tree as argument and returns the number of data items held in the tree as its result. In HOPE this might be written as:

data $tree(\alpha) == tip(\alpha) ++ node(tree(\alpha) \# \alpha \# tree(\alpha))$;

dec $size : tree(\alpha) \rightarrow num$;

--- $size(tip(i)) <= 1$;
--- $size(node(t_1, i, t_2)) <= plus\ (1, plus(size(t_1), size\ (t_2)))$;

'tip' and 'node' in this example are called *constructors* since they serve only to build (construct) data structures. They have no associated rewrite rules.

The 'size' function has two rewrite rules which respectively state that the size of a tree which is a single tip is one, and the size of a tree with a data item at its root is one more than the sum of the sizes of its sub-trees. For example,

size (node (tip(i2), i1, tip(i3))) = 3

A picture of the argument is the tree:

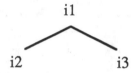

Underlining the redex(es) chosen for re-writing at each stage, reduction of the graph representing this expression proceeds as follows:

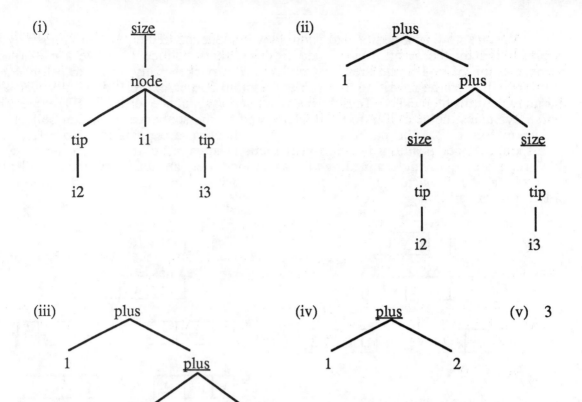

Figure 1 Graph reduction of the expression
size(node(tip(i2), i1, tip(i3)))

2.2   Representation by packets

A node in an expression graph may be represented by a *packet* which is a record divided into fields of the form

Identifier	Function	Argument List	Secondary Fields

The Identifier field simply labels the packet uniquely so that it can be referenced by other packets (see below). It is typically implemented as the *address* of the location in computer storage of the packet, thereby not appearing explicitly in the packet itself. The Function field identifies the function associated with the node represented by the packet, and in practice would be the address of the code of a user defined function or the identifier of a primitive function. The Argument List represents the outgoing arcs from the node, and so consists of a list of identifiers of other packets (representing the top nodes of the argument sub-graphs). The length of the list is variable, so that conceptually packets too have variable length. (In practice packets would normally be of fixed length, providing for a given maximum number of arguments, m say. Function applications with more than m arguments would be implemented by linking together a sufficient number of packets to hold the extra argument-packet addresses). The secondary fields will be discussed later as they become necessary; they contain control information used by the evaluation mechanism.

We are now in a position to show how a sequence of graph reductions may be implemented by the creation and updating of packets. Since we have a one-to-one representation of nodes and arcs by a collection of packets, any graph transformation (corresponding to the rewriting of a sub-expression) can be expressed equally well and uniquely in terms of packets. Thus the above reduction sequence for the HOPE expression which evaluates the size of a tree is implemented by the sequence of packet collections shown in figure 2. The packets within any collection are positioned to reflect the corresponding node positions in the graph reduction shown in figure 1, but the topology of that graph is uniquely determined by the packet identifiers and their argument fields; the packets may be physically located at arbitrary positions in storage, i.e. the identifiers (addresses) are arbitrary.

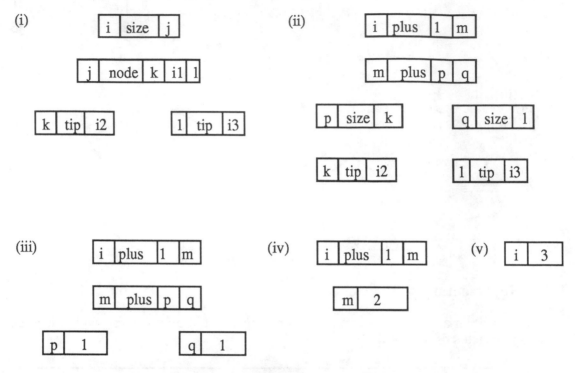

Figure 2   Packet representation of graph reduction

In the main part of this paper we do not consider higher-order functions, but they are supported quite simply in our packet-based model. Higher-order functions are handled at two levels. First, all higher-order functions are translated by the compiler into *partial applications* of a function to a smaller number of arguments than it has formal parameters. This is done by replacing any references to parameters of "outer" functions in a function's defining expression by *new* parameters of this function. (This is equivalent to *lambda-lifting*, [JO85]). Secondly, ALICE supports partial applications by creating *suspensions*, which are packets that indicate the number of missing arguments together with the arguments it has already collected by application of previous suspensions. The application of a suspension to an argument either just appends the argument to its argument list (for later evaluation) or else causes a normal packet rewrite if the argument is its last one.

2.3   Packet communication

Clearly the reduction sequence shown in figure 2 will evaluate the size of the tree correctly, but we have not yet specified how this particular sequence can be generated in the machine executing it. To do this we need a mechanism for indicating the packet (or packets) which corresponds to the next redex (or set of redexes) selected by the chosen evaluation order. A selected redex-packet is easily indicated by a status bit (and/or attaching the identifier of the packet to a "job list" of rewritable packets maintained somewhere in the machine's control system), and then only rewritable packets will be selected for reduction. It therefore remains to determine and mark these packets at each stage in the reduction sequence.

Now, an application of a user-defined function is selected as a redex according to the specified evaluation order, and to show the potential for parallelism, we use an "all redexes in parallel" rule. This will reduce a redex to its Normal form, but may also initiate some non terminating computation, which we will not worry about for the present. For an application of a primitive function, the corresponding delta rule will determine which arguments are needed to permit rewriting. The *number* of arguments needed is stored in the Pending Signals secondary field of the packet representing the primitive function's application, call this packet P, and only the packets representing the required argument-expressions are marked as rewritable in their status fields. After evaluation of an expression, represented by packet Q say, if this is an awaited argument of the primitive function application represented by P, the packet P must be "signalled" that one of its awaited arguments has been evaluated. This is done by having included the identifier of packet P in the Signal Set secondary field of packet Q at the time Q was generated (to cause the communication), and by reducing the Pending Signals field in P when the signal from Q is received. If this becomes zero, the packet P is marked rewritable. Note that the number of packet identifiers in the signal-set is variable; another reason why packets are conceptually of variable length.

The second configuration in the reduction sequence of Figure 2 is elaborated to show the signalling information in Figure 3.

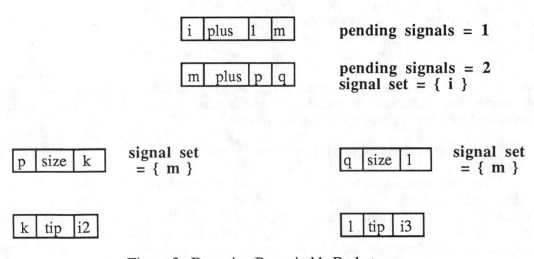

Figure 3   Detecting Re-writable Packets

The signalling mechanism as so far described implies a *control flow* scheme, whereby a signal merely indicates the availability of the result of an argument evaluation. The result itself remains in the signaling packet as per figure 4(a). (Of course if the result is a large structure, access to it would be indirect through the packet which would hold only a pointer.)

A more efficient scheme uses a *data flow* mechanism, whereby the data which is the result of the argument evaluation (or pointer to a structure) is sent to the waiting packet as the signal. The signal set information now has to be augmented to show to which *argument position* in the signalled packet the data must be sent, as well as the packet's identifier. This scheme is illustrated in figure 4(b).

Notice that the redex selection policy described so far will attempt to evaluate all processible packets (redexes) which corresponds to the *eager* evaluation rule. The disadvantage of eager evaluation is that it may result in wasted effort if it turns out that the value of the packet is not ultimately required. As an alternative to eager evaluation *lazy* evaluation only evaluates a packet when the value of that packet is known to be required. For example when evaluating the application of a strict operator such as "+" we know that both of its arguments will be required and so their evaluation can proceeed concurrently. This introduces far less parallelism than eager evaluation (in fact it introduces the minimum possible parallelism whereas eager evaluation generates the maximum possible parallelism) but we at least know that all evaluations which take place will ultimately be useful. To maximise the flexibility of the architecture ALICE allows a complete spectrum of evaluation orders with lazy and eager evaluation being the two extremes. The general scheme relies on *anticipatory* evaluation in which a simple integer (the *anticipation coefficient*) is attached to each packet to indicate how 'deep' a structure it is allowed to generate; this is rather like a 'lookahead' factor. Also associated with the packet is a *pending demands* field which indicates the number of times the packet must be demanded before its evaluation is initiated; this is set to 0 for eager evaluation and 1 for lazy evaluation, as we would expect. When the evaluation of a packet is eventually started the packet evaluates to a depth determined by the anticipation coefficient. This is set to 1 for lazy evaluation and 'maxint' for eager evaluation ('maxint' is the maximum allowable coefficient which in the implementation is treated as an infinite coefficient). If the anticipation coefficient is some 0<n<maxint then the packet will be allowed to generate a data structure of depth n before further evaluation is suspended; in our 'size' example, this would correspond to generating a tree of depth n with the leaves of the trees containing suspended packets (i.e. packets with an anticipation coefficient of 0). Only when the resulting structure has been consumed and more of the structure explicitly demanded will the suspended packet evaluations be resumed, this being achieved by restoring the initial anticipation coefficient of a suspended packet when the first demand for that packet is made. This initial coefficient is also stored in the packet. Note that the anticipation coefficient inherited by the argument packets of a constructor node must be one less than that of the redex packet which generated that constructor node (unless of course the coefficient is 'maxint' in which case it remains unchanged); the initial coefficient, however, always remains unchanged.

2.4 An abstract ALICE architecture

We now have enough information to present an abstract design for our architecture, customised to execute functional, or applicative, expressions: the Applicative Language Idealised Computing Engine with acronym ALICE, [DR81]. There are essentially only three types of component in the abstract machine. Two of these are a *pool* containing a homogenous set of packets and a *collection of processing agents,* each of which repeatedly selects (or is assigned by some server) any rewritable packet from the pool, rewrites it and returns the updated redex-packet to the pool along with any newly generated packets. The whole process proceeds asynchronously until eventually the packet which originally represented the redex of the top-level expression has been fully evaluated and contains the result. This architecture is illustrated in figure 5.

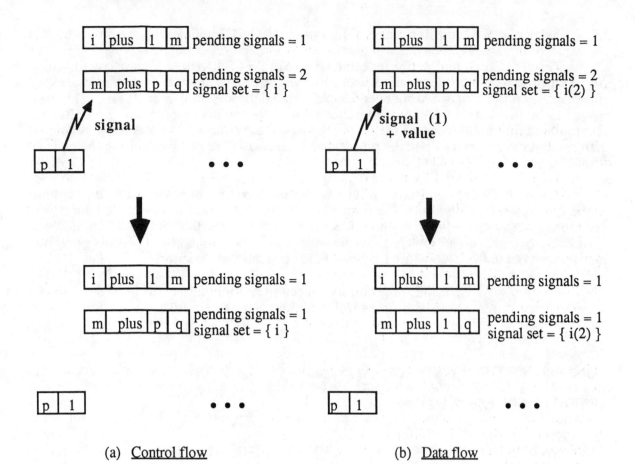

(a) Control flow   (b) Data flow

Figure 4   Signalling Mechanism

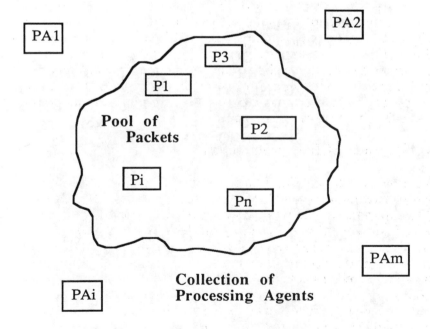

Figure 5   Abstract ALICE Architecture

2.5. The ALICE Compiler Target Language (ALICE CTL)

The ALICE Compiler Target Language (ALICE CTL) is the lowest level of user programming access to the machine and the target code for all compilers. Its most important ferature is that it is independent of the underlying implementation. This has proved to be invaluable because it has allowed us to provide a *stable base* for software development that has decoupled the system software and compiler writers from the many changes that have been made to the physical architecture of the machine during the course of the project.

An ALICE CTL program is built from *constructor operator declarations* and *rewriteable operator definitions*. The former are analogous to the data statements found in a Hope program and the latter to the collections of equations that define a function. A rewriteable operator definition specifies the actions to be performed by a processing agent in order to process a packet whose Function field contains that operator.

A sample ALICE CTL program which rewrites applications of the size function considered in our previous examples follows, the various primitive instructions being explained below.

```
CONSTRUCTOR   tip($1), node ($1, $2, $3)

REWRITEABLE   size($1)

SEQ_DO
      SNAPSHOT_PACKET($1: OPERATOR, OPERAND())
      SEQ_ALT
            IS_CONSTRUCTOR($1)
            ALT
            $1 IS tip($T1)
            REWRITE_$PBP(!1)
                  $1 IS node($T1, _, $T2)
                        SEQ_DO
                        GENERATE_PACKET(&1: size($T1))
                        GENERATE_PACKET(&2: size($T2))
                        GENERATE_PACKET(&3: plus(&1, &2))
                        REWRITE_$PBP(plus(!1, &3))
                        END_SEQ_DO
            END_ALT
      TRUE
            DO
      UPDATE_PACKET($1:
            PENDING_DEMANDS = --1,
            SIGNAL_SET = ++ (CONTROL_FLOW($PBP,
                  WHEN_CONSTRUCTOR)
            )
      )
            RESTORE_$PBP(PENDING_SIGNALS = 1)
            END_DO
      END_SEQ_ALT
END_SEQ_DO
```

The 'brackets' ALT, END_ALT and SEQ_ALT, END_SEQ_ALT enclose alternative actions, only one of which is performed. Each alternative is "guarded" by a boolean expression. In an ALT group, all the guards are evaluated (in any order or indeed concurrently) and if more than one evaluates to true a programmer-defined arbitration method chooses just one alternative. In a SEQ_ALT the guards are evaluated in their textual order and the first alternative whose guard evaluates to true is chosen.

The brackets DO, END_DO and SEQ_DO, END_SEQ_DO enclose actions to be performed. Actions enclosed by DO and END_DO may be performed in any order or indeed concurrently. Those enclosed by SEQ_DO and END_SEQ_DO must be performed in the order specified.

Names beginning with the '$' symbol refer to arguments of the packet being processed, including the components of arguments which are composite data. The special name '$PBP' refers to the packet being processed itself. Names beginning with the '&' symbol refer to new packets generated during the course of the rewrite.

In section 3.4 below we describe how a 'size' packet is processed. The reader will be able to relate the steps taken to the above ALICE CTL very easily.

3. Design of the prototype machine

In this section we describe a physical realisation of the abstract architecture given in the previous section; a *concrete architecture*. The ideal machine would ultimately be constructed with customised VLSI chips, but a prototype, built from off-the-shelf programmable components, to emulate this architecture was favoured partly in order to shorten the delivery time, partly for reasons of cost and funding, but more importantly to achieve a high degree of flexibility in the design and control of the machine. In this way, much post-construction experimentation becomes possible, and indeed advisable, from which the design of a future VLSI machine would be greatly assisted. The prototype comprises three distinct types of boards of electronic components, corresponding to the logical components of the abstract machine, viz. *agent boards* (to perform asynchronous packet rewriting), *memory boards* (to provide a distributed packet pool) and an *interconnection network* (to provide fast, reliable communication between the agents and memories. The concrete architecture, showing these three basic constituents, is illustrated in figure 6.

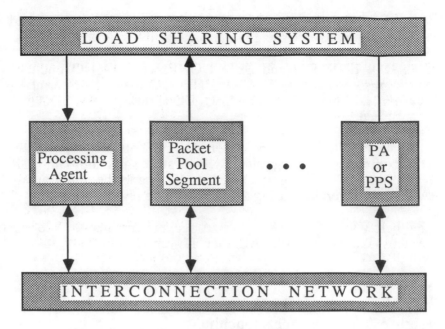

Figure 6   Concrete ALICE Architecture

A further type of communication is in general necessary, in order to implement a *load sharing system*, and at present this is also provided for by the interconnection network. This system is used to distribute work amongst the processing agents and the packet pool segments according to the current load on each such element. The additional communication is necessary in order to maintain and make available the appropriate information, although if load sharing is done on a purely *random* basis, no such communication is necessary; this is precisely what has been implemented in the initial version of the prototype. For expressions with high levels of potential concurrency, for which most processors can be kept busy for most of the time, one would expect the random algorithm to be efficient. This, we shall see in section 6, was found to be the case. However, the converse was also found to hold, expressions evaluating with a large degree of sequential behaviour giving poor performance without improved load sharing.

The designs of each of the three types of physical component are discussed in the following sub-sections, and section 3 closes with a description of the sequence of tasks performed during the evaluation of a functional expression, to illustrate the machine's principles of operation.

3.1   Agent boards

The processing agent component of the abstract architecture is realised by five INMOS transputers on a single board in the prototype machine. Two of these perform the packet rewriting (packet rewriting units, abbreviated to PRUs); one manages the local cache storage which holds the function definitions required by each PRU (function definition management unit, abbreviated to FDU); one serves as an input buffering device, handling all incoming transactions from the network and routing them to the appropriate PRU; and one serves as an output buffering device similarly. The logical organisation of these devices is shown in figure 7, the supporting hardware being omitted.

Each PRU has 64k of RAM and is devoted to the task of rewriting packets, according to their ALICE CTL code which is guaranteed to be in the local memory of the PRU by the FDU (see below). The ALICE CTL code exists in compiled form, in a lower level "Implementation Specific Language " or ALICE ISL. This language represents an idealised instruction set for a PRU, and is what is actually used in the prototype; the transputers, running OCCAM programs, *emulate* a PRU and *interpret* ISL code. Of course this is not the most efficient implementation, but it is the most suitable for the purposes of prototyping. Now, the cycle involved in the rewriting of a packet involves a number of *network transactions*; to fetch a rewritable packet and argument packets, to generate an updated packet, to signal packets, etc, as may be seen in the sample ALICE CTL program of section 2.5 and in section 3.4. The amount of local processing is fairly small, and a PRU would spend a large proportion of time awaiting responses from the packet pool segments. This problem is avoided in the conventional way by *multiprocessing* a number of *virtual PRU*s (VPRUs or "virtual agents") in the PRU, so that when one VPRU is awaiting a response, another may be processing. If the number of VPRUs multiprocessed is v, the buffering transputers each multiplex 2v processes.

The processors which provide the network interfaces are the External Request Unit transputer (ERU) which has 8k of RAM and buffers incoming transactions, decoupling the PRU pair, and the External Transmission Unit transputer (ETU) which performs the complementary task of handling outgoing transactions generated by the PRU pair. It is the ETU which initiates and manages the network communication, and the appropriate *process* executing in it is marked explicitly as NCU (Network Connection Unit) in Figure 7.

Finally, the FDU is responsible for managing the function definition caches of the two PRUs. When a packet arrives in the ERU destined for a PRU, call it A, it is first passed to the FDU which inspects the function field and checks if there is a copy in A's 64k of RAM. If there is, then the packet is passed on to A. If there is a copy in the other PRU's cache, a copy of this is written into A's cache. Otherwise further network transactions are scheduled through the ETU to fetch the function definition from the central function store, residing in the packet pool memory. Now, the ALICE CTL comprising a function-definition is generated by a compiler, written in HOPE for example, as an ordinary data structure in terms of constructor functions. It is therefore compiled into packets in the usual way, and so a function-definition also may be distributed in any way over the packet pool segments. Thus to obtain a function's definition, the FDU schedules a sequence of packet-fetches. When the packets containing the code defining the rewrite rules have all arrived (through the ERU), and been written into A's cache, the original redex-packet is sent to A (by the FDU) which can then perform the rewriting. The states of the caches of the two PRUs are held in tables in the FDU's 8k of RAM.

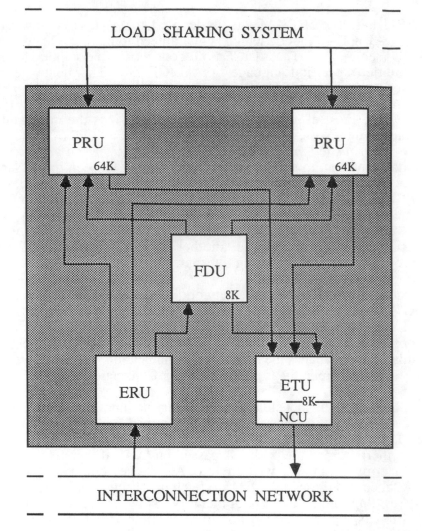

LOAD SHARING SYSTEM

PRU
64K

PRU
64K

FDU
8K

ERU

ETU
8K
NCU

INTERCONNECTION NETWORK

Figure 7   Processing Agent Board

3.2   Packet Pool Segment Boards

The packet pool is distributed over a number of *packet pool segments* (PPSs) in the prototype machine, each segment being built on one board. The segments form one address space. The most significant bits of a packet's identifier are used to specify the segment in which it is stored and the remaining bits provide the offset within that segment. The processing performed by a packet pool segment is rather simpler than that of an agent, comprising in the main the transmission of network transactions in response to incoming messages from PRUs. The major part of the board is allocated to memory chips, providing two megabytes for each segment, controlled by a transputer called the packet management unit (PMU). This transputer also handles the buffering of inputs from the network via a high priority process which has access to enough input buffer space to accommodate one message from *every* virtual agent. Thus incoming network transactions can never be blocked and deadlock cannot occur. As with the processing agent boards, there is a separate ETU transputer to buffer the outgoing transactions and decouple the PMU. The incorporation of input buffering into the PMU avoids the need for a separate ERU, so saving one transputer per PPS board. This is feasible because the computing tasks required of a PMU are sufficiently small, whereas the same is not true of the PRUs, which would become overloaded if they also had to support high-priority buffering processes. The layout of a PPS board is shown in Figure 8.

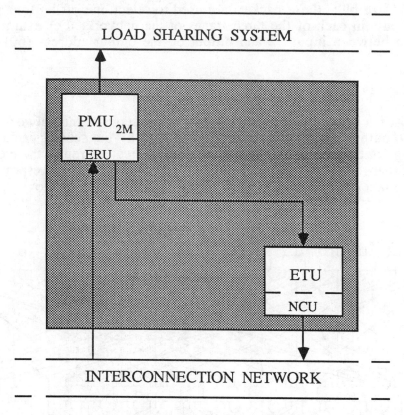

Figure 8   Packet Pool Segment Board

3.3   Communication and the interconnection network

The interconnection network provides bi-directional communication between any processing agent and any packet pool segment. Its ideal implementation would be a *crossbar switch* but such are impractical for all but small numbers of inputs and outputs, their complexity being proportional to the square of the number of connected devices. A *multi-stage switching network* with a *generalised- cube* topology still allows any input to be connected to any output but is far more cost effective; when there are N input and output ports the complexity is proportional to NlogN. Such networks are the subject of [SI85]. Their disadvantage is that the routes from two different inputs to two different outputs may share some intermediate link, thus forcing one communication to have to wait for the other; this is known as *blocking*. There are many types of interconnection networks, the one used in the prototype machine is a *delta network* [Pa79]. The basic building block in such a network is a b x b crossbar switch; in the ALICE machine this is a custom-designed 4 x 4 switch fabricated in Emitter Coupled Logic (ECL) and known as the XS1 [FC85]. In general, multi-stage network with b^n inputs and outputs is built from n *stages* of b^{n-1} switches. The links between the switches in successive stages are arranged so that each of the b^n inputs to the network "sees" a complete 1-to-b^n decode tree encompassing all the b^n

outputs. The ALICE interconnection network consists of three stages of 4 x 4 crossbars giving 4^3=64 connections in total and is shown in Figure 9.

In order to route a message from any input link to output link k the address, k, is partitioned into three two-bit packets (in general $\log_b N$ packets each of $\log_2 b$ bits for a network of size b^n); these packets are used to select one of the four possible crossbar switch outputs in each of the three stages of the network. For example, to establish a connection between input 22 and output 60 the output address (60) is partitioned as follows:-

$$60 = 111100 \rightarrow 11,11,00$$

the leftmost packet (11) is used to select the first stage of the network which routes the message to output 3 of the relevant crossbar switch; the second packet (11) selects the second stage of the network similarly; the third packet (00) routes the message to output 0 of the crossbar reached in the final stage of the network; this corresponds to the network output link labelled 60, as required. The established path is shown as a dotted line in Figure 9.

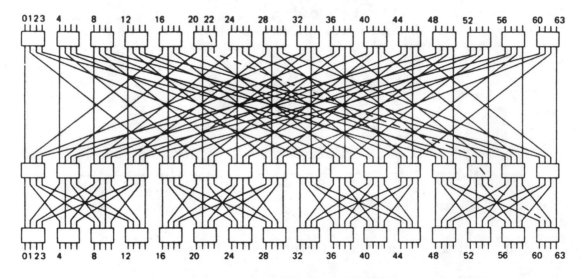

Note: Connection between input 22 and output 60 shown dotted.

Figure 9   The Interconnection Network

In order to keep the engineering complexity of the network within managable bounds we use *bit-serial* communication. The network in the prototype machine uses a *circuit switching* communication protocol so that when a source processor wishes to transmit a message, it first establishes a path through the network that links its ETU (output buffer) to the destination's ERU (input buffer) and then initiates a direct end-to-end transfer of the data. Circuit switching is inherently simpler to implement than packet switching owing to the lack of message buffers in the switch. The low transistor count required to implement circuit switching enabled the component switches to be fabricated in ECL without significant power dissipation problems (1.3W per device).

The structure of each component switching chip (XS1) is shown in Figure 10. This shows the switch to be divided into four identical 'slices' each with a five-wire interface at both input and output sides. To establish a channel through the network the requested network output address is loaded into a shift register which forms part of the *network interface* and a negative transition is placed on the request input (RI) to the crossbar slice associated with that interface. This transition causes a three-pulse burst clock signal to be transmitted back to the source component (on the BO link). At the interface, the first burst clock pulse is used to generate a 'start bit' and the remaining two are coupled to the shift register clock input and have the effect of extracting the first two-bit packet from the register. The start bit, followed by the two crossbar select bits are transmitted back to the switch (on the DI wire) together with the original burst clock (on the CI wire). The signals on the CI and DI inputs are phase-matched to enable the burst clock to be used to latch the two address bits inside the Address Generation Unit without synchronisation problems.

When both address bits have been successfully latched a transition is made on the Acknowledge line (AO) by passing an 'address valid' signal (ADV) through a 5-1 multiplexer unit; this prepares the source interface to receive the next Burst clock sequence. These two bits, validated by a second address valid signal (ADVS), are sent to the Arbitration Unit which then attempts to route the request through to the addressed switch output. If the output is currently free then the five input wires are coupled to the corresponding wires of the address switch output effectively making the switch transparent. This is achieved by appropriately setting the Select signals (S) which activate pass and multiplexer units accordingly. The process is then repeated, this time with the source interface in communication with the selected crossbar in the second stage of the network. When the final stage of the network has been selected the addressed destination responds by transmitting an end-of-path signal to the source which has the effect of coupling the serial links of the source and destination Transputers. The network appears transparent to the Transputers which communicate using their standard handshaking protocol.

In the event of the addressed output port being busy (indicated by the Engaged status lines E), the partial path established is *held* rather than released, although the latter alternative is provided for in the hardware (by setting RI - this can be done asynchronously). A blocked request essentially 'waits' at the input of the blocking switch which is polled on every cycle of a 4-phase, non-overlapping clock ($\phi0..\phi3$ generated from the source ϕx) within the switch to prevent more than one message being allocated the same output simultaneously. When the output required by a blocked message becomes free, the input/output coupling is completed as described above. Thus all contention is internal in switches, there is no queueing, and deadlock cannot occur.

Communication over the network is monitored by fault detection mechanisms that check for misrouted or corrupted messages although we have yet to see any such errors during normal operation. The required 48 switching chips and their supporting electronic components (forming the interfaces) are distributed over 8 boards.

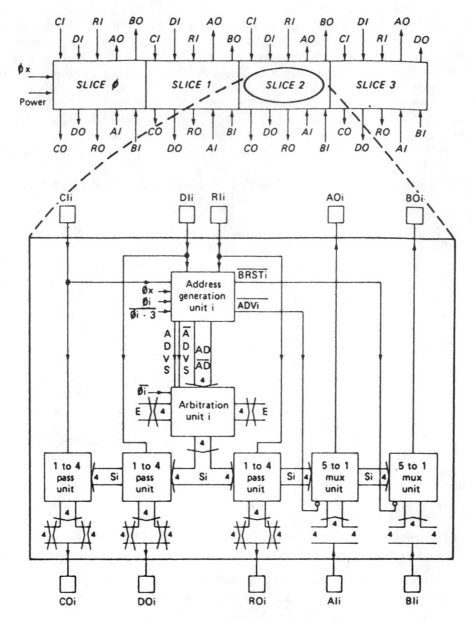

Figure 10   XS1 Circuit Details

316

3.4   Principles of operation

We have seen how functional expressions are evaluated in the abstract architecture, and how the primitive logical elements of this architecture can be realised in a prototype. It is now an easy task to describe the operational principles of ALICE in terms of the *network transactions* generated in the rewriting of a reducible packet residing in one of the PPSs.

First, a packet is *fetched* by any of the idle virtual agents (VPRUs) which issues a request for a reducible packet to one of the PPSs, chosen by the VPRU *at random* (recall we have only random load sharing at present). A reducible packet, if one is present in the PPS, is sent back to the VPRU as a response - otherwise the response indicates that there are no reducible packets, and the transactions are wasted if there are reducible packets elsewhere. Such wasted transactions may or may not significantly affect performance (as we discuss in section 5), but intuitively would be less frequent and have less effect in evaluations having more parallelism, where more processing elements are likely to be busy.

Once a rewritable packet arrives at the ERU of its destination agent board it is passed on to the FDU which ensures that the code defining the function is present in the requesting PRU's cache, by fetching the code via further network transactions if necessary, as discussed in section 3.1. The FDU then sends the redex-packet to the appropriate PRU, addressed to the requesting VPRU. The remainder of this VPRU's operations and network transactions are fully defined by the ALICE CTL associated with the function appearing in the packet. This may involve fetching argument-packets from given addresses (i.e. the PPS and location within its memory), updating and re-storing the redex packet at its original address and generating new packets. A new packet is stored in the RAM of a PPS which is selected at random by the VPRU, at an address which is sent back to the VPRU as an acknowledgement by the PPS. (If the RAM happened to be full, an error code would be returned and the VPRU would try another PPS.) The only other main operation that the VPRU performs is to rewrite a packet with a *primitive function* in its function field.

An illustration of these operations is given by the ALICE CTL code for the rewrite rules of the size function in section 2.5. Having received a size packet to rewrite, the VPRU first fetches the argument-packet, $1. If this is a constructor, the argument has been evaluated (in a lazy implementation) and the packet can be re-written. If the constructor is "tip", the result is the constant 1 and if it is "node" two new packets are generated to evaluate the sizes of the sub-trees. Their addresses, &1 and &2, are bound when the acknowledgements are received from the chosen PPSs. A third packet is then generated which adds the results of packets &1 and &2, and has its address bound to &3. The redex-packet ($PBP) is then updated so as to evaluate the sum of 1 and the result of packet &3. If the argument-packet is not a constructor, then its evaluation must be initiated. This is accomplished by first decrementing its Pending Demands field (this will have been 1 in the lazy implementation), then inserting the identifier of the redex-packet into its Signal Set together with an indication that the signal is to be transmitted when its function field becomes a constructor (i.e. when the packet has been evaluated), and then re-storing it in the packet pool. The control flow signalling scheme is used in this example. The redex-packet is then re-stored with its Pending Signals field set to 1; to be awoken on receipt of the signal from its newly updated argument-redex-packet.

3.5   Other Features

There are a number of supporting features which should be mentioned. These include the diagnostic and monitoring system, Input-Output facilities and garbage collection. The diagnostic and monitoring system provides sophisticated fault detection and location tools and enables detailed data on the behaviour of the system to be collected for analysis; this data will be used in the design of any successor machine. The Input-Output system provides an Ethernet link to the machine, which is used as a high-speed application load and monitor data dump route. This is shown in Figure 11.

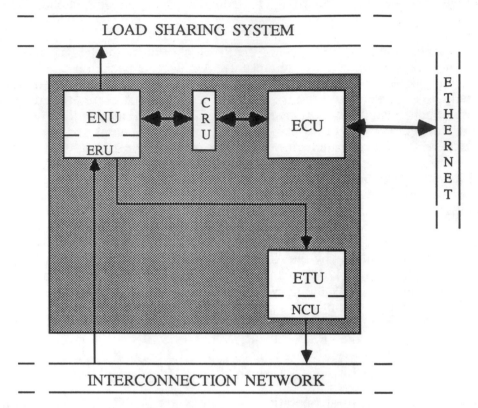

Figure 11   Input-Output Board

As a computation proceeds, many intermediate results are generated. When these are finished with, i.e. are no longer arguments of any function application, the packets they occupy can be reused. This reclaiming process is known as *garbage-collection*. A count, known as the *reference count*, is maintained in all packets, and records how many times the value held in a packet is used by other parts of the computation, i.e. how many times a packet's identifier appears in the Argument List field of other packets. Each time a new reference to a packet is generated the reference count of the packet is incremented by one. Similarly, each time a redex evaluation is completed, the references to its argument-packets disappear and their reference counts are decremented by one. If the reference count of a packet reaches zero, no part of the computation requires its value and so the packet can be reclaimed. This is known as *reference count garbage collection*, and on ALICE this is performed concurrently with expression evaluation. Reference count updating is performed by PRUs as part of the packet rewriting process, but is not shown in the ALICE CTL code given in section 2.5 for the function size.

4.   Parameterisation by an analytical performance model

From the discussion of the previous section, it should be clear that a correctly operating prototype ALICE machine could be constructed using any numbers of agent boards, say p, and PPS boards, say m, together with a large enough delta network, i.e. one that provides at least (p + m)-way communication, and supporting hardware. A major design problem, therefore, is to determine the optimum ratio, p : m, given a constraint on the total size of the machine. In practice the constraint was essentially the size of the rack, which could in fact accommodate 40 processor and memory boards, i.e. p + m = 40. The total number of transputers, the most expensive of the electronic components, was also limited.

A second design issue concerned the degree of multiprocessing of VPRUs in each PRU, the parameter v in section 3.1. Assuming for the moment that memory size is unlimited, the mean packet rewriting rate will always increase with v, provided that there are sufficiently many reducible packets, i.e. at least 2pv, the total number of VPRUs. However, since at most 2p PRUs can be processing at any time, the gains in performance will diminish as v continues to be increased beyond a certain level, and an asymptote will be approached. If now memory is also taken into account, the more VPRUs multiprogrammed, the less local RAM will be available for the function definition cache, and so the greater will be the "miss rate" encountered by the FDU. Thus the number of remote function store accesses will increase, *degrading* performance. There is also the 'microscopic' storage problem of *addressing* of the VPRUs - whenever v increases through a power of 2, an extra addressing bit is required. So what value should we choose for the number of VPRUs in each PRU transputer? Other questions which arise are 'What will be the throughput of a given configuration (in terms of p, m and v as well as other parameters like device processing rates)?'. 'Where will the bottlenecks occur?'. 'How many PRUs should be supported on a single agent board?'.

Rough intuitive guesses could be made for all of these questions, based on the experience of the engineers and using timings of the OCCAM code in which the controlling firmware was written. These guesses suggested that p should be a bit less than m, v should be about 4, throughput might be around 10-20k rewrites of the Fibonnacci function per second (the "NFIB" rate discussed in section 5) and that either the PRUs or PMUs would form the bottleneck. It was possible to be a little more precise regarding the further question of the number of PRUs, n say, to put on an agent board. At low utilisations, one is enough. In a high-loading situation, recall that all of the incoming work for each PRU first passes through the ERU (and FDU in the case of a new redex-packet). Therefore if the mean time delay for an incoming message in the ERU is T_e and in a PRU is T_p, then we should aim to have $T_p = nT_e$ so that the throughputs of the ERU and the combined set of PRUs match (and any bottleneck is then shared between the ERU and PRUs, giving best performance). If $n > T_p/T_e$, performance will not degrade, but the cost of the machine will increase. If $n < T_p/T_e$ performance will suffer.

In order to make precise, reliable predictions for the other quantities of interest, a *performance model* was constructed. In view of the number of components in the concrete architecture, and other disadvantages, a simulation model was rejected, and an analytical model was adopted, [HF86]. An analytical model which represented every transputer individually would also be expensive to run, and a method of aggregating like components was developed using decomposition methods [CO77]. This resulted in a queueing network model with five servers having queue length dependent service rates, which was solved using the standard Convolution Algorithm, see for example [SC81]. The five different servers represented the corresponding five collections of all (a) PMUs; (b) PPS board ETUs; (c) combined ERUs and FDUs on agent boards; (d) PRUs; (e) agent board ETUs. The service rate functions of the aggregate servers were calibrated using the mean service times estimated by OCCAM timings for the associated transputers, and mean DMA transmission times. In addition, each service rate depends on the number of devices aggregated, and number of processes multiprogrammed in them in cases (c), (d) and (e). Thus, formulae for the service rate functions of the five aggregate-servers were given in terms of the mean service times referred to above and respectively m, m, (p and 2v), (2p and v) and (p and 2v) for a prototype with p agent boards and m PPS boards. In each case, the service rate for any queue length is proportional to the rate of an individual server in the aggregate, given by the reciprocal of the estimated mean service time. When the queue length is *n*, the service rate function, $R(n)$, assuming that individual transputer service rates are unity, is as follows (see [HF86]):

Cases (a) and (b): $\quad R(n) = mn/(m+n-1)$

Cases (c) and (e): $\quad R(1) = 1, \ R(n) = \{(2(p-1)v-n+1)/(2pv-n+1)\}R(n-1) + 2pv/(2pv-n+1) \quad (n{\geq}1)$

Case (d): $\quad R(1) = 1, \ R(n) = \{((2p-1)v-n+1)/(2pv-n+1)\}R(n-1) + 2pv/(2pv-n+1) \quad (n{\geq}1)$

The model gave predictions for (amongst other quantities) throughput, for various parameterisations, assuming highly parallel execution in which all virtual agents are always busy. A graph of throughput versus number of agent boards, p, where p + m = 40, shown in Figure 12, indicated that little more performance improvement can be obtained for v > 8, optimum performance then being obtained for p = 16 and m = 24, giving throughput of approximately 120k network transactions per second. The service rate of a single PRU transputer was estimated to be 4, so that this performance prediction is quite close to the theoretical maximum of p.2.4 = 128 transactions per second, obtained when no PRU is idle at any time.

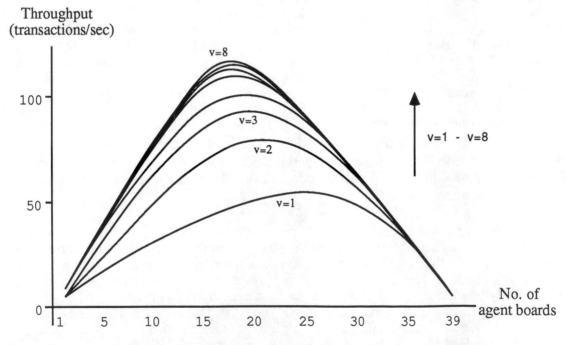

Figure 12 Performance Versus Number of Agent Boards (40 Board Machine)

In order to be able to make a prediction for the number of *function-rewrites* per second performed by the machine, we need information about the form of the functions' definitions. In general, this requires a *workload model also*, but for the purposes of benchmarking we can just inspect the ALICE CTL of the functions concerned to find the number of transactions involved in a rewrite. Our main benchmark is based on the fibonnacci function and has HOPE defining equations

        --- NFIB (1) <= 1;
        --- NFIB (2) <= 1;
        --- NFIB (succ(succ(n))) <= 1 + NFIB (succ(n)) + NFIB(n);

This function has the property that the total number of function calls made to NFIB in the evaluation of an application of NFIB is equal to the result (the addition of 1 includes the top-level call). This property follows immediately by induction on the argument, using the recursive equations. Thus, mean NFIB-function-rewrite rate can be estimated by applying NFIB to any argument and dividing the result by the measured execution time - we call this the 'nfib-rate'. However, this will only give the same answer for every argument if the ratios of the numbers of calls to "plus", NFIB-base-case (NFIB(1) or NFIB(2)) and NFIB-non-base-case are always the same. Moreover, in computing the total number of network transactions involved, we need to know separately the numbers of these different types of call. These results can be derived quite simply as follows. First define the class of functions f_{ij} $(i,j \geq 0)$ by

$$f_{ij}(1) = f_{ij}(2) = i, \text{ and } f_{ij}(n+2) = j + f_{ij}(n+1) + f_{ij}(n) \quad (n \geq 1)$$

Thus f_{10} is the normal Fibonnacci function, *fib* say, and it follows at once that for all $n \geq 1$, $i,j \geq 0$, $f_{i0}(n) = i.f_{10}(n)$ and $f_{ij}(n) = f_{i+j,0}(n) - j$. Now fixing the argument $n =$ N, and writing F to denote *fib(N)*, in the evaluation of the expression NFIB(N) = f_{11}(N) = 2F - 1, we have that

(i)   The number of base-case calls to NFIB is F

(ii)   The number of non-base-case calls to NFIB is f_{01}(N) = F - 1

(iii)   The number of calls to "plus" is f_{02}(N) = 2F - 2

These results again follow by simple induction, and we note as a check that the total number of function calls must be f_{13}(N) = 4F - 3, by similar reasoning, remembering to count two pluses and the top-level call in the recursive defining equation. This total is the same as the sum of (i), (ii) and (iii) as required. We have therefore established that the numbers of calls to "plus" , base-case-NFIB and non-base-case-NFIB are effectively equal to 2F, F and F respectively for even moderately large N, and that our nfib-rate will be the same for all N.

Since applications of NFIB have well-balanced expression graphs, NFIB is 'highly parallel' in that for a sufficiently large argument, there will be enough redexes to ensure that none of the virtual agents need be idle throughout most of the computation. Thus the assumptions of the model are acceptable for this benchmark. We assume use of the *eager* evaluation order for NFIB(N) in which every sub-expression that *can* be rewritten is marked reducible, and the data-flow mode of signalling between packets. In this way, all rewritable packets have their arguments in *immediate* form. Now, for the rewrite of a non-base-case-NFIB packet, there are 5 network transactions: fetch a reducible packet; generate two packets to evaluate NFIB applied to the smaller arguments; generate a packet to add the results of these two packets; and rewrite the redex-packet to add the immediate data value 1 to the result of this packet. For the rewrites of a "plus" or a base-case NFIB packet, there are 3 transactions: fetch a reducible packet; send the result as data to the packet with identifier in its signal set; and rewrite the redex-packet (although an optimisation would omit this transaction which is not necessary in the data-flow mode). Thus the total number of network transactions in the evaluation of NFIB(N) is $5(F-1) + 3(2F-2) + 3F \cong 14F$, and so the predicted maximum nfib-rate is approximately $2F/(14F/120,000) \cong 17k$ rewrites per second.

The model predicts further that near the optimal parameterisation of the system, a 10% increase (or decrease) in the service rate of the PRUs results in a decrease (or increase) of 1 in the optimum value for the number of agent boards, p (when the total number of boards, p + m = 40). These predictions are displayed in the graph of Figure 13, which shows the performance curves near the optimum number of agent boards for individual PRU transputer service rates between 3.6 and 4.6. In fact at the optimum point, we really had $p \cong 17$, but it is expected that the PRU code can be optimised significantly, increasing the service rate of the PRU server. Hence the conclusion that the ideal numbers for p and m are 16 and 24 respectively.

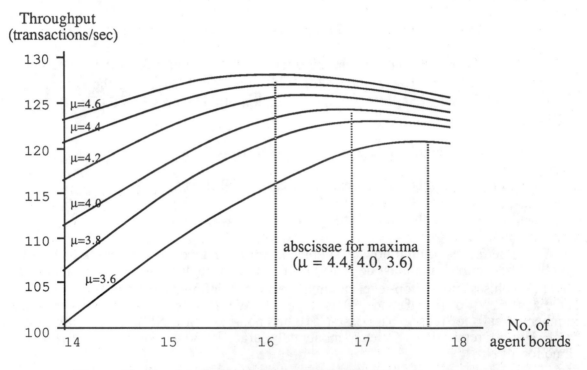

Figure 13 Sensitivity Curves Near the Optimal Parameterisation for PRU service rates between 3.6 and 4.6

The model also predicted the mean queue lengths and utilisations of the transputers, and the result of the bottleneck analysis was that with the optimal parameterisation, the PRU and PMU transputers are *necessarily* joint bottlenecks.

5.   ALICE performance and current status

The ALICE prototype is now operational. At present, RAM images of a computation's initial packets (the top-level expression, its data and the ALICE ISL of the associated functions) are compiled off-line and loaded by the Ethernet link into storage addresses generated by the compiler. However, it is intended to mount a small operating system so that the machine can be made stand-alone. Currently application-level input-output is limited to a keyboard and screen, but it is planned that this will be extended to include a high-bandwidth link via the Ethernet. The source language used is HOPE, which is compiled into ALICE CTL, and a second compilation translates ALICE CTL code into ALICE ISL. It is expected that the parallel logic programming language, PARLOG, will also be compiled into ALICE CTL soon, providing an alternative application language, [DR83].

A number of functional programs have been monitored during their execution on ALICE. The main benchmark is the NFIB function, defined by the HOPE equations given in Section 4. As already noted there, applications of this function have well-balanced graph representations and so great potential for exploiting parallelism. Thus, when applied to a large enough argument, all VPRUs can be kept busy for the large majority of the execution time, and so the prototype machine can be expected to come close to giving its maximum performance. Measurements indicate this to be about 16000 NFIB-rewrites per second, or 32000 function rewrites per second if the contributions from the additions are also included. It has also been observed that, as the machine is scaled down, using fewer than 40 boards in total but always in the optimum ratio, performance decreases linearly with size - i.e. the NFIB rate is about 1k rewrites per second per agent board, e.g. 2k when there are two agents and three PPSs. In fact we also observe 1k when there is one agent and two or more PPSs. This follows since any PPSs in excess of 1.5 are wasted in that the PRUs are then the bottlenecks and become saturated. The linearity of performance with machine size observed for evaluation of NFIB applications is simply a consequence of the high degree of parallelism. In the next example, as the machine size increases, not all VPRUs (and PRUs) can be kept busy and performance does not increase significantly.

The second test function solves an optimal route-planning problem called "Mike's-tour" after Mike Reeve's travelling exploits. This evaluates in a very sequential fashion, and originally exhibited the anomalous property that as machine size increased, execution time *also increased*! The cause was soon discovered to be a limitation of the very naive implementation of "random load sharing". On becoming idle, a VPRU immediately issues a request to a (randomly selected) PPS for a packet to rewrite. If the PPS has none, it indicates thus in its response. The VPRU then chooses a PPS randomly again and the cycle will repeat until a reducible packet is located. Unfortunately a function application may have inherently sequential execution characteristics, i.e. may have a biased rather than balanced reduction graph; consider the factorial function, for example. In such a case, there will be few reducible packets at any time, and large numbers of network transactions will be generated as most VPRUs repeatedly request packets and receive the null response. "Mike's tour" is such a function, and the problem is compounded by the use of lazy evaluation which limits the number of rewritable packets to a minimum. Thus the DMA channels associated with network transactions saturate, and the PRUs and PMUs doing useful work become underutilized. In queueing model terms, the bottleneck has moved due to the sudden decrease in the mean service times of the PRU and PMU servers; although this results in *increased* transaction rate, most transactions do not represent useful work.

The problem of the saturation of the DMA channels with useless messages is easily solved. When a PPS receives a request for a packet to rewrite, but has none, it should *not* send a response until it does have a reducible packet, which it *then* sends. The useless message traffic is thereby removed, and the only problem now occurs when a VPRU is blocked waiting for its destination PPS to acquire a reducible packet when there *are* such packets in other PPSs. However, in a low-load situation, other VPRUs will rewrite these packets, and in a high-load situation a reducible packet will soon arrive in any given PPS. The solution therefore appears effective.

The final function application we consider illustrates the non-deterministic properties of parallel implementations. The example is the function that merges two lists, and can be written non deterministically in a HOPE style using equations with overlapping left hand sides thus:

--- merge (x :: y, z) <= x :: merge(y, z);
--- merge (y, x :: z) <= x :: merge(y, z);

The symbol :: denotes CONS, and the type declarations and base case equations have been omitted. Two lists will merge non deterministically in ALICE if the above equations generate new packets in a *parallel* ALT block in the ALICE CTL defining the rewrite rules for merge. Alternatively, by using SEQ_ALT, biased or alternating merges can be achieved.

6.   Future plans and conclusions

A great deal of experimentation and enhancement is planned for the ALICE prototype in the near future, with the particular intention of aiding the design of a customised VLSI-version. This work will be considered in the categories of modelling, experimentation and machine enhancements.

There is an important role for modelling in the design of complex architectures, as we saw in section 4 for example. The development of reliable analytical models requires systematic validation, and the availability of a flexible experimental machine provides a rare opportunity for this. Conversely, the availability of a reliable model greatly enhances the prospects for the successful design and implementation of significant enhancements, as well as for the design of future machines. Indeed we expect to employ such models in the design of the customised successor to ALICE, so that ALICE herself will not only aid this design through direct experimentation, but also indirectly by assisting in the development of modelling techniques.

Regarding machine enhancements we have already noted in previous sections that a more sophisticated load sharing system than the random one should be developed, with the aim of allocating newly generated packets to the less utilised PPSs and ensuring that requests from VPRUs for reducible packets are addressed to PPSs which have them. A further improvement would then ensure that the reducible subset of packets is also evenly distributed amongst the PPSs in order to reduce the queueing of packet requests at overloaded PPSs. Any improved load sharing will require information to be available about the distribution of work in the system, which itself will require inter-PPS communication, which can be provided by the delta network. A more radical suggestion is to have the packet rewriting cycles initiated by the PMUs, which would choose VPRUs to which to send redex packets. This, some claim, facilitates more balanced load sharing.

An anticipated problem which is inherent in the pure abstract architecture is that of a *grain size* which is too small. In other words, the amount of computation devoted to expression evaluation performed by a VPRU between network transactions is small compared with the latency of the transactions, i.e. the round-trip response time associated with requests sent to the PPSs. In order to recover this lost performance, a very high degree of parallelism may be required. However, excessive parallelism will overload the set of VPRUs which are limited in number to 2pv, or 256 in ALICE. Thus we should exploit *locality* where possible, for example by increasing the sizes of function bodies. Other ways of reducing the number of network transactions would be to allocate packets for rewriting to PRUs which already have the required function definitions in their caches, and for a VPRU to retain at least one packet that it generates in *reducible* form for rewriting later. The second technique should also increase the effect of the first; consider a recursive function definition.

A further machine enhancement we mention concerns the delta network. Although this does *detect* faults it is not fault-tolerant. However, extra stages could be added to provide alternative routes in the normal way, see for example [SI85].

There are also a number of possible language-related enhancements. The prototype machine has been organised to provide for the parallel implementation of a number of languages. However, it is planned to optimise the transputer OCCAM control programs to handle purely functional expression evaluations only, with maximum efficiency. This might also lead to *compiling* ALICE CTL into OCCAM which would execute directly in the PRUs, rather than into ALICE ISL which is currently interpreted.

Finally, we briefly address the conflict between laziness and strictness. A strict (call-by-value) implementation can generate much more parallelism than the lazy scheme, but may also generate non-terminating computations. A solution under investigation is to provide a *strictness analyser* in the compiler which will identify strict arguments in function applications, i.e. those which will *definitely* be needed and so can be pre-evaluated. This would be the perfect solution if *all* such arguments could be detected. However, this cannot be done in general, but current research is very encouraging and it may be possible to identify an extensive class of strict arguments without too much compile-time effort.

To conclude, the experience gained by all concerned in the development of ALICE, from an ideal for the advancement of functional programming to an operational prototype machine offering great flexibility for experimentation, has been invaluable. The ultimate long-term goals are still some way off, and apart from building the successor machine in VLSI, we are also investing a substantial effort in the design of an enhanced functional language, HOPE+, and in the development of a transformation-based programming support environment. But in the arrival of ALICE, we have reached a significant milestone on the way to the attainment of a functional-language-based system for solving the complex computer applications of today and tomorrow.

Acknowledgements

There have been several others involved in the work described in this paper, and we wish to acknowledge the efforts of the members of the Functional Programming Research Section led by Professor John Darlington in the Department of Computing, Imperial College, and of the ALICE Team at ICL's Mainframe Systems Division, West Gorton.

References

[BM80]   R. M. Burstall, D. B. MacQueen, D. T. Sannella, "HOPE: An Experimental Applicative Language", 1st International LISP Conference, 1980.

[CF86]   M. D. Cripps, A. J. Field, M. J. Reeve, "An Introduction to ALICE: A Multiprocesor Graph Reduction Machine", In 'Functional Programming: Languages, Tools and Architectures', ed. S. Eisenbach. Ellis Horwood Limited, 1987.

[CO77]   P. J. Courtois, "Decomposability", Academic Press, 1977.

[DR81]   J. Darlington, M. J. Reeve, "ALICE : A Multiprocessor Reduction Machine for the Parallel Evaluation of Applicative Languages", ACM/MIT Conference on Functional Programming Languages and Computer Architecture, 1981.

[DR83]   J. Darlington, M. J. Reeve, "ALICE and the Parallel Evaluation of Logic Programs", 10th Annual Symposium on Computer Architecture, 1983.

[FC85]   A. J. Field, M. D. Cripps, "Self-Clocking Networks", International Conference on Parallel Processing, 1985.

[SI85]   H. J. Siegel, "Interconnection Networks for Large-Scale Parallel Processing: Theory and Case Studies", Lexington Books, 1985.

[GH84]   H. W. Glaser, C. L. Hankin, D. Till, "Principles of Functional Programming", Prentice-Hall, 1984.

[HF86]   P. G. Harrison, A. J. Field, "Performance Modelling of Parallel Computer Systems", PERFORMANCE '86/ACM SIGMETRICS, 1986.

[JO85]   T. Johnsson, "Lambda Lifting: Transforming Programs to Recursive Equations", Conference on Functional Programming and Computer Architecture, 1985.

[KO79]   R. A. Kowalski, "Logic for Problem Solving", North Holland, 1979.

[MO82]   I. W. Moor, "An Applicative Compiler for a Parallel Machine", SIGPLAN Symposium on Compiler Construction, 1982.

[PA79]   J. H. Patel, "Processor-Memory Interconnections for Multi-Processors", 6th Annual Symposium on Computer Architecture, 1979.

[RE81]   M. J. Reeve, "An Introduction to the ALICE Compiler Target Language", Research Report, Dept. of Computing, Imperial College, 1981.

[SC81]   C. H. Sauer, K. M. Chandy, "Computer Systems Performance Modelling", Prentice-Hall, 1981.

The Four-Stroke Reduction Engine

Chris Clack and Simon L Peyton Jones

Department of Computer Science
University College London,
Gower St, London WC1E 6BT, England

Abstract

Functional languages are widely claimed to be amenable to concurrent execution by multiple
processors. This paper presents an algorithm for the parallel graph reduction of a
functional program. The algorithm supports transparent management of parallel tasks with no
explicit communication between processors.

1. Background

A major challenge facing computer science today is the effective exploitation of
parallelism. Functional languages offer a powerful lever on the programming of parallel
machines, and the most promising model for implementing these languages is graph reduction.

Many current research projects are investigating parallel architectures [Kell85] [Darl81]
[Hudak85] [Peyt85]. Parallel hardware can readily be built using conventional technology,
but designing the system so that parallelism gives worthwhile gains, and so that harnessing
this parallelism is easy for the programmer, represents a greater challenge.

This paper is concerned with the design of a parallel graph reduction algorithm that will
transparently administer the scheduling and synchronisation of concurrent tasks in a parallel
functional-programming machine. The algorithm that we present can be coded as a finite state
machine. This enables us to produce a simple and efficient implementation.

1.1 Functional languages and parallelism

Why not program in a conventional language which supports multiple tasks, such as Ada? In
a conventional language, the programmer must explicitly code the program for parallel
evaluation. The behaviour of the program will depend on the scheduling of the tasks, and the
programmer must ensure that parallel evaluation does not alter the semantics of the program.

The absence of side effects in a functional language means that the execution of one task
cannot affect the outcome of the execution of another task. This implies that task
administration and synchronisation are inherently easier for a functional language.

Functional programs do not require explicit parallel programming. No extra language
constructs are needed to write parallel functional programs, and the result of the program is
guaranteed to be independent of task scheduling (though this may have an impact on
efficiency).

There should be no need for the programmer to give directions concerning details of scheduling and communication, but the programmer must still design the algorithm with concurrency in mind; we can only get the full benefits of parallelism if the algorithm is coded to give gross parallel structure (e.g. using a divide-and-conquer approach).

An automatic compile-time analysis of the source (called "strictness analysis") will often detect much of the inherent parallelism [Clack85], but this is still a research area and programmer annotations may be used in preference or to give additional hints to the compiler.

The resultant parallel tasks can be managed automatically at run-time, and our aim is that the entire business of administering parallel tasks should be hidden from the programmer.

1.2 Graph reduction

A functional program is a single expression which has a natural representation as a syntax tree. In general, there will be sharing of nodes, and so the syntax tree will be a **graph**, which may be cyclic.

A functional program may be evaluated by manipulating the syntax graph. The evaluation proceeds by means of simple steps, each of which performs a local transformation to the graph. Each step is called a reduction, and the process is known as "graph reduction" [Turn79]. A reducible expression is often referred to as a **redex**.

Reductions may take place concurrently, since they cannot interfere with each other, and evaluation is complete when there are no further reducible expressions (normal form).

The curried application of a function "f" to two arguments x and y is represented like this:

where "@" represents an application cell, containing pointers to function and argument.

Consider the following functional program:

```
LET     f x = AND x x
IN      f (NOT TRUE)
```

(the LET introduces a definition of the function f, which takes a single argument x. Function application is denoted by juxtaposition, thus (NOT TRUE) denotes the function NOT applied to the argument TRUE).

The figure below shows how it would be evaluated. Notice that after each reduction the root of the redex is overwritten with the result of the reduction.

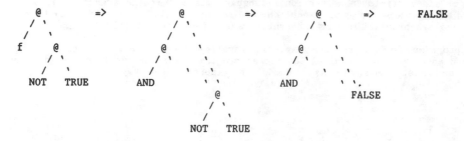

2. A model for parallel graph reduction

Our proposal for parallel graph reduction has the following features:

(i) The reduction of the graph is performed by the concurrent execution of many **tasks**, each of which has access to any part of the graph.

(ii) A task performs a **sequence of reductions,** performed in **normal order.**

(iii) The purpose of a task is to reduce a particular (sub)graph to a normal form in which there is no top level redex - we call this Weak Head Normal Form **(WHNF)** [Peyt86]. A task is therefore completely defined by a pointer to the root of this subgraph.

(iv) During its execution a task may anticipate that it will require the value of a subgraph. In this case it may create a new task to evaluate the subgraph concurrently. To create a new task, a task descriptor is placed in a task pool. We call this **sparking** a task.

(v) There are a number of **agents,** each of which executes a task. Typically an agent will be implemented by a physical processor, although one processor may be timesliced to implement more than one agent.

(vi) There are one or more **task pools,** which may be accessed by the **agents.** A task pool holds a number of tasks which are ready for execution. These tasks may have been created by other tasks, or they may be tasks that have been temporarily suspended and subsequently resumed. Unemployed **agents** will send requests to the task pool for work to be done.

2.1 Parallelism

One of the major issues that must be faced by any parallel implementation is the generation of new tasks. When should a new task be sparked? There are two broad approaches:

(i) Spark a new task to evaluate a sub-graph when it is **certain** that the sub-graph will eventually be evaluated **(conservative parallelism).** This ensures that all tasks are doing useful work.

(ii) Spark a new task to evaluate a sub-graph when it is **possible** that the sub-graph will eventually be evaluated **(speculative parallelism).** This offers maximum opportunities for parallelism.

The danger of speculative parallelism is that machine resources may be consumed evaluating pieces of graph which will eventually be discarded. Speculative tasks need particularly complicated management, since vital tasks must be distinguished from non-vital tasks, and since tasks that are no longer needed must be garbage-collected [Peyt86]. We therefore assume that only conservative parallelism will be exploited.

2.1.1 Creating new tasks in a conservative regime

Suppose that a function F was known to (eventually) require the value of its argument (that is, it is "strict" in that argument). Then a conservative scheduler could safely spark concurrent evaluation of its argument whenever F is applied.

In the case of primitives (functions such as "+" that are built in to the implementation) it is easy to know which arguments will be required. However, in the case of user-defined functions matters are not so clear. Certainly we do not want to work it out at run-time, so we **annotate the function** with information describing which arguments it is sure to need.

These annotations may either be introduced by the programmer or added by a compiler pass which uses strictness analysis to deduce which arguments the function is sure to need

[Clack85]. Annotations should be added with care; if the evaluation semantics are altered, non-termination may result.

Merely annotating functions in this way is not sufficient. Some functions may be strict in a particular argument for one application, but not for another application. Consider the definition of a function F as:

F x y = y 3 x

Clearly, F is not strict in x, because the function argument y may not be strict in its second parameter. Now suppose that elsewhere there occurs the expression

...(F E +)...

where E is some complex expression. In this application of F the second argument is +, so E will certainly be evaluated subsequently. In this particular context, therefore, we can safely spark evaluation of E, and we can indicate this fact by annotating the **application node.**

At first it appears that the second sort of annotation subsumes the first. However, there are situations in which each is uniquely appropriate. The two forms of annotation are complementary, and neither can be omitted without loss [Peyt86] [Hank85] [Burn85]. For example, consider the expression

(IF E_1 f g) E_2

where f is strict in its argument but g is not. We cannot know until run-time whether f or g will be applied to E_2, so we cannot annotate the application node. We can, however, annotate the function f so that E_2 will be evaluated in parallel if f is eventually applied to it.

To summarise, we derive parallelism from

(a) **primitives** - we use innate knowledge about the strictness of primitives, and we require that the implementation has some method for annotating primitive functions with this strictness information.

(b) **user functions** - we use strictness analysis to determine this information, and we require that the implementation has some method to annotate user functions.

(c) **applications** - we use strictness analysis to determine those situations where an application is strict: we require a method to annotate an application node.

2.2 Colouring the graph to synchronise tasks

During the course of evaluation, two tasks may attempt to evaluate a common subgraph simultaneously. Notice that no mutual exclusion is required (since they will both arrive at the same result). In practice, however, it is highly desirable that only one task should evaluate a piece of graph at a time, to avoid duplicated work. The main aim of our algorithm is to achieve this mutual exclusion painlessly.

The idea behind the algorithm is that that as a task traverses the graph it "paints" the nodes that it is working on. After working on a section of graph, a task will "unpaint" the nodes that are no longer being used.

If one task attempts to access a node that has been painted by another task, the intruding task will be **blocked** until the required cell has been unpainted. Thus, if two tasks share the same subgraph, there will be no duplicated effort.

Consider, for example, the following program:

```
LET f   = g 6
    g x = + (-x)
IN
    + (f 3) (f 1)
```

We might spark two tasks to evaluate the (f 3) and (f 1) sub-graphs, which share a common sub-graph f:

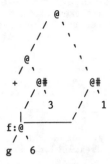

```
                    @
                  /   `
                 /      `
                /         `
               @            `
             /   `           `
            +     @#           @#
                /   `        /   `
               /     3      /     1
              |_____ /
            f:@
            /   `
           g     6
```

The "+" might spark the nodes marked "#" thus creating two new tasks to evaluate the arguments to the "+". The first of these tasks to try to evaluate the node labelled f will paint it (let us suppose it is the left hand task in the picture). When the second task tries to evaluate this node it will be blocked. Meanwhile the first task will reduce the f node to WHNF by applying g to 6, and overwriting the node with the result (+ (-6)). Then, having evaluated the arguments (-6 and 3) it will add them, remove the paint from the f node as it pops the node from its stack, and overwrite the left node marked "#" with the result (-3). Now the second task can proceed, so it will access the f node, where it will see the (+ (-6)). It will never know that there was once a (g 6) redex there.

We intend that parallel tasks should be blocked and later resumed in a way that is **entirely transparent** to the agents, and at low overhead to the implementation. There is no explicit communication between agents or between tasks - synchronisation between tasks is mediated entirely through the graph. The result of a reduction is communicated to the graph as a **single, indivisible operation,** (that is, the overwriting of the root node of the redex) and the reduction appears to all other tasks to take place instantaneously. The graph never appears in an intermediate state, and the interlocking of agents becomes totally hidden from the programmer.

2.2.1 Blocking and resumption

As mentioned above, for efficiency reasons we would like it to be possible for one task to be **blocked** by another. We will now consider the blocking mechanism in more detail, with the help of an example. Suppose a task is evaluating the expression

$(+ \ E_1 \ E_2)$

where E_1 and E_2 are complicated expressions. Now, we know that "+" will need the values of both of its arguments, so the task can spark a child to evaluate one argument (say, E_1) and evaluate the other argument (E_2) itself.

When it has finished evaluating E_2, the parent task will look again at E_1, to make sure that it has been evaluated. E_1 can now be in one of three possible states:

(1) **It has not been evaluated yet** (perhaps because the system has been busy executing other tasks). In this case, the parent task should proceed to evaluate E_1 itself. Eventually, another agent will try to evaluate E_1 (remember, E_1 was sparked, so the child task is in the task pool) but this child task will die immediately upon discovering that E_1 has already been evaluated.

(2) **It has been evaluated already.** In this case, the parent task can immediately proceed to apply the function "+" to the two evaluated arguments.

(3) **It is still in the process of being evaluating.** Now the root node of E_1 will have been "painted" by the child task and the parent task will be blocked until E_1 has been evaluated.

What should happen to a task when it is blocked? There are two main alternatives:

(a) It could simply be returned to the pool of tasks awaiting execution. In due course an unemployed agent looking for work will resume execution of the task. It will very soon encounter the node that blocked the task before. If this node is still painted, then the task is again blocked, and returned to the pool, otherwise it can continue to execute normally.

(b) It could somehow be suspended, so that it is not considered for execution by unemployed agents, and be resumed when the node which blocked it has its paint removed. Reawakening the task would consist of putting it in the pool of tasks awaiting execution.

The first method has the advantage of simplicity, but it is rather inefficient, since repeated attempts are made to execute a task which is still blocked for the same reason.

In order to implement the second method we would somehow have to attach the blocked task to the painted node. Then when the paint is taken off the node, the blocked task can be put back in the task pool as a **resumed** task.

2.3 The task pool

A new task is created by adding a task descriptor to the task pool. What happens when more and more tasks are sparked? If tasks are being added to the task pool faster than they are being taken out, then the task pool may run out of space.

As we showed in section 2.2.1, after a parent sparks a child task to evaluate a strict argument it **always** subsequently returns to evaluate the argument itself. Hence, all **sparked** tasks in the task pool are entirely disposable (even the program root, as long as the I/O mechanism is informed, or automatically tries again later).

Once a task has started, it will block its parent (see section 2.2.1). Therefore, it is **vitally important** that we do not throw away **resumed** tasks.

So a good strategy for administering the size of the task pool would seem to be:

(i) set a limit somewhat below the real limit of the task pool.
(ii) once the task pool has reached that size, **ignore** all sparks until the task pool shrinks again, but
(iii) be careful **not to ignore** any resumptions of tasks.

2.3.1 Task scheduling

When an unemployed agent sends a request to the task pool, which task should be returned out of all those in the pool? A decision must be made on how best to schedule the available tasks.

Although the details of scheduling tasks from the task pool are not yet well understood, we can offer the major comfort that with conservative parallelism **the scheduling of tasks is guaranteed not to affect the result.**

However, scheduling may have a considerable effect on efficiency. Most tasks will cause the graph to grow before it can shrink again, so a bad choice of scheduling algorithm could mean that many tasks will expand a subgraph and then be blocked before the shrinking occurs. This might result in the implementation running out of memory, so that the computation grinds to a halt.

Simple strategies like last-in-first-out (LIFO), or first-in-first-out (FIFO) may give acceptable results and merit some investigation. For instance, a FIFO strategy corresponds to breadth-first evaluation of the graph, and may therefore result in the sparking of more parallel tasks than a depth-first LIFO strategy. Indeed, switching between the two strategies could give useful dynamic control of the production and consumption of tasks.

Another strategy may be always to schedule **resumed** tasks first, since we can be sure that they will be doing useful work (whereas a sparked task may find that its subgraph has already been evaluated), and since they could be blocking other tasks.

3. An implementation of parallel graph reduction

The four-stroke reduction engine assumes that we are implementing graph reduction using a **global heap** of cells, each with three fields; **tag, head** and **tail**. The head and tail fields may each contain either a data object or a pointer to another cell. The tag field is used to identify the type of cell - for instance, an application cell or perhaps a "cons" cell. The hardware should also support the **indivisible update** of a heap cell.

We present an algorithm that is applicable to all forms of graph reduction. We describe how the scheme works both for primitives and for user functions. Our preferred representation for a user function is the supercombinator, although the algorithm is adaptable to other representations.

3.1 Task execution and the 2-stroke cycle

We assume that reductions are carried out in **normal order**, which specifies that **the leftmost outermost redex should be reduced first**. The expression to be evaluated can only be of the form

$$f \ E_1 \ E_2 \ \dots \ E_n$$

where f is a data object (such as TRUE), built-in function (such as AND), or user-defined function, and there are zero or more arguments E_i, which denote arbitrarily large expressions. The graph of this expression looks like this:

Suppose that f takes m arguments; the leftmost outermost redex will be the application of f to its arguments E_1, E_2,...E_m. Before the graph reduction machine can reduce this redex it must find f: it goes down the left branch of each application node from the root until it finds a non-application node.

This left-branching chain of application nodes is called the **spine** of the expression.

It is therefore rather easy to find the next redex to reduce. We descend the spine, painting the spine nodes as we go, until we find a function. Then, based on the function we find, we go back up the spine, collecting the arguments E_i and unpainting the spine nodes as we go, to find the root of the redex. Now the function and all its arguments are available and the reduction may be carried out; the result overwrites the root of the redex.

In order to minimise the overheads of task-switching, we prefer not to remember the argument stack in the task state descriptor. Thus, collecting the arguments **must** wait until we go back up the spine, since it· is only when ascending that we can guarantee never to be blocked.

After completing a reduction, the task again descends the spine and the process repeats. When the task finds that a function does not have enough arguments on the spine, or the expression is now a data object, then the subgraph has reached WHNF and the task dies.

This "down-up" cycle is somewhat reminiscent of a piston engine, and we call it the **2-stroke cycle**. In fact, we only use this method to reduce user functions and primitives with no strict arguments: for all other primitives we need to use four strokes, as we discuss later.

3.1.1 Representation of a task

When a task is not being executed by an agent it must be represented in some way in store. The representation of a task must contain all the information required to continue executing the task from the point at which it was last blocked. In conventional multi-tasking operating systems this representation is often called a Task Control Block, and contains information such as the task's stack pointer, its program counter and the state of the task's registers.

By contrast, in our parallel reduction model a task could be represented completely by a single pointer to the root of the subgraph it is evaluating. **The complete state of a partially completed task is held in the graph,** so that a pointer to the root of its subgraph suffices to represent a task **at any stage in its life** (not only when it is newly sparked).

At any moment an agent can stop performing reductions on a task, put its root pointer back into the task pool, and begin executing another task.

The only trouble with this representation of a task is that if a task is blocked and subsequently resumed the agent has to descend the spine of the subgraph from the root. This is due to the fact that no information is saved about the state of a task - the agent must look in the graph to see how far the task got before being blocked.

We may choose to save more state information in each task descriptor (held in the task pool), and a technique called **pointer reversal** gives us a way to save enough state to allow the task to continue from where it was suspended, i.e. **without** having to descend the subgraph from the root again. Furthermore, pointer reversal allows us to save this much state using just **two pointers!**

3.1.2 Pointer reversal

An evaluator can descend the spine of an expression without using a stack by reversing pointers in the spine as it goes. This pointer-reversing technique is described by Stoye et al [Stoye84].

For example, to descend the spine of $(+ \ E_1 \ E_2)$, we use two pointers "B" (for Backward) and "F" (for Forward). B and F point to two adjacent nodes on the spine; spine nodes below F have undisturbed pointers pointing down the spine to the next node, whereas spine nodes above B have reversed pointers that point up the spine to the previous node. To descend the spine, we read the function pointer in the "F" cell - this becomes the new "F", and we overwrite the cell's function pointer with the old B. The old "F" becomes the new "B":

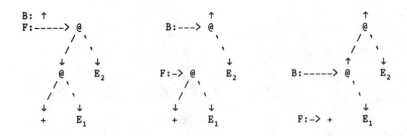

The act of descending the spine using pointer-reversal is sometimes called **unwinding** the spine. Conversely, ascending the spine is called **rewinding**.

At first it appears that this is totally unworkable in a parallel machine, since the pointer-reversed graph is in a "peculiar state" which will be incomprehensible to other tasks. However, pointer reversal only reverses **the painted nodes**. No other task will look inside a pointer-reversed node, and it is therefore safe to use this technique.

The complete state of a task can now be represented by two pointers, the F and B pointers. When a blocked task is resumed, the F and B pointers are already pointing to the area of the graph which is of interest.

In a sequential implementation, pointer-reversal is not as efficient as using a stack, since the pointers have to be re-reversed when rewinding the spine. However, in a parallel implementation which uses the graph-colouring scheme to synchronise tasks, nodes have to be "unpainted" as the spine is ascended, and there will probably be little extra cost to re-reverse the pointers as well.

We conclude that pointer reversal may save repeatedly unwinding the spine each time a task is blocked, and adds very little to the overheads of task switching.

3.1.3 Sparking tasks

Recall from section 2.1.1 that the parallelism information is conveyed to the evaluating agents by two forms of **annotated** graph nodes, namely annotated functions and annotated application nodes. We implement the second form of annotation by means of the tag field in a cell - special kinds of application tags show whether the application node is strict in its argument.

Annotations to application cells can be discovered and sparked on the way **down** down the spine, whereas annotations to primitives and user functions cannot be discovered until we reach the bottom of the spine, and so strict arguments must be sparked on the way **up** the spine. Of course, we must be careful not to spark an argument twice, which would be wasteful. This is easy to achieve, by altering the tag of a spine node when its argument is sparked.

3.2 Task synchronisation

We saw above how task synchronisation could be achieved by "colouring" the graph. Now we are in a position to describe our implementation of such a synchronisation scheme:

3.2.1 How to colour the graph

We implement the "colouring" idea with special values of the tag attached to each node. At each stage of reduction, a task will check the cell tag it wishes to reference, and the value of this tag will determine the future computation. We assume that memory is cheap enough that the extra memory space required is not profligate. The scheme need not be especially wasteful of time, since we can design intelligent memory units to implement special read-modify-write instructions that depend on the value of the tag of the cell (thus allowing us to access the cell, check to see if it is already painted, then paint it if it wasn't before - all in one indivisible operation).

3.2.2 The blocking mechanism

How do we achieve the blocking of multiple tasks on one painted node? We could achieve this by adding an extra field to every application node. This points to a list of tasks which should be reawakened when the paint on the node is removed. This is the approach taken by the ALICE machine [Darl81].

Attaching an extra field to every application node seems rather wasteful, since most of them will not have any tasks blocked on them. Our proposal is to overwrite the head of the application node with a pointer to a list of blocked tasks (we call this a **task queue**), and remember the old head in the tail of the list. Some mechanism would then be required to indicate that there were blocked tasks queued up on a painted node - for instance, yet another special value for the cell tag.

It is only the unwind and rewind operations that affect the blocking and resumption mechanisms. When a task unwinds it may be blocked and will be added to a task queue. When the blocking task finally rewinds back up the spine, it will come across a cell with an attached task queue and all blocked tasks in the queue will now be added to the task pool.

One advantage of the mechanism described here is that it is sufficiently simple and low-level that it can be implemented in hardware (e.g. VLSI), and that as such it can form part of an **Intelligent Memory Unit** - if the agents talk to memory via high-level operations there is **absolutely no need for them** to **know about this blocking mechanism!** If an agent is executing a task that is blocked, it only needs to know that the task cannot continue, and that the task pool should be consulted for more work.

3.3 4-stroke reduction

The four-stroke reduction engine is named after the fashion in which it reduces primitives applied to their arguments. In contrast with user functions (and primitives with no strict arguments), a primitive application like $(+ E_1 E_2)$ cannot be reduced any further until the strict arguments E_1 and E_2 have been evaluated. Therefore, a task must **ensure** that all strict arguments have been evaluated (either by itself, or by another task). To be more specific, any primitive which has at **least one** strict argument will need four "strokes" (instead of two) to reduce:

(1) **inlet stroke**
unwind the spine to determine which primitive is being applied, sparking any strict applications on the way.

(2) **compression stroke**
rewind to the topmost strict argument, sparking strict arguments on the way

(3) **power stroke**
unwind the spine again, evaluating strict arguments one at a time on the way down (and reversing pointers as before).

(4) **exhaust stroke**
finally rewind to the root of the redex, collecting the now-evaluated arguments, perform the reduction and overwrite the root of the redex with the result.

We illustrate four-stroke reduction using the example "$+ E_1 E_2$":

(i) Inlet Stroke

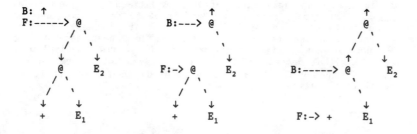

(ii) Compression Stroke

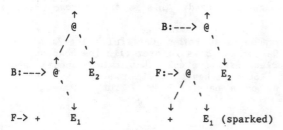

336

(iii) Power Stroke

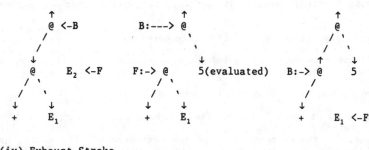

(iv) Exhaust Stroke

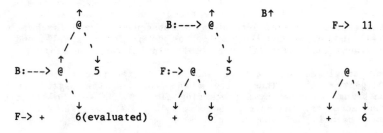

3.4 Optimisations

A disadvantage of the blocking scheme outlined above is that it risks unnecessary serialisation.

Consider the case of a shared subgraph that is already in WHNF, as might be the case with a commonly used partial application. As one task unwinds into the subgraph it paints the top node, thus blocking any other tasks from unwinding into it. **But if the subgraph is already in WHNF, there is no point in making other tasks block.** It is perfectly safe to allow any number of tasks simultaneous access to the subgraph!

This is a specific instance of a general rule: once a sub-graph is in WHNF it will never be altered, so it is quite safe for many tasks to have (read only) access to it.

Our implementation allows many tasks to access a subgraph in WHNF, by requiring that tasks do not use pointer reversal when traversing WHNF subgraphs (they can never be blocked when doing so).

4. Finite State Machine

Perhaps the most satisfying feature of our algorithm is that it can be represented as a finite state machine. This is possible because of the way that we use graph-colouring in order to synchronise tasks.

- The execution of each **task** is governed by a finite state machine.

- Each **agent** executes a finite state machine (physically, the same code will run on all processors in a multiprocessor machine).

- The tasks can each be in any one of a fixed, small number of states.

- The first action of an agent at each stage of the finite state machine will be to access a cell in the shared graph. Each agent holds the B and F pointers that represent the current task. If the current state is one that descends the spine, then the cell accessed will be the F cell. In an ascending state, the B cell will be accessed.

- The value of the tag of the accessed cell will determine the subsequent action (such as sparking the tail of the cell just read, and the painting or unpainting of a cell) and will specify the next state transition (often this will be to stay in the same state).

- In a real implementation, knowledge of actions and state transitions can be incorporated in the intelligent memory. Thus, with a knowledge of the particular high-level memory operation being requested by a processing element, and of the value of the tag of the cell being accessed, the intelligent memory can itself take care of administrative details such as painting and unpainting.

It is important to realise that the value of **both** tags is required to determine the next state transition; the value of one of the tags is **implied by the current state**, and the value of the other tag must be determined by reading from the graph.

How do we define the different states? They are derived from a combination of

(i) the direction of pointer-reversal (are we unwinding or rewinding?)
(ii) the value of the "known" tag (B if going down the graph: F if going up).
(iii) the number of strict arguments still to be collected (compression stroke only), and
(iv) the total number of arguments left to be rewound past (exhaust stroke only).

What happens when a task is resumed? Since a task can only be blocked during the inlet or power strokes, then (iii) and (iv) above do not apply. It also follows that the task must be unwinding. The only condition left is (ii), so directly after resuming a task the first thing that an agent must do to establish the state of the task is to read the value of the B tag.

Our finite state machine currently has a total of 12 states (including the optimisation of using a stack to traverse shared subgraphs in WHNF), and there are 22 different kinds of tag – 11 of which are application nodes in various guises!

5. Conclusion and project status

This algorithm has been implemented as part of the Alvey-funded GRIP project. GRIP (Graph Reduction In Parallel) is a parallel machine based on about 120 processing elements, a fast asynchronous bus, and about 30 intelligent memory units. The finite state machine has now been coded (in C) and we have a running simulator of a parallel graph reduction machine. It is intended that the code executed by an agent should be ported **without change** onto the actual processing elements in GRIP. Our experience has shown that implementing parallel graph reduction is by no means trivial, and we could not have progressed as far if the algorithm had not been represented as a finite state machine. As evidence of this, we found that debugging the simulator has consisted almost entirely of remedying typing errors rather than changing the algorithm. The simulator is now producing results which will help us with the final stages of the hardware design.

References

[Burn85]   Burn G, Hankin CL and Abramsky S, "Strictness analysis of higher order functions", Science of Computer Programming (to appear); also DoC 85/6, Dept Comp Sci, Imperial College London, April 1985.

[Clack85]   Clack CD and Peyton Jones SL, "Strictness analysis - a practical approach", Functional Programming Languages and Computer Architecture, ed Jouannaud, LNCS 201, Springer Verlag, pp35-49, August 1985.

[Darl81]   Darlington J, Reeve M, "ALICE - a multiprocessor reduction machine for the parallel evaluation of applicative languages", Proc ACM Conf on Functional Programming Languages and Computer Architecture, New Hampshire, pp65-75, Oct 1981.

[Hank85]   Hankin CL, Burn GL and Peyton-Jones SL, "An approach to safe parallel combinator reduction", Dept Comp Sci, Imperial College, Oct 1985.

[Hudak85]   Hudak P, "Functional programming on multiprocessor architectures - research in progress", Dept Comp Sci, Yale University, November 1985.

[Kell85]   Keller RM, "Rediflow architecture prospectus", UUCS-85-105, Dept Comp Sci, University of Utah, Aug 1985.

[Peyt85]   Peyton Jones SL, Clack CD, Salkild J and Hardie M, "GRIP - a parallel graph reduction machine", Dept Comp Sci, University College London, November 1985.

[Peyt86]   Peyton Jones SL, "Implementation of Functional Programming Languages", Prentice Hall (to be published), 1986.

[Stoye84]   Stoye WR, Clarke TJW, Norman AC, "Some practical methods for rapid combinator reduction", ACM Symposium on Lisp and Functional Programming, Austin, pp159-166, August 1984.

[Turn79]   Turner DA, "A new implementation technique for applicative languages", Software Practice and Experience 9, pp31-49, 1979.

The FFP Machine—A Progress Report

Gyula Magó and David Middleton

Department of Computer Science
University of North Carolina at Chapel Hill

Abstract

This paper describes a multiprocessor being developed for the direct execution of the FFP (Formal Functional Programming) languages of Backus. The FFP machine is a small-grain multiprocessor comprising a large number of simple (typically bit-serial) processing elements of two kinds interconnected to form a binary tree. These processing elements do not know the FFP language, they respond to a much simpler, low-level, concurrent language in which the primitives of the FFP language are specified.

The machine is a "late-binding" one: program and data are mapped onto the hardware at runtime, without any planning by the programmer or software. As a result, the programmer is able to invoke large-scale MIMD parallelism with ease. The FFP machine is not plagued by the program decomposition problem: instead of having to fit program and data to the hardware, the (small-grain) hardware is dynamically reconfigured during execution to fit the changing requirements of program and data. A detailed software simulator of the machine is now operational. This simulator, together with analytical performance studies, indicates that the FFP machine can deliver high performance.

1. Introduction

The FFP machine project at the University of Carolina at Chapel Hill is aimed at constructing a parallel computer that would not only execute programs at high speed, but could also be programmed in a machine independent fashion.

The FFP machine was first described in 1979 [MA1], and it was first implemented in software by Danforth in 1983 [DA1]. Since about 1976, a considerable amount of effort was spent on predicting the performance of the FFP machine by analytical means. The results are promising enough to justify the construction of a hardware prototype for further evaluation of the machine, and to this end, work has been in progress to refine the design. This paper provides an overview of recent progress made in the development of the FFP machine.

2. Overview

The complexity of an operational description of the FFP machine encourages the issues involved to be introduced gradually, in several stages.

2.1 Objectives

High performance on the one hand, and ease and generality of programming on the other, are equally important objectives. (This is in contrast with projects in which high speed of execution is more important than programmability, and consequently machine dependent programming is tolerated.) Because of the flexibility and generality built into the FFP machine, it is not expected to match in all cases the speed of special purpose parallel computers in their respective areas of specialization.

2.2 Some desirable properties of programmable multiprocessors

The twin demands for increased computer performance and increased generality of programming have long been recognized. However, realizing these objectives simultaneously has proved so difficult that many researchers still strive for high performance in limited contexts, hoping that programmability (of a sufficient generality) can be "added on" later. The failure of so many architectural experiments because of lack of programmability rather than lack of speed should lead one to conclude that programmability cannot be added on; it must be designed into the computer system.

The following have become recognized as desirable (many would argue necessary) in promoting programmability of a parallel computer: (1) MIMD organisation, (2) language based design, and (3) support of dynamic computations.

MIMD organization is clearly an important requirement. Using a design *based on a language that is capable of expressing large-scale parallelism* is essentially a top-down approach to the construction of a parallel computer, because it takes an all-encompassing view of the computations that the computer system might be called to perform. Explicitly requiring the *support of dynamic computations* is an effort to focus attention on the need to execute well the most general, data dependent, unpredictable and irregular computations.

As to performance, we consider *exploitation of fine grain parallelism* and *exploitation of locality in computations* as being crucial to improving the performance of programmable parallel computers.

2.3 Small-grain programmable multiprocessors

A useful concept in discussing multiprocessors is the *granularity* of the machine. We shall distinguish between large-grain and small-grain multiprocessors as follows: in a *large-grain* system each processor is capable of performing nontrivial computations autonomously (each is, in fact, a von Neumann computer), whereas in a *small-grain* system a processor must cooperate with other similar processors to do so. In hardware terms, each processor of a large-grain system typically contains a reasonably powerful ALU, a substantial instruction set and many thousand words of memory; each processor of a small-grain system would typically contain a bit-serial ALU, a small instruction set and a few words of local storage.

The central hypothesis of the FFP machine project is that small-grain multiprocessors will prove superior to large-grain ones in supporting general purpose parallel computation. This goes against the widely held belief that the generality of a multiprocessor necessarily increases with its grain size [SE1]. Such a belief properly appreciates the role of the flexibility and generality of individual PEs, but overlooks the role of flexibility and generality in the *cooperation among PEs*.

By virtue of their granularity, small-grain programmable multiprocessors are expected to have a number of advantages over large-grain ones (over and above the advantage of their regularity and low engineering complexity, which they share with special purpose small-grain parallel processors).

(1) They have a better chance of exploiting fine-grain parallelism, simply because in them an ALU serves only a few "memory locations" (they may be viewed as "logic-in-memory" systems, in which processing power is evenly distributed over memory). A resulting disadvantage of small-grain systems is that they need more communication to bring operands together.

(2) They can more easily afford to move data on a large scale, thereby being able, for example, to preserve locality in computations. This is again because small-grain systems have a relative abundance of processing power.

(3) They have a chance of *fitting hardware to program and data*, and thus do not have problems with program decomposition, allocation and scheduling. In contrast, large-grain systems must fit program and data to the rigid boundaries of their hardware, and they must find solutions to the resulting program decomposition, allocation and scheduling problems.

2.4 General description of the FFP machine

The FFP machine project is an experiment in computer architecture, whose purpose is to explore the possibility of constructing a programmable parallel computer in the form of a small-grain multiprocessor. This section contains a list of the salient features of the FFP machine.

(1) It is a small-grain multiprocessor, whose PEs, or *cells*, form a binary tree. There are two kinds of cells in the machine, the leaf (L) cells, and the internal or tree (T) cells. The machine has no predetermined size; one with a few thousand L cells is expected to be at the low end of useful sizes.

(2) It has a language-based design derived from the requirements of the FFP language of Backus [BA1]. Issues of parallel programming and software have been taken into consideration from the inception of the project.

(3) It is a reduction machine that directly executes FFP programs. Program and data are "rewritten" at runtime, which makes possible the support of dynamic computations.

(4) It exploits parallelism, including fine-grain parallelism, on several levels: on the FFP language level (by working on different user programs concurrently, and working on all innermost applications of each user program concurrently), within FFP primitive operations (by implementing each with a distributed computation on groups of small-grain PEs), and within machine-wide operating system functions, such as partitioning and storage management. Since the innermost applications are independent computations, the machine is an MIMD one.

(5) It preserves locality in computations by maintaining a representation that keeps all symbols of any innermost application together, and then exploits this locality in various ways. It maintains locality via a machine-wide storage management, which uses global information to force the best allocation of resources on the machine.

(6) It works in a cyclical manner, each machine cycle ending with storage management (which is the remapping of the changing program and data onto the hardware). The operation of the machine can be stopped several times in each cycle, which should ease the testing and monitoring of the machine.

(7) It is able to *fit* the small-grain *hardware to* the dynamically changing *program and data* (by a process called partitioning). It does not suffer from program decomposition, allocation and scheduling problems.

3. The current design of the FFP machine

This section concentrates on the current architecture of the FFP machine, restricting description of implementation to tradeoffs that affect speed.

3.1 Fitting hardware to programs

Within each resident FFP program, there will be active computations called *innermost applications* available for execution. The network of processors in the FFP machine allocates a subnetwork to each one. Figure 1 shows how the machine might appear after one particular such allocation. Every innermost application is given its own tailor-made PE; we can view the machine as having variable sized processors targeted for the particular computation each contains. The semantics of FFP allows the innermost applications to be evaluated in isolation and in parallel. (Innermost applications are self-contained, holding all the information they need to generate the result.)

3.2 Requirements of the FFP language

The resident FFP programs are stored as one string of symbols in the machine. Within each tailored PE, or *area*, the processors cooperate in replacing the innermost application with its result, but individual processors behave differently depending on which part of the application they hold. For example, usually the symbols constituting the operand are modified to reflect the effect of the application's function while the symbols constituting the function

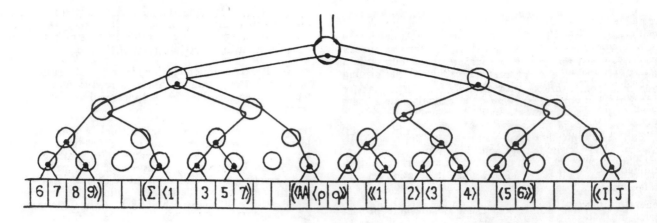

Figure 1. Fitting hardware to programs: allocating areas to computations

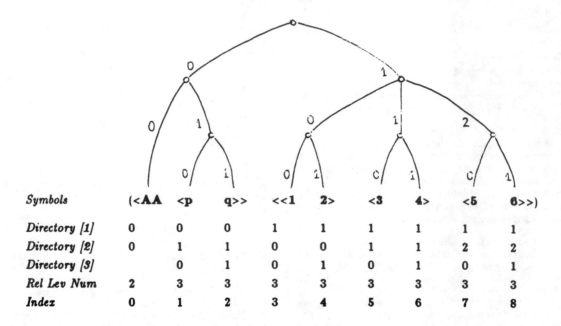

Symbols	(<**AA**	<p	q>>	<<1	2>	<3	4>	<5	6>>)
Directory [1]	0	0	0	1	1	1	1	1	1
Directory [2]	0	1	1	0	0	1	1	2	2
Directory [3]		0	1	0	1	0	1	0	1
Rel Lev Num	2	3	3	3	3	3	3	3	3
Index	0	1	2	3	4	5	6	7	8

Figure 2. Addresses in an FFP application

(i)   (<**AA**   <p   q>>   <<1   2>   <3   4>   <5   6>>)
           a   b   c   d   e   f   g   h   i

(ii)   (<p   q>   <1   2>   <3   4>   <5   6>)

(iii)   (<p   q>   <1   2>   <3   <3   <3   4>   <5   <5   <5   6>)
           a   b   c   d   e   f1   f2   f3   g   h1   h2   h3   i

(iv)   (<p   q>   <1   2>   <p   q>   <3   4>   <p   q>   <5   6>)

(v)   < (<p   q>   <1   2>)   (<p   q>   <3   4>)   (<p   q>   <5   6>) >

Figure 3. Stages in reducing an FFP application

342

are deleted. The behavior of each processor depends on the position, or *address*, of its symbols. This address, comprising a directory, relative level number and index, is shown for one example application in Figure 2. We define the *directory* of a symbol as a vector which describes its position in the parse tree by identifying the path from the root to that symbol. This example only needs three levels of resolution in the parse tree, and in general the directories are only generated to four levels. Figure 2 also shows the relative level number and index parts of the address. Within the parse tree, the relative level number shows how deep a symbol is, and the index is the position in a left-to-right numbering of the symbols.

Each processor in the area holding this application will generate a piece of the result based on the initial local information and on values communicated within this area. How it generates this result is described by a small program called a *microcode segment*. Each segment is intended for all processors holding text in some subtree of the parse tree, and so is tagged with a directory. Figure 3 shows how the application in Figure 2 might be reduced within its isolated area. The initial text in Figure 3ii is transformed into the result in Figure 3v in the following fashion. First, those brackets that group the individual parts together are removed. The surrounding parentheses provide a cocoon to hide this intermediate disorder from the rest of the machine. Processors at the start of each second level operand, labelled *f* and *h*, will request space into which the function string < *p q* > can be copied; and then suspend operation until that request is satisfied. Those processors holding part of the function to be copied jointly arrange telling these processors what size to request. Their requests are satisfied by replicating their contents, for reasons which are explained in Section 3.5.4 . Given a structure like Figure 3iii, the processors holding < *p q* > broadcast their contents. These symbols are picked up in order by the replicated processors to give the pattern in Figure 3iv. It remains for parentheses and brackets to be added, building structure around the new string, to yield the result.

3.3 Interconnections of the FFP machine

We have chosen the tree network of Figure 4 to support this style of reduction. (A tree is not the only network that might be chosen; see for example [KE1]). The tree is not constrained to be balanced and so a machine of any size can be built.

The bulk of computation is performed by a linear array of processors called *L cells*. The linear nature of FFP expressions maps naturally onto this *L array*. Communication among the processors is provided by a tree of communication cells, or *T cells*, connecting the L cells through its leaves. From Figure 1, we can see that during execution an individual T cell can be divided into parts serving separate areas. The three trees that we have seen so far, the parse tree in Figure 2, the hardware tree of T cells in Figure 4b, and the area trees shown in Figure 1 are independent, serving different purposes.

The root of this tree is connected to a controller which terminates or initiates the distributed operations. The ends of the L array are connected to virtual memory, a pair of stacks which hold excess symbols during execution.

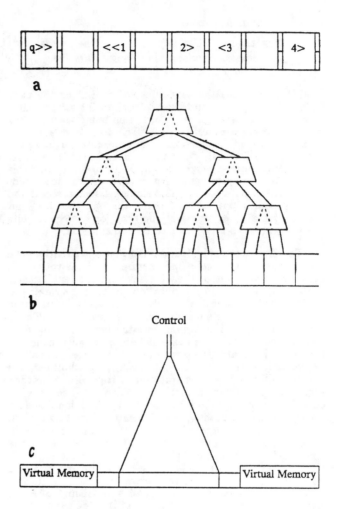

Figure 4. Machine layout

3.4 Machine cycle

The cells of the machine cooperate in a regular cyclic manner. The machine cycle is divided into three phases: partitioning, execution and storage management. Partitioning divides the machine into disjoint areas. The execution phases works independently on the individual applications. Storage management reunites the machine to perform global resource management for the storage requests.

The phases support the following broad functions:

Partitioning:

> *Decomposing the tree of Figure 4b into the separate areas of the form in Figure 1.*

Execution (independently and concurrently within each area):

Initialization:
> *Generate addresses of Figure 2.*
> *Load the set of code segments into the L cells.*

Run:
> *Execute local instructions in the L cell.*
> *Participate in communication operations.*
> *Request extra space and suspend execution.*

Storage management:

> *Preparation. (Globally determine the new layout.)*
> *Movement. (Horisontal shifting to use the*
> *empty space.)*

Figure 5 shows the sequence of events along the path from an arbitrary L cell to the controller. This representative path is chosen because information must be condensed in order to get a useful picture. The horizontal axis represents time and the vertical axis represents height in the hardware tree. We will describe the behavior of the area reducing our example program. The T cell at the root of this area is chosen to represent all such roots and is shown midway up the vertical axis. The sloping lines represent the waves of particular values moving through the tree, and the horizontal lines represent the time for subsequent bits of these values to arrive in a serial transmission.

The first sweep of information in Figure 5 partitions the machine. Certain T cells find themselves at the root of an area tree, and some of those detect that the text in their area forms an innermost application. Behind this wave, and confined to the area just created, comes the information about the function name and the symbol addresses. The T cell at the root of this area queues the function name on a separate output tree to an external library of microcode segments, and initiates the downsweep of address generation. While this isolated area is calculating the addresses, the external library fills a separate input tree with microcode segments for all new reductions. When an L cell has received the address for its symbol and the function name for its area, it begins reading the segments being broadcast on the input tree. It selects the segment that matches its directory and FFP function, and executes that segment while ignoring the rest. In the Apply-to-All example of Figure 3, the L cells determine the size of $< p\ q >$, the expression to be copied, in the first message wave (as described in Section 3.5.5). L cells f and h request this amount of space and suspend execution until they get it. The second message wave transmits the expression $< p\ q >$ to this space. Our message scheme always synchronises the L cells of an area, so this message wave hangs because L cells f and h are suspended. At some point the controller decides to perform storage management (under a policy described in Section 3.6.4), and interrupts all the isolated executing areas.

The tree is reunited as a single network (the partitioning is abandoned), and storage preparation takes place. This prescribes for each L cell a distance to shift its contents so that those L cells that requested space can replicate their contents (as cells f and h do in Figure 3iii). Following the subsequent shifting, the machine returns to the beginning of the cycle. (For ease of description the cycle in Figure 5 has been unrolled). Again, the whole tree undergoes partitioning. The example application, having moved in the L array, receives a different area tree. This area (as with all other partially completed reductions) already has its code segments and addresses and so immediately resumes the interrupted message wave. L cells f and h, having expanded into L cells $f1$, $f2$, $f3$, and $h1$, $h2$, $h3$, join in the restarted second message wave, and the expression $< p\ q >$ is copied into the cells $f1\ f2$ and $h1\ h2$. Inserting parentheses and outer brackets, under the direction of different segments, yields the final result, as seen in Figure 3v. Deleting the cocoon of the original parentheses exposes these three innermost applications to partitioning and then reduction.

In certain FFP functions the number of messages in a message wave depends on the length of the operand. Long message waves must be interrupted for the storage management to satisfy requests for space in other areas. For such message waves a cycle devotes the entire execution phase from partitioning until the interrupt to accomplishing as much communication as possible.

3.5 System functions in the FFP machine

The reduction of FFP expressions relies on certain functions which are normally assigned to an operating system. Here we look at the algorithms for partitioning, address generation, storage management and providing communication.

3.5.1 Partitioning

The intention is to configure the T cells (by setting some channel switches) to accomplish the decomposition illustrated in Figure 1. Even as partitioning decomposes the machine and in particular the L array into areas, it decomposes the FFP program too. The aim is to separate the innermost applications from the rest of the text and allocate areas to them. The machine needs a distributed recognition procedure which works with the limited information

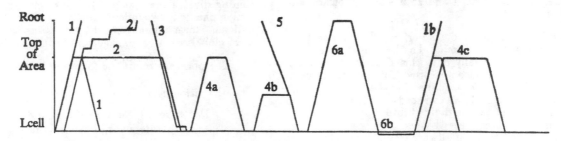

Figure 5. Machine cycle

1 Partitioning   2 Request of FFP function, and address generation in new area

3 Broadcast of segments to new reductions   4a Message wave within area

4b Second message wave blocked and interrupted   5 Interrupt

6a Storage management preparation   6b Storage movement in L array

1b Repartitioning   4c Second message wave restarts and completes available to each subtree. For this section, let *strings* refer to the fragments of the FFP program that partitioning creates. These strings span the text between consecutive parentheses. At each end, a string includes one parenthesis when the available parenthesis opens into the string. Thus the FFP text "..5)(+ < 6 7 >) 8 >) 9 .." is partitioned into five strings: "..5)", " ", "(+ < 6 7 >)", "8 >)", and "9 ..". The ".." emphasizes that this local operation is part of a global scheme distributed over the machine.

A T cell is concerned with at most three areas. It sees the machine as three pieces, two subtrees reached through its children and the rest of the machine reached through its parent. Areas that are entirely in one of these pieces don't need any help from this T cell due to the locality of FFP. This T cell is only concerned with those areas that span more than one piece. Such areas cross one of the three boundaries shown in Figure 6.

Figure 7 shows the four cases for areas crossing these boundaries, and the form that the T cell must take for each. In Figure 7a, three separate areas involve this T cell. The middle area requires a message processor to handle the two streams of messages from the subtrees, but doesn't require a connection to the outside world. The outside areas don't need a message processor because their messages have already been combined in lower T cells, but they do need a connection to the rest of their area outside this subtree. Figure 7e shows the configuration of the T cell for this case.

In Figure 7b, a single area crosses both the central and right boundaries. In this case, all the messages from the right subtree belong in this area and so move through the message processor which is connected on the inside channel. Here they meet the messages from this area's part of the left subtree before the combination is transmitted to the rest of the area outside this tree. As before, the messages of the left area need a channel to join the cells within the tree to those outside; in this case, the T cell is configured as Figure 7f. Figures 7c and 7g show the mirror image of this case.

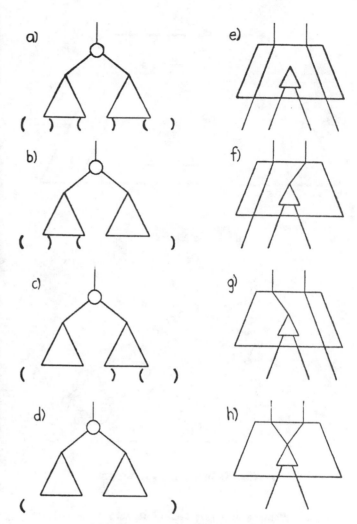

Figure 7. T cell configurations

In the final case, a single area crosses all three boundaries. In this instance, all messages from both subtrees are combined in the message processor before being sent to the parent. That channel should be the parent's inside one, but which channel that is depends on which child this cell is. Instead of the T cell determining whether it is a left or right child, it just sends messages on both parent channels, because the other channel (on the outside) is always unconnected.

Figure 8 shows the form of the T cell (in the main hardware tree) used during the execution phase. The partitioning process is creating one of the configurations 7e through 7h by setting the switches. Whether the left subtree contains parentheses distinguishes cases 7a and 7b from cases 7c and 7d. The left switch in Figure 8 is set outwards exactly when the left subtree contains parentheses. Similarly, the right switch in Figure 8 is set outwards when the right subtree contains parentheses. Partitioning is thus accomplished by having all the subtrees, beginning with single L cells, send a flag indicating "I contain parentheses". Each T cell uses each received flag to set the appropriate switch and then sends the logical OR of the flags to its parent.

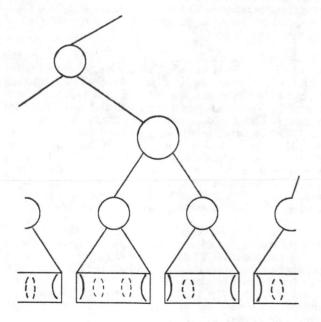

Figure 6. T cell involvement

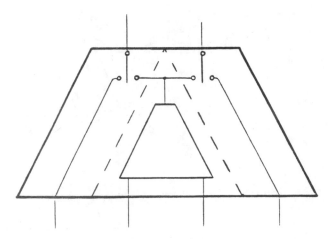

Figure 8. Configurable T cell

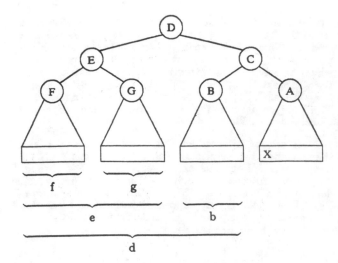

Figure 10. Solving recurrence

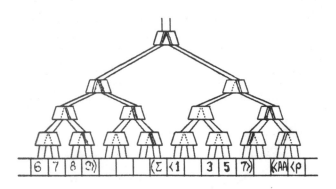

Figure 9. Fitting T cells to programs

Figure 9 shows how this technique actually partitions the machine to conform to some FFP text. In this partitioning method, various inactive substrings of the FFP expression, ones which do not belong to innermost applications, have been allocated areas from otherwise unused resources. Each area uses two bits to determine whether its substring is an innermost application. These bits describe the parentheses enclosing the substring; active areas are those which have correctly matching parentheses.

Since partitioning leaves the T cells in their final setting during the upsweep, it is possible to start generating addresses immediately in the wake of the partitioning bits. This means that partitioning appears to each cell to require a constant three gate delays for fitting the hardware to the FFP programs.

3.5.2 Generation of addresses

Between partitioning and storage management, system functions are confined to a single area within the main hardware tree. An address within the FFP expression consists of three different values, as described in Section 3.2, yet they are all calculated using the same recurrence scheme. The generic scheme will be described, followed by the particular combining functions and initial values used in specific parts of the address generation.

We want the area tree to compute all the addresses concurrently. Figure 10 shows generating the address for a particular L cell X. T cell A sends towards X a description for the string 'd'. T cell C sends this value to A by combining the partial values 'e' from D with 'b' from B. In this fashion, if every T cell knows the information for the substring in its left subtree, it can combine that information with information received from its parent to give the value for its right subtree. The information it gets from its parent also applies directly to its left child. T cells gather the information about their left subtrees in a preceding upsweep. For example, cell E combines the partial values for 'f' and 'g' received from its subtrees and sends this value for 'e' to D.

Given this recurrence scheme, we return to the particular application, that is generating the addresses of the symbols in the area. This requires specifying the particular combining functions and the initial values sent from the L cells, that are to be plugged into the recurrence scheme just described.

The index counts the number of symbols preceding the L cell. Each partial value in the recurrence scheme is the length of the substring in some subtree. The combining function is addition and non-empty L cells send initial values of 1. Figure 11 shows one particular area tree from Figure 1. (Even in complete binary hardware trees, areas are typically unbalanced). Figure 11a shows the upsweep with the T cells keeping the values from their left subtree. Figure 11b shows the downsweep with each T cell sending the value from its parent to the left, and the sum of that value and the stored one to the right. The value each L cell receives is the index for its symbol. (Empty L cells receive values from their parents but are inactive otherwise).

The relative level number counts the number of nested sequences containing the symbol. This is equal to the number of unmatched left brackets preceding the symbol. The relative level number is calculated by using an initial value of 1 for each left bracket and -1 for each right bracket, and again addition is the combining operation. This yields the difference between the number of left and right brackets preceding each symbol.

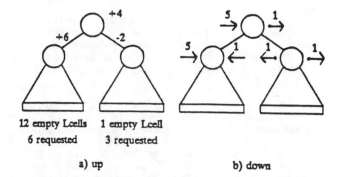

a) up b) **down**

Figure 12. Storage management preparation

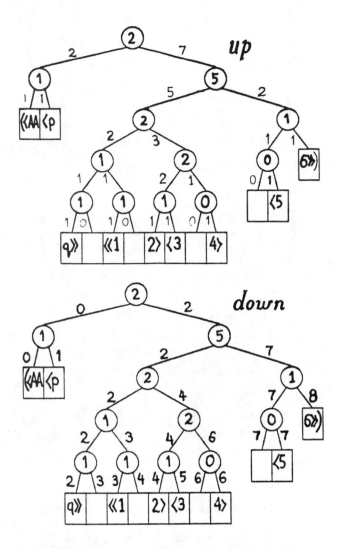

Figure 11. Calculating index using recurrence scheme

The operation to build directories is more complex, and so is only broadly described; more details are available elsewhere [DA1]. Each entry gives the number of left siblings for the ancestor of the symbol's node at that level in the parse tree. Each sibling is an FFP subexpression which is an arbitrary number of FFP symbols in an arbitrary number of further subexpressions. In general, partial values describe properties preceding a symbol. In directories, a subexpression precedes a symbol when its closing bracket also precedes the symbol, and so partial directories are concerned with counting the number of closing brackets at each level of the parse tree. Each entry counts only left siblings, not left cousins. This means that a closing bracket should reset the count of all prior brackets corresponding to deeper subexpressions. Combining two partial directories should reflect this by ignoring all brackets in the left partial directory that are deeper than some bracket in the right partial directory.

3.5.3 Loading microcode segments

Within each active area, every L cell needs instructions directing the manipulation of its symbol. This set of in-

structions is the microcode segment. Every FFP primitive function is evaluated by the distributed execution of a fixed set of such segments. The sets of segments are stored in an external library. The function symbol is sent from the operator part of the innermost application to the T cell at the root of the area. From here, the symbol is broadcast within the area to all L cells and also queued on the output tree to an external library. The library responds by broadcasting all the segments for each function requested. Every segment is tagged with the function name and directory of the L cells where it is to be executed. Every L cell watches the stream of segments until one arrives that matches its function and directory. Ignoring subsequent segments, the L cell begins executing this one.

3.5.4 Storage management

The problem is that some L cells ask to replicate their contents enough times to create space for inserting FFP symbols. The difficulty is that the space may not be nearby in the machine, and using distant space (through pointers, for example) would destroy locality. The solution is to shift unrelated expressions to bring that space nearby, and this is the purpose of the storage management phase.

Storage preparation calculates the necessary symbol flows, as shown in Figure 12. The upsweep determines where empty L cells are and where they are needed, and the downsweep calculates the flows between L cells to satisfy these needs.

Storage movement involves the contents of L cells (which may be partially executed segments and values), shifting through the L array. This allows those L cells requesting space to replicate their contents in adjacent L cells. By allocating space in this fashion the allocated L cells already contain a (partially executed) microcode segment and previously generated intermediate values. In order that the different copies can behave differently (for example, select a different packet in a stream), they are distinguished by the variable *clone-id* which identifies their position in the set of copies.

Prior to storage management, the independently executing areas need to be suspended, the messages flushed from the area tree, and the T cells reunited into a single area. This is initiated by an interrupt from the controller.

3.5.5 Communication

Different FFP functions have different communication requirements to be supported by the message system. In some cases, functions want an aggregate of data that are distributed over the area. At other times they want to copy blocks of symbols. Communication occurs in the absence of centralized control; no cell has knowledge about the source (or destination) of information it needs (or sends). Cells can only glean this information from the messages themselves. We present the message system operation and show two examples of its use.

Within a reduction, communication is divided into message waves, each involving all cells of the area. Within a message wave, messages are transmitted in ordered streams containing an arbitrary number of packets. Each T cell combines the two streams rising from its subtrees into a single stream that it sends to its parent. The single stream emerging from the root of the area is broadcast back to the L cells.

A packet contains three groups, the *key*, the *value* and the *baggage*. The T cells use the *key* field to order the incoming packets. When two packets have the same *key*, they are merged through a small ALU. The ALU determines its operation from the leading field in the *value* group. The *baggage* group is provided for carrying extra information in some transfer operations.

T cells see no finer detail in the packets, but for the L cells these groups contain subfields. The *value* group contains a distinct operator and operand, and the *key* group contains two numeric subkeys and a small key for system use. The final packet in a stream uses the latter key to mark the end of the stream. The T cells cannot detect the difference from ordinary packets, but the L cells use that packet for some system functions.

The message wave begins with the L cells sending to their parent at most one ordinary packet followed by the end of stream packet. Each L cell then begins executing a *filter* which is a block of instructions that is applied to each incoming packet. This filter selects certain packets and then combines their values. This allows generality in the use of the message system to combine information.

This message system evolved to satisfy a number of needs. Every source L cell sees an echo of its message that acknowledges this packet has been broadcast from the root of the area. This allows the system to continue a message wave midstream following an interrupt. Those cells not receiving an acknowledgement before the interrupt must resend in the following cycle. The message system also synchronizes L cells to the same message wave, because it requires each one to have sent some packet, if only the end of stream marker.

Most importantly, as will be shown in Section 3.6.1, this scheme results in message processors that can pipeline messages, that don't need to arbitrate their arrival order, and for which the routing is fixed at machine design time.

Some examples will be used to demonstrate the uses of the message system. Consider taking the transpose of a list of job records shown in Figure 13a, where the result is to be written over the initial matrix. While transposing a matrix of numbers uses a symmetrical permutation, heterogeneous matrices such as Figure 13a, require quite arbitrary permutations. Packets of L cell contents will be sorted as they rise in the message wave, so that the stream emerging from the top of the area is in the row major order of the result. This stream is laid out on the operand from left to right by having every L cell count packets and keep the one that corresponds to its original index. For simple

(a) Example matrix and its transpose

```
<<M 46    <J    W>> <S    37    <P    D>>>

<<M S>    <46    37>    <<J    W>    <P    D>>>
```

(b) Example matrix and its transpose in FFP

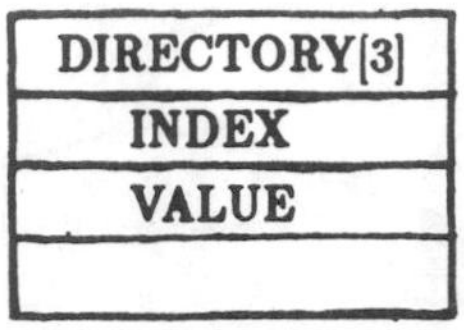

(c) Message packet in FFP transpose primitive

```
<M    <46    <<J    W>    S>    37>    <P    D>
```

(d) Symbols with new brackets before reordering

Figure 13. Example: transposing a matrix

matrices, the second and third entries of a directory are the row and column numbers, and so could be used for the ordering. However, when a matrix element comprises many symbols, their directory elements may be the same, and so cannot be used for ordering. The message packet that each cell sends is shown in Figure 13c. The third element of the directory, used as the first key, causes the symbols to be sorted by column. The index, used as the second key, causes the symbols of each column to be ordered from left to right. This preserves both the row order between separate entries, and the symbol order within a single entry. The value field holds the symbol and the baggage carries the brackets for composite matrix elements. Figure 13d shows how the brackets encompassing rows are modified before the message wave to reflect the changed structure of the result.

Figure 14 demonstrates a sorting operation that is similar to standard hash table sorting, but which takes linear time in the number of distinct values rather than in the range of the values. In this case, the symbols being sorted are transmitted in the key field of the message packets. The value field holds the number of occurrences of that symbol (initially one on leaving the L cells) tagged with the operation addition. The stream of packets reaching the root of

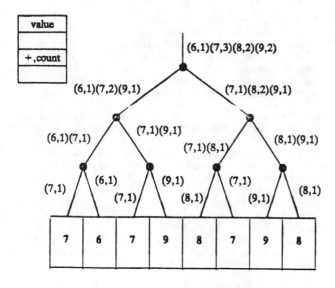

Figure 14. Example: sorting

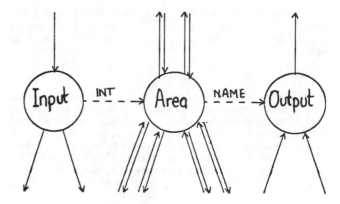

Figure 15. Hardware T cell

the area corresponds to the original values in the L cells, ordered and with common values merged. L cells receiving this stream accumulate occurrences until the sum exceeds their position (given by their index). The packet causing this contains as its key, the symbol destined for this L cell.

3.6 Hardware

Some parallelism is achieved by distributing individual system functions in many cells and by overlapping separate system functions in time. Exploiting such parallelism affects the design of individual cells.

3.6.1 T cell

The FFP machine contains three communication trees, whose nodes are shown in Figure 15. The message tree isolates the area during computation. The input tree provides the broadcast facilities used to load microcode segments. The output tree is used to transfer function names to the external library as requests for microcode segments. The last two trees can also be used to carry the interrupt to the isolated areas, and to remove results from the machine.

The message processor provides the system functions of partitioning, address (and function name) generation, storage preparation and of course message handling. It is this node, shown in Figure 8, that is apportioned to distinct areas during execution. The hardware to accomplish the partitioning and address generation is reasonably obvious in light of the algorithms described above.

The message processor consists of a small amount of hardware as shown in Figure 16, with the ALU capable of performing simple integer operations. As the *keys* come into the processor, it transmits their minimum to the parent, while two buffers store them for possible re-use. The ALU provides control signals to indicate if either key was larger. In that case, no more of that message is accepted, the rest of the other message is transferred unmodified, and the larger key is then compared with the following message from the other subtree. When the two keys are identical, the ALU will combine the packets. The ALU examines the first field of the *values* as they pass, to determine how

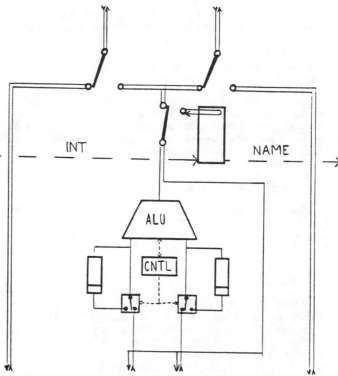

Figure 16. T cell message processor

to combine the operand fields, and neither key will be reused. The results of differing operators or combining *baggage* fields is undefined. The only constraint on the size of a packet in this scheme is the upper limit on the *keys* imposed by the size of the buffers.

A complication arises in the downsweep of storage preparation. Consider the case in Figure 12 where the parent only needs this tree to accept one symbol from the left and none from the right. The left subtree with six available spaces can accept five symbols from the right subtree which can only provide two. When the flows would disagree like this, the T cell chooses the flow with the minimum absolute value. This computation involves both addition and comparison which would prefer (in the absence of buffering) the least significant and the most significant bit respectively to arrive first. A standard binary representation would prevent pipelining this calculation. Pipelining can be accomplished by using a redundant representation for the flows [AV1].

3.6.2 L cell

The easiest way to describe the L cell is to compare it with a microprocessor. The L cell is much like a microprogramming machine, being without stacks, complex addressing calculations, operating system support (such as memory mapping and privileged instruction modes), or high level instructions. It has only direct addressing to access a few hundred bytes of program and data. Certain locations hold the FFP symbol, brackets, parentheses, message buffers, and addresses; the other locations are available for local storage.

System functions are performed by joining hardware interfaces to adjacent cells, and a software monitor that initiates and terminates the functions. The monitor also performs actions such as the participation of empty L cells in message waves. Once a microcode segment has been loaded, it assumes control, returning to the monitor not only on completion, but also for the handling of space requests, communication, and interrupts.

Using separate hardware for execution and loading microcode segments allows the L cell to proceed with its area's operation even as other areas are still receiving their segments. Separating the selection of packets, and their processing in the filter improves operations such as primitive matrix multiplication.

3.6.3 Virtual memory

Execution sees the virtual memory as a pair of stacks that can hold extra FFP symbols during the computation. The total system sees virtual memory as a pair of double ended queues allowing the insertion of programs and the extraction of results.

3.6.4 Controller

The controller is the terminator for the various system operations. It allows certain broad tuning of the FFP machine, for example, by deciding the levels of empty L cells to allow in the L array. It also determines the policy for interrupts. The tradeoff is between delaying areas that have requested space or completed, and interrupting and relocating areas that are performing productive communication.

4. What is known about the FFP machine

4.1 Software model and simulator

The first software implementation of the FFP machine by Danforth [DA1,DA2] was written in a concurrent programming language (C extended with abstract data types [ST2]). It is a detailed model of the FFP machine describing the T cell, L cell, virtual memory and controller in considerable detail. For example, independent processes represent the different parts of a partitioned T cell. After creating instances of the T and L cells, and placing the FFP program to be executed into virtual memory, the software model begins its operation by moving the FFP program from virtual memory into the L cells. During its operation, the model faithfully recreates all inter-cell communications

that would take place in the real machine. It was, therefore, possible to extend it to collect information about the execution times of programs running on the FFP machine. This software model runs under UNIX on a VAX11/780, able to simulate machines with up to 128 L cells. In addition, it is also being used to study the effects of certain design modifications of the cells.

This software implementation represents an important milestone in the development of the FFP machine. Not only does it incorporate the details that were missing in the first description [MA1,MA2], but it also contains a number of important improvements. For example, it is more asynchronous: it is possible for different parts of the machine to be in the partitioning, execution and storage management phases all at the same time. (Storage management is initiated in all L cells by the downsweep of storage management preparation. After finishing its part in storage management, the L cell begins partitioning, and if it already has a microprogram segment, will immediately resume execution too.)

This implementation demonstrates that the FFP machine *works*, and it works exactly as described by the earlier publications: large numbers of cells do indeed cooperate harmoniously, and the large scale parallelism involved in the operation of the machine can be turned into execution speed. The most important issue now is to determine whether simple enough devices can produce this behavior.

4.2 Performance

Since a language-based parallel computer must execute all kinds programs, be they good or bad, efficient use of such a machine is a *programming problem*. Either the user, or an optimizer may be responsible for constructing efficient programs. Both would rely on using high-level guidelines (such as "reduce copying," or "reduce storage management") for improving execution times, and there is typically a large variety of ways to follow such guidelines.

Considerable effort was expended in studying the *execution times* of specific FFP programs. The execution times of static and regular computations (e.g., matrix computations [KO1, MA5, TO2], grid computations such as the solution of elliptic PDEs [MA4,PA1], associative searches [ST1,WI1]) can be determined analytically, using techniques much like those used to study the performance of a von Neumann computer. Such analyses are possible because the FFP program (if alone in the machine) and its initial layout uniquely determine execution time. The method for such analyses uses a model of the machine (it serves the same purpose as the RAM model [AH1] does for the von Neumann computer): execution of the program in question is traced on this model, and *upper and lower bound* expressions are constructed to describe execution time (the execution time of the program in question will be between these bounds for all initial layouts of the FFP expression). These expressions contain hardware parameters (e.g., the pipeline delay through the tree) whose possible values are yet to be determined. When hypothetical but plausible values are substituted for these parameters, the upper and lower bound expressions indicate that high performance (e.g., gigaflops on large machines) can be achieved.

There are many computations that cannot be analyzed in a satisfactory manner on either a von Neumann computer or the FFP machine. They typically involve irregular data structures (e.g., unification and other symbolic computations, sparse matrix computations and graph computations), or unfold in time in an unpredictable and data dependent manner (e.g., adaptive computations). The FFP machine is expected to be suited to execute such computations, because the reduction-style execution, supported by the machine-wide distributed resource management, allows a great deal of freedom at runtime. However, only a large simulator or hardware prototype will be able to provide detailed information about the execution times of such programs on the machine.

The performance of the FFP machine (just as that of a data flow [AG1], reduction or other programmable parallel computer) must be evaluated in a broader context than that of special purpose parallel computers—its programmability and flexibility must be considered as well as its performance. Although the FFP machine aims to deliver high performance on a large variety of computations, it cannot be expected to match in all cases the performance of special purpose parallel computers. For example, our analyses show that the performance of the FFP machine is asymptotically optimal on certain computations (e.g., solving linear recurrences [PA1], retrieval operations [WI1]), it gives no speedup on others (e.g., inner product of two vectors [MA5]), and its performance is between these two extremes for most computations (e.g., solving linear systems of equations [MA5]).

4.3 Extensions

A variety of design alternatives have been investigated [KE1,TO1,MA3], some of which are expected to be incorporated into the first prototype. Among the ongoing efforts is an investigation of the methods for, and the effectiveness of, *routing data items* through the tree *along shortest paths* (rather than through the root of areas). The first step in this direction was taken by Presnell and Pargas [PR1]. Such a capability would improve the performance of the FFP machine on a variety of computations including finite difference methods used to solve certain partial differential equations (such capability was assumed in the performance studies of Pargas [PA1,MA4]).

4.3.1 Virtual memory systems

A considerable amount of work has been done on developing ways to have the FFP machine execute programs that are larger than the capacity of the L array [FR1,FR2,SI1]. Attention was focused on schemes that are *transparent* to the programmer i.e., require no planning on his behalf. The simplest of the virtual memory schemes investigated so far treats the machine as a window on a larger expression; the FFP machine typically is kept as full as possible, but it may "overflow" on either side into this memory, which is a double ended queue. This virtual memory system can also be used to enter new programs and data into the machine, while the tree network can be used for output and certain input purposes. (A variant of this scheme has been implemented by the software model of the machine.)

4.3.2 Other languages on the machine

The FFP machine promises to be able to support programming languages other than FFP either via translation or via interpretation. Smith [SM1] has described recently how the FFP machine could support *logic programming* with a language such as Prolog. Ways to support lambda calculus based languages (including graph reduction) are also being investigated.

5. Conclusions

The attractive architectural properties of the FFP machine provide a strong incentive to construct a VLSI prototype so that the strengths and weaknesses of the machine could be evaluated in greater detail. Work is in progress towards the construction of such a prototype in cooperation with the Computer Systems Laboratory of Washington University, Saint Louis, Missouri.

The viability of the FFP machine will depend most importantly on how simple its building blocks (the T and L cells) can be made. Also, being a small-grain multiprocessor, it must do especially well in performing inter-cell communications, and moving data around within the machine on a large scale. This explains why exploitation of pipelining and asynchrony are expected to play such an important role in constructing the hardware prototype. Our cooperation with the Washington University group is, in fact, motivated by their extensive experience in designing and building asynchronous hardware systems.

Although the FFP machine is in an unexplored part of the design space, its granularity and low engineering complexity make it possible to build a prototype with a relatively modest investment of resources.

References

[AG1] AGERWALA, T. and ARVIND, Data flow systems. *Computer* **15**, 2 (1982), 10-13.

[AH1] AHO, A. V., HOPCROFT, J. E. and ULLMAN, J. D. *The design and analysis of computer algorithms*. Addison-Wesley, 1974.

[AV1] AVIZIENIS, A. Signed-digit number representations for fast parallel arithmetic. *IRE Transactions on Electronic Computers* **EC-10**, 9 (1961), 389-400.

[BA1] BACKUS, J. Can programming be liberated from the von Neumann style? A functional style and its algebra of programs. *Communications of the ACM* **21**, 8 (1978), 613-641.

[DA1] DANFORTH, S. DOT, a distributed operating system model of a tree-structured multiprocessor. *Proceedings of the 1983 International Conference on Parallel Processing*, pp. 194-201.

[DA2] DANFORTH, S. DOT, a distributed operating system model of a tree-structured multiprocessor. Ph.D. dissertation, University of North Carolina at Chapel Hill, 1983.

[FR1] FRANK, G. A. Virtual memory systems for closed applicative language interpreters. Ph.D. dissertation, University of North Carolina at Chapel Hill, 1979.

[FR2] FRANK, G. A., SIDDALL, W. E. and STANAT, D. F. Virtual Memory Schemes for an FFP Machine. *International Workshop on High-Level Computer Architecture 84*.

[KE1] KEHS, D. R. A routing network for a machine to execute reduction languages. Ph.D. dissertation, University of North Carolina at Chapel Hill, 1978.

[KE2] KELLMAN, J. N. Parallel execution of functional programs. Technical report UCLA-ENG-83-02, UCLA Computer Science Department, 1982.

[KO1] KOSTER, A. Execution time and storage requirements of reduction language programs on a reduction machine. Ph.D. dissertation, University of North Carolina at Chapel Hill, 1977.

[MA1] MAGÓ, G. A. A network of microprocessors to execute reduction languages. Two parts. *International Journal of Computer and Information Sciences* **8**, 5 (1979), 349-385, **8**, 6 (1979), 435-471.

[MA2] MAGÓ, G. A. A cellular computer architecture for functional programming. Digest of Papers, *IEEE Computer Society COMPCON* (Spring 1980), pp. 179-187.

[MA3] MAGÓ, G. A. Copying operands versus copying results: a solution to the problem of large operands in FFP's. *Proceedings of the 1981 ACM Conference on Functional Programming Languages and Computer Architecture*, pp. 93-97.

[MA4] MAGÓ, G. A. and PARGAS, R. P. Solving partial differential equations on a cellular tree machine. *Proceedings of the 10th IMACS World Congress*, Montreal, Aug. 8-13, 1982, vol. 1. pp. 368-373.

[MA5] MAGÓ, G. A., STANAT, D. F. and KOSTER, A. Program execution in a cellular computer: some matrix algorithms (in preparation—draft available from authors).

[PA1] PARGAS, R. P. Parallel solution of elliptic partial differential equations on a tree machine. Ph.D. dissertation, University of North Carolina at Chapel Hill, 1982.

[PR1] PRESNELL, H. A. and PARGAS, R. P. Communication along shortest paths in a tree machine. *Proceedings of the 1981 Conference on Functional Programming Languages and Computer Architecture*, Oct. 18-22, 1981 Portsmouth, New Hampshire, pp. 107-114.

[SE1] SEITZ, C. L. Ensemble architectures for VLSI—a survey and taxonomy. *Proceedings, MIT Conference on Advanced Research in VLSI*, 1982, pp. 130-135.

[SI1] SIDDALL, W. E. Virtual memory algorithms for tree-structured processors. Ph.D. dissertation in preparation, University of North Carolina at Chapel Hill.

[SM1] SMITH, B. Logic programming on an FFP machine. *Proceedings of the 1984 International Symposium on Logic Programming*, Febr. 6-9, 1984, Atlantic City, New Jersey, pp. 177-186.

[ST1] STANAT, D. F. and WILLIAMS, E. H. Jr. Optimal associative searching on a cellular computer. *Proceedings of the 1981 ACM Conference on Functional Programming Languages and Computer Architecture*, Oct. 18-22, 1981, Portsmouth, New Hampshire, pp. 99-106.

[ST2] STROUSTRUP, B. Classes: an abstract data type facility for the C language. *SIGPLAN Notices* **17**, 1 (1982), 42-51.

[TO1] TOLLE, D. M. Coordination of computation in a binary tree of processors: a machine design. Ph.D. dissertation, University of North Carolina at Chapel Hill, 1981.

[TO2] TOLLE, D. M. and SIDDALL, W. E. On the complexity of vector computations in binary tree machines. *Information Processing Letters* **13**, 3 (1981), 120-124.

[WI1] WILLIAMS, E. H. Jr. Analysis of FFP algorithms for parallel associative searching. Ph.D. dissertation, University of North Carolina at Chapel Hill, 1981.

Chapter 8: Hybrid Systems

Background

Dataflow and reduction architectures are radically different from von Neumann architectures and introduce a different style of programming. These architectures are going through the same period of refinement that conventional architectures have been going through for the past 30 years. Furthermore, these architectures have not yet taken advantage of recent advances in very large scale integration. Some researchers have already started synthesizing the data-driven and demand-driven computation models to create a hybrid model that takes advantage of both models. Their common aim is to create a general purpose parallel computer that can be programmed in a language that does not have explicit parallel constructs. The software and hardware implicitly take advantage of parallelism in the application. These parallel machines will be scalable and have comparable cost/performance ratio with conventional machines.

Some parallel von Neumann architectures based on a shared-memory model, such as Sequent Balance [13] and Alliant [11] have overcome the cost/performance ratios and do provide implicit parallelism in a multi-user environment. In these systems, *independent* tasks are distributed across a pool of processors. However, parallelizing a single application is a manual task. The distributed memory architectures such as the Intel iPSC [12] are extremely tedious to program [7] and are not really a general purpose parallel architecture, but may be suitable for some numerical applications.

The dataflow and reduction architecture research projects mentioned earlier show some of the limitations of the approaches. The two main concerns with the dataflow model is cost effectiveness and problems in single assignment languages [14]. Most dataflow machines are based on a tagged-token dataflow model to allow for recursion, iteration, and data structures. However, this implies use of an associative memory, which is more expensive than conventional memory. Data structures are handled by using structure stores as a result of refinement of the model and awaits evaluation. The dataflow model requires application to contain enough parallelism to use all of its resources efficiently, and this may make it less cost effective as a general purpose parallel machine.

Reduction architectures are based on functional languages that have a sound mathematical foundation and a higher order function for the expression and manipulation of data structures, and the demand-driven computation model ensures that no unnecessary computation will be done and that independent sub-expressions can be evaluated in parallel. However, a demand-driven computation model can cause many unnecessary accesses between the memory and processor during the evaluation of expression where the arguments are not defined.

Thus, given that both the data-driven and demand-driven models have some good features, it may be possible to combine them to create a hybrid model. The papers in this chapter are based on an attempt to create a machine based on such a hybrid model.

Article Summary

Treleaven et al., in "Combining Dataflow and Control Flow Computing," describe a combined model of computation that integrates the concepts of pure dataflow computation with those of *multi-thread* control flow computation. In the computation model, data are passed indirectly between instructions, via updatable memory cells. Separate control signals then cause an instruction to execute. The program organization is presented at several levels of abstraction, progressing from the *combined* model of computation, through a discussion of problems of program representation in dataflow machines, to a logical description of a computer architecture implementing this organization.

Keller, in "The Rediflow Prospectus," describes Rediflow architecture, which is based on the concept of concurrent execution of small tasks based on graph reduction and incorporates a form of dataflow evaluator. Keller addresses the hardware issues involved for assembling such an architecture, the granularity of task that can be executed with minimum overheads, interconnection issues, and load distribution and balancing. The results of preliminary simulations are presented.

Ashcroft, in "Eazyflow Architecture," describes the Eazyflow architecture, which combines eager and lazy evaluation models of computation and executes a LUCID [2] code directly. Ashcroft develops a new model of program representation called operator nets, which is a network of operators. Unlike the dataflow graphs, the operator nets do not specify operational techniques in the networks. Operator nets [4] are graphical representations of LUCID programs. A hybrid computation model called *eazyflow* (EAger and laZY dataFLOW) is developed for execution of operator nets. A multiprocessor architecture for this model is presented.

Watson et al., in "Parallel Data-Driven Graph Reduction," describe the Flagship project, which is an attempt to combine some features of the Manchester dataflow machine and ALICE to produce a general-purpose parallel machine. The paper describes a packet rewrite model that is similar to ALICE but maintains the properties of dataflow in that the computational resources are only allocated when a task can be completed without external reference from the processor. The granularity of the operations is fine grain unlike ALICE, and the pattern matching is not implemented in hardware. The functional definitions are compiled into simple operations, which are then evaluated by using appropriate operational technique (data driven or demand driven).

Additional material can be found in references 1, 3-6, and 8-10.

References

[1] Ashcroft, E.A., Jagannathan, R., Fustini, A.A., and Huey, B., "Eazyflow Engines for LUCID—A Family of Supercomputer Architectures Based upon Demand-Driven and Data-Driven Computation," *Proc. lst Int'l. Symp. on Supercomputing Systems*, Computer Society of the IEEE Press, Washington, D.C., 1985, pp. 513-523.

[2] Ashcroft, E.A. and Wadge, W.W., "The Syntax and Semantics of LUCID," *Technical Report No. CSL 146*, SRI International, Menlo Park, Calif., March 1985.

[3] Ashcroft, E.A., "Data and Eduction: Data-Driven and Demand-Driven Distributed Computation," *LN in Computer Science*, Springer-Verlag, New York, N.Y., 1986, pp. 1-50.

[4] Ashcroft, E.A. and Jagannathan, R., "Operator Nets," *Fifth Generation Computer Architectures*, edited by J.V. Woods, Elsevier Science Publishers B.V., Amsterdam, The Netherlands, 1986, pp. 177-202.

[5] Dettmer, R., "Flagship: A Fifth-Generation Machine," *Electronics and Power*, March 1986.

[6] Jagannathan, R. and Ashcroft, E.A., "Eazyflow: A Hybrid Model for Parallel Processing," *Proc. 1984 Int'l. Conf. on Parallel Processing*, Computer Society of the IEEE Press, Washington, D.C., 1984, pp. 514-523.

[7] Kallstrom, M. and Thakkar, S., "Experiences with Three Parallel Programming Systems," *Proc. COMPCON S'87*, Computer Society of the IEEE Press, Washington, D.C., 1987, pp. 344-349.

[8] Keller, R.M. and Lin F.C.H., "Simulated Performance of a Reduction-Based Multiprocessor," *Computer*, Vol. 17, No.7, July 1984, pp. 70-82.

[9] Keller, R.M., Lin, F.C.H., and Badovinatz, P.R., "The Rediflow Simulator," *Technical Report*, University of Utah, Salt Lake City, Ut., March 1985.

[10] Keller, R.M., "Notes on Implementation of Logic Programming in Functional Programming for Rediflow Execution," *Technical Report*, University of Utah, Salt Lake City, Ut., May 1986.

[11] Perron, R. and Mundle, C., "The Architecture of the Alliant FX/8 Computer," *Proc. COMPCON S'86*, Computer Society of the IEEE Press, Washington, D.C., 1986, pp. 390-393.

[12] Ratner, J., "Concurrent Processing: A New Direction in Scientific Computing," *Proc. AFIPS 1985 National Computer Conf.*, AFIPS Press, Reston, Va., 1985, pp. 157-166.

[13] Thakkar, S.S., Gifford, P., and Fielland, G., "Balance: A Shared Memory Multiprocessor," *Proc. 2nd Int'l. Conf. on Supercomputing*, Springer-Verlag, New York, N.Y., 1987.

[14] Watson, I., Watson, P., and Woods, J.V., "Parallel Data Driven Graph Reduction," *Fifth Generation Computer Architectures*, edited by J.V. Woods, Elsevier Science Publishers, B.V., Amsterdam, The Netherlands, 1986, pp. 203-220.

Combining Data Flow and Control Flow Computing

Philip C. Treleaven, Richard P. Hopkins and Paul W. Rautenbach

Computing Laboratory, University of Newcastle upon Tyne, Newcastle upon Tyne, NE1 7RU, UK

A model of program organization for a parallel, data driven computer architecture is presented which integrates the concepts of pure data flow computation with those of 'multi-thread' control flow computation. In a data flow organization, data is passed directly from the instruction generating it to those instructions consuming the data, and the availability of input data signals an instruction to execute. In a control flow organization, data is passed indirectly between instructions, via updatable memory cells, and separate control signals cause an instruction to execute. This program organization is presented at several levels of abstraction, progressing from the 'Combined' model of computation, through a discussion of the problems of program representation (e.g. iteration, procedures and resource managers) in data driven computers, to a logical description of a computer architecture implementing the organization. Our objective in developing this Combined model is to investigate how the data flow and the control flow concepts interact.

INTRODUCTION

In this presentation we will use the term 'program organization' as describing the way computation is managed in either a computer or a programming language.

The von Neumann program organization, with its sequential control flow form of computation, totally dominates the design of general-purpose computers. A major reason, and one of the main strengths of the von Neumann organization often overlooked by its critics, is the 'general-purpose' nature of its program organization. It is not just Universal in the sense of a Turing machine, but is able to support effectively a spectrum of styles of programming language and efficiently model a variety of algorithm structures.

However there are two major weaknesses of the von Neumann program organization. Firstly, its lack of useful mathematical properties, which complicates such tasks as program verification, and secondly its inability to represent and utilize parallelism. This has led a number of researchers, notably John Backus[1] and Jack Dennis[2] to question the continuing adequacy for present day computing of the von Neumann organization. To quote from John Backus 1977 ACM Turing Lecture,[1] 'Conventional programming languages are growing even more enormous, but not stronger. Inherent defects at the most basic level cause them to be both fat and weak . . .'.

To overcome the lack of useful mathematical properties in conventional programming languages, reflecting the von Neumann organization, new simpler forms of programming are under investigation. The most well developed such class of very high level languages is functional, or so-called applicative, languages in which program transformations are simply the result of applying functions to their arguments. Traditional examples include LISP and the combinator constructs of APL. More modern language examples include FP,[1] SASL,[3] LUCID,[4] ID[5] and VAL.[6] The program organization concepts in functional languages conflict with those in von Neumann computers, thus implementations are bound to be inefficient.

The second major inadequacy of the von Neumann program organization is its difficulty of specifying parallelism. The pressure on computer architects to utilize the potential parallelism that exists in many problems, has long been motivated by the requirement of increased performance. Recently the need for such parallel computers have received additional motivation from VLSI,[7,8] with the interest to design and program computers built from large numbers of identical and interconnected microprocessors. Functional languages provide an obvious means of programming these computers since parallelism and serialism are both implicitly represented in these languages.

Computing science seems to require a new 'general-purpose' parallel program organization for computers which allows them to support efficiently both functional and conventional programming languages.

Three principal classes of program organization are contenders, namely data flow,[2,9-18] multi-thread control flow[13,19] and the various types of reduction.[1,3,20-24] These models are distinguished by the way in which data is communicated between instructions and by the way in which the execution of instructions is initiated. In a data flow model, when an instruction generates a partial result, the result is passed directly to an instruction that consumes the value. If the result is required as input to more than one instruction then separate copies are created and dispatched. The availability of a complete set of inputs for an instruction causes the instruction to execute and consume the set, after which the inputs are deleted.

In a control flow model a partial result is passed indirectly between instructions via a shared memory cell. Once stored, the result may be read an unspecified number of times. Execution of an instruction, in a sequential control flow model is caused by the availability of a control signal—flow of control. In multi-thread models execution is caused by the availability of a complete set of control signals. Lastly, in reduction models an instruction is executed when a result it generates is required by the invoking instruction. This result is usually passed directly between instructions.

Each model is suited to the representation of a particular class of programming language, because of the way it communicates data and control information. For

355

Reprinted from the *Computer Journal*, Volume 25, Number 2, 1982. Copyright © 1982 by Heyden & Son Ltd.

instance data flow and reduction seem most suited to functional languages, while control flow seems most suited to conventional languages. To obtain a truly general-purpose program organization we believe it is necessary to integrate the concepts underlying these three models into a single model. The program organization presented below shows our attempt to integrate data flow and control flow, both regarded by us as data driven organizations. (We are currently working on the inclusion of reduction which may be viewed as a demand/need driven organization.) This paper discusses our 'Combined' organization and its implications for parallel program representation and execution. Another document[13] describes the hardware simulator we built to support this program organization.

MODELS OF PROGRAM ORGANIZATION

A study of data flow, control flow and reduction models of program organization reveals that two mechanisms seem fundamental to their program organization. First, there is the *control mechanism* by which one instruction causes the execution of other instructions. Second, there is the *data mechanism* by which an instruction obtains the data it requires and communicates data to other instructions. These control and data mechanisms can be regarded as consisting of two basic pairs of mechanisms. The two types of control mechanism that we have identified are the 'by availability' mechanism, in which the availability of operands triggers the execution of the operation to be performed on them, and the 'by need' mechanism, in which the requirement for an operand triggers the operation that will generate it. Similarly, we distinguish two types of data mechanism, i.e. that in which data is communicated directly between operations 'by value' and that in which it is indirectly 'by reference' to a shared named data container.

Data flow and control flow, as we will see below, have 'by availability' control mechanisms. This is one of the main reasons why we have been able to combine these previously separate models into a single fairly simple program organization. Before presenting the control and data mechanisms of this 'Combined' program organization we will consider the mechanisms provided in certain other organizations, namely data flow, our own form of 'multi-thread' control flow called generalized control flow (GCF),[19] and the traditional von Neumann organization. These form logical subsets of the Combined organization.

Figure 1 shows how the assignment statement '$x := (y + 1)*(y - z)$' would be represented by (a) a pure data flow model, (b) a multi-thread control flow (GCF) model, and (c) a single-thread control flow (von Neumann) model. In Fig. 1 the program fragments are viewed as directed graphs, where the rectangular nodes represent instructions, the circles represent stored data and the arcs define flows of information between instructions. A solid arc defines a flow of both data and control information while a dotted arc defines a flow of control. An identifier, such as '$I1$:' in Fig. 1, prefixing an instruction or data item is viewed as the name of the corresponding memory cell in which the item is stored.

In the pure data flow model the control mechanism and the data mechanism are supported by a single scheme. *Data tokens* are used to pass data values from

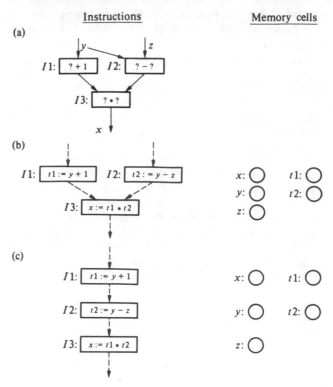

Figure 1. Program organizations for $x := (y + 1)*(y - z)$: (a) data flow; (b) multi-thread control flow; (c) von Neumann control flow.

one instruction to another and also cause the activation of instructions. An instruction is activated when a data token has arrived on each of its input arcs. (In Fig. 1(a) each '?' symbol indicates that a data token is required as input by the instruction.) The instruction removes the set of data tokens from its input arcs and performs the operation on this input data. The results are then released as a set of data tokens on the output arcs. When an instruction generates data it passes the data directly to the instructions that consume the data as inputs. If more than one instruction wishes to consume an item of data, multiple copies are generated. (Constant data as with the '1' in Fig. 1(a) is embedded in the instruction.) This is the 'by value' data mechanism. Further details of the data flow model can be found in the references.[2,10,11]

Data flow program organizations have caused considerable interest in recent years, largely through the pioneering work of Jack Dennis at MIT.[2,10,11] This presumably is because data flow provided one of the first parallel alternatives to the von Neumann organization. However we have shown, elsewhere, that multi-thread control flow program organizations are also viable for parallel computers.[19]

In a control flow model the data mechanism communicates data via named memory cells, with the name of the cell being shared by the instruction generating the data and those instructions consuming it. This common name is embedded in the instruction, as illustrated in Fig. 1(b and c) by identifiers appearing within the rectangles. If the data is constant it is often embedded in the instruction—like the '1' in Fig. 1(b)—replacing a name. When a control flow instruction is activated it uses its embedded names to reference its input data in memory cells, and also to output results to the memory cells. This data mechanism is the 'by reference' mechanism discussed above and is used by both multi-thread and von Neumann program organizations. The control mechanism of these organizations is based on *control tokens* which, like data tokens, are passed to successor instructions signalling them to execute. A control token may be viewed as a data token carrying no data.

In a multi-thread control flow model, in particular the GCF[19] model, the control mechanism is based on multiple control tokens which may signal a number of instructions to execute concurrently. An instruction is activated when a control token is present on each of its input arcs. When an instruction is activated, it removes the set of control tokens from the input arcs, performs the specified operation and releases a set of control tokens onto its output arcs, to activate subsequent instructions. In Fig. 1(b) instructions $I1$ and $I2$ are each activated by a single token, whereas instruction $I3$ requires the presence of two tokens. In the case of instruction $I3$ the two control tokens will signal that $I1$ and $I2$ have executed and that the input data is available in memory cells $t1$ and $t2$.

When a set of control tokens activates an instruction, the assumption is that all the required input data has been computed and that the contents of memory cells used for results may be overwritten. In addition it is assumed that the instruction is safe to execute in parallel with any other instructions that are already executing. For instance, if instructions $I1$ and $I2$ in Fig. 1(b) both assigned their result to memory cell $t1$, the effect of their concurrent execution would be indeterminate. In a multi-thread control flow model, the required pattern of instruction execution is obtained by optimizing the control flow arcs. Hence the traditional von Neumann model, illustrated by Fig. 1(c), is a special case of the multi-thread model in which there is a single thread of control tokens. In a von Neumann organization the single control token, passed from instruction to instruction, is represented by the contents of the computer's program counter, which is automatically updated during each instruction execution.

Having examined the data flow and control flow program organizations, the question to be asked is which organization is the most general-purpose; suitable for efficiently modelling a variety of algorithm structures. Each organization has particular advantages and disadvantages. For instance data flow, with its 'by value' data mechanism, is at an advantage when invoking procedures with value parameters and when evaluating arithmetic expressions, which forms a large percentage of most calculations. Its main disadvantages stem from a lack of updatable memory (in that data structures such as arrays are difficult to implement and variable values which are constant throughout a loop must be regenerated) and from a lack of control flexibility (particularly during the evaluation of conditional expressions).

A control flow organization, with its 'by reference' data mechanism, has advantages where data structures such as arrays are to be shared amongst a number of instructions, where a variable remains constant within a loop, and where inputs might not be used during execution. The main disadvantage of passing data via a memory cell is that additional writes and reads to the memory cell are incurred, thus decreasing performance. Interestingly, the advantages/disadvantages of data flow and control flow are similar to the corresponding procedure parameter passing mechanisms of call-by-value and call-by-reference.

Rather than being competitive, the attributes of data flow and control flow program organizations appear complementary. Thus we, at least, believe that the two forms of program organization can be usefully synthesized. This will allow a compiler writer to obtain the advantages of both organizations. For instance a compiler might generate part data flow and part control flow code for an assignment statement as shown in Fig. 2.

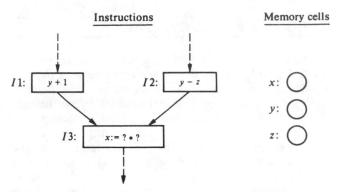

Figure 2. Combined organization for $x := (y + 1)^*(y - z)$.

Figure 2 illustrates the style of program organization supported by our Combined model in which we have attempted to integrate data flow and control flow. This organization is based on a distinction between the roles of the control mechanism and that of the data mechanism. The control of execution of a particular instruction is caused by the availability of a specific set of tokens, which may be data, control or a mixture. The input data for an instruction may come from data tokens or from items embedded in the instruction, both of which may be literal values or the names of memory cells.

Thus in the Combined model a token may be viewed as carrying one of three possible types of operand, i.e. value, name or null. A *data token* can communicate a partial result as either a direct value or as a name used to access a memory cell storing the partial result, while a *control token* can be thought of as a data token carrying a null value. When a set of tokens is complete, and activates an instruction, only data from the data tokens are passed to the instruction as inputs. Instructions activated solely by a set of control tokens do not receive any input values from tokens.

In the data mechanism of the Combined model there are two ways in which an instruction may obtain its inputs, namely (i) by receiving *tokens* which may either carry a literal value or a name of a memory cell, or (ii) by means of *embedded arguments* stored in the instruction which, like the tokens, may be values or names. When an instruction is activated the token arguments and embedded arguments are merged to produce a set of values and names. The names providing inputs are then de-referenced and replaced by their corresponding values from memory. The resulting executable instruction then has a complete set of arguments from which to compute the results.

When the results have been obtained, the outputs of the instruction are generated. Three types of output are provided by the model, namely (i) data tokens, (ii) control

357

tokens, and (iii) data to be stored in memory. These outputs are specified by the instruction and may use both arguments and results. It is thus possible to pass on values received as inputs to succeeding instructions.

The above presentation has given an overview of the Combined model of program organization and the subsidiary data flow and control flow models which it attempts to integrate. In the next section we discuss the representation of parallel programs in the Combined model.

PROGRAM REPRESENTATION

In computers with parallel program organizations, such as the Combined model, special precautions must be taken in a program's representation (style of machine code generated) to ensure that the naturally asynchronous execution does not lead to unwanted indeterminacy. This is basically a problem of synchronizing the usage of shared resources, such as the use of a name associated with a token or a memory cell. The problems of synchronization and program representation can be illustrated by examining the support of iteration, procedures and resource managers in a parallel computer.

Iteration

Iteration becomes a potential problem for the Combined model because program fragments with loops may lead to cyclic graphs, in which each successive iteration of a loop could execute in parallel giving the possibility of multiple tokens on an arc or a single data name (memory cell) being associated with a sequence of values. Three possible schemes may be used to control potentially concurrent iteration. Firstly, the feedback of tokens can synchronize the usage of names. Secondly, the iteration can be represented as recursion, and thirdly, a special iteration number field[16,18] may be included in a (token or memory cell) name. In the Combined model either of the former two schemes may be used, but the latter scheme is not supported because it is only applicable for one level of iteration. Figures 3 and 4 illustrate the feedback and the recursive schemes using as an example a program fragment which calculates the 100th number in the Fibonacci series:

$$(f2, f1) := (1, 1);$$
$$\text{FOR } i := 3 \text{ TO } 100 \text{ DO}$$
$$(f2, f1) := (f2 + f1, f2)$$
$$\text{OD};$$
$$\text{answer} := f2;$$

The loop in this fragment, which uses concurrent assignment, consists of two calculations: one which is producing the Fibonacci series as the successive values of $f2$, and the other which is incrementing the iteration count i. These two calculations may execute in parallel, since i is not used within the DO ... OD.

The first scheme for supporting iteration, shown in Fig. 3, has a direct correspondence to the program fragment. Here the feedback of tokens synchronizes the usage of names, thereby ensuring that only a single token can be on an arc or a single value be associated with a data name. For example in Fig. 3 the code testing for

termination of a loop ensures that all calculations within the loop have terminated before feeding back the tokens for the next iteration.

For the purpose of illustration, the directed graph used in Fig. 3 falls into two parts. The part on the left calculates the sequence of Fibonacci numbers using a data flow representation, while the part on the right performs the iteration count using a control flow representation. In this example a SWITCH instruction is used to synchronize the successive iterations by feeding back tokens. A SWITCH takes two types of inputs, one being the set of tokens to be switched and the other a TRUE/FALSE data token which selects the set of outputs onto which the inputs are released. At the beginning of each iteration the TEST instruction releases a TRUE/FALSE token. If the token is FALSE the other tokens are fed back into the iteration. When the iteration is complete a TRUE token is released causing the data $f2$ to be switched to 'answer', and the other tokens to be discarded, as shown by the 'earth' symbols. If the initial values (i.e the data tokens $f2 = 1$ and $f1 = 1$, and the stored data $i := 3$) are themselves part of a loop then it would be necessary for the release of answer to feedback a signal allowing the loops to be re-entered.

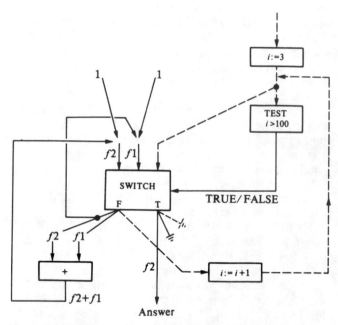

Figure 3. Supporting iteration using the feedback of tokens

The second scheme for supporting iteration is based on the procedure mechanism of the Combined model, which allows concurrent invocations of a single procedure. This mechanism, discussed in detail below, is essential to provide a distinct naming context for each procedure invocation where the stored data and tokens belonging to one invocation will have distinct names, and thus be isolated from those belonging to any other invocation. Figure 4 shows the second iteration scheme which makes use of this isolation mechanism by transforming the iteration into the equivalent recursion:

$$\text{FUNCTION fib}(f2, f1, i)$$
$$= \text{IF } i > 100 \text{ THEN } f2$$
$$\text{ELSE fib}(f2 + f1, f2, i + 1) \text{ FI};$$
$$\text{answer} := \text{fib}(1, 1, 3);$$

Procedures

In the Combined model, as in a conventional computer, before a procedure is invoked, a new distinct context is created for it, in which its instructions can safely execute. The procedure is activated as a process and executes asynchronously with the other active processes.

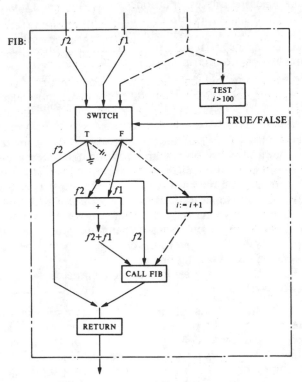

Figure 4. Supporting iteration using recursion.

In a parallel computer each active process requires a unique process name 'P' which specifies the context of the process.[25,26] This P is obtained dynamically when the process is created and is logically prefixed to the static names 'I', embedded at compile time in the code of the process, to give a set of unique runtime object names $P \cdot I$. This also allows the code of the process to be used re-entrantly.

At a logical level there are two instructions involved in procedure invocation, as shown by Fig. 5. In the calling process, say, $P1$ there is a CALL instruction which first obtains a new (globally unique) process name, say, $P2$ and then changes the context of the input parameters

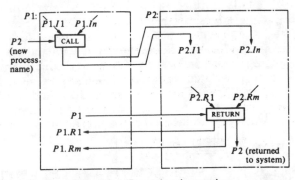

Figure 5. Process creation/Procedure invocation.

from $P1$ to the new context $P2$. At the end of the called procedure there must be a RETURN which changes the context of the results computed by the procedure back to the calling context $P1$, and to achieve this the CALL instruction must provide, as an extra parameter, the caller's process name $P1$.

Resource managers

Although one of the main purposes of using process names in procedure invocation is to allow the procedure code to be used re-entrantly, re-entrancy is not always appropriate. As for example when a procedure directly accesses a peripheral. In addition, accesses that change a resource, such as writing to a file, must be synchronized. Hence the Combined model must support the concept of a resource manager[13,25] to restrict the usage of certain names dynamically. In a situation where a resource manager is used, a number of asynchronous and independent processes may attempt to use a non-sharable resource in parallel. It is the task of a resource manager to ensure that only one process at a time may use its critical region. This is achieved by using a semaphore, supplying a ticket which may only be possessed by a single process. There are two ways in which we might support such a semaphore within our model: (1) a shared *memory cell* which must be tested and set in a single atomic action; (2) a *token* which non-deterministically matches with only one of a possible group of tokens from processes wishing to use the resource. The use of a 'semaphore' token seems to be the most natural way to implement resource managers in a system in which the matching of tokens is the normal instruction activation mechanism.

Figure 6 shows the logical operation of a resource

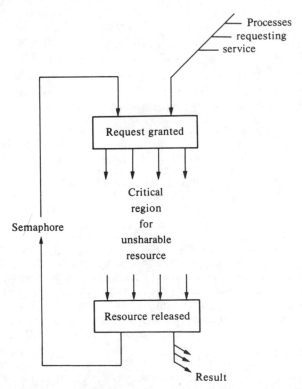

Figure 6. A resource manager.

manager. Each process wishing to invoke the critical region sends a 'request' token, containing the process's name, to the resource manager. This leads to a number of tokens with identical destination names. The semaphore token will non-deterministically match with one of these request tokens, allowing that request token to enter the critical region. When the request has been processed through the critical region, the 'result' tokens are sent back to the requesting process and the semaphore token is released allowing another request to enter.

In the Combined model a resource manager will generally be represented by a separate process which is created and deleted, and communicates with the other processes. In fact the model supports the view of a resource manager as being an invocation of a procedure or function, mapping a stream of requests into a stream of results.

In the remainder of this paper we give a concise description of the Combined program organization in terms of a logical computer architecture. This includes specifications of the computer's information structures, in terms of a BNF syntax, and its machine organization. We start by describing, in more detail, the structure of processes.

PROCESS STRUCTURE AND MANAGEMENT

We use the term process to mean a computation executing in a particular *context* comprising all the objects directly accessible to it. The context is organized into three groups of objects: the process's ⟨code space⟩ is the instructions it is executing, its ⟨stored data space⟩ is the stored data values referenced by those instructions, and its ⟨token space⟩ is the token sets controlling activation of those instructions. Associated with a process is its unique ⟨process name⟩ which is established when the process is created and is attached to all information generated by the execution of the process. This ⟨process name⟩ identifies the ⟨object space⟩s forming the context within which names generated by the process are interpreted.

⟨process name⟩ : : = ⟨code space⟩ ⟨stored data space⟩
⟨token space⟩

Each object is referenced using a two-part ⟨object name⟩, identifying the ⟨object space⟩ and the ⟨relative name⟩ of the particular object within that space.

⟨object name⟩ : : = ⟨object space⟩ · ⟨relative name⟩
⟨object space⟩ : : = ⟨code space⟩|
⟨stored data space⟩|
⟨token space⟩

The purpose of organizing the context of a process into three ⟨object space⟩s and providing two-part ⟨object name⟩s is to support partial sharing of objects between different processes, allowing processes to have 'overlapping contexts'. For example, two invocations of a procedure would have two process names which identify the same code space to allow code sharing, but different data spaces and token spaces to separate the actual executions. When one of these processes accesses an object, such as a stored data value, the ⟨relative name⟩ used is statically embedded in the shared code, whereas

the separate, dynamic, ⟨process name⟩ identifies the particular ⟨object space⟩ in which the ⟨relative name⟩ is interpreted.

By associating a single code, a single stored data, and a single token space with a process, we have clearly restricted the complexity of sharing, but this is in keeping with our overall aim of keeping the program organization and its resulting machine implementation very simple. In a machine implementation we can view the ⟨process name⟩ as indexing into centralized tables that identify the corresponding ⟨code space⟩, ⟨stored data space⟩ or ⟨token space⟩. In addition the system can manage processes by maintaining certain information relating to the use of each ⟨process name⟩ and ⟨object space⟩, such as how many processes are sharing a particular ⟨code space⟩. The following operators illustrate such process management.

(1) ROUTE—this operation changes the ⟨process name⟩ of an object and is used for interprocess communication, such as passing parameters to a new process and returning results to a calling process.
(2) ME—this operation allows a process to obtain and pass its own name to another process so that, say, results can be returned at the end of a procedure call.
(3) NEWP—this operation creates a new ⟨process name⟩ for a calling process.
(4) KILL—this operation returns a ⟨process name⟩ to the system.

To illustrate the use of these operations we will examine the invocation of a process: creating it, the communication of parameters, and the deletion of the process. Figure 7 shows this cycle for a process P2 created by a calling process P1. In the calling sequence the NEWP instruction allocates a process name P2 for the new process and any other resources required to support the process. (In an implementation these will be its local memory cells and some memory space in which to temporarily store its tokens as they are produced.) The ME instruction yields the caller's process name, as required for returning the results. For each input parameter to be passed to P2, a ROUTE instruction in the calling sequence is used to change the context of its second input token to that given by its first input token. The returning sequence is just a ROUTE instruction for each result returned.

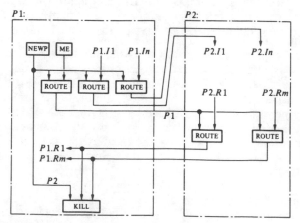

Figure 7. Process creation, parameter passing and process deletion.

When all the results have been returned to the calling process, the called process $P2$ is deleted by the KILL instruction. The effect of deleting a process is to free all machine resources held by the process so that they can be re-allocated in subsequent NEWP instructions. Not only will any memory space be freed for re-allocation but so also is the process name itself, since we presume there is only a finite supply of such globally unique identifiers. In contrast to all data flow computers, in such machine implementations it is unnecessary to insist on program graphs being 'self cleaning'—consuming all their tokens—after all results have been returned there may be some residual tokens belonging to $P2$ which are discarded by the explicit KILL instruction.

One important feature of the use of the primitives NEWP, ROUTE etc. is that they provide both a 'piecemeal' and an 'atomic' form of procedure activation. In the piece-meal form, shown in Fig. 7, the process $P2$ can start work as soon as any one of its input parameters is available and it will return each output result as soon as it is available so that subsequent work in the calling process can start as soon as possible. This allows concurrency between successive iterations in the Fibonacci example of Fig. 4.

In the alternative, more common, 'atomic' form of procedure invocation a procedure cannot start executing until all its input parameters are available and will not return any results until all have been computed. In this form of procedure invocation, as in Fig. 5, the CALL and RETURN are effectively single actions, which is achieved in our architecture by adding some extra synchronization. In Fig. 7 this would reduce the concurrency exhibited and also reduce the period during which the resources used by $P2$ were occupied.

MACHINE ORGANIZATION

Before presenting the machine's information structures and operation it is appropriate to outline the form of an instruction and the instruction execution cycle of the machine, which is based on a packet communication organization.[2] Packet communication is a simple strategy for allocating work to resources in a parallel computer. In a packet communication organization each packet of work to be processed by the computer's resources is placed in one of some number of 'pools of work' with similar packets. An idle resource takes a packet from its input pool, processes the packet and places a modified packet in its output pool. The particular form of packet communication organization described below is similar in concept to that employed in the Manchester Data Flow system,[16, 17] in that instruction execution is based on the 'matching' of sets of tokens.

An instruction consists of an operator, a number of arguments (each distinguished by its argument position), and *mode* information for interpreting the arguments. Activation of an instruction is caused by the availability of a specific set of tokens. Any data from these tokens is carried forward and inserted in vacant argument positions in a copy of the activated instruction. Other argument positions may already contain data embedded in the instruction. At this stage certain of the arguments may be values and the remainder names. Input mode information causes specific names to be de-referenced

and replaced by their corresponding values. Next the operator is applied to arguments in specific positions to produce some results. Finally, output mode information causes certain of the arguments and results to be combined to produce the outputs from the instruction.

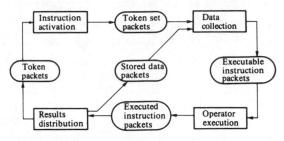

Figure 8. Instruction execution cycle.

Figure 8 illustrates the instruction execution cycle which consists of the following four stages:

(1) Instruction activation—this stage supports the control mechanism of the model. Individual token packets are formed into token sets for a particular destination instruction and are released when the set is complete. This ⟨token set packet⟩ consists of the instruction name and any data from the tokens.

(2) Data collection—this stage supports the data mechanism of the model. It provides a memory for the instructions and data and generates an ⟨executable instruction packet⟩ by inserting the arguments into a copy of an activated instruction. These arguments come from three sources, namely (i) data tokens, (ii) constants embedded in the instruction, and (iii) dereferenced memory cell names.

(3) Operator execution—this stage applies the operator to certain of the arguments and appends the results to produce an ⟨executed instruction packet⟩.

(4) Result distribution—at this stage the outputs are generated by combining certain of the arguments and results. The three types of output packet are (i) data tokens, (ii) control tokens, and (iii) stored data for memory.

MACHINE INFORMATION STRUCTURES

There are basically two kinds of elements in the Combined program organization (i) dynamic *packets* which flow around the logical machine, directly passing information between the stages and (ii) relatively static *objects* which are stored in memory for reference by the packets. The packets and objects have the form of name-value pairs and are of three types—stored data, tokens and instructions. In the following definition of these packets and objects, the BNF syntax uses braces {. . .} to indicate zero or more repetitions of the enclosed material. Also some redundant keywords and punctuation are included to improve the legibility of the examples.

Stored data

An item of ⟨stored data⟩ consists of a ⟨data name⟩ and a ⟨value⟩, and once generated the data may be accessed any number of times without the value being deleted. The name field of an item of data defines the ⟨stored data space⟩—the group to which the data belongs—and the ⟨relative name⟩ of the object within the group of stored data objects. When an item of data is generated any previous stored data with the same ⟨data name⟩ is deleted. (The traditional semantics of control flow.)

⟨stored data⟩ : : = ⟨data name⟩ : ⟨value⟩
⟨data name⟩ : : = ⟨stored data space⟩ · ⟨relative name⟩

A stored data item is generated by a ⟨stored data packet⟩ consisting of a ⟨process name⟩, a ⟨relative name⟩ and a ⟨value⟩ field. The ⟨stored data space⟩ associated with this packet's ⟨process name⟩, together with the packet's ⟨relative name⟩ give the ⟨data name⟩ for the ⟨value⟩.

⟨stored data packet⟩ : : =
            ⟨process name⟩ · ⟨relative name⟩ : ⟨value⟩

Tokens

A ⟨token set⟩ is a grouping of tokens that is temporarily stored until the set is complete, at which stage it is released as a ⟨token set packet⟩ to activate a particular destination instruction. The ⟨token set⟩ has the form of a name-value pair where the ⟨token set name⟩ defines the ⟨token space⟩ and the ⟨relative name⟩ of the token set. The 'value' part consists of the ⟨token⟩s which have been absorbed into the set, the ⟨count⟩ of the total number of tokens for the complete set and the ⟨process name⟩, which must be passed on as part of the ⟨token set packet⟩ when it is released.

⟨token set⟩ : : = ⟨token set name⟩ :
            ⟨process name⟩/⟨count⟩ [{⟨token⟩;}]
⟨token set name⟩ : : = ⟨token space⟩ · ⟨relative name⟩

The ⟨token set packet⟩ identifies the destination instruction, providing a ⟨process name⟩ and a ⟨relative name⟩ identifying a particular instruction within the ⟨code space⟩. Since this ⟨relative name⟩ is unique, as an implementation convenience, it is also used as the ⟨relative name⟩ for identifying the ⟨token set⟩ activating the instruction. The ⟨token packet⟩ specifies a particular token set, provides the ⟨count⟩ (which is the same for all packets contributing to the same set), and provides one or more ⟨token⟩s whose places in the set are defined by unique ⟨position⟩s.

⟨token set packet⟩ : : =
    ⟨process name⟩ · ⟨relative name⟩ [{⟨data token⟩;}]
⟨token packet⟩ : : =
    ⟨process name⟩ · ⟨relative name⟩/⟨count⟩
    [{⟨token⟩;}]

It might seem from the description of the Combined model in section 2 that each ⟨token packet⟩ should contain a single ⟨token⟩. This is true for the majority of tokens. However for program fragments such as resource managers where tokens cannot be uniquely named, it is necessary to ensure that a group of arguments output by one instruction and destined for another instruction are, in fact, placed in the same ⟨token set⟩. This is achieved by placing the arguments in a single ⟨token packet⟩.

    ⟨token⟩ : : = ⟨data token⟩|⟨control token⟩
    ⟨data token⟩ : : = ⟨position⟩ : ⟨value⟩

⟨control token⟩ : : = ⟨position⟩
⟨position⟩ : : = 1|2|3 . . .
⟨count⟩ : : = 1|2|3 . . .

Instructions

An ⟨instruction⟩ is a name-value pair stored in the memory space. The ⟨instruction name⟩ defines the ⟨code space⟩ and the ⟨relative name⟩ for an instruction object, while the ⟨instruction template⟩ gives the value part of the object.

⟨instruction⟩ : : = ⟨instruction name⟩ :
                        ⟨instruction template⟩
⟨instruction name⟩ : : = ⟨code space⟩ · ⟨relative name⟩
⟨instruction template⟩ : : =
    (⟨embedded data⟩ ⟨input mode⟩ ⟨operator⟩
                        ⟨output mode⟩)

Data used in the execution of an instruction consists of a number of ⟨argument⟩s, identified by ⟨position⟩s, and comes either from ⟨embedded data⟩ or as token data from the ⟨token set packet⟩. The set of arguments from these two sources will form a complete set for an instruction, with each occupying a unique ⟨position⟩. Next, the ⟨input mode⟩ lists the ⟨position⟩s of arguments that are to be treated as names and de-referenced. That is, each such ⟨argument⟩ is replaced by the ⟨value⟩ of the stored data item with the name '⟨stored data space⟩ · ⟨argument⟩' where the ⟨stored data space⟩ used is that associated with the ⟨process name⟩ in the ⟨token set packet⟩. The result of this de-referencing is an ⟨executable instruction packet⟩.

Each ⟨operator⟩ is defined as a function from the values at specific argument positions to some result values, each of which is identified by a result (RES) position. For example the ADD operator is defined as:

$$RES\ 1 : = ARG\ 1 + ARG\ 2$$

Thus the definition of operators has been largely separated from the input and output of operands. When the ⟨executable instruction packet⟩ is processed an ⟨executed instruction packet⟩ is generated in which the operator is replaced by a ⟨result list⟩.

⟨executable instruction packet⟩ : : =
    ⟨process name⟩ : (⟨argument list⟩ ⟨operator⟩
                        ⟨output mode⟩)
⟨executed instruction packet⟩ : : =
    ⟨process name⟩ : (⟨argument list⟩
                        ⟨result list⟩ ⟨output mode⟩)
⟨embedded data⟩ : : = {ARG ⟨argument⟩;}
⟨argument list⟩ : : = {ARG ⟨argument⟩;}
⟨result list⟩ : : = {RES ⟨argument⟩;}
⟨argument⟩ : : = ⟨position⟩ : ⟨value⟩
⟨input mode⟩ : : = {DE-REF ⟨position⟩;}
⟨operator⟩ : : = ADD;|MULTIPLY;| . . .
⟨position⟩ : : = 1|2|3 . . .

Finally, the ⟨output mode⟩ defines the stored data and token packets to be emitted by the instruction. This specification identifies the positions of particular argument and result values which are to be combined to form the name and value of a stored data or token object. For instance EMIT-SD(ARG 4, RES 1) specifies a stored data object whose ⟨relative name⟩ is supplied by the argument at position 4 and whose ⟨value⟩ is supplied by the result at position 1.

⟨output mode⟩ ∷ =
  {⟨emit stored data⟩|⟨emit data token⟩|
      ⟨emit control token⟩}
⟨emit stored data⟩ ∷ =
  EMIT-SD (⟨ARGorRES⟩, ⟨ARGorRES⟩);
⟨emit data token⟩ ∷ =
  EMIT-DT (⟨ARGorRES⟩, ⟨ARGorRES⟩);
⟨emit control token⟩ ∷ = EMIT-CT (⟨ARGorRES⟩);
⟨ARGorRES⟩ ∷ = ARG ⟨position⟩|RES ⟨position⟩

Values

The types of operand which may appear as the value part of a data token or stored data value, or as the arguments or results of an instruction are defined by ⟨value⟩. The four types are ⟨basic value⟩, ⟨special value⟩, ⟨reference⟩, and ⟨instruction template⟩. The ⟨basic value⟩s are those on which normal computations are performed, and they are supplemented by the two ⟨special value⟩s NULL and ERROR which deal with exceptional conditions. NULL represents a missing value, as for instance a reference to a non-existing stored data value when an instruction argument is re-referenced. ERROR is the value produced as a result of an erroneous computation, such as division by zero.

⟨value⟩ ∷ = ⟨basic value⟩|⟨special value⟩|⟨reference⟩|
      ⟨instruction template⟩
⟨basic value⟩ ∷ = ⟨boolean⟩|⟨integer⟩|
      ⟨bit string⟩|...
⟨special value⟩ ∷ = NULL|ERROR

The ⟨reference⟩ values can be stored and communicated like any other type of value, but their use is in generating object names. An instruction refers to objects using reference values which can be provided either statically, as embedded data, or dynamically, via data tokens or stored data. In this set a ⟨process name⟩ references a process, an ⟨object space⟩ identifies a group of objects, a ⟨relative name⟩ specifies an object within a group, while a ⟨token reference⟩ defines all of the information for an emitted token, apart from the process name and value.

⟨reference⟩ ∷ = ⟨process name⟩|⟨object space⟩|
      ⟨relative name⟩|⟨token reference⟩
⟨token reference⟩ ∷ =
      ⟨relative name⟩/⟨count⟩[⟨position⟩]

In the next section we follow through the execution of an example program fragment to illustrate the logical machine operation supporting these information structures.

MACHINE OPERATION

To illustrate the machine operation and its instruction execution cycle we will examine the execution of the assignment statement '$x := (y + 1)*(y - z)$'. Figure 9 shows a directed graph and a corresponding 'machine code' representation for the statement. The 'machine code' is given in terms of the above BNF syntax.

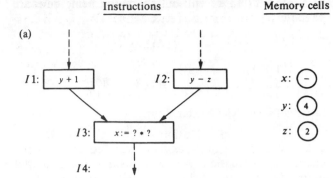

(a)

(b)

I1: (ARG 1:y; ARG 2:1; ARG 3:I3/2[1];
      DE-REF 1;
      ADD;
      EMIT-DT (ARG 3, RES 1);)

I2: (ARG 1:y; ARG 2:z; ARG 3:I3/2[2];
      DE-REF 1; DE-REF 2;
      SUBTRACT;
      EMIT-DT (ARG 3, RES 1);)

I3: (ARG 3:x; ARG 4:I4/1[1];
      MULTIPLY;
      EMIT-SD (ARG 3, RES 1);
      EMIT-CT (ARG 4);)

Figure 9. Representations of $x := (y + 1)*(y - z)$: (a) directed graph; (b) machine code.

Execution starts with the independent arrival of two control ⟨token packet⟩s $P \cdot I1/1[1;]$ and $P \cdot I2/1[1;]$ at the instruction activation stage. Since both packets have a ⟨count⟩ of '/1', both belong to ⟨token set⟩s of one and are released as ⟨token set packet⟩s $P \cdot I1[]$ and $P \cdot I2[]$ to the data collection stage. Here executable instructions are formed. At this stage a ⟨token set packet⟩ contains the name of the destination instruction and any token data; the ⟨position⟩ fields of control tokens and the ⟨count⟩ field having been deleted.

At the data collection stage the ⟨process name⟩ and ⟨relative name⟩ in the ⟨token set packet⟩s identify the two instructions I1 and I2. A copy of each ⟨instruction template⟩ is taken and the ⟨process name⟩ is carried over from the token set to the activated instruction. There is no token data to insert in the instructions. Next the argument ⟨position⟩s listed by the ⟨input mode⟩, DE-REF 1 in I1 and DE-REF 1 & 2 in I2, are de-referenced. Each listed argument is considered a ⟨relative name⟩ in the ⟨stored data space⟩ associated with the ⟨process name⟩ P. These listed arguments are replaced by their corresponding data ⟨value⟩s to produce an ⟨argument list⟩ for the ⟨executable instruction packet⟩s.

P: (ARG 1:4; ARG 2:1; ARG 3:I3/2[1];
      ADD;
      EMIT-DT (ARG 3, RES 1);)
P: (ARG 1:4; ARG 2:2; ARG 3:I3/2[2];
      SUBTRACT;
      EMIT-DT (ARG 3, RES 1);)

At the operator execution stage the ⟨operator⟩ in the ⟨executable instruction packet⟩ is applied as a function to designated arguments in the ⟨argument list⟩ to produce the results in the ⟨result list⟩. In the example these ⟨result list⟩s replace the operators to produce ⟨executed instruction packet⟩s.

P: (ARG 1:4; ARG 2:1; ARG 3:$I3$/2[1];
RES 1:5;
EMIT-DT (ARG 3, RES 1);)
P: (ARG 1:4; ARG 2:2; ARG 3:$I3$/2[2];
RES 1:2;
EMIT-DT (ARG 3, RES 1);)

At the result distribution stage the ⟨stored data packet⟩s and ⟨token packet⟩s are generated from ⟨executed instruction packet⟩s using their ⟨output mode⟩ fields. For each output the ⟨output mode⟩ specifies an ARG or RES ⟨position⟩ for the ⟨relative name⟩ and, apart from control tokens, specifies an ARG or RES ⟨position⟩ for the ⟨value⟩. For our example in Fig. 9 the two data tokens released are $P\cdot I3$/2[1:5;] and $P\cdot I3$/2[2:2;]. These two tokens are formed into a ⟨token set⟩—with temporary storage being provided at the instruction activation stage for the first token to arrive— to activate instruction $I3$.

The ⟨token set packet⟩ released by the instruction activation stage $P\cdot I3$[1:5; 2:2;] supplies data for arguments ARG 1 and ARG 2 of instruction $I3$. At the data collection stage, this token data is merged with the ⟨embedded data⟩ in a copy of $I3$ to form the following ⟨executable instruction packet⟩.

P: (ARG 1:5; ARG 2:2; ARG 3:x; ARG 4:$I4$/1[1];
MULTIPLY;
EMIT-SD (ARG 3, RES 1););
EMIT-CT (ARG 4);)

The multiply is applied to ARG 1 and ARG 2 at the operator execution stage and the resulting ⟨executed instruction packet⟩ is released.

P: (ARG 1:5; ARG 2:2; ARG 3:x; ARG 4:$I4$/1[1];
RES 1:10;
EMIT-SD (ARG 3, RES 1);
EMIT-CT (ARG 4);)

Finally, at the result distribution stage the ⟨output mode⟩ in the packet causes the release of a ⟨stored data packet⟩ $P.x$:10 and a control ⟨token packet⟩ $P.I4$/1[1;].

CONCLUSION

The work reported here forms part of a larger project investigating the design of highly parallel computer architecture. In particular it involves the identification of a truly general-purpose, parallel model of program organization. In this paper we have presented in significant detail a parallel program organization, referred to as the Combined model, which integrates the concepts of the pure data flow computation with those of a 'multi-thread' form of control flow computation. This Combined model was presented at several levels of abstraction progressing from the program organization model, through a discussion of the problems of program representation (e.g. iteration, procedures and resource managers) in parallel computers, to a description of a logical computer architecture that supports this Combined program organization.

The main problem area in the Combined model, as we might expect, concerns stored data and its passive nature. For instance we specify that any ⟨stored data packet⟩s output by an instruction are released first, and update memory before any of the ⟨token packet⟩s are released. These tokens may then signal the availability of the stored data. However in any real implementation it is impossible to update a memory cell instantaneously, but the model seems to require that we know precisely when a cell has been updated. Fortunately in an implementation[13] we can support such semantics.

Although this paper concentrates on the important concepts of the Combined model of program organization, we have implemented a simple multiprocessor computer system that supports the model. This computer[13] is built from dedicated Motorola M6800 systems that are connected and communicate by hardware FIFO queues. (The computer is similar to the system in Fig. 8.) Although the implementation of the computer is relatively simple, its logical architecture contains a number of interesting features frequently absent in comparable parallel (e.g. data flow) computers. These include mechanisms for (i) re-entrant code, (ii) handling asynchronous processes, (iii) resource management, (iv) avoiding the need for 'self-cleaning' graphs, and (v) compiling. As a research vehicle the main advantage is that such a computer may be programmed as if it were a pure (without memory) data flow computer, or as a 'multi-thread' control flow computer, or more interestingly as some combination of these two.

Acknowledgements

The ideas and computer design presented in this document owes much to the support and encouragement of our colleagues at the University of Newcastle upon Tyne. In particular, Edward Farrell, Noordin Ghani and Simom Jones who participated in the design, David Brownbridge who programmed a simulator for the computer, and Brian Smith and T. L. Wat who constructed the multiprocessor computer. Brian Randell, Graham Wood and the referees are thanked for their penetrating comments on earlier versions of this paper. The Computer Architecture Group has also been greatly aided by the Distributed Computing System Panel of the UK Science Research Council, which funds this research.

REFERENCES

1. J. Backus, Can programming be liberated from the von Neumann style? A functional style and its algebra of programs. *Communications of the ACM* **21** (No. 8), 613–641 (August 1978).

2. J. B. Dennis, The varieties of data flow computers. *Proceedings of the First International Conference on Distributed Computing Systems*, 430–439 (October 1979).

3. D. A Turner, A new implementation technique for applicative languages. *Software—Practice and Experience* **9**, 31–49 (1979).

4. A. Ashcroft and W. W. Wadge, LUCID, a nonprocedural language with iteration. *Communications of the ACM* **20** (No. 7), 519–526 (1977).

5. Arvind et al, *The Id Report: An Asynchronous Programming Language and Computing Machine.* Technical Report 114, Department of Information and Computer Science, University of California, Irvine (May 1978).

6. W. B. Ackerman and J. B. Dennis, *VAL—A Value-oriented Algorithmic Language (preliminary reference manual)*, Technical Report MIT/LCS/TR–218, Laboratory for Computer Science, MIT (June 1979).

7. C. Mead and L. Conway, *Introduction to VLSI Systems*, Addison Wesley, Reading, Massachusetts (1980).

8. C. Seitz (Ed.), *CALTECH Conference on Very Large Scale Integration.* (January 1979).

9. A. L. Davis, The Architecture and system methodology of DDMI: A recursively structured data driven machine. *Proceedings of the Fifth Symposium on Computer Architecture*, 210–215 (April 1978).

10. J. B. Dennis, First version of a data flow procedure language, in *Lecture Notes in Computer Science*, Vol. 19, pp. 362–376. Springer-Verlag, New York (1974).

11. J. B. Dennis and D. P. Misunas, A preliminary data flow architecture for a basic data flow processor. *Proceedings of the Second Symposium on Computer Architecture*, 126–132 (1975).

12. M. Cornish *et al.*, The TI data flow architectures: the power of concurrency for avionics. *Proceedings of the Third Digital Avionic Systems Conference*, 19–25 (November 1979).

13. R. P. Hopkins *et al.*, *A Computer supporting Data Flow, Control Flow and Updateable Memory*, Technical Report 144, Computing Laboratory, The University of Newcastle upon Tyne (September 1979).

14. M. P. Lecouffe, MAUD: a dynamic single-assignment system. *Computers and Digital Techniques* **2** (No. 2), 75–79 (April 1979).

15. J. C. Syre *et al.*, Pipelining and Asynchronism in the LAU system. *Proceedings of the 1977 International Conference on Parallel Processing*, 87–92 (August 1977).

16. P. C. Treleaven, Principal components of a data flow computer. *Proceedings of the 1978 Euromicro symposium*, 366–374 (October 1978).

17. I. Watson and J. Gurd, A prototype data flow computer with token labelling. *Proceedings of the AFIPS Conference*, Vol. 48, 623–628 (1979).

18. Arvind and K. P. Gostelow, A computer capable of exchanging processors for time. *Proceedings of the IFIP Congress 1977*, 849–853 (August 1977).

19. E. P. Farrell *et al.*, A concurrent computer architecture and a ring based implementation. *Proceedings of the Sixth Symposium on Computer Architecture*, 1–11 (April 1979).

20. K. J. Berkling, Reduction languages for reduction machines. *Proceedings of the Second International Symposium on Computer Architecture*, 133–140 (April 1975).

21. R. M. Keller *et al.*, A loosely-coupled applicative multiprocessing system. *Proceedings of the AFIPS Conference*, Vol. 48, 861–870 (1978).

22. W. E. Kluge, *The Architecture of a Reduction Language Machine Hardware Model*, Technical Report ISF-Report 79.03, Gesellschaft fur Mathematik und Datenverarbeitung MBH Bonn (August 1979).

23. G. A. Magó, A network of microprocessors to execute reduction languages. *International Journal of Computer and Information Sciences* **8** (No. 5) and **8** (No. 6), (1979).

24. P. C. Treleaven and G. F. Mole, A multi-processor reduction machine for user-defined reduction languages. *Proceedings of the Seventh International Symposium on Computer Architecture*, 121–129 (1980).

25. Arvind *et al.*, Indeterminacy, monitors and dataflow. *Proceedings of the Sixth ACM Symposium on Operating Systems Principles*, pp. 159–169 (November 1977).

26. G. S. Miranker, Implementation of procedures on a class of data flow processors. *Proceedings of the 1977 International Conference on Parallel Processing*, 77–86 (August 1977).

Received February 1981

REDIFLOW ARCHITECTURE PROSPECTUS

Robert M. Keller

August 1985
(date of last revision: 5 April 1986)

Technical Report No. UUCS-85-105

Department of Computer Science
University of Utah
Salt Lake City, UT 84112

(801) 581-5554
Keller@Utah-20.arpa

1. Introduction

Rediflow is intended as a multi-function (symbolic and numeric) multiprocessor, demonstrating techniques for achieving speedup for Lisp-coded problems through the use of advanced programming concepts, high-speed communication, and dynamic load-distribution, in a manner suitable for scaling to upwards of 10,000 processors. An initial physical realization is proposed employing 16 nodes (initially in a hypercube topology), with processor, memory, and intelligent switch at each node.

Rediflow is based on the concept of concurrent execution of small tasks based on *graph reduction*. Reduction is a fundamental problem-solving technique: successively reduce a complex problem to a combination of simpler problems. The idea of *graph* reduction (as opposed to *string* or *tree* reduction) means that simpler sub-problems need be solved only once, rather than multiple times. The graph here alludes to problem representation in which tasks are represented by nodes, and data dependence is represented by arcs. A common sub-problem shows up as a node which has an output arc directed toward more than one other node. We have explored extensively, through simulation, the intimate relation between such problem graphs and a normal-order Lisp execution model, as a basis for multiprocessing [19, 27].

Rediflow has been a top-down language-driven development. The relation to Lisp was mentioned above. During the course of research, it was discovered that processor technology is best exploited by integration of forms of data flow and von Neumann-style processing with the reduction model. These discoveries led to the proposed Rediflow evaluation model.

Rediflow intends to exploit hardware technology for effective multiprocessing. An essential part of its development is a *high-speed intelligent switch* which achieves communication, and assists in special *deferred-evaluation object handling* and *load-balancing*. This switch is designed with *low-latency* in mind, to permit Rediflow to compete effectively with shared-memory architectures.

Rediflow achieves *locality* of information processing through effective use of *saturation control*, in which tasks do not migrate when the system is operating at full processor capacity. Saturation control is integrated with the *completely decentralized load-distribution mechanism*.

Rediflow software will support convenient exploitation of the multiprocessor, with optional use of special concurrency constructs. Through the use of high-level language constructs (i.e. functional and logic programming) with a Lisp-based front-end, determinate execution of programs can be guaranteed despite internal variations in message delays and system technology. The front-end does not require that determinate constructs be used exclusively; if constructs are used which could lead to indeterminacy, the programmer will be so advised. The integrated system conception also entails *distributed dynamic storage management*.

2. Rediflow Rationale

Multiprocessing systems promise to improve speed and reliability over advances achievable simply through advanced device technology. This proposal emphasizes design and exploitation of multiprocessors with a large number (say, in the thousands) of processors, but with a high degree of generality, especially for the accommodation of problems with *irregular* or *dynamic structure*. At the same time, a prime consideration is *minimal intellectual overhead* on the application programmer's part to benefit from such a system. We view our techniques to be especially relevant to rapid prototyping of applications codable in Lisp.

The applicability of multiprocessor organizations rests on the successful solution of problems relating to *communication*. Two main schools of thought seem to exist on this subject. The first, "shared memory" , opts for uniform processor-memory access paths and uniform latency. The second, *partitioned memory* (also sometimes called "loosely-coupled"), opts for non-uniform access paths and latency. Grounds for taking this approach are based on several hypotheses:

1. **Locality** of processor-memory references, even in a less than optimal distribution, will provide gains through reduced latency when a very large number of processors is involved.

2. **Granularity** of processing can be made sufficiently coarse to require a small enough amount of communication vs. computation to avoid slow-down due to channel delay.

3. **Synchronization** necessary for multiple accesses to common memory objects is vastly simplified if each memory module has a specific processor as master. (This circumvents the problem of "cache coherence," for example.)

4. **Cost of hardware** should increase at worst linearly with the number of processors.

5. **Dynamic allocation** of processor load is a necessity due to problem irregularity.

Rediflow is being designed to combine best aspects of shared and partitioned memory organizations. Consider that any scalable architecture is interconnected by hardware units of limited fan-out and communication capacity. This holds true for the interconnection switch of shared memory machines. Non-local references in such machines must traverse some usually-fixed number of smaller switches, and the delay is proportional to the number traversed. One viewpoint of Rediflow is that each such switch contains a processor and memory, so that the average non-local access can be faster than the worst case, and locality can thus be exploited. A second viewpoint is that Rediflow is a partitioned memory machine. However, unlike current such designs, Rediflow's switch will enable communication equivalent to that in shared memory, due to a high-speed design which uses very little buffering, and certainly no slow memory as buffering. Despite a physical memory partitioned for the above reasons, overall system-wide addressability is maintained in Rediflow. This is a key part of our approach for maintaining communication linkages in a distributed system, including those corresponding to large data structures, independent parts of which are concurrently mutable by many processors.

3. Architectural Technical Characteristics

3.1. Overall Motivation

Successful scalable multiprocessors must address the following considerations:

      1. Processors must communicate with memory.

      2. Work must be distributed among the processors.

      3. In machine intelligence applications, it is generally impossible to pre-plan
         the distribution of work.

Responding to the criterion of scalability requires the use of a uniform construction of simple replicable units. If one chooses the *shared* memory configuration, then there are three identifiable units: processors, memories, and switches. Switches are connected into a network permitting any processor to access any memory. For large numbers of processors, the switching network increases latency and complicates usage of fast processor caches. In addition, the switch components must be matched to processor/memory technology, so as not to cause bottlenecks. Trivial switches, such as buses, are known to saturate at numbers of processors far lower than our scalability criterion would dictate.

In contrast, the *partitioned* memory strategy pairs processors one-to-one with memories in nodes. Communication among nodes is achieved by a switch network. Here the technology used in the network has a less important role than in a shared memory system, since significant local processing can be accomplished without using it. It is usually assumed that global information accesses are likely to occur at rates on the order of 1 per 100 instructions, or more, rather than 1 per instruction. Given the latency associated with a shared memory configuration, programs without much inherent concurrency suffer much less under a partitioned memory configuration.

In Rediflow, a processor, memory, and switch are packaged into a replicable unit called a *Xputer* (readable as "transputer"). Rediflow is a collection of Xputers, in which the average non-local access is expected to be faster than the worst case, and locality can thus be exploited. Rediflow will enable communication equivalent to that in shared memory, since the high-speed switch construction will use very little buffering, and certainly no slow memory as buffering. The Xputer switch also plays a major role in load balancing, in addition to its role in routing of data, data requests, and tasks. This will be further described (in Section 3.8) after introduction of the tasking model.

3.2. Graph Reduction Evaluation Model

The evaluation model to be implemented is based on the need to distribute, with low overhead, medium-granularity work among the processors. Rediflow is based on the concept of graph reduction. This seems particularly true for the level of granularity usable by machine intelligence applications, as well as a number of others.

As an example of where graph reduction is useful in spawning concurrent work, consider the Common Lisp function map, which funcalls a function f on a list of lists. Suppose, for example, map is called as follows (using syntax of Common Lisp [33]):

```
(map 'list f (list x1 x2 x3 x4 x5 x6 x7 x8)
            (list y1 y2 y3 y4 y5 y6 y7 y8))
```

which effectively expands into

```
(list   (funcall f x1 y1)
        (funcall f x2 y2)
        (funcall f x3 y3)
        (funcall f x4 y4)
        (funcall f x5 y5)
        (funcall f x6 y6)
        (funcall f x7 y7)
        (funcall f x8 y8))
```

with each component of the resulting list evaluable in parallel. To see how such parallelism is accomplished, consider a semantic definition of map for the special case of two lists for simplicity:

```
(defun map-list (fun list1 list2)
     (if (null list1)
           nil
           (cons (funcall   fun (car list1) (car list2))
                 (map-list fun (cdr list1) (cdr list2)))))
```

This definition is translated into a graph production rule which, during execution on a pair of large lists, "unravels" to yield concurrently-executable funcalls of fun on corresponding pairs from the two lists, as shown in Figure 3-1.

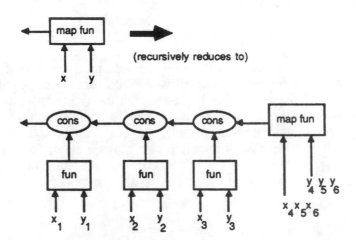

Figure 3-1: Unravelling of the map function

A related form of concurrency is divide-and-conquer, as is exemplified by the Common Lisp function *reduce*. Here we add a keyword argument :associative which, when true, indicates that the function argument is associative, meaning that it can be applied to argument groupings in any order. For example, the following shows a corresponding graph expansion for divide and conquer execution of the reduce function, with concurrent evaluation of the binop's at each level.

370

```
(reduce binop (list x1 x2 x3 x4 x5 x6 x7 x8) :associative t)
```

implemented as

```
(funcall binop
        (funcall binop
                (funcall binop x1 x2)
                (funcall binop x3 x4))
        (funcall binop
                (funcall binop x5 x6)
                (funcall binop x7 x8)))
```

Common Lisp includes *sequence* as a generic type. This permits, in addition to the usual list and array representations, other internal representations such as *virtual concatenation* which are optimized for divide-and-conquer manipulation. System-optimized functions such as *map* and *reduce* will exploit these representations, and generate highly-parallel execution code, as suggested by Figure 3-2. This is one of our principal sources of concurrency, obtained without explicit effort by the programmer.

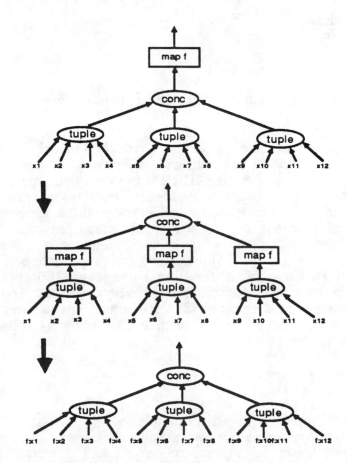

Figure 3-2: Concurrency arising from the use of conc data structures

Using graph reduction, compositions of sequence functions such as a map feeding a reduce are computed with maximal asynchrony. For example, it is not necessary for a map application to be completed before a reduce application begins operating on its result. This is shown graphically in Figure 3-3, and is only one of many variations available under the low-level synchronization provided by graph reduction.

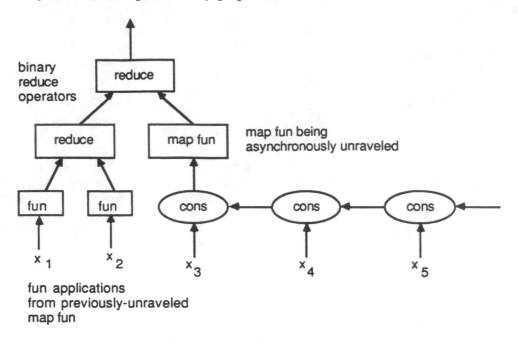

Figure 3-3: Asynchrony in graph-reduction through deferred evaluation

We have experimented with the basic graph reduction model for some time [19, 27] and have come to understand its strengths and weaknesses. While our method of using code blocks as templates achieves the efficient run-time construction and splicing of function graph bodies, it is most appropriate for data structures which are semi-permanent in terms of the lifetime of the computation and less appropriate for transient ones. Thus, our first method refinement is to short-circuit pure graph reduction for computations involving temporary values, in favor of more conventional code in such instances. This idea has been used in one form [2, 16] to achieve what appears to be the fastest existing sequential implementation of a functional language (competitive with Lisp implementations), so the outlook for its use here is very favorable. To this technique, we add the use of *pre-constructed* templates for semi-permanent structures [19]. We hope to gain further speed improvements by this technique. The following example illustrates this effect. Consider the function

```
(defun example(x y)
       (cons (cons x y) (cons y x)))
```

and suppose we are computing (map 'list example list1 list2). Using the approach of [2, 16], each cons operation would require separate allocation and pointer manipulation. With the code-block approach used in [19], the compiler produces a template (code-block) which contains a relocatable graph structure, the nodes of which do not have to be linked individually.

3.3. Dataflow Evaluation Model

A second aspect of our evaluator is the incorporation of a form of dataflow. With lazily-evaluated streams [4, 12, 22], it is already possible to capture the semantics of dataflow, namely graphs of operators which are interconnected by virtual channels, with each operator incrementally consuming its input streams, performing a function, and producing output streams. Our optimized form of dataflow achieves this through Kahn processes, a type of communicating sequential processes, which have a functional semantics [17]. This form is further extended within our model to allow indeterminate processes, as described in [18], for the purpose of resource sharing.

Kahn processes are implemented using conventional sequential code, as discussed in the preceding paragraph, with the addition of stream read/write primitives. The input/output streams are implemented by the construction of linked lists, just as in the graph reduction implementation. Code is immediately re-usable (in contrast to the destructive execution effects of pure graph reduction or the combinator approach), and in the one-output stream case, the linked-list cell is re-used as well. This means that we do not incur a storage recycling overhead for stream-based communication as we would with pure reduction. In the multiple output stream case, some generation of linked-list cells may be necessary to account for differences in consumption rate. This is a subtle problem [27]. Attempts to solve it with fixed buffering, as some proposed dataflow implementations do [8], have been observed to alter the expected stream semantics and introduce deadlock. For this reason, we adhere to an implementation that preserves graph reduction semantics.

3.4. Native-Code Compilation

To produce the fastest possible execution, we will follow [16] in compiling graph reduction to native microprocessor code. The use of such code in a high-performance microprocessor appears to us to be superior to the design of a specialized reduction machine which is merely an interpreter. Our work will extend that of [16], in that we must produce a translation for a concurrent machine, rather than a sequential one.

3.5. Task Basis

Motivated by the above discussion, the following is a brief summary of how tasks (non-primitive function calls) are handled in our evaluation model. Sub-computations are triggered by *demand* for results. At any moment, many demands may be outstanding, and are represented as addresses on one of several queues (one per processor, and further sub-divided by type). Each address points to a node in memory representing a function application that will yield the desired result. Demands can be generated as need determines ("lazily"), or by anticipation of need ("eagerly").

Each processor multiplexes its attention among tasks. If a task needs remote data, the processor generates a request for that data. Meanwhile, it processes other tasks, as selected from its queue. The outstanding remote request is designated by a waiting node in memory. When the response to the request comes back, it is targeted for that node, and a task is again generated. This "wake-up" action allows the task to proceed. Ultimately, the node in memory representing the task itself is overlaid with a result. This result is forwarded to any outstanding requestors of the result, which will re-activate those tasks as identified by the target locations. Figures 3-4 and 3-5 suggest the logic introduced within the Xputer to enable high-performance processing of such task control based on memory-requests.

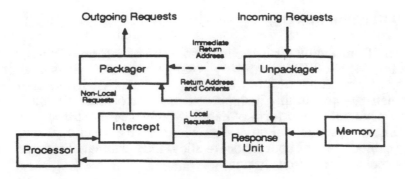

Figure 3-4: Xputer memory reference data flow

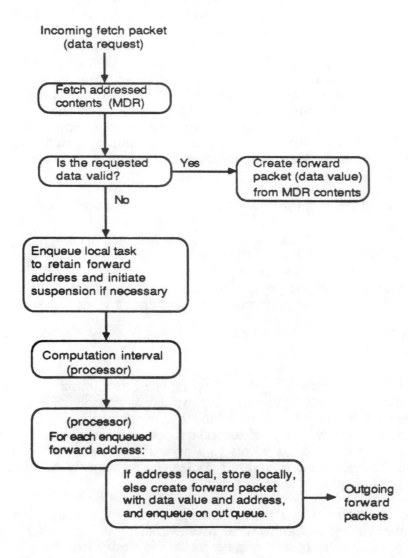

Figure 3-5: Xputer memory reference logic

Typically, a task performs local operations on registers, and may generate further nodes (e.g. cons-cells or arrays) in graph memory (which in our case is just "ordinary" memory, for uniformity). The system-wide graph memory is linked together by a uniform logical address space, permitting data-structures to span many physical Xputers, and thereby be manipulated concurrently. The speedup achieved by Rediflow is due to this concurrent manipulation of graph structure, and the attendant concurrent execution of local operations. Efficient use of partitioned memory relies on the achievement of a sufficiently high ratio of local to remote operations, and on the aforementioned intra-processor task multiplexing. One needed refinement of the task model is a form of priority control for tasks, so that essential tasks can take precedence over speculative ones, at least on a local basis.

3.6. Task Distribution

In certain instances, graph "reduction" is really "expansion," i.e. when we replace a function application with the meaning of that application. Function applications thus define a natural unit of task granularity, in that data within them usually form a logically-related unit. For this reason, we also use this quantum for work distribution. More precisely, any sufficiently complex function (say on the order of a few hundred machine instructions) is considered migrable to a processor other than the one on which it was invoked.

The migration of function applications takes place in the form of an apply task, which is a small packet of information containing:

> 1. **closure descriptor**: A pair of items representing a function together with its static context (bindings of free variables), i.e.
>
> > a. code block number: This designates a block of code for the function, which prescribes the evaluation of its body.
> >
> > b. import: This designates a value, or tuple of values, which the function uses from its static scope. Thus it forms an efficient environment structuring mechanism.
>
> Closures are the key to the implementation of higher-order functions and combinators, as well as being a practical device for keeping argument lists of manageable size.
>
> 2. **argument**: This designates the actual argument to the function. If the function has more than one argument, this information designates a tuple of arguments, the components of which are fetched by the function's code.
>
> 3. **result location**: This indicates where the result of the function is to be sent when complete.
>
> 4. **Xputer target** (optional): A specific target Xputer may be specified for the function's execution.
>
> Examples of pragmas for achieving such targetting are presented below. If this field is not specified, the load-balancer will choose the target dynamically.

Hence an apply task fits in a fixed-length packet, long enough to hold only about four addresses (it being assumed that the combined length of code block number and Xputer number are not longer than an address).

We have developed [19] a dynamic linkage mechanism which enables apply tasks to be free floating, i.e. they can be done locally or transmitted to any other Xputer. Once a resting place has been found for such a task, storage is allocated and linkage is accomplished in the global address space. The invocation of a function causes the creation of a local task which is a pointer to an instruction in the code block. As remarked earlier, numerous local tasks are multiplexed within an Xputer. This serves two purposes:

1. A local task may spawn another task which will likely soon lead to an apply task which is migrable, thereby achieving parallel execution.

2. Latency due to non-local memory requests is absorbed by having the processor switch to a different local task. If a local task becomes blocked due to a non-local request for some data, a notifier pointer is set in the location for that data so that the task can be reactivated when the memory request is acknowledged, by simply putting the notifier back onto the local task queue. Non-local requests and acknowledgments are implemented by packets containing the addresses of the requested location and requesting task, which are routed by the switching network.

3.7. Logical Configuration Pragmas

The optional use of pragmas as mentioned above to place tasks permits Rediflow to be used to dynamically configure networks of processes, for example as would be found in a "systolic array." For example, the RediLisp code below Figure 3-6 recursively defines a simple standard form of digital filter. By annotating the code with the "eval-on" pragma [29], the network can be optimally set up to conform to any physical configuration in which a rectangle can be embedded. An incomplete list of pragmas is given below:

(my-num-neighbors)	Evaluates to the number of neighbors for this Xputer
(num-neighbors x)	Evaluates to the number of neighbors of Xputer x
(my-index)	Evaluates to the index of this Xputer
(my-neighbor i)	Gives the index of the i-th neighboring Xputer (error if i > (my-num-neighbors))
(eval-on x expression)	Evaluate expression on Xputer with index x. Value is that of expression
(evaluate-here expression)	Evaluate expression on this Xputer
(attract expression)	The value of expression attracts to itself any functions having it as an argument (to avoid moving large expressions); attract has identity semantics
(repel expression)	The value of expression repels away from itself functions having it as an argument (to enhance concurrency); repel has identity semantics
(xputer expression)	Evaluates to the xputer on which the root of the structure-valued expression resides

Once the described linkage is in place, function execution may begin. Ultimately, a result of some kind, e.g. an integer or a pointer to a structure or function closure, is sent back to the point of invocation. A special case occurs when the structure establishes a logical dataflow channel, to be used for repeated fetching from a source process in one Xputer to a target process in another, as suggested by Figure 3-7. A preliminary implementation of this form of communication is described in [34].

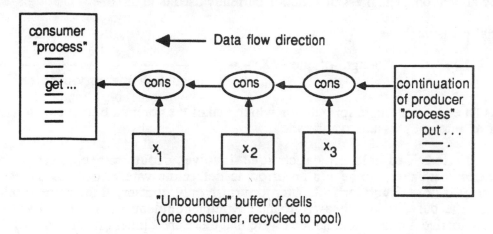

Figure 3-7: Data flow using the channel idiom

3.8. Task Migration by Diffusion

In order to avoid bottlenecks when the system size is scaled upward, we do not rely on a centralized queue from which processors obtain work. Instead, one of our requirements is that the method for distributing work must itself be distributed. As stated earlier, the smaller the grain, the more effectively load balancing can be performed. To avoid granularity so small that communication delays become significant, we aim at "medium" granularity.

The approach taken in Rediflow is to distribute reduction-tasks based on the notion of pressure. We consider each Xputer to have an internal pressure, indicating to the outside world its degree of busyness, i.e. how unreceptive it is toward additional work. The strategy for system workload distribution makes use of the dynamic pressure gradient which is locally sensed by each Xputer [31]. Figure 3-8 suggests how this might be viewed, with the vertical bars corresponding to a "barometer" at each node. We emphasize that this view is only conceptual, and that no processor maintains such a global pressure state.

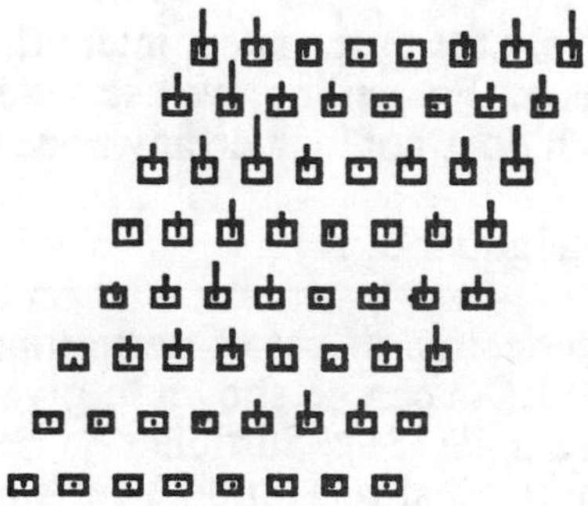

Figure 3-8: Pressure gradient determined by individual pressures

At present, the contributions to internal pressure are the number of packets on an Xputer's local and apply queue and the fullness of the Xputer's memory. However, the average utilization is also a candidate for a slightly different indicator of pressure. Memory is important because the reduction model inherently relies on readily available memory for dynamic allocation. The pressure function currently used is

internal-pressure(X) =

$$\text{length-of-queue}(X) + \frac{c}{1 - \text{fraction-of-memory-occupied}(X)}$$

There is an equivalent logic formulation which makes the computation even simpler when comparing internal pressure to a threshold.

Our distributed load-balancing technique involves Xputers exchanging pressure information with one another, in an effort to determine where to route excess tasks. However, it is not enough for an Xputer to furnish only its internal pressure to others. If this were the case, then a heavily-loaded Xputer could be surrounded by a wall of nominally-loaded Xputers, and not be aware that there are Xputers outside the wall which could accept some of the extra load. Therefore, we introduce the notion of propagated pressure, which is what an Xputer indicates to its immediate neighbors. The propagated pressure of an Xputer is a function of both its own internal pressure and also the external pressure, which is in turn a function of the propagated pressures of its neighbors.

When an Xputer's internal pressure sufficiently exceeds the external pressure, some packets from its apply queue may issue forth into the interconnection network, where they are distributed to Xputers with lower pressures. The Rediflow switch is capable of directing packets along the pressure gradient to find such low points. When a packet reaches an Xputer with a local pressure minimum, it is absorbed into its apply queue. This tends to raise the pressure of that Xputer, and lessen the likelihood that it will receive more packets, until its internal pressure again becomes lower due to completion of work.

This treatment of pressure is obviously heuristic, in that the frequency of updating affects the performance of the system, but not the logical behavior of the functional program being computed. One heuristic function which seems to work moderately well is to define the propagated pressure in terms of the equation

$PP(X) = $ if $PI(X) < $ threshold
        then 0
        else $\min[1 + PE(X), \text{ceiling}]$

where PP, PI, and PE are respectively the propagated, internal, and external pressures, and threshold is a controllable parameter. For ceiling, we use 1 + the diameter of the network (the length of its longest path which does not include any node twice), and for PE we use

$PE(X) = \min\{PE(Y) \mid Y \text{ is a neighbor of } X\}$

The above function produces the desired effect of permitting packets to flow toward a minimally-loaded node. In fact, PE(X) can be shown to give the number of links which need to be traversed to reach such a node [31]. Sufficiently-frequent computation of PP(X) for each X resembles a form of numerical relaxation. Simulation evidence suggests that this can actually be done sufficiently infrequently so as to be relegated to the Rediflow switch and not dilute normal packet processing. Indeed, it need not be done at all in the case of saturation, described next.

3.9. Locality Enhancement Mechanism

As already mentioned, primitive operations are clustered within function code bodies so that costly dispersion of minor operations to separate processors does not occur when these operations are closely related. This is one of our locality enforcement mechanisms. Another such mechanism exploits the phenomenon of saturation which occurs when all Xputers are sufficiently busy that any attempt to migrate apply-packets would be futile, despite pressure differentials. The Rediflow load balancing mechanism detects such saturation by placing a ceiling on the value of propagated pressure, as described above. When the external pressure of an Xputer reaches the ceiling, migration attempts cease. There is no point in arbitrarily spreading out work and data accesses when all Xputers are busy.

As mentioned earlier, an advantage of the reduction model of computation is that concurrently-executable work is easily spawned for migration to other processors. In effect, demand propagation grows a "spanning tree" which corresponds to a single expression from which the "output" of the running program is extracted on a continuing basis. The default mode of servicing each Xputer's apply queue is FIFO, which generates the tree breadth-first and thus has the virtue of reaching concurrently executable nodes earlier. To prevent generation of additional work during saturation, an Xputer switches to LIFO to give depth-first generation, in order to throttle its rate of packet production, as suggested in Figure 3-9. This is helpful for avoiding queue overflows and for reducing the possibility of over-commitment of memory space, which could result in a form of deadlock. (This technique was also utilized in [5].) In saturated mode, operators which would normally demand arguments concurrently are changed to demand them sequentially. This turns out to be easy to do within our particular reduction implementation; pre-demand instructions are ignored, and wait instructions cause both demand and wait.

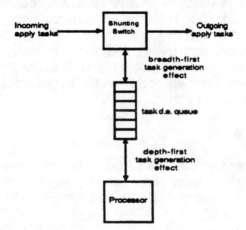

Figure 3-9: Load-dependent modes of task generation

3.10. Code Distribution

When a functional application is begun, the associated code block is either recognized as having been cached locally, or is fetched from another known location, then cached. Although initial experiments will probably entail loading code for each function into each Xputer, in full operation, we intend that this will be done on demand, so as to better handle large programs. Code blocks will be cached, and managed on a least-recently-used strategy, in each Xputer.

3.11. Arrays and Other Structures

The evaluation model directly supports structured data such as arrays. These are considered to be important both in the case of numerical sub-computations and for fast database (e.g. hashed) access. There are two types of arrays, which we called *delimited* and *fixed*. Delimited arrays are accessed through a descriptor which specifies a base address, offset, length, and a tag for defining classes of objects represented by them. Delimited arrays are passed as values by passing their descriptor, but may also be copied wholesale when desired by a special copy instruction. Fixed arrays are passed by their base address only. They are only accessed by fixed indices or record offsets, so there is no need for bounds checking using a descriptor. Lisp cons cells are just fixed arrays of length two.

Arrays also are used to implement the local storage required by closures. This is an efficient means of uniformly implementing both higher-order functions and Kahn processes. In the latter case, after the closure runs, it returns itself with possibly modified local variables, rather than causing an additional closure to be allocated. The closure device may also be used to achieve the effects of object-oriented programming. Here the closure code runs whenever a message is sent to it; sending a message is analogous to applying a function, with object corresponding to function and message to argument.

Arrays may have suspended component values, which means that the value has not yet been computed. The first request for such a value triggers its computation. Subsequent requests either get the value itself, or are queued at the location until the value has been computed. This concept is essentially the same as "I-structures" [1], futures [11], and suspensions [9].

An important technique for dynamically generating arrays is the primitive function make used in the Rediflow simulator [25, 26] which makes an array of specified length, the values of which are specified by a function argument. For example, this permits one to construct fast-access applicative caches [24], and other structures amenable to concurrent traversal [20]. For example, several of the generic functions for sequences have fast divide-and-conquer implementations which rely on the use of make.

3.12. General Packet Flow

A rough overview of the organization of an Xputer as explained above may be found in Figure 3-10. This diagram assumes that pressure sampling information is sent through the switching layer in the form of pressure packets, which are intermingled with packets of other varieties (e.g. data and tasks).

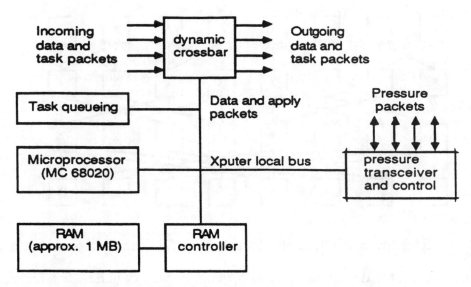

Figure 3-10: Xputer logical information flow

Rather than buffering entire packets in the switch, we plan to use a scheme whereby forwarding of an arriving packet begins as soon as there is sufficient header information to enable routing to occur. This will help to minimize latency in the switch. With proper technology, it is possible to out-perform the global memory-access speed of a shared-memory configuration, since we do not generally incur the worst-case number of hops.

3.13. Topology

The system level aspects of Rediflow are not very topology-sensitive. For large configurations, we plan a form of "butterfly". Our scheme differs in several ways from the BBN Butterfly [32]. For one, we have a processor at every node, rather than at just one rank. For another, our processor does not wait for the response to a request, as it does that of the BBN machine. Indeed, a key part of the Rediflow distributed reduction mechanism is that a request has a "remote procedure call" effect in triggering a demand for production of data, so that quite often there will be a significant gap between request and response. During this interval, the requesting processor is multiplexed to do other work. Lastly, the Rediflow switch will wait or queue rather than re-try, if there is a conflicting request for one of its outgoing channels. The routing tables will be loaded to satisfy a non-deadlocking criterion. For example, Figure 3-11 demonstrates a 24-node butterfly, with fanout of 4, where one should identify the rows of processors on the top and and bottom as being the same. For the 16-node prototype, we will use a binary hypercube network, with each node having 4 bidirectional channels. Further discussion of topologies may be found in [5].

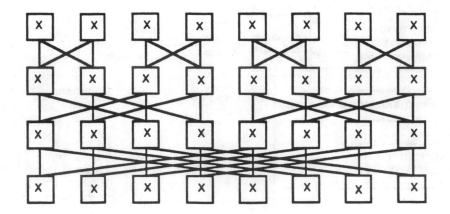

Figure 3-11: Rediflow in the form of a 24 node butterfly (identify top and bottom rows)

Message routing is table-driven, using local memory in each switch node which is down-loaded at system start-up. The table is indexed by a prefix of the physical address of the message target, which means that individual routing decisions will be high-speed. This soft-routing scheme, plus the ability to physically reconnect nodes, also permits experimentation with topology. A sufficient condition for avoidance of message deadlock can be obtained from the ordered resource scheme from operating system theory. It is not difficult to route a butterfly topology or a hypercube topology to achieve deadlock avoidance. The work of [30] shows this for the case of the hypercube.

The following argument demonstrates that the Rediflow partitioned-memory approach is, under equivalent technological assumptions, at least as fast as a shared memory approach. Simply replace each node of the shared-memory switch with a Rediflow node, which contains both a switch, processor, and memory. In Rediflow, the processor only participates if messages are intended for it; in other cases, it is completely bypassed. The electrical delay in the resulting system is thus no more than that in the original system, and may be less, since the number of nodes reachable within distance k in the latter is exponentially increasing with k up to saturation, whereas the number in the former is 1 for $k < \log(n)$, and n for $k = \log(n)$.

The following minimal topological assumptions are all that are necessary for effective operation of the Rediflow scheme:

1. Addressability: There must be a means for uniquely addressing any memory location in the entire system. This is used by Rediflow to establish the necessary argument and result linkages between functions concurrently-executing in different Xputers.

2. Routability: Given a request to fetch or store from a specified memory location, the switch must be able to determine in which direction to route the request. This is used for communication of data once the linkages are established.

3. Deadlock Avoidance: Considering each unilateral link between Xputers as a resource, there is an ordering of these resources such that each end-to-end message route is consistent with the ordering.

3.14. Reliability and Recovery

Although fault-tolerance is not the principal thrust of our architecture, there are several aspects of the latter which can be seen to have a positive effect. First of all, with the proposed switching topology, the complete failure of any node would have negligible effect on the net processing power, since multiple routes around the node are possible. Assuming a dead-start, the routing tables can simply be loaded to reflect the topology resulting after failure. Similarly, fairly-traditional checkpointing mechanisms can be used to avoid complete re-computation.

A more interesting problem is how to achieve recovery from a failure while the computation is in progress. Here considerations are necessary at both the hardware and software levels. From the hardware viewpoint, there are several modes of failure, with the following means of recovery:

1. Link failure: Periodic packets are sent from a node to each of its neighbors, in times of otherwise idle transmission. The lack of such a transmission indicates that the link has failed, and the active node to which the link is connected will modify its own routing table accordingly.

2. Switch failure: This would be manifest to neighboring nodes as a failure on each connecting link, and handled as above.

3. Processor failure: This can be detected by the switch, which is itself a processor sharing memory with the main processor. In this case, the switch informs other nodes attempting communication that failure has occurred.

4. Memory failure: This can also be detected by the switch, and other nodes informed.

Software recovery is a more interesting problem, and one of active research. We are working on a means of using the nodes of the underlying computation graph to permit local-recomputation in the event failure is detected [31]. Also, if the failure is due to a processor, but not memory, then an attempt can be made to use the memory's contents to reduce the amount of recomputation to a minimum.

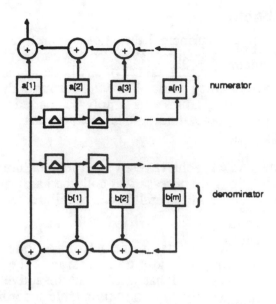

Figure 3-6: "Form II" filter defined by the Redilisp code below, suitable for systolic mapping

```
% performs the "recursive" digital filter with rational z
% transform given by
%                 a[1] + a[2]*z**-1 + a[3]*z**-2 + ....
%                -------------------------------------
%                 b[1]*z**-1 + b[2]*z**-2 + ....
% on stream input

(def ((recfilt a b) input)
     ((numerator a) ((denominator b) input)))

(def (numerator a) (ladder a 1))

(def ((ladder coefficients i) x)
     (if (= i (tlength coefficients))
         (scale (tselect i coefficients) x)
         (++ (scale (tselect i coefficients) x)
             ((ladder coefficients (+ i 1))
              (delay x)))))

(def (denominator coefficients)
     (group
       (result aux)
       (def (aux x)
             (addseq x ((ladder coefficients 1)
                         (delay (aux x)))))))
```

4. Programming Aspects

The language-driven aspect of Rediflow has already been discussed extensively. Here we simply summarize the treatment of some remaining issues.

4.1. Source Language

The source language which drives Rediflow is a dialect of Lisp, called RediLisp. It is a derivative of a previous "publication language" (FEL), which was earlier used to drive the Rediflow simulator (cf. [7, 14, 19, 20, 21, 23, 25]). Some language constructs which implicitly generate concurrent tasks have already been described. Experimentation will take place using these, as well as more explicit constructs, such as are described in [6, 10, 11, 14, 15, 23]. We anticipate using an existing sequential Common Lisp front-end for software development tools.

4.2. Storage Reclamation

An important part of a machine to support Lisp is the storage reclamation scheme. We prefer the copying style garbage collector [3], since it (i) allocates quickly (no free list is required), (ii) compacts, (iii) requires time proportional only to the amount of storage actually accessible, rather than the overall amount of computation (as with reference counting) or to the amount of total memory (as with mark-scan), and (iv) can be done in real-time.

We intend to distribute the two half-spaces evenly across all Xputers, so that each has its own mini-half-space. This permits a high-degree of concurrency can be exploited in the garbage collection process as well as in the computational process. When copying, we do not move objects across Xputers, so that the spread necessary to support parallelism in the computational process will not be destroyed. A similar running implementation has been reported [11]. Most parallel garbage collectors have been described in the shared-memory context. The novelty of ours will be that it is distributed, and achieves coordination by message-passing. A discussion of inter-Xputer synchronization requirements may be found in [13].

5. Results of Technical Analyses

The performance of the Rediflow architecture is being evaluated using simulation. As with most studies in their formative stages, we have begun evaluating speedups using an introspective model, i.e. one in which speedups are measured against a single processor with the same technological assumptions, architecture, and evaluation model as the multiprocessor.

Shown below are speedup measurements for small application programs run on simulated small test configurations. These are mainly to show concept feasibility, rather than be an indication of production quality. The current simulator unfortunately utilizes memory sub-optimally, prohibiting very large examples from being run. Also, the configurations simulated assumed much greater switch latency than is planned for the prototype.

The runs are briefly described as follows:

Logic Programming	simple prolog-like interpreter, using "or-parallel" search.
Signal Correlation	correlates two complex-valued signals, as would be produced by antennae. It entails moving-window weighted inner-product computation.
Image Convolution	local summation of weighted terms over an image array
Six Queens	the standard six-queens search problem, producing all solutions
FFT	8-point fast-Fourier transform and inverse
Matrix Multiply	product of two 16x16 matrices using quad-tree representation
Relational Database	performs retrieval and update queries on a small relational database represented as a set of linked lists
D-and-C	generating and summing a 1024 node tree

The programs for signal processing and logic programming (in RediLisp) are given in Appendices I and II. The figures for "average concurrency" indicate an upper bound on the speedup under ideal circumstances. This will generally be unachievable, since it measures very fine-grain concurrency, with an infinite number of processors. Nonetheless, it indicates something about the nature of the program run.

These examples employ the dynamic load-distribution scheme mentioned earlier. They do not employ the native-code or data-flow optimizations. Also, additional performance can be gained by better tuning of the load balancing mechanism. A series of experiments is planned toward this end. Generally speaking, the pressure-distribution and saturation-detection mechanisms of Rediflow have been observed to work correctly, but are in need of further understanding and tuning.

Rediflow Simulated Speedups

Application	Config.	Proc.	Speedup	Efficiency
Logic programming	hyper	4	3.61	.9
(avg. conc 20.92)	hyper	8	6.43	.8
"	hyper	16	9.55	.6
Signal correlation	hyper	4	3.59	.90
(avg. conc 79.36)	hyper	8	6.67	.83
"	hyper	16	12.17	.76
"	hyper	32	20.5	.64
"	hyper	64	28.05	.44
Image convolution	mesh	9	5.77	.64
"	mesh	4	2.74	.76
Six queens	hyper	8	7.45	.93
(avg. conc. 8.9)				
FFT (avg. conc. 13.5)	hyper	8	4.82	.60
Matrix multiply (partitioned)	hyper	8	7.4	.93
Relational database	hyper	8	6.15	.77
(average conc. 16.8)	cube	27	8.88	.33
D-and-C	grid	4	3.6	.9
(average conc. 223)	grid	9	8.0	.88
	grid	16	12.0	.75
	grid	25	15.9	.64
	grid	36	23.2	.64
	grid	49	28.1	.57
	grid	64	30.3	.47

I. Code for a logic-programming application

```
% Parallel Solver in Redilisp

(result (seq (consume test)))

% control bits
(def or_control lazy)        % eager or lazy
(def production_control lazy) % eager or lazy

(def (atom? x) (or (null? (tail x)) (atom (tail x))))

% Instances of "solve" can be considered "and" nodes in the search tree.
% Each goal in goals must be solved successively.
(def (solve env goals level)  % solve list of goals in env
  (group
   (result (if (null? goals)
               (list env)
               (find_and_append_solutions solve2 rules)))
    % Solve goal by appending solutions for each rule in rules
    % By the "solution for a rule", we mean the solution of the
    % list of goals consisting of the body of the rule after unification
    % and any residual goals from the parent goal list.

    % Instances of "find_and_append_solutions" can be considered "or"
    % nodes in the search tree

    (def goal (head goals))
    (def more_goals (tail goals))
    (def functor (head (tail goal)))
    (def rules (get_relevant_rules functor))

    (def (solve2 rule) (group              % generate new "and" node
      (def newenv (unify1 env (cons level (head rule)) goal))
      (result (if (impossible? newenv)     % see if unifiable
               failure
               (solve newenv new_goals (+ 1 level))))
     (def new_goals (add_levels (tail rule)))

     (def (add_levels lis)
          (if (null? lis)
              more_goals % continuation
              (cons (cons level (head lis)) (add_levels (tail lis)))))
              )) ))

(def (find_and_append_solutions f x)
     (appendl (or_control (mapcar f x))))

(def (appendl x) % combines appendl, mapcar, and or_control
     (if (null? x)
         nil
         (app (head x) (appendl (tail x)))))

(def (unify env x y)    % unify x and y in env, returning new env
     (if (impossible? env)
         env
         (unify1 env (varview env x) (varview env y))))
```

```
(def (varview env x) % dereference to find ultimate binding of var
   (if (var? x)
         (if (null? (vassoc x env))
             x                            % unbound in env ==> leave as is
              (varview env (tail (vassoc x env)))) % recur
        x))                              % not var ==> expand later

(def (vassoc var env)
      (if (null? env)
          []
            (if (and (eq (head var) (head (head (head env))))
                     (eq (tail var) (tail (head (head env)))))
                (head env)
                 (vassoc var (tail env)))))

(def (unify1 env x y)   % unify, without viewing in env
   (cond (equal x y)    env
         (var? x)        (newbind x y env)
         (var? y)        (newbind y x env)
         (atom? x)       (if (and (atom? y) (eq (tail x) (tail y)))
                             env
                              "impossible")
         (atom? y)       "impossible"
         (unify_complex env x y)))

(def (unify_complex env x y) % unify iteratively over lists
  (group
    (def xlev (head x))
    (def ylev (head y))
    (def xterm (tail x))
    (def yterm (tail y))
    (result (cond (atom? x) (unify env x y)        %handle list tails
                  (atom? y) (unify env x y)
                   (impossible? newenv) "impossible"
                   (unify_complex newenv (cons xlev (tail xterm))
                                         (cons ylev (tail yterm)))))
    (def newenv (unify env (cons xlev (head xterm))
                          (cons ylev (head yterm))))  ))

(def (var? x) % test whether variable
     (and (eq (typeof (tail x)) 'string) (eq (head (tail x)) '_)))

(def (vars term acc)    % get variables in untagged term
     (cond  (plain_var? term)  (if (memq term acc) acc (cons term acc))
            (or (null? term) (atom term))  acc
            (vars (head term) (vars (tail term) acc))))

(def (plain_var? x)   % "plain" means untagged here
     (and (eq (typeof x) 'string) (eq (head x) '_)))

(def (newbind var expr env) % make new environment with var bound to exp
     (cons (cons var expr) env))

(def top_level 0)

(def (produce f) (production_control (f)))
```

```
(def (test)
    (group   % test by solving goal; print solutions
        (def solutions (solve nil (list (cons top_level test_goal)) 1))
      (result (produce res))
      (def (res)
            [eol eol "Goal: " (fmtSexp test_goal) eol
              (if (null? solutions)
                  ["no" eol]
                    (report_solutions (mapcar extracter solutions) 1)) ])

        (def goalvars (vars test_goal nil))

        (def (extracter env)
          (group             % function to extract variables in env
            (def (pair_with_view goalvar)
                  (cons goalvar (view env (cons top_level goalvar))))
              (result (mapcar pair_with_view goalvars))))))

(def (report_solutions sols n) % format stream of numbered solutions
    (if (null? sols)
      eol
      (cons (format_solution (head sols) n)
              (report_solutions (tail sols) (add 1 n)))))

(def lazy (lambda x x))
(def failure []) % failure is [], so as to compress out in appendl
(def nil [])

(def (remdups atoms)     % remove duplicates from a list of atoms
    (if (null? atoms)
        nil
        (if (memq (head atoms) (remdups (tail atoms)))
            (remdups (tail atoms))
            (cons (head atoms) (remdups (tail atoms))))))

(def (view env x)
    (cond    %   assert env is not impossible
      (var? x)   (if (null? (vassoc x env))
                     x
                      (view env (tail (vassoc x env))))
      (atom? x) (tail x)
      (cons (view env (cons (head x) (head (tail x))))
              (view env (cons (head x) (tail (tail x)))))))
```

II. Code for a signal-correlation application

```
(result (fir 5 (sgcorr left right 200 100 2 10 25)))

(def (tvalues f FS t0 n)
    (group
      (def cexp (* -2 pi f))
      (def (tval scal tm0 i) (cterm (/ (* cexp (+ tm0 i) scal))))
      (result (|| (tval FS t0) (range0 n-1 1)))))


(def (sgcorr yls yrs n s f t0 FS)
    (if (or (= yls []) (= yrs []))
```

```
          []
          (sgcorrl (offset s yls) yrs n f t0 FS)))

(def (sgcorrl yls yrs n f t0 FS)
  (if (or (= yls []) (= yrs []))
      []
      (group
        (def [tyls tyrs]   [(tail yls) (tail yrs)])
        (def [ylb yrb]     [(fir n yls) (fir n yrs)])
        (def [rcj icj]     (caddseq (\\ cmul (tvalues f FS t0 n))
                                    (\\ corr [ylb yrb])))
        (result [(/ rcj FS) (/ icj FS) (sgcorrl tyls tyrs n f t0 FS)]))))

(def (caddseq x)
    (if (= x [])
      [0 0]
      (cadd (first x) (caddseq (rest x)))))

(def (offset s yls)
      (if (= yls [])
        []
        (if (= 0 s)
            yls
            (offset (- s 1)  (tail yls)))))

(def (laircrft n ampl s0) (emitters n ampl s0))

(def (raircrft n ampl s0 shift noise)
      (group
        (def estr (emitters n ampl s0))
        (result (shmittrs shift noise n ampl s0 estr))))

(def (emitters n ampl s0)   .... input sequence ....)

(def (shmittrs shift noise n ampl s0 estr)   ... input sequence ....)

(def left (laircrft 0 100 10))

(def right (raircrft 0 100 10 20 0.1))

(def (fir n  x)
      (if (= n 0)
        []
        (fby (head x) (fir (- n 1) (tail x)))))

(def pi   3.1415927)

(def (cadd [xr xi] [yr yi])   [(+ xr yr) (+ xi yi)])

(def (cmul [xr xi] [yr yi]) [(- (* xr yr) (* xi yi))
                             (+ (* xr yi) (* xi yr))])

(def (conjug xr xi) [xr (minus xi)])

(def (corr [x y])   (cmul x (conjug y)))

(def (cterm x) [(cos x) (sin x)])
```

III. References

[1] Arvind and R.E. Thomas. I-structures: an efficient data type for functional languages. Technical Report MIT-LCS-TM-178, MIT Laboratory for Computer Science, Sept., 1980.

[2] L. Augustson. A compiler for lazy ML. In Symposium on Lisp and Functional Programming, pages 218-227. ACM, August, 1984.

[3] H.G. Baker, Jr. List processing in real time on a serial computer. CACM 21(4):280-293, April, 1978.

[4] W.H. Burge. Recursive programming techniques. Addison-Wesley, 1975.

[5] F.W. Burton, M.R. Sleep. Executing functional programs on a virtual tree of processors. In Functional programming languages and computer architecture, pages 187-195. October, 1981.

[6] F.W. Burton. Controlling speculative computation in a parallel functional language. Distributed Computing Symposium, May 1985.

[7] A.L. Davis and R.M. Keller. Dataflow program graphs. IEEE Computer 15(2):26-41, February, 1982.

[8] J.B. Dennis. Data flow supercomputers. IEEE Computer 13(11):48-56, November, 1980.

[9] D.P. Friedman and D.S. Wise.   CONS should not evaluate its arguments.   In Michaelson and Milner (editors), Automata, Languages, and Programming, pages 257-284. Edinburgh University Press, 1976.

[10] R.P. Gabriel and J. McCarthy.   Queue-based multi-processing lisp.   In Symposium on Lisp and Functional Programming, pages 25-44. ACM, August, 1984.

[11] R.H. Halstead, Jr. Implementation of multilisp: Lisp on a multiprocessor.   In Symposium on Lisp and Functional Programming, pages 9-17. ACM, August, 1984.

[12] P. Henderson. Functional programming. Prentice-Hall, 1980.

[13] P. Hudak and R.M. Keller. Garbage collection and task deletion in distributed applicative processing systems. In Proc. Conf. on Lisp and Functional Programming, pages 168-178. ACM, August, 1982.

[14] B. Jayaraman and R.M. Keller.   Resource control in a demand-driven data-flow model. In Proc. International Conference on Parallel Processing, pages 118-127. IEEE, 1980.

[15] B. Jayaraman and R.M. Keller. Resource expressions for applicative languages. In Batcher, et al. (editors), International Conference on Parallel Processing, pages 160-167. IEEE, Aug, 1982.

[16] T. Johnsson. Efficient compilation for lazy evaluation. In Symposium on Compiler Construction, pages 58-69. ACM, June, 1984.

[17] G. Kahn. The semantics of a simple language for parallel programming. In Information Processing 74, pages 471-475. IFIPS, North Holland, 1974.

[18] R.M. Keller. Denotational models for parallel programs with indeterminate operators. In E.J. Neuhold (editor), Formal description of programming concepts, pages 337-366. North-Holland, 1978.

[19] R.M. Keller, G. Lindstrom, and S. Patil. A loosely-coupled applicative multi-processing system. In AFIPS Conference Proceedings, pages 613-622. June, 1979.

[20] R.M. Keller. Divide and CONCer: Data structuring for applicative multiprocessing. In Proc. 1980 Lisp Conference, pages 196-202. August, 1980.

[21] R.M. Keller and G. Lindstrom. Hierarchical analysis of a distributed evaluator. In Proc. International Conference on Parallel Processing, pages 299-310. August, 1980.

[22] R. M. Keller. Semantics and Applications of Function Graphs. Technical Report UUCS-80-112, University of Utah, Computer Science Department, 1980.

[23] R.M. Keller and G. Lindstrom. Applications of feedback in functional programming. In Conference on functional languages and computer architecture, pages 123-130. October, 1981.

[24] R.M. Keller and M.R. Sleep. Applicative caching: programmer control of object sharing and lifetime in distributed implementations of applicative languages. In Conference on functional languages and computer architecture, pages 131-140. October, 1981.

[25] R.M. Keller. FEL (Function Equation Language) Programmer's guide.   Technical Report 7, University of Utah, Department of Computer Science, AMPS Technical Memorandum, 1982.

[26] R.M. Keller and F.C.H. Lin. The Rediflow simulator. December, 1983. unpublished memorandum, University of Utah.

[27] R.M. Keller and F.C.H. Lin. Simulated performance of a reduction-based multiprocessor. Computer 17(7):70-82, July, 1984.

[28] R.M. Keller, F.C.H. Lin, and J. Tanaka. Rediflow Multiprocessing. In IEEE Compcon '84, pages 410-417. Feb., 1984.

[29] R.M. Keller and G. Lindstrom. Approaching Distributed Database Implementations through Functional Programming Concepts. In Proc. 5th International Conference on Distributed Computing Systems, pages 192-200. IEEE, Denver, Colo., May, 1985.

[30] C.R. Lang, Jr. The extension of object-oriented languages to a homogeneous, concurrent architecture. PhD thesis, California Institute of Technology, May, 1982.

[31] Frank C.H. Lin. Load balancing and fault tolerance in applicative systems.   PhD thesis, University of Utah, August, 1985.

[32] R.D. Rettberg. Development of a voice funnel system. Technical Report 5284, Bolt Beranek and Newman, Inc., April, 1983.

[33] G.L. Steele, Jr. Common Lisp. Digital Press, 1984.

[34] J. Tanaka. Optimized concurrent execution of an applicative language. PhD thesis, University of Utah, March, 1984.

Eazyflow Architecture

E.A. Ashcroft

Computer Science Laboratory
SRI International

SRI Technical Report CSL-147

April 1985

333 Ravenswood Ave. • Menlo Park, CA 94025
(415) 326-6200 • TWX: 910-373-2046 • Telex: 334-486

Abstract

This report describes a multiprocessor architecture that embodies a novel computation strategy combining demand-driven and data-driven evaluation. The architecture is directly programmed with a high-level language, Lucid.

1 Introduction

SRI proposes to develop a new class of computer architectures, called eazyflow engines. Most members of this class are specialized for particular applications but are variants of one standard architecture which can handle all the applications, but not as efficiently as the specialized machines. This standard architecture will be the main subject of this report.

The main features of all the eazyflow engines are:

- The machines are all operational realizations of a mathematical algorithm specification model called operator nets.

- The computational model employed is a hybrid of demand-driven and data-driven evaluation. (Essentially, data-driven evaluation is what is normally called dataflow. Demand-driven evaluation we will call "eduction".) The hybrid is called eazyflow.

- The different machines will all be programmed using different dialects of the language Lucid. These will be the assembly languages of the machines. (We will see that the choice of Lucid is very natural, because Lucid programs are essentially the textual forms of operator nets.)

- Lucid is a very high-level language, but, since it is the assembly language of the machines, it is very close to the basic architecture of the machines. Other languages can be run on the machines in the normal way, that is, by using compilers that compile into the assembly languages of the machine in question, that is, into the appropriate dialect of Lucid.

- The architectures are all based on the successful architecture of the Manchester Dataflow Machine. They use unidirectional pipelined rings that carry data packets. The data are "tagged".

- The machines will all be composed of several 'submachines' that are joined together by having their rings intersect through a switch. Because the rings are heavily pipelined, the delay through the swich will not reduce the performance of the machines.

- The architectures can incorporate a high degree of fault-tolerance, and thus be intrinsically reliable. To some extent the fault-tolerance technique depends crucially on demand-driven evaluation. (In fact, if fault-tolerance is the over-riding consideration, the machine may have to be completely demand-driven.)

The rest of this report will mainly concentrate on the standard eazyflow engine. It will be a multiprocesssor machine that embodies a combination of dataflow (data-driven "eager" evaluation) and eduction (demand-driven "lazy" evaluation). (EAger plus laZY makes EAZY.) We propose to construct a small-scale prototype of the standard eazyflow engine which will have at least 128 processors. Using off-the shelf, relatively slow components, to speed up construction, and parallel transmission of 128-bit packets, it should be a forty megaflop machine, approximately. Going to parallel transmission of only 32-bit packets (to speed up construction even more), but still using off-the-shelf components, should give a ten megaflop machine.

The variants of the standard eazyflow engine will have roughly the same performance as the standard engine. The reason for having different variants is that it will be easier to program the variants for the different applications, and the variants will better exploit the inherent parallelism in the different applications. The performance ratings given above assume that there is enough parallelism in the programs the machine is given to fully exercise the machine. For the small-scale machine proposed, this should not be a problem, and the standard engine is adequate. If much greater performance than this is needed in subsequent machines, one of the specialized machines may be more appropriate, in order to exploit much more parallelism. (The decrease in performance from forty megaflops to ten, mentioned above, is caused by using four packets where one could have done the job if sufficient ring bandwidth were available. The amount of parallelism exploited is the same in both cases.)

Justification for constructing a prototype eazyflow engine will come from comprehensive analysis and simulation that should confirm the performance ratings predicted above. In the process, several applications will be studied, and one of the big advantages of the machine, the ease with which it can be programmed, should be amply confirmed.

In order to give the background for this report, it will be necessary to describe what has already been done by the Architecture Group of the Computer Science Laboratory at SRI, which has been looking at dataflow. The results that have already been achieved all stem from a willingness to reexamine the basic concepts in this area of asynchronous, highly parallel computation in the light of usability, and, in particular, programmability. At the same time, mathematical elegance and simplicity have been goals, particularly for models and languages. One result of this is that the conventional ideas of dataflow have been found wanting, and the operational concept of "dataflow network" has had to be replaced. The approach taken now, which is simpler and yet is an extension, is to take, instead, the mathematical concept of "operator net" as the most basic idea. The problem of giving operational interpretations to operator nets is a separate problem to the problem of what the nets mean, mathematically speaking, and different modes of operational behavior can be studied. This allows different operational interpretations to be compared; it has permitted the Group to design a novel operational interpretation that is a hybrid of two of the basic interpretations, to get the advantages of both while largely avoiding their drawbacks.

The hybrid operational interpretation, called eazyflow, is the basis for the architecture that SRI proposes to study and simulate. A small-scale prototype of the architecture will be built also. The architecture is based on several "submachines" joined together through an interconnection switch. The architecture should be "scaleable" in the sense that the number of submachines can be increased without the performance of the individual submachines being degraded. It would be the main purpose of building a small-scale prototype to confirm this property, and to do this we propose that the prototype should have eight submachines. Since each submachine will have at least sixteen processors, the "small-scale" prototype will have at least 128 processors, not "small-scale" by conventional standards, but, hopefully, much smaller than the maximum size that this architecture can comfortably deal with.

We will start by looking at the proposed operator net model, and, towards the end of this section, compare it to dataflow networks, and justify the abandonment of the latter.

2 The Operator Net Model

An *operator net* is a structured directed graph in which most of the nodes are associated with operators or user-defined "functions". The graph is "structured" because it is built up from subgraphs, called *sub-nets*. (Effectively, subnets are used to specify subcomputations.) The only nodes that are not associated with operators are *split* nodes. Operation nodes (i.e., the ones with associated operators or user-defined functions) have the same number of incoming edges as the "arity" of the associated operator or user-defined function, and have *one* outgoing edge. *split* nodes have one incoming edge and two or more outgoing edges.

There may be edges in a subnet that do not come from any node in the subnet -- these are called *input edges* of the subnet. Edges of a subnet that do not go to any node of the subnet are called *output edges* of the subnet. (The nodes of a subnet of a net N are nodes of N.)

The so-called user-defined functions are named operator nets with the right number of input edges and exactly one output edge. (The "right number" is the number of incoming edges to all the nodes in the total operator net that are associated with the user-defined function in question, what we called the "arity" of the defined function.) The operator nets for user-defined functions may contain subnets, and they may refer to other user-defined functions, or even to themselves (i.e., recursive functions are allowed). An operator net is thus really one main graph, and several subsidiary graphs, one for each user-defined function.

Syntactically, the main difference between operator nets and dataflow networks is that there are no operation nodes with more than one outgoing edge. This seems a trivial difference, but it has far-reaching implications. It means that nodes can be associated with true operators or functions, and, consequently, it is possible to assign mathematical meanings to operator nets. Also, the syntax is simpler and more uniform. It also means, however, that there is nothing in the syntactic form of operator nets to specifically deal with conditional evaluation; conditional evaluation has to be embodied in the actual operators, in the semantics. To do this, it must be possible for some of the operators to be nonstrict. (A strict operator or function is one that requires all its arguments to be defined in order for the result of applying the operator or function to be defined.) As we shall see, this has far reaching implications for the ways in which operator nets can be given operational interpretations.

As we have indicated, it is possible to assign mathematical meaning to operator nets (under certain general circumstances). That is, nets will be mappings from "inputs" to "outputs". Moreover, if the operators associated with operator nodes include such things as addition, testing equality and "if-then-else", together with a few "time dependent" operators, the operator net model is powerful enough to specify arbitrary computable mappings from inputs to outputs.

Meaning is assigned to operator nets in a mathematical way, using "fixpoint" theory. Each operator net is associated with a set of mathematical equations that has a designated unique solution. This solution is taken as the meaning of the net. (This technique is based on the pioneering work of Gilles Kahn [8].)

2.1 Operational Semantics of Operator Nets

There are several ways in which operator nets could be given operational meanings. All of these involve the idea that data-items travel along the edges. We will call these elements of data *datons*; the particle-physics metaphor is amusing and also strangely appropriate. The possible operational meanings of operator nets all require that the the operator or user-defined function at each operation node act upon the datons arriving on its incoming edges, producing new datons that leave the node along its single outgoing edge. (Also, the *split* nodes simply copy their incoming datons, sending them on along *all* the outgoing edges. In addition, user-defined functions are invoked by replacing the node in question by the operator net that defines the function.) The operators of the various nodes can all be being evaluated at the same time, if there are datons available for them to work on, with no synchronization between them. Thus, parallel processing naturally comes into play.

2.1.1 Piped vs. Tagged Evaluation

There are two radically different ways in which operator nets can be interpreted operationally. One is to consider the edges in the operator net to be pipes along which datons flow, in a first-in, first-out manner; in other words, they are queues acting as buffers between the nodes. (Often, these queues have to be of bounded length, but we will not discuss the pros and cons of this here.) We will call this the *piped* method of evaluation. (Architecture based on this is often called *static* architecture.)

The other way is to have the edges in the operator net simply indicate the routes that datons must take. The buffers between the nodes then are not queues; they are unordered multisets. (These multisets are generally considered to be unbounded.) Some discipline must be imposed on the order in which a node takes the datons from the incoming edges; this is achieved by associating the datons with *tags*, so that the node looks for datons with appropriate tags. (If we consider the tags as well as the datons, the buffers are sets, not multisets. Datons may be identical, but they will have different tags.) This method of interpreting operator nets is called the *tagged* method of evaluation. (Architecture based upon tags is often called *dynamic* architecture.)

Often the tag simply indicates the order in which the datons were added to the set. If the operator then can only take datons from the set in increasing order of tag, and the datons produced have the same tag as the datons consumed, tags simply simulate pipes. On the other hand, if we want to allow the operator to be applied simultaneously to many datons and the operator terminates sooner for some inputs than others, the tag can no longer correspond to the order in which the datons produced are added to the buffer, as indicated by the following example.

2.1.2 Example showing benefit of tags

Consider, for example, an operator net that computes the sum of some time-consuming operator f applied to the integers from one to one thousand. The node corresponding to this operator will be in a cycle in the network, and the integers from one to one thousand will be fed into this node. The time-consuming operator f will be a bottleneck in the computation, and, to relieve this, it would be advantageous if we could let the operator f be applied to successive integers without waiting for the earlier applications to terminate, i.e., if we could have many applications of f running in parallel. Since addition is associative, we can do this by simply adding the results produced by f to some accumulator which is initially zero. (The order in which these results are added to the accumulator does not matter.)

Suppose, however, that we do not require a simple sum of the values of f applied to the integers from one to one thousand. Suppose that the results are to be "incorporated" into the initially-zero accumulator in a special way: namely, if the result is larger than the accumulator, it is *subtracted* from the accumulator, and if it is smaller it is *added*. The results of the operator have to be "incorporated" into the accumulator in a specific order, using the ordering on the arguments, first $f(1)$, then $f(2)$, and so on. The results of f can be combined only in the order mentioned, if the correct answer is to be produced. If the operator sometimes is evaluated quicker for some integers than it is for preceding integers, the results will be produced in a different order than they are needed. This is a situation that needs the tagged-token technique. The results are tagged with the same tag as had the arguments to which the operator was applied, and the node which is going to do the incorporation into the accumulator will be tag-sensitive, so that it incorporates results in the correct order. In this way we get the benefit of reduced execution time, by having many evaluations of the operator proceeding in parallel, without requiring any serialization or synchronizing of these evaluations. (The "special sum" is, of course, artificial and was devised only to give a simple example of a situation in which the tagged-token idea is very beneficial. However, the situation that it illustrates is one that crops up in very many applications.)

Thus we have seen that there are reasons for wishing to abandon the idea that the tag indicates the order in which items are added to a set. Rather, the tag indicates the position of the daton in the *conceptual* sequence of items emitted by a node. Thus it is still useful to think of sequences of datons, but we needn't think that a node must consume the datons in order or produce them in order.

The above example showed that tags can allow more parallelism and, hence, increased efficiency. There also are cases where tags are *essential*, where the piped method gives incorrect results. This happens if some of the operators or user-defined functions are nonstrict. Piped evaluation is unable to handle such operators. This is because all their arguments must be evaluated, in order for the node to receive the later arguments that will come down the pipe, and the arguments that are not needed right now might well be undefined (the result of an evaluation that does not terminate).

Thus, with nonstrict operators or user-defined functions, piped evaluation could cause nonterminating computation in some cases where the mathematical semantics of the operator net implies that there is a defined result. Nonstrict operators are essential for general computation, so piped evaluation (or, at least, exclusively piped evaluation) is inadequate. (This difficulty is avoided in dataflow networks by not allowing nonstrict operations. Conditional evaluation is handled by using nodes that are associated with operations that are not operators in our sense, that is, that have more than one outgoing edge.) In the rest of this report, unless otherwise stated, we will assume that tagged evaluation is being used.

One way of avoiding the difficulty with piped evaluation might be to find a way of aborting computation that has already started. If we could do this, it would be possible to have an *if-then-else* node that works in a piped manner. When a daton for the first argument, the test, arrives at the node, the appropriate one of the other two incoming edges is selected and its daton is passed on. We then need to abort the computation in the part of the net leading to the other edge, because any value it produces will not be needed. To do this we might use a new sort of "particle"; we might send *backwards*, up this unwanted edge, a sort of "killer token" which will annihilate the first daton it sees. This token we might call a *lethon*. Lethons are anti-datons -- they annihilate each other when they meet, rather like anti-matter.

The way in which lethons behave, "lethon physics", is not too difficult to work out, but there are some nets for which lethons are not the answer, because lethon deadlock can be set up. Piped evaluation still is not acceptable. Lethons, on the other hand, *may* be useful, in particular for implementing Prolog in terms of operator nets. This will be discussed later.

2.1.3 Data-driven vs Demand-driven Evaluation.

There are two more ways in which the computations of operator nets could be driven, orthogonal to the other two; they could be based on *data-driven* evaluation or on *demand-driven* evaluation. The data-driven method says that the operator or user-defined function of a node will be performed as soon as there is a daton on each of the necessary incoming edges of the node. (The word "necessary" allows for nonstrictness. If the operator is the ternary *if-then-else* operator, for example, and the daton on the first incoming edge is *true*, only that and the daton on the second edge are necessary.) This is what is usually called *dataflow*.

In demand-driven mode, the operator of a node will be performed only if, as before, there are datons on each of the necessary incoming edges and if, in addition, there is a *demand* for the result of the operator. If there is a demand but there is a necessary incoming edge of the node that does not have a daton on it, then a demand for a daton is made of the node at the beginning of that edge. When, as a result of such demands, there is a daton on each necessary incoming edge, the operator of the node is performed (consuming the inputs), and its result is sent out along the node's outgoing edge.

The demands can be vizualized as traveling through the net in the backwards direction, from the ends of edges to their beginnings. We will call these "particles" *questons* (from the word "request").

If a node is associated with a user-defined function, the node is replaced with the operator net defining the function when there is a demand for the result of the function, *not* when there are datons on all the incoming edges. (This latter is what must happen in dataflow; in dataflow user-defined functions must be strict, and the "parameter passing mechanism" must be call-by-value.)

This evaluation technique we have called *eduction*. According to the Oxford English Dictionary, eduction means "the action of drawing forth the results of calculations from the data", a quite good description of demand-driven evaluation.

Demand-driven evaluation is relatively easy to define for operator nets; it is difficult to define for dataflow networks. It is simple for operator nets because every node that is not a *split* has one outgoing edge. It is then relatively easy to say what happens when a queston comes in the reverse direction along that edge. It is not clear what to do, in dataflow networks, with nodes that have two or more outgoing edges to which the incoming datons are selectively *distributed*. If a queston arrives along one outgoing edge, somehow a queston must be generated for inputs that will cause that edge to be the one along which the daton is to be sent. (It is partly the difficulty of defining demand-driven evaluation for dataflow networks that made the Architecture Group seriously consider a different model.)

We have indicated that piped evaluation is inadequate for general operator nets, because of nonstrict operators. How do data-driven and demand-driven evaluation cope? Data-driven evaluation in the presence of nonstrict operators is not very efficient, because all the arguments of such an operator will be evaluated, whether they are needed or not. This can result in a lot of wasted computation, especially if the value of an unnecessary argument is undefined. With demand-driven evaluation, on the other hand, evaluation is quite efficient, because only the needed operands are evaluated. Thus, in the presence of nonstrict operators, both tagging and demand-driven evaluation appear to be necessary. (Nonstrict user-defined functions require both tagging and demand-driven evaluation also.)

The demand-driven approach does have some drawbacks. Firstly, just in propagation of questons, work must be performed before any operators actually get executed. Secondly, the amount of parallel activity seems less than would be produced by the data-driven approach, because operators are only executed after it has been determined that their results are definitely needed. It appears that there must be a sequential *ebb and flow* effect. Questons are propagated, from the edges leading out of the operator net, back through the net until they reach the nodes representing constants (nullary operators) or edges leading into the net from outside (along which inputs arrive). This is followed by a wave of computed values that go roaring forwards through the net until datons finally come out along the edges that lead out of the net. Another wave of questons then flows in the backwards direction (resulting from demands for the next output values), and so on. The operators that will eventually lead to a subsequent output value cannot be performed until the computations that lead to the previous output value have been completed. This contrasts sharply with data-driven computation, where these different computations can be proceeding simultaneously, in different parts of the net.

This *ebb and flow* effect is actually caused by not demanding an output until the previous output has been produced; the effect would disappear if demands for output were made spontaneously, that is, if computations were made to result from an endless stream of demands for output being autonomously injected into the net. By this means, several ebbs and flows can propagate through the net simultaneously. The rate at which these demands for output are injected into the net could be crucial in terms of getting as much parallelism from the demand-driven approach as can be obtained from the data-driven approach.

2.1.4 Operator Nets vs. Dataflow Networks

We have seen that the simple syntactic difference between operator nets and dataflow networks, the requirement for only one outgoing edge for each node (other than *splits*), has made a significant difference in the operational interpretations of the two models. In operator nets, demand-driven evaluation is essential in many cases, for efficiency, whereas in dataflow networks it is never used. Since dataflow networks have been used for years, one must ask if there really are any drawbacks to dataflow networks that would be good reasons for choosing operator nets instead.

Although we said that demand-driven evaluation is never used in dataflow networks, in fact some demand-driven evaluation does take place, to produce constants. In operator nets, constants are just nullary operators, operators with no arguments. In dataflow networks, constants are unary constant operators; they take one argument, but that argument is ignored and the constant value is produced. The argument is used simply as a "trigger". This trigger is essentially a *demand* for the constant.

One big problem with dataflow networks is that the operators in nodes must be strict. This makes it difficult, if not impossible, to translate some languages into dataflow networks.

Even with languages that do not need nonstrict operators other than *if-then-else*, dataflow networks are not easy to write programs for. That is, it is difficult to automatically translate programs into dataflow networks, even programs in languages that are designed for exactly that. This is partly because it is not simple for an automatic translator to discover appropriate triggers for constants. Also, it can be difficult for an automatic translator to express complicated interrelationships between conditional expressions, for example, in terms of *select* and *distribute* nodes, the nodes that are available for expressing the desired conditional-evaluation behaviour.

Another drawback to dataflow networks is that not all networks, constructed from the different types of nodes, are meaningful or represent an expressible computation. The different types of nodes must be put together in certain ways in order to make sense. For example, one combination of *select* and *distribute* nodes will give the effect of "if then else", and another will give the effect of looping, but others may make no sense at all.

Another problem with dataflow networks is that it is difficult to handle data structures. Consider a program that uses a one-dimensional array A. If there are places in the program where elements of the array are referred to, say by expressions $A[I]$ and

A[J], the normal dataflow behavior would send copies of *A* (*all* of it) to the parts of the network corresponding to these expressions. This is clearly inappropriate. What is really needed is that the values of *I* and *J* be used to produce *demands* for particular elements of *A*, and that no copies of *A* be made. The array *A* must be stored somewhere and referred to, which goes against the normal idea of dataflow.

We have seen that, in dataflow, user-defined functions must be strict; the parameter-passing mechanism must be call-by-value. There are definite reasons why, in some languages, the parameter-passing mechanism must be call-by-need. These languages can not easily be implemented using dataflow, and this is another reason why dataflow can be inadequate.

All these problems with dataflow networks do not arise with operator nets, and are compelling reasons for studying the latter model.

2.1.5 Expressing Demand-driven by Data-driven

There has been some work on translating demand-driven dataflow networks into conventional data-driven networks (Pingali and Arvind [10], for example). This work is intended to show that data-driven evaluation is more general, and that, therefore, demand-driven evaluation need not be considered when designing dataflow machines.

The translated networks are all much more complicated than the originals, because they must express all the mechanism of demand-propagation. Moreover, they may not have properties that useful dataflow networks normally have. For example, the networks produced by the translation in [10] do not have the "self cleaning" property, which should ensure that all spurious datons are "eaten up" (but this may have been corrected in subsequent revisions of the algorithm). How the translation avoids the use of storage, which appears to be an inevitable consequence of demand-driven evaluation, and how the problem, mentioned earlier, of sending questons back through *distribute* nodes, is not clear to the authors without further study. Nevertheless, even if there are no problems with these things, the translation does not make demand-driven evaluation unnecessary for dataflow machines, because there still remains the problem of the impossibilty of having nonstrict operators in dataflow. (This could be solved, perhaps, by expressing the nonstrict operators as user-defined functions, in terms of *if-then-else*, but this requires that non-strict user-defined functions be handleable by the translation algorithm, something which may not be possible.)

All in all, it seems simpler to consider operator nets rather than dataflow networks. There are some drawbacks to demand-driven evaluation, principally the cost of performing queston propagation. For this reason, a hybrid technique has been developed, which we hope will combine the advantages of demand-driven and data-driven evaluation, while avoiding their drawbacks. It has been called "eazyflow", and will be the architecture most closely studied in this report.

3 Eazyflow

The name "eazyflow" comes from "EAger and laZY dataFLOW", where we are using "eager dataflow" to mean conventional, data-driven dataflow, and "lazy dataflow" to mean unconventional, demand-driven lazy evaluation. The name and technique were invented by Jaggan Jagannathan, who is part of the Architecture Group.

We have seen that, in operator nets, nonstrict operators prevent the efficient use of data-driven evaluation. Nonstrict operators are just special cases of operators that have this effect. The general cases are those that we call "unpredictably heedless". Predictably heedless operators are those for which there is a finite set of times such that it is possible, in general, at each time, to predict the times at which datons that are about to arrive at the node are needed for the next value to be produced by the operator. This has to be predicted only from whether or not the time in question is in the finite set of times . (Here "time" is part of the information in tags. It needn't be related to actual time.) It is a compile-time decision, if you will.

(*Some* nonstrict operators are predictably heedless, such as an operator that takes as its first output the first value on its first incoming edge and all subsequent outputs from the values that come along its second incoming edge. These operators *can* be used efficiently with data-driven evaluation.)

The unpredictably heedless operators can cause much more redundant computation than can nonstrict operators, if they are used in a data-driven evaluation mode. For example, an operator that passes on the values on its (single) input until that input becomes negative, and nothing after that, would be disastrous in data-driven evaluation. Values would be produced as input to this operator long after the operator's job is done.

The eazyflow evaluation technique is based on a division of operator nets into parts, so that part of the net will be data-driven and part will be demand-driven. The division depends crucially on the operators associated with the nodes, in particular on whether or not the operators are unpredictably heedless. The easiest way to visualize it is to imagine that the edges are to be coloured. Values that are eagerly generated (by data-driven evaluation) travel along green edges, and those that have to be demanded before they are produced come along red edges. An edge leaving a node is red if the node is associated with an unpredictably heedless operator or one of the edges arriving at the node is red. (There are a few other cases that need not concern us here.) The rest of the edges are green. (The set of red edges of an operator net is the smallest set of edges having the above property.)

The coloring of the edges determines how evaluation proceeds. If the edge leaving a node is green, that node will be data-driven. When datons arrive at the node, the operator is applied and the results sent out along the outgoing edge. If the leaving edge is red, that node will be demand-driven. Nothing happens until a queston arrives (along the leaving edge, in the reverse direction), and then, if some of the necessary datons on the incoming edges are not yet present, questons are sent back along those edges; if there are already enough datons there, the operator is applied to them. (If a node has already sent demands back for datons, when these arrive the operator of the node will be applied automatically, as in data-driven evaluation.)

The eazyflow evaluation technique needs one more feature. If green edges lead to nodes with unpredictably heedless operators, there can be a large build-up of unnecessary values on this edge, because the values will be generated automatically. There needs to be some way to prevent this. This is done by imposing a bound on how far these values can be generated ahead of their actual use by the node. Details of this will become clearer when we consider an architecture embodying the eazyflow model.

4 A Programming Language for Operator Nets: Lucid

If we are abandoning dataflow networks, we should be sure that the replacement, operator nets, are as useable as dataflow networks for the specification of algorithms. We want to know that operator nets can be programmed relatively easily. Nets are two-dimensional objects, at best, and it is difficult to display them on terminals, write them into files, etc. What is needed is some textual representation, a language. In addition to this, we need to know that this language can express useful computations.

As it happens, there *is* a programming language that corresponds exactly to operator nets. This language is called Lucid. Lucid programs can be thought of as linearized forms of operator nets (and operator nets as graphical forms of Lucid programs). The translation from one to the other is trivial (in marked contrast with the difficult translation of other programming languages, or even Lucid, into dataflow networks). Lucid is actually a family of languages, a particular member of this family being determined by the data-objects that the programs use and the basic operations on these objects that are available. In operator net terms, this corresponds to choosing which datons are going to pass along the edges of the operator nets and which operators are available to be associated with nodes. In the rest of this report we will be assuming that the element of the Lucid family that we will be concerned with will be the language that is currently implemented in C, running under UNIX* on a VAX [6].

Lucid was invented and developed by Drs. Edward Ashcroft and William Wadge. They have written several papers on early versions of the language [1], [2], [3]. Details of the current version of the language can be found in a recent SRI Technical report [4]. Also, a book has just been published by Academic Press [11], that is concerned with this latest, and final, version of the language, the version that is most directly equivalent to operator nets.

---

*UNIX is a trademark of AT&T Bell Laboratories

Although it looks imperative at first sight, Lucid is actually a functional language. Therefore, as with all functional languages, it is concerned with the values of variables, and these values do not change with time. However, as we will see, Lucid can often be viewed as a language that deals with objects that change with time, even though it is a functional language.

The (unchanging) values of variables in Lucid are actually infinite sequences, but the variables should be thought of as objects that change with time. For example, the Lucid definition

```
x = 1 fby x+1;
```

(the operator fby means followed by) defines the value of x to be the sequence $<1, 2, 3, 4, ... >$ but it is natural and useful to think of the value of x as an object, which is initially 1 and subsequently changes to 2, 3, 4, etc.

This simple idea has many consequences. It means that the language enjoys all the advantages of a functional language, such as referential transparency, provability etc., while retaining an operational iterative flavor. It means that defined functions in Lucid are functions from infinite sequences to infinite sequences, which, in operational terms, means that they are *filters* that produce outputs as inputs are fed in. Moreover these filters do not need to act 'pointwise' -- the output at any time need not just depend on the input at that time, it can depend on all the previous inputs. For example, we can write a function that produces a running sum of its inputs, as follows

```
Sum(x) = s where
         s = first x fby s + next x;
         end;
```

Operationally, the filter sum keeps around a local variable s (for each invocation of sum, i.e., for each expression sum(*e*)), which "remembers" the running sum (of *e*).

It also means that all Lucid programs are essentially continually operating programs, which are given infinite sequences of inputs and produce infinite sequences of outputs. This doesn't mean that Lucid is only suited to special applications like signal processing, process control, or data processing; it just means that the operating system would have to take special action if a Lucid program were to be a "one off" job, if it were required to give only a single result. In the current implementation of Lucid [6] [5], this action is invoked when the system gets *eod* as input. (*eod* stands for *end-of-data*.)

Lucid is a high-level language with several interesting characteristics. There are no concepts of "flow of control" and sequencing, and computations are naturally 'distributed', since there is nothing to stop computations from proceeding in different places at the same time. With the emphasis on iteration rather than recursion, the language can be programmed in very conventional ways; yet it can also be programmed in ways that take advantage of some of its more unusual features, such as coroutines. Semantically speaking, the language is based on the idea of infinite sequences, and continuous, unending operation. It is not surprising that it turns out to be the linearized form of operator nets.

5 An Eazyflow Architecture

The eazyflow computational model for operator nets is the basis of a multiprocessor architecture, which we shall call "the eazyflow engine". The eazyflow engine is programmed directly using textual representations of operator nets (by which, of course, we mean Lucid programs).

When given an operator net (i.e., a Lucid program), the eazyflow engine acts like the network, in the sense that the appropriate operations are performed on the appropriate data, with appropriate degrees of parallelism.

The basic idea in eazyflow, the coloring of edges in operator nets to correspond to the parts of the net that can be data-driven and the parts that muust bedemand-driven, when expressed in terms of Lucid results in the variables in programs being partitioned into two sets. Certain variables in the Lucid program, the *eager variables*, can be eager-evaluated (that is, they can be computed in a data-driven manner) and the rest, the *lazy variables*, must be lazy-evaluated (that is, they must be computed in a demand-driven manner). This partitioning is done automatically on the basis of the definitions of the variables; it is not decided by the programmer.

The data-driven computation is controlled by demands for other variables that must be lazy-evaluated. When a demand is made for a lazy variable that needs eager variables, demands will be produced for some or all of the eager variables. This is the only way in which it happens that eager variables are demanded. When an eager variable X is demanded at time i, and that time is "close" to the limit of the values of X that have been, or will be, produced, the limit for X is increased by a fixed number N, and eager-evaluation is triggered for the most basic variables on which the eager variable depends. (These variables are necessarily eager.) Only N values of these variables will be produced. (To get more produced, there must be another demand for X, for a time that is "close" to the new limit for X.) The values of N and "close" are parameters of the system, and good values for them will be found by experiment.

The machine is composed of submachines, connected to each other through a switch. The number of submachines is arbitrary, larger numbers requiring larger switches, but, for the small-scale prototype machine, we propose to have eight submachines. Each submachine is itself an elementary eazyflow engine, with its own set of processors.

5.1 A Single Submachine

Each submachine essentially consists of three intersecting rings, one for handling demands, one for applying operators to the results of demands (we shall call these the "eduction rings") and one for computing values in a data-driven manner (the "dataflow ring"). The dataflow ring is essentially the same as the single ring of the dataflow machine at Manchester, and the second eduction ring also is somewhat similar to the ring of the Manchester machine, since once an operator has been demanded it works in a data-driven way. The whole design is a generalization of the proven architecture of the Manchester machine. In fact, Ian Watson, one of the two designers of the Manchester machine, made great contributions to the tentative design when he was working with Ed Ashcroft at SRI, for the month of September, 1983. We propose to have Dr Watson as a consultant to the project.

The rings constituting a submachine are unidirectional pipelines, around which tagged tokens flow in a quasi-synchronized manner. Each ring contains a queue. The three rings are interconnected because the demand ring can produce results for the application ring, and the application ring can produce demands (when nonstrict operators are tentatively applied, as when the *if-then-else* operator produces a demand for one of the branches after it receives the result of the test). The demand ring can affect the dataflow ring (when data-driven evaluation is initiated or resumed as a result of a demand), and the dataflow ring can produce results for the demand ring (when a value is produced, in a data-driven manner, for an eager variable that occurs in a lazy definition).

Each ring will be described separately. Each ring picks up processors from a pool of processors, and we propose to use one pool for all the rings. (This is not essential; simulations may show that it is advantageous to use a separate pool for each ring. In this case, the latter design will be the one used. No difficulty is expected in making this change, if it is deemed advisable.) The structure of the submachine is shown in Figure 1. A quite detailed description of the design of the submachine can be found in the Appendix.

Now we will consider the way in which the switch (that is common to all the submachines) allows the submachines to act in concert as a single machine.

5.2 The Whole Machine

The Appendix describes the architecture for a single submachine. In fact there will be several such submachines (we have arbitrarily chosen eight), and they are connected together by using the same switch, as indicated in Figures 1 and 2. Packets are routed to particular submachines by the switch, depending on the tags or the return addresses in the packets. For some packets, such as result packets, skeleton packets, store packets and insert packets, the submachine to go to is specified directly in the packet. For demandpackets and value packets, the submachine is determined by the tag, using a fixed random hashing function. (All submachines use the same hashing function.) The hashing distributes the computational activity among the submachines in a random way and balances the load on the various processors.

Eazyflow Subengine

Comprised of three intersecting rings that share the processor pool: application ring, demand ring, and dataflow ring

Subengines are interconnected via the switch

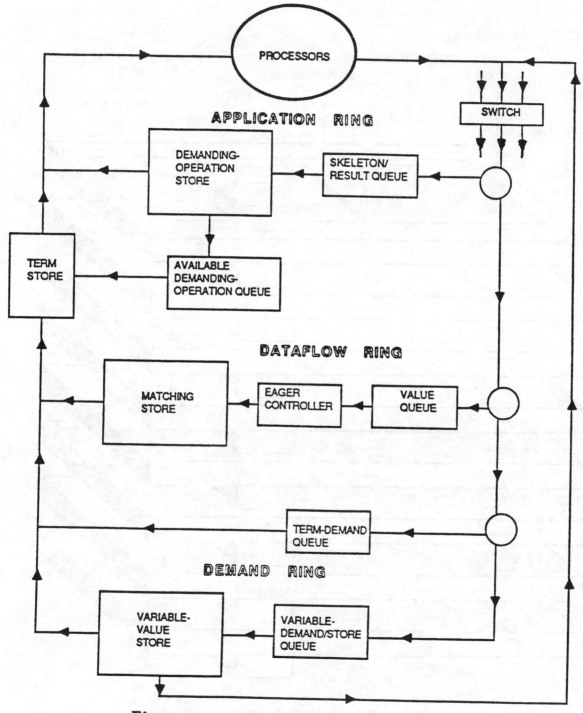

Figure 1: An Eazyflow Engine Submachine

Eazyflow Engine

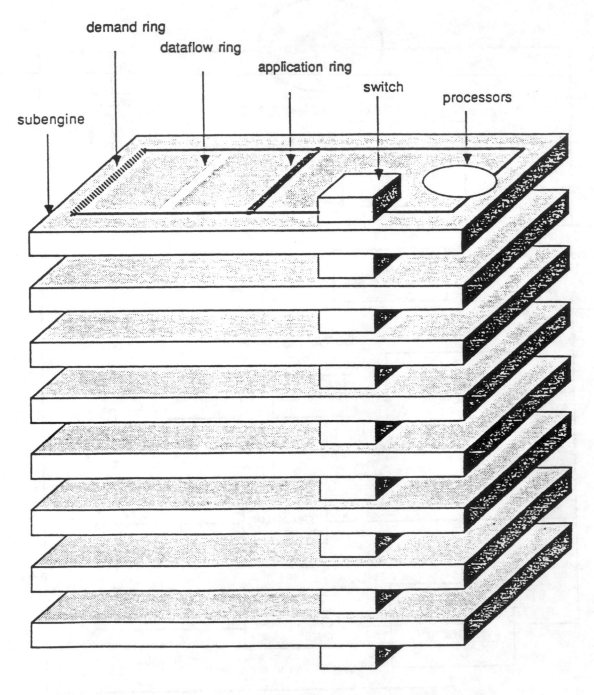

Figure 2: The Whole Machine

6 Storage Management

The overall architecture of submachines is inadequate in one respect: values are never removed from the pool of variable values, even though the value may never be demanded again. In practice, the architecture will be somewhat different from that described above, because it will have storage management built in to it. It will embody a management scheme employing a "future usage count" that is able to remedy the above defect; a (tagged) value will be thrown away when its future usage count gets down to zero.

The current Lucid interpreter handles this problem with a "retirement age" scheme [5]. If a tagged variable value passes retirement age, i.e., has not been demanded for some time (measured in terms of the number of garbage collections it has survived), it retires at the next garbage collection. The retirement age is adjusted dynamically if tagged values have to be recomputed because they are demanded after they have been retired.

A heuristic method of handling a similar problem has been proposed by Keller and Sleep [9]. They want to avoid recomputing terms like $f(e)$, in applicative languages, and propose that the programmer supply an *initial count function* which, depending on the value of e, gives an initial usage count for $f(e)$. If, after the count reaches zero, and the value of $f(e)$ has been thrown away, $f(e)$ is subsequently demanded, it can be re-evaluated from the definitions, so no real harm results from choosing an incorrect initial count function.

In contrast to the above two schemes, the usage count scheme is not heuristic. In Lucid it is possible to devise an algorithm using usage counts that ensures that, when a value is thrown away, it will never be demanded again. Initial experiments by Tony Faustini have indicated that the scheme can indeed drastically reduce the storage requirements for Lucid programs, and also give at least an order of magnitude decrease in running time.

7 Reliability

It wasn't incorporated in the machine design outlined in the Appendix, but the eazyflow engine can be simply adapted to give a high degree of hardware fault-tolerance. With hundreds of processors, the possibility of processor failure is quite high, and building fault-tolerance into such a machine is probably crucial. The addition of tolerance of processor faults requires that the number of processors used be doubled, but the other components of the machine would remain substantially unchanged, if the possibility of other sorts of faults can be ignored. The fault-tolerance scheme has not been incorporated into the prototype design, because the prototype will use only about 128 processors, but it easily could be, if required. It would increase the hardware cost by about 30%. The way that tolerance of processor faults would be incorporated is follows.

It is assumed that the main faults to be tolerated are failures of processors, either failure to give any results at all, or failure to give the correct results. It is also assumed that these failures will be so rare that the possibility of two failures, in different processors, at the same time, or within a short time of each other, is so remote as to be not worth considering.

The idea behind the fault-tolerance technique is simply this: when a processor has to be picked up, to execute a basic operation, modify a tag, produce new demands, etc., *two* processors should be picked up, rather than one, and both should be set to work doing the same calculation. In a few microseconds both processors should be finished. (If either of them is not finished within a reasonable time, it can be assumed that the processor has failed, and the corresponding result will be taken to be some failure flag.) The two results can be compared by a third, distinct, processor. If they both give the same result, this result is sent off around the appropriate ring. If they disagree, a fourth, necessarily reliable, processor should be immediately grabbed and set to work on the same minute computation. In a few microseconds it, too, will have finished, and its result is the result which is sent around the rings. (This result can also be used to determine which of the two original processors was in error (or even if the third, arbitration processor falsely indicated that the first two processors disagreed). The errant processor can then be immediately removed from its pool of processors, or flagged as suspect.) The computation can then proceed with a delay of only a few microseconds, well within the limits imposed by the most stringent of fault-detection requirements.

One of the advantages of this technique, over the "conventional" fault-detection technique for Von Neumann machines, is that only double redundancy, not triple, is required. (We are not counting the arbitration processor because it does not need to have all the capabilities of the other processors; all it does is check whether two bit-strings are identical.) Only when a fault is detected, by two processors disagreeing, is it necessary to call for a fourth, distinct, processor. (This should happen rarely.)

It is possible to do this because of the way that the eazyflow engine, like dataflow machines, naturally breaks its computations into minute pieces, and because there are no side-effects of evaluating these pieces. The only result of such an evaluation is a single value, which can easily be compared with the result of a duplicate evaluation. If the results disagree, no effects will have occurred to prevent a third processor from performing a fresh evaluation, from the original data.

Another advantage is that the eazyflow engine, like dataflow machines, naturally has several processors, and if one processor becomes defective and has to be taken out of service, the machine will be essentially unchanged, and be ready to detect more errors. Only when a large fraction of the total number of processors has been removed from service will the machine become too slow to be able to function effectively.

The eazyflow engine consists of more than just pools of processors; it has several other components, and data packages will be transmitted around the rings in great numbers. Can not errors occur in the rest of the machine? The answer, of course, is yes, but these errors will be different in kind to the errors produced by defective processors. These errors could be transmission errors, or they could be memory faults. In both cases, if they produce changes in only one bit, they could be detected, and corrected, by conventional single error correction codes. The special-purpose processors needed to do this error detection and correction can be built into the hardware of the machine, with enough redundancy to be immune to faults.

There could also be faults that cause whole packets to be lost, whole blocks of memory to go bad, and single faults that put whole components out of commission, for example. These can be handled by a modification to the architecture of the machine that detects (using a time-out mechanism) when one of these faults may have occurred, and then institutes investigative measures. When the fault has been confirmed, recomputation is initiated. It is one of the great advantages of the demand-driven approach to computation is that this can be done. (The technique has been developed by Jaggan Jaganathan of the Architecture Group.) Although it was not one of the requirements for a fault-tolerance technique when Jagannathan started looking at the problem, it turns out that the technique that he has developed can even handle the loss of a complete submachine!

(There has to be some level at which possible faults are disregarded. For example, in this discussion we are assuming that the communication channels between components of the machine are not going to be broken.)

8 Hardware

The main processing power of the eazyflow engine lies in the processors in the processor pools, but each of the components in the rings has a rudimentary form of intelligence. For example, if we follow the precedent of the Manchester machine, in each submachine the variable-value store will be interrogated using hardware hashing; dealing with collisions that the hardware hashing can not handle will be the responsibility of some simple dedicated processor. Because of the unidirectional, sequential nature of the rings, only one variable value will be requested at one time, and a single dedicated processor is adequate for handling any collisions that may occur. If we decide to use genuine associative memory, intelligence is built into the memory.

The switch, which routes packets from ring to ring, will be a normal multistage switch, perhaps a delta-network, with buffering between the stages. The transit time across the switch will depend logarithmically on the number of rings. This will not limit the number of rings that can be used, because the number of stages in the pipelines is increased accordingly, and the pipelines should be full. The only problem with the switch is that contention could result in gaps in the pipelines, but analysis shows that a random distribution of packet destinations (i.e., an equal probability of wanting to go between any two rings) should result in about 75% of the maximum possible throughput. Choosing the best hashing function for determining which ring to go to will probably be a major factor in fine-tuning the machine for optimum performance.

It may turn out that locality properties inherent in Lucid programs will allow a much simpler kind of switch, which would give the machine the property of scalability, the ability to be expanded in terms of the number of processors used, etc, without requiring changes in existing hardware other than simple additions.

Solving the switch/hashing function issue is one of the reasons for building a pilot machine using tried-and-true techniques. This will allow us to get a machine quickly to experiment with, and to determine how a much better, production machine could be built in the future.

The number of processors that can be used effectively in each processor pool is bounded by the ratio of the average number of packets per second that are fed into the processor pool to the average number of such packets that a single processor can process in one second. This can be expressed as follows. For each ring i, let t_i be the time taken by the slowest stage in the pipeline, on average, and let p_i be the average fraction of the number of packets that leave the switch that go around ring i. Let t and p be the values of t_i and p_i such that $t_i p_i$ is maximized, over all the rings. If β is the throughput of the switch (that is, the maximum average "fullness" of the pipelines entering the switch that the switch can handle) and T is the average time taken by the processors to handle a single packet, the bound on the number of processors that a submachine can effectively use is given by

$$M = T/(t(1-\beta+\beta p)).$$

For example, if T is four microseconds, t is five hundred nanoseconds, p is one third (0.33333..) and β is 0.75, the value of M is sixteen.

This bound can not be determined with any accuracy at this stage of the design. It would depend on the actual choice of processors, and the particular details of the hardware hashing mechanism, for example. Tentatively, we are proposing that each submachine have a pool of sixteen processors (but this could be modified very easily if analysis and simulation show that another number would be more appropriate). This is not a very large number, and is far short of the hundreds or thousands of processors that are often postulated for dataflow machines. The eazyflow engine will get its real power by the use of many submachines. We are proposing that eight submachines be used in the prototype, but the design is the same for any number. It probably would be better to use sixteen, so that meaningful experiments be conducted to see how the behavior and performance of the machine vary with the number of submachines. Such a machine would be very expensive to construct, and perhaps its construction should be delayed until preliminary results are obtained for eight submachines. We are proposing to construct a switch big enough for sixteen submachines, so that, if the go-ahead is given later for a sixteen submachine prototype, or if the cost of constructing each submachine turns out to be less than expected, extra submachines just need be constructed and "plugged in". The eight submachine eazyflow engine has a total of one hundred and twenty eight processors, not counting the dedicated, simple processors that are part of the components like variable-value stores, etc. Experience with the Manchester machine has shown that the processors in that machine are performing useful work about 90 to 95% of the time. If this holds true for the prototype eazyflow engine, and using three microseconds as the average time for processing a floating point operation, the prototype should be a thirty eight megaflop machine, approximately.

This preceding calculation assumed that, as in the Manchester machine, the rings and switch are "wide enough" to take a whole packet at once. The packets, with values, tags, return addresses, etc., can get quite long and will be well over 100 bits. Moreover, at this stage, it is probably not a good idea to fossilize the size and format of packets in hardware. Probably what should be done is break the packets up into 32-bit chunks. This will make it easier to use off-the-shelf components, and speed up construction of the prototype. It will also slow the machine down by about four times, to just less than a ten megaflop machine, but in later versions of the machine, which may be engineered for raw power, this simplification may be dropped.

9 The Advantages of the Machine

To a large extent the Manchester machine can be considered to be a precursor of the eazyflow engine proposed here, and lessons can be learned from the experience with that machine. Evidence from use of the Manchester machine [7] indicates, by extrapolation, that the eazyflow engine should be able to utilize its processors efficiently, and thus be a very fast machine. The actual performance of the machine can not be predicted before more details of the hardware, such as the processors to be used and the hardware hashing technique to be employed, have been settled. Nevertheless, it can be confidently predicted that the unidirectional pipeline structure of submachines will work, and the main unknown is how effective is the connection of submachines. This can really be determined only by actually building a machine, but some indications should come from analysis of the simulations we propose to carry out.

The Manchester evidence is that there should be no difficulty finding problems with enough parallelism to exercise the computing power of the machine. In fact, the problems do not have to be regularly structured (as they must for vector machines) or even numerically oriented.

Apart from its effectiveness, another reason for designing this machine is that it will be the first eazyflow engine, and we confidently expect that analysis of our simulations will show that eazyflow is better than straight (data-driven) dataflow in most cases, both for programmability and speed of computation.

One of the advantages of an eazyflow engine of the type described is that it will run Lucid very efficiently. This is important, but more important is the fact that it is *designed* to run Lucid, and thus will be a machine with a very high-level assembly language. This will enable programmers to write programs that are close to the problem in question and close to the machine, at the same time.

Since the machine is designed to run Lucid, certain features that depend crucially on properties of Lucid can be built into the architecture. Two such features are:

- The usage count scheme of storage management, which promises to make Lucid a practical language even on conventional von Neumann machines

- Certain links between the structure of tags and the syntax of programs, which promise to simplify the possible communication between submachines (because the tag will be the crucial factor in determining which submachines packets are routed to), allowing simpler switches and, it is hoped, a truly scalable machine, that is, one in which the effort required to connect two equal-sized machines together to give one of (almost) twice the power is independent of the size of the machines.

One advantage of basing the machine on Lucid is that it can have an operating system rather like UNIX. Lucid and the UNIX shell language are very compatible, with Lucid functions acting very much like UNIX filters, with composition of functions corresponding to the joining together of filters to form pipes. In a sense, the operating system will be very similar to Lucid itself, which means that, for this machine, there will be little difference between ordinary programming and systems programming.

We have emphasized here that the machine will be a Lucid machine, but, in fact, the actual design of the machine will not have Lucid itself built into the hardware. (The meanings of the tag-manipulating operators, i.e., the Lucid operators, and the system operators, *will* be built in, but as firmware not hardware.) The machine could also be used as a machine for many other high-level languages. It could also be used for pure LISP, or KRC, or Hope, or VAL, or ID, or SISAL, for example. (These languages can all be thought of as equivalent to subsets of Lucid, especially if the tagging mechanism is used, as it can be, to handle higher-order functions (functions that take functions as arguments). Also, most of full LISP can be handled, by using the usage count technique.) The possibility of using the machine for Prolog is being investigated also.

10 Analysis of the Architecture

The architecture will be analyzed in three different ways, which give increasing levels of confidence in the realism of their results.

1. The first attack on the analysis problem will be via the construction of a formal model of the architecture that will allow quantitative results to be

generated about the performance of the architecture when applied to particular classes of problems.

2. The second line of attack will be to simulate the architecture, at the level of functional units, using event-based simulation.

3. The third line of attack is to emulate the architecture (mimicking its operation so precisely that it will really provide an implementation of Lucid) and instrument it so that it will give performance measurements for the machine that is being mimicked.

The first approach, of constructing a formal model of the architecture, can be pursued at many levels. In the section on hardware, an expression is given for the number of processors that a single submachine can effectively use. This expression was derived using a simple model in which an "average" traffic is postulated, including an "average" division of this traffic between rings, an "average" processor evaluation time, an "average" time taken for each stage in the various pipelines and an "average" throughput of the switch. All these things could be analysed in detail using more sophisticated models, and these models could be used to investigate such questions as the "average" lengths of the various queues and the variance in such lengths. One crucial set of results to come from application of the formal model will relate to the overall or "average" performance of the machine.

The second approach will be used basically to check the validity of the results given by the formal model. The simulations will be written using such simulation packages as Oasis, which uses SIMULA. These packages are designed to simulate multiprocessor architectures, and it should be relatively straightforward to do the simulations. The simulation will give figures that are more obviously related to "real life" than does the model. However, to some extent, the assumptions made by one will be made by the other (concerning "average" programs for various applications, for example). Thus, some residual doubt may remain about the validity of the results, which should be removed by results obtained by applying the third approach.

Most of the analysis work done so far has been devoted to the third approach. One emulation is being programmed, at the moment, using the Waterloo Port multiprocessor operating system, which allows flexible multiprocessor structures to be set up that correspond to the various components in the rings of the eazyflow engine. The computing power that Port can muster is comparatively modest, but, nevertheless, it should be possible to establish the correctness of the architecture as an implementation of Lucid. In another emulation experiment, the architecture that is being used is that of the HEP. The HEP architecture fits very well with the eazyflow engine architecture. The advantage of using the HEP, of course, is that the computing power is substantial, and the enormous amount of computation required for emulation should be tractable.

One advantage of emulation over simulation is that actual programs are analysed, and none of the assumptions, that were needed for the model or for the simulation, will need to be made. The results will closely correspond to reality. Another advantage is that, if the operating system or the architecture of the machine on which the emulation is to be performed is close to the eazyflow architecture (as are Waterloo Port and the HEP) the effort required to construct a simulator can be quite small.

11 Some Applications

It is a characteristic of dataflow architectures that their proponents claim that they are applicable, with high efficiency, thanks to expected effective use of multiple processors, to all types of computation. Eazyflow is no different in this respect. The eazyflow architecture should be particularly effective in three areas: signal processing, symbolic computing and multifunction processing.

11.1 Signal Processing

There are two reasons why an eazyflow engine should be useful for signal processing. First of all there is the fact that the language Lucid, and thus the machine itself, is based on the idea of processing unending sequences of data items (that in this context could be signals). Secondly, these signals may arrive without being demanded, so the data-driven aspect of the machine would be useful here. The demand-driven aspect is necessary to be able to selectively expend more effort on processing certain signals in critical situations. In the data-driven approach, even when all processing power should really be dedicated to getting the airplane, or whatever, out of a particularly tight situation, processors will still be grinding away processing non-critical signals like air temperature. Using demand-driven evaluation, certain tasks can be given high priority when necessary, and the lower priority tasks would automatically go on the "back burner", to be resumed when more resources are available.

It can be argued that real time is of the essence in signal processing, and any degree of demand-driven computation is going to destroy the link with real time. This can be avoided by associating, or marking, the incoming signals with the actual time (absolute or relative) at which theyd were received. In fact, this might well be a useful thing to do anyway, to allow for different, or non-constant, sampling rates of the sensors. This will be explained in more detail.

In a Lucid program, the values of variables are actually infinite sequences, and these sequences are generated as the computation of the program progresses. Variables with no definitions are *input variables*, which take a sequence of values from the "outside world". For real-time applications, the input variables should be taken as eager variables, in most cases. (The exceptions will be those readings that are made at unpredictable intervals, when needed. These will be lazy variables.) The elements in the sequence for an eager input variable will be inputted in order. Every eager input variable v will have associated with it another variable v_t which records the actual times (in milliseconds since system start-up) at which the elements of v are inputted to the program. This, too, will be an eager variable. Using these variables it is possible to make the behavior of the program depend on actual time.

Here is a simple program fragment which takes readings from an accelerometer and produces values for velocity and distance (in the same direction as the acceleration is measured). The original velocity and distance, when the readings of the accelerometer are started, are V_0 and D_0, respectively.

```
vel = V₀ fby vel + acc*delta;
dist = D₀ fby dist + vel*delta;
delta = (next acc_t - acc_t)/1000;
```

The variable `delta` will give the times (in seconds) between successive readings of the accelerometer. (It probably will be constant, i.e. be a constant sequence, but the program works just as well if it is a varying sequence.) The variables `acc`, `delta`, `vel` and `dist` can be used in any way one wishes. For example, if the program contained the following definition

```
avg(x) = mean
            where
              mean = x fby mean + d;
              d = (next x - mean)/(index + 2);
            end;
```

(the Lucid constant `index` is the sequence $<0,1,2,...>$) then the expression `avg(vel)` will give the running average velocity, which may well be a useful thing to know. If there were readings of the rate of fuel consumption, taken at the same times as the accelerometer readings, represented by a variable `fuel_rate`, then `vel/fuel_rate` will give the instantaneous "milage" (actually feet per gallon) and `avg(vel/fuel_rate)` will give the average milage. If the fuel tanks originally hold F gallons of fuel, the expression

```
vel/fuel_rate*left
    where
      left = F fby left - fuel_rate*delta;
    end
```

will give the distance that can be traveled if the present velocity is maintained. (Actually, if the present fuel consumption is maintained.)

Thus there are many values that will be calculated, in a continuous way. It is possible to have values that are conditionally updated. For example, we could keep track of the distance travelled, once every five seconds. (This would be appropriate for a visual display, which would be unreadable if it changed as often as the accelerometer produced readings.) This could be defined by

```
display = if sawtooth eq 0 then dist else display fi
            where
              sawtooth = 0 fby if sawtooth >= 5 then 0
                              else sawtooth + delta fi;
            end;
```

We now must consider the operational behavior of the eazyflow machine produced by these definitions. The example is rather simple because it is based on the assumption that the readings for the two input variables, acc and fuel_rate, are made at the same times, and because only pointwise operators are used. This means that the values of the other variables will correspond to the same real times as do the values of acc and fuel_rate. The times at which they are calculated will differ, but the logically they correspond to the real times given by acc_t. If the the inputs came at different times, or nonpointwise operators were used, the program would have to be more complicated, making appropriate uses of the variables giving the real times at which the readings were made.

The meaning of the program is independent of whether the input variables are data-driven or demand-driven. This may seem strange, but the anomaly is removed once it is realized that the values of acc_t) will differ in the two cases, and the difference will take care of the differences in the values of acc and fuel_rate. Of course, it must be assumed in the second case that the demands for output are made at sufficiently great intervals of time to allow the computation of each output to be completed before the next demand for output is made, and in the first case that inputs are provided at sufficiently great intervals, for the same reason.

There can be a problem when one of the outputs required involves conditional evaluation, as is the case with display here. If the variable dist were a lazy variable and were not used anywhere else, it would only be demanded when display needs it, namely once every five seconds, and the required value would not have been generated automatically, by data-driven evaluation. To get the required value of dist, all the intervening values of dist must be calculated, corresponding to the times since dist was last needed, five seconds previously. This will be a longer calculation than usual, and may, in fact, be too long, and overlap with the next demand for output. In situations like this, the program should be carefully written to ensure that the lazy variables are kept to a minimum.

We have just demonstrated that data-driven evaluation is preferred in signal processing applications. Nevertheless, there are situations in signal processing where having demand-driven evaluation is an advantage. The advantage of demand-driven computation is that we can have different types of demands. We can have urgent demands, for values needed right now, and we can have less urgent demands, and we have the values that are produced in a data-driven manner. All of them are calculated using processors taken from the same processor pool, and priority can easily be given to the urgent demands by allowing them to "jump the queue", and by holding up packets arriving at the processor pool from parts of the machine that are temporarily out of favor. Also, it will be natural in practice to have some values whose speedy evaluation is more critical than others, and this naturally fits in better with a multi-priority demand-driven evaluation scheme than with a single priority data-driven scheme. (It is more natural to have a multi-priority demand-driven scheme than a multi-priority data-driven scheme because the urgency attached to a particular computation comes from the top, from the use that is going to be made of the results of the computation, rather than from the bottom, from the basic operations comprising the computation.))

One of the attractive features of Lucid in this application is that the definitional nature of the language allows one to simply state that, for example, the velocity of the airplane is the running sum of the accelerometer reading multiplied by the time between readings, and the distance travelled is the running sum of the velocities multiplied by these same times between readings. This is stated in two lines in Lucid, and these calculations are then done automatically, continually.

This application has not yet been investigated in detail, but it shows a great deal of promise.

11.2 Symbolic Processing

We will consider symbolic processing to be any non-numeric processing, not just processing of strings of symbols. The eazyflow engine can be used directly for applications that can be expressed in any applicative language, like pure LISP, or Hope. This is not surprising, and also, perhaps, not very interesting, since most non-numeric applications use the *non*-applicative features of (impure) LISP. What *is* surprising is that the eazyflow engine can handle most programs written in this way, too. What is required is that there be some discipline in the ways that the side-effect producing operations of LISP, RPLACA and RPLACD, are used. (The details are too involved to be described here.) The use of the PROG feature of LISP to give iteration is easily handled by Lucid.

One benefit of the Lucid way of handling LISP-like programs is that garbage collection, for data structures, is not needed. Because the LISP-like version of Lucid does not allow cyclic structures to be constructed from noncyclic structures, storage management can be handled with a reference-count technique. This would be an advantage in a single processor machine, but it is of paramount importance in a multiprocessor machine; it means that storage management is then distributed and no central management "authority" is needed.

The fact that eazyflow engines can run LISP-like programs is not, of itself, reason for doing so. What needs to be established is that an eazyflow engine can run such programs much faster than a conventional sequential machine, such as a LISP Machine. For this, some performance analysis needs to be done of the appropriate eazyflow engine, and of the parallelism in the sorts of LISP-like programs that would be run on it.

A very important application area for symbolic computation is inferential or logic programming. The most widely used logic programming language is Prolog. The most direct way of making the eazyflow engine applicable to logic programming is implement

Prolog, by writing a compiler for Prolog that compiles into the assembly language of the machine, that is, into Lucid. (This compiler also should be *written* in Lucid if the compilation is to be done on the machine.) This compiler could implement normal sequential Prolog, but it should be possible also to implement an unconventional Prolog in which advantage is taken of the parallel nature of the machine.

There are three places where parallelism can be used in Prolog, or in the unconventional Prolog that we are considering. First of all, parallelism could be used in implementing unification. Then there could be and-parallelism (the simultaneous attempt to attain the goals in a clause) and or-parallelism (the simultanous exploration of several branches of the search tree). And-parallelism is difficult to implement because of the interaction between the computations that are attempting to solve goals, because of the sharing of variables between goals. The implementation of or-parallelism may be much easier. What it seems to require is the use of a nonsequential "parallel-or" operator. (A nonstrict operator is sequential if the arguments of a call to the operator can be evaluated one at a time, the arguments to evaluate being determined by the values of the arguments evaluated so far. The parallel-or operator is nonsequential because it returns *true* if any of its arguments is true, even if some are undefined, and the arguments can not be evaluated one at a time. The *if-then-else* operator, on the other hand, *is* sequential.) If the eazyflow machine were modified to handle nonsequential operators, in particular, parallel-or, "parallel Prolog" programs could be easily translated into Lucid programs that use it.

The problem with handling a nonsequential operator in the eazyflow machine is easily seen by considering the operator nets of Lucid programs that use it. The problem is similar to the problem of using nonstrict operators, like *if-then-else*, in piped evaluation. Somehow evaluation must be aborted for the arguments of the operator that have been found to be unnecessary. As with nonstrict operators in piped evaluation, what are needed are lethons. It has been found that there are flaws in "lethon physics", but these are caused by programs that would not result from compiling Prolog programs, and there does appear to be a chance of making them work in this case. (The implementation of and-parallelism may require similar techniques.)

The details have not been worked out, but a variant of the eazyflow engine could be used as the target architecture of a Prolog compiler that should effectively use the and- and or-parallelism in "parallel Prolog" programs.

11.3 Multifunction Processing

There are several applications for which an eazyflow engine could be constructed, for example, signal processing, scientific calculations (MHD, nuclear physics, etc.), expert systems, non-numeric processing in general, graphics, and so on. These machines would differ mainly only at the microcode level, the general structure of the machines would be the same. With some loss of efficiency, these machines could be unified to give a single machine that could be used (with still exceptional performance) in any of these applications. Even better, the machine could perhaps be used in applications that really straddle two or more of the basic applications, for example giving three-dimensional graphic display of the developing weather pattern of the Earth, as it is being predicted.

This scenario appears quite feasible, because all the machines will basically be programmed in different extensions of the same language. The unified machine would be programmed in a "super" extension that has each of the individual extensions as subsets. The "straddling" programs would be programmed in this super extension (but not in any individual extension).

The whole multifunction processor problem is not just a language design problem, but solving the language problem, the design of a uniform "super" extension, will go a long way towards solving the architectural problems.

This discussion of applications has, in each case, ended up talking about specialized versions of the eazyflow engine. This agrees with the current conventional wisdom that different applications call for different specialized machines. In this case, however, all of these machines are based on the general eazyflow engine described above, and it is this general machine which we propose to analyze, simulate, emulate and eventually build a prototype for. Nevertheless, the applications that are most appropriate for different variants of the machine will be characterized and analyzed.

I. A Single Submachine

The operation of a submachine will be explained in a very general, incomplete, and simplified way.

I.1 The Demand Ring

The demand ring is the most involved, and will be described first. Actually the ring for handling demands is really two rings, because demands for terms that are simply variables are handled differently than demands for terms that are operators or user-defined functions applied to operands or actual parameterse. Thus there are *two* queues used here, so that three of the main components in the rings are the previously mentioned pool of processors, the term-demand queue and the variable-demand queue. In addition there is a *variable-value store*, and a *term store*, in which programs are stored in the form of intermediate code. (This intermediate code is very simple. It is basically a linearized form of the parse tree of the program in question. One feature of the intermediate code is that the address of the term defining a variable or function, or the term occurring in the declaration of a variable, will be used to identify the variable or function in the intermediate code, and in the variable-value store.)

The whole operation of the eduction rings can be simply explained by describing what happens to the demand packets that come off the term-demand queue and the variable-demand queue.

A *demand packet* represents a demand for the tagged value of a term that is not a basic constant. A demand packet is of the form (a,t,r). a is the address in the term store of the term being demanded (together with two bits to indicate whether the term is a variable, or a basic operator applied to operands, or a function applied to actual parameters, or a Lucid or system operator applied to operands); t is the tag; and r is the return address. The latter, r, is both the address of the *demanding-operation* that has been promised the result of the demand, and an indication of the position, in the demanding-operation, into which the result is to be put. (Demanding operations also contain return addresses.)

The demand packets are routed to the appropriate queue as a result of inspecting the two bits in the address of the term.

Each demand that comes off the variable-demand queue goes to the value store, where the tagged value of the variable is located, if it has such a tagged value. This value is sent to the result queue, which we will consider later. If there is no value, but there is an indication that the value is "being computed", the return address of the demand is put on a list of return addresses associated with the variable value, in the value store. If there is no value at all for the tagged variable, an indication that the variable is "being computed" is left in the value store, and then different things happen depending on the type of variable it is.

If the variable is a lazy variable, after the demand is modified by incorporating the variable-value store address of the variable, the demand travels on to the term store.

If the variable is an eager variable, the return address of the demand is put on the list of return addresses, just as though the "being computed" indication were there to start with.

In all cases, if the time for which an eager variable is demanded is "close" to the limit for this variable (the limit being kept in the variable-value store), the limit will be increased and a *trigger packet*, containing the variable and the tag, sent on to the term store.

Each demand that comes off the term-demand queue goes directly to the term store.

When a trigger packet for a variable X arrives at the term store, trigger packets are made for each of the basic variables on which X depends. (A list of the basic variables will be kept in the term store, as part of the intermediate code of the Lucid program. It is interesting to see how the intermediate code of the program reflects the partition of the program into data-driven and demand-driven parts. For lazy variables, the term store will give the operator and the addresses of the code for the operands. For the eager variables used in eager definitions, the term store will give the operator and the addresses of the variables that *use* this variable. For eager variables used in lazy definitions the term store will give the operator and a list of all the basic variables dependent on this variable. For eager variables used in both sorts of definitions the term store will contain both sorts of information.) The trigger packets are sent directly to the eager controller.

When a demand arrives at the term store, the following things happen. First of all a packet is constructed, consisting of the contents, c, of address a, together with the demand itself. Next, if the term is a basic operator applied to operands, or is simply a variable, an address, s, of an available demanding-operation is taken from the queue of addresses of available demanding-operations, and put in the new packet. Finally, this packet is sent to the processor pool.

At the processor pool, a processor is chosen, and this processor then performs various actions, depending on the sort of term being demanded.

If the term is a defined function applied to actual parameters, so that c denotes the address in the term store of the defining term of the function, the tag is modified by adding the address a to the "calling sequence" embodied in the original tag t. A demand is then sent off to the demand queue for the value of c with this new tag, and with the original return address r.

If the term is a basic (pointwise) operator applied to arguments (which means that c denotes the operator) several things happen: namely, demands are made for the values of the operands of the operator, and space is set up to hold these values until they have all been produced and the operator can be applied. This will be explained in more detail.

The first thing that happens is that a *skeleton* is created for a *demanding-operation*. The skeleton will consist of the address s of the demanding-operation, the operator c that will wait there for operand values, and the return address r to which the result of the operator will eventually be sent. The skeleton is sent around the application ring (the queue that holds results also will hold skeletons), and, when it gets to the demanding-operation store, it causes the appropriate demanding-operation to be set up at address s.

A demanding-operation contains the op-code for the operator that is eventually to be performed (in this case c), the return address of the demand that generated the demanding-operation (in this case r), and space in which to put the values of the arguments when they are eventually produced. (In practice there should be a bound on the number of arguments that an operator can have, so demanding-operation storage can be divided into fixed-size blocks. This will simplify storage management.)

For nonstrict basic operators, like if-then-else-fi, essentially the same thing happens, only the space for operand values in demanding-operations will also be used to hold pointers to the arguments which are to be evaluated later, as well as the tag for which they are to be evaluated. (Actually this will be a pointer to a separate block of storage in which the original demand is put, since this demand will give all the relevant information.)

The other thing that happens, when c is a basic operator, is that demand packets are created for the necessary arguments of the basic operator, and are sent to the demand packet queue. The addresses of these operands will be obtained from the address a by simply adding an offset corresponding to the operand number, and the return addresses of these demands will be s together with the positions, in the demanding-operation at s, in which the results of these demands are to be put. The tags of the demands will be t.

If any of the arguments are basic constants, like ▪3▪ or ▪[A B C]▪, the demand is not sent off to the demand queue. (Remember that demands in the demand queue should not be demands for constants.) In fact the demand packet will not be constructed. Instead a result packet is constructed using c (which will be the value of the constant, or, as in the second example, a pointer to the value) and the return address. This is sent around the application ring, to the demanding-operation store.

If the operator c is a Lucid (nonpointwise) operator, or a system operator, the processing of the demand is completely different. No demanding-operation is created. Instead, a new demand packet is set up for an argument of the Lucid operator or system operator, with the same return address, but with a different tag. For example, if the term is next E, the new demand will be for E, with the tag increased by 1. If it is E fby F, and the tag corresponds to Lucid-time 0, the new demand is for E, with tag corresponding to Lucid-time 0; if the tag corresponds to a Lucid-time greater than 0, the new demand is for F, with the Lucid-time (tag) decreased by one. (Since all other Lucid operators can be defined in terms of next and fby, using recursion, we do not need to consider them here. However, we could put special actions into the machine to handle them directly.) The systems operators, for dealing with subcomputations, references to global variables, etc., produce demands for the same term but with a different tag, also. In all cases, the new demand is sent to the demand packet queue.

If the term is just a variable, a tagged value of that variable must have been absent in the variable-value store, and now a demand has to be sent off for the term defining the variable (namely that addressed by c), with tag t and return address s. Before doing this, a skeleton must be sent off to the demanding-operation store, for the special operator, *store*. The demanding-operation is put in location s. The demanding-operation will contain the address in the variable-value store of the variable that is being demanded. (This was picked up, by the demand, at the time the "being computed" flag was set.)

No other cases need be considered here, for the actions of the processor dealing with a demand. (We have glossed over the system operators, which occur in the intermediate code, for manipulating tags. These deal with subcomputations (the effects of "is current"), with references to global variables of functions, and with references to formal parameters, which must give access to the actual parameters via tag modification and reference to the intermediate code. These features, though crucial and distinctive to this implementation of Lucid, are too complicated to be explained simply here. See Faustini and Wadge [5].)

I.2 The Application Ring

We will now consider the operation of the application ring. We saw that the values of already-calculated variables, when demanded, are sent to the result queue, and it is with the result queue that we will start.

The result packets on the result queue consist of data values together with return addresses. (The demand for the already-calculated variable, mentioned in the last paragraph, came with a return address, and this return address was combined with the variable value to give the result packet that was sent to the result queue.) As these result packets come off the result queue, they go to the demanding-operation store, where the data value is put into the correct demanding-operation, at the correct place, as indicated by the return address.

If this data value completes the set of operands for the demanding-operation, the information in the demanding-operation is made into a packet which is sent to the processor pool. (The address of the demanding-operation is added to the list of addresses of available demanding-operations.)

When a completed demanding-operation packet reaches the processor pool, it takes a processor, which then applies the appropriate operator to the data values in the packet. The result is made into a result packet by adding the return address of the demanding-operation, and this is added to the result queue. The only exception to this is when the operator in question is *store*. In this case, the operator performed is the identity function, but there is another effect as well as the production of a result packet. The value, which is the argument of the *store* operator, together with the address in the variable-value store of the tagged variable (that address being found in the demanding operation), is made into a packet (a *store packet*). This store packet is sent off to the variable-value store. (The variable-demand queue can also hold store packets.)

When this packet reaches the variable-value store, the value is put into the appropriate address and the value is used to make result packets for all the suspended demands for the variable that have been kept in the variable-value store. These result packets are sent to the result queue.

This completes the description of the eduction rings. We will now consider the dataflow ring.

I.3 The Dataflow Ring

The dataflow ring contains a matching store, exactly like the matching store of the Manchester machine. It also contains a *value queue* and a stage called the "eager controller", that will be explained shortly. It is to the eager controller that triggers are sent from the term store. Also arriving at the eager controller are values produced by processing completed packets from the matching store. These packets contain operators to be performed, together with their operand values, the tag that the result is to have, and the destinations to which the results are to be sent. Each value produced will be an ordinary data value, like those stored in the variable-value store, together with a tag and the destination to which it is to be sent. A destination consists of the operator to be performed and the address in the term store of the variable whose definition contains the occurrence of the operator in question and an indication of whether this is the value of one of the basic eager variables on which the values of other eager variables depend.

When a value packet arrives at the eager controller, if the destination indicates that the value is not one for a basic eager variable, the packet is passed on to the matching store. If the value *is* one for one of the basic eager variables, the relevant part of tag is compared with the limit for this variable. (The limit is stored in the eager controllerf.) If the relevant part of the tag is less than the limit, the packet is passed on to the matchingf store. If the relevant part of the tag is greater than the limit, the packet is stored in the eager controller.

When a value packet reaches the matching store, a search is made for a packet in the matching store that has the same operator and variable address as given by the destination field in the value packet, and has the same tag. If one is found, the value is put into this packet at the appropriate point. (What is the appropriate point is part of the destination also.) If one isn't found, such a packet is created, and the value is put in it at the appropriate point. If doing either of these things results in a packet in the matching store that has a full complement of operands (the operand is bound to be predictably heedless, so "fullness" is easily determined), the full packet travels to the term store. There the packet is changed to several packets, one for each of the places where the result of applying the operator is to be used in an eager definition. (This information is contained in the term store, as mentioned earlier, and is found by using the address of the variable in question.) These packets then travel to the processor pool, where a processor is used to apply the operator to the operands, yielding a result packet that travels to the eager controller.

If the variable in question is used in lazy definitions (possibly in addition to being used in eager definitions), a packet is created, at the term store, which contains the operator, the operands, the variable, and the tag. When this gets to the processor pool, the operator is applied to the operands and the result is combined with the variable name and the tag to produce what we call an *insert packet*. This insert packet is sent to the variable-value store, where the value is given to the appropriate variable with the appropriate tag. (This is done using an associative match, unlike the other way of giving values to variables, via store packets, which uses actual addresses in the variable-value store.) If there is nothing in the variable-value store for that variable and tag, a place is created. If there *is* something there it will be an indication that it is "being computed", and there will be at least one demand for the variable and value being held there. As happens with store packets, these values are sent to the application ring, and put in the demanding-operation store.

When a trigger for a variable arrives at the eager controller, the limit number for that variable and tag (ignoring the time in the tag) is increased to be N plus the time in the tag in the trigger, if this is greater than the current limit. Also, the values for that variable that are being held by the eager controller (and are below the new limit) are sent off to the matching store.

This completes the description of the dataflow ring, and thus completes the description of the whole submachine. The description is quite complicated, but it is basically a relatively complete description of an interpreter for the high-level language Lucid, expressed as an architecture. Language interpreters are generally complicated things, and usually no attempt is made to describe them relatively precisely *in English*, as we have done here. The fact that we could do it indicates that there is a good match between the language's syntax and semantics and also that the language is simple and elegant.

References

[1]   Ashcroft,E.A., and Wadge,W.W.
        Lucid - A Formal System for Writing and Proving Programs.
        SIAM Journal on Computing (3):336-354, September, 1976.

[2]   Ashcroft,E.A. and Wadge,W.W.
        Lucid, a Nonprocedural Language with Iteration.
        CACM (7):519-526, July, 1977.

[3]   Ashcroft,E.A. and Wadge,W.W.
        Structured Lucid.
        Technical Report CS-79-21, University of Waterloo, June, 1979.
        Revised May 1980.

[4]   Ashcroft, E.A. and Wadge, W.W.
        The Syntax and Semantics of Lucid.
        1985.
        SRI Technical Report CSL-146.

[5]   Faustini A.A. and Wadge W. W.
        The development of the pLucid System.
        To be submitted to the Journal of Software Practice and Experience.

[6]   Faustini, A.A., Matthews S.G. and Yaghi AG A.
        The pLucid Programmer's Manual.
        Technical Report TR83-004, Computer Science Department, Arizona State
            University, Oct., 1983.

[7]   Gurd,J. and Watson,I.
        Preliminary Evaluation of a Prototype Dataflow Computer.
        In *Information Processing (IFIP) 83*, pages 545-551. North Holland, September,
            1983.

[8]   Kahn,G.
        The Semantics of a Simple Language for Parallel Processing.
        In *Proceedings of IFIP Congress 74*, pages 471-475. International Federation for
            Information Processing, 1974.

[9]   Keller, R.M., and Sleep, M.R.
        Applicative Caching: Programmer Control of Object Sharing and Lifetime in
            Distributed Implementations of Applicative Languages.
        In *Proceedings of the 1981 Conference on Functional Programming Languages
            and Computer Architecture*, pages 131-140. ACM, October, 1981.

[10]   Pingali, K., and Arvind.
        Efficient Demand-driven Evaluation(I).
        To appear in TOPLAS.

[11]   Wadge,W.W. and Ashcroft.E.A.
        Lucid, the Dataflow Programming Language.
        Academic Press U.K., 1985.

Fifth Generation Computer Architectures, J.V. Woods (ed.)
Elsevier Science Publishers B.V. (North-Holland)
© IFIP, 1986

PARALLEL DATA-DRIVEN GRAPH REDUCTION

Ian Watson, Paul Watson and Viv Woods

Dept. Computer Science,
University of Manchester,
MANCHESTER M13 9PL,
ENGLAND.

The search for efficient, wide purpose, highly extensible parallel computers continues. There have been many
interesting experiments in this area over the last fifteen
years but few ideas, which can be termed general purpose,
have reached commercial maturity. This paper examines most
of these major experiments and attempts to suggest that the
way forward is a synthesis of Dataflow and Graph Reduction
principles together with a serious look at the lessons which
can be learned concerning cost-performance from more conventional approaches.

INTRODUCTION

It has now become widely accepted that, despite occasional claims
that a breakthrough in technology is imminent, computing machines of the
future will need to exploit parallelism in order to achieve significant
increases in speed. There have been many attempts to build machines
which make use of regular data structure manipulations which are
believed to exist in a large number of scientific computations; both
array and vector processors [1],[2] can be regarded in this category.

The apparently more flexible parallel structure which consists of a
number of conventional machines, each running a section of a program and
communicating when necessary, has appeared in many forms from C.mmp [3]
to Transputers [4] and the Cosmic Cube [5].

More recently, there have been experiments in computer architecture
which depart from the conventional views of computation which are still
fundamental to the above approaches. The most widely known of these is
Dataflow and there are now a number of operational Dataflow machines
which have been evaluated [6],[7].

The most recent proposals are for machines which are built with the
intention that they should be vehicles for the implementation of a particular programming style; either single assignment [8], functional [9]
or logic [10]. As yet, there is little or no information about the
performance of these approaches in practice although much simulation and
analysis has been performed.

This paper examines the strengths and weaknesses of all these major
approaches to parallel computer architecture in terms of their performance, efficiency, general applicability and the ease with which they
can be programmed. It becomes apparent that all current approaches have
limitations in at least one of these areas and that a synthesis of
packet based graph reduction and Dataflow may be the most promising avenue for further exploration, particularly if the inherent implementation
inefficiencies can be overcome.

AN ANALYSIS OF CURRENT APPROACHES .

It is worthwhile listing the idealized properties of any parallel machine in order to evaluate how far current approaches have succeeded. The following is considered to be a reasonably complete list :-

(1) The power of a parallel machine should be a linear function of the hardware resources provided.

(2) The linear power function should apply over an infinite range. i.e. the machine should be infinitely extensible.

(3) There should be no large constants in the above function. i.e. a parallel machine should have a comparable cost/performance ratio with conventional machines.

(4) A parallel machine should be resilient to hardware failure; isolation of faulty components (ideally automatically) should enable the machine to function with a small degradation in performance.

(5) The machine should be general purpose and be able to exploit any form of parallelism which exists in a problem.

(6) The programming of the machine should involve no more (ideally less) conceptual complexity than current approaches.

(7) The programming task should not require any knowledge of the physical machine structure or its underlying mechanisms.

(8) The languages in which the machine is programmed should be general purpose and be capable of expressing all forms of computation. Ideally this should be a single language.

Vector and Array processors are, in theory anyway, linearly extensible over a wide range and also cost-effective. However, they are not resilient nor are they able to support wide varieties of parallelism and a wide variety of applications. The programming task requires knowledge of the physical structure, particularly if good use of resources is to be achieved. The conceptual complexity of problem specification is probably not much greater than currently required but algorithm design can require a great deal of thought.

If problems could be partitioned in such a way that inter-process communication were reduced to an absolute minimum then conventional multi-processors would be able to achieve extensible linear speedup in a cost effective manner. Unfortunately, the evidence is that both communication bottlenecks and idle resources waiting for communication severely degrade practical performance. The programming of these machines usually requires a language which includes explicit inter-process communication facilities. Not only does this introduce a considerable degree of complexity, but also requires an intimate knowledge of the machine in order that the process partitioning can be done. Although, in principle, the machines are resilient, removal of hardware will usually require re-programming. The machines can be regarded as general purpose if partitioning strategies can be achieved.

Dataflow machines are an attempt to produce general purpose multi-processor structures which overcome many of the problems of the conventional approach by introducing fine grain dynamic processor allocation. Processor resources are only allocated when computational effort is required and thus they do not become idle. The processes have all input available before allocation and produce output when complete. As a result, machine structures require only uni-directional communication. Although this communication has very high bandwidth requirements, its uni-directional nature facilitates the design of communication structures. These properties combine to produce machines which are highly extensible with linear speedup characteristics and are able to exploit wide varieties of parallelism. There is a close relationship between

Dataflow models of computation and a simple functional programming style. As a result, most Dataflow machines are programmed in a single assignment language where there is no necessity to express parallelism explicitly. The complexity of the programming task is, due to the functional nature of the languages, arguably easier than for a conventional machine. The structures are resilient in that processing and storage resources can be removed (at least manually) without need for re-programming.

It is in the areas of cost-effectiveness and the expression of general problems at the language level that Dataflow has limitations. Most practical machines make use of the tagged Dataflow model where the data carries a large amount of context information. This is necessary in order that recursion, iteration and data-structures can be handled. This requires a large amount of store in a physical implementation but more seriously implies an associative mechanism in order that the availability of data at the input to a computational operation can be detected. In the Manchester machine [11] this has been implemented using a hardware hashing mechanism which is both complex and expensive.

The language issue concerns the need for either explicit storage or infinite structures in order that full expressive power is available. The first destroys the functional nature and introduces the necessity for synchronization of access. The latter requires the concept of demand driven evaluation which is not a natural part of the Dataflow model. It should be mentioned at this point that most Dataflow projects have recognized the necessity to accommodate a demand-driven element and features such as 'matching functions' [12] and structure stores [13] have been added in an attempt to achieve it. There are, as yet, no comprehensive evaluations of these modifications but there is some evidence that, because they are 'add-ons' rather than a fundamental part of the approach, they will not provide a totally acceptable solution.

Finally we will examine those approaches which have been proposed with a view to the implementation of particular programming styles. Most of these have similarities to Dataflow but incorporate demand driven features. The Eduction [8] model described by Ashcroft is very similar to tagged Dataflow but has a demand phase which builds a dynamic dataflow graph. It is specifically aimed at the implementation of LUCID [14] and therefore has a firmer software base. It shares many of the properties of normal Dataflow implementations and, in particular, still requires an associative mechanism.

Details of parallel machines which are specifically aimed at logic programming are scarce. The ALICE machine [9] is primarily intended for functional language implementation, but it has been demonstrated that such a packet based rewrite model can also implement at least a usable subset of logic programming. It is believed that much of the work in this area is derived from ALICE and that the properties of these machines are broadly similar.

ALICE uses a dynamic processor allocation strategy, but the process size is somewhat larger than Dataflow, being at the level of a complete language function definition at least during the rewriting phase. This is, in principle, a sensible decision because it reduces the dynamic process allocation overheads and is likely to lead to a significant reduction in the communication bandwidth requirements. An AGENT is allocated a packet which contains a specification of a function which is to be applied to arguments which are contained in the packet. These arguments may either be atomic values or pointers to further packets which reside in a PACKET POOL store. These further values may be CON-STRUCTORS which are general evaluated structures or they may require further processing to become evaluated. The AGENT process will produce a set of new packets which represent the body (Right Hand Side) of the function which has been specified. These new packets may themselves be immediately processable or they may reside in the PACKET POOL in a state where they will only become processable if their value is required as arguments by a function which is being processed. The AGENT will contain a set of REWRITE RULES for the function which specify the structure of the new graph and the modes in which the new packets are to be produced.

The first point to note is that a recursive definition will result in a new copy of the function body for each recursive call. There are no environment tags and the need for associative storage mechanisms is removed. It may appear that a copying mechanism is inefficient in both time and space, but in practice the absence of tags and the re-tagging function interface required for Dataflow, more than compensate.

The major drawback of current proposals in this area is a result of the process size. The majority of functions will contain conditional computation either explicitly or in the form of pattern matching (which is implemented directly in the current ALICE prototype). Unless the arguments are present as values in the packet to be rewritten, the process will require accesses to the PACKET POOL in order to proceed. There is clearly a conflict here; the forcing of evaluated arguments before a function rewrite is attempted is not possible in a demand driven environment but allocating a process before it is complete results in idle processor time and bi-directional processor store communication.

Packet based graph reduction or rewrite rule machines can exploit wide varieties of parallelism. They share with Dataflow the properties that parallelism is not explicit at the programming level and that there is no need for a knowledge of the machine structure. The languages are potentially more general purpose than those used for Dataflow machines and have a firm mathematical foundation. They are also resilient.

By removing the need for associative storage they are potentially more cost-effective than Dataflow, but it is doubtful whether their cost-performance is comparable with conventional machines in their current form. There is a major question concerning their extensibility, because they have departed from some of the major principles which were fundamental to the linear speedup properties of Dataflow, it is unlikely that they will achieve the same results in this area.

What should we conclude from all these observations ? Both vector and array processors are essentially 'hardware first' approaches and, if it were possible to program these machines to exploit their potential on a wide variety of problems, they would undoubtedly provide a very cost-effective solution. It is likely that they will remain prominent in the narrow application areas to which they are suited.

Conventional multi-processors are again a 'hardware first' approach, but an attempt to be more general purpose. It would appear that they are one of the least promising in that not only does the programming task become more complex but there is little hope of achieving hardware efficiency.

Dataflow tries to strike a balance halfway between software and hardware. The underlying computational model provides features which lead to an efficient but not cost-effective implementation. Using a simple functional programming style eases considerably the programming task, but by not addressing the issues of demand-driven computation directly, there are some questions about the general applicability.

Eduction shares most of the properties of Dataflow but introduces demand driven computation as a fundamental part of the model and as such accommodates those features required by a 'language first' approach. However, the hardware implementation requires associative storage and is therefore unlikely to be cost-effective.

The packet based graph reduction approach is also 'language first'. By adopting a code copying mechanism it removes some of the hardware complexity but, due to its non data driven process allocation strategy, may not result in highly extensible machines.

Given this wealth of information and experience, it should be possible to extract the best features from all of the above approaches and the work described in this paper is an attempt to do this. Although the title of data-driven graph reduction implies that the major input has come from the 'language first' / dataflow ideas, there are serious lessons to be learned from the fact that the 'hardware first' approach generally leads to a more cost effective, if not generally applicable, solution. However, there is already deep concern about the 'software crisis' which has resulted from the complexity of current programming approaches and any further increase in complexity in a search for parallelism would be foolish. The opportunity to program high speed parallel machines in language styles which are mathematically sound is too attractive to dismiss. For that reason our approach is definitely 'language first'.

A COMMENT ON DATA STRUCTURES

Before proceeding with a description of the synthesis of ideas, there are some serious software issues which have been 'glossed over' in the preceeding sections. In any attempt to advance the cause of parallel computer architecture, we must recognize that there are widely varying opinions about the applicability of various programming styles. There are extreme opposing views from those who claim that current logic / functional languages (in some areas the difference between these two camps is also extreme, but that is a different issue) with only their recursive data structures are applicable to all known programming tasks, to those who claim that no sensible program can ever be written without the facility of explicitly updatable arrays. Of course, the truth lies somewhere in-between. It is not an issue of whether things can be expressed in a particular style, but whether it is natural to do so and whether the resulting program can be executed with any degree of efficiency. So the claims in the previous section that the 'language first' approach is generally applicable must be treated with a degree of scepticism.

In order to achieve a programming style which requires no explicit expression of parallelism, we must think in terms of complete data objects which when operated on become new objects. Any attempt to specify computation in terms of updating elements of an object in a parallel environment immediately introduces the need for explicit synchronization and seriously complicates the programming task, this is clearly undesirable. If we adopt this view, it is then necessary to consider how such things can be implemented at the execution level; creating new objects implies that the whole object is copied. Lists and trees etc. are attractive because, as long as we limit ourselves to the correct set of object operations, it is easy to devise updating mechanisms which create only small sections of a new structure and share existing portions, which are unchanged, via pointers. Arrays, because they are accessed by a relative offset from the base of the structure cannot be treated in this way and complete copies must be taken. We must also realize the limitations of 'acceptable' structures; adding an element to the end of an N element list is probably more inefficient at an implementation level than updating the Nth. element of an N element array by complete copying.

It is important to realize that this is a fundamental problem to which there is no easy solution. It is difficult to argue that there are not a good number of programming tasks which require such facilities although the use of arrays in current programming practice is not a good measure of their necessity. Even then we must not assume that all programs which appear to have a natural array structure are going to cause problems. For example there are a large number of scientific applications such as signal processing where at a global level we are taking a complete array structure and computing a new value for each element and thus naturally creating a new structure. Although we may introduce additional store management problems by excluding in-place updating, the overall implications are nowhere near as serious as the true random access case. If we require random access to structures and wish to maintain the clean language level view, there are only a small number of alternatives.

The first is to find a representation for structures which allows random access with minimum penalty. Balanced trees, for example, have a logN penalty for random access and a logN penalty for an update if we represent a single dimensional N element array in this form. If we have very heavy use of such a structure then this may not be acceptable, an additional criticism is that all accesses must go through a root which may become a bottleneck in a parallel implementation.

Another possibility is to maintain the clean language level view but detect any synchronization requirements at a lower level. This may take the form of compiler analysis and the production of suitable code but it could also be the subject of specialized hardware mechanisms. The Manchester Dataflow team have had some success in this area in the implementation of the SISAL [15],[16] language.

An alternative form of hardware support might introduce specialized copying functions at the implementation level. It is certainly possible to envisage autonomous store to store block copying operations which could operate considerably faster than the same task done by normal processor operation.

This issue has been around for some time in the Dataflow world but has largely been ignored by the 'language first' camp. This is due to the fact that Dataflow was initially targetted at scientific computation where array usage is considered mandatory whereas non-numeric applications are more used to a list based style and this is the area for which functional / logic language systems are intended. It remains to be seen if current LISP programmers will be happy without their 'rplac' operations. It is the most serious hurdle in the search for a truly general purpose parallel computer system which can be programmed without resort to the unacceptable techniques of language level synchronization.

The purpose of raising this issue is to indicate that the search for an ideal parallel system is more complex than the initial analysis suggested. The model presented here does not tackle this issue other than to note that that it exists. We can of course achieve the tree structured approach but believe that, before a real machine is constructed, the issue of more direct support for random access structures must be addressed.

A NEW LOOK AT PACKET REWRITE ARCHITECTURES

As we have already described, packet based architectures such as ALICE use a dynamic process allocation scheme where the process size is at the level of a complete language function. The desire to implement demand driven computation leads to a situation where, in many cases, such a process cannot proceed until store accesses have been made to determine the form of those arguments. Even if they are already evaluated, there is a penalty in wasted processor time and bidirectional processor store communication. In many cases, further evaluation of the arguments may be required before any decisions can be made. In that case the attempt to rewrite must be suspended and reactivated when that evaluation has completed.

The problem is that, in general, the amount of computation between decision points in most programs is very small. If we try to raise the task allocation size in a parallel architecture above that level we will encounter the problems already described. We must, therefore, consider the basic computational model at a fine grain level. This suggests the need for very high bandwidth communication and the presence of process allocation overheads as in current Dataflow machines. We will try to suggest later that there is a difference between the level at which we view the basic computational model and the level at which we need to implement it in a physical realization. If the physical machine structure is correct, many of these apparent disadvantages disappear.

We are trying to implement a packet rewrite model which is similar to ALICE, but maintain the properties of Dataflow whereby computational resources are only allocated when a task can be completed without any external reference from the processor. We believe that in order to do this, the individual processor operations must be at a similar level to current Dataflow, that is at the level of ADD's, SUBTRACT's etc.. One fundamental change from the ALICE view is that we will not attempt to implement language level pattern matching directly and require that all such constructs are compiled into simple conditionals.

The general principles of the approach are best illustrated by example. Take the simple definition of factorial written in a pattern matching form :-

```
fac(0) <= 1;
fac(n) <= n * fac (n-1);
```

We adopt the approach of compiling a function into a set of skeleton packets, rather than a specification of how those skeleton packets are to be produced. We feel that this facilitates the addition of information concerning the modes in which the packets are to be produced at rewrite time. The following would, in outline, represent the above definition :-

```
(0)    | ITE | ^1 | ^2 | ^3 |
(1)    | CEI | $2 | I0 |    |
(2)    | ATO | I1 |    |    |
(3)    | MUL | $2 | ^4 |    |
(4)    | fac | ^5 |    |    |
(5)    | SUB | $2 | I1 |    |
```

The notation is fairly straightforward, the first field is either a basic operation :-

```
ITE = if _ then _ else
CEI = compare equal integers
ATO = atomic constructor
MUL = multiply
SUB = subtract
```

or a function identifier which is used to select the applicable rule set. The pointer notation ^n means 'when taking a copy of this packet, insert a pointer to the address of the packet which is a copy of the n th. packet'. The I notation indicates a literal integer which will appear in the copy. A $n indicates that the n th. field of the packet which represents a call to this function is to be inserted here. The issue of packet modes has not yet been addressed, we will assume initially that packets can be produced in two basic forms, either they are immediately processable (we will use the term RE-WRITABLE to be consistent with ALICE terminology) or in a state in which they will not be processed until they are triggered by a demand for their value, we will term this DORMANT. These states will be indicated both in the skeleton packet set and the copied packets by a single letter annotation R or D. Note that in the skeleton set the annotation is a statement about the mode which will be given to a generated packet, whereas in a copied packet it is control information used in subsequent evaluation. The skeleton set is now :-

```
(0)  R  | ITE | ^1 | ^2 | ^3 |
(1)  D  | CEI | $2 | I0 |    |
(2)  D  | ATO | I1 |    |    |
(3)  D  | MUL | $2 | ^4 |    |
(4)  D  | fac | ^5 |    |    |
(5)  D  | SUB | $2 | I1 |    |
```

It should be noted that by generating the head packet with a RE-WRITABLE tag and all others with a DORMANT tag we will achieve an outermost evaluation order. Mechanisms by which other evaluation orders can be achieved will be discussed later. One further detail requires discussion before we proceed with the example. The value of any function must always have been demanded before evaluation is attempted, in the simplest case we can regard this as an outer level demand from the user, but in general it will be a value required by a field of another packet. Any REWRITABLE packet must therefore carry with it a RETURN ADDRESS which is a packet address together with a field number.

If we started with a packet which required re-writing of the form :-

```
        R  | fac | I2 |    |    | RA |
```

we would produce the following graph :-

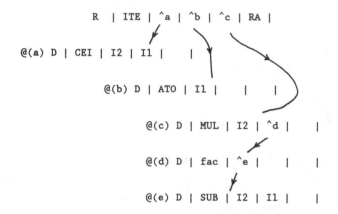

```
        R   | ITE | ^a | ^b | ^c | RA |

@(a) D | CEI | I2 | I1 |      |

     @(b) D | ATO | I1 |    |    |

        @(c) D | MUL | I2 | ^d |    |

        @(d) D | fac | ^e |    |    |

        @(e) D | SUB | I2 | I1 |    |
```

Note that the RETURN ADDRESS of the original packet has now been inserted in the head packet of the newly created graph. In the same way as in ALICE we envisage creating packets representing the complete right hand side of the function in a single processing step. The difference being that this RHS contains all the information about conditional computation required to select the applicable part of the function. Once this graph has been constructed, further computation takes place at a fine grain level. A REWRITABLE basic operation is inspected to see if arguments that it requires are in the correct form, in the example given here that form will be embedded integer or boolean values. If the required arguments are in the form of a pointer to other packets, a DEMAND will be sent to the packet(s) requesting its value. The demanding packet will become SUSPENDED with a count attached of the number of values which it requires before it is a candidate for further processing. When all these replies have been received, the packet again becomes REWRITABLE. The DEMAND will contain the RETURN ADDRESS of the demanding packet and field number. On receipt of this demand the demanded packet will become REWRITABLE. At this point we should note that the situation will occur where DORMANT packets are pointed to from more than one place. To accommodate the sharing of any forced evaluation, we introduce the concept of a GHOST packet. Any DORMANT packet which becomes REWRITABLE will leave a GHOST in the storage location which it occupied, the RETURN ADDRESS of the demand will be left in the GHOST and the newly REWRITABLE packet will have the GHOST address attached as its RETURN ADDRESS. In this particular case, the return address will not have a particular field number, the GHOST will attain the form of any returned packet. Any demands which encounter a GHOST packet (conceptually) add their RETURN ADDRESS to a 'waiting list'.

We are now in a position to follow the execution of the example.
The rewritable ITE packet requires its first boolean argument field
before any further processing can occur. Combining several of the above
steps we will obtain the graph :-

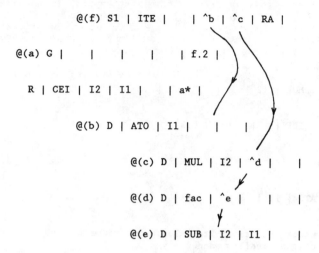

```
        @(f) S1 | ITE |     |  ^b |  ^c | RA |

@(a) G |    |    |    |    | f.2 |

 R | CEI | I2 | I1 |    | a* |

        @(b) D | ATO | I1 |    |    |

                @(c) D | MUL | I2 | ^d |    |

                @(d) D | fac | ^e |    |    |

                @(e) D | SUB | I2 | I1 |    |
```

and later :-

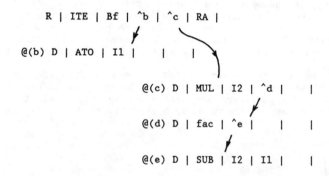

```
    R | ITE | Bf | ^b | ^c | RA |

@(b) D | ATO | I1 |    |    |

            @(c) D | MUL | I2 | ^d |    |

            @(d) D | fac | ^e |    |    |

            @(e) D | SUB | I2 | I1 |    |
```

The left hand branch can now be discarded (garbage collected) and the
ITE becomes an identity operator on the right hand branch :-

```
  @(g) S1 | IDE |    |    | RA |

    @(c) G |    |    |    | g.2 |

        R | MUL | I2 | ^d |    | c* |

        @(d) D | fac | ^e |    |    |

        @(e) D | SUB | I2 | I1 |    |
```

The MUL will now suspend and activate the fac packet. Note that when the
new recursive call is replaced by its RHS, the argument which is
inserted in all The $2 positions will be a pointer to the (e) packet and
it will therefore be shared. Its evaluation will initially be forced by
the compare operation which in this case will return a boolean true

value and select the left branch of the conditional. If we had started with a larger initial value, so that the right branch was selected the GHOST mechanism would have been invoked with a waiting list. Omitting the detail of several intermediate steps the graph becomes :-

```
@(g) S1 | IDE |    |    |    | RA |

    @(c) G |    |    |    |    | g.2 |

    @(h) S1 | MUL | I2 |    |    | c* |

    @(x) S1 | IDE |    |    |    | h.3 |

    @(y) G |    |    |    |    | x.2 |

        R | ATO | I1 |    |    | y* |
```

Rewriting a constructor results in its value being returned and the execution will proceed in a Dataflow manner.

In the form shown here there are obviously a number of inefficiencies. A large number of ghost packets have been introduced which were largely unnecessary, for example, in a simple atomic evaluation of this sort it would be possible to force the evaluation of the argument of 'fac' before the rewrite was attempted. In that case no pointer sharing would result and the ghost mechanism would be unnecessary. The example was presented in this form to indicate the most lazy mode of evaluation.

Both arms of the conditional were copied at each rewrite step even though it was inevitable that one of them would be discarded. This can be avoided by introducing auxiliary functions and a special atomic function value which is returned as a value by a conditional. In this case the code would be :-

```
(0)  R  | ^1  | $2 |    |    |
(1)  D  | ITE | ^2 | *3 | *4 |
(2)  D  | CEI | $2 | I0 |    |

(3)  D  | ATO | I1 |    |    |

(4)  D  | MUL | $2 | ^5 |    |
(5)  D  | fac | ^6 |    |    |
(6)  D  | SUB | $2 | I1 |    |
```

Now no redundant packets are copied because the conditional is evaluated and the alternative set of rules for the appropriate auxiliary function selected.

Many simple atomic calculations of are, of course, perfectly safe to execute in an eager manner. In the above example, all the communication involved in the demand phase is unnecessary. If we introduce the SUSPENDED annotation and a mechanism for specifying return links into the rewrite-rules, it is possible to 'pre-compile' the demands and thus avoid the overheads. The code would become :-

```
(0)  S1  |     | $2 |    |    |
(1)  S1  | ITE |    | *3 | *4 | 0.1 |
(2)  R   | CEI | $2 | I0 |    | 1.2 |

(3)  R   | ATO | I1 |    |    |

(4)  S1  | MUL | $2 |    |    |
(5)  S1  | fac |    |    |    | 4.3 |
(6)  R   | SUB | $2 | I1 |    | 5.2 |
```

Now as soon as the copy has been made with the appropriate insertion of pointers, the Dataflow evaluation can proceed immediately.

This brief description is intended only to give an outline of the model. We have not discussed general constructor handling nor higher order function mechanisms. The first is relatively obvious, the latter involves a packet based supercombinator [17] technique. There are many implementation issues concerning physical packet size, the handling of waiting lists etc. A discussion of these issues is beyond the scope of this paper.

SOME COMMENTS ON MACHINES

Before proceeding with an outline picture of a physical machine which might implement the above model, there are some general issues concerning parallel machine architecture which need discussion.

As we have already observed, array and vector processors, if their potential can be realized, provide a cost-effective solution. In general the 'language first' approaches appear to be far less cost-effective. It is worthwhile examining the reasons for this.

In the more conventional approaches the selection of the next step in the computation is selected by sequential control, i.e. a program counter, and the total amount of information required is very small. In more general parallel structures, a process is able to nominate its successors by local information held within the process. For example, in Dataflow, each data token carries with it the computational node to which it is directed and each computational node has the destinations of its output attached. This represents a significant amount of information in relation to the 'real' data. However, it is difficult to envisage a flexible distributed system which does not use a similar technique. Of course, the larger the process, the smaller the overhead but we have already argued against large process sizes for a variety of reasons.

The model described above is no different in that the arguments in a packet are potentially global addresses in the storage structure of the machine, although the rewrite-rule code can use a much compacted form. One challenge of a physical implementation is to reduce this overhead as much as possible.

For many years, conventional processors have been very closely coupled to the store(s) with which they communicate. Vector and array processors are essentially no different; although local processors may have their own store, it is essential that the majority of accesses are local. Many proposals in the area of both conventional and unconventional multi-processors have departed from this view, this includes both Dataflow and ALICE. Many researchers have been seduced by the idea of cheap microprocessor like building blocks in a structure which supports a number of processing elements from the bandwidth of a single store. This, of course, introduces problems of communication, arbitration and distribution and may account for some of the cost-performance problems. In the meantime the newer conventional microprocessors are moving in exactly the opposite direction; the devices are starting to include on chip cache store in an attempt to overcome the limitations of main store bandwidth.

It is now apparent that the 'small but many' building block approach was an aberration brought about by a narrow view of a particular stage of technological development. Unless there is a major breakthrough in storage technology, a return to closely coupled store processor structures is inevitable.

The above statements require further qualification. It is necessary to define the scale of the structures involved. At some level it must be possible to view any multi-processor system as composed of a homogenous collection of building blocks. In the Manchester Dataflow machine it is a single ring, in ALICE it is a single packet pool with its associated agents. It is below this level that parallelism in processing is probably a mistake. However, it should be noted that we have identified blocks of considerable complexity containing large amounts of store (megabytes). The other mistake is to accept the principle of the above arguments but to restrict oneself in practice to a store processor building block whose size is severely limited by the desire to implement it on a single VLSI chip.

In the same way that execution models should be driven by the programming requirements, then implementations should reflect the requirements of the model. The true engineering skill is to use technology to build what is required in a cost-effective manner not to develop technology and then attempt to find a use for it !

AN OUTLINE PHYSICAL ARCHITECTURE

It has been stated that the graph reduction model described is data-driven, it is probable that this terminology needs explanation. In our terms, an execution model is data-driven if resources are allocated only to processes which have a complete set of inputs and this condition is normally achieved by the arrival of data at a point where other process information is stored. It is also necessary that the resources are released as soon as processing is completed. We do not distinguish between 'real' data and control data. Being data-driven is therefore a property of an execution mechanism rather than a computational model. Dataflow is a particular example of a computational model where there is an obvious translation to a data-driven implementation. It is believed that data-driven properties are essential to an efficient implementation but that Dataflow is only one of a number of models for which this can be achieved.

Once this property has been established then the major features of Dataflow machines, which have been highly successful in their quest for speedup as a linear function of hardware resources, can be exploited. The major feature which we feel is still applicable is the pipelined uni-directional communication structure. Although there are, as yet, few published practical results in this area, there have been many simulations which verify the effectiveness of this approach. Initial results are now available from a small scale but nevertheless real implementation of such a structure which has been built at Manchester and the preliminary results show speedups which are very close to linear for a machine containing sixteen rings [18].

An architecture to support the data-driven graph reduction model is, in outline, very simple, it is shown in Figure 1.

The storage functions have been split in order that some pipelined parallelism can be exploited in the access of Rewritable packets, the access of the skeleton rewrite rules and the main packet store. The processor is assumed to contain storage management hardware in addition to the packet processing functions. The storage management involves the allocation of packet addresses and garbage collection using a distributed reference count mechanism.

The Delta Network switch is the interconnection point for a number of store-processor configurations.

The packet addresses are (in principle) global to the whole architecture but a processor will know which are locally available and which are not. Reference to a global address will involve the sending of a

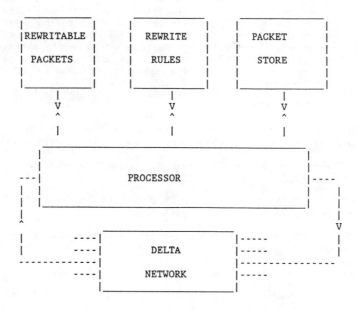

Figure 1. The Outline Architecture

message via the communication network. However, we would envisage the rewriting of complete function bodies as taking place in a single store/processor. In that case a large amount of the communication would take place as local store-processor accesses.

The purpose of this approach is to maintain the flexibility of the low level model but in practice, by using large closely coupled building blocks, to achieve the virtues of a larger process allocation unit. This approach still retains the information overhead associated with small process size unless it is possible to compact local addresses. In terms of address width, it is unlikely that the local addresses will be significantly shorter than the global ones. If it were possible to achieve storage allocation strategies which ensured that, for example, all packets for a particular rewrite copy were located within a single page of a paged memory system, then a significant reduction in address size could be achieved.

Most of these issues are not resolved and we do not yet have a detailed design of a practical machine. However, we believe that this general approach has the ability to produce efficient general purpose parallel machines which have a more realistic cost-performance ratio than most of the 'language first' approaches currently proposed.

CONCLUSIONS

General purpose parallel machines are not yet a reality. There are a number of special purpose structures which perform well on problems to which they are suited.

The programming of parallel machines can be a complex task and given the problems which occur with the reliability of conventional approaches, any further complexity is very undesirable. The expression of explicit parallelism is felt to be the major weakness of many multi-processor structures. The use of Declarative languages avoids the necessity for any explicit expression of parallelism and reduces the overall complexity of the programming task.

We feel that parallel machines based on a Declarative approach are the only practical route to general purpose parallel computing, but that there are many problems, particularly in the areas of cost-performance, in most of the current proposals.

Rewrite rule models appear to provide the facilities required for language implementation but there are many lessons to be learned from Dataflow and more conventional machines when it comes to implementation. It has been demonstrated that a data-driven execution mechanism can be devised for a rewrite-rule model by adopting a fine grain packet based approach. If the correct decisions are made concerning the physical machine structures then many of the apparent disadvantages of this approach can be overcome.

REFERENCES

[1] Reddaway S.F., DAP - A Distributed Array Processor, 1st. Annual Symposium on Computer Architecture, Gainesville, Florida, 1973.

[2] Cray Research Inc, CRAY-1 Computer System Reference Manual, Cray Research Inc, Minneapolis, 1976.

[3] Wulf W A and Bell C G, C.mmp - A multi-mini-processor, Proc. AFIPS FJCC, vol.41, September 1972, p765.

[4] Brain S., The Transputer-"exploiting the opportunity of VLSI", Electronic Product Design, December 1983.

[5] Seitz C.L., The Cosmic Cube, CACM Vol 28, No 1, Jan 1985.

[6] Gurd J. R. and Watson I., Preliminary Evaluation of a Prototype Dataflow Computer, Proc. IFIP83, September 1983

[7] Amamiya M, Takahashi N, Naruse T and Yoshida M, A Data Flow Processor Array System for Solving Partial Differential Equations, Proc. International Symposium on Applied Mathematics and Information Science, Kyoto University, March 1982.

[8] Ashcroft E.A., Eazyflow Architecture, SRI Technical Report CSL-147, Apr 1985.

[9] Darlington J. & Reeve M., ALICE- A Multi-Processor Reduction Machine for the Parallel Evaluation of Applicative Languages, Proc of 1981 ACM Conf on Functional Programming Languages & Computer Architecture.

[10] Murakami K., Kakuta T. and Onai R., Architectures and Hardware Systems : Parallel Inference Machine and Knowledge Base Machine. Proc. International Conference on Fifth Generation Computer Systems, TOKYO 1984.

[11] Da Silva J.G.D. and Watson I., A Pseudo Associative Store with Hardware Hashing, Proc IEE, Part E, 1983.

[12] Catto A.J., Nondeterministic Programming in a Data Driven Environment, PhD. Thesis, University of Manchester, 1981.

[13] Sargeant J., Efficient Stored Data Structures for Dataflow Computing, PhD. Thesis, University of Manchester, 1985.

[14] Ashcroft E.A. & Wadge W.W., LUCID, a Non-Procedural Language with Iteration, CACM Vol 20 No 7 p519-526 July 1977.

[15] McGraw et al. SISAL - Streams and Iteration in a Single Assignment Language, Lawrence Livermore Laboratory, M-146, University of California, 1985.

[16] Bohm A.P.W. and Sargeant J., Efficient Dataflow Code Generation for SISAL, Parallel Computing 85, Berlin 1985, To be Published.

[17] Hughes R.J.M., Graph Reduction with Super-Combinators, Oxford University Programming Research Group, Technical Monograph PRG-28, 1982.

[18] Foley J., A Multi-Ring Dataflow Machine PhD. Thesis, University of Manchester, In Preparation.

(Continued on inside back cover)

Other Computer Society of the IEEE Texts

(Continued on inside back cover)

For Further Information:
Computer Society of the IEEE, 10662 Los Vaqueros Circle, Los Alamitos, CA 90720
Computer Society of the IEEE, 13, Avenue de l'Aquilon, B-1200 Brussels, BELGIUM